D1504437

Prague

timeout.com/prague

Published by Time Out Guides Ltd, a wholly owned subsidiary of Time Out Group Ltd.
Time Out and the Time Out logo are trademarks of Time Out Group Ltd.

© Time Out Group Ltd 2006
Previous editions 1995, 1997, 1998, 2000, 2002, 2004

10 9 8 7 6 5 4 3 2 1

This edition first published in Great Britain in 2006 by Ebury Publishing
Ebury Publishing is a division of The Random House Group Ltd,
20 Vauxhall Bridge Road, London SW1V 2SA

Random House Australia Pty Limited 20 Alfred Street, Milsons Point, Sydney, New South Wales 2061, Australia
Random House New Zealand Limited 18 Poland Road, Glenfield, Auckland 10, New Zealand
Random House South Africa (Pty) Limited Isle of Houghton, Corner Boundary
Road & Carse O'Gowrie, Houghton 2198, South Africa

Random House UK Limited Reg. No. 954009

Distributed in USA by Publishers Group West
1700 Fourth Street, Berkeley, California 94710

Distributed in Canada by Penguin Canada Ltd
10 Alcorn Avenue, Toronto, Ontario, Canada M4V 3B2

For further distribution details, see www.timeout.com

ISBN 1-904978-63-0 (until January 2007)
ISBN 9781904978633 (after January 2007)

A CIP catalogue record for this book is available from the British Library

Colour reprographics by Wyndeham Icon, 3 & 4 Maverton Road, London E3 2JE

Printed and bound in Germany by Appl

Papers used by Ebury Publishing are natural, recyclable products made from wood grown in sustainable forests

Time Out Guides Limited
Universal House
251 Tottenham Court Road
London W1T 7AB
Tel + 44 (0)20 7813 3000
Fax + 44 (0)20 7813 6001
Email guides@timeout.com
www.timeout.com

Editorial
Editor Will Tizard
Deputy Editor Edoardo Albert
Listings Editors Hela Balinová, Radka Slabá, Iva Skochová
Proofreader Tamsin Shelton
Indexer Anna Norman

Editorial/Managing Director Peter Fiennes
Series Editor Ruth Jarvis
Deputy Series Editor Lesley McCave
Business Manager Gareth Garner
Guides Co-ordinator Holly Pick
Accountant Kemi Olufuwa

Design
Art Director Scott Moore
Art Editor Pinelope Kourmouzoglou
Senior Designer Josephine Spencer
Graphic Designer Henry Elphick
Digital Imaging Dan Conway
Ad Make-up Jenni Prichard

Picture Desk
Picture Editor Jael Marschner
Deputy Picture Editor Tracey Kerrigan
Picture Researcher Helen McFarland

Advertising
Sales Director Mark Phillips
International Sales Manager Ross Canadé
International Sales Executive Simon Davies
Advertising Sales (Prague) ARBOmedia.net Praha
Advertising Assistant Kate Staddon

Marketing
Group Marketing Director John Luck
Marketing Manager Yvonne Poon
Marketing & Publicity Manager, US Rosella Albanese

Production
Group Production Director Mark Lamond
Production Manager Brendan McKeown
Production Coordinator Caroline Bradford

Time Out Group
Chairman Tony Elliott
Managing Director Mike Hardwick
Financial Director Richard Waterlow
TO Magazine Ltd MD David Pepper
Group General Manager/Director Nichola Coulthard
TO Communications Ltd MD David Pepper
Group Art Director John Oakey
Group IT Director Simon Chappell

Contributors
Introduction Will Tizard. **History** Jonathan Cox, Paul Lewis (*Blazing resistance* Kristina Alda, *God's civil servants* Peter Konunczuk). **Prague Today** Drew Harris, Will Tizard (*How to get rich* Iva Skochová). **Architecture** Barbara Frye, Andy Markowitz (*Top this* Will Tizard). **Literary Prague** Will Tizard. **Beer** Will Tizard. **Where to Stay** Jacey Meyer, Jen Perez, Theodore Schwinke, Mark Nessmith, Dinah Spritzer. **Sightseeing** Carole Cadwalladr, Jonathan Cox, Frank Kuznik, Will Tizard, Emma Young. **Restaurants** Will Tizard. **Cafés, Pubs & Bars** Will Tizard. **Shops & Services** Jacy Meyer, Jennifer Sokolowsky, Theodore Schwinke (*Dressing for dark; Powergifting; Saps and gems* Jacy Meyer). **Festivals & Events** Will Tizard. **Children** Mark Nessmith, Alena Živnůstková. **Film** Raymond Johnston, Will Tizard. **Galleries** Mimi Rogers. **Gay & Lesbian** Wendy Wrangham. **Music** Frank Kuznik, Will Tizard (*No summer blues* Frank Kuznik; *Monkey Business, Sound Czech* Will Tizard). **Nightlife** Will Tizard (*Tram from hell* Frank Kuznik). **Sport & Fitness** Sam Beckwith (*Get in-line* Iva Skochová). **Theatre & Dance** Lizzie Lequesne, Frank Kuznik (*Breaking barriers* Frank Kuznik). **Trips Out of Town** Jonathan Cox, Pavla Kozáková, Iva Skochová, Will Tizard. **Directory** Mark Baker, Hela Balinová, Dave Rimmer, Will Tizard.

Maps by JS Graphics (john@jsgraphics.co.uk)

Photography Elan Fleisher, except: page 10 Peter Turnley/CORBIS; pages 12, 13, 16 akg-images; page 14 Milan Paumer; page 15 Bettmann/CORBIS; page 18 AP Photo/Libor Hajsky/CTK; page 22 Camera Press/David W Cerny; page 36 Pavel Hořejší; page 84 Stapleton Collection/CORBIS; pages 128, 158, 170, 216, 222 Rene Jakl; page 204 Will Tizard; pages 211, 212 2Media.cz; page 219 Katerina Sedova; pages 264, 267, 271, 277, 281, 282/283 Czech Tourism.

The following images were provided by the featured establishments/artists: pages 56, 67, 186, 215, 228, 235, 238, 255, 272, 274, 278, 284, 286, 287.

The Editor would like to thank the *Prague Post*, the Archa Theatre, Czech Tourism and especially Hela Balinová for the tireless help, and all contributors to previous editions of *Time Out Prague*, whose work forms the basis for parts of this book.

Contents

Introduction 6

In Context 9

History 10
Prague Today 22
Architecture 27
Literary Prague 34
Beer 37

Where to Stay 41

Where to Stay 42

Sightseeing 71

Introduction 72
Map: Key Sights 74
Hradčany 75
Map: Prague Castle 77
Malá Strana 88
Staré Město 98
Nové Město 115
Further Afield 127

Eat, Drink, Shop 135

Restaurants 136
Cafés, Pubs & Bars 162
Shops & Services 177

Arts & Entertainment 199

Festivals & Events 200
Children 205
Film 210
Galleries 215
Gay & Lesbian 224
Music 228
Nightlife 241
Theatre & Dance 250
Sport & Fitness 256

Resources A-Z 296
Vocabulary 313
Further Reference 314
Index 316
Advertisers' Index 322

Trips Out of Town 263

Getting Started 264
Day Trips 266
Overnighters: Town & Village 276
Overnighters: Country 284

Maps 323

Trips Out of Town 324
Prague Overview 325
Street Maps 326
Street Index 334

Directory 289

Getting Around 290

Prague Metro 336

Introduction

Czechs these days have success on their minds. It's proving to be an idea that takes getting used to. It's easy to look successful, of course – in fact the country's top new magazine recently advised its readers that this is a great first step to actually becoming successful.

This Dale Carnegie-style thinking is decidedly not what Bohemians are used to (though a surprising number of them are into mysticism of many flavours and any stripe of it that's useful in acquiring a BMW would surely be a hit in Prague). In fact, it's good to check twice before venturing across the street in the city's money-mad Nové Město district, lest a freshly minted executive flatten you while enjoying the trappings of corporate life.

Pedestrianised Staré Město is a safe bet, though. Feel free to crane your neck while walking around its blackened Gothic churches, pubs and townhouses. You're at little risk of loss of life. The only thing likely to flatten you here is a pack of beautiful young things headed off for a night of clubbing. In few other places in the world, except possibly Russia, are the newly on-the-go so eager to snap up status items and then put them on public dispay. Invariably good for a laugh, you may swear you've just stumbled into a fashion shoot for *Cosmopolitan* or *GQ* when you run into one of these impossibly good-looking bon vivants.

Fortunately the city's signature architecture isn't yielding so quickly to the more livable and efficient glass and steel shopping malls and offices. They're popping up, of course, but the old centre of town, with its timeless, even melancholy feel, will probably never surrender fully to the free market.

Or, as one hack recently put it (and it was one who actually produces books, rather than just tossing concepts about in pubs with the rest of us), the city's not really so tragic. There are many that have suffered far worse fates from centuries of occupation in this part of Europe. Rather, Prague has 'a gravity'. Readers of Kafka would certainly agree to that.

An odd quality in a place that's so clearly on the move. Perhaps, for all the quantum leaps in efficiency, customer service, reliability, transparency, healthy living and democratic reforms, life in Prague manages to remain well grounded somehow. In times of such tectonic change, that's a blessing indeed – and may be the only way to stay sane.

Whatever the case, in their race to be as Westernised as humanly possible, Czechs do generally manage to keep things wonderfully in perspective. No matter how demanding the new career, mortgage, shopping and dressing up (or down), there's always time for a beer or five with a friend. And no job yet has caused anyone to stop flirting, joking or debating the latest cocktail.

So here's your chance to get the scoop they've all been seeking – and no crushed ice, fresh mint or Cointreau is required. This killer intoxicant is simply known as Prague.

ABOUT THE TIME OUT CITY GUIDES

The seventh edition of *Time Out Prague* is one of an expanding series of around 50 Time Out City Guides produced by the people behind the successful listings magazines in London, New York, Chicago and other cities around the globe. Our guides are all written by resident experts who have striven to provide you with all the most up-to-date information you'll need to explore the city or read up on its background, whether you're a local or a first-time visitor.

THE LOWDOWN ON THE LISTINGS

Above all, we have tried to make this book as useful as possible. Addresses, opening times, websites, telephone numbers, admission prices, transport information and credit card details are included in our listings, as are details of selected other facilities, services and events. All were checked and correct at press time. However, owners and managers can change arrangements with little notice. Before you go out of your way, we strongly advise you to call and check the opening times, dates of exhibitions and other relevant particulars. While every effort has been made to ensure the accuracy of this guide, the publishers cannot accept responsibility for any errors that it may contain.

PRICES AND PAYMENT

The Czech Republic joined the European Union in 2004 and, all being well, it intends to adopt the euro as the national currency in 2010. However, you'll find that some hotels already accept payment in euros. We have listed prices in *koruna česká* or Czech crown (Kč) through-out, and we have noted whether venues take credit cards, detailing which of the major credit cards – American Express (AmEx), Diners Club (DC), MasterCard (MC), Visa (V) – each establishment accepts. Some shops, restaurants and attractions will also take travellers' cheques.

The prices given in this guide should be treated as guidelines, not gospel. Fluctuating exchange rates can cause prices to change rapidly. But if they vary wildly from those that we've quoted here, please write and let us know. We aim to give the best and most up-to-date advice, so we always want to know when you've been badly treated or overcharged.

THE LIE OF THE LAND
We have divided the city into areas and the relevant area name is given with each venue listed in this guide. Wherever possible, a map reference is provided for venues, indicating the page and grid reference for where it can be found in the street maps at the back of the book.

TELEPHONE NUMBERS
To dial Prague from outside the Czech Republic, first dial the international code, then 420 (for the Czech Republic and Prague) and finally the local number (always nine digits in Prague). To dial a mobile phone number from outside the Czech Republic, just call the international code, then 420, then the mobile number. For more information on telephones and codes, turn to p309 in the Directory chapter.

ESSENTIAL INFORMATION
For all the practical information you might need for visiting Prague, including emergency phone numbers and details of local transport, turn to the Directory chapter at the back of the guide. It starts on page 289.

LANGUAGE
Most Czechs living in Prague speak at least a little English, and while street signs are in Czech, most tourist information and menus are available in English. The majority of places are referred to by their Czech names but we have also included the English name where useful.

MAPS
At the back of this guide (and within each of the Sightseeing chapters) you'll find a series of maps providing overviews of the greater Prague area and its neighbourhoods in relation

to each other, along with detailed street maps of Hradčany, Malá Strana, Staré Město, Nové Město and some of the more outlying areas, including Žižkov and Vinohrady. There's also a comprehensive street index, a map showing the key tourist sights, a map of the region for planning trips out of town, a plan of Prague Castle and its environs, and a map of the Metro. The street maps start on page 326, and pinpoint the locations of the hotels (**❶**), restaurants (**❶**), and cafés, pubs and bars (**❶**) that are featured elsewhere in the guide.

LET US KNOW WHAT YOU THINK
We hope you enjoy *Time Out Prague*, and we'd like to know what you think of it. We welcome tips for places that you consider we should include in future editions and take note of your criticism of our choices. You can email your comments to us at guides@timeout.com.

There is an online version of this guide, and guides to over 140 international cities, at **www.timeout.com**.

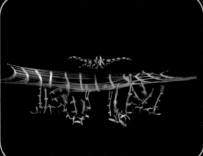

In Context

History	10
Prague Today	22
Architecture	27
Literary Prague	34
Beer	37

Features

Blazing resistance	14
God's civil servants	19
Key events	21
Still crazy How to get rich	24
Prague by numbers	26
Still crazy Top this	31
Under *Giraffe*'s spots	36
One-degree brew	39

Astronomical Clock. *See p101*.

The **Velvet Revolution**. See p19.

History

Between powers.

Bohemia's roots go deep: in 400 BC a Celtic tribe called the Boii occupied the region where the Czech Republic now lies. The Boii successfully repelled attacking armies for the best part of 1,000 years, but they were eventually driven out by the Germanic Marcomanni and Quadi tribes who, in turn, were wiped out by Attila the Hun in AD 451. Slavic tribes moved into the area sometime during the seventh century, ruled over by the Avars whose harsh regime provoked a successful Slavic rebellion.

IN THE BEGINNING

Czechs had to wait until the eighth century and the founding of the Přemyslid dynasty for real independence. One of the dynasty's origin myths relates that, in the absence of a male heir, Čech tribe leader Krok was succeeded by his soothsaying daughter Libuše. When the indignant men of the tribe told her to find a husband, she went into a trance and sent her white horse over the hills to find a ploughman with two spotted oxen. His name was Přemysl.

Prague's own origin myth holds that, standing atop Vyšehrad, Libuše foretold the birth of 'a city whose splendour will reach to the stars'. This time a craftsman making a door sill (*práh*) was found, for, as Libuše said, 'mighty Lords bend before a low door'. His workshop was promptly declared the site of the Praha and hence Prague was born.

In the ninth century Charlemagne briefly occupied the region. The realignment of power this caused allowed the foundation of a Slavic state in Moravia. The second king of Great Moravia, Rastislav (AD 846-70), cemented its cultural and historic importance by asking the Byzantine Emperor Michael III for Slavic-speaking Christian apostles to help end the worship of sun gods. The emperor sent Greek monks, the brothers Cyril and Methodius, who not only converted the people but developed the Cyrillic alphabet still used in many Slavic nations.

Slav leader Svatopluk (AD 871-94) sided with the Germans and seized power, building an empire that encompassed Moravia, Bohemia and

Slovakia. After his death the Magyars took a piece of Slovakia and held on to it until the early 20th century, disrupting all attempts to unite Slovaks and Czechs.

ON THE FEAST OF STEPHEN

Over the next four centuries Bohemia rode a rollercoaster from chaos to political supremacy in Central Europe. Although there are Christmas carols that still sing his praises, many Czech nobles felt that 'Good King' Wenceslas (actually Prince Václav or Wenceslas, 921-35) sold out to the Germans. They backed Wenceslas's brother, Boleslav the Cruel (935-67), who had Wenceslas murdered in 935 in the present-day town of Olomouc. Prague was made a bishopric in 973, thus completing the Christianisation of Bohemia, but internal fighting soon broke out.

National prestige reached new heights with Přemysl Otakar II (1253-78) grabbing Cheb from the Germans and briefly controlling an empire that stretched from Florence to Poland. An invasion by Holy Roman Emperor Rudolf of Habsburg in 1276 soon supplanted the Přemysls when the last one, Václav III, was assassinated in 1306.

German emigration to the Czech lands flourished, and the new arrivals assumed great influence over the Church and the trades, dividing Prague into three autonomous areas: Malá Strana, Hradčany and Staré Město (Old Town). Malá Strana's Jewish community was forced into a ghetto in Staré Město.

> ## 'King John attempted to recreate the Knights of the Round Table by inviting all the great paladins of Europe to the city. Unfortunately, no one came.'

By the 14th century Czech and German nobles were in conflict, as they would be from that time on. In 1310 John of Luxembourg, the 14-year-old son of the Holy Roman Emperor, was elected king of Bohemia, but his contribution was limited to attempting to re-create the Knights of the Round Table by inviting all the great paladins of Europe to the city. Unfortunately, none turned up, though Prague did gain a town hall, became the dominant centre of Bohemia and scored an archbishopric in 1344.

After John died in a kamikaze charge against Welsh archers at the Battle of Crécy, his son Charles IV was elected Holy Roman Emperor in 1346, which made his position as king of Bohemia unassailable. With that prestige behind him, Charles (1346-78) launched a

golden age and Prague even managed to escape the Black Death in 1348. Laying claim to a Přemyslid lineage through his mother, the 'Father of his Country' brought the 23-year-old Swabian architect Peter Parler to Prague to build the Charles Bridge and to work on St Vitus's Cathedral. In 1348 he established Central Europe's first university, then founded the Nové Město (New Town) along modern grid principles, unlike the warren of workshops that was Staré Město.

Charles declared the union of Bohemia, Moravia, Silesia and Upper Lusatia indissoluble and grafted bits of Germany on to Bohemia.

NOT-SO-GOOD KING WENCESLAS

His incorrigible son, Wenceslas IV (1378-1419), was at least champion of the common man. He would go out shopping dressed in commoners' clothing and execute any swindlers; soon Prague was crime-free.

He also railed against the Church, however, and at his christening he was alleged to have urinated into the holy water. He is said to have spent his last years in a drunken stupor and barely escaped imprisonment by the nobles.

In 1403 the rector of Prague University, Jan Hus, took up the campaign against Church corruption. German academics left for Leipzig to found their own university and the Church deemed Hus's arguments heretical.

In November 1414 Hus was summoned by Wenceslas's brother, Sigismund, King of Hungary, to appear before the General Council at Constance. Hus went in good faith but on arrival was arrested and ordered to recant. He refused and on his 46th birthday was burnt.

Hus became a martyr to two vital Czech hopes: reform of the Church and independence from German dominance. His motto 'truth will prevail' – still chanted during the Velvet Revolution of 1989 – became a rallying cry for his followers.

HUSSITES GIVE 'EM HELL

A mob of several hundred Czech nobles stormed the Nové Město town hall on 30 July 1419 and threw the mayor and his councillors through the window to their deaths, thus minting that quintessentially Czech form of protest, defenestration.

When Wenceslas died in an apoplectic fit a few days later, Hussite mobs marked the occasion by rioting and sacking the monasteries. Sigismund elbowed his way on to the Bohemian throne, but radical preachers such as Jan Želivský furiously denounced him and Rome. The Pope called for a holy crusade against Bohemia, while in return radical Hussites burnt alive nine monks in Prague.

Rudolf II.

suppress Protestant dissidents, while inviting the Society of Jesus to Bohemia to spearhead the Counter-Reformation.

AT THE CENTRE OF EMPIRE

In 1583 the Habsburg Rudolf II (1576-1611) moved his court from Vienna to Prague and, for the first time in 200 years, the city became the centre of an empire. But the Empire badly needed a man of action, vision and direction to deal with Turkish invaders raging to the south and the demands of Bohemia's Protestants. What it got was a dour, eccentric monarch engrossed in alchemy, who tended to ignore everyone except Otakar, his pet lion. While Europe headed towards the Thirty Years' War, Prague became a surreal fantasy world.

Yet Rudolfine Prague was a dazzling confluence of art, science and mysticism, host to scores of brilliant or mad creatives. As word of Rudolf's sponsorships spread, the flood began. One recipient was Tycho Brahe, the Danish astronomer who first shattered Aristotle's theories, had a metal nose and died of an intestinal implosion after overeating. As Turkish armies thrust northwards, however, and an attack on Vienna loomed, a coterie of archdukes concluded that Rudolf had to go. His brother Matthias picked up the reins.

THROUGH THE WINDOW

Neither Matthias nor his successor, Ferdinand II, both strong Counter-Reformation Catholics, did much to win over Protestants. In Prague, on 23 May 1618, an assembly of Protestants marched to the Old Royal Palace at Prague Castle. They were met by the emperor's die-hard Roman Catholic councillors, Slavata and Martinic, who were then thrown out the window but landed in a dung heap and survived.

Prague's most famous defenestration turned out to be the first act of the Thirty Years' War. Then Frederick of the Palatinate, son-in-law of James I of England and Scotland, was elected to the Bohemian throne and failed spectacularly to rally the Protestant princes of Europe to defend Bohemia. On 8 November 1620 the Protestants were trounced at the Battle of White Mountain (Bílá Hora) on the outskirts of Prague.

On the first anniversary of the defenestration, 27 Protestant leaders were beheaded on Old Town Square, their heads then skewered on the towers of Charles Bridge.

Ferdinand maintained that it was 'better to have no population than a population of heretics'. Soon Bohemia lost three-quarters of its native nobility, along with its eminent scholars and any remaining vestige of national independence. War further reduced its population from three million to 900,000. Three-quarters of the land in

Rome's call to arms against the heretic nation was taken up all over Europe and the Czechs were soon surrounded. They were united, however, behind a powerful moral cause and their brilliant one-eyed general, Jan Žižka. He not only repelled the enemies from Vítkov hill in what is now Žižkov in Prague, but, by 1432, he and his Warriors of God were pillaging all the way up to the Baltic coast. Women fought and died alongside men.

Most Hussites, known as Praguers, were moderate and middle class and their leaders were based at Prague University. The more extreme group, known as Táborites, were based on a fortified hillside. They banned all class divisions, shared their property and held religious services only in Czech.

Unable to win a holy war, the Pope invited the Czechs to discuss a peace settlement, but that proved unnecessary when, in 1434, the Praguers marched their army down to wipe out 13,000 Táborites at the Battle of Lipany.

BOHEMIA'S FIRST KING

During the Hussite wars, the Church's power was devastated and the vacuum filled by the nobles, who seized Church property and ruled, with considerably less mercy than the monks, over the peasants. The new Czech king, George of Poděbrady (Jiří z Poděbrad), tried to restore order by choosing successors from the Polish Jagellon dynasty. But after George's death in 1471, Vladislav II, then Ludvík, ruled ineffectually in absentia. After Ludvík's death, the Estates of Bohemia elected the Habsburg Duke Ferdinand I king of Bohemia. This foreign Catholic monarch sent troops into Prague to

Bohemia was seized to pay war expenses. All Protestants who refused to abandon their faith were driven from the country and the towns and villages filled with German immigrants. Jesuits swarmed in to 're-educate', and the peasants were forced to stay and work the land.

General Wallenstein (or Valdštejn), a Bohemian-born convert from Protestantism, became leader of the Imperial Catholic armies of Europe and scored spectacular victories, but the emperor's Jesuit advisors conspired to have him dismissed. Wallenstein, whose palace still covers much of Malá Strana and who had been secretly negotiating with the Swedish enemy, then joined the Protestants.

'Czech heritage now rested entirely with the enslaved and illiterate peasantry.'

After he entered Bohemia in 1634 Czech hopes for a Wallenstein victory were dashed when a band of Irish mercenaries jumped him in Cheb, stabbed him and dragged him down the stairs to his death. The Thirty Years' War petered out on Charles Bridge in 1648, as Swedish Protestants scuffled with newly Catholicised students and Jews.

CZECHING IN
By the mid-17th century German had replaced Czech as the official language of government. The lifeline of Czech heritage now rested entirely with the enslaved and illiterate peasantry. Meanwhile, the oppression resulted in the construction of Prague's most beautiful baroque palaces and churches.

During the 18th century Empress Maria Theresa centralised Bohemia with a new wave of Germanisation in schools and government. Maria Theresa's successor, the enlightened despot Joseph II, had little patience with the Church, though, and kicked out the Jesuits. He nationalised the education system, freed Jews from the ghetto and expanded the Empire's bureaucracy. As the industrial revolution began, this was all good news for the Czechs.

Though the Czech language had gone underground, a revival gradually took root. By the end of the 18th century, suppressed works were published, notably Balbín's *Defence of the Czech Language*; the Bohemian Diet began to whisper in Czech; the Church, seeing rows of empty pews, started to preach in Czech; and Emperor Leopold II even established a chair in Czech Language at Prague University.

The cultural revival continued under Ferdinand V (1835-48), with Josef Dobrovský's *Detailed Textbook of the Czech Language* and František Palacký's *History of the Czech Nation*, while Prague's theatres staged patriotic dramas.

1848: AN EMPIRE SHAKEN
Finally, the Czechs demanded equal rights for their language in government and schools. As the 1848 revolutions swept Europe, Emperor Ferdinand V tossed promises Prague's way.

Jan Hus. *See p11.*

Blazing resistance

Czechs by and large have coped with occupation by lying low and biding their time. So the armed resistance to, and desperate escape from, communist oppression by the Mašín group still provokes bitter controversy.

During their two-year struggle in the early 1950s, the band led by the Mašín brothers stole weapons, distributed anti-communist pamphlets, attacked police stations and committed acts of sabotage. They also killed four people while escaping across the border to avoid being imprisoned by the authorities.

The two Mašín brothers, Josef and Ctirad, along with another member of the gang, Milan Paumer, successfully reached West Berlin, 250 kilometres (155 miles) away, despite being hunted by thousands of soldiers and police. Two other members of the group were arrested on the way and later executed.

Demonised by the communists for decades, even today some call the Mašíns murderers. Others argue that their deeds were justified and indeed constituted the only way to successfully fight the pre-1989 regime.

Petitions to the state by organisations such as the Political Prisoners Confederation that call for the Mašíns to be decorated for valour have repeatedly met with failure.

Not everyone is afraid of the Mašín controversy, however. By way of celebrating the group's escape across the Iron Curtain, five Czechs set out in October 2005 to re-enact the escape. The ten-day journey, most of it on foot, took them from the Czech-German border to what was once Checkpoint Charlie in Berlin.

'It's important to keep reminding people of the communist past,' said one of the project organisers, Ondrej Karas. 'Many Czechs today aren't aware of the horrors committed by the regime in the 1950s.'

'Czechs like their heroes to be passive victims,' said Pavel Novák, another of the five travellers. 'But the communist regime declared a war on the Czech people. Actively fighting back was not only justified but heroic.'

So why do so many Czechs still believe the Mašíns were essentially terrorists? Some attribute the tarnishing to the remaining hold of the Communist Party, which still vilifies the brothers and won around 20 per cent of the vote in the last two parliamentary elections, most recently in summer 2006.

It's all too familiar to Josef Mašín, the younger of the brothers, who is now 73 and lives in California. 'Czech society won't find any closure so long as communists continue to abuse democratic processes to promote their own goals,' he says, 'which have cost society tens of millions of lives in the past.'

But Paumer, another surviving member of the group, finds hope in the willingness of young Czechs today to commemorate the escape. 'It's never too late,' he says.

But the Habsburg general, Prince Windischgrätz, fired on a peaceful gathering in Wenceslas Square, provoking a riot to give himself an excuse for wholesale suppression. The new emperor, Franz Josef (1848-1916), came to the throne on 2 December 1848 on a tidal wave of terror, then declared all Habsburg territories to be one entity.

A group known as the Young Czechs attacked the more moderate Prague establishment for pursuing a 'policy of crumbs'. Adopting Jan Hus as their hero and supported by Realist Party leader Professor Tomáš Garrigue Masaryk, they swept the 1891 elections to the Diet.

Czechs finally began to forge the political, social and economic infrastructure of a nation. Rapid industrialisation transformed the region, and an efficient rail network linked the Czech lands to the European economy. Industrialisation also gave rise to working-class political movements and Czech arts flourished. The era produced composers Smetana, Dvořák and Janáček, and painters such as Mucha. The Czech Academy of Sciences and Arts also achieved renown.

Professor Masaryk.

WORLD WAR I

The Czechs assumed during World War I that they could win concessions on a federal constitution in return for support for the war effort. The Empire didn't agree, and the Czechs soon realised that their best hopes for autonomy lay in the downfall of the Empire itself. Czechs deserted to the other side and in Prague an underground society, which was known as the 'Mafia', waged a campaign of agitation against the imperial regime.

Masaryk and Edvard Beneš drummed up Allied support for an independent state. Europe's elite hardly signed up to that, but the United States took the lead, and granted de jure recognition to a provisional Czechoslovak government under Masaryk.

On 28 October 1918 a National Committee member, Antonín Švehla, marched into the Corn Institute and announced that the Committee was going to take over food production. Later that day the Habsburg government sent a note to the American president, Woodrow Wilson, acquiescing to Czechoslovak independence.

INDEPENDENCE AND ETHNIC TENSIONS

With little damage from the war, a well-developed industrial base, coal and iron, an efficient communications infrastructure and a highly-trained and educated workforce, the new Republic of Czechoslovakia bloomed into a liberal democracy.

Slovaks, however, were largely an agricultural people long ruled by Hungarians rather than Habsburgs and, unlike the Czechs, they looked upon the Catholic Church as a symbol of freedom.

The Jews, who comprised only 2.5 per cent of the population, formed a significant part of the intelligentsia, but spoke German, which created Czech resentment. The Germans, who formed 23 per cent of the population, presented the biggest obstacle to a united nation. Still powerful, though now resentful of being in a minority, they were spread throughout the Czech lands but concentrated in Prague and the Sudeten area near the German border.

Konrad Henlein, head of the pro-Hitler Sudeten German Fatherland Front, cashed in on all these tensions. By 1935 the Sudeten Party was the second largest parliamentary bloc. In 1938 the Sudeten Nazis demanded union with Germany. British Prime Minister Neville Chamberlain, for whom the Sudeten crisis was a 'quarrel in a faraway country between people of whom we know nothing', went to Munich with the French premier to meet both Mussolini and Hitler. All of the parties involved (except Czechoslovakia, which wasn't invited) agreed that Germany should take the Sudetenland in exchange for Hitler's promise of peace.

With Poland and Hungary also eyeing its borders, Czechoslovakia found itself encircled, and abandoned by its allies. Six months later Hitler took the rest of the country, with Poland snatching Těšín and Hungary grabbing parts of southern Slovakia. On 14 March 1939, a day before Hitler drove into Prague, the Slovaks declared independence and established a Nazi puppet government.

DARKNESS DESCENDS

In Czechoslovakia, now the Reich Protectorate of Bohemia and Moravia, everybody except for Jews and Gypsies fared better under occupation than did people in most other European countries. A National Government of Czechs was set up to follow Reich orders. Hitler had often expressed his hatred of 'Hussite Bolshevism', but he needed Czech industrial resources and skilled manpower for his war machine.

Hitler made fierce examples of resisters; 1,200 students were sent to concentration camps for demonstrating, and all Czech universities were closed. Reinhard Heydrich, later to chair the infamous Wannsee Conference on the Final Solution, was appointed Reichsprotektor and began rounds of calculated terror, while enticing workers and peasants to collaborate.

Beneš fled to London where he joined Jan Masaryk (son of Tomáš) to form a provisional Czechoslovak government in exile. There they were joined by thousands of Czech soldiers and airmen, who fought alongside the British forces. Czech intelligence agents passed approximately 20,000 messages on to London, including the details of Germany's ambitious plans for the invasion of the Soviet Union.

Beneš, with the help of the British Special Operations Executive, hatched a plan for the assassination of Heydrich using British-trained Czech parachutists. Jan Kubiš and Josef Gabčik were dropped into Bohemia and, on 27 May 1942, successfully ambushed Heydrich's open-top Mercedes, fatally injuring the hated Reichsprotektor.

The assassins and their accomplices were hunted down to the crypt of the Orthodox Cathedral of Ss Cyril and Methodius. Anyone with any connection to the paratroopers was murdered. The villages of Lidice and Ležáky were mistakenly picked out for aiding the assassins and razed to the ground; the men were murdered, the women were sent to concentration camps (in Ležáky they were shot) and the children were 're-educated', placed with German families or killed. The transportation of Jews to concentration camps was stepped up.

Occasional acts of sabotage continued, but the main resistance took place in the Slovak puppet state, where an uprising that began on 30 August 1944 lasted four months. The Czechs' act of defiance came in the last week of the war. In May 1945 5,000 died during a four-day uprising in Prague. The US forces that had just liberated Pilsen (Plzeň) to the west were only a few miles from Prague. But Allied leaders at Yalta had promised the Soviets the honour of liberating Prague, so General Eisenhower ordered his troops to pull back. General Patton was willing to ignore the order and sent a delegation to the leaders of the Prague uprising, asking for an official request for the American troops to liberate the capital. The communist leaders refused. Although communist power was not consolidated until 1948, the country already found itself inside the Soviet sphere of influence.

More than 300,000 Czechoslovaks perished in the war, the majority of them Jews. The Jewish population of Czechoslovakia was destroyed. Most Jews were rounded up and sent to the supposedly 'model' Theresienstadt (Terezín) ghetto. Many died there, but the remainder were transported to Auschwitz and other concentration camps. In fact, around 90 per cent of Prague's ancient Jewish community was murdered.

For at least 1,000 years the community had been walled into a ghetto in Staré Město, where life was characterised by pogroms, poverty and mysticism. Between the late 18th century, when they left the ghetto, and the arrival of the Nazis, Jews had dominated much of Prague's cultural life. Now the rich literary culture that had produced Franz Kafka had been wiped out. Indeed, Kafka's family perished in Auschwitz. The only thing that saved some of Prague's synagogues and communal Jewish buildings from destruction was the Nazis' morbid intention to use them after the war to house 'exotic exhibits of an extinct race'.

The Czech government under the Reich Protectorate actively supported the

extermination of its Romany citizens and helped to run dozens of concentration camps for Gypsies all over Bohemia and Moravia. An estimated 90 per cent of the region's Czech Romany died in Nazi concentration camps, mostly in Germany and Poland. Beneš's faith in liberalism had been dented by the way the Western powers had ditched his country. He began to perceive the political future of Czechoslovakia as a bridge between capitalism and communism. His foreign minister Jan Masaryk was less idealistic, stating that 'cows like to stop on a bridge and shit on it'.

Beneš needed a big power protector and believed that, if he could win Stalin's trust, he could handle the popular Communist Party of Czechoslovakia, while keeping the country independent and democratic. During the war he signed a friendship and mutual assistance treaty with the Soviet Union, and later on he established a coalition government comprising principally communists and socialists. In 1945 Stalin knew that a straightforward takeover of a formerly democratic state was not politically expedient. He needed Beneš as an acceptable front in order to buy time. For all his tightrope diplomacy, Beneš was effectively shuffling his country into Soviet clutches.

COMMUNIST TAKEOVER

The Soviets and Czech communists were widely regarded as war heroes and won a handsome victory in the 1946 elections. Klement Gottwald became prime minister of a communist-led coalition. Beneš, still hoping that Stalinist communism could co-exist in a pluralistic democracy, remained president. The communists made political hay, setting up workers' militias in the factories, installing communist loyalists in the police force and infiltrating the army and rival socialist parties.

One of the first acts of the government, approved by the Allies, was to expel more than 2.5 million Germans from Bohemia. It was a popular move and, as Klement Gottwald remarked, 'an extremely sharp weapon with which we can reach to the very roots of the bourgeoisie'. Thousands were executed or given life sentences and many more were killed in a wave of self-righteous revenge.

In 1947 Czechoslovakia was forced to turn down the American economic aid promised by the Marshall Plan. Stalin knew that aid came with strings, and he was determined to be the only puppetmaster. In February 1948, with elections looming and communist popularity declining, Gottwald sent the workers' militias on to the streets of Prague. The police occupied crucial party headquarters and offices, and the country was incapacitated by a general strike. Beneš's

diplomatic skill was no match for the brutal tactics of Moscow-trained revolutionaries. With the Czech army neutralised by communist infiltration and the Soviet army casting a long shadow over Prague, Beneš capitulated and consented to an all-communist government. Gottwald now became Czechoslovakia's first 'Working Class President'.

Shortly after the coup Jan Masaryk fell to his death from his office window. The communists said it was suicide. But, when his body was found, the window above was tightly fastened. The defenestration had a distinctly Czech flavour, but the purges that followed had the stamp of Moscow. They were directed against resistance fighters, Spanish Civil War volunteers, Jews (often survivors of concentration camps) and anyone in the party hierarchy who might have posed a threat to Moscow. The most infamous trial was that of Rudolf Slánský, a loyal sidekick of Gottwald who had orchestrated his fair share of purges. After being showered with honours, he was arrested just a few days later. In March 1951 Slánský and ten senior communists (mostly Jews) were found guilty of being Trotskyite, Titoist or Zionist traitors in the service of US imperialists. They 'confessed' under torture, and eight were sentenced to death.

PRAGUE SPRING

Gottwald dutifully followed his master, Stalin, to the grave in 1953 but the paranoia that had gripped Prague took a long time to ease. By the 1960s communist student leaders and approved writers on the fringes of the party hierarchy began tentatively to suggest that, just possibly, Gottwald and Stalin might have taken the wrong route to socialism. Slowly, the drizzle of criticism turned into a shower of anger and awkward questions. Then, on 5 January 1968, an alliance of disaffected Slovak communists and reformists within the party replaced Antonín Novotný with a reformist Slovak communist named Alexander Dubček.

For the next eight months the whole world watched the developments in Prague as Dubček rehabilitated political prisoners and virtually abandoned press censorship. Understandably, Moscow was alarmed and tried to intimidate Dubček by holding full-scale military manoeuvres in Czechoslovakia, but still the reforms continued. On 27 June 70 leading writers signed the widely published *Two Thousand Word Manifesto* supporting the reformist government. Suppressed literature was published or performed on stage and Prague was infused with the air of freedom. Dubček called it 'socialism with a human face'.

Soviet leader Leonid Brezhnev failed to influence the Czechoslovak leader. On the night of 20 August 1968 nearly half a million Warsaw

The face of socialism: the Soviet invasion of 20 August 1968.

Pact troops entered the country, took over Prague Castle and abducted Dubček and his closest supporters. The leaders fully expected to be shot, but Brezhnev needed some sort of a front for his policy of repression with a human face, so Dubček was returned to Prague eight days later.

Meanwhile, on the streets of Prague, crowds of thousands of people confronted the tanks. Free radio stations using army transmitters continued to broadcast, and newspapers went underground and encouraged Czechs to refuse any assistance to the occupiers. Street signs and house numbers were removed, and the previously Stalinist workers' militia found a way to defend a clandestine meeting of the national party conference.

'An era of grey, everyday totalitarian consumerism had begun.'

The resistance prevented nothing. Dubček stayed in power for eight more months and watched his collaborators being replaced by pro-Moscow ministers. In April 1969 Dubček too was removed in favour of Gustav Husák, who was eager to push for more of Moscow's 'normalisation'. Husák purged the party and state machinery, the army and the police, the unions, the media, every company and every other organ of the country that might have a voice in the nation's affairs. Anyone who was not for Husák was assumed to be against him. Within a short time every aspect of daily Czechoslovak life was dictated by Husák's many mediocre yes-men. Without firing a shot, Husák was able to subdue the nation back into apathy by permitting an influx of consumer goods.

SUICIDE OR MARTYR?

On 16 January 1969 a 21-year-old philosophy student called Jan Palach stood at the top of Wenceslas Square, poured a can of petrol over himself and set himself alight. He died four days later. A group of his friends had agreed to burn themselves to death one by one until the restrictions were lifted. On his deathbed Palach begged his friends not to go through with it, though some did.

Palach's death symbolised, with malicious irony, the extinguishing of the flame of hope. As Václav Havel wrote: 'People withdrew into themselves and stopped taking an interest in public affairs. An era of apathy and widespread demoralisation began, an era of grey, everyday totalitarian consumerism'.

Instead of mass arrests, tortures and show trials, the communists now bound up the nation in an endless tissue of lies and fabrications, and psychologically bludgeoned all critical thought by rewarding people for not asking awkward questions and punishing them for refusing to spy on their neighbours. Punishment could mean spells in prison and severe beatings, but for most it meant losing a good job and being forced into menial work. During this time, Prague had an abnormally high percentage of window cleaners with PhDs.

There were some, however, who refused to be bowed. A diverse alternative culture emerged in which underground (*samizdat*) literature was circulated around a small group of dissidents. In December 1976 a group led by Václav Havel issued a statement demanding that leading Czechoslovak authorities should observe human rights obligations, and Charter 77 became a small voice of conscience inside the country, spawning a number of smaller groups trying to defend civil liberties. In 1989 it had 1,500 signatories. But there seemed little hope for real change unless events from outside took a new turn. Then, in the mid 1980s, Mikhail Gorbachev came to power in the Soviet Union and initiated his policy of *perestroika* and *glasnost*.

THE VELVET REVOLUTION

The Soviet leader came to Prague in 1988. When his spokesman was asked what he thought the difference was between the Prague Spring and *glasnost*, he replied '20 years'. In the autumn of 1989 the Berlin Wall came down and then the communist regimes of Eastern Europe began to falter. The Czechoslovak government, one of the most hardline regimes in Eastern Europe, seemed firmly entrenched until 17 November, when police violently broke up a demonstration on Národní třida commemorating the 50th anniversary of the closure of Czech universities by the Nazis. A rumour, picked up by Reuters news agency, said that a demonstrator had been killed. Another demonstration was called to protest against police brutality.

On 20 November, 200,000 people gathered in Prague to demand the resignation of the government. The police behaved with restraint and the demonstrations were broadcast on television. The government announced that the man who had allegedly been killed on the 17th was alive, but many were sceptical. Some months after the revolution it emerged that the KGB had probably been behind the rumour as part of a plan to replace the government with something in line with Soviet *glasnost*.

That there had not been a death made little difference ultimately. A committee of opposition groups formed itself into the Civic Forum (Občanské fórum), led by Václav Havel, who addressed the masses in Wenceslas Square. On 24 November 300,000 people assembled there to see him, joined by Dubček. The government had lost control of the media and millions watched the scenes on television. Students from Prague raced out to factories and farms to galvanise the workers into supporting a general strike on the 27th. Workers' militias had put the communists into power in 1948; it was crucial that they chose not to stand by communism in its final hour.

The acting communist prime minister, Adamec, also appealed to the crowds and further purges within the Communist Party followed. The party then declared that it felt

God's civil servants

Lord knows how the Czech Republic's going to sort out its biggest employment headache: 2,800 priests who technically work for the state. Along with Slovakia, this is the only country in the world where padres are government employees. The situation dates from the communist regime's seizure of all Church assets, including its staff, in 1949. As part of his strategy to control all facets of life the communist dictator Klement Gottwald put every cleric into state employment.

Now, although the Czech Republic has returned most of the churches and church land it confiscated to the Catholics and other denominations, it still employs most of the priests. And, at monthly wages of just 13,600 Kč, they're not happy about their employer.

Not surprisingly, this has led to rows. The Czech Culture Ministry, which administers clerical salaries, says that the Church claimed pay for 17 more priests than it actually has last year. Church officials deny this, one quipping that the state 'falsely accused the Prague archbishopric of having committed the crime of trade in dead souls'.

Furthermore, says Cardinal Miloslav Vlk, the country's most senior Catholic, his Church,

the country's biggest religious denomination, receives 28 million Kč less than it should.

The feud is only the latest wrinkle in an adversarial relationship the Church has had with the state, oh, since about 1620, when the Catholic Habsburgs beat back an uprising by the Protestant Czechs. Thus, there's a long tradition of baiting priests in Bohemia that certainly didn't improve under communism, which gleefully made use of this history to weaken religious loyalties. But with the Church often associated with foreign oppressors, a majority of Czechs even today are agnostics or atheists.

As for the pay dispute, Prime Minister Stanislav Gross, who has since stepped down owing to the controversy over his alleged unexplained income, at least managed to take decisive action on this unholy row while still in power. He ordered the Culture Ministry to pay 3.5 million Kč to the Prague archbishopric from government reserves.

The Czech system could eventually be scrapped as part of a wider restitution with the church, but until it is, the state is stuck paying priestly wages and insurance that totals around 818 million Kč a year.

that the 1968 Soviet invasion had been wrong after all, promising free elections and a multi-party coalition. It was all too late. A new government of reformist communists was proposed, but rejected by Civic Forum. Talks continued between the communists and Civic Forum for weeks until 27 December, when a coalition of strongly reformist communists and a majority of non-communists – mainly from Civic Forum – took power with Havel as president. Not a single person died. Havel's co-revolutionary Rita Klímová called it the Velvet Revolution. But in some ways, given the KGB's involvement in the handover of power, it might as well have been called the Velvet Putsch.

INTO THE WILD, WILD WEST

For months after the revolution Prague floated in a dream world and the playwright-president captured the world's imagination, but the serious issues of economic transformation were put off. In the summer of 1992 the right-of-centre Civic Democratic Party (ODS), led by Václav Klaus, a no-nonsense free-marketeer, was voted into power. But, just as Klaus got down to the business of privatisation and decentralisation, calls for Slovak independence were taken up by Vladimír Mečiar's Slovak separatist HZDS party.

Slovaks had always resented what they had felt was a benign neglect by Prague, and Havel had never been popular among them. One of his first acts as president was to abandon the arms trade, dealing a big blow to the Slovak economy. Slovaks complained that economic reforms were going too fast. But Klaus would not compromise and had a mandate from Czech voters to press on. Mečiar upped his separatist threats until, with Machiavellian manoeuvring, Klaus called Mečiar's bluff and announced that he would back Slovak independence.

> **'Highly educated Czechs set up successful internet businesses, leaving the countries further east to promote themselves on the back of cheap labour.'**

The two leaders divided up the assets of the state, and the countries peacefully parted ways on 1 January 1993 without so much as a referendum. Havel was elected president of the new Czech Republic, but Klaus had also outmanoeuvred him, forcing Havel into a predominantly ceremonial role.

Klaus indicated that he had little time for a policy of flushing out communists from

responsible positions (known as 'lustration'). Thus communists successfully dodged the spotlight amid a blizzard of accusations and counter-accusations. A significant number of Czechs seemed to have skeletons in their cupboards, and it became nearly impossible to untangle the good from the bad. Dissidents watched helplessly while communists remained in charge of the country's largest factories.

The first four years of the Czech Republic under Klaus's leadership produced massive privatisation changes, however, which helped make the Czechs the envy of the East. Foreign investors and businesses, along with a few savvy locals, quickly capitalised on the huge opportunities for profit and development.

ON A WORLD STAGE

Economic differences have increased drastically since 1992 but the Czech Republic has taken its place on the world stage. First came membership of NATO in 1999, then entry into the European Union in 2004. Klaus himself was forced out of power in 1997 following a campaign funding scandal, but returned as president in 2004.

With the country's moral leader, Václav Havel, now out of power, attention has shifted to more prosaic questions such as foreign investment, and the modernisation of the courts and the banks. Foreign investors still decry the lack of transparency and incentives (the tortuous bankruptcy system, for example, encourages start-up directors to take the money and run when businesses go bad) and Klaus's conservatives looked poised to take back control of Parliament.

The Social Democrats have fallen into scandals of their own as voters and journalists grow more accustomed to demanding accountability. Two Social Democrat prime ministers have lost their seats of late, with Stanislav Gross driven out in 2005 over alleged unexplained income and business contracts his wife landed. Meanwhile, the third prime minister of the party's reign, Jiří Paroubek, has set precedents in actually firing members of his cabinet who were caught in corruption probes, and in appointing a pitbull of a health minister, David Rath, to modernise the money-haemorrhaging national healthcare system. Pension and labour reforms remain huge obstacles as society is slowly weaned out of state care from the cradle to the grave.

In 2006 the economy remained bullish, with the information sector accounting for most growth as highly educated Czechs set up successful internet businesses, leaving the countries further east to promote themselves on the back of cheap labour.

Key events

c400 BC Celtic Boii tribe occupies Bohemia.
AD 600s Slavic tribes settle in region.
c700 The Přemyslid dynasty begins.
863 Cyril and Methodius bring writing and Christianity to Great Moravia.
929 'Good King' Wenceslas is killed by his brother and becomes a martyr and the Czech patron saint.
973 Prague is made a bishopric.
1235 Staré Město gets a Royal Charter; Jews forced into the ghetto.
1253 Otakar II becomes king.
1306 Přemyslid dynasty ends with the murder of Václav III.
1346 Charles IV becomes Holy Roman Emperor and king of Bohemia; founds Central Europe's first university in Prague.
1352 Swabian architect Peter Parler begins work on St Vitus's Cathedral.
1357 Foundations laid for Charles Bridge.
1378 King Wenceslas IV crowned.
1389 3,000 Jews killed in pogrom.
1403 Jan Hus, rector of Prague University, begins preaching against Church corruption.
1415 Hus, having been excommunicated and declared a heretic, is burned at the stake.
1419 Hussite mob throws the mayor out of new town hall window; Hussite wars begin.
1420s-30s Hussites repel all attacks.
1434 Moderate Hussites wipe out the radicals and the Pope agrees to allow them considerable religious freedom.
1458 Czech noble George of Poděbrady becomes the 'People's king', but is soon excommunicated by the Pope.
1471-1526 Jagellon dynasty rules Bohemia.
1526 Habsburg rule begins with Ferdinand I.
1556 Ferdinand invites the Jesuits to Prague to counter fierce anti-Catholicism in Bohemia.
1583 Habsburg Emperor Rudolf II moves the court to Prague for the next 20 years.
1609 Tycho Brahe's work leads to his *Laws of Planetary Motion*; Rudolf concedes some religious rights to Bohemia's Protestants.
1618 Protestants throw two Catholic councillors from a window in the castle, thus starting the Thirty Years' War.
1620 Protestants lose the Battle of White Mountain.
1621 27 Protestant leaders executed in Old Town Square.
1648 The Thirty Years' War ends on Charles Bridge as the citizens of Prague repel the invading Swedes.

1740 Maria Theresa becomes empress.
1743 French attack Prague.
1757 Prussians attack Prague.
1781 Emperor Joseph II abolishes the Jesuits and closes monasteries.
1848 Revolutions in Europe; unsuccessful uprisings in Prague against Austrian troops.
1893 Clearing of the Jewish ghetto begins.
1914 Outbreak of World War I; Habsburgs refuse concessions on federalism and Czech soldiers desert to the Allies.
1918 Czechoslovak Republic founded with Tomáš Masaryk as its first president.
1938 Chamberlain agrees to let Hitler take over the Sudetenland.
1939 Hitler takes all Czechoslovakia.
1942 Czech paratroopers assassinate Reichsprotektor Reinhard Heydrich. Nazis destroy villages Lidice and Ležáky in revenge.
1945 Prague uprising; the Red Army arrives.
1948 The Communist Party assumes power under Klement Gottwald.
1951 The Slánský show trials and mass purges take place.
1968 Reformist communist Dubček becomes first secretary and promotes 'socialism with a human face', but the Prague Spring is crushed by Warsaw Pact troops.
1969 Philosophy student Jan Palach immolates himself in protest.
1977 The underground movement Charter 77 is established to monitor human rights abuses.
1989 Student demos turn into full-scale revolution and the communist regime falls.
1990 Poet, writer and anti-communist activist Václav Havel elected president of Czechoslovakia.
1993 The Slovak Republic and the Czech Republic divide and become separate, independent states.
1996 Michael Jackson's statue briefly takes up the spot vacated by Stalin's in Letná Park, as part of his History tour.
1998 The largest demonstrations since the Velvet Revolution sweep the city to celebrate the Czech ice hockey team winning an Olympic gold.
2000 The largest demonstrations since the Olympics fill Wenceslas Square to demand the ousting of Prime Minister Miloš Zeman and ODS head Václav Klaus.
2004 Havel steps down and the Czech Republic is admitted to the European Union.

Václav Klaus.

Prague Today

Real change is afoot – if you look very carefully –
and we don't mean malls.

Officially, 2006 was the year the Social Democrats fell from power. Tired of unkept promises that the old, the sick, labourers and students would finally be treated with some respect (and corruption in high places rooted out), the electorate gave the nod to the conservatives. They did it by a minuscule margin, it's true, but nevertheless, the party founded by Thatcherite, EU-bashing Václav Klaus was given the reins – or at least the prime minister's seat. Parliament, to everyone's annoyance, split 100-100 between the left- and right-wing blocs.

But what really happened on 2 and 3 June of that year, after an election campaign that often reached the level of farce, was not to be found in the 'Stalemate' headlines about Klaus's qualified victory and the confusion all around. The official story was one of cautious reform, and the move away from creaking systems and structures that the Czechs are used to but sick of. So nothing very different since 1989 threw all the gates open.

However, something significant did happen, but it was on the sidelines of the elections – as significant events often are in election years. The Green Party, for the first time in Czech history, made it into Parliament – just barely. That's not the telling event, though. What is, is how they did it. The party, of course, has been around for years, trying without much success to stir folks up about the importance of preserving open space in the city rather than giving it over unconditionally to traffic and developers in the name of boosting the economy. Occasionally, they also point out things like local zoning councils on the take or that returning to coal as an energy source will damage air quality, even if it does make the country less dependent on Russian natural gas.

Interesting, admittedly, but hardly the stuff of political success. Then came Martin Bursík.

A bored rich kid who won back a mansion in the centre of Prague through restitution, the process by which the state has slowly returned property confiscated from families by the old regime, Bursík took one look at the bickering Greens and saw gold. As an experienced marketer and successful businessman, he was not the dreadlocked, bike-riding flower child you might think of as a natural for the party. But he clearly knows how to create a hit brand and that's just what he did: Czechs were thoroughly disgusted with the existing political parties in Parliament and none of the efforts to revitalise their images was working. (One party even took to a guerrilla sticker campaign in which they plastered the city with mysterious messages suggesting a grassroots protest movement – 'It's legal to be a loser' was by far the most popular. The purple stickers, which covered streetlamps and tram stops, turned out to be just another product of an ad agency, one hired by the Freedom Union, a bunch of centre-right folks who'd split off from the more successful Civic Democrats, and the voters banished them in disappointment.)

Bursík had a more ingenious idea: what about rebranding the Greens as young people who care about the earth, something dear to the pastoral Czechs, but who also favour private enterprise and the free market? Who cares that balancing these philosophies is no small trick? Instead of protesting like losers outside unsafe chemical factories, they'd jump into bed with the business-friendly (and powerful) Civic Democrats, the party founded by Klaus.

It worked like a charm. Voters gave them well over the required five per cent of popular votes needed to get into Parliament – in fact, they gave them 6.92 per cent, a figure mighty impressive for a new entry into the halls of the deeply fractious Chamber of Deputies. And the share of seats they won, six, was just enough to prevent the left from controlling Parliament. Members of the Green Party looked perplexed at finding themselves in with the suits, but it was Bursík's show and that's where he wanted them. It added up to one big, but effective compromise. Metaphors, anyone?

A bit of context: Czechs tend to be careful people, not prone to radical change and reform – even if it's clear that much of the social network created by the pre-1989 regime is falling apart or wildly dysfunctional. Ask any Praguer on the street what they think of the pension, health, labour and education systems and they won't hesitate to tell you that they're *v prdeli* or, basically, arsed. Now ask them what should be done about it. They shrug. *Všechno jsou stejní hajzlové*, they'll say. 'They're all the same crap.'

If you're in politics, then, by definition you're corrupt. That's only natural, right?

With this kind of fatalism prevalent only 17 years into a democracy so many risked their lives and livelihoods to bring about, real, systemic change is not going to happen overnight. What's more, when politicians are expected to lie, cheat and steal for all they're worth, they're generally happy to live down to those sorts of expectations.

Yet, when a truly novel voice comes along, or a party not yet tainted by corruption scandals, it seems all hope is not dead among the voters. The 2006 general election featured some of the highest voter turnout since the first democratic vote after the Velvet Revolution. Granted, much of that was protest voting against the Social Democrats and Prime Minister Jiří Paroubek, also known by his moniker 'the steamroller'. Paroubek, the third leader of his party in as many years, had been brought in when his predecessor, Stanislav Gross, left office in spring 2005 after being unable to explain how he paid for his luxury flat.

'Most Czechs admit they believe in something – they just don't know quite what.'

Paroubek seemed a breath of fresh air at first, making dramatic statements and reshuffling his cabinet when corruption was exposed, at least when the cabinet member in question was expendable. In time, of course, it emerged that two of the most suspicious appointees in the administration weren't going anywhere: a justice minister who had helped a Qatari prince convicted of child molesting avoid Czech prison time remained in place despite the national outcry, and a health minister, David Rath, was given enormous powers to shake up the admittedly dysfunctional healthcare system despite having been caught charging drug companies millions of crowns for ads in the official magazine of the Czech Medical Chamber while he was its president.

Business as usual, in other words. Interestingly, though, instead of just tolerating it, voters tossed out the Social Dems and made the Greens kingmakers – or very nearly.

They say people take comfort in the familiar, even when they realise it's not particularly healthy or beneficial. That's certainly true of Czech voters: they didn't give anyone enough votes to empower real, dramatic changes in social care or, for that matter, business conditions. But they made a statement that they want new ideas and energy.

Still crazy How to get rich

Now that Czechs are becoming more comfortable with the lures of capitalism, fast realising that increasing income gaps are quite pleasant as long as you're the one digging it, so the strategies for getting rich quick are getting more creative.

They have to be, alas: the years when ordinary people got fields, castles or at least art deco apartment buildings returned to them in compensation for the property seizures of the old regime are long gone.

Becoming a member of the Czech nouveaux riches these days actually (gasp!) takes work. Fortunately, Czechs are inventive and ingenious – and the post-'89 generation is particularly so when it comes to avoiding hard work.

In a recent article, the weekly news magazine *Týden* offered 101 tips for getting rich, quite insightfully asserting that there has never been a better time to do so. Though any time's a good time for acquiring lucre, this particular survey seems to capture the zeitgeist.

Some more creative tips include making money through your children. There's always demand for hockey players (think sons) and models (insert daughter here). If you have a problem with child exploitation, remember that Jaromír Jágr is arguably the

world's best-paid hockey player and Karolina Kurková the most expensive model.

Other tips include strategies that already work successfully abroad: suing large corporations, bankrupting companies, buying the property of bankrupt companies cheap, positioning yourself to score hefty EU subsidies, or – if you crave all that and golden handshakes too – running for public office.

There are more traditional suggestions as well, ranging from investing in fast food and gourmet specialities, to buying the Canadian dollar (now that's living dangerously) and exporting antique cars.

Tip 101, for the worst-case scenario, is the 'hard work method'. This, of course, will not get you much street cred around the Prague of the 21st century. The old-school idea of starting with an entry-level job, working your way up through middle management and, finally, at age 49, arriving at a position that looks tolerable on a business card, somehow doesn't resonate with most young Czechs.

For the more visionary types, *Týden* suggests that you might just get rich by looking rich. So get out there with your designer togs, stick to the top-shelf liquor, run up those credit card bills and start living beyond your means. Welcome to capitalism.

Clearly, folks are searching. Could it be that they're seeking something they can believe in?

The Czech Republic is known for being one of the most agnostic nations on earth – with a *Chicago Tribune* story in April 2006 claiming that only 19 per cent of the populace profess any belief in God, although other polls find more than double that percentage to be theists. Whichever statistic is correct, the *Tribune* report went on to point out that most Czechs, when pressed, will admit that they believe in something – they just don't know quite what. This 'somethingism' has prompted enormous interest in Eastern religions, mysticism, Kabbalah and the occult. Meanwhile, hundreds of state-owned churches stand empty and falling apart in Bohemia and Moravia. With small congregations and not enough funds for shoring them up, the Catholic Church has said it doesn't want the state to return them. It can't afford the upkeep. Thus, the bishops say, they're just fine with seeing them turned into museums, hotels, even nightclubs.

It's not such a stretch after all – it's obvious that young Czechs are looking for something

to elevate their lives and clubs might seem to offer that in the short term. At least they'd be back in a church while doing so. But searches for meaning and fulfilment can be hazardous.

The levels of hard drug use among Czechs are chilling these days: health studies showed a ten per cent rise in the use of crystal meth, known locally as *pervetin*, among young people in 2005. The stuff is easily made from over the counter cold medicine, which contains the vital ingredient pseudoephedrine. Hardly relegated to the poor and disenfranchised, it's considered a bargain high by thousands of kids who come from middle-class families.

Others search elsewhere for thrills and easy money. The Czech porn business has all but eclipsed Hungary's, which was long considered the foremost centre for production in Europe. Surveys, meanwhile, indicated that a large percentage of youth in Prague consider 'sex for money' to be nothing unusual.

There are many forms of paying for thrills, of course. Czechs now congregate in gleaming citadels of chrome capitalism like the malls at Černý Most, Palác Flora and Nový Smíchov, all of which feature international chain stores along with signatures of Western teen life, like fast food courts and modern multiplex movie theatres. Citizens have also skipped past the phone-in-the-home phenomenon and gone directly mobile. Foregoing the bureaucracy of landline installation, many small businesses use no regular phone line at all.

Meanwhile, visitors to Prague's greatest shrine of art nouveau, the fin-de-siècle Municipal House (*see p118*), during the next year are bound to be breathing some dust as what is sure to be the biggest mall yet goes up in a former baroque barracks across the street. And all of this construction is happening only a block away from what was until now the biggest, swishest shopping mall in town, Slovanský dům on Na Příkopě.

'Czech voters finally roused themselves from drugs, porn and shopping to get to the ballot box.'

In a society undergoing such fundamental shifts, and where civic leaders are no more respected than most parents, who long ago had to learn compromise to survive, is any of this really surprising? Sadly, probably not.

Nor is the apparent need to reach back into the comfortable while at the same time taking faltering steps forward: a recent social critic had a Czech audience of hundreds in hysterics with his own take on Morgan Spurlock's *Super-Size Me*. Instead of eating only McDonald's food for 30 days, one Karel Gustav Bozan decided to try a diet made up exclusively of beer, *smazný sýr* (fried cheese) and goulash. The results: Bozan claimed to look and feel better than ever – actually, he lost six kilograms (13 pounds), although doctors involved in the experiment advised against trying it at home. Apparently, Bozan had been living on a diet that was even unhealthier before his gastronomic conversion.

Around the same time as this story circulated in the Czech press, another proclaimed some less happy news. The Chamber of Deputies effectively killed off any chance that Czech workers will get an extra day off in the spring by failing to pass a proposed law that Good Friday become a new public holiday. Although there was virtually no religious call behind the effort, the idea of another day off to augment the 12 national holidays Czechs already enjoy was the main appeal. Alas, the killjoys in Parliament felt obliged to point out that the bill, basically a populist pre-election measure put forward by the Social Dems together with the Communists, would place a burden of nine billion Kč on the economy.

Czechs go wild in the city.

Though it came close to passing, it seems that even in Bohemia folks have become resigned to the need to move on from the times of coddling cradle-to-grave state care and insulation from cold, hard market realities.

As local wag and British columnist Sam Beckwith pointed out on his Prague.tv blog, if the Czech Republic had voted itself a thirteenth day off each year it would have put the country ahead even of France, with 12 national holidays, and the Netherlands, with 11. But it wasn't just laziness, there was a certain logic to the argument for another holiday: when a British public holiday falls on a weekend, UK workers, like those in the USA, get a weekday off instead – something that doesn't happen for Czechs.

But what really struck readers was that the politicians voting on the decision – and who in the end decided against on the grounds of lost productivity – get around ten weeks off every year, and pay themselves a basic monthly salary of 57,600 Kč – vastly above the national average wage.

Looks like Czech voters have finally been angered enough to rouse themselves from drugs, porn and shopping for long enough to cast a vote for change, at least a moderate one.

But some things will likely never change. Czechs will continue to drive like lunatics, drink beer for breakfast and insist that grey pâté made from mutilated chicken organs really does taste great. But if Prague is, as the late great founding editor-in-chief of the *Prague Post*, Alan Levy, once famously put it, 'Second Chance City', then one thing is clear: Czechs are determined to make the most of theirs.

Prague by numbers

On the ground

1.2 million population of Prague
10.3 million population of the Czech Republic
78,866sq km (30,450sq miles) area of Czech Republic
1,600sq km (618sq miles) of Czech land confiscated in 1918 that the Lichtenstein royal family claims

Ethnic divisions

94.4 per cent Czech
1.9 per cent Slovak
0.6 per cent Polish
0.5 per cent German
0.3 per cent Romany
0.2 per cent Hungarian
1 per cent other

Religions

59 per cent Unaffiliated
26.8 per cent Roman Catholic
2.1 per cent Protestant
8.8 per cent other

Lifestyle

99 per cent literacy
73 average life expectancy for a Czech male
80 average life expectancy for a Czech female
20 per cent decline in Czech population predicted in 50 years due to low birth rate
£10,570 ($19,500) GDP per capita
9.1 per cent unemployment rate
15,000 Kč average monthly wage in the Czech Republic
1st ranking of taxes and insurance in expenses of an average Czech family

250,000 number of Czechs struggling to pay household loans
450 billion amount in Kč that Czechs owe in consumer loans
158 litres (41.73 gallons) amount of beer drunk annually by the average Czech
292,000 number of internet users
6 the multiple by which car traffic has increased in Prague since 1990s

Housing

8 per cent predicted rise in regulated rents over next four years
4,600 number of homeless in Prague
560 beds available for homeless in Prague

Sex

900 number of brothels in the Czech Republic
3,000-6,000 estimated Prague street prostitutes
0.1 per cent HIV/AIDS infection rate

Crime

2 average ranking of fatal accidents per car on the road in Europe (Slovakia is No.1)
1,127 number of traffic fatalities in the Czech Republic in 2005
70 metres (230 feet) amount of 'new' StB secret police files from before 1989 discovered in 2005
1 rank of car theft among crimes committed in the Czech Republic
17 teenage girls a Qatar prince was convicted of molesting before being sent home without jail by Justice Minister Pavel Němec in 2005
57 million Kč amount two Czech women tried to defraud from the EU in May 2006

Municipal House. *See p32.*

Architecture

A symphony in stone.

If there's one thing about Prague that isn't culturally (or commercially) compromised, it's architecture. All right, gargantuan shopping malls have gone up all over town. But, since the city has been fully built up since the Middle Ages, the malls have generally been constructed within magnificent old structures. And thus, like Paris's Musée D'Orsay or London's Tate Modern, the retail havens installed at Nový Smíchov and on the edge of Staré Město at Náměstí Republiky have had little choice but to have wonderful exteriors, with their original façades preserved and the necessary parking secreted and, hence, secretive, beneath the ground.

That's because Prague is well aware that it is a story told in stone. A flavour of every period from Romanesque to postmodernism is proudly set out, as if at an epic building buffet, all within a half hour's walk of Old Town Square. The city's architectural fairytale, written in cycles of repression and strife, has indeed managed to resolve most of them with happy endings.

While it's true that communist central planners left the city centre crammed with monstrosities like the former Federal Assembly (*see p116*), which is now the headquarters of Radio Free Europe, most of even these have now been prettified at least a little and turned over to commercial or office use, reflecting the city's boom times. Reconstructed in the late 1960s from the former Stock Exchange building, the Federal Assembly is one of the last truly ugly holdouts, a block of black steel and smoked glass with a protruding two-storey addition plopped on top. Glowering down on Wenceslas Square from between the splendid State Opera (*see p232*) and the grand National Museum (*see p206*), it's a building that seems like a three-dimensional act of spite.

But most architects working here today say their greatest challenge is to create something new, while not desecrating a virtually sacred cityscape. It's a daunting task – harmonising these is an elusive, if not impossible, task. Some think the Dancing Building comes close; it's certainly the one recent structure to achieve iconic status, its playful post-1989 exuberance representing its time in the same way that the landmarks highlighted below sum up their own eras. Modern, market-driven Prague may not have yet developed an epoch-defining signature

St George's Basilica. *See p29.*

style, but the city's architecture has a way of roaring back after periods of war and foreign occupation. So there's no reason why the post-communist period can't do the same in the end.

BEGINNINGS
Property development in Prague dates from the seventh century, when Slavic tribes began building settlements along the Vltava river.

A couple of hundred years later the prototype of Prague Castle was built on an outcrop above the river, and the race was on. The city proper began taking shape around the castle, Vyšehrad and Staré Město (Old Town) in the 11th and 12th centuries; the most extensive surviving structure from the era is St George's Basilica (*see p79*) in the castle complex. Behind the creamy baroque façade thrown up in 1671 are the heavy arches, sly windows and thick pillars of the basilica's Romanesque roots. Walk around the back for a look at the round towers, built in 1142 by some of the first of the Italian craftsmen who would have a major hand in shaping the city for centuries to come.

The early Romanesque period also meant rotundas, and two survive more or less intact: St Martin's Rotunda at Vyšehrad (*see p132*), and Staré Město's Rotunda of the Holy Cross (*see p108*), both mutely evocative links to a dim and distant past.

GOTHIC
The French-reared Gothic style appeared in Bohemia around 1230, adding ribbed vaults, flying buttresses, pointed arches and lacy trefoils to the architect's quiver. The Old-New Synagogue (*see p110*), built around 1280 and one of the best-preserved medieval buildings in Europe, offers a concentrated dose. Two octagonal columns support its ribbed, nine-metre-high (30-foot) vaulting; above the portal is a tympanum with a gorgeous carving of a vine-covered tree of life. Little natural light penetrates the two oriel windows and 12 narrow stained-glass windows, which match the still-used synagogue's modest dimensions – building size was severely limited in the densely packed Jewish ghetto.

Other examples of the period include: St Agnes's Convent (*see p113*), the city's earliest Gothic structure; the House at the Stone Bell (*see p218*) on Old Town Square and the Church of Our Lady Before Týn (*see p101*) towering above it; the austere Powder Tower (*see p100*) and the east tower of the New Town Hall (*see p123*); and, of course, Charles Bridge (*see p107*).

RENAISSANCE
Bloodied by the Hussite Reformation in the first half of the 15th century, Prague entered the 16th century in relative calm. The city's architects began looking to the burgeoning Italian style for inspiration, creating buildings that celebrated humanity instead of reaching towards heaven. The soaring vertical spaces of Gothic cathedrals gave way to airy, horizontal palaces. The Renaissance arrived with the Belvedere (*see p81*) in Prague Castle's Royal Gardens, one of the first summer palaces built outside Italy. Paolo della Stella's arcaded exterior and Ionic columns, which were interspersed with reliefs of mythological scenes, make it a perfect Renaissance specimen, but its roof, shaped like an inverted ship's keel, makes it like no other building in Prague. Sadly, it's a grimy specimen, and the metal bars inserted between the columns to help it carry the load of the upstairs gallery mar its grandeur.

'The Church of St Nicholas may be history's most sumptuously sheathed iron fist.'

Further examples of the Renaissance period are the Schwarzenberg Palace (*see p86*), a riot of gables and sgraffito (unfortunately, it is closed for reconstruction until 2007, but you can still stand in front and gawk) and the neighbouring Martinic Palace (Hradčanske náměstí 67, Hradčany, Prague 1), its symmetrical coupled windows and biblical etchings combining the simplicity of the early Renaissance with the flourish and dash of the latter part of the period.

BAROQUE
When the smoke cleared from the Thirty Years' War the Catholics were back in charge with a vengeance. The Counter-Reformation wasn't the only force behind the building wave that remade Prague in the 17th and 18th centuries, but it's hard to miss the message in the city's baroque magnum opus, the Church of St Nicholas (*see p88*). The crowning achievement of father-and-son architects Christoph and Kilián Dientzenhofer, St Nicholas's may be history's most sumptuously sheathed iron fist. The enormous verdigris dome lords it over Malostranské náměsti; and beneath it, the elaborate curves and decoration testify not so much to the majesty and mystery of the Church as to its power. The locals converted in short order.

Elsewhere you'll find the formidable Clementinum (*see p105*), Prague's other major signifier of Jesuit ascendancy; the Wallenstein Palace (*see p90*), Renaissance style carried into baroque spectacle by dint of its patron's ego; Old Town Square's Golz-Kinský Palace

(*see p101*) and Villa Amerika (*see p124*) in Nové Město (New Town), among other splendid chocolate boxes; and the gloriously over-the-top Loreto (*see p86*), the triumphant Church's potent cocktail of blood-soaked mysticism and gratuitous wealth.

NEO-CLASSICAL

The enlightened absolutist Joseph II was having none of that rococo nonsense when he took the throne in 1780, and the Premonstratensians of Strahov Abbey saw the rationalist handwriting on the wall. The result is the Strahov Monastery Library (*see p87*), a politically adroit flanking manoeuvre (the wily monks brought in books by the ton to convince the monastery-closing monarch they ran an educational institution). Architecturally, the building is a bridge into the classically minded Age of Reason, its

baroque frills tempered by a soaring façade of capital-topped pilasters. Inside the stunning Philosophical Hall the bookcases and balustrades rise to a frescoed ceiling, science meeting art in religious drag.

To seek out further neo-classical style head to Anton Haffenecker's imposing, Corinthian-fronted Estates Theatre (*see p251*), home to the première of *Don Giovanni* – and don't you forget it – and U Hybernů (Na Poříčí 3, Nové Město, Prague 1), with its Doric columns and cornices showing off the high Empire style of the Napoleonic era.

REVIVALISM

Few 'national' buildings are as worthy of the name as the National Theatre (*see p232*), dreamt up by the cream of the National Revival movement and paid for entirely with public contributions. In May 1868 50,000 people

Still crazy Top this

Stalin once glowered from the most prominent promontory in Prague, the clifftop edge of Letná park in Holešovice above the Vltava river just north and downstream of the Malá Strana district. Endless myths surround the massive granite monument, which was years in the building and yet stood for only seven before Russia's greatest mass murderer was discredited and the thing had to be dismantled in 1962. It took 800 kilograms (1,763 pounds) of explosive to bring down the 17,000-ton statue. One of the most persistent rumours is that Uncle Joe's head is still secreted in someone's Prague apartment.

It would have to be quite a penthouse suite: the Stalin statue weighed thousands of tons and was 50 metres (64 feet) high. It also included a crush of grateful peasants. (A joke asked why Stalin was smiling. The answer: he's reached the front of the queue.)

These days, a few Australians with an idea for an ocean theme park and a competing Austrian crystal company have ideas of their own for the space.

Underwater World Oceanarium, though not heard from much lately, at one point promised to bring the ocean to Prague by 2007. Its plan: an ocean park on an 8,000-square-metre (86,111-square-foot) site behind and under the Letná metronome. That's the rust-red spike you can now see atop Letná, the work of former dissident artist David Černý (it's meant to be ticking, symbolising eternity, but usually it's stuck at two o'clock).

The $27.8-million investment in massive tanks, up to 4,000 fish species and 300 mammals, other attractions and underground infrastructure has been predicted by UWO to be profitable within a decade – but first it will have to get past some rather bothersome environmental issues.

Though Prague council would have to make major zoning changes to allow the oceanarium, which it says would be too disruptive and cause traffic problems, one argument in a developer's favour is the current state of the plinth: it's fenced off, cracked and weed-covered and the city says it has no funds for repairs.

On the other hand, though, Prague already has newish aquariums, one at the Prague Zoo, and one called Mořský svět, or Sea World, at Prague 7s Výstaviště exhibition grounds.

More likely to pass muster is a plan by the crystal giant Swarovski for a cultural and historical museum atop Letná, which is said to be favoured by Prague mayor Pavel Bém. The crystal plan, admittedly, has a lot more to do with Bohemia, a world capital of quality glass, than an aquarium in the land-locked Czech Republic. Also it would, perhaps wisely, celebrate the scientific discoveries Johannes Kepler made at Prague Castle (he believed the universe to be constructed of five different crystal shapes) and thus have a strong educational component – all for the bargain-basement cost of just $10.2 million. Better still, there's very little chance it would leak.

The Old-New Synagogue. See p29.

Rudolfinum (*see p218*) and Schulz did the honours for the grandiose National Museum (*see p206*), an impressive if not bombastic shrine to civic pride but breathtaking by night.

ART NOUVEAU

Erected just as the Austro-Hungarian Empire melted down, the gaudy, glitzy Municipal House (*see p118*) dazzles like a gilt-trimmed butterfly emerging from a chrysalis. The 'ding-dong, the witch is dead' vibe is unmistakable, but it took more than incipient independence to create the jewel of Prague's flamboyant art nouveau, festooned with stained glass, floral motifs and other decorative filigree. Production and population were booming, fuelling a business fund with a taste for symbolism and style. Architects Antonín Balšánek and Osvald Polívka, aided by the leading artistic lights of the day, harnessed the new energies into an extraordinary catalogue of patriotic pomp (stately Smetana Hall) and swirling, swinging optimism (the Alfons Mucha-designed Mayor's Hall), oozing aspiration from every floor.

> **'Prague architecture c1948-89 suggests the communists' puzzling inability to recognise that even workers like to be surrounded by beauty.'**

Other examples of art nouveau worth seeking out are Polívka's colourfully ornamental Prague Insurance Building and Topič Building (Národní 7 and 9, Nové Město, Prague 1); the Grand Hotel Evropa (*see p63*) on Wenceslas Square, with its gleaming façade undimmed by years of communist neglect inside; the grand row of apartment houses running down Masaryk Embankment; and Josef Fanta's original Hlavní nádraží (Main Train Station, Wilsonova, Nové Město, Prague 2; *see p290*) – tatty yet still carrying a whiff of opulence.

MODERNISM

Cubism, functionalism and constructivism all stamped themselves on to the cityscape in the first decades of the 20th century, but the city's most striking modern building is none of the above. Following no one's uncompromising theoretical blueprint, the Church of the Sacred Heart (*see p132*) sprang whole from the febrile imagination of Slovene architect Josip Plečnik, who also gave Prague Castle a between-the-wars touch-up. With its enormous clock-face rose window beaming over the great brick block of a church down on a Vinohrady square,

marched in a procession behind the foundation stone. The theatre opened 13 years later to the strains of Smetana's patriotic opera *Libuše*, then promptly burned down. The public dug deep again and the whole thing was rebuilt in two years, with Josef Schulz adapting mentor Josef Zítek's original plan and the 'National Theatre generation' of artists contributing the painting and statuary, which strikes a fittingly heroic note atop the lofty arched portico. The gold-crowned oblong dome is one of the icons of the Czech nation; the bucking horses atop the balustrade are pretty dramatic too.

Zítek and Schulz also lent their neo-Renaissance stylings to the monumental

Plečnik's creation mixes and matches with abandon, bathing the chilly geometry of modernism in a warm, Gothic-tinted glow.

Modernist architecture is also represented by the constructivist mass of Holešovice's Veletržní palác (Trade Fair Palace); c1911 Koruna Palace's (Wenceslas Square and Na Příkopě, Nové Město, Prague 1) futurism is pulled off with a Babylonian twist; the clean lines and practical spaces of 1930s housing estate Baba (above Podbabská 15-39, Dejvice, Prague 6); and functionalist landmark Mánes gallery (*see p221*), its river-spanning rectilinear slab outfitted with modern art and somehow blending in with the 15th-century water tower next door.

COMMUNISM

Prague architecture c1948-89 suggests the communists' puzzling inability to recognise that even workers like to be surrounded by beauty. Most relics of the period are blocky and grim, but the communist-era building Praguers most love to hate is the streamlined Žižkov Tower (*see p133*), a fusillade of television antennae built atop an old Jewish cemetery.

At 216 metres (709 feet), it's the tallest structure in Prague – you might have stood in line for bread but, by God, you were going to have good reception. Completed just before the revolution, it does manage to muster a sort of charm on misty evenings, with artist/provocateur David Černý's climbing black babies silhouetted in the twilight.

Ringing the city, the ubiquitous prefab *panelák* housing estates (Metro Zličín or Háje) still house much of the population, while local governments try to break up their grey monotony with two-tone paint jobs. Kotva department store (*see p178*), with its odd angles and brown panelling, and the Česká Typografie building (Na Poříčí and Na Florenci streets, Nové Město, Prague 1) – formerly the office of the communist newspaper *Rude právo*, which the party made sure was the tallest building in Prague 1 when it opened in 1989 – still ring out their communist-era foundations.

POST-COMMUNISM

Architects no longer labour under communist overlords, but they work under the watchful eyes of preservationists and impatient investors instead. In gritty Karlín, the riverside Danube House (River City Prague, Rohanské nábřeží, Karlín, Prague 6) office building won kudos from the esteemed *Architectural Review* even before it opened in autumn 2003. Its ship's-prow shape is unquestionably contemporary, but its architects chose materials that resemble the soft sandstone of many neighbouring buildings and

the magazine's judges likened its large atrium to crystals set in 'solid stone volumes', with a nod to traditional Czech glass-making skills.

Other post-communist treats include the eye-catching Dancing Building (*see p123*), nicknamed 'Fred and Ginger' by its designers, US superstar Frank Gehry and Croatian Vlado Milunic, and the Euro Palace (Václavské náměstí 2, Nové Město, Prague 1), which was designed as a 21st-century counterpart to Koruna Palace (*see p117*) on the other side of Wenceslas Square. Judge for yourself if this glass-sheathed construction is worthy of its situation right at the nexus of Prague's flourishing high-street shopping district.

The world's only Cubist lamp-post, 28 Řijna.

Literary Prague

City as muse.

Let's be honest: no one is likely to come to Prague for the light. So, since itinerant painters are a no no, it's just as well that the city has provided a home and inspiration for so many writers through the years. Now, though, with the cost of living approaching West European levels, living frugally in a garret while writing that novel is no longer so feasible for impecunious scribblers. Nevertheless, for a city this size there is a surprisingly vital and concentrated literary scene, supported by writerly cafés, journals that welcome submissions from new authors, a thriving small press or two and several impressive festivals.

One group still keeping the spirit of Kafka alive is **Alchemy** (www.alchemyprague.com), an informal gathering of writers and poets with regular slam nights at which new work is trotted out twice monthly. Inspired by a medieval tract called *Rules for the Practising Alchemist*, this band of writers, poets and musicians has been meeting in Prague for longer than anyone can remember, seeking to turn words into literary gold. The Monday night readings, currently held at Tulip Café (*see p155*), have little more than a mission statement as structure, but that openness seems to work.

The inclusive approach is something that, for better or worse, has predominated in the Prague literary scene, at least for English speakers, since not long after the Velvet Revolution. Before that the canon belonged to the likes of Václav Havel, whose absurdist parodies of life under communism (*The Memorandum*, *The Garden Party* and *Audience*) landed him in jail, and a host of contemporary writers and artists such as Ivan Klíma, Ludvík Vaculík and Jiří Kolář.

Their forerunners can be traced to the first of the Czech-language publishing successes (always risky in Habsburg-ruled Prague), during the city's literary National Revival of the mid 19th century. Božena Němcová, known as *Babička*, or Grandmother, inaugurated a new era for writing in colloquial Czech with morbid, tender fairytales still read to children today.

Jaroslav Hašek, author of *The Good Soldier Švejk*, is credited with personifying Czech political dissent in his main character, who never misses an opportunity to get an order wrong, a strategy that helps him to make it through World War I intact while driving his supposed superiors out of their minds. Prague's German-speaking Jewish community of the early 20th century couldn't have known a more troubled cauldron, but the period produced luminary work by, of course, Prague's most famous son, Franz Kafka (*see p111* **Still crazy**). But he was not the only Jewish writer of the period. His contemporaries include the poet, Max Brod, who was instructed to burn Kafka's manuscripts upon his death, novelists Paul Leppin (*Severin's Journey into the Dark*) and Gustav Meyrink (*The Golem*), both of whom wrote enthralling accounts of the last days of the Habsburg Empire. Add to this list Holocaust survivors like Jiří Weil and Arnošt Lustig and it's easy to see how much Czech letters were enriched by the contribution of this marginalised group of writers. What's more, all have been translated into English.

> ## 'Novelist Jáchym Topol cast Prague as a sleazy, noirish place of jackals in *City, Sister, Silver*.'

The poet Vitězslav Nezval, who founded the Czech Surrealists in the 1930s, was part of a wave that encompassed much Bohemian art in every medium. Nezval was a member of the seminal *Devětsil* avant-garde movement, as was Nobel laureate poet Jaroslav Seifert.

After the communists seized power in 1948, independent-minded writers were forced underground. Other writers continued working secretly, publishing *samizdat* manuscripts, illicitly distributing individually typewritten pages among themselves. Aside from Havel, Zdeněk Urbánek (*On the Sky's Clayey Bottom*) and the scientist-poet Miroslav Holub (*Vanishing Lung Syndrome*) were part of that network. The novels of Bohumil Hrabal (*Closely Observed Trains, I Served the King of England*) are too fantastical to fit the label dissident, though he was clearly suspect for his quirky tales of paper

recyclers, scrap metal gatherers and railroad clerks who somehow transcend their drab worlds. Hrabal died in 1997 after a fall from a fifth-floor window while feeding pigeons – just as a character in one of his books did.

The post-Velvet Revolution Czech writers are difficult to categorise, but a good survey of their work in translation can be found in the imprints of the publisher, Twisted Spoon (www.twistedspoon.com). These lush books, on good paper, with original illustrations and fresh translations of both new and classic Czech writing, are a gold mine for readers.

One Czech writer early out of the gates, the poet and novelist Jáchym Topol, cast Prague as a sleazy, noirish place of jackals in *City, Sister, Silver*, but in a town changing as fast as this one, his depiction, barely five years old, already seems to have little in common with Prague. Lukáš Tomin's introspective *Ashtrays, The Doll* and *Kye* are open-ended poetic collections, which are true to the perpetually tangled life of a Prague intellectual.

Titles from all of the above are available at Prague's two literary oases, the **Globe Bookstore & Coffeehouse** (*see p181*) and **Shakespeare & Sons** (*see p175*). **Big Ben Bookstore** (*see p181*) is also an excellent source of indie titles and collections of short stories by international writers, such as *This Side of Reality* (Serpent's Tail). For information on where to get Czech literary journals, *see p304*.

FESTIVALS

Writers love to schmooze and, indeed, no city's finer for it than Prague, with its countless cafés and dens of wine-soaked debate. In summer, not a month goes by without an important writers' gathering.

Local scribe and poet Louis Armand is behind the triennial **Prague International Poetry Festival** (www.geocities.com/prague poetryfestival), which takes place next in May 2007, jointly co-ordinated by the *Prague Literary Review*, Shakespeare & Sons, Twisted Spoon Press and the InterCultural Studies Programme at Charles University. The ambitious scope of the festival is indicated merely by listing a few of the talents attending: Sudeep Sen of India, Charles Bernstein from the US, Franz Josef Czernin of Austria, Trevor Joyce of Ireland, Tadeusz Pioro of Poland, John Kinsella of Australia, Drew Milne of the UK and Anselm Hollo of Finland.

The more established **Prague Writers' Festival** (*see p200*) in March has been a star-studded series in the past, with writers like Martin Amis, Margaret Atwood and William Styron, but seems a bit more muted these days, with less-commercial talents on the roster.

Under *Giraffe*'s spots

Praguer Jonathan Ledgard was inspired by the city's dark past in writing his first novel, *Giraffe*, a many-faceted work that reads like a cross between a dark Bohemian fairytale and a spare Cold War thriller. The book grew from his discovery of a secret operation in 1975 involving the extermination of the largest captive herd of giraffes in the world in a zoo in Czechoslovakia, purportedly because of the risk of contagion.

Where did the idea for Giraffe *first take root?*
Jonathan Ledgard: I was a Central and Eastern Europe correspondent of *The Economist* at the time. One day, around 2001, I came across a snippet in one of the Czech papers. It was just a line in an interview with someone who later defected, to the effect that he had filmed the birth of a giraffe for Czechoslovak state television, but that the footage had disappeared after secret police had shot dead all the giraffes in that zoo. Could this be true? I was captivated.

The research was a kind of three-dimensional journalism: I wanted the facts, but I also wanted the feelings. The feelings were most important. I managed to track down many of those involved. I interviewed zookeepers, veterinarians, retired secret police officers, butchers, former dissidents, biochemical warfare specialists and others. The highlight came right at the end when, quite by chance, I met with the hunter who was brought in by the secret police to shoot the giraffes. We spent a day in his cabin in the mountains talking through what happened. He had never spoken about it before. He still had nightmares about it. I asked him, for example, what kind of rifle strap he had, how he wore it, how the moonlight played on the corrugated iron roof of the giraffe house, and what was the sound of the body of a giraffe hitting concrete.

He answered everything, thoughtfully, and although he did not wish to be identified, he spoke with a great sense of relief, as if he had been waiting to unburden himself. We walked away from his hut. It was summer, the grass in the meadows was high, all the snow melted, even in the shadows, and I felt moved almost to tears because I knew that I had finally got under the skin of that one single suffering.

Is the phrase 'communist moment' something commonly used, or did you coin it for Giraffe*? If so, why do you think it works?*
JL: It's a phrase I coined. I'm interested in time and space. The ČSSR in 1975 was a communist moment. I was trying to get at the brevity of communism and yet how it seemed, in 1975, that it would go on for a long time.
There's a lot of melancholy and resignation in your main character, Emil, the haemodynamicist, that is, as you describe, someone who specialises in blood flow in vertical creatures like giraffes and man. Was that a function of the time or is that something still in the atmosphere of Prague?
JL: Both, I think. In writing terms, there's a deliberate flatness about Emil. You can't really say if he's good or bad, successful or failing: he's compromised and he's haunted – just like Prague.
What was the most surprising piece of zoology you came across in your research?
JL: Definitely the verticality of the giraffes (and all of its physiological implications). There are so few beasts that are pushed up from the earth (rather than stretched along the face of it).
You seem equally fascinated by science and myth. Is there some relation between the two? Perhaps in the questing?
JL: Truth is indivisible. If there are angels, powers, principalities, then they are also subject to science, a certain biology; if there are not, then the absence is a mystery every bit as tantalising.

Beer

'Beer is proof that God loves us and wants us to be happy'
– Benjamin Franklin.

The undisputed Czech national treasure (and that includes ice hockey champions, supermodels and crystal) is *pivo*. Better known to foreigners as beer, the stuff is the glue that holds Czech society together – or perhaps keeps it so addled that it can't be bothered to fall apart.

Fermented brews in Bohemia date back to the Middle Ages, from which time proverbs survive about beer – a favourite being '*Unus papa Romae, una cerevesia Raconae*', or 'one pope in Rome, one beer in Rakovnik'. In fact, King Wenceslas II granted 260 families in Pilsen the right to brew beer in 1290. But the golden lager that put the Czech lands on the map was the one developed in Pilsen in 1842, using the breakthrough bottom-fermenting process. So successful was the combination of texture, taste and colour that the brew had to be branded as Pilsner Urquell, or Original Pilsener, because German brewers almost immediately copied the process.

Fights over great Czech beer names continue to this day, one of the longest-running and most expensive being between the old Czech label Budvar, or Budweisser in German, and the American mass market brewery of the same name. There's no connection between the two companies – as their respective beers make abundantly clear – but the big guns of the US brand have been demanding exclusive use of the name for many years, while at the same time endeavouring to buy out the Czech brewer Budvar. But the state-owned South Bohemian brewery is definitely not for sale at any price. It seems that, unlike hundreds of castles, churches and national park areas across the country, this is one national treasure that Czechs have no interest in selling off to make some quick cash.

Not that the industry isn't consolidating here. Just as everywhere, corporations are expanding fast and gobbling up small producers, resulting in more homogeneous, widely available products, but far less character.

Many passionate Bohemian beer drinkers are concerned with the way the giant multinationals are affecting Czech beer. Staropramen, for one, is now owned by Interbrew, which has been frightfully successful at pushing (gasp!) Stella Artois on to the Czech market. Young trendies can be seen sipping it at Old Town's fashionable bars, apparently under the impression that it makes them seem worldly and more European. But this bland factory-made imitation of a Pilsner doesn't even rate with standard Staropramen ten-degree brew. And in Prague, Staropramen is consistently voted one of the least interesting home-grown tastes around. Partly to remedy that, Staropramen launched a ruby-coloured brew with more nutty, fruity notes, called Granat, which has had some success among younger drinkers.

'Pining for the perfect pint.'

The trouble seems to be that for many in the post-1989 generation Czech beer is still deeply associated with their grizzled dads and uncles sitting in the local nicotine-stained *hostinec* every night, downing cheap pint after cheap pint while grousing about the government.

Many younger Czechs, in fact, eschew beer altogether and have developed a taste for wine. For years they were satisfied with the vinegary plonk that came from badly neglected local vineyards, but these days reasonably priced French and Italian vintages are common and it seems that the local Frankovka is finally getting its just desserts. For many others, however, it seems that beer is still all right, especially for young males, but perhaps it shouldn't be the beer your father drinks.

Thus, where you once saw beer taps for Budvar, Pilsner, Kozel, Staropramen and maybe Platan or Branik at the corner pub, market consolidation means you now see just one major Czech beer on tap, usually alongside a global brand like Stella or Guinness. Can Sam Adams and Foster's be far behind?

Meanwhile, the one old Czech brew everyone still respects, Pilsner Urquell, is now being made outside of Pilsen (if only for foreign markets), which is also troubling to many.

But not all developments are for the worse and there is one that is brightening up the lives and livers of Prague's beer drinkers: the new wave of microbreweries that have opened.

In Prague and around the region, a visionary in this field is Jan Suran. He lived abroad for many years, pining for the perfect Czech pint,

One-degree brew

Pivovar U Bulovky doesn't look like anything special from the nondescript street it stands on in the Palmovka district of Prague 8, east of Holešovice. In fact, if there's anything notable about this part of town, it's that it's where British-trained Czech resistance fighters assassinated Hitler's enforcer in the Protectorate of Bohemia and Moravia, Reinhard Heydrich, in 1942. Nevertheless, this transitional neighbourhood is on the radar of the country's most discerning beer fans. That's because of the above-named solidly neighbourhood pub on Bulovka street (Bulovka 17, Prague 8, 284 840 650), and the beers, brewed by brewmaster and inventor František Richter, that can be supped here. In typically Czech fashion, for Richter the prize-winning beer that is microbrewed on the spot is as much a philosophical statement as a beverage.

'Things should never be more than one degree removed from nature,' says the former punk rocker and returned émigré, who at the last count had created 125 varieties of beer. While Richter has no problem with traditional bottom-fermented Pilsener, the national passion and art, he believes beer should be broader than that. His trademark cloudy 'yeast beer', more orange than gold and with a less firm head, has been described by one overheated reviewer as having 'a fragrant hops scent and warming malt notes to the nose, with a crisp citrus and slightly yeasty initial taste followed by perfectly balanced bittersweet flavours'.

What's more, Richter provides a taste of what beer used to be like before modern technology arrived to protect us from ourselves. Most beer these days has had the live yeast that formed it killed off through pasteurisation, a process widespread for hygiene reasons. Bubbles are then put back into the beer at the serving tap, usually through carbonation. But not at Pivovar U Bulovky.

which he set about brewing when he came home. Pivovarský dům (*see p171*), his Nové Město microbrewery, certainly pours a traditional great, but it also has whatever exciting brews he finds from around the country and abroad. Following Pivovarský dům's lead, a number of microbreweries have cropped up in places around the country, like Lipnik and Frydek-Mistek.

Another returning émigré, František Richter (*see above* **One-degree brew**), has brought the same magic to the otherwise blighted district of Prague 8. His Richter Brewery, which opened its doors just recently, has caused beer fans from all over Europe to make the trip out to the north-eastern reach of the city.

One reason is his flavourings, something still uncommon or unknown, apart from hops, in the Czech lands. Like Germany, whose pure beer laws dating from Renaissance times ban the addition of anything but barley malt, hops, water and yeast, most Czech brewers are serious traditionalists. Thus, natural flavourings such as nut extract, orange peel, stinging nettles, pepper or rosehips are still virtually unknown locally. But unlike Germany, there's no law forbidding the practice in the Czech lands, other than 500 years of tradition, which seems to do the job just as thoroughly.

Exceptions are a handful of slightly more adventurous, if still traditional, pubs where spiced beer like Ferdinand's Sedm kuli is on tap. One such place, Ferdinanda, just off

Wenceslas Square (Opletalova 24, Nové Město, Prague 1, 222 244 302) is an unpretentious and very local place to try this brew. Restaurace Černý slon (Týnská 1, Staré Město, Prague 1, 222 329 353), meanwhile, is a cosy, old-fashioned place in a cosy, old-fashioned hotel, located, amazingly, just off Old Town Square.

But the traditional methods of Czech brewers are a good thing, certainly. Even big, successful Pilsner, for example, keeps alive a cooper's guild, into which the first apprentice in 30 years was inducted in 2006. The giant, modern brewery keeps a workshop out back where a small crew builds and maintains giant oak barrels in which beer is fermented just as it has been for centuries. Although this makes for a popular attraction on brewery tours, it serves a serious purpose: the Pilsner brewed the old, natural way in the oak casques is tasted alongside the mass-produced modern stuff as a quality control measure (some tasters confess they still think the barrelled stuff is better, though others swear it's identical to what consumers get – only those who visit the brewery will know for sure; they're allowed a taste of the brew made the old way).

It's a comfort to know that the great Czech traditions are still treated with reverence by some. Otherwise the appearance of such marketing moves as the big Stella push might become too depressing. But in the end there's always one way to appreciate Czech beer: try a foreign brew. The difference is golden.

Where to Stay

Where to Stay   **42**

Features

The best Hotels   42
Beats room service   46
Palatial *palács*   59

Aria Hotel. *See p47*.

Where to Stay

Czech in.

The sleeping situation in Prague is, like the rest of the city, in hyperspeed transition, with just about every hotel and pension boasting upgraded amenities. Room prices, traditionally high, haven't officially changed much, but competition has spurred so many promotional deals, usually found on hotel websites, that it pays to book yourself. And, while service continues to be an issue (sigh), modern hotel amenities are now common in Prague. And rest assured, long gone are the days when toilet paper was rationed and the heating was turned off at night to save a few crowns.

In fact, ambitious Czechs have pulled ahead of their Central and Eastern European counterparts with modern, often outlandishly 'designer', lodgings popping up like mushrooms after rain: the **Hotel Yasmin** has gone sci-fi (with critically lauded restaurant); **987 Prague** is affordably cool; and **Floor Hotel** has hip rooms for backpackers and grown-ups.

Meanwhile, the flagship hotels continue to refine their appeal, with **Le Palais** drawing film stars, **Aria** hosting rockers and the **Hotel Josef** becoming a scribbler's retreat. With over four million visitors trekking to Prague annually, it's obvious this massive, city-wide overhaul is working. And there's good news for those on a budget: the Czech capital still offers good value for the most basic accommodation. Backpackers can choose from dozens of hostels and hundreds of spare rooms, many of which flower like dandelions every summer only to wither with the autumn. However, Prague's appeal among frugal travellers means that finding an empty room often involves quite a bit of schlepping from hostel to hostel.

Finding a room somewhere between opulence and austerity is now an enjoyable pursuit after years of lagging in this sector. Families can find deals at the **Mövenpick**, **Marriott** or **Dorint Don Giovanni**, while couples can nestle without breaking the bank at cosy charmers like the **Julian**, **U Žluté boty**, **Hotel Anna** or the lovely **Hotel Černy Slon** just off Old Town Square. And family-owned inns, such as **Residence Řetězova** or **Pension Vyšehrad** lie in the centre or within a ten-minute tram ride of it. Though indie innkeepers are being squeezed by competitive forces, for the time being those same forces keep drawing new entrants to the game.

Availability and price can vary hugely with seasons. An absence of comfortable weather and business conferences makes the months from October to March and a few weeks in later summer the most competitive times of the year among the best hotels. Hostels tend to stay full from May to September.

INFORMATION AND BOOKING

Varying strategies maximise buying power at renovated or brand-new hotels, medieval family-run inns and giant, corporate-owned multi-star hotels. Many give discounts to groups and for longer stays (normally around ten days or more); rooms are generally 20-40 per cent cheaper off-season, and many deluxe hotels give 10-20 per cent discounts in July and August. Smaller places may offer a significant reduction for cash payment, or a hefty credit card surcharge, depending on how you look at it. Try to establish this, preferably with hard-copy confirmation, before you arrive. Internet booking discounts are also plentiful, so check the web frequently for these special deals.

Service at the higher-end hotels is comparable to that in any European capital. That is not the case at some of the more moderate hotels, where

The best Hotels

For cosy comfort
Dům U velké boty (see p45), **Hotel Anna** (see p68), **Hotel Villa Schwaiger** (see p67).

For family-friendly deals
Dorint Don Giovanni (see p67), **Ibis Praha City** (see p70), **Marriott** (see p63), **Mövenpick Hotel** (see p67).

For fine dining
Bellagio Hotel Prague (see p55), **Four Seasons Hotel Prague** (see p53), **Radisson SAS Alcron** (see p62).

For old European style
Hotel Elite (see p63), **U zlaté studny** (see p58).

For romantic weekending
Residence Řetězova (see p58), **Romantik Hotel U Raka** (see p45).

Spend the night with *Figaro* at the **Aria Hotel**. *See p47.*

the staff can give the impression that it is your privilege to stay with them. As is the case at luxury hotels worldwide, you can get hit with ludicrous charges for both local and international phone calls. Watch out also for the taxis that cluster around the hotel entrances: for these hustlers, a taxi meter is a jackpot that always pays out. If the hotel has its own fleet, it's a better option, although charges may still be double those set for city taxis. Hotels are also infamous for refusing to call honest taxi services for guests, such as AAA or Profi (*see p293*), because they're in on the game.

Even with all the new accommodation that has sprouted in the city, rooms in Prague have still not caught up with the huge summer demand. If you come to the city in peak months without a reservation, expect to pound the pavement for hours before you find a clean, well-lit place. Even off-peak, it's still wise to book ahead. All deluxe hotels have English-speaking staff; those at cheaper establishments may struggle, though you can usually make yourself understood. Many hotels can arrange airport pick-ups for a fixed price, which will save you time, money and hassle.

PRICES AND CLASSIFICATION

Hotels are classified below according to their cheapest double room; prices include breakfast, unless stated otherwise. Note that these prices are usually only available off-season and also be aware that some of the more upmarket hotels fix their room rates in euros or US dollars. For ease of use we have converted all prices into Czech crowns, but exchange-rate fluctuations may affect these prices.

Hotels are listed by area and our price categories work as follows: a Deluxe hotel is one in which the cheapest double room costs 8,000 Kč or more per night; an Expensive hotel costs 6,000-8,000 Kč; Moderate is 3,000-6,000 Kč; Budget hotels cost under 3,000 Kč; and all Hostels are grouped together. All the rooms listed in the 'Deluxe' and 'Expensive' categories have an en suite bathroom. This also applies to the 'Moderate' category, unless otherwise stated in the listings.

Facilities in other categories vary – it's always best to check exactly what you'll be getting when you book. A selection of hotels that are particularly welcoming to gay guests is listed in the Gay & Lesbian chapter.

Accommodation agencies

Agentura Kirke

Moskevská 25, Vršovice, Prague 10 (271 725 898/ fax 271 723 726/www.agentura-kirke.cz.). Metro Náměstí Míru/tram 4, 22. **Open** 8.30am-5pm Mon-Fri. **No credit cards.**
British expat Nicholas Kirke's eponymous agency offers long- and short-term rentals on flats (minimum lease one year). All flats are unfurnished.

Prague Accommodations

Petřínská 4, Prague 5 (608 228 999/fax 251 512 502/www.pragueaccommodations.com).
It makes no sense to visit this apartment and pension company in person, either book by phone or online before you come. The agency's properties include some of the most centrally located and elegant historic buildings you could possibly stay in. Prices range from cheap to moderate, depending on how many people stay in one apartment.

Stop City

Vinohradská 24, Prague 2 (222 521 233/fax 222 521 252/www.stopcity.com). Metro Muzeum or Náměstí Míru/tram 11. **Open** *Apr-Oct* 10am-9pm daily. *Nov-Mar* 10am-8pm daily. **Credit** AmEx, MC, V. **Map** p331 P8.
Helpful staff will book you into a pension, hotel, private room or apartment starting at around 483 Kč per person. Rooms range from the slightly dodgy to slightly above average, with a wide range of price options. They don't handle hostel bookings but are willing to make reservations for callers from abroad, provided a credit card number is given via fax. The booking office is closed on Sundays.

Hradčany

Staying within the shadow of Prague Castle does limit your culinary and nightlife options, and not everyone is up for a hike up the hill at the end of the day. But rooms here come with bragging rights and the backstreets hold some treasures.

Deluxe

Hotel Savoy

Keplerova 6, Prague 1 (224 302 430/fax 224 302 128/www.hotel-savoy.cz). Tram 22, 23. **Rooms** 61. **Rates** 10,900-13,900 Kč singles and doubles. Extra bed 2,550 Kč. **Credit** AmEx, MC, V. **Map** p326 A3 **❶**
Stepping into the dignified lobby, complete with reading room and fireplace, it may seem hard to imagine this isn't a haven for prima donna celebs such as Tina Turner and Princess Caroline of Monaco. But this is a peaceful bastion of first-class service with tasteful, modern rooms. Standard rooms are spacious, and the deluxes amount almost to a suite. Concierge service is top notch. How's this for a pleasant surprise: breakfast and minibar are included in the price of the room, as use of the fitness centre.

Business centre. Concierge. Disabled: adapted room. Gym. Internet (dataport). No-smoking rooms. Room service (24hrs). TV: pay movies/satellite.

Expensive

Hotel Neruda

Nerudova 44, Prague 1 (257 535 557/fax 257 531 492/www.hotelneruda.cz). Metro Malostranská/tram 12, 20, 22, 23. **Rooms** 73. **Rates** 7,040-8,320 Kč single; 7,840-9,600 Kč double. *Extra bed* 1,400 Kč. **Credit** AmEx, DC, JCB, MC, V. **Map** p326 D3 **❷**
Hotel Neruda might only have served as a hotel for the past six years, but it's still a building with history, the main building dating from 1348. The hotel's success has meant the addition of a new, Bořek Sípek-designed, wing, bringing the number of rooms to 73. Expect lots of free-floating curves from the Czech Republic's top glass artist and architect. Rooms in the older building are comfortable but a little plain, so be sure to ask for one with a view of Nerudova street. Attentive, friendly service.
Bar. Internet (dataport). No-smoking rooms. Parking (call ahead to reserve). Restaurant. Room service (until 11pm). TV: satellite.

Romantik Hotel U raka

Černínská 10, Prague 1 (220 511 100/fax 233 358 041/www.romantikhotel-uraka.cz). Tram 12, 22, 23. **Rooms** 6. **Rates** 4,840-5,123 Kč single; 6,260-6,833 Kč double. **Credit** AmEx, DC, JCB, MC, V. **Map** p326 A2 **❸**
Dating from 1739, this small, rustic pension is a good choice for couples who have lots of time to spare. Located just down the hill from the castle and within earshot of the bells of the Loreto, U raka has tons of personality but still boasts the polish and service you'd expect in this category. There are just six rooms available – two in the main house and four adjacent cottages – plus a beautiful breakfast room/café/reading room with brick hearth. Reserve well in advance. No children under 12. No bar.
Internet. Parking. Room service (8am-11pm).

Moderate

Dům U velké boty

Vlašská 30, Prague 1 (257 532 088/fax 257 533 234/www.dumuvelkeboty.cz). Metro Malostranská/ tram 12, 20, 22, 23. **Rooms** 8. **Rates** (excl breakfast) 1,800 Kč single; 3,000-3,760 Kč double; 4,100 Kč suite. *Extra bed* 500 Kč. **No credit cards.** **Map** p326 D4 **❹**
The Rippl couple have a secret jewel in the heart of Malá Strana, popular with visiting writers and actors (there's no sign, just press the buzzer marked 'Jan Rippl'). The eight-room house, which dates from 1470, is filled with appropriately period furniture. The Rippls look after guests like they're members of their own family, which leads many guests to return time and again to the House at the Big Boot. Breakfast is an extra 200 Kč.
Gym. Internet (wireless).

Where to Stay

Beats room service

Bar flies who trawl the watering holes
of Prague today might have difficulty
imagining that in the glory days of the First
Czechoslovak Republic following World War I
Prague boasted some of the swankiest,
swingin'est bars on the Continent. In fact,
well before that, under the Habsburg Empire,
the city had as many grand, brassy bars,
filled with swells and ne'er-do-wells, as any
cosmopolitan European capital. A full cast of
artists, intellectuals, moguls and good-time
gals populated this world of the night. Often
they were in characterful old hotels like the
Alcron, off Wenceslas Square (today the
Radisson SAS Alcron; see p62), where
Josephine Baker, Louis Armstrong and
Duke Ellington partied after shows.

Successive Nazi and Soviet occupations
didn't do a lot for bar culture, or anything
else, but, since the Velvet Revolution, there's
been considerable attention paid to reviving
the best of the gems, and to creating some
equally good new hotel bars.

The Alcron itself, as it's still known to old
timers, was badly neglected under the old
regime and, though the Radisson's installed
art deco wood and sculpted, frosted glass
throughout, the Be-Bop lobby bar has a name
that's more fun than the actual place itself.
Even with live jazz and quality gin it can't
really escape its new role as a business
hotel – although it's a damn good one.

That Jazz Age spirit can still be found in
a handful of hotels that offer sophisticated,
clubby, environs for an assignation and a
single malt. One of the best is in the Aria
Hotel (see p47). The grand piano, jazz theme,
crimson accents and serious cocktails make
the Coda a great hideout.

An even more discreet destination, with
a gourmet menu to boot, is Le Papillon, the
bar at Le Palais (see p66), a secret film biz
hideout with old-school green leather chairs
and a fine collection of Scotch. There's also
a grand terrace view of the Nusle Valley just
outside – the trade-off for being out of centre.

Hotel Questenberk

*Úvoz 15, Prague 1 (220 407 600/fax 220 407 601/
www.questenberk.cz). Tram 22, 23.* **Rooms** 30.
Rates 3,120-4,540 Kč single; 3,690-5,680 Kč double;
4,830-8,520 Kč junior suite. **Credit** AmEx, MC, V.
Map p326 B4 ❺
The baroque building that houses the Questenberk
was established in the 1660s as the Hospital of St
Elisabeth and St Norbert. Keep the address handy
when you're looking for the hotel – you may walk
right by, thinking it's a cathedral (what with the dramatic stone crucifix at the entrance). Inside, rooms
are standard for this category of hotel, but you're
paying for the location, just 500m from the castle.
Internet. No-smoking rooms. Parking. TV: satellite.

Pension Corto II

*Nerudova 27, Prague 1 (224 215 313/fax 224 235
779/www.corto.cz). Metro Malostranská/tram 12, 20,
22, 23.* **Rooms** 13. **Rates** 1,700-2,950 Kč single;
2,060-3,400 Kč double; 3,200-4,900 Kč apartment.
Extra bed 400-600 Kč. **Credit** AmEx, DC, JCB, MC,
V. **Map** p326 D3 ❻
The rooms are neat, clean and quite large, if a bit
plain. But no matter: the Corto II offers some of the
best value accommodation in this part of the city. A
gem for budget travellers intent on staying near the
castle. What's more, breakfast is included in the price.
TV: satellite.

U Červeného Lva

*Nerudova 41, Prague 1 (257 533 832/fax 257 532
746/www.hotelredlion.com). Metro Malostranská/*
tram 12, 22. **Rooms** 8. **Rates** 3,500-6,300 Kč single;
3,900-6,900 Kč double. *Extra bed* 800-1,000 Kč.
Credit AmEx, MC, V. **Map** p326 D3 ❼
There are few small hotels on the Royal Route leading up to the castle that can boast such authentic
17th-century decor, including hand-painted vaulted
ceilings. This reconstructed burgher's house provides guests with a sense of Renaissance Prague.
Service is adequate, though a bit lethargic.
Bar. Restaurants (3). TV: satellite.

U Červeného Lva II

*Nerudova 42, Prague 1 (257 535 538/fax 257 535
539/www.starshotelsprague.com). Metro Malostranská/
tram 12, 22.* **Rooms** 20. **Rates** 3,500-6,300 Kč
single; 3,900-6,900 Kč double. *Extra bed* 800-1,000 Kč.
Credit AmEx, MC, V. **Map** p326 D3 ❽
A low-key, sister hotel to U Červeného Lva, the Lva
II is just across the street. Originally built in the
1460s, the house was badly damaged in a 1541 fire,
and then reconstructed several times in subsequent
centuries. There's a lift as an alternative to the winding, 16th-century stairs. All the rooms are non-smoking. 10% discount for cash.
*Internet connection. Parking (off-site). Restaurants
(3). TV: satellite.*

U krále Karla

*Úvoz 4, Prague 1 (257 532 869/fax 257 533 591/
www.romantichotels.cz). Metro Malostranská/tram 12,
22.* **Rooms** 19. **Rates** 3,400-6,100 Kč single; 3,900-
6,900 Kč double; 7,500-7,900 Kč suite. *Extra bed* 1,100
Kč. **Credit** AmEx, MC, V. **Map** p326 D3 ❾

Solid oak furnishings, painted vaulted ceilings, stained-glass windows and various baroque treasures lend this hotel the feel of an aristocratic country house. In fact, it was once owned by the Benedictine Order. *Bar. Parking (call ahead to reserve). Restaurant. Room service (until 10pm). TV: satellite.*

U Žluté boty

Jánský vršek 11, Prague 1 (257 532 269/fax 257 534 134/www.zlutabota.cz). Tram 12, 20, 22, 23. **Rooms** 7. **Rates** 2,800-3,300 Kč single; 3,150-3,900 Kč double; 3,700-5,200 Kč apartment. *Extra bed* 900 Kč. **Credit** AmEx, MC, V. **Map** p326 D3 ⑩
Located on a quiet alley in the heart of Malá Strana, the U Žluté boty offers visitors all the rustic charm – and some of the drawbacks – of old Prague. Despite a renovation in 2001 some guests still complain of intermittent hot water on the top floor, and connecting doors between rooms so thin you can hear all about the cathedrals and pubs your neighbours visited that day. Still, the gorgeous, wood-lined building, which was built in the 1630s, has an antique charm and many guests have enjoyed their stays. Breakfasts come highly recommended.
Internet (wireless in reception).

Zlatá Hvězda

Nerudova 48, Prague 1 (257 532 867/fax 257 533 624/www.starshotelsprague.com). Metro Malostranská/tram 12, 22. **Rooms** 26. **Rates** 3,500-7,700 Kč single; 4,900-8,300 Kč double. **Credit** AmEx, MC, V. **Map** p326 C3 ⑪
The Zlatá Hvězda (Golden Star) dates from 1372, but a reconstruction in 2000 added lifts and modern bathrooms to the five-storey house's original architectural elements, including vaulted ceilings and a spiral staircase. A couple of tips: rooms ending with a 5 are spacious and feature huge bathrooms, and discounts for longer stays can sometimes be negotiated via the website. There's a tour desk on site.
Internet. Parking (off-site). Restaurant. TV: satellite.

Budget

Golden Horse House

Úvoz 8, Prague 1 (257 532 700/fax 257 532 700/www.goldhorse.cz). Metro Malostranská/tram 12, 20, 22, 23. **Rooms** 10. **Rates** 711-1,423 Kč single; 853-1,847 Kč double. *Extra bed* 284 Kč. **No credit cards.** **Map** p326 C3 ⑫
In the combination of prime location and low prices, the Golden Horse House is hard to beat. Rooms, with their own bath and toilet, are on a par with the better pensions or hostels. Breakfast costs 100 Kč.
Internet (wireless). TV: satellite.

Malá Strana

The Lesser Quarter feels like a small town in its own right. If you book well ahead, it's quite doable to score a bargain room on a cobbled, hilly lane straight out of a Dickens tale – or, perhaps, a Jan Neruda story.

Deluxe

Alchymist Grand Hotel & Spa

Tržiště 19, Prague 1 (257 286 011/fax 257 286 017/www.alchymisthotel.com). Metro Malostranská/tram 12, 20, 22, 23. **Rooms** 46. **Rates** 6,830-9,110 Kč double; 9,680-12,000 Kč junior suite. **Credit** AmEx, MC, V. **Map** 327 E4 ⑬
Relive Prague in its Habsburg days at the Alchymist, with antique furniture, ornately carved ceilings and sweeping, gauzy curtains. Formerly housing the Ježíšek Palace, built in the 16th century, the hotel is a short walk from the throngs on the Charles Bridge, but the on-site spa boasts an experienced team of masseuses to rub out those aching muscles. Finish the day with a dip in the hotel's indoor pool, or grab some maki at the sushi bar.
Gym. Internet (dataport). Restaurant. Spa. TV: Satellite.

Aria Hotel

Tržiště 9, Prague 1 (225 334 111/fax 257 334 666/www.ariahotel.net). Metro Malostranská/tram 12, 20, 22, 23. **Rooms** 52. **Rates** 9,100 Kč single; 9,950-12,084 Kč double; 15,000-27,300 Kč suite. **Credit** AmEx, MC, V. **Map** 327 E4 ⑭
First, let's dispel any notion that the music-themed Aria Hotel is a mere theme hotel. The amenities, service and location are all tremendous. The rooms are comfortable and jammed with features, including computers, DVD players, fresh orchids and fruit, and custom-designed furniture from Spatium. Now for the music: the floors are divided by genre – classical, opera, contemporary, jazz – and each room is dedicated to an artist. The computer in every room features a custom site with bio and songs from its namesake. There's a music lending library in the lobby with CDs, books and DVDs. That's where the Aria's musical director, the charming and knowledgeable Dr Ivana Stehlikova, holds court. The roof terrace may just be the best view in the city. Request a room facing the baroque gardens. **Photo** *p43.*
Bar. Business services. Concierge. Gym. Internet (high-speed). No-smoking rooms. Parking. Restaurant. Room service (24hrs). TV: satellite.

Expensive

Hotel Hoffmeister

Pod Bruskou 7, Prague 1 (251 017 111/fax 251 017 120/www.hoffmeister.cz). Metro Malostranská/tram 12, 18, 22. **Rooms** 41. **Rates** 4,820-7,372 Kč single; 6,000-8,500 Kč double; 8,213-16,860 Kč suite. *Extra bed* 1,445 Kč. **Credit** AmEx, MC, V. **Map** p327 G1 ⑮
The Hoffmeister is perhaps better suited to explorations of romantic and artistic Prague than more prosaic pursuits like closing a business deal, particularly since the hotel offers a head start by being filled with original works by the artist Adolf Hoffmeister. The rooms are spacious and tastefully decorated, and the soundproofed windows cut out the noise from the busy junction below. Under-fives stay for free, those between six and 11 are half price.

Bar. Disabled: adapted room. Internet (dataport). Parking. Restaurant. Spa. TV: pay movies/satellite.

Residence Nosticova

Nosticova 1, Prague 1 (257 312 513/516/fax 5731 2517/www.nosticova.com). Metro Malostranská/ tram 12, 22. **Rooms** 10. **Rates** 6,109-7,672 Kč suite; 8,089-10,360 Kč large suite. **Credit** AmEx, MC, V. **Map** p327 F5 ⑮

A classy little nook for those who plan to stay longer, this recently modernised baroque Ďresidenceí is on a quiet lane just off Kampa Island. The suites range from ample to capacious and come with antique furniture, baths big enough to swim in and, best of all, fully equipped kitchenettes. Two have working fireplaces and one a rooftop terrace. If you don't feel like cooking your own, continental breakfast is served for an extra 12 euros (341 Kč).

Internet (access in lobby, dataport in rooms). Parking. Restaurant. TV: satellite.

Moderate

Best Western Kampa Hotel

Všehrdova 16, Prague 1 (257 320 508/fax 257 404 333/www.praguekampahotel.com). Metro Malostranská/ tram 6, 9, 12, 20, 23, 22. **Rooms** 84. **Rates** 5,113-5,672 Kč single; 4,254-6,097 Kč double. *Extra bed* 879-1,984 Kč. **Credit** AmEx, DC, JCB, MC, V. **Map** p327 G6 ⑰

Located on a quiet backstreet in Malá Strana, the Kampa Hotel has retained its 17th-century architecture and style through recent renovations and the rooms are elegantly arranged. The vaulted 'Knights Hall' dining room and adjacent pub provides food, mounted weapons, a knights' tourney and dancers. The 60 Kč beers aren't worth the money, though.

Bar. Internet (dataport). Parking. Restaurant. TV: satellite.

Hotel Čertovka

U Lužického semináře 2, Prague 1 (257 011 500/fax 257 534 392/www.certovka.cz). Metro Malostranská/ tram 12, 22, 23. **Rooms** 21. **Rates** 3,663-4,232 Kč single; 4,886-5,624 Kč double. *Extra bed* 1,278 Kč. **Credit** AmEx, MC, V. **Map** p327 G4 ⑬

Located on a quiet, winding street near Charles Bridge, Hotel Čertovka is named after the canal on which it sits. Formerly a baroque mansion, it was transformed by the Richmond Group in 2000 into a comfortable hideaway with reasonable prices. You can request a room looking on to Prague Castle or the Charles Bridge tower (No.10 has the best view). The most romantic room, albeit with a shower rather than a bath, fronts the canal. Furnishings are tastefully modern with hints of 18th-century poshness. Warm and attentive staff.

Disabled: adapted room. Internet (dataport). Parking (off-site). Restaurant. TV: satellite.

Hotel Pod Věží

Mostecká 2, Prague 1 (257 532 041/fax 257 532 069/www.hotelpodvezi.cz). Metro Malostranská/tram 12, 22, 23. **Rooms** 12. **Rates** 4,055-6,068 Kč single;

5,082-8,000 Kč double; 6,780-9,020 Kč suite. *Extra bed* 1,000 Kč. **Credit** AmEx, DC, MC, V. **Map** p327 G4 ⑲

There's one thing that stands the Pod Věží in particularly good stead: its location at the end of Charles Bridge. That seems to have led to a certain complacency in other areas. For this category of hotel one would expect more than standard rooms and soft mattresses, but the location trumps such considerations. Try it as a second choice if you're keen to find a place to stay near Charles Bridge.

Internet (dataport). Parking (guarded). Restaurant. Room service (11am-11pm). TV: pay movies/satellite.

Hotel Waldstein

Valdštejnské Náměstí 6, Prague 1 (257 533 938/fax 257 531 143/www.certravel.cz). Metro Malostranská/ tram 12, 18, 22, 23. **Rooms** 30. **Rates** 2,640-6,600 Kč single; 3,630-7,920 Kč double; 4,290-8,910 Kč triple. **Credit** AmEx, MC, V. **Map** p327 F3 ⑳

The newly reconstructed Hotel Waldstein boasts a Renaissance vault where hearty buffet breakfasts are served. The lobby features stone tile floors and vaulted ceilings, and rooms have antique furniture and 17th-century ceiling frescoes, if no lifts. Budget travellers can opt for the Waldstein annexe, next door, with 11 apartment rooms and one suite that are rather plainer, but still classy. Rates vary greatly by season.

Internet. No-smoking hotel. Parking. TV: satellite.

Janáček Palace Hotel

Janáčkovo Nábřeží 19, Prague 1 (226 201 910). Tram 6, 9, 22, 23. **Rooms** 17. **Rates** 3,100-4,900 Kč 1 bedroom apartment; 4,049-5,903 Kč 2 bedroom apartment; 4,788-11,657 Kč 3 bedroom apartment. **Credit** AmEx, MC, DC, V.

It might claim to be a palace, and the impressive riverside location and gabled exterior support the billing, but the rooms themselves, despite being comfortable and airy, don't live up to the name. More money spent on design would turn an exceptional building into an exceptional place to stay, but the Janáček still offers a taste of fine Bohemian living.

TV: satellite.

Rezidence Lundborg

U Lužického semináře 3, Prague 1 (257 011 911/fax 257 011 966/www.lundborg.se). Metro Malostranská/ tram 12, 20, 22, 23. **Suites** 13. **Rates** 4,537-22,400Kč. **Credit** AmEx, DC, MC, V. **Map** 327 G4 ㉑

With a prime view of Charles Bridge, and built on the site of the older Juditin Bridge, this Scandinavian-owned hotel exudes luxury and charm. An example of the executive residence/hotel hybrid, Rezidence Lundborg pampers its guests with 13 suites, each a distinct and tasteful blend of reconstructed Renaissance decor and modern business amenities. It's a major splashout, but every conceivable need has been anticipated, from wine cellar to internet-connected computers in every room. The desk will efficiently arrange anything else you can think of asking for, and arrange golf programmes in Karlštejn or Konopiště resorts during summer.

Bar. Internet. Parking. Room service. TV: satellite.

U Karlova mostu

Na Kampě 15, Prague 1 (257 531 430/fax 257 533 168/www.archibald.cz). Metro Malostranská/tram 12, 20, 22, 23. **Rooms** 26. **Rates** 3,300-5,700 Kč single; 3,300-7,500 Kč double; 4,500-9,000 Kč apartment. *Extra bed* 1,000-1,200 Kč. **Credit** AmEx, DC, JCB, MC, V. **Map** p327 G5 ②

Formerly named Na Kampě 15, this hotel 'At Charles Bridge' affords some fine views of the bridge and Old Town, yet it's situated at a sufficient distance from the self-same bridge to provide its guests with some peace and quiet. The management here has done a sensitive restoration job on what used to be a 15th-century tavern that brewed one of the city's pioneering beers. The rooms are attractive, featuring wood floors, exposed beams and garret windows alongside modern furnishings. The two cellar pubs (which are ingeniously named Pub I and Pub II) and the beer garden out the back offer a reasonably varied menu, a good assortment of Czech and French wines and, of course, excellent Czech beer on tap. Be sure to check the hotel's website before booking a room, as it sometimes lists last-minute bargains. Service is very welcoming and friendly.

Bar. Internet (wireless in reception). Restaurants (2). No-smoking rooms. TV: satellite.

U Kříže

Újezd 20, Prague 1 (257 312 272/fax 257 312 542/ www.ukrize.com). Tram 6, 9, 12, 20, 23, 22. **Rooms** 22. **Rates** 2,400-3,700 Kč single; 2,800-3,900 Kč double; 3,300-5,600 Kč suite. **Credit** MC, V. **Map** p327 F6 ②

A popular choice, U Kříže provides great value for money in this price category. The rooms are clean and pleasant and the location is strategic: it's across the street from Petřín Hill, a quick walk to Kampa Island, one tram stop to the National Theatre, two stops to Malostranské náměstí, and just a few feet from Bohemia Bagel! A hotel that ticks all the right boxes. Be sure to ask for a room facing the atrium. Other rooms face Petřín Hill (which is great) but also the tram tracks (not so great).

Bar. Internet (dataport in reception). No-smoking rooms. Parking (covered).

U Páva

U Lužického semináře 32, Prague 1 (257 533 360/ fax 257 530 919/www.romantichotels.cz). Metro Malostranská/tram 12, 20, 22, 23. **Rooms** 27. **Rates** 4,600-6,700 Kč single; 4,800-7,200 Kč double; 7,500-8,200 Kč suite. *Extra bed* 1,400 Kč. **Credit** AmEx, DC, MC, V. **Map** p327 H3 ②

The dark oak ceilings and crystal chandeliers don't synthesise as well here as at U krále Karla (which is also owned by Karel Klubal; *see p46*), where the elegance is seamless, but U Páva's ideal location in a serene corner of Malá Strana should make visitors quite forgiving. When booking ask for suite 201, 301, 401 or 402, which all look on to the castle. Some rooms are not accessible via lift, so, if you need it, say so. Some rooms have a fireplace. **Photo** right.

No-smoking rooms. Parking. Restaurant. Room service (7.30am-10pm). TV: satellite.

U Tří Pštrosů

Dražického náměstí 12, Prague 1 (257 288 888/fax 257 533 217/www.upstrosu.cz). Metro Malostranská/ tram 12, 22, 23. **Rooms** 18. **Rates** 3,900-4,900 Kč single; 5,100-6,900 Kč double; 8,500-10,500 Kč suite. *Extra bed* 1,200 Kč. **Credit** AmEx, MC, V. **Map** p327 G4 ②

The prime location of U Tří Pštrosů at the foot of Charles Bridge may scare away some who fear a non-stop cacophony of tourists shrieking, 'This is just like Disney World!', but inside the hotel the noise factor is a non-issue thanks to soundproof windows. What is an issue is the iffy service. The rooms are pretty, though, with original ceiling beams giving a rustic feel, but the stairs are steep, so it's not a good choice for the less agile visitor. Rooms with a view of the bridge cost a bit more.

Bar. Internet (wireless). Parking. Restaurant. Room service (7am-midnight). TV: satellite.

U Zlaté Studně

U Zlaté studně 4, Prague 1 (257 011 213/fax 257 533 320/www.zlatastudna.cz). Metro Malostranská/ tram 12, 22, 23. **Rooms** 20. **Rates** 4,113-5,680 Kč double; 4,824-6,390 Kč deluxe double. *Extra bed* 993 Kč (in deluxe rooms only). **Credit** AmEx, DC, MC, V. **Map** p327 F2 ②

Hotel U Zlaté Studně is nestled on a secluded street in Malá Strana. Rooms in this tasteful high-end hideaway feature wood floors and ceilings and stylish furniture. If you love to soak, ask for one of the rooms with a huge tub. You can eat breakfast on a terrace that boasts a fine view of the city. The outlook from the dining area is tremendous as well. **Photo** *p52*.

Internet. Parking. TV: satellite.

Budget

Blue Key

Letenská 14, Prague 1 (257 534 361/fax 257 534 372/www.bluekey.cz). Metro Malostranská/tram 12, 22, 23. **Rooms** 28. **Rates** 2,267-3,970 single; 2,833-4,817 Kč double; 4,675-7,662 Kč suite; under-14s free with 2 adults. **Credit** AmEx, MC, V. **Map** p327 G3 ②

The Blue Key is located in a 14th-century townhouse just a minute or so from Malostranské náměstí in one direction, and Malostranská metro station in the other. Ask for a room facing the courtyard rather than one overlooking busy Letenská, which hosts a tram line and a steady stream of traffic. Double rooms are quite spacious and are equipped with kitchenettes. Some rooms are accessible only by stairs, so if you need the lift, say so. Repeat guests can take advantage of discounts.

Bar. Business services. Internet (wireless). No-smoking rooms. TV: satellite.

Hotel William

Hellichova 5, Prague 1 (257 320 242/fax 257 310 927/www.euroagentur.cz). Tram 12, 20, 22, 23. **Rooms** 42. **Rates** 2,640-4,785 Kč single; 2,970-5,115 Kč double. *Extra bed* 1,980 Kč. **Credit** AmEx, MC, V. **Map** p327 F5 ②

Would **U Páva** have a room in gold or crimson? *See p50.*

A taste of old Prague. **U Zlaté Studně**. *See p50.*

Opened in 2001, the William is an inconspicuous hotel set in a great location, a quick walk to the funicular up Petřín Hill, and just one tram stop from Malostranské náměstí. The interior, however, is definitely memorable, the interior decorators having gone a wee bit overboard trying for a 'castle feel'. The rooms, however, are comfortable and good value for money. Ask for one at the back of the hotel, away from the noise of the trams.
Internet (wireless). No-smoking rooms. Parking. TV: satellite.

Pension Dientzenhofer
Nosticova 2, Prague 1 (257 311 319/fax 257 320 888/www.dientzenhofer.cz). Metro Malostranská/ tram 12, 20, 22, 23. **Rooms** 9. **Rates** 1,900-3,250 Kč single; 2,500-4,100 Kč double; 1,950-6,900 Kč suite. **Credit** AmEx, DC, MC, V. **Map** p327 G5 **㉙**
The quiet courtyard and back garden of this pension offer a lovely respite in the midst of Malá Strana. Rooms are not tremendously posh, but they are bright and airy, and the staff are friendly. This 16th-century house is the birthplace of baroque architect Kilian Ignaz Dientzenhofer, whose work fills this quarter of the city. Book well ahead as it invariably fills up for summer. Note that it shares the building with Hostel Sokol (*see below*). **Photo p55.**
Bar. Disabled-adapted rooms. Internet. Parking. TV: satellite.

Hostels

Hostel Sokol
Nosticova 2, Prague 1 (257 007 397/fax 257 007 340). Metro Malostranská/tram 12, 20, 22, 23. **Open** 24hrs daily. **Beds** 104. **Rates** (per person) 300-350 Kč dormitory; 700-900 Kč double. **No credit cards. Map** p327 G5 **㉚**
Find Hostel Sokol, hidden in the yard behind Sokol sports centre (follow the signs to reception), and you've found the thirsty student travel nexus of Prague. There's a great beer terrace for alleviating that thirst, but many of the bunks are in a large gymnasium. The hostel is situated close to the castle and Charles Bridge, but breakast is not included in the price. Book rooms ahead via the phone number above, or e-mail hostelsocool@seznam.cz.
No-smoking rooms. Parking.

Staré Město

Sleeping in the heart of things can be managed and won't necessarily break the bank, though you'll pay more for food and drink. New inns are always opening and major hotels often offer discounts to build up business.

Deluxe

Four Seasons Hotel Prague
Veleslavínova 2A, Prague 1 (221 427 000/fax 221 426 000/www.fourseasons.com/prague). Metro Staroměstská/tram 17. **Rooms** 161. **Rates**

8,880-19,733 Kč single; 9,367-20,300 Kč double; 21,302-41,200 Kč suite. **Credit** AmEx, MC, V. Euros accepted. **Map** p328 J4 **㉛**
The only fault to be found with the Four Seasons is that it's too perfect. While the hotel is a seamless melding of restored Gothic, baroque, Renaissance and neo-classical buildings, guests will be hard-pressed to catch even a whiff of musty history. Of course, there's no shortage of that just outside the walls, so you might as well enjoy the pampering surroundings and service. Vista-seekers will want to reserve the top-flight rooms with sweeping views of Prague Castle and Charles Bridge. Excellent breakfast available in the restaurant.
Bar. Disabled: adapted rooms. Internet (dataport). Gym. Parking. Restaurant. Room service (24hrs). TV: pay movies/satellite.

Iron Gate
Michalská 19, Prague 1 (225 777 777/fax 225 777 778/www.irongate.cz). Metro Staroměstská or Národní třída/tram 6, 9, 18, 21, 22, 23, 26. **Suites** 43. **Rates** 6,951-9,790 Kč studio; 10,921-17,000 Kč suites. *Extra bed* 994 Kč. **Credit** AmEx, MC, V. Euros accepted. **Map** p328 L5 **㉜**
Antiquarians wanting authentic places to stay, take note: the Prague Municipality recognised the Iron Gate as the best historic reconstruction in 2003. The two buildings date from the 14th and 16th centuries and preserve the original painted ceiling beams and frescoes. To maintain the Gothic look, the suites' kitchenettes are discreetly tucked inside antique armoires. The Tower Suite is over the top in more ways than one: stashed away on three floors of the building, it features a heart-shaped bed, jacuzzi built for two, and a study suitable for the astronomer Johannes Kepler, with views of the Old Town Hall, Prague Castle and acres of orange roof tiles.
Bar. Concierge. Gym. Internet (wireless). Restaurant. Room service. TV: satellite.

Expensive

Casa Marcello
Řásnovka 783, Prague 1 (222 310 260/fax 222 313 323/www.casa-marcello.cz). Metro Náměstí Republiky/ tram 5, 8, 9, 14. **Rooms** 32. **Rates** 7,670 Kč single and double; 9,374 Kč junior suite; 11,074 Kč apartment (for up to 6 people). **Credit** AmEx, DC, JCB, MC, V. Euros accepted. **Map** p329 N2 **㉝**
Adjacent to the Convent of St Agnes, this hotel occupies an impossibly charming corner of Old Town. The labyrinthine hallways and grotto-like rooms reflect the twisting alleys and hidden courtyards outside. Like an ageing old eccentric, Casa Marcello is unapologetically old-fashioned and showing a bit of wear around the edges, but always charming.
Bar. Gym. Internet (dataport). No-smoking rooms. Restaurant. TV: satellite.

Grand Hotel Bohemia
Králodvorská 4, Prague 1 (234 608 111/fax 222 329 545/www.grandhotelbohemia.cz). Metro Náměstí Republiky/tram 5, 8, 9, 14. **Rooms** 78.

Rates 5,534-7,229 Kč single; 6,100-7,665 Kč double; suites from 11,780 Kč. *Extra bed* 1,704 Kč. **Credit** AmEx, MC, V. **Map** p329 N4 ❸❹

An understated art deco masterpiece, the Bohemia goes quietly about its task of providing top-notch service with Habsburg-like stateliness. One would never guess that the hotel's subterranean ballrooms once hosted some pretty scandalous Jazz Age excesses. Nowadays guests are mainly preoccupied with business and the odd moment of serenely gazing down on the city from the upper floors. Children aged up to nine can stay here free of charge.

Bar. Disabled: adapted rooms. Internet (wireless). No-smoking floors. Restaurant. TV: satellite.

Hotel Rott

Malé náměstí 4, Prague 1 (224 190 901/fax 224 216 762/www.hotelrott.cz). Metro Staroměstská/tram 17. **Rooms** 83. **Rates** 5,537 Kč single; 6,530 Kč double; 7,760 Kč triple; 7,000-8,400 Kč apartment. **Credit** AmEx, JCB, MC, V. **Map** p328 L4 ❸❺

There's definitely nothing rotten in the heart of Old Town, but there are some surprisingly plain rooms. The Rott takes its name from the ornately frescoed building next door, but the hotel feels a little unfinished: add to the plainly-decorated rooms some that lack air-conditioning, although portable units will suck away any Czech heatwaves. Though there are some fine views of Prague Castle and the spires of Týn Church from the housetop maisonette.

Bar. Business services. Concierge. Disabled: adapted room. Gym. Internet (dataport). No-smoking rooms. Restaurant. TV: pay movies/satellite.

Pachtův Palace

Karolíny Světlé 34, Prague 1 (234 705 111/fax 234 705 112/www.pachtuvpalace.com). Metro Můstek/tram 6, 9, 17, 18, 22, 23. **Rooms** 50. **Rates** 6,980-9,963 Kč studio; 9,680-15,820 Kč suite. **Credit** AmEx, DC, MC, V. **Map** p328 J5 ❸❻

With 50 deluxe, just-modernised apartments and managers for various big-shot corporations already moving in, you're in some powerful company at Pachtův Palace. The former residence of Count Jan Pachta is now a swank place to stay, where business amenities, a classy bar and babysitting go along with the timbered rooms and, well, stunning palatial public areas. The buzz about this grand villa is persistent among Prague's elite.

Bar. Internet (dataport). Gym. Restaurant. Room service (24 hrs). TV: satellite.

Moderate

Apostolic Residence

Staroměstské náměstí 26, Prague 1 (221 632 222/ fax 221 632 558/www.prague-residence.cz). Metro Staroměstská/tram 17, 18. **Rooms** 3. **Rates** 3,590-5,990 Kč single; 4,290-6,990 Kč double; 5,990-8,990 Kč apartment. *Extra bed* 1,500 Kč. **Credit** AmEx, V. **Map** p328 L4 ❸❼

Amazingly, this enchanting and reasonably priced Renaissance-era inn overlooks Old Town Square. With just three rooms (a double room and two flats)

and this central location, it's no surprise that the Apostolic needs to be booked well ahead. But bedding down on the Apostolic's antique dark wood beds, in quarters that boast original ceiling beams and thick cream-coloured walls, and staff that offer efficient service, is surely worth planning ahead for. One advantage to the heavy ancient masonry is that it effectively muffles most of the all-night noise that can drift up from Old Town Square below.

Bar. Internet (wireless). Parking (off-site). TV: cable.

Bellagio Hotel Prague

U Milosrdných 2, Prague 1 (221 778 999/ fax 221 778 900/www.bellagiohotel.cz). Metro Staroměstská/tram 17/133 bus. **Rooms** 46. **Rates** 5,000-6,000 Kč single; 5,120-6,600 Kč double; 5,900-8,110 Kč suite. **Credit** AmEx, MC, V. **Map** p328 L2 ❸❽

This Italian-style hotel in Josefov features a grand, winding stairwell leading guests into fine rooms that boast modular, sensible furniture, and brown and burnished gold touches. Noted chef Lars Sjöstrand used to serve up cuisine at Kampa Park and other upmarket eateries; now he dedicates his time to the Bellagio, crafting Italian and world cuisine for the hotel's Restaurant Isabella. A no-nonsense cocktail bar and conference room boost this gem's attribute list, as does the prime location. **Photo** *p56.*

Bar. Internet (high-speed). Restaurant.

Pension Dientzenhofer. See *p53.*

Bellagio Hotel Prague. See p55.

Černá Liška

*Mikulášská 2, Prague 1 (224 232 250/fax 224 232
249/www.cernaliska.cz). Metro Staroměstská/tram
17, 18.* **Rooms** 12. **Rates** 2,700-3,500 Kč single;
3,500-4,600 Kč double; 4,800-5,500 Kč suite. *Extra
bed* 720-950 Kč. **Credit** MC, V. **Map** p328 L4

Though a location right on Old Town Square is not
for everyone, the Black Fox offers excellent value in
the medieval centre of Prague, with the accent, in the
neat rooms, on locale rather than charm. Wake up
to the sound of the Týn church bells (and the rum-
ble of tourist traffic), then stumble out for some
gallery-hopping, pubbing and clubbing, without
ever needing to risk your budget on Prague's infamous taxis. Note: the tiny lifts were apparently built
for the people of Jan Hus's time, who were much
smaller. Not the best choice around here, but certainly a good backup.

Disabled: adapted room. Restaurant. TV: satellite.

Cloister Inn

*Konviktská 14, Prague 1 (224 211 020/fax 224
210 800/www.cloister-inn.com). Metro Národní
třída/tram 6, 9, 18, 22, 23.* **Rooms** 75. **Rates**
3,100-4,600 Kč single; 3,300-4,500 Kč double;
3,800-5,000 Kč triple. **Credit** AmEx, DC, JCB,
MC, V. **Map** p328 K5

The Cloister Inn has a lot going for it: attentive staff,
great location, good prices and a nearby house full
of nuns in case you're in need of redemption. Rooms
are bright and cheery, and in the lobby you'll find a

computer with free internet access, plus free coffee
and tea, and a lending library. Prices have risen of
late, but keep your eye on its website for deals.

*Concierge. Internet. No-smoking rooms. Parking
(paid). TV: satellite.*

Floor Hotel

*Na Příkopě 13, Prague 1 (234 076 300/fax 234 076
112/www.floorhotel.cz). Metro Můstek.* **Rooms** 43.
Rates 2,420-3,700 Kč single; 3,130-4,840 Kč double.
Credit AmEx, MC, V. **Map** p328 M5

Floor is a newly opened luxury hotel sitting conveniently on Prague's marquee shopping promenade,
Na Příkopě. Half the rooms are designed with traditional luxury in mind, the remainder go for the sleek,
modern look. Only four storeys high, it features an
upscale Italian restaurant with an impressive menu,
and a large, crystal-chandeliered conference room
for the business traveller.

Bar. Internet (high-speed). Restaurant. TV: cable.

Hotel Josef

*Rybná 20, Prague 1 (221 700 111/fax 221
700 999/www.hoteljosef.com). Metro Náměstí
republiky/tram 5, 8, 9, 14.* **Rooms** 109. **Rates**
4,236-5,800 Kč single; 4,235-6,822 Kč double. *Extra
bed* 1,421 Kč. **Credit** AmEx, MC, V. Euros accepted.
Map p329 N3

Definitely the hippest, if not the only, designer hotel
in Old Town, the Josef opened in 2002. The flash
interiors, and unique fabrics and glass bathrooms
(superior-class rooms only) are the work of London

based designer Eva Jiřičná. The hotel is in the thick of the historic centre, with the top-floor rooms in the 'Pink House' having the best views. Children aged under six are invited to stay for free. **Photo** *p58*.
Bar. Business services. Concierge. Gym. Internet (wireless). No-smoking floors. Parking. Room service. TV: satellite.

Hotel Liberty

28 Října 11, Prague 1 (224 239 598/fax 224 237 694/www.hotelliberty.cz). Metro Můstek/tram 6, 9, 11 18, 21, 23. **Rooms** 32. **Rates** 4,694-8,391 Kč single; 4,967-9,941 Kč double. *Extra bed* 1,136 Kč. **Credit** AmEx, DC, MC, V. **Map** p328 M5 **43**
Don't you just love PR speak: 'Where the rooms have not only a number – but also a soul'. Come on, it's a hotel, not a human being. What the Liberty does have is superb service, a central location and dignified rooms tailored to affluent business travellers. Three suites have balconies and one has an exceptional view of the castle. Just stop anthropomorphising four walls and a ceiling.
Internet (dataport). Gym. No-smoking rooms. Parking. TV: pay movies/satellite.

Hotel Mejstřík Praha

Jakubská 5, Prague 1 (224 800 055/fax 224 800 056/www.hotelmejstrik.cz). Metro Náměstí Republiky/tram 5, 14, 26. **Rooms** 29. **Rates** 3,600-5,500 Kč single; 4,400-6,200 Kč double; 7,300-8,300 Kč suite. *Extra bed* 900-1,200 Kč. **Credit** AmEx, DC, MC, V. **Map** p329 N3 **44**
The Mejstřík, handily located in the heart of Old Town, is now back in the hands of the family that founded it in 1924. Individually decorated rooms are a hybrid of ubiquitous modern hotel decor and 1920s style. Art deco elements and wood trim are a nice touch and corner rooms offer great vantages for spying on streetlife and gables.
Bar. Business service. Disabled: adapted rooms. Internet (dataport). No-smoking rooms. Parking. Restaurant. TV: satellite.

Hotel Metamorphis

Malá Štupartská 5 (Ungelt Square), Prague 1 (221 771 011/fax 221 771 099/www.metamorphis.cz). Metro Náměstí Republiky/tram 5, 14, 26. **Rooms** 24. **Rates** 4,680-6,870 Kč single; 4,980-7,170 Kč double; 5,580-8,070 Kč suite. *Extra bed* 1,320-1,600 Kč. **Credit** AmEx, DC, JCB, MC, V. **Map** p328 M3 **45**
The former Pension Metamorphosis has metamorphosised not into a beetle, but into the Hotel Metamorphis. Each room is different, but all are tastefully done, featuring wood floors and an array of comforts, and some ceilings have original beams from the end of the 15th century. The once-empty square on which the Metamorphis stands has become a tourist mecca, jammed with craft shops, a respectable bookstore and cafés, and one of the best is on the ground floor of the Metamorphis itself. Ask for a view of Týn Church. Check website for deals.
Bar. Internet (dataport). Parking. Restaurants (2). TV: pay movies/satellite.

Hotel Paříž Praha

U Obecního domu 1, Prague 1 (222 195 195/ fax 224 225 475/www.hotel-pariz.cz). Metro Náměstí Republiky/tram 5, 8, 9, 14. **Rooms** 95. **Rates** 4,800-5,760 Kč single; 5,120-6,080 Kč double; suites from 8,000 Kč. *Extra bed* 1,920 Kč. **Credit** AmEx, DC, JCB, MC, V. **Map** p329 N3 **46**
If any hotel captures the spirit of Prague's belle époque, it's the Hotel Paříž Praha. Immortalised by Bohumil Hrabal's *I Served the King of England*, the Paříž is ageing with remarkable grace. Guests who are weary of cookie-cutter hotels will appreciate the patina of the historic rooms and carefully preserved Jazz Age dining room and café. Is money no object? Then be sure to reserve (well in advance) the Royal Tower Suite, with its 360-degree view of the city.
Bar. Internet (dataport). No-smoking floor. Restaurant. Spa. TV: satellite.

Hotel U Klenotníka

Rytířská 3, Prague 1 (224 211 699/fax 224 221 025/www.uklenotnika.cz). Metro Můstek/tram 6, 9, 11, 18, 21, 23. **Rooms** 11. **Rates** 2,100-2,500 Kč single; 3,100-3,800 Kč double; 3,100-4,500 Kč double with extra bed. **Credit** AmEx, DC, MC, V. **Map** p328 L5 **47**
A burgher house from the 11th century situated on a narrow street lined with historic façades. U Klenotníka is perfect for night owls, situated as it is right between Wenceslas and Old Town Squares. The rooms are sparse but tidy and clean, and the bathrooms have been newly renovated. The quietest rooms face the back of the hotel: doubles 11 and 21, and singles 12 and 22. The tiny lift is only for luggage, so this is not a good choice if you're uncomfortable climbing stairs.
Bar. Internet (dataport). Parking (guarded, off-site). Restaurant. TV: satellite.

Hotel U Prince

Staroměstské náměstí 29, Prague 1 (224 213 807/ fax 224 213 807/www.hoteluprince.cz). Metro Staroměstská/tram 17, 18. **Rooms** 24. **Rates** 4,480-5,990 Kč single; 4,190-6,190 Kč double; 5,600-7,190 Kč junior suite; 7,990-10,990 Kč suite. *Extra bed* 1,200 Kč. **Credit** AmEx, MC, V. **Map** p328 L4 **48**
An authentic slice of history smack in the centre of Old Town Square. Opened in 2001, the hotel is a reconstruction of a 12th-century building and boasts huge rooms with antiques and individually designed canopy beds and armoires. The marble bathrooms make for splendid decadence. There are several eateries, including a seafood cavern. Its rooftop restaurant offers a dazzling view of most of Prague's landmarks. As with many hotel eateries, however, it's probably best to just enjoy a coffee or cocktail, then dine elsewhere. Still, even subtracting points for the obnoxious squawking parrots in the lobby, this is one of the most interesting and best-located hotels that you'll find in the city.
Bar. Internet (dataport). No-smoking room. Parking. Restaurants (3). Room service (24hrs). TV: satellite.

Hotel Josef. *See p56.*

Inter-Continental Praha

Náměstí Curieovych 43-45, Prague 1 (296 631 111/ fax 224 811 216/www.intercontinental.com). Metro Staroměstská/tram 17, 18. **Rooms** 372. **Rates** 3,380- 8,250 Kč single and double; 8,636-11,650 Kč suite. **Credit** AmEx, MC, V. **Map** p328 K2

Celebrating its 33rd anniversary in 2007, the Inter-Continental Praha may at last be getting it right. While visual traces of communist design were expunged during a $50-million refurbishment in the 1990s, only recently does the transformation seem to have taken hold in earnest, with courteous service and no reminders of the C word in sight. All rooms have a dataport for your laptop and the entire hotel will soon be a wireless hotspot. The negative? One side of the hotel faces a garish neon-lit casino, and there's an extra charge if you want a room facing the river. Children eat for free.

Bar. Business services. Disabled: adapted room. Gym. Internet (wireless). No-smoking floors. Pool. Restaurants (2). Room service (24hrs). TV: pay movies/satellite.

Residence Řetězova

Řetězova 9, Prague 1 (222 221 800/fax 222 221 800/www.residenceretezova.com). Metro Staroměstská/ tram 17, 18. **Rooms** 9. **Rates** 3,550-5,830 Kč single, double; 4,840-8,260 Kč suites. **Credit** AmEx, MC, V. **Map** p328 K5

The Residence Řetězova features nine bright and airy apartments on one of the city centre's quieter, tourist-friendly streets. Just a stone's throw from Charles Bridge, the double rooms have more character than most hotel rooms in town, with warm

wood accents and soft, neutral tones. Fireplaces and vaulted ceilings are the norm for the suites, as are bidets and comfy sitting areas.

Internet (high-speed). No-smoking rooms. Parking (off-site). TV: cable.

U Tří Bubnů

U radnice 10, Prague 1 (224 214 855/fax 224 236 100/www.utribubnu.cz). Metro Staroměstská/tram 17, 18. **Rooms** 18. **Rates** 2,800-4,900 Kč double; 3,400-5,300 Kč suite. *Extra bed* 600-1,100 Kč. **Credit** MC, V. **Map** p328 L4

The U Tří Bubnů is just 50m from Old Town Square, but despite the location the rooms are quiet, thanks to ancient, thick walls. And while those rooms might have few frills, the wood furniture and ceilings lend the hotel the atmosphere of old Prague. The service is worthy of the days of old as well. The attic suites are huge, perfect for a family stay.

Internet. TV: satellite.

U zlaté studny

Karlova 3, Prague 1 (222 220 262/fax 222 221 112/www.uzlatestudny.cz). Metro Staroměstská/ tram 17. **Rooms** 6. **Rates** 3,750-4,900 Kč double; 4,500-5,600 Kč suite. **Credit** AmEx, MC, V. **Map** p328 K4

Fans of the arcane will delight in this 16th-century building and the well in its cellar that gives the hotel its name. Exquisitely decorated and furnished with Louis XIV antiques and replicas, the four suites and two double rooms are positively cavernous by Old Town standards. Sightseers, once they get their bearings, will appreciate its location halfway between Charles Bridge and Old Town Square on the Royal Route. Children aged up to 15 stay for free. *Internet point. Restaurant. TV: satellite.*

Ventana Hotel

Celetna 7, Prague 1 (866 376 7831/www.epoque hotels.com). Metro Náměstí Republiky/tram 5, 8, 9, 14. **Rooms:** 30. **Rates** 3,730-6,600 Kč single; 4,450-7,750 Kč double. *Extra bed* 1,150 Kč. **Credit** AmEx, V. **Map** 328 M4 ⑬
Another charming new entry just off Old Town Square, the Italian marble, elegant detail work, soft lighting and high, stuccoed ceilings show a sense of understated style. The library and bar are welcoming, and rooms have Philippe Starck touches, café au lait colour schemes and big beds. Service is also sharp, as at other Epoque Hotel properties.
Bar. Concierge. Internet (dataport). Room service (24hrs). TV: satellite.

Budget

Betlem Club

Betlémské náměstí 9, Prague 1 (222 221 574/fax 222 220 580/www.betlemclub.cz). Metro Národní třída/tram 6, 9, 18, 22, 23. **Rooms** 22. **Rates** 1,900-3,000 Kč single; 2,800-4,500 Kč double; 3,200-5,100 Kč suite. *Extra bed* 350-900 Kč. **Credit** MC, V. **Map** p328 K5 ⑭
Like a number of hotels in Prague, the Betlem Club trades more on its location – a twist and a turn from Charles Bridge in one direction, a hop and a skip to

Old Town Square in the other – than its design, although the single rooms in the attic remain good bargains. The rooms have an air of faded elegance, the chintzy modern touches serving only to highlight the decline, rather like an ageing socialite who's struggling to recapture her sparkle with cheap jewellery and stale perfume. Modern bathrooms are a saving grace, however. Whoever 'decorated' the lobby must have scored a crate of replica swords on the cheap. Under-fives stay for free.
TV: satellite.

Botel Albatross

Nábřeží Ludvíka Svobody (adjacent to Štefánik Bridge), Prague 1 (224 810 541/fax 224 811 214/www.botelalbatros.cz). Metro Náměstí Republiky/tram 5, 8, 14, 26. **Rooms** 86. **Rates** 1,021-1,986 Kč single; 1,306-2,497 Kč double; 1,929-3,239 Kč triple. **Credit** AmEx, MC, V. Euros accepted. **Map** p329 O1 ⑮
Essentially a floating prefab apartment, the Albatross has seen better days. Still, it's hard to beat the price for a quiet room in Old Town, especially if you're going to spend most of your time ashore anyway. The rooms are humble, the facilities modest and the staff somewhat salty.
Bar. Parking. Restaurant. TV: satellite.

Hotel Černy Slon

Tynská 1, Prague 1 (222 321 521/fax 222 310 351/www.hotelcernyslon.cz). Metro Staroměstská/tram 17, 18. **Rooms** 16. **Rates** 2,075-4,462 Kč single;

Palatial *palács*

Come to a fairytale city, stay in a palace. The logic's inescapable. So, then, assuming you've got your expense account in order...
 Pachtův Palace (*see p55*) was once home to Count Jan Pachta, who hosted Mozart. Now this oasis for the well-heeled, with 50 apartments, each with distinct decor, is managed by the capable MaMaison residences. The rooms are indeed decadent, with fireplaces, exposed beams and frescoes, but the epic, imperial glamour pretty much ends at the lobby and common areas. Still, Pachtův has impeccable service and wall-to-wall character, 24-hour room service, and comes with bragging rights.
 Janáček Palace Hotel (*see p49*), across the River Vltava in the Malá Strana district, despite its name, has nary a regal connection to its past – but who needs to know that? The clean rooms, more affordable if far less inspired, come with views of the pantiled rooftops all around. If your friends press you for historic details, just mutter something about an Archduke Ferdinand.

The **Alchymist Grand Hotel & Spa** (*see p47*) doesn't even have 'palace' in its name, but just have yourself photographed in the entrance and you'll silence any sceptics. This baroque pile is as much a stately home as any pedigreed lord ever scored in the Czech lands – and it comes with vaulted ceilings, frescoes, four-poster beds, Balinese massage, and a pool and a sushi bar.
 The **Hotel Palace Praha** (*see p61*), though long known for its capable service and reliable facilities for business folks, is not, truth be told, a palace at all, despite a lovely fin-de-siècle façade and much brass and marble within.
 Le Palais (*see p66*), however, more than lives up to the name, with movie stars, deep carpets, a fine brandy with truffles in the clubby bar, and service so discreet you could plot a coup here. Who cares that it was once a meatpacking house? If it lacks pedigree, it more than makes up for that with a palace conception cut from whole cloth and brought off as successfully as anyone might hope for.

HOTEL METAMORPHIS ★★★★
Malá Štupartská 5/636, Prague 1

The hotel is situated directly in the heart of the historical centre of Prague, in the UNESCO listed area of Ungelt. The building history dates back to 17th century, formerly the building served as custom house during a florishing business period..

The hotel offers accommodation in 24 rooms incl. appartements and suites, which are sensitively built into the former spaces. Rooms are equipped with bath and/or shower, WC, minibar, SAT-TV, direct-dial-phone, safe, tea and coffee making facitilities. Most of them air-conditioned, accessible by lift.

The hotel offers 2 restaurants – Café and Club Restaurant, possibility of meetings and social events, parking and concierge services.

Reception / Reservations:
Tel: +420 221 771 011,
Fax: +420 221 771 099
E-mail: hotel@metamorphis.cz,
Website: www.metamorphis.cz

HOTEL · CLUB · RESTAURANT
METAMORPHIS

Hotel Athena Palace is new hotel located in the centre of Prague surrounded by well known hisorical sights and places such as Wenceslav Square, Charles Square, Old Town Square, Astronomical Clock, National Museum. We could offer to you luxury accommodation for good price. Rooms are furnished with antique furniture, TV sat, direct telephone, safebox, minibar. You could use our conference facilitites for meetings, weddings, parties etc... We would like to wish you nice stay in Prague

★★★★
Hotel Athena Palace

Salmovská 10, Praha 2,
Tel.: +420 224 900 634
Fax: +420 222 513 516
E-mail: info@hotelathenapalace.com
http://www.hotelathenapalace.com

2,842-5,400 Kč double; 4,349-6,700 Kč triple.
Extra bed 950 Kč. **Credit** AmEx, MC, V.
Map p328 M3 ⑱
With an incredible location in the shadow of the Týn Church just off Old Town Square, this cosy 16-room inn is ensconced in a 14th-century building that is on the UNESCO heritage list. Gothic stone arches and wooden floors go along with the smallish but comfortable rooms laid out with basic amenities. Windows look out on the cobbled mews of Old Town, with a constant parade of characters. Fortunately, it's on one of the district's quieter lanes, despite being just metres from the tourist hordes rampaging in Old Town Square.
Bar. Parking (off-site). Restaurant. TV: satellite.

U krále Jiřího
Liliová 10, Prague 1 (221 466 100/fax 221 466 166/ www.kinggeorge.cz). Metro Staroměstská or Národní třída/tram 6, 9, 17, 18, 21, 22, 23, 26. **Rooms** 12.
Rates 1,650-2,750 Kč single; 2,500-4,250 Kč double; 3,750-7,550 Kč apartment. *Extra bed* 1,100-1,850 Kč. **Credit** AmEx, MC, V. **Map** p328 K5 ⑰
This simple pension is named for King George of Poděbrady, who kept a house nearby. An easy walk from Old Town Square and Charles Bridge, it's a fair choice for tourists who want to get the most out of their time. For a drink, pop next door to Prague's original Irish pub, the James Joyce.
Bar. Restaurant. TV: satellite.

U Medvídků
Na Perštyně 7, Prague 1 (224 211 916/fax 224 220 930/www.umedvidku.cz). Metro Národní třída/tram 6, 9, 18, 21, 22, 23, 26. **Rooms** 33. **Rates** 1,550-3,000 Kč single; 2,300-4,500 Kč double; 3,100-6,000 Kč triple. *Extra bed* 400-1,000 Kč. **Credit** AmEx, MC, V. **Map** p328 L6 ⑱
The Little Bears hearkens back to a number of Dark Ages. The iron doors on some rooms may remind visitors of Gothic dungeons, while the rudimentary bathrooms evoke the benighted years of communism. The traditional inn's pub – one of the first to serve Budvar – keeps a constant stream of tourists and locals fed on roasted pig, but the prices of food and drink could be lower.
Bar. Restaurant. TV: satellite.

Hostels

Travellers' Hostel
Dlouhá 33, Prague 1 (224 826 662/663/fax 224 826 665/www.travellers.cz). Metro Náměstí Republiky/ tram 5, 14, 26. **Open** 24hrs daily (all branches).
Rates (per person) 650-750 Kč double; 500 Kč triple; 450 Kč 4-6-bed rooms; 2,100-2,400 Kč 2-4-bed apartment; 2,500-3,000 Kč 2-room apartment; 390 Kč dormitory. **Credit** MC, V. **Map** p329 N2 ⑲
The two constants at the Travellers' Hostel on Dlouhá street are good value and English-speaking backpackers. You'll find internet access, drinks and sandwiches for sale in the lobby. In addition to dorm beds, this location also now features five apartments and a surprisingly romantic double suite complete

with beamed ceilings. Both the apartments and the suite feature kitchens and offer outstanding value. Make sure to book ahead. The hostel also functions as a booking office connecting travellers to a whole network of hostels (www.czechhostels.com). The seventh night stay comes free.
Internet. No-smoking hotel.
Other locations: throughout town. Check website or the phone book for your nearest.

Nové Město

Prague's New Town lacks the medieval charm of Old Town, but more than makes up for it with lower prices, more rooms and better dining. And you're still only streets away from the centre, but also near the happening neighbourhoods of Vinohrady and Žižkov.

Deluxe

Ambassador Zlatá Husa
Václavské náměstí 5-7, Prague 1 (224 193 111/fax 224 226 167/www.ambassador.cz). Metro Můstek/ tram 3, 9, 14, 24, 26. **Rooms** 161. **Rates** 7,700 Kč single; 9,000 Kč double; 10,200 Kč suite. **Credit** AmEx, DC, MC, V. **Map** p328 M5 ⑳
The address alone is enough to get most people to book, and while the amenties are right, service is quite iffy for the price and some may be disappointed in the 'nothing special' rooms. Apartments are good-sized, however, and there is the built-in casino and plush strip club. Check the website before you book, it often lists decent specials.
Bar. Concierge. Disabled: adapted rooms. No-smoking rooms. Restaurant. Room service (24hrs). TV: pay movies/satellite.

Hotel Palace Praha
Panská 12, Prague 1 (224 093 111/fax 224 221 240/www.palacehotel.cz). Metro Můstek/tram 3, 9, 14, 24, 26. **Rooms** 124. **Rates** 6,920 Kč single; 8,200-10,080 Kč double; 11,100-21,560 Kč suites; 25,600-32,000 Kč presidential apartment. *Extra bed* 1,400 Kč. **Credit** AmEx, MC, V. **Map** p329 N5 ㉑
Off Wenceslas Square, yet still close to everything, especially the city's smarter Na příkopě, the Palace almost seems to belong in another part of the city. Understated but tasteful is how one could describe both the rooms and the staff. You won't be oohing and ahhing, but you won't miss anything either.
Bar. Business services. Disabled: adapted rooms. Internet (dataport). No-smoking floors. Restaurant. TV: satellite.

K+K Fenix
Ve Smečkách 30, Prague 1 (225 012 222/fax 222 212 141/www.kkhotels.com). Metro Muzeum/tram 3, 9, 14, 24, 26. **Rooms** 130. **Rates** 7,504 Kč single; 8,064 Kč double. *Extra bed* 1,400 Kč. **Credit** AmEx, MC, V. Euros accepted. **Map** p 331 N7 ㉒
The Fenix looks a bit out of place on this quiet street off Wenceslas Square. But once you're inside, the clean, simple look will be soothing. Owner K + K

Grand Hotel Evropa on the outside, not so grand within. *See p63.*

operates a number of hotels around Europe, and seems to have the service thing down pat. The rooms have an almost austere quality to them, with light wood and colours predominating.
Bar. Concierge. Disabled: adapted rooms. Gym. Internet (high-speed). No-smoking floors. Parking (16 euros/night). TV: satellite.

Expensive

Hotel Yasmin

Politických vězňů 12, Prague 1 (234 100 100/fax 234 100 101/www.hotel-yasmin.cz). Metro Mustek/tram 3, 9. **Rooms** 209. **Rates** 6,260-7,400 Kč single; double; 7,400-8,540 Kč suite. **Credit** AmEx, DC, MC, V. **Map** p329 O6 ⑥³
This ultra-modern hotel opened up in early 2006, bolstered by its just off Wenceslas Square location and easy access to public transit. Rooms are all clean lines and cutting-edge design, while the lobby and restaurant, Noodles, combine high fashion and a retro 1970s flair via lots of glass and geometric shapes. Includes more than 100 non-smoking rooms and several rooms for people with disabilities.

Bar. Business services. Disabled: adapted rooms. Gym. Internet (dataport). No-smoking rooms. Restaurant. TV: satellite.

Radisson SAS Alcron

Štěpánská 40, Prague 1 (222 820 000/fax 222 820 100/www.radisson.com/praguecs). Metro Muzeum/tram 3, 9, 14, 24, 26. **Rooms** 211.
Rates 6,270-8,850 Kč single and double; 10,050 Kč suite. *Extra bed* 1,500 Kč. **Credit** AmEx, DC, MC, V. Euros accepted. **Map** p331 N7 ⑥⁴
Originally known as a jazz hotel when it was built in 1930, the Radisson SAS Alcron has kept that part of its history preserved, as well as being one of the city's first luxury hotels. It still is widely believed to be one of the best hotels in town, with well-blended art deco style and Radisson service. The higher up your room, the more beautiful the views, but the high ceilings and period furnishings in all the rooms make each one a true classic.
Bar. Concierge. Disabled: adapted rooms. Gym. Internet (dataport). No-smoking floors. Parking. Restaurant. Room service (24hrs). TV: pay movies/cable/satellite.

Moderate

Andante

*Ve Smečkách 4, Prague 1 (222 210 021/fax 222
210 591/www.andante.cz). Metro Muzeum or IP
Pavlova/tram 4, 6, 10, 11, 16, 22, 23.* **Rooms** 32.
Rates 2,800-4,060 Kč single; 3,920-4,4480 Kč double;
4,760-6,160 Kč suite. *Extra bed* 700-860 Kč. **Credit**
AmEx, MC, V. Euros accepted. **Map** p331 N8 ⑮
The spartan exterior of the Andante hides a warm
and welcoming interior. Add that to an excellent
location and cheerful staff and you have ample reason for booking, even if the rooms are a little small.
*Concierge. No-smoking rooms. Restaurant. TV:
satellite.*

Carlo IV

*Senovážné náměstí 13, Prague 1 (224 593 111/fax
2224 593 000/www.boscolohotels.com). Metro Hlavní
nádraží/tram 5, 9, 26.* **Rooms** 152. **Rates** 3,800-
10,500 Kč single; 3,800-14,400 Kč double; 12,200-
28,800 Kč suite. **Credit** AmEx, DC, MC, V. Euros
accepted. **Map** p329 P4 ⑯
Italian opulence slightly misplaced, that's how we'd
describe the Carlo IV. The displacement comes from
its location in a well-placed but not particularly pretty street. The luxury comes thanks to the Boscolo
Hotels chain, which did a lot of work on this former
bank/post office to turn it into the luxury hotel of
today. There's a cigar bar, indoor swimming pool,
wooden floors and a soothing colour palette of sage,
gold and mahogany. A relaxing place to stay.
*Concierge. Internet (dataport). Gym. No-smoking
rooms. Parking (350 Kč/night). Pool (indoor).
Restaurant. Spa. TV: pay movies/cable/satellite.*

Grand Hotel Evropa

*Václavské náměstí 25, Prague 1 (224 228 117/
fax 224 224 544/www.evropahotel.cz). Metro
Můstek/tram 3, 9, 14, 24, 26.* **Rooms** 92 (52
en suite) **Rates** 2,990 Kč single; 3,990 Kč double;
4,990-5,200 Kč suite. **Credit** AmEx, MC, V.
Map p329 N6 ⑰
The art nouveau façade of the building is noticeable
– sticks out like a sore thumb, actually – among the
souvenir shops of Wenceslas Square. Once inside,
you'll appreciate the exterior. Some rooms still come
in tattered Louis XVI style, although the renovated
ones are more pleasant. If you want a laugh, and a
chance for inside and out photos to show folks back
home, try 'economy class' accommodation: rooms
have a basin that share a bathroom. **Photo** *left.*
Concierge. Parking. Restaurant.

Hotel Adria Prague

*Václavské náměstí 26, Prague 1 (221 081 111/
fax 221 081 300/www.hoteladria.cz). Metro
Můstek/tram 3, 9, 14, 24, 26.* **Rooms** 88.
Rates 3,332-5,572 Kč single; 3,556-6,692 Kč
double; 4,480-8,092 Kč suites. **Credit** AmEx,
DC, MC, JCB, V. **Map** p328 M6 ⑱
Once a Carmelite convent but now in the heart of Sin
City on Wenceslas Square, the Adria offers decent
value for the location and comes with the attached
Fransiscan Gardens. A complete renovation brought
it up to modern snuff in 2003 and has modernised
this veteran nicely with cool designer tones. And
then there's the faux grotto cellar restaurant.
*Bar. Concierge. Disabled: adapted rooms. Gym.
Internet (high-speed). No-smoking rooms. Parking.
Restaurant. Room service (24hrs). TV: pay
movies/cable.*

Hotel Elite

*Ostrovní 32, Prague 1 (224 932 250/fax 224 930
787/www.hotelelite.cz). Metro Národní třída/tram 6,
9, 18, 21, 22, 23, 26.* **Rooms** 79. **Rates** 3,400-5,200
Kč single; 3,800-5,950 Kč double; 4,300-6,500 Kč suite.
Credit AmEx, MC, V. **Map** p330 L7 ⑲
The Elite is a member of the Small Charming Hotels
group, and that is the perfect way to describe it. The
14th-century building has been carefully renovated
to retain the ancient architectural features, with the
suite protected by the Town Hall as a historical monument. The location is slightly off the track, but convenient nonetheless, and provides a good base for
exploring the restaurants and bars of the neighbourhood. To top it off, friendly and helpful staff.
*Bar. Concierge. Internet (wireless). Parking.
Restaurant. TV: satellite.*

Hotel Opera

*Těšnov 13, Prague 1 (222 315 609/fax 222 311
477/www.hotel-opera.cz). Metro Florenc/tram 8, 24.*
Rooms 67. **Rates** 2,730-4,200 Kč single; 3,360-5,760
Kč double; 3,800-6,500 Kč triple; 5,880-7,600 Kč suite.
Credit AmEx, DC, MC, V. **Map** p329 Q2 ⑳
You can't miss the towering pink building of the
Hotel Opera, just steps from the Florenc metro station. The rooms are small, but everything's quite
new as the hotel was severely damaged in the floods
of 2002. Close to Old Town, but in an emerging area
full of different places to discover.
*Bar. Gym. Internet. Parking. Restaurant. TV:
satellite.*

Marriott

*V Celnici 8, Prague 1 (222 888 888/fax 222 888
889/www.marriotthotels.com). Metro Náměstí
Republiky/tram 5, 8, 9, 14.* **Rooms** 293. **Rates** 5,700-
7,300 Kč single/double; 9,600-13,300 Kč suites; 41,600
Kč presidential suite. **Credit** AmEx, DC, MC, V.
Map p329 P3 ㉑
Safety and comfort, Marriott style. You know what
to expect for the money, and sure enough you get
the same excellent service here as you would at any
other Marriott. A good location and amenities make
it a fine choice for the business traveller.
*Bar. Business services. Concierge. Disabled: adapted
rooms. Gym. Internet (dataport). No-smoking floors.
Parking. Pool. Restaurant. Room service (24hrs).
TV: pay movies/satellite.*

Mercure Prague Centre Na Poříčí

*Na Poříčí 7, Prague 1 (221 800 800/fax 221 800
881/www.mercure.com). Metro Náměstí Republiky/
tram 5, 8, 9, 14.* **Rooms** 174. **Rates** 4,000 Kč single;
4,500 Kč double; 9,500 Kč suite. **Credit** AmEx, DC,
MC, V. Euros accepted. **Map** p329 O3 ㉒

The bright white lobby and sweeping staircase you see when you get inside will match the expectations born of the building's beautiful neo-baroque exterior. The rooms themselves, though, are basic, but efficient staff ensure a pleasant stay. Literary tourists, take note: Franz Kafka worked in the building when it housed an insurance company, and the bar/library is a tribute to Kafka and other Czech writers.
Bar. Concierge. Disabled: adapted rooms. Internet (dataport). No-smoking rooms. Restaurant. Room service. TV: satellite.

987 Prague

Senovažné náměstí 15, Prague 1 (255 737 100/ fax 222 210 369/www.designhotelscollection.com). Metro Hlavní Nádraží/tram 3, 9, 14, 24. **Rooms** 80. **Rates** 4,287-8,433 Kč singles and doubles; 6,003-9,720 Kč suite. **Credit** AmEx, DC, MC, V. **Map** p329 P4 ⑦
The newest property in Spanish hotel chain Design Hotels Collection, 987 Prague owes its übercool design mainly to Philippe Starck. Originally a 19th-century apartment building, the architects kept the outside while allowing Starck to infuse the interior with contemporary brightness. There's a bit of a '60s/'70s retro feel, but it's brought off in a more effective, sleek and comfortable way than many other hotels in Prague have managed. Opened in Febuary 2006, 987 Prague gives the block a fresh look and is well situated between Wenceslas Square and Old Town. Check website for deep discounts.
Bar. Concierge. Internet connection. Restaurant. TV: pay movies/satellite.

Renaissance Prague Hotel

V Celnici 7, Prague 1 (221 822 111/fax 221 822 200/www.renaissancehotels.com). Metro Náměstí Republiky/tram 5, 8, 9, 14. **Rooms** 310. **Rates** 4,400-8,000 Kč single and double; 8,000-15,000 Kč suites. **Credit** AmEx, MC, V. Euros accepted. **Map** p329 P3 ⑦
Like its sister the Marriott across the street, the Renaissance emphasises consistency. Thus it makes for an excellent choice for the business traveller, with meeting rooms online and high-speed wi-fi. Guest rooms are well kept and decorated, offering a bit more warmth than others in Prague, even in this price category. And of course, they have all the executive amenities, including the chain's well-hyped new beds featuring custom duvets, big pillows and luxurious linens. Breakfast not included, however.
Bar. Business services. Disabled: adapted rooms. Gym. Internet (wireless). No-smoking floors. Parking. Pool. Restaurant. TV: pay movies/satellite.

Budget

Hotel 16 U sv. Kateřiny

Kateřinská 16, Prague 2 (224 920 636/224 919 676/fax 224 920 626/www.hotel16.cz). Metro IP Pavlova/tram 4, 6, 10, 11, 16, 22, 23. **Rooms** 14. **Rates** 2,300-2,500 Kč single; 2,400-3,500 Kč double; 2,800-4,700 Kč apartment. **Credit** MC, V. **Map** p330 M10 ⑦

A bit off the beaten path, this small hotel is great for people looking for a quiet bargain within walking distance of Wencelas Square. Located right next to the Botanical Gardens, it's a peaceful place with friendly staff, and even offers some 'big' hotel amenities like babysitting and airport transfers.
Bar. Parking. TV: satellite.

Jerome House

V Jirchářích 13, Prague 1 (224 933 207/fax 224 933 212/www.jerome.cz/jerome-house.html). Metro Národní třída/tram 6, 9, 18, 21, 22, 23, 26. **Rooms** 65. **Rates** 2,268-3,100 Kč single; 2,800-3,600 Kč double; 3,472-4,800 Kč triple. **Credit** MC, V. **Map** p330 K7 ⑦
The Jerome House has 52 normal en suite rooms but, for a cheaper deal if you're travelling in a group, ask about the special rates for the nine rooms with shared facilities. The location isn't typical for tourist hotels, although Wenceslas Square is nearby, which means that there are plenty of local restaurants and shops waiting to be discovered.
Business centre. Disabled: adapted room. TV: satellite.

U Šuterů

Palackého 4, Prague 1 (224 948 235/fax 224 911 23/www.usuteru.cz). Metro Můstek/tram 3, 9, 14, 24, 26. **Rates** 1,690-2,590 Kč single; 1,990-3,490 Kč double; 2,090-4,090 Kč apartment. **Credit** MC, V. **Map** p330 M7 ⑦
A winner for those looking for small and cosy near Wenceslas Square. The building goes back to 1383, but rooms were renovated in 2004. The interior, from the rooms to the lobby, is tastefully decorated with understated elegance, and the pub downstairs is popular throughout the city for its goulash. **Photo** *p66*.
Bar. No-smoking rooms. Restaurant. TV: satellite.

Hostels

Charles University Dorms

Voršilská 1, Prague 1 (224 933 825/fax 224 930 361). Metro Národní třída/tram 6, 9, 18, 21, 22, 23, 26. **Rates** 200-500 Kč per person, double. **No credit cards. Map** p330 K7 ⑦
True budgeteers should check out the university's dormitories. Be warned, though: some locations are a bit out of town, and at others you will be roughing it. The downtown office arranges accommodation in hundreds of dorm rooms scattered throughout the city; prices vary according to location.

Klub Habitat

Na Zderaze 10, Prague 2 (tel/fax 224 921 706/ 224 918 252). Metro Karlovo náměstí/tram 4, 10, 16, 22, 23. **Rooms** 7. **Rates** 390-500 Kč per person, quadruple. **No credit cards. Map** p330 K8 ⑦
It's spic and span, all proceeds go to charity and you get free lemonade. Suspicious? Don't be. It's simply outstanding value, great service, good location – and in overwhelming demand. Book ahead.
Bar.

U Šuterů. *See p65.*

Further afield

Staying a bit out of the centre (which is small, so all of the below are within 10-15-minute public transport range) can mean fresher air, lots more neighbourhood character and a chance to mix with locals. It can also save you a bundle.

Deluxe

Le Palais

U Zvonařky 1, Vinohrady, Prague 2 (234 634 111/ fax 222 563 350/www.palaishotel.cz). Metro IP Pavlova or Namĕstí míru/tram 4, 10, 16, 22, 23. **Rooms** 72. **Rates** 8,260-11,060 Kč single; 8,960-12,040 Kč double; 12,880-67,200 Kč suites. **Credit** AmEx, DC, MC, V. Euros accepted. **Map** p331 P12 80

Surprise, surprise, this beautiful belle époque palace used to be a meat-processing plant. Now it's a quiet hotel situated in an idyllic corner of Vinohrady. Originally decorated by renowned Czech artist Luděk Mařold in exchange for rent, many of the original touches remain, including the frescoed ceilings and staircase. Service is premium and the rooms are well decorated, but could maybe use a little improvements – carpets especially are showing their age. A large and well-equipped fitness centre, a fine restaurant and a beautiful summer terrace with an excellent view make Le Palais a good choice. **Photo** *p69.*

Bar. Concierge. Disabled: adapted room. Gym. Internet (dataport). No-smoking rooms. Parking (660 Kč/day). Restaurant. Room service (24hrs). TV: satellite.

Prague Hilton

Pobřežní 1, Karlín, Prague 8 (224 841 111/fax 224 842 378/www.hilton.com). Metro Florenc/tram 8, 24. **Rooms** 788. **Rates** 7,710-9,600 Kč single; 8,040-9,930 Kč double; 11,190-12,450 Kč suite; 23,790 Kč family apartment. **Credit** AmEx, MC, V.

Hello, it's the Hilton. This massive behemoth is very un-Prague on the outside but it hides a beautiful atrium and five-star luxury on the inside. Decorated in typically Hilton fashion, you won't want for much, except maybe some of the more off-beat elements of Prague's charm. But it's just east of the centre, convenient for public transport options and close to the river, so an escape is easy to make. The popular and well-respected CzecHouse restaurant is located here.

Business centre. Disabled: adapted rooms. Gym. Internet (dataport in business-class rooms only). No-smoking floors. Pool. Restaurant. TV: satellite.

Expensive

Andel's Hotel Prague

Stroupežnického 21, Prague 5 (296 889 688/fax 296 889 999/www.andelshotel.com). Metro Anděl/tram 4, 6, 7, 9, 10, 12, 14. **Rooms** 239. **Rates** 6,580-8,400 Kč single; 7,140-9,100 Kč double; 8,960 Kč junior suite; 10,640 Kč suite. **Credit** AmEx, MC, V.

Sleek and contemporary is the aesthetic of Andel's Hotel Prague, yet another ripple of the 'design hotels' wave, this one crafted by British architects D3A and designers Jestico+Whiles. And, sure enough, all the 'design hotel' boxes are ticked: clean lines, lots of glass and media amenities. It's set in a handy Smíchov district location, with a shopping mall nearby and two cinemas. But is there anything here to suggest that you're in Prague? What's more, service lags behind the appearance, and comfort-wise, it's no better than many a more reasonable option. Metro and tram stops are close by, and it's an excellent option for those driving into Prague. There is a nicer than hotel-average fitness centre.

Business centre. Concierge. Disabled: adapted rooms (2). Gym. Internet (dataport). No-smoking floors. Parking (covered). Restaurants (2). TV: satellite.

Arcotel Hotel Teatrino

Bořvojova 53, Žižkov, Prague 3 (221 422 211/ fax 221 422 222/www.arcotel.at). Metro Jiřího z Poděbrad/tram 5, 9, 11, 26. **Rooms** 75. **Rates** 4,600 Kč single; 6,300 Kč double. **Credit** AmEx, MC, V. **Map** p333 C2 81

Žižkov is a unique part of Prague, and this hotel fits right in to the area's atmosphere. Austrian designer, architect and painter Harald Schreiber is the man to credit for the interior decoration and artistic design, and his work faces you the moment you walk in to the lobby. There you'll see his painting of 100 people – Kafka, Smetana, Mozart, Rilke among others – with its strong links to the city. All told, Arcotel

is an odd combination of styles, with each room decorated differently in an attempt, apparently, to 'animate the hotel's guests for a journey through the art and history of the city'. Interesting.
Internet (dataport). Parking. Restaurant. Room service. TV: pay movies/satellite.

Diplomat Hotel Praha

Evropská 15, Dejvice, Prague 6 (296 559 111/ fax 296 559 215/www.diplomatpraha.cz). Metro Dejvická/tram 2, 20, 26. **Rooms** 398. **Rates** 6,100-7,260 Kč single; 6,580-8,250 Kč double; 10,080-14,850 Kč suite. **Credit** AmEx, MC, V.

The Diplomat is a good choice for those who prefer some distance from the hustle of tourist central, but not so much distance that they can't take advantage of its benefits. Located just outside the Hradčany district in Prague 6, a quick metro ride brings you to the centre of town. The hotel is only 20 minutes by car from the airport, and its excellent meeting rooms and other amenities make it a positive choice for business travellers. Diplomat is also popular with families, both because of its periodic specials and the ample room to roam outside. Helpful and friendly staff add to the recommendation.
Bar. Business services. Disabled: adapted rooms. Gym. Internet (dataport). No-smoking floors. Parking. Restaurants (2). Room service (6am-midnight). TV: pay movies/satellite.

Moderate

Bohemia Plaza

Žitná 50, Prague 2 (224 941 000/fax 224 943 000/www.bohemiaplaza.com). Metro IP Pavlova or Muzeum/tram 4, 6, 10, 11, 16, 22, 23. **Rooms** 5 rooms, 15 suites. **Rates** 4,480-5,600 Kč single and double; 3,360-7,000 Kč suite. **Credit** MC, V. **Map** P330 L8 ⑫

Located between Wenceslas Square and Vinohrady, the quiet elegance inside forgives the noisy street outside. This is a mainly suite hotel, and each one is decorated in a different theme – take the No.9 apartment with its Chinese wedding theme and shockingly pink walls, or the Russian Imperial design of apartment 14, decorated with original oil paintings. Most of the rooms aren't as fancy, but the owners have taken care with the antique furniture in each one. Monthly rates available.
Bar. Concierge. Internet (wireless). No-smoking rooms. Parking. Restaurant. Room service (24hrs). TV: cable/satellite.

Corinthia

Kongresová 1, Vyšehrad, Prague 4 (261 191 111/ fax 261 255 011/www.corinthia.cz). Metro Vyšehrad. **Rooms** 544. **Rates** 3,100-7,500 Kč single and double; 10,800-15,150 Kč suite. **Credit** DC, MC, V.

This high-rise hotel is a bit outside the centre, but adjacent to Vyšehrad, a picturesque sight not to be missed. The Corinthia group has a reputation for outstanding service, and the one in Prague is no exception. The 24-storey building offers five non-smoking floors and a range of suites, as well as run

of the mill rooms for the normal folk. Basic hotel room decor, but a swimming pool on the 26th floor, a bowling alley and casino should be enough to lure you out. Good motorway access.
Bar. Disabled: adapted rooms. Gym. Internet (dataport). No-smoking floors. Pool. Restaurant.

Dorint Don Giovanni

Vinohradská 157A, Žižkov, Prague 3 (267 031 111/fax 267 036 717/www.dorint.de). Metro Želivského/tram 10, 11, 16, 19, 26, 35. **Rooms** 397. **Rates** 4,400-7,600 Kč single and double; 5,600-8,400 Kč suite. **Credit** AmEx, MC, V.

Although the location isn't terribly picturesque by Prague's high standards, the Don Giovanni makes up for that with its interior. The lobby looks positively futuristic, while the room furnishings border on the whimsical. Service is top notch. This is also a good family hotel, as two children can stay for free in the parents' room, and there are indoor and outdoor playgrounds to help them let off steam.
Bar. Business services. Concierge. Disabled: adapted rooms. Gym. Internet (dataport). No-smoking floors. Parking. Restaurants (2). Room service (24hrs). TV: pay movies/cable/satellite.

Hotel Villa Schwaiger

Schwaigerova 3, Bubeneč, Prague 6 (233 320 271/ fax 233 320 272/www.villaschwaiger.cz). Metro Hradčanská/131 bus. **Rooms** 22. **Rates** 2,660-4,200 Kč single; 3,360-7,112 Kč double; 4,480-8,232 Kč suite. *Extra bed* 600 Kč. **Credit** AmEx, MC, V.

Those who are looking for peaceful elegance that's close to a beautiful park will do no better than booking a room at Hotel Villa Schwaiger. Designed for comfort rather than style, the rooms are simple but tasteful, the staff pleasant and you'll be sleeping in the heart of ambassador row.
Bar. Parking. Restaurants (2). TV: pay movies/ satellite.

Mövenpick Hotel

Mozartova 1, Smíchov, Prague 5 (257 151 111/fax 257 153 131/www.movenpick-prague.com). Metro Anděl/tram 4, 7, 9. **Rooms** 436. **Rates** 3,100-6,420 Kč single and double. *Extra bed* 1,140 Kč. **Credit** AmEx, MC, V.

It's all supposed to be about location, but the Mövenpick is the exception that proves the rule. It may be out of the city centre, but the combination of surrounding natural beauty, excellent service and top-class amenities proves that even a hotel can overcome a less than ideal location. In fact, there's actually two buildings, with the executive wing only accessible by cable car: its breathtaking views and fine dining attract many a Czech celebrity. Rooms are comfortable, although a little nondescript. The peaceful park that lies below the hotel makes for a relaxing place to stroll.
Concierge. Disabled: adapted rooms (4). Gym. Internet (dataport). No-smoking floors. Parking (covered). Restaurants (2). Room service (24hrs). TV: pay movies/satellite.

Budget

Alpin penzion

Velehradská 25, Žižkov, Prague 3 (222 723 970/ fax 222 723 551/www.alpin.cz). Metro Jiřího z Poděbrad/tram 11. **Rooms** 28. **Rates** 1,270-1,600 Kč single; 1,370-1,700 Kč double; 1,970-2,300 Kč triple. **Credit** MC, V. **Map** p333 C3 ⑥

Contrary to what the name suggests, this is no half-timbered cottage with a flaxen-haired shepherdess tending the hearth. Rather, it's a bare-bones, institutional-looking pension, but the staff are friendly and the prices reasonable. Located in the heart of Žižkov's pavement café district. Breakfast included.
Disabled: adapted room. Parking.

Ametyst

Jana Masaryka 11, Vinohrady, Prague 2 (222 921 947/fax 222 921 999/www.hotelametyst.cz). Metro Náměstí míru/tram 4, 10, 16, 22, 23. **Rooms** 84. **Rates** 2,500-4,600 Kč single; 2,900-6,200 Kč double. *Extra bed* 800-1,600 Kč. **Credit** AmEx, MC, V. **Map** p331 Q11 ⑥

Located on a quiet Vinohrady street, the hotel's German owners and Austrian manager ensure a steady stream of their countrymen booking. The hotel offers its decorations of original oil paintings and pastel drawings for sale, meaning an ever-changing look. This and the comfortable rooms are probably the best things about the hotel, as the staff can't be considered overly helpful or friendly.
Bar. Concierge. Disabled: adapted room. No-smoking floors. Restaurant. TV: pay movies/satellite.

Botel Admiral

Hořejší nábřeží, Smíchov, Prague 5 (257 321 302/ fax 257 319 516/www.admiral-botel.cz). Metro Anděl/tram 4, 6, 7, 9, 10, 12, 14, 20, 26. **Rooms** 87. **Rates** 1,880-2,980 Kč single; 2,000-3,130 Kč double; 3,490-5,400 Kč quad. **Credit** AmEx, DC, MC, V. Euros accepted.

The joy of staying on the high waters of the Vltava. The Admiral (a boat hotel) has excellent views across and down river, a fun restaurant and a bar. A decent, and decidedly unusual, place to stay.
Bar. No-smoking rooms. Parking. Restaurant. Room service. TV: satellite.

City Penzion

Zahřebska 16/Belgická 10, Vinohrady, Prague 2 (tel/fax 222 522 422/www.citypenzion.cz). Metro Náměstí Míru/tram 4, 10, 16, 22, 23. **Rooms** 21. **Rates** 1,500-1,900 Kč single; 1,900-2,500 Kč double; 2,500-3,300 Kč suite. **Credit** AmEx, MC, V.

Formerly known as Hotel City, the hotel shut for extensive renovations and repairs in 2005. Now reopened and renamed the City Penzion, it offers friendly, helpful service in a quiet, tucked-away corner of Vinohrady. Everything is new, including the light wood furniture and colourful painted walls. There are 'classic' and 'economy' rooms; economy class entails sharing a bathroom with another room. For Prague, its email response is excellent.
Internet (dataport). Parking. TV.

Hotel Abri

Jana Masaryka 36, Vinohrady, Prague 2 (222 515 124/fax 224 254 240/www.abri.cz). Metro Náměstí Míru/tram 4, 10, 16, 22, 23. **Rooms** 25. **Rates** 2,300-2,700 Kč single; 2,800-3,400 Kč double. *Extra bed* 400 Kč. **Credit** AmEx, MC, V.

Hotel Abri is a small but lovely hotel well situated in a quiet Vinohrady neighbourhood, about five minutes from the metro station, and two minutes from a tram stop. The staff are excellent: it is, after all, unusual for the receptionist to be genuinely quite distressed when a room is not available for the entire length of the requested stay. The rooms themselves are large and airy, the lobby spacious and the terrace is a restful respite in warm weather.
Disabled: adapted room. Parking (220 Kč/night). Restaurant. TV: satellite.

Hotel Anna

Budečská 17, Vinohrady, Prague 2 (222 513 111/ fax 222 515 158/www.hotelanna.cz). Metro Náměstí Míru/tram 4, 10, 16, 22, 23. **Rooms** 24. **Rates** 1,900-2,500 Kč single; 2,500-3,100 Kč double; 3,300-3,900 Kč triple; 3,500-4,200 Kč suite. **Credit** AmEx, MC, V. **Map** p333 B4 ⑥

The Anna brings one back to yesteryear, with its late 1800s building and art nouveau interior, all set on a quiet, tree-lined street in Vinohrady. Rooms are simply but classily furnished, and anything a recreational traveller may need is available.
Internet (wireless). Parking. TV.

Hotel Tosca

Blanická 10, Vinohrady, Prague 2 (221 506 111/fax 221 506 199/www.hotel-tosca.cz). Metro Náměstí Míru/tram 4, 10, 16, 22, 23. **Rooms** 27. **Rates** 2,380-4,600 Kč single; 2,660-4,920 Kč double; 3,480-4,920 Kč apartment. *Extra bed* 800-1,000 Kč. **Credit** AmEx, MC, V. **Map** p333 A4 ⑥

Forgive the noisy road it sits on, and you'll enjoy the Hotel Tosca. There's a huge and welcoming bar area when you enter, and friendly staff. The rooms won't win any decorating prizes, but they are comfortable and contain what you need.
Bar. Concierge. Internet (dataport in reception). Parking (320 Kč/day). TV: cable/satellite.

Hotel Tříska

Vinohradská 105, Žižkov, Prague 3 (222 727 313/ fax 222 723 562/www.hotel-triska.cz). Metro Jiřího z Poděbrad/tram 11. **Rooms** 57. **Rates** 1,300-1,890 Kč single; 1,700-2,310 Kč double; 2,450-3,150 Kč triple. **No credit cards. Map** p333 C3 ⑥

A style all its own. That's the best way to describe the Tříska's combination of Czech murals, art deco and empire furnishings. The rooms each have their own decorating scheme, but it's obvious the owners took time over the interior and take pride in what they've done. The area has many good restaurants and pubs, and this hotel is an ideal base from which to explore the city. If possible, request a courtyard-facing room as the street can get quite noisy.
Bar. Disabled: adapted room. Parking. Restaurant. TV: satellite.

You wouldn't think **Le Palais** was once a meat-processing plant. *See p66.*

Ibis Praha City

*Kateřinská 36, Nové Město, Prague 2 (222 865 777/
fax 222 865 666/www.accorhotels.com). Metro IP
Pavlova/tram 4, 6, 10, 11, 16, 22, 23.* **Rooms** 181.
Rates 1,932-3,350 Kč single; 2,268-3,950 Kč double.
Credit AmEx, MC, V. **Map** p331 N9 ⑩
For those looking for familiarity and reliability when
travelling, but not up for shelling out for a Marriott
or Hilton, the Ibis will take care of you in efficient
style. The location is good, rooms classic hotel and
staff know their customer service.
*Bar. Gym. Parking. Pool. Restaurant. Room service.
TV: pay movies/cable/satellite.*
Other locations: Ibis Praha Karlin, Šaldova 54,
Karlin, Prague 8 (222 332 800/fax 224 812 681).

Julian

*Eliíšky Peškové 11, Smíchov, Prague 5 (257 311 150/
fax 257 311 149/www.julian.cz). Tram 6, 9, 12, 20.*
Rooms 32. **Rates** 2,680-4,100 Kč single; 2,980-4,400
Kč double; 3,800-5,300 Kč suite. *Extra bed* 700-1,000
Kč. **Credit** AmEx, MC, V.
A bit of luxury in up-and-coming Smíchov. The
Julian features a drawing room with fireplace and
library, both wonderful places to relax and unwind
after a day spent about town. The hotel has a separate breakfast room for smokers, and its lobby bar
is non-smoking, which is a rarity here. All rooms are
decorated in a light, understated style, there are
apartments with kitchenettes as well as a family
room, complete with toys. Not dead in the centre, but
a ten-minute tram ride away.
*Bar. Gym. Internet (dataport). No-smoking rooms.
Parking. TV: pay movies/satellite.*

Pension Vyšehrad

*Krokova 6, Vyšehrad, Prague 2 (241 408 455/
fax 6122 2187/www.pension-vysehrad.cz). Metro
Vyšehrad.* **Rooms** 4. **Rates** 1,000 Kč single;
1,700 Kč double; 2,100 Kč triple. **No credit cards.**
If you want to live like a local, here's your best bet.
Located in a residential area, the family-run pension
is full of home-style hospitality. The rooms are lovingly decorated, and there's a beautiful green garden for sunny days. Two metro stops and you are
in the centre, but you have the luxury of staying
away from the crowds. Pets stay free.
Parking.

Hostels

A&O Hostel Prague

*U Vystaviště 1, Holešovice, Prague 7 (220 870 252/
fax 220 870 251/www.aohostels.com). Metro
Holešovice/tram 5.* **Open** 24hrs daily. **Beds** 140.
Rates 900-990 Kč single; 570-660 Kč double; 330-450
Kč dormitory; breakfast 130 Kč. **No credit cards.**
Map p332 E1 ⑪
Dormitory, single and double rooms in a great loca-
tion in the Holešovice area, with good tram and
metro services to the city centre. There's no curfew,
24-hour service, big American breakfasts and a bar
in an 18th-century cellar.
Bar. Internet (in reception). No-smoking hotel. Parking.

Clown & Bard

*Bořivojova 102, Žižkov, Prague 3 (222 716 453/
www.clownandbard.com). Metro Jiřího z Poděbrad/
tram 5, 9, 11, 26.* **Open** 24hrs daily. **Beds** 143.
Rates 250-450 Kč dorm; 400 Kč per person in 4-6-
person apartments (with kitchen and private bath).
No credit cards. Map p333 B2 ⑫
Set in the colourful Žižkov neighbourhood, the Clown
& Bard's bar certainly does its best to contribute to
the local fun index. Not the place for a quiet stay, but
if you want to party, this is the hostel for you. No
lockout, no reservations. Breakfast available.
Bar.

Hostel Boathouse

*Lodnická 1, Modřany, Prague 4 (241 770 051/fax
241 766 988/www.aa.cz/boathouse). Tram 3, 17, 21.*
Open 24hrs daily. **Beds** 56. **Rates** 360-460 Kč per
person. **No credit cards.**
This is the place for those who want to escape to the
country while visiting the city. Set on the banks of
the Vltava, it'll take you about 20 minutes by tram
to get to the centre. However, the hostel is friendly,
it has all the hostel amenities and it offers golf, tennis, bikes for rent, and will arrange canoeing and
hiking trips. Breakfast and bed linens are included.
Internet (dataport in reception). Parking.

Miss Sophie's Prague

*Melounova 3, Vinohrady, Prague 2 (296 303 530/
fax 296 303 531/www.miss-sophies.com). Metro
Karlovo náměstí/tram 4, 6, 10, 16, 22, 23.*
Beds 25. **Rates** 360-440 Kč per person in dorm
(up to 5 people); 900-1,500 Kč single; 1,300-1,700 Kč
double; 1,500-2,000 triple; 1,100-2,400 Kč apartment.
Credit MC, V.
Dorms, private rooms and apartments, all in smart
Vinohrady? Yep, Miss Sophie's covers the spectrum
with style. The apartments that have full kitchens
are located across the street. Dorm rooms are sparse
with wooden floors; private rooms have elegant marble bathrooms and the owners have done an amazing job with antique touches (the staircase is a
marvel). Boasting both a terrace and a brick cellar
lounge, Miss Sophie's is a stylish addition to the
Prague hostel/hotel scene.
Internet (high-speed).

Sir Toby's Hostel

*Dělnická 24, Holešovice, Prague 7 (283 870 635/
fax 283 870 636/www.sirtobys.com). Metro Vltavská
or Nádraží Holešovice/tram 1, 3, 9, 12, 15, 25.*
Open 24hrs daily. **Beds** 70. **Rates** 250-390 Kč
per person in dorm (up to 8 people); 320-400 Kč
triple; 450-525 Kč double. **Credit** AmEx, DC, MC, V.
Map p312 E2.
The friendly, accommodating staff make Sir Toby's
Hostel a sure winner. The art nouveau building has
been stylishly redecorated, and the interior almost
makes you forget you're staying in a hostel. The
Holešovice neighbourhood is happening, and there's
easy access to the centre of town. Both shared and
private rooms available.
Internet (wireless in reception). Parking.

Sightseeing

Introduction	**72**
Hradčany	**75**
Mala Straná	**88**
Staré Město	**98**
Nové Město	**115**
Further Afield	**127**

Features

What lies beneath	83
Who did Brahe?	84
Walk this way Mala Straná idylls	94
Walk this way Old Town art	102
Still crazy Franz Kafka	111
Reclaiming Wenceslas	125
Still crazy Žižkov	128

Maps

Key sights	74
Prague Castle	77

Vladislav Hall. *See p79.*

Introduction

Open the box of delights.

Prague's compact old centre will take you on a visual trip through every period of the last millennium. Within blocks of each other you'll encounter palaces, galleries, cellar pubs and mysterious passageways, only to emerge into the formal gardens of some count or other, in a scene straight out of *Amadeus*.

A bend of the Vltava river arcs through the heart of the city, gracing it with nine dramatic bridges, all scaled perfectly for a stroll from one side of Prague to the other. The river eventually runs north to the Baltic after curling around Letná, the high country on the left bank that first provided a strategic vantage to Stone Age peoples. The neighbouring hill of **Hradčany** (*see p75*) gave the first Czech princes, the Přemyslids, their castle foundations, which still exist today under **Prague Castle** (*see p76*). Head here for a heart-stopping overview of the town below.

Between Hradčany and the Vltava, the **Malá Strana** district (*see p88*) is a tapestry of its former histories: a craftsmen's quarter during the medieval period, prize real estate granted to nobles for supporting the crown during the late Renaissance, and a hotbed of poets bristling against foreign domination in coffeehouse cabals during the 19th century. Cottages, fabulous palaces and smoky cafés from each era stand side by side today on its narrow streets.

On the right bank, the river is also responsible for the unique underworld of flat **Staré Město** (*see p98*), Old Town, with its subterranean drinking holes, cinemas, music halls and

galleries. These countless vaulted, stone-walled spaces were once at street level, but constant flooding of the Vltava during the 13th century prompted city fathers to raise the streets one storey to the level at which they lie today. This means that ordinary-looking doorways to pubs and clubs often lead to underground labyrinths.

Prague's layers are such that no matter how deep you dig, you're constantly making new discoveries. People who have lived here for years still stop in amazement when an old passage between favourite streets is reopened. Many of these walkways through building courtyards haven't seen the light of day for over 50 years but now host designer shops and smart bars. Prague is rediscovering itself, as it digs out from its grey pre-Velvet Revolution days.

Bordering Staré Město to the south and east is **Nové Město** (*see p115*), New Town, the first area of the city to be laid out with broad streets, planned by Charles IV in 1348. This is where the city's commerce gets done and is also where the uniquely Czech form of political dissent known as defenestration was perfected. All of Europe was plunged into the chaos of the Thirty Years' War after the tossing out the window of city mugwumps from the New Town Hall. Nové Město's Wenceslas Square is very much the heart of modern Prague and the adjoining Na příkopě street is the place to shop for lifestyle essentials. South of the National Theatre, the area sometimes known as SONA is still blooming as a fashionable, hedonistic quarter.

To the east of the city centre lies the tumbledown district of **Žižkov** (*see p132*), boasting the highest number of pubs per capita in the world. It's also the place to see phenomenal regional music acts and indie artists trying to create conceptual cuts, and meet up with irascible Prague characters. The hippest clubs outside Staré Město are also here.

The good-value **Prague Card** (690 Kč adults, 560 Kč concessions), available at American Express (Václavské náměstí 56, Nové Město, Prague 1, 224 219 992), is valid for three days of public transit and entry to museums, including Prague Castle.

The whole city is, of course, one great outdoor museum, with free sights aplenty in the centre. For in-depth guided tours, try **City Walks** (608 200 912), which departs from the St Wenceslas equestrian statue, Wenceslas Square, at 9.45am daily (450 Kč, 300 Kč concessions).

Essential Prague...

...in two days

Style it up with art and live jazz

● Wander the **baroque gardens** of Malá Strana (*see p90*).

● Soak up the live jazz at **U Malého Glena** (*see p239*), sample some Czech rock at **Malostranská beseda** (*see p236*), or brush up your Mozart at the **State Opera** (*see p232*), **National Theatre** (*see p232*) or **Rudolfinum** (*see p230*).

● Take your child, or inner child, to the **Aquarium**, **Prague Zoo** or the **National Technical Museum** (for all, *see p236*).

● Get a taste of Bohemian style at the **Museum of Decorative Arts** (*see p114*).

...in three days

Art, architecture – and more beer

● Get the ghostly perspective or Kafka's angle on Staré Město with a guided **City Walk** (*see p72*).

● Take a crash course in 20th-century architecture with a stroll down **Wenceslas Square** (*see p115*) and lunch at **Jáma** (*see p155*).

● Catch Prague's particular own brand of mannerist/erotic Renaissance/Old Masters art up the hill at the castle: **St George's Convent** (*see p82*), the **Prague Castle Picture Gallery** (*see p76*) and **Sternberg Palace** (*see p85*).

● Wander through **Nové Město**'s attractions then come down to earth at the chilling **Police Museum** (*see p124*) and the sobering **Church of SS Cyril & Methodius** (*see p126*).

● Go on a proper crawl through these Žižkov pubs: **Akropolis**, **Blind Eye**, **Park Café**, **U Sadu** and **U vystřelenýho oka** (for all, *see p175*).

...in four days

Go for detail

● The best of outlying **Holešovice**: peruse cosmic modern art at **Veletržní palác** (*see p127*), refresh at **Výletná** beer garden, **Fraktal** or **La Bodega Flamenca** (for all, *see p173*), then explore the extraordinary **Bílek Villa** (*see p86*).

● Seek out the **cubist architecture** of Staré Město and Nové Město (*see p98*).

● Investigate the amazing obscurantism of **Strahov Library** (*see p87*).

● Vow to stay longer and start planning a trip to the beautiful **Šumava** region or Czech paradise (**Český ráj**) (for both, *see p284*).

Left bank in one day

The key sights

● Breakfast at the **Globe Bookstore & Coffeehouse** (*see p181*), or a mimosa at **Café Slavia** (*see p169*) in Nové Město.

● Stroll toward the Vltava river past the **National Theatre** (*see p232*), an icon of Czech national identity.

● Cross the **Most Legií** (Legionnaire's Bridge; *see p74*), taking in the city's best view of the Charles Bridge and Prague Castle.

● Walk through **Kampa park** in Malá Strana and catch the cosmic works by František Kupka at Kampa Museum.

● Make your way up the Castle Steps, skipping touristy Nerudova street, to **Prague Castle** (*see p76*).

● Catch the **changing of the Prague Castle guard** at the Hradčanské náměstí gate (best show at noon; *see p76*).

● Reward yourself with a perfectly tapped Kozel beer at **U Černého vola** (*see p163*).

● Catch the **No.22 tram** (*see p292*) down the hill from Hradčany, the best scenic tour of the city.

Right bank in one day

● In **Staré Město**, exit at the Novotného lavka stop and walk across the **Charles Bridge** (*see p107*); make a wish at the **Lorraine cross**.

● Continue across to Malá Strana for lunch with wonderful views at **Kampa Park** or **Hergetova Cihelna** (for both, *see p143*).

● Cross back into **Staré Město** to visit the **Jewish Museum** (*see p112*).

● Stroll on to Dušní and Vězeňská streets to take in the monument to literary Prague, the surreal **Franz Kafka statue** (*see p110*).

● Take Pařížská down to **Old Town Square** (*see p100*), checking out the state of early 21st-century capitalism in Bohemia.

● Catch the dancing figures of the Apocalypse on the **Old Town Hall Astronomical Clock** (on the hour 8am-8pm daily; *see p101*).

● Nearby are some of Prague's most unusual permanent and temporary exhibition spaces, including the **Museum of Communism** (*see p124*), **Municipal House** (*see p118*), the **House of the Black Madonna** (*see p98*), **House at the Stone Bell** (*see p101*) and the **Galerie Rudolfinum** (*see p218*).

● Consider more beer and an improbably filling dinner at a classic like **U Medvídků** (*see p169*) or **U Pinkasu** (*see p156*).

Sightseeing

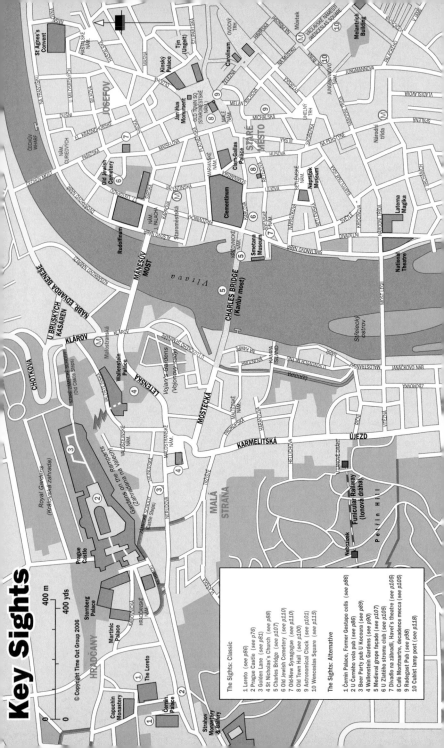

Key Sights

0 — 400 m
0 — 400 yds

© Copyright Time Out Group 2006

The Sights: Classic

1 Loreto (see p86)
2 Prague Castle (see p76)
3 Golden Lane (see p81)
4 St Nicholas's Church (see p88)
5 Charles Bridge (see p107)
6 Old Jewish Cemetery (see p110)
7 Old-New Synagogue (see p110)
8 Old Town Hall (see p100)
9 Astronomical Clock (see p101)
10 Wenceslas Square (see p115)

The Sights: Alternative

1 Černín Palace, Former Gestapo cells (see p86)
2 U Černého vola pub (see p86)
3 Beer Party pub U Kocoura (see p89)
4 Wallenstein Gardens (see p90)
5 Medieval grope façade (see p107)
6 U Zlatého stromu club (see p105)
7 Divadlo na zábradlí, Havel's theatre (see p105)
8 Café Montmartre, decadence mecca (see p105)
9 Radegast Pub (see p98)
10 Cubist lamp post (see p116)

Hradčany

The castle on the hill.

Maps p326 & p327

The roots of the Czech nation take tangible form in **Prague Castle**, at the centre of the Hradčany district. You can't help but be affected by the dizzying heights of its Gothic spires and the flying buttresses of St Vitus's Cathedral, no matter how often you've seen them before. The coronation of Charles IV and the Nazis' march through the gates are just two moments in Hradčany's 1,000-year history that are likely to give you goose bumps. Nowhere else in Prague resonates with as much national identity and symbolism, increased by the pride Czechs take in having the castle finally returned to them in 1989. Locals and foreigners alike, wanting to escape the hordes that come here by day, will be seen rambling through late at night or on drizzly days when the long-departed spirits of Hradčany are most strongly felt.

The castle itself has recently undergone a major makeover, with a dozen rooms newly opened to the public beneath the Old Royal Palace, the first real display addition since 1989 worthy of such a national treasure.

The rest of the district comprises the surrounding streets, which stretch north and west from the castle across the hilltop. It's quiet, enchanting and less touristy than the castle itself, and the Nový Svět, or New World, pocket of streets is particularly enchanting.

The castle grounds themselves demand lengthy strolling, but you'll find a fair number of options for refuelling in the near vicinity.

Prague Castle

Founded some time around 870 by Přemysl princes, the impressive if somewhat sombre collection of buildings that makes up the castle – including a grand palace, three churches and a monastery – has been variously extended, torn down and rebuilt over the centuries. The final touches, including the present shape of **St Vitus's Cathedral** (*see p77*), were not added until the early 1900s, thus the castle can feel like an enormous festival of architectural styles, stretching all the way back to the Romanesque.

The grandiose façade enclosing the complex is the result of Empress Maria Theresa's desire to bring some coherence to the jumble of mismatched parts that the castle had become by the mid-18th century. But the outcome of Nicolo Pacassi's monotonous design concept is uninspiring – 'an imposing mass of building in the factory style of architecture', as one 19th-century commentator put it. After Maria Theresa's son, Joseph II, attempted to turn the castle into a barracks, it was largely deserted by the Habsburgs. Václav Havel chose not to live here, although his presidential office was installed in the castle. He did his best, however, to enliven the palace, opening it to the public and hiring the costume designer from the film *Amadeus* to remodel the guards' uniforms. You really can't get away without spending at least half a day up at the castle. Unfortunately, this is impressed on every visitor to the Czech capital. The result is a notable lack of any real city life and an awful lot of chattering tour groups and whirring video cameras. To avoid the worst of the crush, come as early or as late in the day as you can. Another frustration is the almost complete lack of labelling in English and lacklustre exhibits on the castle tour – the St Vitus crypt looks more like a concrete bunker, despite being the final resting place for the nation's most hallowed forefathers. But most of the female volunteers installed around the castle and its palaces are friendly, English-speaking and forthcoming.

The first & second courtyards

The grandest entrance to the Prague Castle complex, through the **Hradčanské náměstí gates**, is overseen from a discreet distance by an approving Tomáš Garrigue Masaryk, the first president of free Czechoslovakia, whose bronze likeness was added during the cultural festival Praha 2000. The gateway has been dominated since 1768 by Ignatz Platzer's monumental sculptures of battling Titans. They create an arresting, if not exactly welcoming, entrance. The changing of the guard takes place in this courtyard, a Havel-inspired attempt to add some ceremonial pzazz to the castle. The change is carried out on the hour every day from 5am to 10pm, but the big crowd-pulling ceremony, complete with band, takes place at noon. The two tapering flagpoles are the work of Slovene architect Josip Plečnik, who was hired by President Masaryk in the 1920s to create a more uniform look for the seat of the First Republic. To reach the second courtyard go through the Matthias Gate (Matyášova brána), a baroque portal dating from 1614, topped by a double-headed German Imperial Eagle that pleased Hitler when he came to stay in 1939. A monumental stairway is visible from inside the passage (on the left-hand side), which leads up to the magnificent gold-and-white Spanish Hall (Španělský sál). It's open to the public only during occasional concerts, but if one occurs during your stay it's worth the effort to attend, if only to see the hall. Built in the 17th century for court ceremonies, the decor was redone in the 19th century, when the trompe l'oeil murals were covered with white stucco, and huge mirrors and gilded chandeliers were brought in to transform the space into a glitzy venue suitable for the coronation of Emperor Franz Josef I.

Franz Josef, however, failed to show up and it was not until the 1950s that the hall was given a new use – it was here that the Politburo came to discuss the success or, more usually, the failure, although that was never admitted, of their latest five-year development plan, protected from assassins by a reinforced steel door. Behind the austere grey walls of the second courtyard lies a warren of opulent state rooms whose heyday dates from the time of Rudolf II. The state rooms of the airy second courtyard, which are rarely open to the public, housed Rudolf's grand art collection and such curiosities as a unicorn's horn and three nails that were supposedly taken from Noah's ark. The bulk of the collection was carried off in 1648 by Swedish soldiers, although some remnants are housed in the **Prague Castle Picture Gallery** (*see p82*) on the north side of the courtyard near the **Powder Bridge** (U Prašného mostu) entrance. A 17th-century baroque fountain and the **Chapel of the Holy Rood** dominate the yard. The chapel now houses a box office for castle tours and concert tickets, and also rents out audio guides.

Prague Castle

Hradčanské náměstí, Prague 1 (224 371 111/ http://old.hrad.cz). Metro Malostranská/tram 12, 22, 23. **Open** *Apr-Oct* 9am-5pm daily. *Nov-Mar* 9am-4pm daily. **Admission** 50-350 Kč; 175 Kč concessions; 520 Kč family. Tickets valid for 2 days. **Credit** AmEx, MC, V. **Map** p327 E2.

There's no charge to enter the grounds of the castle, but you will need a ticket to see the main attractions. An audio guide (available in English) costs extra; pick one up from the information centre in the second courtyard. One ticket covers entrance to the Old Royal Palace – which now features an extensive museum on palace life – the Basilica of St George, the Golden Lane, the Powder Tower and the choir, crypt and tower of St Vitus's Cathedral (except Jan-Apr & Oct-Dec, when the tower is closed and the Golden Lane is free). Entrance to the art collection of St George's Convent (*see p82*) and the Toy Museum (*see p85*) is extra. Be warned that it's a stiff walk up the hill to the castle from Malá Strana's Malostranská metro station. The least strenuous method of approach is to take the No.22 tram and get off at the Pražský hrad stop. There are a handful of adequate cafés within the castle complex, if you don't mind paying high prices.

St Vitus's Cathedral

The third courtyard – the oldest and most important site in the castle – is entirely dominated by the looming towers, pinnacles, spires and buttresses of St Vitus's Cathedral (Katedrála sv. Víta). Entry is free to the nave and chapels, but a ticket is required for the rest. Although the cathedral was only completed in 1929, exactly 1,000 years after the murdered St Wenceslas was laid to rest on the site, there's no doubt the awe-inspiring building is the spiritual centre of Bohemia. This has always been a sacred place: in pagan times Svatovít, the Slavic god of fertility, was worshipped on this site, a clue as to why the cathedral was dedicated to his near namesake St Vitus (svatý Vít in Czech) – a Sicilian peasant who became a Roman legionnaire before he was thrown to the lions. Right up until the 18th century young women and anxious farmers would bring offerings of wine, cakes and cocks. The cathedral's Gothic structure owes its creation to Charles IV's lifelong love affair with Prague. In 1344 he managed to secure an archbishopric for the city, and work began on the construction of a cathedral under the direction of French architect Matthew of Arras. Inconveniently, Matthew died eight years into the project, so the Swabian Peter Parler was called in to take up the challenge. He was responsible for the Sondergotik or German late Gothic design. It remained unfinished until late 19th-century nationalists completed the work according to

Parler's original plans. The skill with which the later work was carried out makes it difficult to tell where the Gothic ends and the neo-Gothic begins, but a close look at the nave, the twin towers and the rose window of the west end will reveal the telltale lighter-coloured newer stone.

From outside, as from anywhere you look in the town below, the **Great Tower** is easily the most dominant feature. The Gothic and Renaissance structure is topped with a baroque dome. This houses Sigismund, unquestionably the largest bell in Bohemia, made in the middle of the 16th century, weighing in at a hefty 15,120 kilograms (33,333 pounds). The clapper alone weighs slightly over 400 kilograms (882 pounds). Getting Sigismund into the tower was no mean feat: according to legend it took a rope woven from the hair of the city's noblest virgins to haul it into position. Below the tower is the Gothic **Golden Portal** (Zlatá brána), visible from the courtyard south of the cathedral.

It's decorated with a mosaic of multicoloured Venetian glass depicting the Last Judgement that, after years of Getty-funded refurbishment, has been restored to its original lustre. On either side of the centre arch are sculptures of Charles IV and his wife, Elizabeth of Pomerania, whose talents allegedly included being able to bend a sword with her bare hands.

Inside, the enormous nave is flooded with vari-hued light from the gallery of stained-glass windows created at the beginning of the 20th century. All 21 of them were sponsored during a period of nationalist fervour by finance institutions including (third on the right) an insurance company whose motto – 'those who sow in sorrow shall reap in joy' – is subtly incorporated into the biblical allegory. The most famous is the third window on the left, in the **Archbishop's Chapel**, created by Alfons Mucha. It depicts the struggle of Christian Slavonic tribes; appropriately enough, the artwork was paid for by Banka Slavia.

On the right is the **Chapel of St Wenceslas** (Svatováclavská kaple), on the site of the original tenth-century rotunda where 'Good King' Wenceslas was buried. Built in 1345, the chapel has 1,345 polished amethysts, agates and jaspers incorporated into its design and contains some of the saint's personal paraphernalia, including armour, chain shirt and helmet. Alas, it's closed to the public – too many sweaty bodies were causing the gilded plaster to disintegrate – but you can catch a glint of its treasure trove over the railings.

Occasionally, on state anniversaries, the skull of the saint is put on display, covered with a cobweb-fine veil. A door in the corner leads to the chamber that contains the crown jewels. A papal bull of 1346 officially protects the jewels, while legend has it that fate prescribes an early death for anyone who uses them improperly. At

Sightseeing

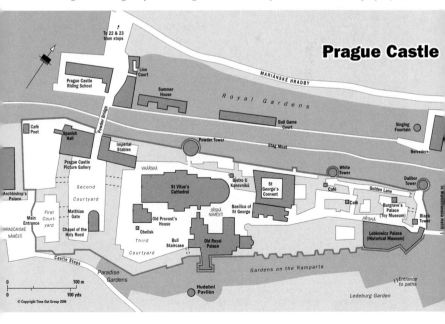

Prague Castle

any rate, the curse seemed to work on the Nazis' man in Prague: Reichsprotektor Reinhard Heydrich tried on the crown and was assassinated shortly afterward by the Resistance. The door to the chamber is locked with seven keys, after the seven seals of the Book of Revelations, each looked after by a different Prague state or Church official.

The most extraordinary baroque addition to the cathedral was the silver **tombstone of St John of Nepomuk**, the priest who was flung from Charles Bridge in 1393 as a result of King Wenceslas IV's anti-clerical wrath. The tomb, designed by Fischer von Erlach the Younger in 1733-36, is a flamboyant affair (the entry ticket is now required to get a proper look at it). An astonishing 2,032 kilograms (two tons) of silver was used for the pedestal, statue of the saint and fluttering cherubs holding up a red velvet canopy. The phrase 'baroque excess' scarcely does it justice. Close by is the entrance to the crypt. Below lie the remains of various Czech monarchs, including Rudolf II. Easily the most eye-catching tomb is Charles IV's modern, streamlined metal affair, designed by Kamil Roškot in the mid 1930s. However, the vault itself, hastily excavated between world wars, has a distinctly cramped, temporary look to it.

The third courtyard

After the cathedral, the second most noticeable monument in the third courtyard is the fairly incongruous 17-metre-high (50-foot) granite obelisk, a memorial to the dead of World War I, erected by Plečnik in 1928.

Close to the Golden Portal is the entrance to the **Old Royal Palace** (Starý královský palác; ticket required). The palace contains three areas of royal chambers above ground level, all with badly photocopied engravings for displays, most with more Russian text than English, and a wonderful, gorgeously presented new permanent exhibition on palace life in the basement. The new displays – which at press time still lacked heating so wrap up if visiting in the winter – inhabit the 12th-century Romanesque remains of Prince Soběslav's residence. Six centuries of kings called the palace home and systematically built new parts over the old. A worthwhile highlight at ground level is the **Vladislav Hall**, designed by Benedict Ried at the turn of the 16th century. The hall, where Václav Havel was sworn in in 1990 as the first democratically elected president since 1948, boasts an exquisitely vaulted ceiling, representing the last flowering of Gothic in Bohemia, while the large, square windows were among the first expressions of the Renaissance. It is here that the National

Assembly elects its new president. The specially designed **Rider's Steps**, at the east end, allowed knights to enter the hall without dismounting. On the floor above is the **Bohemian Chancellery** and the window through which the victims of the defenestration of 1618 were ejected. In the chamber above the Habsburgs inflicted their payback – 27 Czech nobles were sentenced to death after the Battle of White Mountain in 1621.

The **Diet chamber** ('diet' essentially means 'parliament', above the Rider's Steps, is the third attraction to the palace, featuring heraldic crests from all the best families of Bohemia and a few editions from the court library, catalogued before numerical systems were invented, using an imaginative system of plant and animal images on the spines.

Just east of the cathedral is Jiřské náměstí, named after **St George's Basilica** (Bazilika sv. Jiří). If you stand far enough back from the basilica's crumbling red-and-cream baroque façade, you'll notice the two distinctive Romanesque towers jutting out behind. The Italian craftsmen who constructed them in 1142 built a fatter male tower (Adam, on the right) standing guard over a more slender female one (Eve, on the left). The basilica, founded by Prince Vratislav in 921, has burned down and been rebuilt over the centuries. Its first major remodelling took place 50 years after it was originally erected, when a Benedictine convent was founded next door. A major renovation in the early 20th century swept out most of the baroque elements and led to the uncovering of the original arcades, remnants of 13th-century frescoes and the bodies of a saint (Ludmila, who was strangled by assassins hired by Prince Wenceslas's mother, Drahomira) and a saint-maker (the notorious Boleslav the Cruel, who martyred his brother Wenceslas by having him stabbed to death). The basilica's rediscovered simplicity seems closer to God than the baroque pomposity of most Prague churches.

On the left of the main entrance is an opening built to give access for the Benedictine nuns from **St George's Convent** next door (now housing part of the National Gallery's vast collections) and to keep to a minimum their contact with the outside world. **Vikářská lane**, on the north side of the cathedral, is where Picasso and Eluard came to drink in the Vikářská tavern, now closed.

It gives access to the 15th-century Mihulka or **Powder Tower** (Prašná věž). Here Rudolf II employed his many alchemists, who were engaged in attempts to distil the Elixir of Life and transmute base metals into gold. Today the tower hosts exhibits (in Czech only) about alchemy and Renaissance life in the castle.

St Vitus's Cathedral. *See p76.*

Elsewhere on the castle grounds

Going down the hill from St George's, signposts direct you to the most visited street in Prague, **Golden Lane** (Zlatá ulička; ticket required Mar-Sept). The tiny multicoloured cottages that cling to Prague Castle's northern walls were thrown up by the poor in the 16th century out of whatever waste materials they could find. Some allege that the name is a reference to the alchemists of King Rudolf's days, who supposedly were quartered here. Others contend that it alludes to a time when soldiers billeted in a nearby tower used the lane as a public urinal. In fact, the name probably dates from the 17th century, when the city's goldsmiths worked here. Houses used to line both sides of the street, with barely enough space to pass between them, until a hygiene-conscious Joseph II had some of them demolished in the 18th century. Although the houses look separate, a corridor runs the length of their attics and used to be occupied by the sharpshooters of the Castle Guard. The house at No.22 was owned by Kafka's sister Ottla, and he stayed here for a while in 1917, reputedly drawing inspiration from the streets for his novel *The Castle*. If he rewrote it today, he'd call it *The Souvenir Shop*. Atmospheric at night, by day the lane is logged with shuffling tourists.

At the eastern end some steps take you under the last house and out to the **Dalibor Tower** (Daliborka), named after its most famous inmate, who amused himself by playing the violin while awaiting execution. According to legend (and Smetana's opera *Dalibor*), he attracted crowds of onlookers who turned up at his execution to weep en masse. Continuing down the hill takes you past a **Lobkowicz Palace** (Lobkovický palác), one of several in the town. This one, finished in 1658, houses the **Historical Museum** (Jiřská 3, no phone, www.nm.cz, closed Mon). Opposite is Burgrave House, home of the **Toy Museum**. The statue of a naked boy in the courtyard fell victim to Marxist-Leninist ideology when President Novotný decided that his genitals were not an edifying sight for the populace and ordered them to be removed. Happily, the boy and his equipment have since been reunited.

The lane passes underneath the **Black Tower** (Černá věž) and ends at the **Old Castle Steps** (Staré zámecké schody), which lead to Malá Strana, as do the **Castle Steps** (Zámecké schody) on Thunovská (accessed from the other end of the castle). Before descending, pause at the top for a view over the red tiled roofs, spires and domes of the Lesser Quarter (*see p88*).

An even better view can be had from the **Paradise Gardens** (Rajská zahrada; *see p90*) on the ramparts below the castle walls (enter from the Bull Staircase or from outside the castle, to the right of the first courtyard).

This is where the victims of the second and most famous defenestration fell to earth. They were fortunate that it was a favoured spot for emptying chamber pots, as the dung heap surely saved the lives of the defenestrated Catholic councillors. The site is now marked by an obelisk, signifying ground consecrated by the victorious Habsburgs after putting down the upstart Czech Protestants.

The gardens, which were initially laid out in 1562, were redesigned in the 1920s by Josip Plečnik. The spiralling **Bull Staircase** leading up to the castle's third courtyard and the huge granite bowl are his work. Their restoration is complete after many years, and you can now make the descent to Malá Strana via the terraced slopes of five beautiful Renaissance gardens, open, like most gardens in Prague, from April to October only. The pride of the restoration is the lovely **Ledebour Gardens** (Ledeburská zahrada), featuring fountains, ornate stone stair switchbacks and palace yards, and emptying you out as to the middle of **Valdštejnská**. Fit hikers might consider ascending to the castle this way as well, though there's a fee of 60 Kč whichever way you go.

The Royal Garden & the Belvedere

Cross over the Powder Bridge (U Prašného mostu) from the castle's second courtyard and you will reach the **Royal Garden** (Královská zahrada), on the outer side of the **Stag Moat** (Jelení přikop). Laid out for Emperor Ferdinand I in the 1530s, it once included a maze and a menagerie, but was devastated by Swedish soldiers in the 17th century.

At the eastern end of the gardens is the **Belvedere**, saved from French fire in the 18th century by a canny head gardener's payment of 30 pineapples. The beautiful Renaissance structure was built by Paolo della Stella between 1538 and 1564 (though work was interrupted by a fire at the castle in 1541). The strangely shaped green copper roof is supported by delicate arcades and columns. The Belvedere was the first royal structure in Prague to be dedicated to pleasure-seeking rather than power-mongering – it was commissioned by Ferdinand I as a gift for his wife, Anne – a loveshack one remove away from the skulduggery of life in Prague Castle. But the long-suffering Anne never got to see 'the most beautiful piece of Renaissance architecture north of the Alps' – as the city's gushing tourist brochures invariably call it. She

Sightseeing

A quiet day for a stroll down **Golden Lane**, Prague's most visited street. *See p81.*

drew her last breath after producing the 15th heir to the throne. The royal couple are immortalised in the reliefs adorning the façade. The Belvedere went on to become the site of all sorts of goings-on: mad King Rudolf installed his astronomers here and the communists later bricked up the windows of the upper level to prevent assassins from getting too close to the president. People come here today to see occasional art shows.

In front of the palace is the so-called **Singing Fountain** (Zpívajicí fontána), created in bronze by Bohemian craftsmen in the 1560s. It used to hum as water splashed into its basin but sings no longer, thanks to overzealous reconstruction.

On the southern side of the garden, overlooking the Stag Moat, is another lovely Renaissance structure, completed by Bonifác Wohlmut in 1563 to house the king's **Ball Game Court** (Míčovna). The elaborate black-and-white sgraffito has to be renewed every 20 years. The last time this was done some decidedly anachronistic elements were added to the allegorical frieze depicting Science, the Virtues and the Elements: look carefully at the lovely ladies on the top of the building and you'll see that the woman seated next to Justice (tenth from the right) is holding a hammer and sickle. On the same side of the garden, by the entrance, is the quaint, mustard-coloured **Dientzenhofer Summer House**, the presidential residence from 1948 to 1989.

During this period, large sections of the castle were closed to the public and huge underground shelters were excavated to connect the exalted president's residence with the remainder of the complex. No sooner were the shelters completed than it was seen that the subterranean passages might help to conceal counter-revolutionary saboteurs, and so the exit shafts were blocked off with enormous concrete slabs.

Prague Castle Picture Gallery

Obrazárna Pražského hradu
Prague Castle (2nd courtyard), Prague 1 (224 373 368/http://old.hrad.cz). Metro Malostranská/tram 18, 22, 23. **Open** 10am-6pm daily. *Tours* Tue-Sun. **Admission** 100 Kč; 50 Kč concessions; 150 Kč family; free under-6s. **No credit cards. Map** p326 D2.
This collection of Renaissance and baroque works is home to Giuseppe Arcimboldo's infamous manner-ist work *Vertumnus*, which cast Rudolf II as a Roman harvest god. The gallery also includes works by Rubens, Tintoretto, Titian, Veronese and lesser-known masters. Though there's no hope of ever piec-ing together the emperor's original collection, which has been scattered to the winds, the castle has bought back a handful of works from the original cache.

St George's Convent

Klášter sv. Jiří
Jiřské náměstí 33, Prague 1 (257 531 644). Metro Malostranská and up the Old Castle steps/tram 18, 22, 23. **Open** 9am-5pm Tue-Sun. **Admission** 100 Kč; 150 Kč family; free under-10s. **No credit cards. Map** p327 E2.

What lies beneath

No one really knows what's underneath Prague Castle. Apart from a brief spurt of archaeological excavations in the 1930s done while sprucing up the grounds of the seat of the first sovereign Czechoslovak republic at the close of World War I very little has been explored to date.

The First Republic didn't last long, thanks to the Nazis, and the post-war Soviet-backed communist regime had a distinct lack of interest in unearthing the roots of Czech history (after all they were out to rewrite history, not uncover it).

And since 1989 there hasn't been much funding available for archeological research. But a brief flurry was caused in mid-2005 when what is believed to be the burial chamber of King Charles IV was discovered under St Vitus's Cathedral. However, because the church is in daily use (and in fact the whole castle complex is a living, administrative centre with added presidential residence), it's yet to be excavated. That's a pity because speculation had been rife for ages about the exact location of Charles's final resting spot. Somehow Bohemia's greatest native son had become misplaced. Although his remains lie in a simple bronze casket visible in the crypt of St Vitus, his fabulous original burial place is still more or less an enigma, although it's thought to be somewhere in front of the main altar, according to Czech press accounts.

Art historian Jana Marikova-Kubkova found traces of the royal burial chamber when she was studying fragments of the former Romanesque church upon which the Gothic cathedral was later built. A probe with a camera then uncovered previously unknown ten-metre-long, interconnected burial rooms under the main altar. Mysteriously, the chamber is almost empty, with only fragments of bones and coffins visible. Historians believe they may be the remains of Charles IV's wives, though that just throws up more questions than answers.

Charles's resting place aside, another set of graves is clearly visible to everyone, their contents far more chilling than the grave of the king: a pagan burial site.

A pre-Christian temple is known to have existed where St Vitus's now stands, where sacrifices of cakes and cocks were made to Svantovit, god of fertility. But until digging began in preparation for the 'Life at Prague Castle' exhibit, no one knew about the graves.

But why is this site chilling? The bodies in it were found buried with hands bound, and weighed down with rocks. It's believed that the practice was intended to ensure that whoever got buried, stayed buried. Seems that Czech palace intrigues are nothing new.

Who did Brahe?

True crime has been a bestselling genre since Truman Capote wrote *In Cold Blood*. No doubt the authors of *Heavenly Intrigue: Johannes Kepler, Tycho Brahe, and the Murder Behind One of History's Greatest Scientific Discoveries* were thinking of *Da Vinci Code* league profits when they set about arguing that Prague's greatest astronomer, Johannes Kepler, may have stolen the research of his mentor, Tycho Brahe (pictured), and murdered him into the bargain.

Americans Joshua Gilder and his wife Anne-Lee assert in their book that Kepler poisoned Brahe to obtain his priceless observation journals, which Kepler then used to formulate his seminal three laws of planetary motion.

They back up this theory with essentially two points: high levels of mercury were found in the moustache hairs of Brahe (who officially died of a collapsed bladder) and the great astronomer was a combative personality (who had lost his nose in a duel, replacing it with a metal one).

Brahe, of course, was one of the most famous astronomers of his time, a favourite son of Denmark lured in the late 1500s to the court of Emperor Rudolf II in Prague, where he was given lavish facilities and a free hand to conduct his observations of the heavens. Brahe did not use telescopes, which were still in their infancy; instead, he employed astrolabes, sextants and other mechanical instruments to make precise measurements of the movement of the planets.

Brahe recruited Kepler, a noted German mathematician, to join him, primarily as a number-cruncher. Given enough data, Brahe was sure calculations would show that his geocentric theory (with the earth at the centre of the solar system) would be proven correct. Kepler believed the solar system was heliocentric.

Igor Janovský, a researcher at the National Technical Museum, takes exception to the Gilders' ideas. First, Brahe was also an alchemist who handled mercury often (more has been found in Isaac Newton's remains than in Brahe's). Second, not enough hair samples were used by the 1996 Swedish forensic team who explored this issue, says Janovský.

Whatever the cause of Brahe's death, which followed a banquet when the courteous astronomer refused to leave the table until the feasting was over, causing his overextended bladder to explode, mercury seems a questionable factor in his untimely end. But one thing is known: the illustrious Dane enjoyed his last days, living it up as the star of one of the most decadent and best-bankrolled courts of Europe.

If anything actually troubled him in his last years, it may have been all the distractions the good life presented to his research. One aspect of his relationship with Kepler is well documented: Brahe often complained about the late-night parties and carrying on by his room mate in the small Hradčany district dwelling that they shared.

St George's Convent features mannerist and baroque art, including paintings from the collections of whacked-out Rudolf II. A highlight is the stylised work of the Antwerp innovator Bartholomaeus Spranger, whose sophisticated colours, elegant eroticism and obscure themes typify mannerism at its best. The baroque selection begins with Karel Škréta, a down-to-earth painter, whose canvases contrast with the feverishly religious work of Michael Leopold Willmann and Jan Krystof Liška. The tendency in baroque painting and sculpture to borrow from each other can be seen in the paintings of Petr Brandl, the most acclaimed Czech artist of the early 18th century. His work is displayed near that of the two great sculptors of the time, Mathias Bernard Braun and Ferdinand Maxmilián Brokof. A workshop was recently opened, offering glimpses of the tools and methods of the masters.

Šternberg Palace

Šternberský palác
Hradčanské náměstí 15, Prague 1 (233 090 570). Metro Malostranská/tram 22, 23. **Open** 10am-6pm Tue-Sun. **Admission** 150 Kč; free under-10s. **No credit cards. Map** p327 C2.
Enlightened aristocrats trying to rouse Prague from provincial stupor founded the Šternberg Gallery here in the 1790s. The palace, located just outside the gates of Prague Castle, now houses the National Gallery's European Old Masters. Not a large or well-balanced collection, especially since some of its most famous works were returned to their pre-war owners, but some outstanding paintings remain, including a brilliant Frans Hals portrait and Dürer's *Feast of the Rosary*. The gallery recently finished renovations, making space for more paintings from the repositories, and restoring ceiling frescoes and mouldings that had long been covered up. It is now fully renovated and open to the public.

Toy Museum

Muzeum hraček
Jiřská 6, Prague 1 (224 372 294/www.muzeum hracek.cz). Metro Malostranská/tram 12, 18, 22, 23. **Open** 9.30am-5.30pm daily. **Admission** 60 Kč; 120 Kč family; free under-5s. **No credit cards. Map** p327 F2.
Part of Czech émigré Ivan Steiger's large collection is displayed on the two floors of this museum in the castle grounds. Brief texts accompany cases of toys, from teddy bears to an elaborate tin train set. Kitsch fans will love the robots and the enormous collection of Barbie dolls clad in vintage costumes throughout the decades. Good for a rainy day but probably better for the young at heart than the actually young, most of whom prefer playing with toys to looking at them from a historical perspective.

Hradčany

Hradčany owes its grand scale and pristine condition to a devastating fire in 1541, which destroyed the medieval district, and the frenzied period of Counter-Reformation building that followed the Protestant defeat at the Battle of White Mountain in 1620. Little has changed here in the last two centuries.

The area's focal point is **Hradčanské náměstí**, one of the grandest squares in the city, lined with august palaces built by the Catholic aristocracy, anxious to be close to the Habsburg court. It was nonetheless cut off from the castle and its temperamental inhabitants by a complicated system of fortifications and moats, which remained until Empress Maria Theresa had a grand spring clean in the mid-18th century. Along with the moat went the tiny Church of the Virgin Mary of Einsedel, which used to stand next to the castle ramp. Lovely as this was said to have been, it's hard to believe that it was lovelier than the superb panorama of Malá Strana, the Strahov Gardens (*see p87*) and Petřín Hill (*see p96*) that the demolition opened up.

Over on the north side of the square, next to the castle, is the domineering 16th-century **Archbishop's Palace** (Arcibiskupský palác). The frothy rococo façade was added in 1763-64.

Next door, slotted between the palace and a lane of former canons' houses, stands the **Šternberg Palace** (Šternberský palác), which houses part of the National Gallery's collection of European art. Opposite stands the heavily restored **Schwarzenberg Palace**

The Loreto. *See p86.*

(Schwarzenberský palác), one of the most imposing Renaissance buildings in Prague. It was built between 1545 and 1563, the outside exquisitely decorated with 'envelope' sgraffito. Alas, thanks to the return of nationalised property, it no longer contains the Military Museum, which long had a comprehensive collection of killing instruments.

Further up Loretánská is the respected pub U Černého vola (*see p163*), a Renaissance building with a crumbling mural on the façade. As a result of some direct action in 1991 – the patrons bought the place – it's one of the few places left in Hradčany where the locals can afford to drink. Its well-worn environs make a just reward after a day of castle-trekking and you don't have to feel guilty about the amount you drink – all profits from the sale of beer go to a nearby school for the blind.

The pub overlooks **Loretánské náměstí**, a split-level square on the site of a pagan cemetery. Half of it is taken up by a car park for the Ministry of Foreign Affairs in the monolithic **Černín Palace** (Černínský palác) – an enormous and unprepossessing structure; its long and imposing grey façade, articulated by an unbroken line of 30 pillars, is telling. Commissioned in 1669 by Humprecht Johann Černín, the Imperial ambassador to Venice, the construction of the palace financially ruined his family. As a result, the first people to move in were hundreds of 17th-century squatters. Gestapo interrogations were later conducted here during the Nazi occupation. Its curse surfaced again in 1948, when Foreign Minister Jan Masaryk, the last major political obstacle to Klement Gottwald's communist coup, fell from an upstairs window a few days after the takeover and was found dead on the pavement below. No one really believed the official verdict of suicide, but no evidence of who was responsible has ever come to light.

Somewhat dwarfed by the Černín Palace is the **Loreto**, a baroque testimony to the Catholic miracle culture that swept the Czech lands after the Thirty Years' War. The façade (1721) is a swirling mass of stuccoed cherubs, topped with a bell tower. Every hour the 27 bells ring out the cacophonous melody 'We Greet You a Thousand Times'. The streets behind the Loreto are some of the prettiest and quietest in Hradčany, and are known as **Nový Svět** (New World). The quarter was built in the 16th century for Prague Castle staff; its tiny cottages are now the most prized real estate in the city. Going down Kapucínská, you pass the **Domeček**, or Little House, at No.10, home to the notorious Fifth Department – the counterintelligence unit of the Defence Ministry. At No.5 on the nearby Černínská is **Gambra**

(Černínská 5, 220 514 527, open Mar-Oct noon-6pm Wed-Sun, Nov-Feb noon-6pm Sat, Sun), a funky gallery specialising in surrealist art. Its owner, the world-renowned animator Jan Švankmajer, lives in the attached house. At the foot of the hill is Nový Svět street itself, full of brightly coloured cottages restored in the 18th and 19th centuries – all that remains of Hradčany's medieval slums. The rest were destroyed in the great fire of 1541. Tycho Brahe, the Danish astronomer known for his missing nose and breakthroughs in accurate observations of planetary orbits, lived at No.1, the Golden Griffin.

Back up from Loretánské náměstí is Hradčany's last major square, **Pohořelec**. The passage at No.8 leads to the peaceful surroundings of the **Strahov Monastery** (Strahovský klášter), which contains some magnificent libraries and religious art.

Bílek Villa

Bílkova vila
Mickiewiczowa 1, Prague 1 (224 322 021). Metro Hradčanská/tram 18, 22. **Open** 10am-5pm Sat, Sun. **Admission** 50 Kč. **No credit cards. Map** p332 A4.
Down the hill on the opposite side of Prague Castle, to the north, is this building, which must be the only one in the world designed to look like a wheat field. Built in 1911-12 by mystic sculptor František Bílek as his studio and home, it still contains much of his work. Bílek went to Paris to study as a painter, but discovered that he was partially colour-blind. He then turned to sculpture and illustration. The wheat field, representing spiritual fertility and the harvest of creative work, was one of his many motifs. The results range from the sublime to the repellent. If the grouping of Hobbit-like wooden figures out front takes your fancy, you should have a look inside.

The Loreto

Loretánské náměstí 7, Prague 1 (220 516 740/ www.loreta.cz). Tram 22. **Open** 9am-12.15pm, 1-4.30pm Tue-Sun. **Admission** 90 Kč; 60 Kč concessions. **No credit cards. Map** p326 B3.
The Loreto is probably the most outlandish baroque fantasy you'll see in Prague. Its attractions include a sculpture of the bearded St Wilgefortis, the skeletons of another two female saints and the highest concentration of cherubs found anywhere in the city. It was built as part of a calculated plan to reconvert the masses to Catholicism after the Thirty Years' War.

At the Loreto's heart is a small chapel, the Santa Casa ('Holy House'), whose history is so improbable that it quickly gained cult status. The story goes that the original Santa Casa was the home of the Blessed Virgin Mary in Nazareth until it was miraculously flown over to Loreto in Italy by angels, spawning a copycat cult all over Europe. This one, dating from 1626-31, boasts two beams and a brick in the 'original', as well as a crevice left on the wall by a divine lightning bolt that struck an unfortunate

Knocking at heaven's door: **Strahov Monastery**.

blasphemer. The red colour scheme makes it look less like a virgin's boudoir and more like a place in which to hold a black mass. The shrine was a particular hit with wealthy ladies, who donated the money for baroque maestri Christoph and Kilian Ignaz Dientzenhofer to construct the outer courtyards and the Church of the Nativity (1716-23) at the back. They also sponsored the carving of St Wilgefortis (in the corner chapel to the right of the main entrance), the patron saint of unhappily married women, who grew a beard as a radical tactic to get out of marrying a heathen, and that of St Agatha the Unfortunate, who can be seen carrying her severed breasts on a meat platter (in the Church of the Nativity). The famous diamond monstrance, designed in 1699 by Fischer von Erlach and sporting 6,222 stones, is in the treasury. **Photo** *p85.*

Miniatures Museum

Muzeum miniatur
Strahovské nádvoří 11 (grounds of Strahov Monastery), Prague 1 (233 352 371). Metro Malostranská/tram 22, 23. **Open** 9am-5pm daily. **Admission** 50 Kč; 20 Kč children. **Credit** AmEx, DC, MC, V. **Map** p326 A4.
With the aid of magnifying glasses and microscopes, you'll be able to see truly tiny works of art – portraiture on a poppy seed, a caravan of camels painted on a grain of millet, a prayer written out on a human hair, and minuscule copies of masterpieces by the likes of Rembrandt and Botticelli. Just as well you can combine this with a visit to the Strahov Monastery: it's not worth the long walk in itself.

Strahov Monastery

Strahovský klášter
Strahovské nádvoří 1, Prague 1 (233 107 749/www. strahovskyklaster.cz). **Open** 9am-noon, 1-5pm daily. **Admission** 80 Kč. **No credit cards. Map** p326 A4.

The Premonstratensian order (or Norbertines) set up house here in 1140 and soon after embarked upon their austere programme of silent contemplation and celibacy. The complex still has an air of seclusion, with fragrant orchard gardens stretching down the hill to Malá Strana. Since 1990 several cowled monks have returned to reclaim the buildings taken from them by the communists in 1948. They can sometimes be seen from Úvoz street walking laps around green fields and meditating, and, in a pointed rejoinder to their one-time communist overlords, the Mass is again being offered in the Church of Our Lady. The church retains its 12th-century basilica ground plan after remodelling in the early 17th century.

The highlights of the complex are surely the superb libraries, which appear on posters in universities all over the world. Within the frescoed Theological and Philosophical Halls alone are 130,000 volumes, with a further 700,000 volumes in storage. Together they form the most important collection in Bohemia. Visitors cannot, unfortunately, stroll around the libraries. They are, however, generously allowed to gawp through the doors. The comprehensive acquisition of books didn't begin until the late 16th century. When Joseph II effected a clampdown on religious institutions in 1782, the Premonstratensians managed to outwit him by masquerading as an educational foundation, and their collection was swelled by the libraries of less shrewd monasteries. Indeed, the monks' taste ranged far beyond the standard ecclesiastical tracts, including such highlights as the oldest extant copy of *The Calendar of Minutae* or *Selected Times for Bloodletting.* Nor did they merely confine themselves to books: the 200-year-old curiosity cabinets house a collection of deep-sea monsters that any landlocked country would be proud to possess.

Elsewhere in the monastery, the Strahov Gallery exhibits a part of the monks' collection of religious art.

Malá Strana

Between the castle and the river.

Maps p326 & p327

Mellow **Malá Strana** has a true left bank feel, in accord with its history as a warren for artists, craftsmen working for the castle, and royal retainers awarded palaces for deeds of empire consolidation. Its quiet lanes lie between the Vltava river and Prague Castle, skirting the hill that makes up Hradčany. Its backstreets reward explorers with old-world embassies, rustic pubs and ornate churches; best of all, the once-private formal gardens are now open to strollers.

Malá Strana was founded by the Přemyslid Otakar II in 1287, when he invited merchants from Germany to set up shop on the land beneath the castle walls. Very little remains of this Gothic town today – the present-day appearance of the quarter dates to the 17th century. The area was transformed into a sparkling baroque district by the wealthy Catholic aristocracy, who won huge parcels of land in the property redistribution that followed the Thirty Years' War. When the fashionable followed the Habsburg court to Vienna in the 17th century, the poor returned to the area.

It has been the home of poets, drunks and mystics ever since, these bohemians living in unlikely juxtaposition with diplomats quartered close to the castle. The British, American, German, Irish, Italian and French embassies, among many others, are situated in Malá Strana.

Today the character of the area is changing rapidly, as accountancy firms, bankers and wine bars set up shop. It's still remarkable,

though, just how few businesses there are in what is one of the most central Prague districts. **Malostranské náměstí** now throbs with life deep into the night, but this is mostly down to overt tourism marketing, and the many bars, restaurants and music venues that draw visitors to the capital. Apart from stores selling souvenirs and cut glass, there is very little shopping in the area.

This lack of development means that the district has preserved its ancient look and the backstreets of Malá Strana are a favourite locale for a stream of film crews shooting period pieces in the city. Local residents are unfazed by the attention, however, and carry on as ever.

Malostranské náměstí & around

The short main drag between Charles Bridge and Malostranské náměstí is **Mostecká**. It's a continuation of the Royal Route – the path taken by the Bohemian kings to their coronation – and is lined with elegant baroque dwellings. The one at No.15 is the **Kaunitz Palace** (Kaunicův palác), built in 1773 for Jan Adam Kaunitz, an advisor to Empress Maria Theresa, who sycophantically had the exterior painted her favourite colours – yellow and white. It's now the embassy of Serbia and Montenegro. Just off Mostecká are the Blue Light jazz pub (*see p163*) and the U Patrona restaurant (Dražického náměstí 4, 257 530 725, www.upatrona.cz), both oases of quality in a stretch that is dominated by naff souvenir shops. At the heart of the quarter is wide, open Malostranské náměstí, a lively square edged by large baroque palaces and Renaissance gabled townhouses perched on top of Gothic arcades. A decidedly modern touch has been added with Square (*see p143*), a sleek and excellent restaurant with modern minimalist design and Mediterranean cuisine. This space was known as Malostranská Kavárna for a century and inspired the tales of one of the city's most beloved Bohemian writers, Jan Neruda, author of *Prague Tales*. Bang in the middle of the square, dividing it in two, is the **Church of St Nicholas** (Chrám sv. Mikuláš), a monumental late baroque affair, whose dome and adjoining bell tower dominate the skyline of Prague's left bank. Built between 1703 and 1755, it's the largest and most ornate of the city's many Jesuit-founded churches. Local residents fought bitterly against the destruction of the two streets, two churches and various other structures that had to be demolished to make room for the church.

The grim block next door at No.25 is yet another Jesuit construction, built as a college for the society's priests and now housing harassed-looking maths students. More appealing is the **Lichtenstein Palace** (Lichtenštejnský palác) opposite, finished in 1791. The Lichtensteins used to be major landowners in Bohemia and the Alpine principality has been battling to regain the palace, which was confiscated in 1918. The palace is currently used as a venue for classical concerts. Also in the square, located in the former town hall at No.21, is the club Malostranská beseda (*see p236*), home to music of a more raucous bent. Opposite the south side of St Nicholas is a parade of pubs and restaurants. The original American backpacker hangout Jo's Bar (*see p163*) is on this stretch, but under new ownership.

Nerudova heads up from the north-west corner of the square towards Prague Castle, and is a fine place to begin deciphering the ornate signs that decorate many of the city's houses: the Three Fiddles at No.12, for example, or the Devil at No.4. This practice of distinguishing houses continued up until 1770, when that relentless modernist Joseph II spoiled all the fun by introducing numbered addresses. The street, which is crowded with restaurants, cafés and shops aimed at the ceaseless flow of tourists to and from the castle, is, as you might expect, named after the poet and novelist Jan Neruda. He lived at No.47, the Two Suns (U Dvou slunců). The house was turned into a pub and during the communist period was a favourite hangout of the Plastic People of the Universe, the underground rock band that was later instrumental in the founding of Charter 77, the petition carried out in December 1976 against restrictions of the regime. Sadly, the place is joyless and full of tourists. Also to be ignored is the turquoise drinking establishment at No. 13 where Václav Havel, in an uncharacteristic lapse of taste, took Boris Yeltsin for a mug of beer. A better bet is U Kocoura (257 530 107) at No.2. It was briefly owned by the Friends of Beer (formerly a political party, now a civic association). Although its political manifesto might be a bit vague, the staff's ability to pull a good, cheap pint is beyond question. The more recent Bazaar Mediterranée restaurant at No.40 offers enviable terrace views for lunch and ridiculous striptease and drag-show entertainments with dinner.

The alley next door leads up to the British Embassy at Thunovská 14, which a diplomatic wag christened 'Czechers'. Leading up from here are the **New Castle Steps** (Nové zámecké

Nothing much has changed in **Maltézské Square**. *See p93*.

schody), one of the most peaceful (and least strenuous) routes up to the castle and a star location in the film *Amadeus*.

There are still more embassies back on Nerudova, the Italians occupying the **Thun-Hohenstein Palace** (Thun-Hohenštejnský palác) at No.20, built by Giovanni Santini-Aichel in 1726 and distinguished by the contorted eagles holding up the portal, the heraldic emblem of the Kolowrats for whom the palace was built. The Italians were trumped for a while by the Romanians, however, who used to inhabit the even more glorious **Morzin Palace** (Morzinský palác) at No.5. Also the work of Santini-Aichel, the façade, dating from 1714, sports two hefty Moors – a pun on the family's name – who hold up the window ledge. Their toes have been rubbed shiny by passers-by who believe that touching them will bring good luck.

Nerudova also leads up to Prague Castle, with the added incentive of a respite from the crowds and a good midway break provided by U zavěšenýho kafe (*see p164*), a mellow pub situated where Nerudova turns into Úvoz. Walking back down Nerudova, if you continue straight down the tram tracks instead of veering off on to Malostranské náměstí, you'll see on your left the **Church of St Thomas** (Kostel sv. Tomáše). Its rich baroque façade is easy to miss, tucked into the narrow side street

Nerudova. See p89.

of Tomášská. Based on a Gothic ground plan, the church was rebuilt in the baroque style by Kilián Ignaz Dientzenhofer for the Augustinian monks. The symbol of the Order, a flaming heart, can be seen all over the church and adjoining cloisters (now an old people's home) and makes a distinct impression, held tightly in the hand of St Boniface, a fully dressed skeleton who occupies a glass case in the nave.

On the corner of Josefská and Letenská is the **Church of St Joseph** (Kostel sv. Josefa), a tiny baroque gem set back from the road and designed by Jean-Baptiste Mathey. Since 1989 it has been returned to the much-diminished Order of English Virgins, who were also one-time owners of the nearby **Vojan's Gardens** (Vojanovy sady), one of the most tranquil spots in the city.

Running parallel to U Lužického semináře is Cihelna, a street named after the former brick factory converted into a restaurant and museums dedicated to Franz Kafka and jewellery. The road provides an opening on to the river and an almost perfect view of the Vltava and Charles Bridge beyond. Back on Letenská, towards Malostranská metro station, is a door in a wall leading into the best-kept formal gardens in the city. The early 17th-century **Wallenstein Gardens** belonged, along with the adjoining **Wallenstein Palace** (Valdštejnský palác), to General Albrecht von Wallenstein, commander of the Catholic armies in the Thirty Years' War and a formidable property speculator.

The palace (which now contains the Czech Parliament) is simply enormous. Designed by the Milanese architect Andrea Spezza in 1624-30, it once had a permanent staff of 700 servants and 1,000 horses. A little-noticed entrance to the palace gardens, just to the right of the Malostranská metro station exit, provides a wonderful way of cutting through the district and leaving tourists behind. You come out on Valdštejnské náměstí, just west of an even more impressive collection of greenery, terraces and baroque arches, the **Paradise Gardens** (Rajská zahrada).

Much of the area of Malá Strana between Malostranská metro station and the square is these days sprouting cosy little bars and cafés, one of the best being **Palffy Palác**. Another, just uphill from Parliament and a new favourite of its members, is restaurant U Zlaté studně (*see p141*), up the tiny street of the same name.

Church of St Nicholas

Kostel sv. Mikuláše
Malostranské náměstí, Prague 1 (257 534 215).
Metro Malostranská/tram 12, 22. **Open** *Nov-Feb*
9am-4pm daily. *Mar-Oct* 9am-5pm daily.
Admission 60 Kč; 30 Kč concessions. **Map** p327 F3.

Wallenstein Gardens: for an afternoon of outdoor order. *See p90*.

The immense dome and bell tower of St Nicholas, which dominate Malá Strana, are monuments to the money and effort that the Catholic Church sank into the Counter-Reformation. The rich façade by Christoph Dientzenhofer, which was completed around 1710, conceals an interior and dome by his son Kilián Ignaz, dedicated to high baroque at its most flamboyantly camp – bathroom-suite pinks and greens, swooping golden cherubs, swirling gowns and dramatic gestures; there's even a figure coyly proffering a pair of handcuffs.

Commissioned by the Jesuits, it took three generations of architects, several financial crises and the demolition of much of the neighbourhood between presentation of the first plans in 1653 to final completion in 1755. Inside, a trompe l'oeil extravaganza, created by the Austrian Johann Lukas Kracker, covers the ceiling, seamlessly blending with the actual structure of the church below. Frescoes portray the life and times of St Nicholas, best known as the Bishop of Myra and the bearer of gifts to small children, but also the patron saint of municipal administration. Maybe this is why St Nicholas's was restored by the communists in the 1950s when the rest of Prague's baroque churches were left to crumble. The church tower also happened to make a favourite spy roost for teams of secret police.

Church of St Thomas

Kostel sv. Tomáše
Josefská 8, Prague 1 (257 530 556). Metro Malostranská/tram 12, 22. **Open** 11am-1pm Mon-Sat; 9am-noon, 4.30-5.30pm Sun. **Admission** free. **Map** p327 F3.

It's worth craning your neck to get a good look at the curvy pink façade of St Thomas's. The lopsided structure is the legacy of an earlier Gothic church built for the Order of Augustinian hermits. After the structure was damaged by fire in 1723, Kilián Ignaz Dientzenhofer was employed to give it the baroque touch. The newly rich burghers of Malá Strana provided enough cash for the frescoes to be completed at breakneck speed (they took just two years) and for Rubens to paint the altarpiece, *The Martyrdom of St Thomas*. They even bought the body of St Boniface. The original altarpiece is now part of the National Gallery's collection on show in the Šternberg Palace (*see p85*) and has been replaced by a copy, but the skeletons of the saints dressed in period costume are still on display. Next door are 17th-century cloisters, where the monks dabbled in alchemy before realising that transforming hops into beer was easier and more lucrative than trying to make gold out of lead. A door on Letenská leads to their former brewery, now a tourist-filled restaurant.

Kampa Island

The approach to Malá Strana from Staré Město via Charles Bridge affords one of the best photo opportunities in the city: the twin towers of the bridge framing an almost perfect view of the Church of St Nicholas and the castle behind. Before continuing, however, take the flight of steps on the left leading down to **Na Kampě**, the principal square of **Kampa Island**. Until 1770, it was known simply as Ostrov or 'island',

Church of St Nicholas. *See p88.*

which understandably led to confusion with the other islands of the Vltava – especially since Kampa's southern end looks as if it's attached to land. A little fork of the Vltava, the burbling Čertovka, translated as Little Devil, runs briefly underground at the south end but resurfaces to slice Kampa from the mainland. It went by the altogether unromantic name of the Ditch until it was cleaned up and rechristened in the 19th century. The communists proposed filling the Čertovka to create a major road but were thwarted by a sudden outbreak of good sense, and this singular place, with its medieval water wheels, has survived.

Kampa is an oasis of calm on even the most crowded August day. Its verdant setting is home to the revamped **Kampa Museum** and at the south end of the island is one of the loveliest parks in the city. This was created in the 19th century, when an egalitarian decision was made to join the gardens of three private palaces and throw them open to the public. Washerwomen once rinsed shirts on the banks – note the **Chapel to St John of the Laundry** (Kaple sv. Jana Na Prádle) near the southern end. Today it's taken up by snoozing office workers and bongo-beating hippies. The river and bridge views are as romantic as they come, while the overhanging chestnut trees make shady spots for reading and recharging. In spring the park is filled with pink blossom. Kampa Park restaurant (*see p143*), one of Prague's classier and pricier places to eat, is at the north end of the island, where the Čertovka

runs back into the river by Charles Bridge, and, no mean feat, offers the finest waterfront view of any dining establishment in town.

Between Kampa & Petřín Hill

Across the tiny bridge on Hroznová that leads to tranquil **Velkopřevorské náměstí** is **Buquoy Palace** (Buquoyský palác), a pink stucco creation dating from 1719, which now houses the French Embassy. Opposite is the **John Lennon Wall**, which in the 1980s became a place of pilgrimage for the city's hippies, who scrawled messages of love, peace and rock 'n' roll across it. The secret police, spotting a subversive plot to undermine the state, lost no time in painting over the graffiti, only to have John's smiling face reappear a few days later. This continued until 1989 when the wall was returned to the Knights of Malta as part of a huge restitution package. The Knights proved even more uptight and were ready to whitewash the graffiti when an unlikely Beatles fan, in the form of the French Ambassador, came to the rescue. Claiming to enjoy the strains of 'Give Peace a Chance' wafting through his office window, he sparked a diplomatic incident but saved the wall. In the summer of 1998 the Knights had a change of heart, the graffiti and crumbling remains of Lennon's face were removed, the wall was replastered and the Beatle's portrait repainted by artist František Flasar. The John Lennon Peace Club is encouraging modest graffiti – preferably in the form of little flowers.

Just around the corner is the quiet and lovely **Maltézské náměstí**. The Knights of Malta lived here for centuries until the communists dissolved the order. The Knights regained great swathes of property under the restitution laws, including the square's highlight, the Church of Our Lady Beneath the Chain. Opposite the church is the excellent little café-restaurant Cukrkávalimonáda (*see p139*) and round the corner on Saska ulička are the prettiest flower shops and boutiques for club clothes in town. Prokopská street is home to the U Maltézských rytířů restaurant (*see p139*), which occupies a Gothic cellar that was once a hospice operated by the Knights. The baroque building on the corner of the square was once known as the Museum of Musical Instruments. It has suffered more than its fair share of misfortune: its priceless Flemish tapestries were given to Von Ribbentrop, Hitler's foreign affairs advisor, and its Stradivarius violins were stolen in 1990; now the museum is closed for good.

Although the museum is gone, the sound of students practising at the nearby conservatory provides a soundtrack for wandering around the area. The strange **Church of Our Lady Beneath the Chain** (Kostel Panny Marie pod Řetězem) is the square's most notable sight, the oldest Gothic parts of which were built by a military-religious order to guard the Judith Bridge, which spanned the Vltava close to where Charles Bridge sits today – bits of the original bridge are visible in the lobby of the **Rezidence Lundborg** (*see p49*). Two heavy towers still stand at the entrance, but they now contain some of the most prized apartments in Prague. The Hussite wars barred the construction of the church and it was never finished. In place of a nave is an ivy-covered courtyard that leads to a baroque addition (dating from 1640-50), built in the apse of the original structure.

At the foot of Petřín Hill runs Újezd, which becomes Karmelitská as it runs north before leading into **Malostranské náměstí**. There are peculiar diversions along the way. The first is at the intersection of Újezd and Vítězná (the border between Malá Strana and Smíchov), where you'll find the popular Bohemia Bagel (*see p138*) spilling rock music and American college kids on to the street. There they mix with Death Metal fans from Újezd next door (*see p246*). Just to the north is the **Michna Palace** (Michnův palác), a fine baroque mansion also built in 1640-50.

It was intended to rival the Wallenstein Palace, which was itself built to compete with the majesty of Prague Castle. With these gargantuan ambitions, Francesco Caratti took Versailles as his model in designing the garden wing of Michna Palace. Today the gardens contain little but tennis courts.

Sightseeing

Kampa Park. *See p92.*

Walk this way Malá Strana idylls

The Malá Strana district has been known for centuries as the home of artists, poets, boozers, dramaturges and musos, from visionary photographers like Jan Sudek to novelists such as Jan Neruda. This walk through their favourite haunts and drinking holes should take a morning or afternoon if you choose to visit and appreciate the works of art at the Wallenstein Riding School gallery as a start. Otherwise, it makes for a reasonably exerting two-hour stroll.

Starting at the Malostranská metro, you'll find it has an exit conveniently leading right to the courtyard of the **Wallenstein Riding School** (see p220). Don't let the name fool you, no one's instructing in the equestrian arts here these days and the former stables are now one of the left bank's finest exhibition halls for Czech artists, run by the National Gallery. The works being exhibited range from sculpture and traditional painting to postmodern multimedia and digital art. Recent shows have celebrated National School masters of the 19th century, but you're just as likely to come across young pioneers yet to be discovered in group shows, some of which include mini art-walks with guides in English (for upcoming events check the Wallenstein website, www.ngprague.cz).

If you'd prefer to skip the art (and we admit that the prospect of postmodern multimedia installations can make the hardiest of tourists quail), or you need to rest your eyes after sampling the latest outpouring of artistic genius, then a stroll through the **Wallenstein Gardens** is the perfect cure. Use the little-noticed entrance in the garden wall to the left of the metro exit, which is on the right as you leave the station. It's only open April to October but makes for a wonderfully unexpected refuge, filled with trimmed shrubs, bronze statuary and, sometimes, outdoor concerts. Exit the gardens at the west end, which takes you past the Czech Parliament, on to Valdštejnská.

Head left on this street for a latte refuelling stop on Malostranské náměstí at **Square** (see p143). Though it's gone the way of many an old Prague bar and become a designer tapas place these days, it was once the Malostranská Kavárna, where the district's most famous author, Jan Neruda, penned his *Malá Strana Tales*, filling it with the neighbourhood characters.

From here head up the hill to the east on the street named after him, Nerudova, taking in the district's signature doorway lintel façades: two suns marking out No.47, the pub **U Dvou Slunců** (*At the Two Suns*) and so on. Turn left at the first set of stairs you come to, which turn into Tržiště street. Head south down this twisting back lane past **Baráčnická Rychta** (see p141), a grand old pub and former lecture salon where, in another sign of the times, these days you're more likely to see Balkan brass bands performing. If Square is a bit rich for your blood or your pocket, then this beerhall is a great, affordable stop for a filling lunch of ye olde Bohemian.

Continue down Tržiště street to Karmelitská, crossing it and continuing east on Prokopská. Take the first left, then turn right at the Church of Our Lady Beneath the Chain and continue west until, imagine, you come to the **Lennon Wall**. This shrine to peace, love and rock 'n' roll is still covered with graffiti tributes 26 years after Lennon's death, although now the writers and artists no longer risk imprisonment by the secret police, as was the case in communist times.

From here continue east to Kampa Island, home to neo-hippies, and, a bit to the south along the Vltava river, Museum Kampa. The museum exemplifies Czech bohemianism with its collections of abstract sculpture by artists such as Otto Gufreund and visiting installations from the likes of Yoko Ono.

At the southern end of the island, where it reconnects with Malá Strana, turn right on Říční and stroll on over to Újezd. Turn right, heading north, and on the right-hand side at No.30 you'll spot the easily overlooked entrance to one of Jan Sudek's former photo studio (he had two, dividing his time between them), **Josef Sudek Atelier** (see p223). This one-armed World War I veteran put Czech photography on the map with his haunting still life, figure and landscape images of Prague. Strolling around the humble building where he spent so many years, making its courtyard and steamed windows world famous, is a treat indeed.

Now reward yourself for your exertions at any of the cafés along Újezd, almost certain to contain at a corner table a bohemian scribbler putting his thoughts into a notebook. And don't be too shocked if you discover that that person is you.

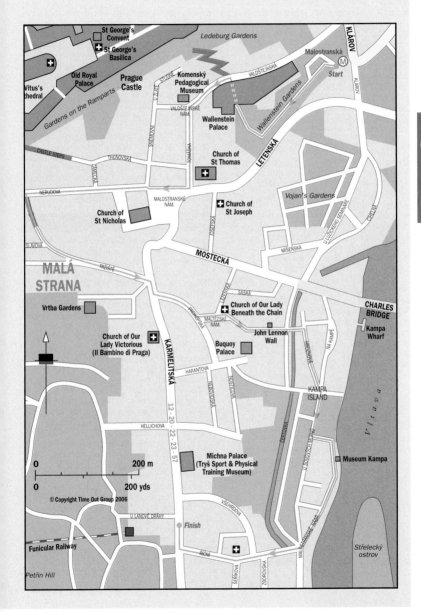

Sightseeing

Just north up Karmelitská, at No.9, is the **Church of Our Lady Victorious** (Kostel Panny Marie Vítězné; *see below*), the first baroque church in Prague (built from 1611 to 1613). It belongs to the Discalced (Barefoot) Carmelites, an order that returned to the city in 1993 and has taken charge of the church's most celebrated relic: the doll-like, miracle-working Bambino di Praga. Porcelain likenesses of the wonder baby fill shop windows for blocks around, and pilgrims from across the globe file into the church.

Heading left up the hill from Karmelitská is **Tržiště**, on the corner of which stands U Malého Glena (*see p164*), which is a convivial jazz pub run by expat American Glenn Spicker. A little further up the hill is the hip St Nicholas Café cellar bar (*see p163*) and opposite it is the cosy little Gitanes (*see p138*), which is the ideal place for a traditional romantic dinner. The 17th-century **Schönborn Palace** (Schönbornský palác), which is now the American Embassy, sits at Tržiště 15. The palace was built by Giovanni Santini-Aichel, who, despite his Mediterranean-sounding name, was, in fact, a third-generation Praguer and one of the descendants of Italian craftsmen who formed an expat community on **Vlašská** just up the hill.

From here, Tržiště becomes a tiny little lane that winds its way up the hill, giving access to some of the loveliest hidden alleys you'll find in Malá Strana. Developers have been busy converting most of the flats here into investment property, but No.22 is a great survivor, Baráčnická rychta (*see p163*). This is one of the most traditional – and certainly the most insalubrious – drinking establishments of the Lesser Quarter.

Vlašská runs on up the hill from Tržiště and contains the **Lobkowicz Palace** (Lobkovický palác) at No.19. One of four Lobkowicz Palaces in Prague, its design (1703-69) is based on Bernini's unrealised plans for the Louvre. In 1989 the gardens sheltered thousands of East Germans, who ignored the verboten signs and scaled the high walls, setting up camp in here until they were granted permission to leave for the West. Until the nationalisation of property in 1948, the Lobkowicz family was another of Bohemia's major landowners.

Vlašská ambles on upwards, fading out as it passes a hospital and chapel founded in the 17th century by the area's Italian community, and eventually leading back on to Petřín Hill.

Church of Our Lady Victorious

Kostel Panny Marie Vítězné
Karmelitská 9, Prague 1 (257 533 646). Tram 12, 22. **Open** 8.30am-7pm Mon-Sat; 8.30am-8pm Sun. **Admission** free. **Map** p327 F4.

The early baroque Church of Our Lady Victorious is entirely eclipsed by its diminutive but revered occupant: Il Bambino di Praga (Pražské Jezulátko). This 400-year-old wax effigy of the baby Jesus draws pilgrims, letters and lots of cash from grateful and/or desperate believers the world over. The list of miracles that the Infant of Prague is supposed to have performed is long and impressive, and over 100 stone plaques expressing gratitude attest to the efficacy of his powers. The effigy, brought from Spain to Prague in the 17th century, was placed under the care of the Carmelite nuns, just in time to protect them from the plague. It was later granted official miracle status by the Catholic Church.

A wardrobe of over 60 outfits befits this dazzling reputation: the baby Jesus is always magnificently turned out, and his clothes have been changed by the Order of English Virgins at sunrise on selected days for around 200 years. While he's said to be anatomically correct, the nuns' blushes are spared by a specially designed wax undershirt. At the back of the church is a shamelessly commercial gift shop, jostling with miraculous souvenirs.

Petřín Hill

Rising up in the west of Malá Strana is **Petřín Hill** (Petřínské sady), the highest, greenest and most peaceful of Prague's seven hills. This area is the largest expanse of greenery in central Prague – a favourite spot for tobogganing children in winter and canoodling couples in summertime. Petřín comes from the Latin word for rock, a reference to the hill's past role as the source for much of the city's Gothic and Romanesque building material. The southern edge of the hill is traversed by the so-called **Hunger Wall** (Hladová zeď), an eight-metre-high (23-foot) stone fortification that was commissioned by Charles IV in 1362 in order to provide some work for the poor of the city.

The lazy (and most fun) way to the top of the hill is to catch the funicular from Újezd, which runs roughly every ten minutes during the summer season (Apr-Oct 9am-11.30pm daily, 14 Kč) and every 15 minutes in winter (Nov-Mar 9am-11.20pm daily, 14 Kč), stopping halfway up by the touristy Nebozízek restaurant (Petřínské sady 411, 257 315 329, www.nebozizek.cz). At the top is a fine collection of architectural absurdities. Ascend the 299 steps of **Petřín Tower** (Rozhledna; *see p97*), a fifth-scale copy of the Eiffel Tower, for spectacular views over the city. The tower was erected in 1891 for the Jubilee Exhibition, as was the neighbouring mock-Gothic castle that houses **Mirror Maze** (Zrcadlové bludiště; *see p97*), which is a fairground-style hall of wacky reflectors. There's a café at the base of the tower and a basic refreshment hut nearby. The third and

least-frequented of the Petřín attractions is
Štefánik Observatory (Hvězdárna), which
is at the top of the funicular.

While children get the most out of the hilltop
attractions, Petřín's meandering paths are the
attraction for grown-ups. You wind through
the trees for hours, seeking the statue of Karel
Hynek Mácha, unofficial patron saint of lovers.
The shadowy bowers are a favourite of his
disciples. **Strahov Monastery** (*see p87*)
and the No.22 tram stop are just a gentle
stroll downhill from here.

Mirror Maze

Zrcadlové bludiště
*Petřín Hill, Prague 1 (257 315 212). Tram 12, 22,
then funicular railway.* **Open** *Jan-Mar, Nov, Dec*
10am-5pm Sat, Sun. *Apr, Sept* 10am-7pm daily.
May-Aug 10am-10pm daily. *Oct* 10am-6pm daily.
Admission 50 Kč; 40 Kč children. **No credit
cards. Map** p326 C6.

Housed in a cast-iron mock-Gothic castle, complete
with drawbridge and crenellations, is a hall of dis-
torting mirrors that still causes remarkable hilarity
among children and their parents. Alongside is a
wax diorama of one of the proudest historical
moments for the citizens of Prague: the defence of
Charles Bridge during the Swedish attack of 1648.

Petřín Tower

Rozhledna
*Petřín Hill, Prague 1 (257 320 112). Tram 12, 22,
then funicular railway.* **Open** *Jan-Mar, Nov-Dec*
10am-5pm Sat, Sun. *Apr, Sept* 10am-7pm daily. *May-
Aug* 10am-10pm daily. *Oct* 10am-6pm daily. Closed
in poor weather. **Admission** 50 Kč; 40 Kč children.
No credit cards. Map p326 C5.

While Parisians were still hotly debating the aesthetic value of their newly erected Eiffel Tower, the
Czechs decided they liked it so much that they constructed their own version out of recycled railway
tracks in a lightning 31 days for the 1891 Jubilee
Exhibition. Its fiercest opponent was Adolf Hitler,
who looked out of his room in the castle and immediately ordered 'that metal contraption' to be
removed. Somehow it survived. It is fairly tatty these
days, but the stiff climb to the top is made worthwhile by phenomenal views of the city. The sight of
St Vitus's Cathedral includes the complete building,
not just the usual vista of a set of spires poking over
the top of the rest of the castle. Just try not to think
about the way the tower sways in the wind.

Prague Jewellery Collection

Pražský kabinet Šperku
*Hergetova Cihelna, Cihelná 2b, Malá Strana, Prague
1 (221 451 400/257 535 510/www.cihelna.info).
Metro Malostranská/tram 6, 9, 22.* **Open** 10am-6pm
daily. **Admission** 60 Kč; 50 Kč concessions.
No credit cards. Map p327 H3.

Housed in a magnificently reconstructed brickyard
on the river and just a stone's throw from Charles
Bridge, this new museum is a collaboration between

the Museum of Decorative Arts and the private COPA
company. The collection brings together an impressive assortment of jewellery and goldsmithing, doc-
umenting the evolution of the art from the 17th century
to the present. Included are Tiffany art works and
Fabergé eggs, along with some Czech pieces once
exhibited at the Expo '58 world's fair in Brussels.

Štefánik Observatory

Hvězdárna
*Petřín Hill, Prague 1 (257 320 540/www.
observatory.cz). Tram 12, 22, then funicular railway.*
Open *Jan, Feb, Nov-Dec* 6-8pm Tue-Fri; 10am-noon,
2-8pm Sat, Sun. *Mar* 7-9pm Tue-Fri; 10am-noon,
2-6pm, 7-9pm Sat, Sun. *Apr-Aug* 2-7pm, 9-11pm
Tue-Fri; 10am-noon, 2-7pm, 9-11pm Sat, Sun.
Sept 2-6pm, 8-10pm Tue-Fri; 10am-noon, 2-6pm,
8-10pm Sat, Sun. *Oct* 7-9pm Tue-Fri; 10am-noon,
2-6pm, 7-9pm Sat, Sun. **Admission** 40 Kč; 30 Kč
concessions; free under-3s. **No credit cards.**
Map p326 D6.

With classic old-regime inconvenient opening hours,
Prague's observatory is nevertheless part of a proud
tradition of historical astronomical connections.
Both the haughty Dane Tycho Brahe and his protégé Johannes Kepler resided in the city. The duo
features in the observatory's stellar displays (which
contain some English). Telescopes offer glimpses of
sunspots and solar transits by Mercury and Venus
during the day, and panoramas of the stars, the planets and the moon on clear nights.

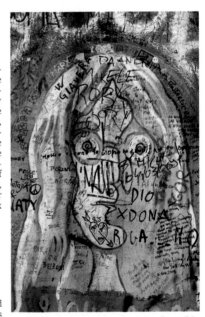

John Lennon Wall: signs of peace. *See p92.*

Staré Město

Old Town.

Maps p308 & 309

Once a walled city, the heart of Prague is still a formidable fortress against the present, with traditional ironmongers and shoe repair shops standing their ground against trendy brewery-licensed restaurants and modern art galleries. In fact, it's possible to see the district as a microcosm of the nation; what was once the scene of bloody martyrdoms, a Jewish ghetto and communist-era neglect is now more hip and more Western European. Yet, like a Kafka tale, the twists and turns will confound you.

The **Powder Gate** (Prašná brána; *see p100*), a Gothic gateway dating from 1475 at the eastern end of Celetná, marks the boundary between the Old and New Towns. It's also the start of the so-called **Royal Route** (Královská Cesta) – the traditional coronation path taken by the Bohemian kings and now a popular tourist track. The first stretch runs west down Celetná, a promenade lined with freshly restored baroque and Renaissance buildings.

A more recent makeover is the **House of the Black Madonna** at No.34, the first cubist building in the city (built in 1913), which now houses, appropriately, the city's first museum of Czech cubism. Kubista (*see p181*), on the ground floor, is a stylish shop selling original cubist pieces and copies made according to the original techniques.

On the opposite side of Celetná an alley leads into **Templová**, where you'll be immersed in a part of town where ancient façades are jumbled with fresh new pastel-paint jobs, and restoration

has revitalised long-dormant lanes. This hub of nightlife is where backpackers, tourists and foreign residents disappear into a warren of bars, clubs and restaurants, most of which, for some reason, have French names: La Provence (*see p144*), Chateau Rouge (*see p165*) and the Marquis de Sade (*see p167*) are all within a block of each other, while the Radegast Pub (*see p169*), unchanged in decades, holds its ground.

Just west is the **Basilica of St James** (Bazilika sv. Jakuba), on Malá Štupartská – a typical baroque reworking of an older Gothic church. The city's best English-language bookshop, Big Ben Bookstore (*see p181*), is across the street. From this lane you can find a sharp contrast to the sleaze of the neighbourhood's popular bars and stroll through the crisply restored, café- and restaurant-lined square of Týn, better known by its German name of Ungelt. The square now houses upscale businesses such as Botanicus (*see p183*) and the Ebel Coffee House (*see p166*). Continuing west takes you past the ominous Church of Our Lady before Týn (Kostel Matky Boží před Týnem; *see p101*), Staré Město's parish church since the 1100s, and on to Old Town Square.

Basilica of St James

Kostel sv. Jakuba
Malá Štupartská 635, Prague 1 (224 828 816).
Metro Náměstí Republiky/tram 5, 14, 26.
Open 9.30am-noon, 2pm-4pm Mon-Sat;
2-3.45pm Sun. **Admission** free. **Map** p328 M3.
St James's boasts a grand total of 21 altars, some fine frescoes and a desiccated human forearm hanging next to the door. The latter belonged to a jewel thief who broke into the church in the 15th century and tried to make off with gems from the statue of the Virgin. The Madonna grabbed the thief by the arm and kept him captive until the limb had to be cut off.

House of the Black Madonna

Dům u Černé Matky Boží
Ovocný trh 19, Prague 1 (224 211 746). Metro
Náměstí Republiky/tram 5, 8, 14. **Open** 10am-6pm
Tue-Sun. **Admission** 100 Kč; 150 Kč family.
No credit cards. Map p329 N4.
Renovated and reopened in November 2003, this fantastic cubist building and collection of paintings and sculptures strive to present a totally plane-defying environment. Worth a visit for the Josef Gočár-designed building alone, the House of the Black Madonna is perhaps the finest example of cubist

Powder Gate. *See p98.*

architecture you'll find in Prague. Considering its new lease on life under the umbrella of the National Gallery, English-language information on displays remains frustratingly scarce – and an hour with an English-speaking guide is a whopping 1,200 Kč.

Powder Gate

Prašná brána
U Prašné brány, Prague 1 (no phone). Metro Náměstí Republiky/tram 5, 14, 26. **Open** *Apr-Oct* 10am-6pm daily. **Admission** 50 Kč; 40 Kč under-10s. **No credit cards. Map** p329 N4.
The Powder Gate, or Tower, is a piece of late 15th-century flotsam, a lonely relic of the fortifications that used to ring the whole town. The bridge that incongruously connects it to the art nouveau masterpiece of the Municipal House (*see p118*) used to give access to the royal palace that stood on the same site during the tenth century. By the mid-14th century Charles IV had founded the New Town, Nové Město, and the city's boundaries had changed. The Powder Gate mouldered until it finally gained a purpose, and a name, when it became a store for gunpowder in 1575. This, unfortunately, made it a target for invading Prussian troops and it was severely damaged during the siege of 1757. It was once again left to crumble until the neo-Gothic master Josef Mocker provided it with a new roof and redecorated the sides in the 1870s.

Old Town Square

For centuries the beautiful **Old Town Square** (Staroměstské náměstí), edged by an astonishing jumble of baroque and medieval structures, has been the natural place for people visiting Prague to gravitate to. This was the medieval town's main marketplace and has always been at the centre of the action: criminals were executed here; martyrs were burnt at the stake; and, in February 1948, huge crowds greeted the announcement of the communist takeover. Most of the houses are much older than they look, with Romanesque cellars and Gothic chambers hiding behind the toy-town, pastel-coloured baroque and Renaissance façades – the communists spent an unprecedented $10 million smartening up the formerly grimy square for the 40th anniversary of the Czechoslovak Socialist Republic.

The west side is lined with stalls selling kitschy souvenirs. The grassy area behind them was provided by the Nazis, who destroyed much of the Old Town Hall on 8 May 1945, when the rest of Europe was celebrating the end of World War II. The town lost most of its archives, though gained a fine vista of the **Church of St Nicholas** (Kostel sv. Mikuláše; *see p230*).

The **Old Town Hall** (Staroměstská radnice; *see p101*) was begun in 1338, after the councillors had spent fruitless decades trying to persuade the king to allow them to construct a chamber for their affairs. John of Luxembourg finally relented, but with the bizarre proviso that all work was to be financed from the duty on wine. He obviously underestimated the high-living inhabitants of Staré Město – within the year they had enough money to purchase the house adjoining the present tower.

Jan Hus Monument. *See p101.*

You can still see what remains of the Old Town Hall after the Nazis did their worst, although trying to decipher the extraordinary components of the **Astronomical Clock** (Orloj; *see p101*) is more rewarding. It was constructed in the 15th century, sometime before the new-fangled notion that Prague revolves around the sun and not vice versa. Undismayed, the citizens kept their clock with its gold sunburst swinging happily around the globe. Perhaps the finest of the houses that make up what is left of the Old Town Hall is the **Minute House** (U Minuty), the beautiful black-and-white sgraffitoed structure on the south-west corner, which dates from 1611. Franz Kafka lived here as a boy; opposite the Astronomical Clock you'll find Café Milena (Staroměstské náměstí 22, 221 632 602), named after Milena Jesenská, the radical journalist who was Kafka's girlfriend. The area teems with other Kafka sites. The writer was born at U Radnice 5, lived for a while at Oppelt's House on the corner of Pařížská and the square (where *Metamorphosis* takes place), went to primary school on nearby Masná and later attended the strict German Gymnasium on the third floor of the Golz-Kinský Palace. This frothy stuccoed affair in the north-east corner of Staroměstské náměstí once contained Kafka's father's fancy goods shop; it now houses the Franz Kafka Bookshop (No.12, 222 321 454), which carries numerous translations of his works. Adjoining the palace is the **House at the Stone Bell** (*see p218*), the baroque cladding of which was removed in the 1980s to reveal a 14th-century Gothic façade. The focal point of the square is the powerful Jan Hus Monument dedicated to the reformist cleric, designed by Ladislav Šaloun and unveiled in 1915 (and received as a passé artistic flop). On the orders of the Council of Constance, Hus was burnt at the stake in 1415 for heresy, although the Catholic Church, some 500 years after the fact, has formally apologised. Hus's fans may at last feel vindicated as they point to the quote on the side of his monument that reads 'Pravda vítězí' ('Truth will prevail'). Those words were also used, somewhat ironically we feel, by President Klement Gottwald, after the communist takeover in 1948. However, Hus's words finally came true during the Velvet Revolution in 1989.

Church of Our Lady before Týn

Kostel Matky Boží pod Týnem
Staroměstské náměstí 604, Prague 1 (222 322 801).
Metro Náměstí Republiky or Staroměstská/tram 17, 18. **Open** *Services* (doors open 30mins before) 6pm Wed-Fri; 8am Sat; 9.30am, 9pm Sun. **Admission** free. **Map** p328 M4.

Old Town Square: the place to be. *See p100.*

The twin towers of Týn are one of the landmarks of Staré Město. The church nave is much lighter and more inviting than its foreboding exterior would lead you to believe. The church dates from the same period as much of St Vitus's Cathedral (late 14th century; *see p77*), but whereas St Vitus's was constructed to show the power of King Charles IV, Týn was a church for the people. As such it became a centre of the Hussite movement in the 15th century before being commandeered by the Jesuits in the 17th. The Jesuits commissioned the baroque interior, which blends uncomfortably with the original Gothic structure, and melted down the golden chalice in the church façade, which was a symbol of the Hussites, recasting it as the Virgin. At the end of the southern aisle is the tombstone of Tycho Brahe, Rudolf II's personal astronomer, who was famous for his false nose-piece and gnomic utterances (*see p84* **Who did Brahe?**). Look closely at the red marble slab and you'll see the former, while the lines above provide evidence of the latter, translating as 'Better to be than to seem to be'.

Old Town Hall & Astronomical Clock

Staroměstská radnice/Orloj
Staroměstské náměstí, Prague 1 (724 508 584).
Metro Staroměstská/tram 17, 18. **Open** *Nov-Mar* 11am-5pm Mon; 9am-5pm Tue-Sun. *Apr-Oct* 11am-6pm Mon; 9am-6pm Tue-Sun. **Admission** 50 Kč. **No credit cards. Map** p328 L4.

Walk this way Old Town art

Prague gets swoons for its architecture from many who wouldn't know a cubist building from a gas station. It doesn't take a scholar to appreciate the sense of ornament to the city. Better still, many of the most beautiful buildings are home to even more breathtaking art, especially in the Staré Město district.

This art and architecture walk should take most of a day if you hit all the buildings and galleries, so feel no compunction to do them all and certainly stop at the beerhalls along the way. Just don't go on a Monday, when the museums and galleries are closed.

Start at the Staroměstská metro and head up Široka street, a block north of you, making a right and continue as it turns into Vězeňská, then little U obecného dvora, which leads to **St Agnes's Convent**, the oldest surviving building in Old Town. The pre-Renaissance attempts at perspective in *The Descent of the Holy Ghost* or the realism in the portraiture of Master Theodoric are a sight to behold.

From here, head south across Haštalské náměstí, down Rybná, turning left on U Obecného domu to **Municipal House**. This gorgeous art nouveau masterpiece has a small gallery on the top floor that consistently features compelling modern work, from photographic shows to the commercial art of Karel Capek's brother, Josef. There's also a Vienna-style coffeehouse on the ground floor, with tinkling piano and little cakes on trollies.

From here, turn west down Celetná, and you'll come to one of the world's architectural rarities: the cubist **House of the Black Madonna**. It's filled with a musuem exploring

the plane-defying form (which the rest of the world, prompted by Picasso and friends, thinks is a 2-D only genre).

Now, go west down Celetná, going left on the open former fruit market Ovocný trh. At the end on the right-hand side is the main building of Charles University, the **Carolinum**. Another well-curated exhibition space, this pillared pile of granite had to shore itself up with glass and brick after being damaged during World War II. Now it is home to varying shows, ranging from the World Press Photo finalists to visual histories of Beckett.

As you exit the Carolinum, turn right down Železná to Old Town Square, or Staroměstské náměstí. Walk past the landmark that is the **Astronomical Clock** and, at the east end of the square next to the **Týn Church**, you'll spot a tall, battered sandstone building with its original Gothic façade still visible, the **House of the Stone Bell**. This lovely old gallery, arranged around an ancient courtyard, goes in for some inspired shows like the Zvon Biennale of Young Artists or digital installations that explore perception and subjectivity.

If that makes your head spin, recharge at the handy Café Ebel just down the unnamed passage between the Stone Bell and the Týn Church for quiche and coffee. Now head north on Týnská to the easily overlooked **House of the Golden Ring**, where art from various media and periods is thoughtfully organised by theme, rather than by artist or country.

Continue up Týnská and go left down Masná until you hit Vězeňská. Have a look to your right and acquaint yourself with Jaroslav

The Old Town Hall, established in 1338, was cobbled together over the centuries out of several adjoining houses, but only around half of the original remains standing today. The present Gothic and Renaissance portions have been carefully restored since the Nazis blew up a large chunk at the end of World War II. The Old Town coat of arms, adopted by the whole city after 1784, adorns the front of the Old Council Hall, and the clock tower, built in 1364, has a viewing platform that is definitely worth the climb. The 12th-century dungeon in the basement became the headquarters of the Resistance during the Prague uprising in 1944, when reinforcements were spirited away from the Nazis all over Staré Město via the connecting underground passages. Four scorched beams in the basement remain as a testament to the Resistance fighters who fell there. On the side of the clock tower is a plaque giving thanks

to the Soviet soldiers who liberated the city in 1945. There's also a plaque commemorating Dukla, a pass in Slovakia where the worst battle of the Czechoslovak liberation took place, resulting in the death of 84,000 Red Army soldiers.

The Astronomical Clock has been tick-tocking and pulling in the crowds since 1490 – even if its party trick is laughably unspectacular, prompting 'is that it?' looks from bemused spectators. Every hour on the hour, from 8am to 8pm, wooden statuettes of saints emerge from trap doors while, below them, a lesson in medieval morality is enacted by Greed, Vanity, Death and the Turk. The clock shows the movement of the sun and moon through the zodiac, as well as giving the time in three different formats: Central European Time, Old Czech Time (in which the 24-hour day is reckoned around the setting of the sun) and, for some reason, Babylonian Time. A par-

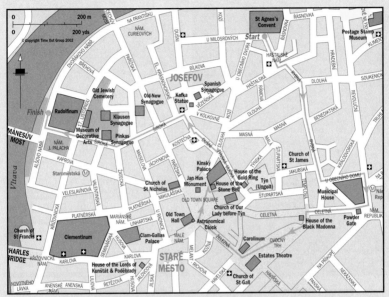

Rona's surrealist sculpture that is Prague's first real tribute to **Franz Kafka** (that is, one not printed on a T-shirt or postcard – Czechs have issues with Kafka), a hulking, dark bronze figure erected in 2002.

Now continue west down Široká street to your last stop, the magnificent but manageable **Rudolfinum**. Prague's greatest *kunsthalle*, and the only significant exhibition space in the city dedicated to this genre of changing major shows, which may be a Chinese art show or a Cindy Sherman photo collection.

Now, after all that art, it's Pilsner time – and you won't have to go far. There's a classically unreformed pub, U Rudolfinum, opposite on Křižovnická, diagonally across from the gallery. What's more, on the corner of Kaprová you're back at the Staroměstská metro.

ticularly resilient Prague legend concerns the fate of the clockmaker, Master Hanuš, who was blinded by the vainglorious burghers of the town to prevent him from repeating his horological triumph elsewhere. In retaliation Hanuš thrust his hands inside the clock and simultaneously ended both his life and (for a short time at least) that of his masterpiece. Below the clock face is a calendar painted by Josef Mánes in 1865, depicting saints' days, the astrological signs and the labours of the months.

Old Town Square to Charles Bridge

The simplest and most direct route from Old Town Square to Charles Bridge is along **Karlova** – the continuation from Celetná of the Royal Route. Twisting and curling as it does, the lane would not be particularly obvious were it not for the crowds proceeding along it.

Before heading down Karlova, fuel up at U Radnice (*see p148*), a traditional cellar restaurant on the west side of the Old Town Hall. To reach Karlova, walk past the Old Town Hall into **Little Square** (Malé náměstí). In the centre is a plague column enclosed by an ornate Renaissance grille and overlooked by the neo-Renaissance Rott House, which was built in 1890 and entirely decorated with murals of flowers and peasants by Mikoláš Aleš. Karlova winds past a succession of souvenir Bohemian glass shops, the third turn arriving at the massive, groaning giants that struggle to hold up the portal of the **Clam-Gallas Palace** (Clam-Gallasıv palác) on Husova. Designed

by Fischer von Erlach and completed in 1719, the palace now houses the city's archives; those that weren't destroyed by backing-up sewers in the flood of 2002, that is. An alternative route to Charles Bridge is Řetězová, a block south of Karlova. This walk, down a narrow lane full of funky smells, takes you past No.7, Café Montmartre (*see p165*), a historic scene of hedonism that's now been revived as a mellow sipping space with embroidered parlour sofas. It was here during the glory days of the inter-war First Republic that opium, absinthe and jazz mixed into a potent cocktail that at one point led to black masses and orgies – or so the owners say, at any rate. A block further west on Anenské náměstí you'll find the little **Divadlo Na zábradlí** (Theatre on the Balustrade; *see p253*), the theatre where a set-builder named Václav Havel first tried his hand at absurdist play-writing and soon landed himself in jail.

Back on Karlova, the vast, looming bulk of the **Clementinum** (Klementinum) makes up the right-hand side of Karlova's last stretch. After Prague Castle, it's the largest complex of buildings in Prague. The Jesuits, the storm troopers of the Counter-Reformation, set up home here and enthusiastically went about their traditional tasks of pedagogy and casuistry. Like much of Staré Město, Karlova is best viewed at night, when tour groups are safely back at their hotels. If you get peckish along the way (and aren't picky), there are two all-night eateries: U Zlatého stromu (222 220 441, www.zlatystrom.cz) at Karlova 6, where there's a non-stop restaurant in a complex that

also includes a hotel, disco and, of course, strip show, and Pizzeria Roma Due at Liliová 18.

At the foot of Karlova, tourists have trouble crossing the road past the continuous stream of trams and cars that race through **Knights of the Cross Square** (Křížovnické náměstí). The eponymous Knights, a bunch of elderly neo-medieval crusaders, have come out of retirement and reclaimed the **Church of St Francis** (Kostel sv. Františka). Designed by Jean-Baptiste Mathey in the late 17th century, the church, which has a huge red dome, is unusual for Prague, not least because its altar is facing the wrong way. The gallery next door houses religious bric-a-brac that the Knights extricated from various museums, and a subterranean chapel decorated with stalactites made out of dust and eggshells, an 18th-century fad that enjoyed unwarranted popularity in Prague. On the eastern side of the square is the **Church of St Saviour** (Kostel sv. Salvátora; *see below*), marking the edge of the Clementinum.

Clementinum

Klementinum
Mariánské náměstí 4, Prague 1 (221 663 111).
Metro Staroměstská/tram 17, 18. **Open** *Library*
Mar, Apr, Nov, Dec 2-6pm Mon-Fri; 11am-6pm Sat,
Sun. *May-Oct* 2-7pm Mon-Fri; 10am-7pm Sat, Sun.
Chapel of Mirrors for concerts only. **Admission**
100 Kč. **Map** p328 K4.
In the 12th and 13th centuries this enormous complex of buildings was the Prague headquarters of the Inquisition, and when the Jesuits moved in during the 16th century, kicking out the Dominicans, they also, unfortunately, retained some of the Holy Office's less savoury practices, including the forcible baptism of the city's Jews, although on the credit side must be placed the Society's commitment to education and learning. They also replaced the medieval Church of St Clement with a much grander design of their own (rebuilt in 1711-15 and now used by the Greek Catholic Church) and gradually constructed the building of today. It is arranged around five courtyards, and several streets and 30 houses were demolished during its construction.

The Jesuits' grandest work was the Church of St Saviour (Kostel sv. Salvátora), whose opulent but grimy façade was designed to reawaken the joys of Catholicism in the Protestant populace. Built in 1578-1653, it was the most important Jesuit church in Bohemia. The Jesuits' main tool was education and their library is a masterpiece. It was finished in 1727 and has a magnificent trompe l'oeil ceiling showing the three levels of knowledge, with the Dome of Wisdom occupying the central space. However, the ceiling started crumbling and, to prevent the whole structure from collapsing, the Chapel of Mirrors was built next door in 1725 to bolster the walls. The chapel interior, decorated with fake pink marble and the original mirrors, is lovely. Mozart used to play here and it is still used for chamber concerts today

Old Town Hall. *See p100.*

Sightseeing

Charles Bridge. *See p107.*

– the only way you can get in to see it. At the centre of the complex is the Astronomical Tower, where Kepler came to stargaze. It was used until the 1920s for calculating high noon: when the sun crossed a line on the wall behind a small aperture at the top, the castle was signalled and a cannon fired.

Charles Bridge

Charles Bridge (Karlův most) is the most popular place in the city to come and get your portrait painted, take photos of the castle, have your pocket picked or pick up a backpacker. The range of entertainment is always dodgy and diverse, from blind folk-singers to the man who plays Beethoven concertos on finger bowls. The stone bridge was built in 1357 (replacing the earlier Judith Bridge that collapsed in a flood in 1342) and has survived over 600 years of turbulent city life. Guarding the entrance to Charles Bridge is the early 14th-century **Old Town Bridge Tower** (Staroměstská mostecká věž), a Gothic gate topped with a pointed, tiled hat. Climb the tower for a bird's-eye view of Prague's domes and spires, the wayward trail of Charles Bridge, the naff Klub Lávka (*see p244*) and the most massive addition to Prague clubbing, Karlovy Lázně (*see p243*), all below on the river and beyond.

The statues lining Charles Bridge didn't arrive until the 17th century, when Bohemia's leading sculptors, including Josef Brokof and Matthias Braun, were commissioned to create figures to inspire the masses as they went about their daily business. The strategy proved more effective than an earlier Catholic decoration – the severed heads of Protestant nobles. More mundane statues were added in the 1800s.

The third statue on the right from the Staré Město end is a crucifixion bearing a mysterious Hebrew inscription in gold. This was put here in 1696 by a Jew found guilty of blaspheming in front of the statue, according to local lore; his punishment was to pay for the inscription 'Holy, Holy, Holy, Lord God Almighty'.

St John of Nepomuk – the most famous figure – is eighth on the right as you walk towards Malá Strana, recognisable by his doleful expression and the gold stars fluttering around his head. Legend has it that John was flung off the bridge after refusing to reveal the secrets of the queen's confession. Actually, he was just in the wrong place at the wrong time during one of Wenceslas IV's anti-clerical rages. A bronze bas-relief below the statue depicts the scene, and people stop and rub it for luck. The statue, placed here in 1683, is the bridge's earliest. Cast in bronze, it has weathered better than the sandstone statues, most of which have been replaced by copies.

Further towards Malá Strana, fourth from the end on the left, is the Cistercian nun St Luitgard, sculpted by Matthias Braun in 1710 and depicted in the middle of her vision of Christ. The statue is considered by many, including Prince Charles, to be the finest work on the bridge; he pledged the money to save her from the elements, which threatened to wipe the look of wonder off her face. On the same side, second from the Malá Strana end, is the largest grouping on the bridge. It commemorates the founders of the Trinitarian Order, which built its reputation by ransoming Christian, held hostage by the Ottomans: SS John of Matha and Felix of Valois (accompanied by his pet stag) share space with a rogue St Ivan, included for no obvious reason. Below them is a lethargic Turk and his snarling dog framing three imprisoned Christians.

If you've fallen for the city, seek out the bronze **Lorraine cross** located on the wall halfway across the bridge on the downstream side, touch it, make a wish – and hey presto, it's guaranteed that you'll return to Prague.

Old Town Bridge Tower

Staroměstská mostecká věž
Křižovnické náměstí, Staré Město, Prague 1 (224 220 569). Metro Staroměstská/tram 17, 18. **Open** *Nov-Feb* 10am-5pm daily. *Mar* 10am-6pm daily. *Apr, May, Oct* 10am-7pm daily. *June-Sept* 10am-10pm daily. **Admission** 50 Kč; 40 Kč concessions. **No credit cards. Map** p328 J4.
Built in 1373, along the shadow line of St Vitus's Cathedral (*see p77*), the Old Town Bridge Tower was badly damaged in 1648 by marauding Swedes, but Peter Parler's sculptural decoration on the eastern side survives. There's a dull exhibit on the tower's history, but the real reason for visiting is to take in the splendid view from the top. Don't miss the medieval groping figures on the tower's outer corners, just visible before you go under the tower coming from Staré Město: each depicts a buxom lass being felt up by a gentleman friend.

Southern Staré Město

Canny German merchants were the first to develop the area south of Old Town Square. They built a church dedicated to St Havel (more commonly known as St Gall) when Charles IV generously donated some spare parts of the saint from his burgeoning relic collection. The onion domes of the existing **Church of St Havel** (Kostel sv. Havla), on Havelská, were added in 1722 by the Shod Carmelites – the Barefooted Carmelites settled on the other side of the river. The opposite end of Havelská is lined with bowed baroque houses precariously balanced on Gothic arcades. Prague's best open market (*see p179*) also stands in this lane.

Between here and Celetná, on Ovocný trh, is one of Prague's finest neo-classical buildings: the **Estates Theatre** (*see p231* and *p251*), dubbed the 'Mozart Theatre'. Unlike Vienna, Prague loved Mozart – and Mozart loved Prague. During the composer's lifetime, the theatre staged a succession of his greatest operas, including the première of *Don Giovanni*, conducted by Wolfgang Amadeus himself. The building was paid for by Count Nostitz, after whom it was named when it opened in 1783 – aimed at promoting productions of works in German. But by the late 19th century most productions were being performed in Czech, and the name was changed to the Tyl Theatre, after the dramatist JK Tyl. His song 'Where Is My Home?' was played here for the first time and later adopted as the Czech national anthem.

The massive oriel window overlooking the theatre belongs to the Carolinum, the university founded by Charles IV (*see p11*). Charles never made a move without consulting the stars and ascertained that Aries was an auspicious sign for the first university in Central Europe, established on 7 April 1348.

Opposite the Estates Theatre is the former Soviet House of Science and Culture. Boutiques, a Ticketpro (*see p230*) and a dubious black light theatre occupy the complex these days.

Around Betlémské náměstí

Once the poorest quarter of Staré Město and a notorious area of prostitutes – whose present-day descendants can be seen lining Perlova and Na Perštýně a few blocks away – this was the natural breeding ground for the radical politics of the late 14th century. On the north side of **Bethlehem Square** (Betlémské náměstí) are the swooping twin gables of the plain **Bethlehem Chapel** (Betlémská kaple), a reconstructed version of the 1391 building where Jan Hus (*see p11*) and other independent Czech preachers passed on their vision of the true church to the Prague citizenry.

Across the courtyard is the Galerie Jaroslava Fragnera (Betlémské náměstí, 222 222 157) – the best place for Czech and English-language design books and magazines in town – while Klub Architektů (*see p144*) serves cheap eats in the basement and, in summer, at tables outside. On the other side of the square is the **Náprstek Museum** (*see p109*). After making his fortune by inebriating the masses, Vojta Náprstek installed a collection of ethnological knick-knacks in the family brewery. A 19th-century do-gooder, he didn't just spend his time hunting down shrunken heads, but also founded the first women's club in the country. The room, untouched for 100 years, can still be

seen, although the peephole he drilled through from his office perhaps draws into question the purity of his motives.

One of the three Romanesque rotundas in the city, the **Rotunda of the Holy Cross** (Rotunda sv. Kříže), is on nearby Konviktská. The tiny 12th-century building was constructed entirely in the round so that the devil had no corner to hide in. If you don't manage to get a look inside, try the Hostinec U Rotundy (Karoliny Světlé 17, 224 227 227). Covered with lovely sgraffito, it's as authentic a pub as you'll find in Staré Město.

On Husova, to the north-east, is the **Church of St Giles** (Kostel sv. Jiljí), a vast Gothic structure that looks like a fortress from the outside. It was built by the Dominicans in 1340-70, a mendicant order that has now returned to reclaim its heritage and inhabit the monastery next door. Nearby is U Zlatého tygra (*see p170*), favourite watering hole of the late Bohumil Hrabal, the author and Nobel Prize nominee who spent half his life inside pubs and the other half writing about what goes on inside them. The pub makes a good refuelling stop before a visit to the Romanesque **House of the Lords of Kunštát and Poděbrady** on Řetězová (Dům Pánu z Kunštátu a Poděbrad); though note that the House of the Lords is currently undergoing work that is expected to be completed by June 2006.

Parallel to Konviktská is the unnaturally quiet **Bartolomějská**. Czechs still avoid its environs – a legacy of the role it played in communist times. Police departments line the street and most dissidents of note did time in the StB (Secret Police) cells in the former convent. The building, now containing the Pension Unitas (Bartolomějská 9, 224 221 802, www.unitas.cz), has been restored to the Sisters of Mercy and you can stay the night in the cell where former President Havel was once locked up to ponder the error of his ways. The river is only a few dozen yards away, and from the west end of this street you have a perfect view across it to Kampa, with the castle high on the hill beyond. Turning right will take you past Novotného Lávka, a group of buildings jutting into the river centred around a 19th-century water tower and a small assortment of bars, and back to Charles Bridge. Turn left at the end of Konviktská to reach the National Theatre and the start of the Nové Město.

Bethlehem Chapel
Betlémská kaple
Betlémské náměstí 4, Staré Město, Prague 1 (224 248 595). Metro Národní třída or Staroměstská/tram 6, 9, 18, 22. **Open** *Nov-Mar* 10am-5.30pm Tue-Sun. *Apr-Oct* 10am-6.30pm Tue-Sun.
Admission 40 Kč; 20 Kč concessions. **Map** p328 K5.

Get a taste of Czech vision at the reconstructed **Bethlehem Chapel**. *See p108.*

The Bethlehem Chapel, a huge barn-like structure dating from 1391, was where the proto-Protestant Jan Hus delivered sermons in the Czech language, accusing the papacy of being, among other things, an institution of Satan. It's perhaps not surprising that he was burnt at the stake in 1415. His last request before being thrown to the flames was for 'history to be kind to the Bethlehem Chapel'. In response, the Jesuits bought up the site and turned it into a woodshed. In the 18th century German merchants moved in and built two houses within the walls. Hus's wish was finally fulfilled under the communists. They chose to look on him as a working-class revolutionary thwarted by the forces of imperialism and spared no expense in the extensive restoration of the chapel. Three of the original walls remain and still show the remnants of the scriptures that were painted on them to enable people to follow the service. Following the fall of communism, religious services have resumed at the chapel. Secular visits are also welcome.

Náprstek Museum

Náprstkovo muzeum
Betlémské náměstí 1, Prague 1 (224 497 500/ 511/www.aconet.cz/npm). Metro Můstek or Národní třída/tram 6, 9, 17, 18, 22, 23. **Open** 10am-6pm Tue-Sun. **Admission** 80 Kč; free under-6s; free 1st Fri of mth. **No credit cards. Map** p328 K5.
The 19th-century nationalist Vojta Náprstek had two passions: modern technology and primitive cultures. While the gadgets he collected are now in the National Technical Museum (*see below*), the ethnographic oddities he acquired from numerous Czech travellers can be seen here in an extension to his house. The displays concentrating on the native peoples of the Americas, Australasia and the Pacific Islands are interesting and exemplarily arranged. Temporary exhibitions tend to favour travelogues of exotic cultures by Czech photographers.

Josefov

The main street of **Josefov** is **Pařížská**, an elegant avenue of designer shops, flash restaurants, expensive cocktail bars and airline offices, which leads from the Old Town Square down to the river. Here you'll find swish places like Barock (*see p153*) and Bugsy's (*see p165*). This is all, however, in sharp contrast to the rest of what was once Prague's Jewish quarter.

The spiritual heart of Josefov, the Old-New Synagogue (Staronová synagoga; *see p110*), stands on a wedge of land between Maiselova and Pařížská. Built around 1270, it's the oldest synagogue in Europe. Legend has it that the foundation stones were flown over by angels from the Holy Temple in Jerusalem on the condition (*al tnay* in Hebrew) that they should be returned on Judgement Day, hence the name Alt-Neu in German and Old-New in English.

Next door is the former **Jewish Town Hall** (Maiselova 18), dating from the 1560s, with a rococo façade in delicate pinks and a Hebraic clock whose hands turn anti-clockwise. The money to build the Town Hall and the neighbouring **High Synagogue** was provided by Mordecai Maisel, a contemporary of Rabbi Löw, and a man of inordinate wealth and discriminating taste. The Town Hall has been the centre of the Jewish community ever since. The High Synagogue, built at the same time as the Town Hall and attached to it, was returned to the community early in 1994 and is now, once again, a working synagogue serving the Jewish community (not open to sightseers).

Further down Maiselova is the **Maisel Synagogue**. This, with the Pinkas, Klausen and Spanish synagogues, and the Old Jewish

Cemetery and Ceremonial Hall, comprises the extraordinary **Jewish Museum** (*see p112*), which has been newly expanded and spruced up with exhibitions for 2006's year-long celebration of the museum's centennial. The Maisel Synagogue was also funded by the wealthy 16th-century money-lending mayor but, sadly, the current building is a reconstruction of the original (apparently, the most splendid synagogue of them all). The first effort burnt down in the great fire of 1689, when all 318 houses of the ghetto and 11 synagogues were destroyed. The present structure dates from 1892 to 1905, and houses a permanent exhibition of Jewish history.

On U Starého hřbitova is the **Old Jewish Cemetery** (*see p112*), a small, unruly patch of ground that contains the remains of thousands upon thousands of bodies. Forbidden to enlarge their burial ground, the Jews buried their dead on top of each other in an estimated 12 layers, so that today crazy mounds of earth are jammed with lopsided stone tablets. To the left of the entrance is the **Klausen Synagogue** (*see p112*), built in 1694 by the same craftsmen responsible for many of Prague's baroque churches. Inside, the pink marble Holy Ark could almost pass for a Catholic altar were it not for the gold inscriptions in Hebrew. Here you'll find displayed various religious artefacts and prints as well as explanations of Jewish customs and traditions. Facing the synagogue is the **Former Ceremonial Hall**, designed in the style of a Romanesque castle at the beginning of this century, which hosts an exhibition of funerary ornaments.

On the other side of the cemetery is the **Pinkas Synagogue**, built as the private house of the powerful Horowitz family in 1607-25. The building is now primarily given over to a memorial to the Jewish men, women and children of Bohemia and Moravia who died in Nazi concentration camps. A communist-era 'refurbishment' once obscured the names recorded on the Pinkas walls, but every one was painstakingly repainted in a two-year project started in April 1997. Josefov's final synagogue, the **Spanish Synagogue**, was built just outside the boundaries of the ghetto in 1868, on Dušní. It was constructed for the growing number of Reform Jews, and its façade is of a rich Moorish design. Since being returned to the community it has been meticulously restored and is now a working synagogue again, featuring a permanent exhibition on Jewish history in the Czech lands up to the beginning of World War II.

Standing just before the Spanish Synagogue is a surreal bronze statue of Franz Kafka, depicted as a gnomish figure riding on the shoulders of a headless, handless, footless giant with a striking resemblance to the Golem of Prague – and, arguably, a certain horror icon known for having bolts in his neck. Incredibly, this creation of Czech sculptor Jaroslav Rona, cast in early 2004, is the first memorial to Kafka ever erected in the city he did so much to mythologise.

Old-New Synagogue

Staronová synagoga
Červená 2, Prague 1 (no phone). Metro Staroměstská/tram 17, 18. **Open** *Apr-June* 9.30am-6pm Mon-Thur, Sun; 9.30am-5pm Fri. *Nov-Mar* 9.30am-5pm Mon-Thur, Sun; 9am-2pm Fri. **Admission** 200 Kč; 140 Kč concessions; free under-6s. **No credit cards. Map** p328 K3.
The Old-New Synagogue is a rather forlorn piece of medievalism. The oldest survivor of the ghetto and the spiritual centre of the Jewish community for over 700 years, it has now been returned to the community and is still used for services. The austere exterior walls give no clues to its peculiar, and distinctly unusual, Gothic interior. An extra rib was added to the usual vaulting pattern to avoid the symbolism of the cross. Instead the decor and structure revolve around the number 12, after the 12 tribes of Israel: there are 12 windows, 12 bunches of sculpted grapes, and clusters of 12 vine leaves decorate the pillar bases. The interior was left untouched for 500 years as a reminder of the blood spilled here during the pogrom of 1389, when the men, women and children who sought sanctuary in the synagogue were slaughtered. The 19th-century neo-Gothic enthusiasts, however, couldn't resist the temptation to 'restore' the original look of the building and slapped a fresh coat of paint over the top.

Oak seats line the walls facing the bema, or platform, protected by a Gothic grille, from which the Torah has been read aloud every day for more than 700 years, with the exception of the period during the Nazi occupation. The tall seat marked by a gold star belonged to Rabbi Löw, who was the most famous inhabitant of the ghetto. The rabbi lived to the age of 97, and a sculpture by Ladislav Šaloun to the right of the New Town Hall in Mariánské náměstí depicts the manner of his death. Unable to approach the scholar, who was always absorbed in study of the scriptures, Death hid in a rose that was offered to Löw by his innocent granddaughter. The rabbi's grave can be found in the Old Jewish Cemetery, recognisable by the quantity of pebbles and wishes on scraps of paper that are placed upon the tomb to this day.

Despite its wealth of historical and religious significance, there's not much to see once you're inside the Old-New synagogue and precious little explanation is provided.

Precious Legacy Tours

Kaprova 13, Prague 1 (222 321 954/www.legacy tours.net). Metro Staroměstská/tram 17, 18. **Open** *Oct-Mar* 9.30am-6pm Mon-Fri, Sun.

Still crazy Franz Kafka

If Franz Kafka was a little ambivalent about his feelings for *Matka Praha*, or Mother Prague – not many sons describe their maternal figure as having claws – she clearly reciprocated.

Outside Czech lands, it's impossible to pick up a literary work on Prague that doesn't refer to Kafka. *The Trial*, *The Castle* and maybe *Metamorphosis* are required reading for any literary student. It's a bit different in Prague itself, though. Ask a Czech to name the country's greatest writers and names such as Bohumil Hrabal, Karel Čapek and Jaroslav Seifert come up.

And Kafka? A troubled look comes with that question, then a polite suggestion something like: 'Well, he's not really Czech...and, besides, I can't make head nor tale of his stories.'

Literature students may secretly be inclined to agree with the latter assessment. Kafka himself was painfully aware that the radical forms of writing he was venturing into were considered, at best, curious. Swept along by the spirit of the new 20th century, it's hard to imagine that Kafka wasn't inspired by other revolutionaries in the arts: Picasso and Scriabin abroad; the cubist architecture of Gočár; and the tone poems of Janáček at home. But his passions were traditional and it's doubtful he set out to redefine literature.

Kafka often read and wrote all night, turning up exhausted to his day job as attorney for the Workers Accident Insurance Company. He consumed Czech, German and Jewish literature and always had works by Shakespeare, Dostoevsky and Tolstoy close at hand.

Still, Kafka didn't need to be a revolutionary wordsmith to be an outsider in Prague at the turn of the 19th century. His difficulty with assimilation was part of a long history of Bohemia's troubled relationships with Judaism, the German language and even Czech identity.

The writer who did much to mythologise Prague and put the city on the world's literary map, who spent most of his life perambulating a few blocks of Staré Město and whose work was inspired by Prague, has only recently been honoured with a statue in the city. Kafka's image is plastered everywhere these days, but, until January 2004, it was all essentially for foreign tourist consumption.

An odd, hulking bronze statue (*see p110*) now stands at Dušní and Vězeňská streets, a surrealist creation by Jaroslav Rona, depicting a Golem-like headless and handless figure carrying a smaller, dapper man on his shoulders. At its base, 'Franz Kafka' is all that's inscribed.

In his own day, Kafka could hardly have ever been well loved. He was born on the wrong side of every major national, cultural and linguistic divide of the age. Kafka arrived in the world on 3 July 1883 in the final days of Prague's Jewish ghetto. This sensitive child of an ambitious social climber, who started out as a butcher in South Bohemia, felt mainly terror at the thought of the teeming Josefov district. As a German speaker in a time of feverish Czech nation-building, his mother tongue symbolised 500 years of foreign oppression to the new powers of Prague – his lover Milena Jesenská chided him in the Czech tongue he never mastered.

And, of course, his apathy toward Judaism did nothing to keep him from being an undesirable to the anti-Semitic German bourgeoisie of Prague. Indeed, had he not died of tuberculosis in 1924, Kafka would almost certainly have ended up in the concentration camps that claimed his sister Ottla.

The sense of alienation that runs through his work is hardly surprising. Yet Kafka captured the spirit of Prague, and arguably of 20th-century alienation in general, better than any other author. Perhaps that's the real reason his name is still bound to chill conversation even among Prague's 21st-century consumer-mad EU-citizenry. His tales hit just a bit too close to the bone.

But one comfort Kafka would surely take is the very discomfiture his work still causes at home. 'Altogether,' he wrote in 1904 to his friend Oskar Pollak, 'I think we ought to read only books that bite and sting us. If the book we are reading doesn't shake us awake like a blow on the skull, why bother reading it in the first place? So that it can make us happy, as you put it? A book must be the axe for the frozen sea within us. That is what I believe.'

Is Kafka's unforgivable sin, then, that his writing is a kind of well that reflects the soul (and the demons) of whoever gazes in? If so, it would take a society of rare courage to be able to embrace such a writer.

Dig deep and see what you find at the **Old Jewish Cemetery**. *See p110.*

Apr-Sept 9.30am-6pm Mon-Fri, Sun.
Admission 300 Kč; *tour with guide* 630 Kč.
No credit cards. Map p328 J3.
This Jewish travel agency purveys tickets for the various Jewish Museum sights, the Old-New Synagogue, tours of Prague and trips to Terezín (*see p275*), a small town that was used in 1941 as a holding camp for Jews destined for concentration camps further east. The English-speaking staff at Precious Legacy Tours are also able to book boat tours, meals in kosher restaurants and accommodation.

Jewish Museum
Židovské Muzeum
*U Staré Školy 1, Prague 1 (221 711 511/
www.jewishmuseum.cz). Metro Staroměstská/
tram 17, 18.* **Open** *Apr-Oct* 9am-6pm Mon-Fri, Sun.
Nov-Mar 9am-4.30pm Mon-Fri, Sun. Closed Jewish holidays. **Admission** 300 Kč; 200 Kč concessions; free under-6s. *Old-New Synagogue* 200 Kč.
No credit cards. Map p328 L2.
These directions, hours and rates apply to the six museum sites listed below; buy tickets at any one for the entire complex.

Former Ceremonial Hall
Obřadní síň
U starého hřbitova 3A, Prague 1 (222 317 191).
Map p328 K3.
The Romanesque turrets and arches of this building at the exit of the cemetery make it appear as old as the gravestones. In fact, the Former Ceremonial Hall was built in 1906 for the Prague Burial Society, which used the building for only 20 years. Today, it hosts fascinating temporary exhibitions on such topics as Jewish customs and traditions, focusing particularly on illness and death.

Klausen Synagogue
Klausova synagoga
U starého hřbitova 3A, Prague 1 (222 310 302).
Map p328 K3.

The great ghetto fire of 1689 destroyed the original Klausen Synagogue along with 318 houses and 10 other synagogues. The existing synagogue, hastily constructed on the same site in 1694, has much in common with Prague's baroque churches, as it was built by the same craftsmen. Its permanent exhibition explores religion in the lives of the ghetto's former inhabitants. The best view of the synagogue is from the Old Jewish Cemetery, where the simple façade rises behind the ancient gravestones, topped by two tablets of the Decalogue with a golden inscription.

Maisel Synagogue
Maiselova synagoga
Maiselova 10, Prague 1 (224 819 456). **Map** p328 K3.
Mordecai Maisel (1528-1601), mayor of the Jewish ghetto during the reign of Rudolf II, was one of the richest men in 16th-century Europe. Legend traces Maisel's wealth to a lucky intervention by goblins, but more realistic historians suggest that Rudolf II granted Maisel a lucrative trading monopoly. The original building on this site, funded by Maisel, was apparently the most splendid of all the quarter's synagogues until it burned down along with most of the others in 1689. The present structure, sandwiched between apartment blocks, has a core dating to the 1690s; the rest was redone between 1892 and 1905. The synagogue houses exhibitions on the Jewish history of Bohemia and Moravia.

Old Jewish Cemetery
Starý Židovský hřbitov
Široká 3, Prague 1 (no phone). **Map** p328 K2.
The Old Jewish Cemetery, where all of Prague's Jews were buried until the late 1600s, is one of the eeriest remnants of the city's once-thriving Jewish community. The 12,000 tombstones that are crammed into this tiny, tree-shaded patch of ground are a forceful reminder of the lack of space accorded to the ghetto, which remained walled until the late 1700s. Forbidden to enlarge the burial ground, the Jews

were forced to bury the dead on top of one another. An estimated 100,000 bodies were piled up to 12 layers deep. Above them, lopsided stone tablets were crammed on to mounds of earth. Burials began here in the early 15th century, although earlier gravestones were brought in from a cemetery nearby. Decorative reliefs on the headstones indicate the name of the deceased or their occupation: a pair of scissors, for example, indicates a tailor. The black headstones are the oldest, carved from 15th-century sandstone; the white ones, of marble, date from the 16th and 17th centuries.

Pinkas Synagogue

Pinkasova synagoga
Široká 3, Prague 1 (222 326 660).
Map p328 K3.
The story goes that a Rabbi Pinkas founded this synagogue in 1479 after falling out with the elders at the Old-New Synagogue. The building was enlarged in 1535, and a Renaissance façade was added in 1625. In the 1950s the names of more than 80,000 men, women and children of Bohemia and Moravia who died in the Holocaust were inscribed on the synagogue's walls as a memorial. In 1967, after the Six Day War, the Czechoslovak government expelled the Israeli ambassador and closed the synagogue for 'restoration'. In the ensuing 22 years, the writing became indecipherable. Not until after 1989 could the museum begin restoring the names, a job completed in 1994. The Pinkas also houses a particularly powerful exhibition of drawings by children interned in Terezín (*see p275*), the last stop en route to the death camps in the east.

Spanish Synagogue

Španělská synagoga
Vězeňská 1, Prague 1 (224 819 464).
Map p328 L2.
The Old Synagogue or Altschul, older still than the Old-New Synagogue, stood on this site as an island in Christian territory, to which Jews could cross from the main ghetto only at certain times. It became a Reform synagogue in 1837, then the prospering congregation rebuilt it in 1868 in the then-fashionable Moorish style. After painstaking reconstruction, the long-decrepit building reopened in 1998. Its lovely domed interior again glows with hypnotic floral designs that are traced in green, red and faux gold leaf, lit by stained-glass windows. It houses varied and inspired exhibitions on Jewish history and, in its upper-floor prayer hall, an exhibition of synagogue silver. It occasionally hosts concerts; tickets are available in the lobby.

Northern Staré Město

The area along the banks of the Vltava wasn't incorporated into the new design of Josefov, and the grandiose buildings there have their backs turned upon the old ghetto. Going down Kaprova towards the river will bring you to **Náměstí Jana Palacha**, a square that was named in memory of Jan Palach, the first of the students who set themselves on fire in 1969 to protest the Soviet bloc invasion (the second student, Jan Zajic, didn't get a square named after him, but he is remembered on the memorial in Wenceslas Square).

Dominating the square is the breathtakingly beautiful **Rudolfinum** (*see p218*), or 'House of Arts', which houses the Dvořák and Suk concert halls. It was built between 1876 and 1884 (and named after Rudolf II) in neo-classical style and entirely funded by the Czech Savings Bank to display its 'patriotic, provincial feelings'. You can see the bank's corporate logo, the bee of thrift, in the paws of the two sphinxes with remarkably ample breasts who guard the riverfront entrance. In 1918 the concert hall became home to the Parliament of the new republic.

When Chamberlain returned to England from meeting Hitler in 1938 disclaiming responsibility for the 'quarrel in a faraway country between people of whom we know nothing', it was here that 250,000 of these people came to take an oath and pledge themselves to the defence of the republic. The Nazis, having little use for a parliament building, turned it back into a concert hall and called it 'the German House of Arts'. Legend has it that a statue of the Jewish composer Mendelssohn was ordered to be removed for obvious reasons, but the workmen, not knowing what Mendelssohn looked like, took their lessons in racial science to heart and removed the figure with the biggest nose – which turned out to be Richard Wagner. Opposite, with its back to the Old Jewish Cemetery, is the magnificent Museum of Decorative Arts (*see p114*).

Few visitors make it over to the streets of art nouveau tenement houses in northern Staré Město – some are still semi-derelict but most have been restored for the last few years – but they are well worth inspection, even without the attraction of **St Agnes's Convent** (Klášter sv. Anežky České; *see p114*), the oldest example of Gothic architecture in the city. Its founder, St Agnes, died a full 700 years before the Pope made her a saint. Popular opinion held that miracles would accompany her canonisation, and, sure enough, within five days of the Vatican's announcement the Velvet Revolution was under way. St Agnes's Convent is now the home to the National Gallery's medieval collection.

Nearby is **Dlouhá** or 'Long Street', which contained no fewer than 13 breweries in the 14th century when beer champion Charles IV forbade the export of hops. These days

Sightseeing

its main attraction is the Roxy (*see p245*) at No.33. It's a thoroughly crumbling cinema that was once the improbable headquarters of the Communist Youth Association and is now, even more improbably, the city's most atmospheric club. Next door is the serene Dahab teahouse (*see p165*), replete with belly dancers and Middle Eastern cheap eats, and above it lies Gallery NoD, a hive of new media artists and one of the city's grooviest internet bars. In the pleasantly quiet streets between Dlouhá and the river lie several more convivial bars and cafés including the French-style Chez Marcel (*see p149*), the impossibly Irish Molly Malone's (*see p167*), the über-hip M1 Secret Lounge (*see p167*), the snazzy Tretter's (*see p169*) and the neo-Bohemian Blatouch (*see p165*).

Convent of St Agnes of Bohemia

Klášter sv. Anežky České
U milosrdných 17, Prague 1 (224 810 628). Metro Náměstí Republiky/tram 5, 8, 14. **Open** 10am-6pm Tue-Sun. **Admission** 100 Kč; 150 Kč family; free under-10s. **No credit cards**. **Map** p328 M2.
The St Agnes's convent, the first Gothic building in Prague, now houses a collection highlighting Bohemian and Central European medieval art from 1200 to 1550. Prague, after all, was at the forefront of European artistic development during the reign of Charles IV (1346-78) and one of the greats of the end of the 14th century was the Master of Třeboň. Here you can see his altarpiece featuring the *Resurrection of Christ* and his *Madonna of Roudnice*, an example of the 'Beautiful Style' that prevailed until the outbreak of the Hussite wars. Gothic remained popular

in Bohemia right up to the 16th century, as seen in the extraordinary wood carving by the monogrammist IP, depicting the skeletal, half-decomposed figure of Death brushed aside by the Risen Christ. The convent is fully wheelchair accessible.

House at the Golden Ring

Dům U Zlatého prstenu
Týnská 6, Prague 1 (224 827 022). Metro Náměstí Republiky/tram 5, 8, 14, 26. **Open** 10am-6pm Tue-Sun. **Admission** 90 Kč; 160 Kč family; free under-6s. **No credit cards**. **Map** p328 M4.
The collection comprises a broad spectrum of 20th-century Czech works, organised intriguingly by themes rather than by artist or period. There's a fine basement exhibition space for temporary installations, often well curated, fresh and international, though the gallery itself has limited space.

Museum of Decorative Arts

Uměleckopr Ěmyslové muzeum
Ulice 17. listopadu 2, Prague 1 (251 093 111/ www.upm.cz). Metro Staroměstská/tram 17, 18. **Open** 10am-7pm Tue; 10am-6pm Wed-Sun. **Admission** 80-130 Kč; free under-10s; free 5-7pm Tue. **No credit cards**. **Map** p328 K3.
This neo-Renaissance museum, built between 1897 and 1900, is a work of art in itself, boasting richly decorated halls, stained- and etched-glass windows, and intricately painted plaster mouldings. Exhibits group objects according to material. In addition to the excellent 20th-century collection, the permanent, pre-20th century collections comprise lavishly crafted pieces including furniture, tapestries, pottery, clocks, books, a beautifully preserved collection of clothing, and fine displays of ceramics and glass.

Museum of Decorative Arts.

Nové Město

Wenceslas Square, sleaze, traffic and streetlife form this district,
Prague's closest equivalent to a modern Western capital.

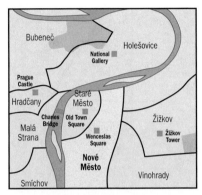

Maps p329, p330 & p331

New Town (Nové Město) may no longer be
an accurate description of the district that
surrounds Old Town (it was created in the
14th century), but Wenceslas Square has
undeniably taken over from Old Town Square
as the living heart of the city. With its mix of
grand architecture, low streetlife, glitzy stores
and crumbling remnants and reminders of life
under foreign oppressors, Nové Město embodies
the zeitgeist of an entire nation seeking to
establish its place in 21st-century Europe.

The area is bounded roughly to the north
and east by Národní, Na Příkopě and Revoluční,
which form the border with Staré Město, Old
Town (*see p98*). The heavy traffic on the
arterial road Wilsonova (which turns into
Mezibranská) forms a natural barrier to the
south. Heading west from there along Žitná
or Ječná takes you through the backstreets
and past some of the more historic buildings
in Nové Město to the Vltava river.

Wenceslas Square

The hub of Nové Město (and for that matter,
the entire city) is **Wenceslas Square**, a
broad, sloping boulevard nearly one kilometre
(0.63 miles) long. Almost every major historical
event of Prague's past century has unfolded
here, or at least passed through. Masses
assembled in Wenceslas Square for the
founding of the Czechoslovak Republic in

1918, and again in 1939, when Nazi troops
marched in to establish the Protectorate of
Bohemia and Moravia. In 1968 the brief hope
of the Prague Spring was born and died here.
And, when the communist regime was finally
toppled by the Velvet Revolution in 1989, the
world watched throngs celebrating in
Wenceslas Square.

Only faint echoes of those events are
discernible now, mostly in the form of
monuments and plaques that are easy to
miss. The tone is commercial, with a busy
mix of hotels, shops, restaurants, clubs and
tourist services. Cabs buzz up and down the
boulevard, which is often cluttered with
construction work, parked cars and police
pulling over traffic violators. The pedestrian
mix is lively and varied. By day, office workers,
shoppers and vendors mingle with the tourist
crowds. After dark, the night people emerge
– hustlers trying to draw people into clubs,
hookers openly soliciting startled passers-by,
and boisterous groups of drunken tourists
careening from pub to pub.

Indeed, night is when Wenceslas Square is
most alive. The glow of neon signs high atop
the buildings; the smell of frying sausages from
the food stands; the mix of languages, laughter
and come-ons as you stroll the broad pavements
– it's like a carnival, with crystal shops and
brightly lit souvenir arcades glittering along
both sides of the central promenade.

A tour of the square

At the top of Wenceslas Square sits the
National Museum (*see p206*), overlooking
the boulevard. Built from 1885 to 1890, this
neo-Renaissance palace is covered in decades
of grime and the street graffiti that has become
common in Prague since the Velvet Revolution.
Nevertheless, the building merits a visit, as
every niche, corner and column top boasts
elaborate nationalist stonework. The soaring
lobby and grand staircase inside are also
worth a look, unfortunately far more so
than the actual contents of the museum.

In front of the museum, twin mounds in
the cobbled street mark the site of two self-
immolations. In January 1969 the Czech student
named Jan Palach set himself on fire to protest
against Soviet oppression. The following month

Wenceslas Square. *See p115.*

another student, Jan Zajíc, did the same. To this day the mounds are usually covered with flowers and candles.

One of the most popular meeting spots in Prague is across Wilsonova in the gigantic form of the Czech patron saint: the statue of Wenceslas astride a horse, surrounded by Saints Agnes, Adelbert, Procopius and Ludmila, Wenceslas's grandmother. (The good king takes a satirical ribbing nearby, inside the Lucerna complex at the corner of Štěpánská, where he hangs from the ceiling in an inverted version, the work of art prankster David Černý.) A few steps below 'the horse', as the stately monument is known, a headstone with the images of Palach and Zajíc stands as a memorial to the victims of communism.

The modern glass-and-stone structure just east of the National Museum was the new Parliament building, where the Federal Assembly met until the split of the Czech and Slovak republics in 1993. It then became the home of Radio Free Europe, although it's better known to the station employees as 'the fortress', owing to the concrete barriers and tight security that surround it. Continuing post-9/11 security concerns – the station's prime focus is broadcasting to Muslim fundamentalist audiences – caused RFE to agree in late 2005 to move to the suburbs, although the move is waiting upon the completion of its new building. These days, the current Czech Parliament is ensconced in the more fashionable Wallenstein Palace (see p90).

The next building along is the State Opera (see p232), which opened in 1888 as the New German Theatre. Stepchild of the city's performing arts establishment, the theatre is perennially underfunded and perpetually trying to compensate with creativity and enthusiasm. It's worth the price of a ticket just to see the sumptuous neo-rococo performance hall.

Just past the State Opera beauty is the beast, Hlavní nádraží (see p290), the city's main train station – also known as Wilsonovo nádraží, or Wilson Station. Way overdue for renovation (one's slated for late 2006), the station no longer retains even faded glamour. Dirty inside and out, it's a haven for the homeless, junkies and cruising rent boys. The upstairs rotunda, which houses a rough café, offers glimpses of bygone glory: dull brass rails, dusty statues and peeling murals that disappear into the dark curve of the dome. The lower level, where escalators connect with the metro, is a prime example of late communist design.

Heading down Wenceslas Square, historical monuments quickly give way to capitalist totems like McDonald's and KFC. At No.56 you'll find Jágr's Sport Bar (224 032 481,

www.jagrsportbar.cz), a Western-style drinking emporium with prices to match, owned by Czech hockey hero Jaromír Jágr.

(If you need a sports fix, though, you're better off going around the corner to Hvězda Sport Bar, which shows more than just hockey and football; see p173).

Along with the upside-down horse, the Lucerna shopping passage offers one of the last survivors of pre-war Czech grandeur. This tattered art nouveau gem is a labyrinth of shops ranging from high-fashion boutiques to a Ticketpro, where you can buy tickets to most entertainment events. Walk through the passage for a flavour of everyday Prague, the small-scale cafés, second-hand camera shops and wedding dress rentals characterising the lifeblood of the city. Take the big staircase from the main lobby up to the Lucerna cinema bar (see p211), a classy, run-down art nouveau relic.

Continuing along Wenceslas Square, the building fronts become more ornate. Sit on any bench, look up, and you'll discover stone angels, griffins, muscular atlantes and all manner of ornamental filigree. There's a particularly impressive set of murals on the Wiehl House (1896) at No.34, while Blecha's Supich Building (1913-16) at Nos.38-40 has likeably bizarre Assyrian-style masks adorning its façade. The second-floor balcony of the Melantrich Building (No.30) became the unlikely venue for one of the most astounding events of the Velvet Revolution: on 24 November 1989, in front of over 300,000 people, Václav Havel and Alexander Dubček stepped forward and delivered a message signifying the end of 21 years of 'normalisation'. Within weeks the entire cabinet had resigned.

For an interior version of gorgeous art nouveau mural and stained-glass work, stop in at the Grand Hotel Evropa (see p63) at No.25, the hotel time forgot. From here, the growing number of Levi's and Nike logos means you're approaching the cobbled walkway at the bottom of Wenceslas Square.

Northern Nové Město

From the end of Wenceslas Square, Na Příkopě runs north-east along what was once a moat surrounding Staré Město, though there's no hint of that now. Instead, the street has some of the city's poshest shops and most impressive examples of 'adaptive reuse' – in this case, turning stately baroque buildings into shopping meccas. Palác Koruna, at the junction of Wenceslas Square and Na Příkopě, is a prime example.

Across the way, the Star Café (224 232 173) at No.3 is noteworthy not for its coffee, but for the blithe manner in which former socialist countries expropriate capitalist symbols. This is no Starbucks, though everything from the green-and-white logo out front to the 'Starpuccino' on the menu inside does its best to blur the distinction. You'll see other examples of this throughout the city, such as the all-Czech Hard Rock Café (220 108 148) a few doors west.

The Prague Information Service (*see p311*) at Na Příkopě 20 is a good place to pick up leaflets, schedules and maps. Just beyond, the swanky and successful Slovanský dům shopping mall seems an improbable renovation of the former offices of the Gestapo and the Communist Party. Somewhere, totalitarians are spinning in their graves over the sushi bar, multiplex cinema and U2-owned Joshua Tree club.

Opposite is one of Prague's cultural treasures, the resplendent **Municipal House** (Obecní dům; *see p118*). The city's finest art nouveau orgy, built from 1905 to 1911, it serves as a multipurpose facility housing the 1,500-seat performance hall of the Prague Symphony Orchestra (*see p228*), galleries, offices, meeting rooms and restaurants. The entranceway is crowned with a dome and arched gable framing a monumental tile mosaic, *Homage to Prague*, by Karel Špillar. The walls and floors inside are also covered with fabulous tile work and murals, some of the latter by Alfons Mucha.

The forbidding Gothic structure attached to the Municipal House is the Powder Tower (*see p100*), built in 1475 and renovated many times since. Originally called New Tower, its current name derives from the storage of gunpowder there beginning in the early 1800s. Centuries earlier, the tower marked the beginning of the Royal Route, which coronation parades took through Staré Město, across Charles Bridge (*see p107*) and up to Prague Castle (*see p76*).

A brief loop around two streets running east from the Municipal House offers a capsule view of a city in transition. V Celnici could be almost anywhere in Western Europe, with the modern Marriott (*see p63*) and Renaissance (V Celnici 7, 218 211 111) hotels facing each other across the street and two upscale shopping malls: Millennium Plaza and Stará Celnice, the latter with a Christian Dior shop.

The street ends at Masarykovo nádraží (*see p290*), the Masaryk train station, a smaller and cleaner version of Hlavní nádraží. Turn right and south and you'll end up in Senovážé námesti. Better to turn left up Havlíčkova, which will bring you to the Café Imperial. The café was being reconstructed at press time but it's slated to reopen soon as a high-ceilinged and high-spirited remnant of First Republic decadence, with eye-popping, floor-to-ceiling ornamental porcelain tile work.

A left on Na Poříčí takes you back toward the Municipal House, past newly polished shops and the hip and airy Café Dinitz at No.12 (*see p170*). Consumer fever can be felt as you reach the bottom of the street, where a massive new shopping mall is going up, replacing a 17th-century barracks. Sharing the building with Dinitz is the YMCA – if it's open, stop in for a look at a working paternoster, a cross between a dumbwaiter and a lift that's a thrilling fright to ride.

Southern Nové Město

Back at Wenceslas Square, 28. Října stretches from the north end of the square south-west to Jungmannovo náměstí. The Adria Palace at No.28, built from 1923 to 1925, is perhaps the city's finest example of rondocubist architecture. Don't miss the Church of Our Lady of the Snows (Kostel Panny Marie Sněžné) – its towering black-and-gold baroque altarpiece is awe-inspiring. Also worth seeking out here is the church's side chapel (accessible via a door on the right in the rear), where you can gawp at the trio of gruesome crucifixes.

Outside the church stands the world's only cubist lamp-post. Everywhere else, cubism was confined to painting; in the Czech Republic it shaped everything from furniture to this bizarre, solitary creation. Leading off in the other direction, a path takes you to the Franciscan Gardens (Františkánská zahrada), an oasis of green and calm.

Heading west from Jungmannovo náměstí along Národní brings you to Tesco (*see p178*), five floors of bustling department-store capitalism. In the basement supermarket expats forage for non-Czech grocery items. Gather here after clubbing to catch a night tram (*see p293*). Across Spálená, you'll find the first of two great cafés. Café Louvre (*see p171*), accessible via a lobby and staircase entrance from the street, was once a hangout for Prague's literary and intellectual crowd. Cleaned up and modernised, it's now the ideal place to people-watch and mix with locals.

Further down the street, Slavia (*see p169*) was a famous dissident meeting place during the 1970s and 1980s, and a storied haven for literati like Tolstoy and Kafka for a century before. There's no plotting now and precious little inspiration, just a pricey menu and one of the best riverside views in town. Grab a window seat for a glamour shot of Prague Castle after dark.

Next to the entrance for Café Louvre, you'll notice photos of Bill Clinton playing saxophone in the basement jazz club Reduta (*see p239*) at No.20. Little of that vibe has been left behind,

Lucerna shopping passage. *See p121.*

though – the club feels like it's still run by the old regime. For a funkier hangout try the adjoining Rock Café (*see p239*) or the basement club Vagon (*see p239*) across the way at No.25.

Národní ends at the Vltava river, where the breathtaking **National Theatre** (Národní divadlo; *see p232*) anchors the nation's culture. Topped by a crown of gold and with statues of bucking stallions lining the balustrade, the building is a product and symbol of the fervour of 19th-century Czech nationalism. It took 20 years to raise the money to begin construction, and from 1868 to 1881 to build it. Then, just days before the curtain was to be raised for the first performance, it was gutted by fire. Construction started all over again, and, in 1883, the building finally opened with *Libuše*, an opera written for the occasion by Smetana. The theatre's hall is only open for performances, but it's a wonderful place, perfect for a swish night on the town.

Just before you reach the National Theatre, you'll see its bastard offspring, Laterna Magika, or Magic Lantern (*see p254*). A frosted-glass monstrosity, it was built from 1977 to 1981 as a communist showpiece. The interior is all made from expensive imported marble – the floors, walls, even the banisters – and every seat is upholstered in leather, now well worn and patched. The black light shows and other multimedia fare that play here are not worth the admission, which is perhaps in keeping with an unintentionally ironic socialist relic.

Directly across the street, however, is a high neo-Renaissance delight: the Czech Academy of Sciences (Akademie Věd) built from 1858 to 1862 as a Czech savings bank. The façade, fashioned after St Mark's Library in Venice, is crowned with an allegorical figure receiving the savings of the people. Inside, stone lions guard the entrance hall, and, in the spacious library beyond, ornate female figures of Economy and Thrift watch over the stacks.

Following the river south takes you past Slovanský Island. In the days before slacking became an art form, Berlioz came here and was appalled at the 'idlers, wasters and ne'er-do-wells' who congregated on the island. With a recommendation like that it's hard to resist the outdoor café or spending a few lazy hours in one of the rowing boats for hire. There's also a fine statue of Božena Němcová, as seen on the front of the 500 Kč note. She was the Czech version of George Sand, a celebrated novelist whose private life scandalised polite society.

The island is home to the newly restored cultural centre Žofin (224 934 400, www.zofin.cz) – a large yellow building dating from the 1880s that hosted tea dances and concerts until just before World War II. Today you'll still find concerts here, but also lectures, along with one of the sweetest riverside beer gardens in Prague. At the southern tip is Galerie Mánes (*see p221*), a 1930s functionalist building oddly attached to a medieval water tower. Named for Josef Mánes, the 19th-century artist and

Enjoy the wildlife along the embankment of the river Vltava.

Senovážé Námesti. *See p118.*

nationalist, the building also houses a restaurant and dance club. The intelligentsia used to gather here between the wars, while in 1989 this was where the Civic Forum churned out posters and leaflets. Some of that spirit lives on in the gallery's shows, which feature mostly contemporary Czech artists.

Back on the riverside, continuing south along Masarykovo nábřeží brings you to the corner of Resslova and the Dancing Building (Tančící dům), a collaboration between Czech architect Vlado Miluniç and American architect Frank Gehry, completed in 1996. Also known as 'Fred and Ginger' – he's the rigid vertical half, she's the swaying glass partner – the project presaged Gehry's later, more prominent work, such as the Guggenheim Museum in Bilbao. According to Gehry, the original inspiration for the pinch in the middle of the glass tower came from wanting to protect a neighbour's view of Prague Castle.

Two blocks further south, Palackého náměstí is dominated by a huge Stanislav Sucharda sculpture of 19th-century historian František Palacký, who took 46 years to write a history of the Czech people. The solemn Palacký sits on a giant pedestal, oblivious to the beauties and demons flying around him. Behind him rise the two modern spires of the altogether more ancient Emmaus Monastery (Klášter Na Slovanech), founded by Charles IV. The spires were added after the baroque versions were destroyed by a stray Allied bomb during World War II.

Around Karlovo náměstí

The streets that lie between the National Theatre and the Dancing Building, moving east back toward Spálená, comprise one of the lesser-known yet more entertaining nightlife areas of the city. The name SONA (south of Národní) was floated for a while but never really stuck, which is probably just as well. Part of this area's charm is its amorphous character; there are interesting pubs and restaurants on almost every street, although they never quite coalesce into a scene. Given that, and the tendency of these places to appear and disappear with alarming regularity, you always feel like you're exploring.

For years the Globe Bookstore & Coffeehouse (see p181) was the centre of expat life in Prague, but now that's not so true. A quick glance at the menus posted outside the entrances of neighbouring restaurants shows one reason why: most are in both Czech and English, an indication of how English-friendly the central city has become. There are also other English-language bookshops in Prague (see p181) and plenty of places to get online (see p301).

U Fleků (see p172), at Křemencova 11, remains a tourist mainstay, mostly for the busloads of Germans who disembark ready to quaff 13-degree dark beer and sing along with the accordion players. Its entrance is marked by a picturesque old clock hung like a tavern sign. But there are plenty of hip, relaxed and far better-value pubs nearby. Walk north to the corner of Opatovická and you'll see a host of places accommodating a variety of budgets and tastes – exchange student heaven Tulip Café (see p155) at No.3 has now become a mecca for the huge numbers of American students doing semesters in Europe. Meanwhile, dullish H2O (No.5, no phone) and Cheers (Křemencova 17, no phone) feature cocktail menus reflecting how worldly (or globally uniform) Prague has become, at least in its boozing. Cuba Libre, Long Island Iced Tea and, of course, the obligatory Sex on the Beach are served at the lot. The more you walk, the more places you'll discover – including, by day, some entertaining antique shops, such as Hamparadi Antik Bazar (see p181).

The south-east corner of the area drops you into Karlovo náměstí, a sprawling square that used to be a cattle market and the site of Charles IV's relic fair. Once a year he would wheel out his collection of sacred saints' skulls, toenails and underwear, causing cripples to throw down their crutches and the blind to miraculously regain their sight.

On the north end of the park that forms the area's spine, the handsome New Town Hall (Novoměstská radnice) dates back to the 14th century, though the current version was built during the 19th and early 20th centuries. This was the notorious site of Prague's first defenestration. Across the square is the splendidly restored Jesuit Church of St Ignatius (Kostel sv. Ignáce), a typically lush early baroque affair, with gold-trimmed cream, pink and orange stucco. Built from 1665 to 1670, it features a wonderful collection of angels in its arches and nave. At the south-west corner of the park sits the Faust House (Faustův dům), an ornate 17th-century building that has more than a few legends attached to it. Edward Kelly, the earless English alchemist, once lived here, as did a poor student who was lured into making a Faustian pact with the Prince of Darkness: the impoverished kid was offered riches in exchange for his soul, which Satan then snatched through a hole in the roof.

Walking east on Ječná will bring you to No.14, where Dvořák died. But rather than staring at the plaque on the wall, go to the **Dvořák Museum** nearby (see p124), where you can catch a chamber recital. It's quartered in a lovely summerhouse designed by Kilian

Sightseeing

Ignaz Dientzenhofer – the Villa Amerika – though these days it's surrounded by incongruous modern bits of concrete.

At the far end of the street is a museum of a very different sort – the **Police Museum** (*see p126*). Brek, the stuffed wonder dog responsible for thwarting the defection of several hundred dissidents, has been given a decent burial, but there are still plenty of gruesome exhibits here to delight the morbid.

If it all gets too much, seek sanctuary in the unusual church next door, dedicated to Charlemagne, Charles IV's hero and role model. The octagonal nave of Na Karlově was only completed in the 16th century, and for years the superstitious locals refused to enter it for fear that it would collapse. The gilt-frescoed walls inside were restored after the building was partially destroyed in the Prussian siege of 1757, but bullets can still be seen embedded in them. From the garden there are extensive views across the Nusle Valley to Vyšehrad on the other side.

A few blocks to the west on Vyšehradská is the Church of St John on the Rock (Kostel sv. Jana Na Skalce), a fine Dientzenhofer structure built in the 1730s, perched at the top of an impressive double stairway. And a little further to the south from that are the delightful, though little-visited, Botanical Gardens (Botanická zahrada), with tranquil terraces.

Walking the other way on Ječná (west, towards the river), the street turns into Resslova and quickly brings you to the baroque **Orthodox Cathedral of SS Cyril and Methodius** (Kostel sv. Cyrila a Metoděje; *see p126*).

Dvořák Museum

Muzeum Antonína Dvořáka
Villa Amerika, Ke Karlovu 20, Prague 2 (224 923 363). Metro IP Pavlova/tram 4, 6, 11, 16, 22, 23, 34. **Open** *Apr-Sept* 10am-5.30pm Tue-Sun. *Oct-Mar* 9.30am-5pm Tue-Sun. **Admission** 50 Kč. **No credit cards.** **Map** p331 N10.
Hidden away behind wrought-iron gates, the Dvořák Museum is housed in an elegant early 18th-century baroque summer palace. This small red-and-ochre villa was built by Kilian Ignaz Dientzenhofer in 1720 for Count Jan Václav Michna, then became a cattle market during the 19th century. It now houses the Dvořák Society's well-organised tribute to the most famous Czech composer. Memorabilia and photographs make up the ground-floor display. Upstairs are further exhibits and a recital hall, decorated with frescoes by Jan Ferdinand Schor. Concerts held here are the best way to appreciate the building's past as a retreat for the composer. Outdoor recitals in warm weather are particularly evocative. Ironically, Dvořák actually spent very little time here as his career was mainly established in the grand concert halls of Western Europe.

Mucha Museum

Muchovo muzeum
Kaunický palác, Panská 7, Prague 1 (221 451 333/ www.mucha.cz). Metro Můstek/tram 3, 9, 14, 24. **Open** 10am-6pm daily. **Admission** 120 Kč. **No credit cards.** **Map** p329 N5.
Opened in 1998, this museum is dedicated to perhaps the most famous of all Czech visual artists, Alfons Mucha (1860-1939). Known for commercial work such as mass-produced decorative panels and posters for Sarah Bernhardt's theatre performances, Mucha exercised his greatest influence through his *Encyclopaedia for Craftsmen* (1902), a catalogue of art nouveau decorative elements, forms and designs. Mucha created a stained-glass window for St Vitus's Cathedral (*see p77*) and the *Slavonic Epic*, a series of gigantic narrative oil paintings, which are now residing in Moravský Krumlov castle, south-west of Brno. The museum also displays lithographs, drawings, sketches, notebooks and a video on his life.

Museum of Communism

Muzeum komunismu
Na Příkopě 10, Prague 1 (224 212 966/ www.museumofcommunism.com). Metro Můstek/tram 3, 9, 14, 24. **Open** 8am-9pm daily. **Admission** 180 Kč. **Credit** AmEx, MC, V. **Map** p328 M5.
Opened in 2001 as the first of its kind in the country, this museum puts the communist era in historical perspective through its ample archive photographs, each with explanatory texts, as well as hundreds of relics on display. Co-founded by American restaurateur and long-time Prague resident Glenn Spicker, the museum has mock-ups of a schoolroom from the period, with Czechoslovak and Soviet flags hanging side by side and a Russian lesson on the blackboard. More eerie is the interrogation room, which is just like those used by the Czechoslovak secret police. And just to keep Lenin spinning, the museum is directly above a McDonald's restaurant and shares a floor in the building with a casino.

Museum of the City of Prague

Muzeum Hlavního města Prahy
Na Poříčí 52, Prague 1 (224 816 773/www. muzeumprahy.cz). Metro Florenc/tram 3, 8, 24. **Open** 9am-6pm Tue-Sun. **Admission** 80 Kč; 160 Kč family; free under-6s; 1 Kč 1st Thur of mth concessions. **No credit cards.** **Map** p329 Q2.
Antonín Langweil spent 11 years of the early 1800s building an incredibly precise room-sized paper model of Prague. Now this museum's prize exhibit, it is the only complete depiction of what the city looked like before the Jewish ghetto was ripped down. Other displays follow the city's development from pre-history through to the 17th century, with some English labels provided in the rooms devoted to medieval and later events. The upstairs galleries host temporary exhibitions and the original of the Josef Mánes painting reproduced inside the Old Town Hall's astronomical clock tower.

Reclaiming Wenceslas

Sadly, Czechs have all but abandoned Prague's signature boulevard, despite it being the setting for historic turning points, both national and international. Let's just look at the highlights: Wenceslas Square was where demonstrators gathered to demand the end of communist rule during the Velvet Revolution (on the balcony of the building that is now home to Marks & Spencer, Václav Havel formally declared the long nightmare of Soviet control to be over). Only 20 years before, in 1968, the square had seen Soviet tanks crushing the bloom of the Prague Spring, thus proving that reformer Alexander Dubček's idea of 'socialism with a human face' was an oxymoron. Further back, in March 1939, the Nazis celebrated their bloodless conquest of Czechoslovakia with a military parade, while October 1918 saw a mass demonstration declaring national independence.

But these days Wenceslas Square is hardly a point of pride: lit by the neon lights of casinos and strip clubs, and lined with parked cars, tourist-targeted crystal shops and sausage stands, the once-grand boulevard is a sorry sight.

Architect Jakub Cigler plans to change all that. Having created the winning plan in a city competition for a Wenceslas Square makeover, Cigler has produced a vision for returning the pride to the pride of the Nové Město district. He foresees more green space and pedestrian areas, far fewer cars, the possible return of the trams that once ran up and down the square, and reconnecting the square with its original crowning glory, the National Museum.

Central planners under the pre-1989 regime cut off the national icon from the rest of Wenceslas Square to create a traffic arterial road, but Cigler wants all those cars rerouted to a ring road that's gradually being built around Prague.

City planners hope to have the new conception finished by 2010, but are well aware that the cost, in the billions of crowns, might make that date look optimistic.

Still, Cigler's ideas are clearly in sympathy with those who yearn for those pre-war days when Wenceslas Square was filled with stylish Czechs, browsing through glamorous stores and lounging in classy cafés.

The new plan 'respects the historical environment and provides modern design as well, which will make the whole of the square more people friendly', says Prague 1 Mayor Vladimír Vihan, who, along with the city council, weighed nine other proposals before choosing Cigler's.

Business owners and hoteliers are breathing a sigh of relief at the scheme, having become tired of having to shoo away the panhandlers, drug dealers and drunken stag parties that can at times infest the square.

Prague lord mayor Pavel Bem, an admirer of New York's mayors Rudolf Giuliani and Michael Bloomberg, says he won't be shy about using more police to fight the crime that attends such streetlife. But even Bem, deferring to another Czech tradition, has qualified his pledge with deference to the Interior Ministry, which would have to foot the bill. Regimes may come and go but bureaucrats live on forever, it seems.

Sightseeing

National Theatre. *See p121.*

Orthodox Cathedral of SS Cyril & Methodius

Kostel sv. Cyrila a Metoděje
Resslova 9, Prague 2 (224 920 686). Metro Karlovo náměstí/tram 4, 7, 9, 12, 14, 16, 18, 22, 24.
Open *Jan-Apr, Oct-Dec* 10am-4pm Tue-Sun. *May-Sept* 10am-5pm Tue-Sun. At other times, ring the administrator's bell to be admitted. **Admission** 50 Kč; 20 Kč concessions. **No credit cards.** **Map** p330 K9.

This baroque church, built in the 1730s, was taken over and restored by the Czech Orthodox Church in the 1930s. A plaque and memorial outside, together with numerous bullet holes, still attract tributes and flowers today, and are a clue to what happened inside during World War II. On 29 December 1941 two Czech paratroopers trained in England were flown into Bohemia, together with five colleagues, to carry out, among other resistance acts, the assassination of Reinhard Heydrich, Reichsprotektor of Bohemia and Moravia, and the man who chaired the infamous 1942 Wannsee Conference on the Final Solution. They succeeded, ambushing Heydrich as he drove to work on 27 May 1942. Gabčik's gun jammed, but Kubiš threw a grenade at the car, which seriously wounded the SS man. Heydrich died in agony on 4 June. Josef Gabčik, Jan Kubiš and their co-conspirators were given sanctuary in the crypt here after the event, until they were betrayed to the Germans. In the early hours of 18 June, 350 members of the SS and Gestapo surrounded the church and spent the night bombarding it with bullets and grenades. The men, who managed to survive until dawn, used their final bullets to shoot themselves.

The incident did not end there. Recriminations were swift, brutal and arbitrary. Hundreds of peo-ple, many of them Jews, were rounded up in Prague and shot immediately, while five entire villages and most of their inhabitants were liquidated, the most famous being Lidice. The events brought about a turning point in the war. Britain repudiated the Munich Agreement and Anthony Eden declared that Lidice had 'stirred the conscience of the civilised world'. The story of the assassination and its after-math is movingly told in the crypt of the church (entrance on Na Zderaze), where the Czech para-troopers made their last stand.

An excellent collection of photos is on display in the church, and you can also see the tunnel through which the assassins tried to dig their way out, in a failed effort to reach the city sewer. They came with-in centimetres of reaching their goal.

Police Museum

Muzeum policie ČR
Ke Karlovu 1, Prague 2 (224 922 183/www. mvcr.cz/ministerstvo/muzeum.htm). Metro IP Pavlova/tram 6, 11. **Open** 10am-5pm Tue-Sun. **Admission** 20 Kč; 40 Kč family. **No credit cards.** **Map** p331 N11.

Prague's surprisingly interesting Police Museum resides in a former convent, which is attached to the Karlov Church. In the section on crime detection techniques you can take your own fingerprints or try to reconstruct events at a creepy scene-of-the-crime mock-up. Children love it here, though parents are warned that some of the photographs are quite graphic. The final room of the museum contains an arsenal of home-made weaponry that would please James Bond: sword sticks, makeshift pistols, pen guns, even a lethal lighter. The texts, unfortunately for visitors, are almost entirely in Czech.

Sightseeing

Further Afield

Where the locals live, play and die.

Maps p332 & p333

Holešovice, Letná & Troja

Holešovice may still show visitors a grimy, neglected façade (although with some pride, it seems) but real estate-mad Czechs are buying properties up at a phenomenal rate. With that comes the trappings of stylish city living but, thankfully, this 19th-century suburb remains a world apart. You can still see Staré Město, the Old Town, to the south over the Vltava river, from Letná park, while the former factories become art spaces, and families and in-line skaters play in Stromovka, Letná park and the surrounding cafés and pubs. And should you want to get away, one of Prague's two international train stations, Nádraží Holešovice (see p291), links to the wider world.

Down towards the river on Kostelní is the **National Technical Museum**, a constructivist building dating from 1938-41, whose dull name belies a fascinating collection of Czechnology that instantly wows children. Five minutes' walk east is Holešovice's main drag, **Dukelských hrdinů**. Here stands a sleeker constructivist building, the modern-looking **Veletržní palác**. Built in the mid 1920s to house the trade fairs that had long outgrown Výstaviště, it was gutted by fire in 1974 but has been splendidly restored. The white-painted atrium rises up seven storeys and is lined with sweeping guard rails, giving it the feel of a massive ocean liner. Pop in to peek at the atrium, even if you don't have time to take in the **National Gallery Collection of 19th-, 20th- and 21st-Century Art** within.

A couple of minutes' walk to the north is **Výstaviště**, a fairground fronted by an unusual wrought-iron pavilion erected for the Jubilee Exhibition of 1891 and considered the first expression of art nouveau in the city. Here, in the **Lapidárium**, you'll find an intriguing collection of reject monuments that once stood around the city. But don't go expecting much laughable communist-era public art: the collection is mainly historic baroque and Gothic statuary, including most of the original statues from Charles Bridge (those there now are almost all copies; see p107), moved here years ago to protect them from the elements. Beyond the pavilion is **Lunapark**, featuring a roller-coaster and Ferris wheel – always a fave with local teens and lovers – from which there are fine views over the woody environs of **Stromovka**, a park to the west, laid out by Rudolf II in the 16th century as a place for him to commune with nature. His favoured companion was English alchemist John Dee, who got the job when he claimed to understand both the language of the birds and the one Adam and Eve spoke in Eden. Today the leafy park makes a wonderful spot for a stroll or picnic – though you may have to dodge the hordes of in-line skaters. Just south of Stromovka lie two of the city's hotbeds of late-night lifestyling: Fraktal, the semi-trashed bar where you'll find performance artists and affable international drunks sitting around tattered, hand-carved furnishings, and La Bodega Flamenca (for both, see p173), the Czech-owned cellar-haven of sangria sipping, one of the area's best after-hours refueling options. For some of Prague's best clubbing, with elbow room and a stylish long bar, try the Holešovice dance favourite known as Mecca (see p244), on the eastern side of the district.

If you need a breath of fresh air, take the half-hour walk back to Staré Město via the sedate embassy-land of **Bubeneč**, just to the west of these bars and clubs, and ramble on past the AC Sparta stadium (see p256) and through **Letná park** (Letenské sady). This was where the biggest demonstration of 1989 took place, attended by nearly a million people. On the edge of the park sits a plinth where a massive

Still crazy Žižkov

Of all the separatist groups in the world, Žižkovites are surely the most fun-loving. Traditionally working class, the area has long attracted bohemian intellectuals. Even now, with high-end boutiques and residential developments moving in, the neighbourhood's irrepressible character remains intact.

In May 2006 Žižkov celebrated the 125th anniversary of being declared an independent town in 1881. At the time, the district, which benefited commercially from its proximity to Prague, was the fourth-biggest town in Bohemia and being upgraded from village status was a great source of pride for residents, who were always fierce patriots – Žižkov patriots, that is.

In fact, since losing its independence and becoming part of Prague in 1922, Žižkov has seen waves of mock campaigns calling for a self-governing Žižkov republic. Thus Žižkovites demonstrated an early appreciation for farce, which was also a favourite pastime of Jaroslav Hašek, author of the classic Czech comic novel, *Good Soldier Švejk* (much of which is said to have been penned in the local pubs).

'The beauty of Žižkov lies in its chaos,' according to Richard Biegel, Žižkov resident and head of Klub za starou Prahu, a Prague historical preservation society. But communists were never fans of chaos and in the 1970s the central planners drew up plans for ugly utilitarian concrete apartment blocks to replace the 18th- and 19th-century tenements that line Žižkov's narrow lanes. Fortunately, they only built a handful at the eastern edge of the area before running out of funds.

The mishmash of Žižkov's influences is especially visible along Seifertova and Husitská streets, the neighbourhood's main arteries. There you'll find an old hardware shop or a pub alongside a Thai massage parlour, a halal butcher, a yoga studio or a swanky bar.

To the south and closer to nearby Vinohrady, Kubelíkova street is a bar hoppers' paradise, with nightspots that include Palác Akropolis, a beacon to concert-goers. The multi-level former movie theatre draws big-name international bands such as the Flaming Lips, the Fall and the Pixies, alongside local bands.

Nad Viktorkou, situated on the hill near the Viktoria Žižkov soccer stadium, is another favourite haunt, as is Parukářka pub, atop Parukářka Hill.

The scene is similar at U vystřeleného oka, a pub near Husitská street below Vítkov Hill. The pub's name – the Shot-Out Eye – pays homage to Jan Žižka, the one-eyed Hussite leader, after whom the district is named. Locals favour its beer garden, where dogs lie under tables, mugs get filled and refilled, and occasionally a train rumbles by on the tracks that run parallel to Husitská street.

The general, reportedly a hard drinker, seems a fitting icon for such a refractory locale.

statue of Stalin once stood. Now it bears a giant metronome. Letná features its own hot new dance space, Výletná (*see p174*), which masquerades as a great garden barbecue pub.

Alternatively, a 20-minute walk north of Stromovka (or bus No.112 from Metro Nádraži Holešovice) brings you to the elaborate **Troja Château** (Trojský zámek), restored after suffering massive damage from the floods of 2002. The inmates of **Prague Zoo** (*see p206*) across the road (rebuilt and expanded since the floods) can only curse their historical mistiming – at Troja, the count's horses were provided with a vast, sumptuous stable block, with marble floors, that was decorated with frescoes of their noble forebears.

National Gallery Collection of 19th-, 20th- & 21st-Century Art

Sbírka moderního a současného umění

Veletržní palác, Dukelských hrdinů 47, Holešovice, Prague 7 (224 301 122/www.ngprague.cz). Metro Vltavská/tram 5, 12, 17. **Open** 10am-6pm Tue-Sun. **Admission** *1 floor* 100 Kč; *2 floors* 150 Kč; *3 floors* 200 Kč; *all 4 floors* 250 Kč. *Temporary exhibitions* 50 Kč; free under-10s. **No credit cards. Map** p332 E3.

This functionalist building, designed by Oldřich Tyl and Josef Fuchs and opened in 1929, hosted trade fairs until 1951; later it served as headquarters for several foreign trade companies. It has housed the National Gallery's collections of modern and contemporary art since its reconstruction in 1995. The 19th-century collection, housed here since 2000, is on the fourth floor. Highlights include paintings by Karel Purkyně, informed by close observation and a thorough knowledge of Old Master techniques, and the mystical strain of 19th-century Czech art represented by symbolists Max Švabinský and František Bílek. Czech art from 1900 to 1930 fills out the gallery's impressive holdings along with French modernist art. The groundbreaking abstract artist František Kupka is well represented too, along with Czech cubists, surrealists and social art from the 1920s. And a better collection of Bohemian art from 1930 to the present, including surrealist works by Toyen and Jindřich Štýrský, would be difficult to find anywhere else in the world. There are also many chilling, sometimes amusing, works of Stalin-era socialist realism and the existentialist Art Informel pieces from around the same period.

National Technical Museum

Národní technické muzeum

Kostelní 42, Holešovice, Prague 7 (220 399 111/www.ntm.cz). Metro Hradčanská or Vltavská/tram 8, 25, 26. **Open** 9am-5pm Tue-Fri; 10am-6pm Sat, Sun. **Admission** 70 Kč; 150 Kč family. **No credit cards. Map** p332 D3.

Don't let the mundane name put you off visiting: this is a fascinating collection, enjoyable for both children and adults. The museum traces the development of technology and science in Czechoslovakia, which, until the stultifying communist era, was among Europe's most innovative and industrially advanced nations. The Transport Hall contains steam trains, vintage motorcycles, racing cars and biplanes, while the claustrophobic 'mine' in the basement has sinister coal-cutting implements in place in mock tunnels. Guided tours of the mine are available in English. There's also an extensive photography and cinematography section, and a collection of rare astronomical instruments.

Troja Château

Trojský zámek

U Trojského zámku 1, Holešovice, Prague 7 (283 851 614). Metro Nádraži Holešovice/bus 112. **Open** *Apr-Oct* 10am-6pm Tue-Sun. *Mar-Nov* 10am-5pm Sat, Sun. **Admission** 120 Kč; 60 Kč concessions. **No credit cards.**

After winning huge tracts of land in the property lottery that followed the Thirty Years' War, Count Šternberg embarked upon creating a house worthy of his ego. An 18th-century Czech nobleman, he was anxious to demonstrate his loyalty to the Habsburg emperor and literally moved mountains to do so. The hillside had to be dug out to align the villa with the royal hunting park of Stromovka, still accessible via footbridge from the embankment, and the distant spires of St Vitus's Cathedral. The result, built by a French architect and Italian craftsmen, is a paean to the Habsburgs, modelled on a classical Italian villa and surrounded by formal gardens in the French style. The château's interior is replete with beautiful trompe l'oeil murals and on the massive external staircase classical gods hurl the rebellious titans down into a dank and dreary grotto. In the Grand Hall the Habsburgs enjoy a well-earned victory over the infidel Turks. This, a fascinating though slightly ludicrous example of illusory painting, is Troja's main attraction. To see it you have to don huge red slippers to protect the marble floors.

Výstaviště

U Výstaviště, Prague 7 (220 103 111/484/ www.incheba.cz). Metro Nádraži Holešovice/tram 5, 12, 17. **Open** 2-9pm Tue-Fri; 10am-9pm Sat, Sun. **Admission** 20 Kč Sat, Sun; free under-6s free Tue-Fri. **No credit cards. Map** p332 D1.

Built from curvaceous expanses of wrought iron to house the Jubilee Exhibition of 1891, Výstaviště signalled the birth of the art nouveau art form in Prague. During the late 1940s it became the site of various communist congresses, but today it is mainly used for trade shows for industries ranging from information technology to pornography. It's worth dodging past the knots of salesmen to see the interior. The industrial feeling of the wrought-iron structure is offset by vivid stained glass and exquisite floral decorations. The best view of the exterior is from the back, where a monumental modern fountain gushes kitschily at night, in time to popular classics and accompanied by a light show. The grounds are filled with architectural oddities such as the Lapidárium and the delightfully dilapidated funfair Lunapark, which pulls in the weekend crowds of Czech families.

Sightseeing

Dejvice & further west

Some of the most exclusive residences in the city are located in **Prague 6**, the suburbs that lie beyond Prague Castle. This neighbourhood is filled with embassies and the former residences of court and republic retainers of all stripes. You'd never guess this, though, from the rather desolate hub of the area, **Vítězné náměstí**, where another statue of Lenin used to stand. Leading north from the square is the wide **Jugoslávských partyzánů** (Avenue of Yugoslav Partisans), at the end of which you'll find the **Crowne Plaza Hotel** (Koulova 15, 296 537 111), formerly known as Hotel International. This monumental piece of 1950s socialist realism is one of the last remaining bastions of Marxist-Leninist decor in the city. The façade over the main entrance features Russian war heroes being greeted by grateful Czech peasants – it feels a bit out of place now, juxtaposed as it is with the bars inside the lobby, which are frequented by yuppies and foreign business folk who look like they regularly use the hotel's new fitness centre. Very much a sign of the times.

On the hill above the hotel are the **Baba Villas** (Přírodní památka Baba), a colony of constructivist houses built after, and inspired by the huge success of, the 1927 Exhibition of Modern Living in Stuttgart. Under the guidance of Pavel Janák, all 33 of the houses were individually commissioned to provide simple but radically designed living spaces for ordinary families. However, they were quickly snapped up by leading figures of the Czech avant-garde and many of them are still decorated with original fixtures and fittings. None, alas, are open to the public, but they are still a must-see for any fan of modern architecture. Take bus No.131 to U Matěje and walk up Matějská to reach the estate.

On the western fringe of the city, just off Patočkova, is the **Břevnov Monastery** (Benediktinské arciopatství sv.Vojtěcha a sv. Markéty, just north of Patočkova at Bělohorská), inhabited by Benedictine monks since 993 and modelled on 'God's perfect workshop'. Since the Velvet Revolution the monks have purged all traces of the Ministry of the Interior, which for the last 40 years had used the **Basilica of St Margaret** (Bazilika sv. Markéty) as a warehouse for its files on suspicious foreigners. This Romanesque church was remodelled by the Dientzenhofer father-and-son act in the early 18th century and is one of their most triumphant commissions, with a single high nave and unfussy interior.

Close by, near the terminus of tram No.22, a small stone pyramid marks the site of **Bílá Hora**, or White Mountain, the decisive first battle of the Thirty Years' War, fought in 1620. In the park is the **Hvězda Hunting Lodge** (Letohrádek Hvězda), a product of the Renaissance, its

Vyšehrad: a rocky outcrop with a few Prague myths to tell. *See p131.*

angular walls and roof arranged in the pattern of a six-pointed star (*hvězda* in Czech). It was built in the 1550s for Archduke Ferdinand of Tyrol, who was obsessed with numerology, and is conceived as an intellectual conundrum.

North of here, off Evropská, is the extensive and wonderfully wild **Divoká Šárka** (*see p261*), a fine place to stroll, swim or cycle, away from the city crowds and fumes. There's a nude sunbathing area in summer by the murky lake.

Smíchov & Barrandov

Smíchov has undergone some changes since Mozart stayed in 1787. Rapid industrialisation rather spoilt the ambience of the aristocracy's summer houses and the area was until recently dominated by factories (such as Staropramen Brewery). Now it has exploded with new malls, multiplexes and office complexes. However, a few remnants of proletarian glories are commemorated in a couple of surviving socialist realist murals in Anděl metro station. To get an idea of what Smichov was once like visit **Bertramka**, the house with lilac gardens that belonged to František and Josefina Dušek, now a museum to their most famous house guest, Wolfgang Amadeus Mozart.

South of Smíchov is **Barrandov**, the Czech version of Hollywood. On the cliffs below there are even white Hollywood-style letters that spell out 'Barrande' – though this is actually in homage to the 19th-century geologist after whom the quarter takes its name. Vast studios were built here in the 1930s, which have been the centre of the Czech film industry ever since.

Mozart Museum

Bertramka
Mozartova 169, Smíchov, Prague 5 (257 318 461/ 7465/www.bertramka.com). Metro Anděl/tram 4, 7, 9, 10. **Open** *Apr-Oct* 9am-6pm daily. *Nov-Mar* 9.30am-4pm daily. **Admission** 110 Kč; free under-6s; concerts 390-450 Kč. **No credit cards.**
Villa Bertramka – a former vineyard manor house that has been restored to its 18th-century glory – is a welcome refuge in its walled park next to the Mövenpick Hotel (*see p67*). Mozart stayed several times as a guest of the villa's owners, composer František Dušek and his wife, Josefina. And it was here, in 1787, that he composed the overture to *Don Giovanni*, the night before its première in the Nostitz Theatre (which is now the Estates Theatre; *see p251*). Bertramka showcases memorabilia of Mozart and the Dušeks, including personal keepsakes, musical instruments, manuscripts and letters. Tranquillity, however, is the villa's greatest asset – mid morning or late afternoon, it is possible to linger over cappuccino in the courtyard café and remain relatively undisturbed by tour groups. There are also occasional evening recitals on the terrace.

National Memorial. *See p133.*

Zbraslav Château

Zámek Zbraslav
Bartošova 2, Zbraslav, Prague 5 (257 921 638). Metro Smíchovské nádraží, then 129, 241 or 243 bus to Zbraslavské náměstí. **Open** 10am-6pm Tue-Sun. **Admission** 80 Kč; 120 Kč family. **No credit cards.**
The Zbraslav Château, a baroque house at the southern tip of Prague, houses the National Gallery's surprisingly extensive collection of Asian art. The Chinese and Japanese holdings are particularly good. There's also a smattering of Indian, South-east Asian and Islamic pieces, plus a handful of Tibetan scrolls. It's a 30-minute bus ride from the metro.

Vyšehrad

Vyšehrad, the rocky outcrop south of Nové Město, the New Town, is where all the best Prague myths were born. Here Libuše, the mythic mother of Prague, fell into a trance and sent her horse out into the countryside to find a suitable spouse, the ploughman called Přemysl, after whom the early Bohemian kings take their name. The more prosaic story is that a castle was founded here in the first half of the tenth century, enjoying a period of importance when King Vratislav II (1061-92) built a royal palace on the rock. Within 50 years, though, the Přemyslid rulers had moved back to Prague Castle and Vyšehrad's short-lived period of political pre-eminence was over.

Sightseeing

Rotunda of St Martin.

Paul (Kostel sv. Petra a Pavla) dates from the beginning of the 20th century. Restoration has brought out the best of the splendid polychrome interior, decked out with art nouveau-style saints and decorative motifs.

Next door is **Slavín**, Vyšehrad's cemetery, conceived by the 19th-century National Revival movement and the last resting place of the cream of the country's arts worthies, including the composers Dvořák and Smetana, writers Karel Čapek and Jan Neruda, and painter Mikoláš Aleš. The Slavin (meaning 'pantheon') was designed by Antonín Wiehl and jointly commemorates further artistic big cheeses such as painter Alfons Mucha and sculptor Josef Václav Myslbek. It is very much sacred ground in Czech intellectual history. Surrounded by Italianate arcades, the cemetery contains an abundance of fine memorials, many of them displaying art nouveau influences. On the south side of SS Peter and Paul are four monumental sculptural groups by Myslbek depicting mythological heroes from Czech history; the couple nearest to the church are Přemysl and Libuše. The park extends to the cliff edge overlooking the Vltava, from where there are lovely views across to Prague Castle.

If you continue down the hill from Vyšehrad along Přemyslova, you'll find one of the city's most outstanding pieces of cubist architecture, a corner apartment block designed by Josef Chochol at Neklanova 30 (1911-13). Some way south is a railway bridge popularly known as the **Bridge of Intelligence** because it was built by members of the intellectual elite who ended up working as labourers after losing their jobs during the purges of the 1950s.

The easiest way to reach Vyšehrad is to take the metro to the Vyšehrad stop, under the enormous road bridge spanning the **Nusle Valley**. Built in the 1970s, the bridge was hailed as a monument to socialism, a description that was hastily dropped when chunks of concrete began falling on passing pedestrians and it became the most popular spot for suicides in the city. Walk away from the towering Corinthia (Kongresová 1, Prague 4, 261 191 111) and past the unappealing, monolithic **Congress Centre** (*see p234*), completed in 1980 as the supreme architectural expression of the Soviet-imposed 'normalisation' years, then through the baroque gateway into the park. The information centre (V pevnosti, no phone) to the right of here can provide maps of the area.

One of the first sights you will pass is the over-restored **Rotunda of St Martin** (Rotunda sv. Martina). Dating from the second half of the 11th century, the Rotunda is the oldest complete Romanesque building in Prague and now hosts evening Mass.

There's been a church at Vyšehrad since the 14th century, but the original was apparently irrevocably damaged when Lucifer, angered by an insubordinate cleric, threw three large rocks through the roof. The granite slabs (known as the Devil Pillars) can be found close to the Old Deanery, but the holes are gone. Joseph Mocker's neo-Gothic **Church of SS Peter &**

Vinohrady & Žižkov

Map p333

Vinohrady came into existence in what the communist guidebooks called the period of Bourgeois Capitalism, and it's an area of magnificent, if crumbling, fin-de-siècle tenements. The heart of the neighbourhood is **Náměstí Míru**, a round 'square' spiked by the twin spires of the neo-Gothic **Church of St Ludmila** (Kostel sv. Ludmily; Náměstí Míru) and faced by the opulent **Vinohrady Theatre** (Divadlo Na Vinohradech; Náměstí Míru 7, 296 550 111). The Radost FX café, gallery and nightclub complex (*see p245*), still one of Prague's premier clubs, is nearby on Bělehradská. The Medúza café (*see p174*) on quiet Belgická is one of the city's cosiest, if threadbare, winter hideout spots and, just over on the border of **Prague 10**, the Café Atelier (*see p160*) on Na Kovárně is one of the most accomplished local eateries. The area south of

Náměstí Miru has become a centre of Prague's gay scene, with bars, clubs and pensions (*see p225*). The main artery of Vinohrady, however, is **Vinohradská**, a little further north. Formerly called Stalinova třída, after one of history's greatest mass-murderers, it saw some of 1968's fiercest street battles against Warsaw Pact troops. Art nouveau apartment blocks line Vinohradská, looking out on to the **Church of the Sacred Heart** (Nejsvětější Srdce Páně; Náměsti Jiřího Z Poděbrad), one of the most inspiring pieces of modern architecture in the city, dominated by its huge glass clock. It was built in 1928-32 by Josip Plečnik, the pioneering Slovenian architect who also redid Prague Castle. Fans of ecclesiastical modernism, if such creatures exist, might also enjoy Pavel Janák's 1930s **Hussite Church** (Husův sbor) on the corner of U Vodárny and Dykova, as well as Josef Gočár's functionalist **Church of St Wenceslas** (Kostel sv. Václava) on Náměsti Svatopluka Čecha.

Near Plečnik's church is the scary **Žižkov Tower** (*see p134*), which was completed in 1989. A couple of nearby venues worthy of note are Hapu (Orlická 8, 222 720 158), a contender for top living-room cocktail bar, and U Sadu (*see p175*), cheap and Czech, with well-located outside seating in the summer.

Down the hill to the north and east is **Žižkov**. This district, notorious for its rowdy pubs and large Romany population, not surprisingly also became known for quirky outlandishness. What is more surprising is that a working-class district became a popular interment place for post-war communist presidents. The massive **National Memorial** (Národní památnik; *see p134*) on top of **Vítkov Hill** is a mausoleum with the largest equestrian statue in the world, a 16,764-kilogram (37,000-pound) effigy of Hussite hero Jan Žižka. The corpses of the communist presidents were ejected from the mausoleum in 1990 and reburied elsewhere or cremated; now it's an eerie place that occasionally hosts raves (if you fancy your chances of attending one, check out www.techno.cz/party).

Further east on Vinohradská are two fine cemeteries. The first, **Olšany Cemetery** (Olšanské hřbitovy; *see p134*), is the largest in Prague. The cemetery extends from the Flora metro station to Jana Želivského, and includes a Garden of Rest, where the Red Army soldiers who died liberating Prague are buried. Since 1989 the cemetery has begun to suffer from graffiti and grave-robbing. Next door is the **Jewish Cemetery** (Židovské hřbitovy), not to be confused with the Old Jewish Cemetery (*see p112*) in Staré Město. Here fans of Franz Kafka come to pay respects at his simple grave (follow the sign at the entrance by Želivského metro station; it's approximately 200 metres/660 feet down the row by the southern cemetery wall). Though founded in 1890, only a fraction has been used since World War II and the neglect is obvious.

Žižkov Tower: don't have nightmares.

National Memorial

Národní památník

U památníku 1900, Prague 3 (222 781 676). Metro Florenc/bus 133, 168, 207. **Open** times vary (advance booking required, minimum 20 people). **Admission** varies. **Map** p333 C1.

This hulking mass of concrete is one of the city's best-known and least-liked landmarks. The immense constructivist block and enormous equestrian statue high up on Vitkov Hill can be seen from around the city. The memorial was built in 1925 by Jan Zázvorka as a dignified setting for the remains of the legionnaires who fought against the Austro-Hungarian Empire in World War I. In 1953 the communist regime turned it into a mausoleum for Heroes of the Working Class. The mummified remains of Klement Gottwald, who was the first communist president, were kept here, tended by scientists who unsuccessfully tried to preserve his body for display, Lenin-style, before the project was abandoned and the decaying remains fobbed off on Gottwald's family in 1990. Opening times of the memorial are unpredictable, but it doesn't really matter as most of what you might want to see is visible from the outside. In front stands the massive equestrian statue of one-eyed General Žižka, who was the scourge of 14th-century Catholics and the darling of the communists, who subsequently adopted him in an effort to establish genuine Bohemian credentials. **Photo** p131.

Olšany Cemetery

Olšanské hřbitovy

Vinohradská 153 at Jana Želivského, Prague 3 (272 739 364). Metro Flora or Želivského. **Open** dawn-dusk daily. **Map** p333 E3.

The overgrown yet beautiful Olšany Cemetery contains impressive memorials to two unlikely bed fellows: the first communist president, Klement Gottwald, who died after catching a cold at Stalin's funeral, and the most famous anti-communist martyr, Jan Palach, the student who set fire to himself in Wenceslas Square in 1969. In death their fates have been strangely linked, as neither's mortal remains have been allowed to rest in peace. Palach was originally buried here in 1969, but his grave became such a focus of dissent that the authorities disinterred his body and reburied it deep in the Bohemian countryside. In 1990 he was dug up and brought back to Olšany. His grave is to the right of the main entrance. Gottwald, too, travelled in death. His remains were first housed in the National Memorial, where scientists tried to mummify him, but following the Velvet Revolution his corpse was removed and returned to his family. His current resting place is harder to locate, hidden away as it is in section five and sharing a mass grave with various other discredited party members.

Žižkov Tower

Mahlerovy sady, Prague 3 (242 418 784). Metro Jiřího z Poděbrad/tram 5, 9, 26. **Open** 11am-11pm daily. **Admission** 60 Kč; free under-5s. **No credit cards. Map** p333 C2.

The huge, thrusting, three-pillared television tower in Žižkov has long been dubbed the *Pražský pták*, or 'Prague Prick', by local fans. Seemingly modelled on a Soyuz rocket ready for blast-off, or maybe something out of *Thunderbirds*, it has been more of a hit with space-crazy visitors than with the locals. The tower also made a guest appearance in *Blade II*. It was planned under the communists (who tore up part of the adjacent Jewish Cemetery to make room for it), completed early in 1989, and no sooner started operating in 1990 than it came under attack from nearby residents who claimed it was guilty of, among other things, jamming foreign radio waves and giving their children cancer. You can take a lift up to the eighth-floor viewing platform or have a drink in the fifth-floor café, but in many ways standing at the base and looking up the 216m (709ft) of grey polished steel is even more scary. More than 20 TV channels broadcast from behind the white plastic shielding that defends against the elements. Transmitters lower down deal with radio stations and emergency services. The tower is now the subject of public art, with several large black babies crawling on its exterior. The intriguing, rather disturbing *Miminka* are the work of Czech bad-boy artist and satirist David Černý.

Jižní Město & Háje

To the south and east of the city centre lies the wilderness of **Prague 4**. Though parts are very old and beautiful, the postcode has come to mean only one thing for Praguers: *paneláky*. Panelák is the Czech word for a tower block made from prefabricated concrete panels. These blocks sprouted throughout the 1960s and 1970s as a cheap solution to the post-war housing crisis. **Jižní Město**, or Southern Town, has the greatest concentration, housing 100,000 people, and now inspires Czech rap music polemics by its more youthful residents. There have been intermittent efforts to individualise the buildings with pastel exteriors, but this has only made the district look like a nightmarish toy town.

Háje, the last metro stop on the red Line C, is a good place to see the worst. Before 1989, Háje used to be known as Kosmonautů, a nod in the direction of the USSR, and a rather humorous sculpture of two cosmonauts is outside the metro station. **Galaxie** (Arkalycká 877, Háje, Prague 4, bookings 267 900 567, programme information 267 900 540, www.cinemacity.cz), Central Europe's first multiplex cinema and perhaps the only place in the world that sells pork-flavoured popcorn, is nearby, as is the popular swimming spot of **Hostivař Reservoir** (Prague 15; take tram Nos.22 or 26 to the end of the line), which is full of semi-clad sun-seekers all summer.

Eat, Drink, Shop

Restaurants	**136**
Cafés, Pubs & Bars	**162**
Shops & Services	**177**

Features

The best Restaurants	136
What's on the menu?	148
Still crazy Tommy Sjöö	157
The best Pubs	163
Shooters	166
Made into runts	172
The best Shops	178
Dressing for dark	186
Saps and gems	190
Powergifting	193

Kubista. *See p181.*

Restaurants

Ye olde Bohemian goes global.

Eating out in Prague is still a sport, but it's no longer the martial art it used to be. The experience can still be an adventure, however, owing mainly to pre-1989 habits in the service department that can offset even the finest cuisine. But even if it's not always smooth, the search for exciting victuals is far more rewarding than it used to be, thanks to a vastly expanded menu. The city's chefs are noticeably growing in confidence, while eating environs are becoming more distinct and conducive. Check out **La Scene**, **Mosaika** or **Monarch** for fine examples of places that make you feel both hungry and stylish the moment you walk in.

The best Restaurants

For celeb-spotting
Make the scene at **Hergetova Cihelna** (*see p143*) and **Siam-I-San** (*see p144*).

For dining with the city at your feet
Enjoy steaks and ravioli among the cliffs and roof gables at **Rio's Vyšehrad** (*see p159*) and **Cowboys** (*see p138*).

For indulgence
Allegro (*see p150*), **U Modré kachničky** (*see p148*) and **La Scene** (*see p147*) all dish the haute cuisine with elegance, making it look easy.

For intimacy
Aromi (*see p161*) and **Le Bistrot de Marlène** (*see p156*) serve it up in warm splendour.

For palatial dining
Palffy Palác (*see p139*) has culinary prowess to match its setting.

For riverside romance
Impress your date at **Kampa Park** (*see p143*), **Střelecký ostrov** (*see p143*) or **Hergetova Cihelna** (*see p143*).

For vegetarian
Radost FX Café (*see p159*), **Country Life** (*see p153*) and **Himalaya** (*see p157*) provide for those daring to defy Czech meat mania.

Of course, style itself is an ambiguous quality. If it has an essence, it probably lies in a distillation of multiple cultures and influences, something that the Czech Republic was denied under communism. But in the last decade an influx of returning émigrés and curious foreigners seems to have provided the critical mass necessary for a definite improvement in cuisine and service. Meanwhile, Prague still offers solid value and, even in the places not newly done over in ochre and red, a collection of incredible settings.

It's not that pizza served with ketchup has been banished, nor have the city's famously negligent waiters all suddenly snapped to attention (and learned to enjoy themselves). It's more like a momentum shift, led by eateries that combine the best of hearty Czech food with lighter, modernised fare. Take the hip and fun-loving **Cowboys**, for example, the latest project of established Prague restaurateur and hipster Nils Jebens. Or the lovely roast duck, eaten riverside al fresco at the **Museum Kampa**. All these add to beachheads already established, like the wood-fired Neapolitan pies at **Hergetova Cihelna** or fiery Thai at tiny **Siam Orchid**.

Then, of course, there's the classic, utterly unchanged neighbourhood pub, invariably serving pork knuckle, schnitzel (known here as *řízek*), beef in cream sauce (*svíčkova*), and endless cheap half-litres of Pilsener beer. These places are a working-class treat to be savoured, where you sit at communal tables, smoke hangs heavy in the air, and your waiter, after working a 12-hour shift, looks about to pass out. Be forewarned that most of these officially close their kitchens at 10pm and may well tell you at 9pm that no more food's available. Even that detail provides a blast from the past in this country, where the communists were recently polling at near 20 per cent. Frankly, this kind of old-school *hospoda* or *hostinec* is a national cultural treasure and one that looks set to long outlive the wave of absurdly haughty designer showcases of recent years.

A few genuine gems at the high end have proven their staying power with elegant, imaginative gusto, such as **Aromi**, **Opera Garden**, the Four Season's **Allegro**, the beloved French **Le Bistrot de Marlène** and the wine bar **Le Terroir**. Prague's venturesome expat community has further

Search for the Philosopher's Stone at **Alchymist**. *See p139.*

enriched the mix with satisfying brunches, bagel shops and Sonoran Mexican food at places like **Radost FX**, the ever-popular **Bohemia Bagel** and **Picante**, a cheap, all-night fast food joint that nevertheless serves the best Mexican in town (for Mex in a more relaxed setting, try **Banditos**). Even vegetarians in this meat-loving town have reasonable options at **Himilaya**, **Country Life** and **Radost FX**.

TIPPING AND ETIQUETTE

At pubs and beerhalls, tables are often shared with other patrons who, like you, should ask '*Je tu volno?*' ('Is it free?') and may also wish each other '*dobrou chuť*' before tucking in. Prague dines with a relaxed dress code and reservations are necessary at only the new generation of upscale spots. Many waiters still record your tab on a slip of paper, which translates at leaving time into a bill. Pay the staff member with the folding wallet in his or her waistband, not your waiter (the phrase '*Zaplatím, prosím*' means 'May I pay, please?'). A small cover charge and extra charges for milk, bread and the ubiquitous and frightful accordion music are still in practice at many pubs, as is tipping by rounding the bill up to the nearest 10 Kč. At nicer places, 10-15 per cent tips have become the rule. While you should have little trouble making a phone reservation in English at modern establishments, just about everywhere else it might be easier to book in person.

Hradčany

Asian

Malý Buddha

Úvoz 46, Prague 6 (220 513 894). Metro Malostranská, then tram 22, 23. **Open** 1-10.30pm Tue-Sun. **Main courses** 100-250 Kč. **No credit cards. Map** p326 B4 ①

The 'Little Buddha' is a teahouse with a difference: great vegetarian spring rolls and noodle dishes go hand in hand with the dozens of teas that are brewed by the laid-back owner, who's always on hand. Sit in candlelight and inhale whiffs of incense with your eggrolls. Mellow doesn't half describe it. There's a no smoking shrine at the back.

Czech

U Císařů

Loretánská 5, Prague 6 (220 519 484/www.ucisaru.cz). Metro Malostranská, then tram 22, 23. **Open** 11am-midnight daily. **Main courses** 200-300 Kč. **No credit cards. Map** p326 C3 ②

This is another favoured location for traditional Czech cuisine that's within a short walk of Prague Castle. At the Emperor's delivers platters of smoked meats, the potato-thyme soup is excellent and the beer is as fine as any you'll find around.

U Ševce Matouše

Loretánské náměstí 4, Prague 6 (220 514 536). Metro Malostranská, then tram 22, 23. **Open** 11am-11pm daily. **Main courses** 180-280 Kč. **Credit** AmEx, MC, V. **Map** p326 B3 ③

Kampa Park. *See p143.*

The classic steakhouse, Czech style, with done to order tenderloins in traditional sauces such as green peppercorns or mushrooms. A short walk east of Prague Castle and in a cosy former shoemaker's workshop (where it was once possible to get your boots repaired while lunching). Reasonable prices given the prime location.

Malá Strana/Smíchov

Americas

Bohemia Bagel

Újezd 16, Prague 1 (257 310 694/www.bohemia bagel.cz). Tram 6, 9, 12, 22, 23. **Open** 7am-10pm Mon-Fri; 8am-10pm Sat, Sun. **Main courses** 180-280 Kč. **No credit cards. Map** p327 F6

The owners of U Malého Glena, the jazz club (*see p239*), created the republic's first true bagel café and it's been packed ever since. Free coffee refills, another breakthrough idea in Prague, help wash down the fresh muffins, breakfast bagels and bagel sandwiches. There's also usually something of interest – courses, places to rent, exhibitions – on the bulletin board. **Other locations**: Masná 2, Staré Město, Prague 1 (224 812 560).

Cowboys

Nerudova 40, Prague 1 (800 152 672/www.kampa group.com). Metro Malostranská/tram 12, 22, 23. **Open** noon-2am Mon-Thur, Sun; noon-3am Fri, Sat. **Main courses** 250-500 Kč. **Credit** AmEx, MC, V. **Map** p326 D3

You might not necessarily believe it, when you see the Stetsons and kinky leather vests in abundance and hottie servers, but Cowboys is actually a great deal classier than the restaurant that previously inhabited this labyrinth of brick cellars. For the location, service and T-bones, not to mention live folk rock, courtesy of crooner Jamie Marshall, it's incredible value, and it's all topped off by a terrace with the most enviable views of the city in this district.

Asian

Nagoya

Stroupežnického 23, Smíchov (251 511 724/www. nagoya.cz). Metro Anděl/tram 6, 7, 9, 10, 12, 14, 20. **Open** noon-3pm, 5-11pm Mon, Wed-Sun. **Main courses** 200-450 Kč. **Credit** AmEx.

Prague's gone Nippon mad. However, this is one foodstuff that costs more in the Czech Republic than it does in London or New York, so beware. If you shell out, we recommend the nagiri and maki.

Balkan

Gitanes

Tržiště 7, Prague 1 (257 530 163/www.gitanes.cz). Metro Malostranská. **Open** noon-midnight daily. **Main courses** 150-290 Kč. **Credit** MC, V. **Map** p327 E4

A bracing taste of spice in traditional, safe Central Europe, this two-room place just off the district's main square serves Yugoslavian favourites like sheep's cheese, stuffed peppers, home-made bread with paprika milk-fat spread, and hearty red wine. Warm service, gingham and doilies give you the feeling you're visiting your Balkan granny's house, only with much cooler music – emanating from speakers hidden in the birdcages. Don't miss the private table available for curtained-off dalliances.

Continental

Alchymist
Hellichova 4, Prague 1 (257 312 518). Metro Malostranská/tram 6, 12, 20. **Open** noon-3pm, 7-11pm daily. **Main courses** 900-1,400 Kč. **Credit** AmEx, MC, V. **Map** p327 F5 ❼
Billed in the local press as 'Baroque pimp', this decorator's orgy – replete with red velvet, alchemical symbols, statues and gilt mirrors – nevertheless does credible French and continental: duck with roast apples and celery or a killer saffron risotto, plus crème brûlée with pistachio. Wine is frankly expensive, but dinner won't be soon forgotten. **Photo** p137.

Bar Bar
Všehrdova 17, Prague 1 (257 312 246/www.bar-bar.cz). Tram 12, 22, 23. **Open** 11am-midnight Mon-Thur, Sun; 11am-2am Fri, Sat. **Main courses** 150-250 Kč. **Credit** MC, V. **Map** p327 F6 ❽
It takes some effort to find Bar Bar, tucked away as it is on a twisty, picturesque Malá Strana backstreet. But the local crowds that will greet you show that the orienteering was effort well spent. The open sandwiches, salads and grill dishes will pass but the savoury crêpes are the real highlight. English-style dessert pancakes with lemon and sugar are priced at a pittance. Waiters are cool and reasonably flexible about substitutions.

C'est la Vie
Říční 1, Prague 1 (721 158 403/www.cestlavie.cz). Tram 12, 22, 23. **Open** 11.30am-1am daily. **Main courses** 300-1,200 Kč. **Credit** AmEx, MC, V. **Map** p327 G6 ❾
Self-billed as a 'trendy eaterie for those who want to be in', this upscale place is geared toward Czuppies. But it may be worth cutting through the attitude for a river embankment table, baked butterfish with mushroom risotto or filet mignon with a cabernet. Service doesn't keep up with the ambitious menu, though.

Cukrkávalimonáda
Lázeňská 7, Prague 1 (257 530 628). Metro Malostranská/tram 12, 22. **Open** 8.30am-8pm daily. **Main courses** 100-300 Kč. **No credit cards. Map** p327 F4 ❿
A hip, yet homely café a block off the main tourist drag leading from Charles Bridge that lets you look out on to a quiet corner of Maltézské náměstí while sipping chardonnay or tucking into one of the daily specials of chicken roulades with heaps of mashed potatoes. Expect tall lattes, casually alert service, designer benches, hanging greenery and slick magazines for leafing through.

David
Tržiště 21, Prague 1 (257 533 109/www.restaurant-david.cz). Metro Malostranská/tram 12, 22, 23. **Open** 11.30am-11pm daily. **Main courses** 400-1,450 Kč. **Credit** AmEx, MC, V. **Map** p327 E4 ⓫
It seems there's nothing touring rock stars like more than a discreet, family-run dining room that knows how to pamper the hungry megastar. The strong suit is definitive Bohemian classics like roast duck with red and white sauerkraut or rabbit fillet with spinach leaves and herb sauce. Booking essential.

Hungarian Grotto
Tomášská 12, Prague 1 (257 532 344/www.hungarian-grotto.cz). Metro Malostranská/tram 12, 22, 23. **Open** 11:30am-11.30pm daily. **Main courses** 250-450 Kč. **Credit** AmEx, MC, V. **Map** p327 F3 ⓬
Much of Czech cooking is derived from Hungarian sources, but only old Magyar places like this are likely to use sufficiently punchy paprika. Robust meat-and-potatoes cuisine straight from Budapest features stuffed mushrooms, tender sirloin and, of course, Egri bikaver red wine.

Pálffy Palác
Valdštejnská 14, Prague 1 (257 530 522/www.palffy.cz). Metro Malostranská/tram 12, 22, 23. **Open** 11am-11pm daily. **Main courses** 350-850 Kč. **Credit** AmEx, MC, V. **Map** p327 F2 ⓭
A supper on the terrace of this neglected baroque-palace-cum-classical-music academy is certainly something to remember in your old age. The owner, Prague clubbing mogul Roman Řezníček, assures top drawer cuisine like quail confit and roebuck marinated in honey and juniper. The crêpes and salads are generous and delicate affairs.

U Malířů
Maltézské náměstí 11, Prague 1 (257 530 000/ www.umaliru.cz). Tram 12, 22, 23. **Open** 11.30am-11.30pm daily. **Main courses** 500-2,250 Kč. **Credit** AmEx, MC, V. **Map** p327 F4 ⓮
Still one of Prague's most expensive restaurants – which is saying something these days – this quaint 16th-century house with original painted ceilings specialises in authentic, quality French cuisine and a clientele that dines to impress. Pâté with Sauternes or sea bass, lobster, lamb and squab. A bottle will double the cost of a meal.

U Maltézských rytířů
Prokopská 10, Prague 1 (257 533 666/www.umaltezskychrytiru.cz). Tram 12, 22, 23. **Open** 11am-11pm daily. **Main courses** 400-1,250 Kč. **Credit** AmEx, MC, V. **Map** p327 F4 ⓯
The Knights of Malta once served as an inn for the crusader monks. Now a restaurant has set up in the candlelit, Gothic cellar and a good one at that, with a fine venison châteaubriand. Mrs Černíková, whose family runs the place, does a nightly narration on the history of the house, then harasses you to eat the incredible strudel. Booking essential.

U Patrona

Dražického náměstí 4, Prague 1 (257 530 725/ www.upatrona.cz). Metro Malostranská/tram 12, 22, 23. **Open** 10am-10pm daily. **Main courses** 350-1,200 Kč. **Credit** AmEx, MC, V. **Map** p327 G4 ⓰
An oasis of quality in an area dominated by naff souvenir shops. Fine dining and delicate conceptions of Czech game classics at just a few tables.

U Zlaté studně

U Zlaté studně 166, Prague 1 (257 533 322/www. zlatastudna.cz). Metro Malostranská/tram 12, 22, 23. **Open** 11am-midnight daily. **Main courses** 400-1,250 Kč. **Credit** AmEx, MC, V. **Map** p327 F2 ⓱
In mild weather, stopping here is the perfect reward for tramping about Prague Castle – you can walk right in from the castle gardens. Now run by the management of the standard-setting Aria Hotel (*see p47*), At the Golden Well offers spectacular views of the Malá Strana district below, sharp service and a menu that starts off with decadent choices like duck livers marinated in armagnac.

Czech

Baráčnická rychta

Tržiště 23, Prague 1 (257 532 461/www.baracnicka rychta.cz). Metro Malostranská/tram 12, 22, 23.

Open noon-11.30pm Mon-Sat; 11.30am-9pm Sun. **Main courses** 180-300 Kč. **No credit cards**. **Map** p327 E4 ⓲
Right out of Jan Neruda's *Prague Tales*, this 19th-century hall is split into two: a small beerhall frequented by hardcore *pivo* drinkers, both of the student and middle-aged variety, and a downstairs music hall that increasingly often these days features live gigs by local rock hopefuls. Obvious tourists may catch the occasional scowl, but in general it is a friendly place.

Na Verandách

Nádražní 84, Smíchov, Prague 1 (257 191 111/ www.ppivovary.cz). Metro Anděl/tram 12, 20. **Open** 11am-midnight daily. **Main courses** 150-300 Kč. **Credit** AmEx, MC, V.
In the mighty Staropramen brewery is hidden a trad Czech restaurant that's about the district's best at combining modern, Western-style service with great pub grub, like smoked meat dumplings, and a brew as well tapped as you'll find in Bohemia.

Petřínské Terasy

Seminářská zahrada 13, Prague 1 (257 320 688/ www.petrinsketerasy.cz). Metro Malostranská/tram 12, 22, 23. **Open** noon-11pm Mon-Fri; 11am-11pm Sat, Sun. **Main courses** 250-550 Kč. **No credit cards**. **Map** p326 D5 ⓳

Everything gleams at **La Scene**, the place to be for lamb lovers. *See p147.*

Nostress. *See p147.*

One of two tourist traps on Petřín Hill, the Petřín Terraces offers exquisite views of Prague Castle and the city, unfortunately at the price of expensive Krušovice and indifferent service.

U Karlova mostu

Na Kampě 15, Prague 1 (257 531 430/www. nakampe15.cz). Metro Malostranská/tram 12, 22. **Open** 11am-11pm daily. **Main courses** 90-200 Kč. **Credit** AmEx, DC, MC, V. **Map** p327 G5 ⑳
What's going on? An unpretentious pub-restaurant serving potato-thyme soup and *topinka* (Czech fried toast with raw garlic) this close to Charles Bridge? Just don't tell the package tourists – and mind that you don't accidentally wind up in the pricey restaurant at this same address. Swing around the corner to the pub with the mustard walls for the real thing. The scattering of outdoor tables on the edge of Kampa park is among the perks.

U Sedmi Švábů

Jánský vršek 14, Prague 1 (257 531 455). Metro Malostranská/tram 12, 22, 23. **Open** 11am-11pm daily; kitchen closes at 10pm. **Main courses** 150-250 Kč. **Credit** AmEx, MC, V. **Map** p326 D3 ㉑
A *krčma*, or Czech medieval tavern, the Seven Swabians is a trippy, if borderline tacky, experience, with occasional live troubadour music, traditional sweet honey liqueur and salty platters of pork knuckle. Only in Prague.

Mediterranean

Café El Centro

Maltézské náměstí 9, Prague 1 (257 533 343/ www.elcentro.cz). Metro Malostranská/tram 12, 22, 23. **Open** noon-midnight daily. **Main courses** 150-280 Kč. **No credit cards. Map** p327 F4 ㉒
An easily overlooked Malá Strana bar just a block off the main square that specialises in mambo soundtracks and tropical cocktails. Efforts to expand into a full restaurant specialising in paella aren't winning over the daiquiri lovers, but the postage-stamp patio at the rear is a boon.

Il Giardino

Mozartova 1, Smíchov (257 154 262/www.moven pick-prague.com). Metro Anděl/tram 4, 7, 9. **Open** 5.15am-10.30am, noon-11pm daily. **Main courses** 350-1,200 Kč. **Credit** AmEx, MC, V.
The Mövenpick's international chefs, top-class reputation, plus family-friendly service and fine views complement the satisfactory Mediterranean cuisine. Excellent lunch specials and swift service (served in 20 minutes with free parking) appeal to the business crowd. The saltimbocca alla romana and bouillabaisse have all won cheers.

Square

Malostranské náměstí 5, Prague 1 (257 532 109/ reservations 800 152 672/www.kampagroup.com). Metro Malostranská/tram 12, 22, 23. **Open** 8am-1am daily. **Main courses** 250-750 Kč. **Credit** AmEx, MC, V. **Map** p327 F3 ㉓

Square it isn't. But it is a celebration of cool, modern design that features running waterfalls and padded, creamy walls. And, naturally, the modish design extends to the fine food. Expect to see items like the house speciality, delicious high-concept Spanish tapas, and nouvelle seafood delights such as tiger prawns and squid fritters.

Střelecký ostrov

Střelecký ostrov 336, Prague 1 (224 934 028/ www.streleckyostrov.cz). Metro Národní třída, then tram 6, 9, 22, 23. **Open** 11am-1am daily. **Main courses** 250-450 Kč. **Credit** MC, V. **Map** p327 H6 ㉔
Sitting on a lovely Vltava river island in the centre of town, this terraced spot caters to the casual with decent pizzas but also manages good wines and a gourmet menu. Previous endeavours at this location have been ruined by floods but the current management is banking on better luck.

Seafood

Café Savoy

Zborovská 68, Smíchov, Prague 5 (251 511 690/ www.cafesavoy.cz). Tram 6, 9, 12, 22. **Open** 11am-10pm Mon-Sat. **Main courses** 300-600 Kč. **Credit** AmEx, MC, V.
Just out of the way enough to merit a walk across the Most Legii from Staré Město, Café Savoy is a bright, high-ceilinged 19th-century café, now streamlined and elegant and stocked with an excellent menu of fresh mussels, courtesy of its new owner, the seafood importer across the street. Classy service and a fashionable crowd.

Kampa Park

Na Kampě 8b, Prague 1 (257 532 685/www. kampagroup.com). Metro Malostranská/tram 12, 22, 23. **Open** 11.30am-1am daily; kitchen closes at 11pm. **Main courses** 280-600 Kč. **Credit** AmEx, MC, V. **Map** p327 H4 ㉕
The location's arguably the finest in Prague – in the shadow of Charles Bridge with a beautiful riverside terrace. Al fresco dining on oysters or Thai tuna steak in summer complements a slick bar-room scene inside, which dependably acts as a celeb lightning rod – seems you can't shoot a feature film in Prague without wrapping at Kampa Park. **Photo** p138.

World

Hergetova Cihelna

Cihelna 2b, Prague 1 (257 535 534/reservations 800 152 692/www.kampagroup.com). Metro Malostranská/tram 12, 22, 23. **Open** 11.30am-midnight daily. **Main courses** 250-450 Kč. **Credit** AmEx, MC, V. **Map** p327 H4 ㉖
Impressive value and creative culinary efforts, which are both signature qualities of owner Nils Jebens, make Hergetova Cihelna a hot reservation even in winter. The obsession with celebs gathering in the upstairs bar is a perfect insight into what

makes Prague tick today, but is less intense than at Jebens' A-list eaterie Kampa Park (*see above*) just next door. Great Belgian ales with killer casual chow plus knock-out riverside tables, complete with cosy blankets for when it's chilly.

Staré Město

Americas

Brasiliero
U Radnice 8, Prague 1 (224 234 474/www.ambi.cz). *Metro Staroměstská/tram 17, 18.* **Open** 11am-midnight daily. **Main courses** 180-450 Kč. **Credit** AmEx, MC, V. **Map** p328 L4 ❷
Part of the local Ambiente group, Brasiliero specialises in hearty Brazilian butchery, with enough chops and fillets to stop any healthy heart. A hit.

Red Hot & Blues
Jakubská 12, Prague 1 (222 314 639). *Metro Náměstí Republiky/tram 5, 14, 26.* **Open** 9am-11pm daily. **Main courses** 120-230 Kč. **Credit** AmEx, MC, V. **Map** p329 N3 ❷
Perhaps best on Sunday mornings for brunch on the patio (assuming you're not trumped by a stag party), Red Hot & Blues, a requisite expat institution, brought Cajun and heaping Mexican platters to Bohemia. With the mood-proviking blues player on a stool by night, and the patio now conveniently heated and enclosed for winter, the restaurant is reliable and relaxed. You're best off avoiding the overpriced drink specials.

Asian

Orange Moon
Rámová 5, Prague 1 (222 325 119/www.orange moon.cz). *Metro Náměstí Republiky/tram 5, 8, 14.* **Open** 11.30am-11.30pm daily. **Main courses** 180-350 Kč. **Credit** AmEx, MC, V. **Map** p328 M2 ❷
Orange Moon offers Thai, Burmese and Indian food in a warm, unpretentious, well-lit cellar space. Eager and efficient servers bring on the curries and Czech beer, a divine combination as it turns out. The restaurant entrance is easy to miss, so just follow the voices of customers telling their Prague tales.

Red Fish
Betlémská 9, Prague 1 (222 220 716/www. redfish.cz). *Metro Staroměstská/tram 17, 18.* **Open** 11.30am-midnight daily. **Main courses** 180-450 Kč. **Credit** AmEx, MC, V. **Map** p328 K5 ❷
The best-priced sushi in town with delightful nagiri and zesty noodles in a setting of comfy wicker chairs, picture windows and pink walls. On a street that's hidden off Betlémské náměstí, it's hard to fault – just mind the tempura Czech veggies.

Restaurance po Sečuánsku
Národní třída 25, Prague 1 (221 085 331). **Open** 10am-11pm daily. **Main courses** 59-220 Kč. **No credit cards. Map** p328 K6 ❷

Tucked away in the Palác metro shopping passage, this is a handy, clean, bright option for Chinese food, with a vast list of *rychlé*, or quick, items for 59 Kč. Kung pao, sweet-and-sour chicken and fried rice all come in these light sizes.

Siam-I-San
Valentinská 11, Prague 1 (224 814 099). *Metro Staroměstská/tram 17, 18.* **Open** 10am-11pm daily. **Main courses** 250-650 Kč. **Credit** AmEx, MC, V. **Map** p328 K3 ❷
Chic Thai, above a designer glassware shop, with the biggest selection of fiery South-east Asian appetisers in town. A favourite among well-heeled expats.

Continental

Bellevue
Smetanovo nábřeži 18, Prague 1 (222 221 438/ www.pfd.cz). *Metro Národní třída/tram 6, 9, 18, 22, 23.* **Open** noon-3pm, 5.30-11pm Mon-Sat; 11am-3.30pm, 7-11pm Sun. **Main courses** 350-1,250 Kč. **Credit** AmEx, MC, V. **Map** p328 J6 ❸
Veal loin in black truffle sauce and fallow venison in juniper reduction go mighty well with Sunday jazz brunch. Formal and traditional but with wonderful views of Prague Castle. Booking essential.

DeBrug
Masná 5, Prague 1 (224 819 283). *Metro Náměstí Republiky/tram 5, 8.* **Open** noon-2am daily. **Main courses** 250-550 Kč. **Credit** AmEx, MC, V. **Map** p329 N3 ❸
First Stella Artois infiltrated Czech beer heaven, now Belgian bistros are spreading through the city. Where will it end? Still, great frites and moules, no getting around that, and a great-looking crowd of international types. Above-average service and modern decor go with the bivalves.

Klub Architektů
Betlémské náměstí 5a, Prague 1 (224 401 214/ www.klubarchitektu.com). *Metro Národní třída/ tram 6, 9, 18, 22, 23.* **Open** 11.30am-midnight daily. **Main courses** 120-350 Kč. **Credit** AmEx, MC, V. **Map** p328 K4 ❸
Down in the cellar of an architecture and design gallery next door to the Bethlehem Chapel (*see p108*) you'll find this great restaurant. At Klub Architektů the value is excellent, the cuisine credible and creative European, the waiters are gracious and friendly, and the speed of service is just right.

La Provence
Štupartská 9, Prague 1 (222 324 801/reservations 800 152 672/www.kampagroup.com). *Metro Náměstí Republiky/tram 5, 8, 14.* **Open** 11am-11pm daily. **Main courses** 250-650 Kč. **Credit** AmEx, MC, V. **Map** p328 M4 ❸
Newly taken over by the Czech Republic's answer to Terence Conran, Nils Jebens, La Provence is a comfortable rural French eaterie that now does fine foie gras, tasty tiger prawns, roast duck and monkfish. This is a good place for a treat.

U Medvídků. *See p148.*

Eat, Drink, Shop

La Scene

U Milosrdných 6, Prague 1 (222 312 677). Metro Staroměstská/tram 17, 18. **Open** noon-2pm, 7pm-midnight Mon-Fri; 7pm-midnight Sat. **Main courses** 280-580 Kč. **Credit** AmEx, MC, V. **Map** p328 L2 ③⑦
A quiet, sleek lounge wine bar with pan-fried foie gras and rhubarb purée, and some of the best lamb in town, served with gingerbread crust. The modern interior complements the 13th-century convent and hall of the National Gallery. **Photo** p141.

La Veranda

Elišky Krásnohorské 2, Prague 1 (224 814 733/ www.laveranda.cz). Metro Staroměstská/tram 17, 18. **Open** noon-midnight Mon-Sat; noon-10pm Sun. **Main courses** 490-1,600 Kč. **Credit** AmEx, MC, V. **Map** p328 L2 ③⑧
A très modern gustatory sanctuary for the newly rich that lays on garlic foam fish ragout soup along with classic old roast duck with thyme. It's also still affordable, if a bit much, what with the minimalist designer decor and servers who scrape and fawn.

Le Café Colonial

Široká 6, Prague 1 (224 818 322). Metro Staroměstská/tram 17, 18. **Open** 10am-midnight daily. **Main courses** 350-1,250 Kč. **Credit** AmEx, MC, V. **Map** p328 K3 ③⑨
An airy restaurant, Le Café Colonial comes with teak accents, delicious miniature quiches, delicate pork and delightful salads. There's more formal dining on the left side in a darker setting, while a veranda with rattan furniture and Matisse colour tones fills out the right side. Resolutely French.

Nostress

Dušní 10, Prague 1 (222 317 004/www. nostress.cz). Metro Staroměstská/tram 17, 18. **Open** 8am-11pm Mon-Fri; 10am-11pm Sat, Sun. **Main courses** 250-550 Kč. **Credit** AmEx, MC, V. **Map** p328 L3 ④⓪
Nostress is an elegant café-cum-lifestyle shop that encourages patrons to have a good look around at the wrought-iron furnishing and hanging lamps. All are, like your espresso and foie gras, for sale. Couches and tables could be a bit much for hand luggage but much of the good stuff is portable and handmade locally. A great spot for lunch. **Photo** p142.

Století

Karolíny Světlé 21, Prague 1 (222 220 008/ www.stoleti.cz). Metro Národní třída/tram 6, 9, 18, 22, 23. **Open** noon-midnight daily. **Main courses** 180-400 Kč. **Credit** AmEx, MC, V. **Map** p328 J6 ④①
Comfortable, capable and imaginative, Století does not waste effort on empty flourishes, but just delivers the goods without fuss. A blue cheese, pear and almond salad named after Valentino, or a spinach soufflé go with the old world decor and swift service.

V Zátiší

Liliová 1, Betlémské náměstí, Staré Město, Prague 1 (222 221 155/www.pfd.cz). Metro Národní třída/ tram 6, 9, 18, 22, 23. **Open** noon-3pm, 5.30-11pm daily. **Main courses** 400-600 Kč. **Credit** AmEx, MC, V. **Map** p328 K5 ④②
Celebs and foodies are often spied slipping into an old townhouse on a narrow lane, apparently seduced by the call of delicate gourmet risottos, sashimi, monk-fish and saffron sauce, venison with rosehip sauce or a maple and herb-crusted rack of New Zealand lamb. Owned by the management of Bellevue (*see p144*), this is one of the city's most elegant dining rooms with consistently bold culinary inspirations and some fine French vintages. Stops short of heaven, however, with unreliable service, always an issue in Prague (sigh), and enthusiastic wine inflation – stick to the imports: at least these are arguably worth the price.

Czech

DaMúza

Řetězová 10, Staré Město, Prague 1 (222 221 749/ www.damuza.cz). Metro Staroměstská/tram 17, 18. **Open** 11am-12.30am daily. **Main courses** 150-300 Kč. **Credit** AmEx, MC, V. **Map** p328 K5 ④③
DaMúza is the official café of the Academy of Dramatic Arts, whose Czech acronym is contained in the restaurant's name. There are no major awards due for the predictable fare, but the garlic soups and schnitzels are fine examples of the form. Six kinds of beer are on tap, as are fairly substantial steaks – an unusual option for a Prague café. Schedules on the tables list the irregular theatre pieces and concerts performed in the cellar. Nice glass-roofed garden.

Kolkovna

V Kolkovně 8, Prague 1 (224 819 701/www. kolkovna.cz). Metro Staroměstská/tram 17, 18. **Open** 9am-midnight daily. **Main courses** 180-450 Kč. **Credit** AmEx, MC, V. **Map** p328 L3 ④④
An art nouveau interior and trad pub grub like potato pancakes and beer-basted goulash attract the bright and beautiful local patrons to a re-creation of old Prague. And it's licensed by the brewery Pilsner Urquell, so you know the beer will be good.

Pivnice u Pivrnce

Maiselova 3, Josefov, Prague 1 (222 329 404). Metro Náměstí Republiky/tram 5, 8, 14. **Open** 11am-midnight daily; kitchen closes at 11.30pm. **Main courses** 120-230 Kč. **Credit** MC, V. **Map** p328 K3 ④⑤
Rough, ready and looking set to stare down the next century unchanged, this pub prides itself on traditional Czech pork and dumplings with above-average presentation. *Svíčková* (beef in lemon cream sauce), duck with sauerkraut and walls covered with crude cartoons guaranteed to offend. Radegast here is well tapped and nicely priced.

U Bakaláře

Celetná 13, Prague 1 (224 817 369/www.ubakalare. euweb.cz). Metro Náměstí Republiky/tram 5, 8, 14. **Open** 9am-7pm Mon-Fri; 11am-7pm Sat, Sun. **Main courses** 40-70 Kč. **No credit cards.** **Map** p328 M4 ④⑥

Eat, Drink, Shop

What's on the menu?

English menus are common at most Czech restaurants and pubs these days – and most even have the same prices as the Czech versions. When visiting an old-school pub or eatery, however, it's handy to know that there are two categories of main dishes: *minutky*, cooked to order (which may take ages), and *hotová jídla*, ready-to-serve fare. The usual accompaniments to these dishes are rice, potatoes or the fried béchamel dough known as *krokety*, all of which should be ordered separately. When dining in pubs, the closest thing served to fresh vegetables is often *obloha*, which is a garnish of pickles, or a tomato on a single leaf of cabbage. Tasty appetisers to try are Prague ham with horseradish or rich soups (*polévka*), while a dessert staple is *palačinky*, filled pancakes.

Meals (*jídla*)

snídaně breakfast; **oběd** lunch; **večeře** dinner.

Preparation (*příprava*)

bez masa/bezmasá jídla without meat; **čerstvé** fresh; **domácí** home-made; **dušené** steamed; **grilované** grilled; **míchaný** mixed;

A life-saver for nearby Charles University students, this Staré Město lunch buffet is a stalwart example of that pre-revolutionary classic, the workers' cafeteria. Situated across the street from one of the university colleges, U Bakaláře is still an excellent standby for a quick, cheap toasted sandwich, savoury pancake or soup when you need to refuel for sightseeing. You'll find communal seating, friendly-ish service and far too much salt in everything.

U Medvídků

*Na Perštýně 7, Prague 1 (224 211 916/www.
umedvidku.cz). Metro Národní třída/tram 6, 9, 18,
22, 23.* **Open** 11am-11pm Mon-Sat; 11am-10pm Sun.
Main courses 150-350 Kč. **Credit** AmEx, MC, V.
Map p328 K6 ⑰

Five centuries of cred as a beerhall make the Little Bears a mecca for Budvar drinkers. The menu is elevated pub grub, with pork in plum sauce and fillets in dark beer reduction. **Photo** p145.

U Modré kachničky

*Michalská 16, Prague 1 (224 213 418/www.
umodrekachnicky.cz). Metro Staroměstská/tram
6, 9, 18, 22, 23.* **Open** 11.30am-11.30pm daily.
Main courses 350-750 Kč. **Credit** AmEx, MC, V.
Map p328 L5 ㊼

One of the most successful little dining rooms since the Velvet Revolution might have the feel of a granny's front room, but food is modern, boasting classics such as roast duck with pears and boar steak.

U Radnice

*U Radnice 2, Prague 1 (224 228 136). Metro
Staroměstská/tram 17, 18.* **Open** 11am-midnight
daily. **Main courses** 50-100 Kč. **Credit** AmEx, DC,
MC, V. **Map** p328 L4 ㊾

U Radnice is one of the last places around Old Town Square with trad food and prices meant for the locals. The tasty Czech specialities such as goulash or beef in cream sauce go for a pittance. Alas, a recent restoration cleaned it up a bit too much, but the communal tables still create a comfy pub atmosphere.

U Sádlů

*Klimentská 2, Prague 1 (224 813 874/www.usadlu.cz).
Metro Náměstí Republiky/tram 5, 8, 14.* **Open** 11am-
1am Mon-Sat; noon-midnight Sun. **Main courses**
180-450 Kč. **Credit** MC, V. **Map** p329 N2 ㊿

OK, it's medieval kitsch – but efficient, tasty and affordable medieval kitsch. A good laugh on a Friday night while having a mead with pepper steak or boar. Reading the illuminated menu by torchlight can be a challenge but there is nice armour in the bar.

Eat, Drink, Shop

na roštu roasted; **pečené** baked; **plněné** stuffed; **smažené** fried; **špíz** grilled on a skewer; **uzené** smoked; **vařené** boiled.

Basics (*základní*)

chléb bread; **cukr** sugar; **drůbež** poultry; **karbanátek** patty of unspecified content; **máslo** butter; **maso** meat; **ocet** vinegar; **olej** oil; **omáčka** sauce; **ovoce** fruit; **pepř** pepper; **rohlík** roll; **ryby** fish; **smetana** cream; **sůl** salt; **sýr** cheese; **vejce** eggs; **zelenina** vegetables.

Drinks (*nápoje*)

čaj tea; **káva** coffee; **mléko** milk; **pivo** beer; **pomerančový džus** orange juice; **sodovka** soda; **víno** wine; **voda** water.

Appetisers (*předkrmy*)

boršč Russian beetroot soup (borscht); **chlebíček** meat open-sandwich; **hovězí vývar**

beef broth; **kaviár** caviar; **paštika** pâté; **polévka** soup; **uzený losos** smoked salmon.

Meat (*maso*)

biftek beefsteak; **hovězí** beef; **játra** liver; **jehně** lamb; **jelení** venison; **kančí** boar; **klobása, párek, salám, vuřt** sausage; **králík** rabbit; **ledvinky** kidneys; **slanina** bacon; **srnčí** roebuck; ▶

French

Chez Marcel

Haštalská 12, Prague 1 (222 315 676). Metro Náměstí Republiky/tram 5, 8, 14. **Open** 8am-1am Mon-Sat; 9am-1am Sun. **Main courses** 200-350 Kč. **No credit cards. Map** p328 M2 ⑤

As thoroughly French as it gets, Chez Marcel invariably attracts a local crowd with its appealing brass plaques, copies of *Le Monde* and views on to a lovely Old Town Square. It also makes the deepest quiche in town, which makes a delicious accompaniment to the big baskets of crispy fries, particularly if dappled with Dijon mustard. By night it is a favourite rendezvous for clubbers, by day it offers highchairs (rare in Prague restaurants) and a non-smoking section.

Other locations: Brasserie le Molière, Americká 20, Vinohrady, Prague 2 (222 513 340).

Francouzská restaurace

Municipal House, Náměstí Republiky 5, Prague 1 (222 002 770/www.obecnidum.cz). Metro Náměstí Republiky/tram 5, 8, 14. **Open** noon-3pm, 6-11pm Mon-Sat; 11.30am-3pm, 6pm-midnight Sun. **Main courses** 250-500 Kč. **Credit** AmEx, DC, MC, V. **Map** p329 N4 ⑤

Though the service is heavy-handed and the cuisine passable, the aesthetics are impeccable. The city's pre-eminent shrine to art nouveau (and one of its top concert halls) was painstakingly renovated, including this space, which acts as its dining room. Service is laid on thick rather than well, as in many an upmarket Prague restaurant, but the rabbit in mustard sauce and the French cheese plate are both treats, and you could spend much more for the same fare elsewhere in Staré Město.

Indian

Rasoi Restaurant/Bombay Café

Dlouhá 13, Prague 1 (222 324 040/www.rasoi.cz). Metro Náměstí Republiky or Staroměstská/tram 5, 8, 14. **Open** *Restaurant* noon-11pm daily. *Bar* 5pm-4am Mon-Thur, Sun; 5pm-5am Fri, Sat. **Main courses** 280-480 Kč. **Credit** AmEx, MC, V. **Map** p328 M3 ⑤

Head to the cellar for tawa lamb tikka or a fiery vindaloo in Prague's tandoori haven. With pan-cooked regional specialities from the Subcontinent, and an appealingly twee dining room, it's also a bar at street level that packs in the Czuppies, drawn by the killer Bombay Gin Martinis.

What's on the menu? (continued)

šunka ham; **telecí** veal; **tlačenka** brawn; **vepřové** pork; **zvěřina** game.

Poultry & fish (*drůbež a ryby*)

bažant pheasant; **husa** goose; **kachna** duck; **kapr** carp; **křepelka** quail; **krocan** turkey; **kuře** chicken; **losos** salmon; **pstruh** trout; **úhoř** eel.

Main meals (*hlavní jídla*)

guláš goulash; **řízek** schnitzel; **sekaná** meat loaf; **smažený sýr** fried cheese; **svíčková** beef in cream sauce; **vepřová játra na cibulce** pig's liver stewed with onion; **vepřové koleno** pork knee; **vepřový řízek** fried breaded pork.

Side dishes (*přílohy*)

brambor potato; **bramborák** potato pancake; **bramborová kaše** mashed potatoes; **hranolky** chips; **kaše** mashed potatoes; **knedlíky** dumplings; **krokety** potato or béchamel dough croquettes; **obloha** small lettuce and tomato salad; **rýže** rice; **salát** salad; **šopský salát** cucumber, tomato and curd salad; **tatarská omáčka** tartar sauce; **zelí** cabbage.

Cheese (*sýr*)

balkán feta; **eidam** hard white cheese; **hermelín** soft, similar to bland brie; **Madeland**

Swiss cheese; **niva** blue cheese; **pivní sýr** beer-flavoured semi-soft cheese; **primátor** Swiss cheese; **tavený sýr** packaged cheese spread; **tvaroh** soft curd cheese.

Vegetables (*zelenina*)

česnek garlic; **chřest** asparagus; **cibule** onion(s); **čočka** lentils; **fazole** beans; **feferonky** chilli peppers; **hrášek** peas; **kukuřice** corn; **květák** cauliflower; **mrkev** carrot; **okurka** cucumber; **petržel** parsley; **rajčata** tomatoes; **salát** lettuce; **špenát** spinach; **žampiony** mushrooms; **zelí** cabbage.

Fruit (*ovoce*)

ananas pineapple; **banány** banana; **borůvky** blueberries; **broskev** peach; **hrozny** grapes; **hruška** pear; **jablko** apple; **jahody** strawberries; **jeřabina** rowanberries; **mandle** almonds; **meruňka** apricot; **ořechy** nuts; **pomeranč** orange; **rozinky** raisins; **švestky** plums; **třešně** cherries.

Desserts (*moučník*)

buchty traditional curd-filled cakes; **čokoláda** chocolate; **dort** layered cake; **koláč** cake with various fillings; **ovocné knedlíky** fruit dumplings; **palačinka** crêpe;

Jewish

King Solomon

Široká 8, Josefov, Prague 1 (224 818 752/www.kosher.cz). Metro Staroměstská/tram 17, 18. **Open** noon-11pm Mon-Thur, Sun (kitchen closes at 10.30pm); 11am-90mins before sundown Fri; open by request with reservation Sat. **Main courses** 200-500 Kč. **Credit** AmEx, MC, V. **Map** p328 L3 ⑤

Just a block from the Jewish Museum, King Solomon is a solid addition to the area: an upscale restaurant with Sabbath menu, Hebrew-speaking staff and certified kosher cuisine, unavailable elsewhere. With the atrium in the back, the long and authoritative Israeli wine list and austere sandstone-and-iron decor, it may be an odd setting for traditional comfort food like *gefilte* fish, chicken soup and carp with prunes, but Solomon's a hit with visiting groups.

Mediterranean

Allegro

Veleslavínova 2a, Prague 1 (221 426 880/www.four seasons.com/prague). Metro Staroměstská/tram 17, 18. **Open** 6.30am-11pm daily. **Main courses** 650-1,800 Kč. **Credit** AmEx, MC, V. **Map** p328 J4 ⑤

The Four Seasons flagship is chef Vito Mollica's shrine to Tuscan-meets-Czech. Veal fillet, pan-fried foie gras and truffles or monkfish saltimbocca have won deserved raves. The restaurant terrace looks out on Prague Castle across the Vltava.

Amici Miei

Vězeňská 5, Prague 1 (224 816 688/www.amicimiei.cz). Metro Staroměstská/tram 17, 18. **Open** 11am-11pm daily. **Main courses** 250-650 Kč. **Credit** AmEx, MC, V. **Map** p328 L2 ⑤

Amici Miei serves outstanding cuisine in a slightly overlit hall that's discreetly curtained off from the street. Come here and expect to receive tender veal scallops, simple, comforting tagliata with parmesan and rocket, and unusually warm and attentive service, plus an excellent wine list.

Don Giovanni

Karolíny Světlé 34, Prague 1 (222 222 060/www.dongiovanni.cz). Metro Staroměstská/tram 17, 18. **Open** 11am-midnight daily. **Main courses** 200-500 Kč. **Credit** AmEx, DC, MC, V. **Map** p328 J5 ⑤

An institution among Italian expats in Prague, Don Giovanni is a formal but understated eaterie that hosts some of the finest Italian dining in town.

pohár ice-cream sundae; **šlehačka** whipped cream; **zákusek** cake; **závin** strudel; **žemlovka** bread pudding with apples and cinnamon; **zmrzlina** ice-cream.

Useful phrases

May I see the menu? Mohu vidět jídelní lístek? **Do you have…?** Máte…? **I am a vegetarian** Jsem vegetarián/ vegetariánka (m/f). **How is it prepared?** Jak je to připravené? **Did you say 'beer cheese'?** Říkal jste 'pivní sýr'? **Wow, that smells!** Páni, to smrdí! **Can I have it without…?** Mohu mít bez…? **No ketchup on my pizza, please** Nechci kečup na pizzu, prosím. **I didn't order this** Neobjednal jsem si to. **How much longer will it be?** Jak dlouho to ještě bude? **The bill, please** Účet, prosím. **I can't eat this and I won't pay for it!** (use with extreme caution) Nedá se to jíst a nezaplatím to.

Takeaway/to go S sebou. **A beer, please** Pivo, prosím. **Two beers, please** Dvě piva, prosím. **Same again, please** Ještě jednou, prosím. **What'll you have?** Co si dáte? **Not for me, thanks** Pro mě ne, děkuji. **No ice, thanks** Bez ledu, děkuji. **He's really smashed** Je totálně namazaný.

Owner Avelino Sorgato oversees the home-made fettuccine, and pappardelle with boar and porcini mushrooms, and the Parma ham is the real stuff. Sample from one of over 30 grappas or stick to the noteworthy, if expensive, Italian wine list.

Kogo Pizzeria & Caffeteria

Havelská 27, Prague 1 (224 214 543/www.kogo.cz). Metro Můstek/tram 6, 9, 18, 22, 23. **Open** 8am-11pm daily. **Main courses** 250-550 Kč. **Credit** AmEx, MC, V. **Map** p328 M4 🚳
Scampi, bruschetta, bean soup and focaccia done fast, stylishly and surprisingly affordably, all served up by foxy Yugoslavian wait staff. What's more, despite the white linen tables it manages never to be stuffy. Nicely topped pizzas and tiramisu.
Other locations: Na přikopě 22, Nové Město, Prague 1 (224 214 543).

Maestro

Křížovnická 10, Prague 1 (222 320 498). Metro Staroměstská/tram 17, 18. **Open** 11am-11pm daily. **Main courses** 130-270 Kč. **Credit** AmEx, DC, MC, V. **Map** p328 J4 🚳
Maestro is much more than a neighbourhood pizza place. There are wicker chairs to sit in, there's baroque trompe l'œil on the walls and, yes, it boasts

proper wood-fired pizzas. The sauce made here is one of the best you'll find in town, service is generally on target and a meal here is still a fair bargain. The chicken cacciatore is definitely inspiring too.

Metamorphis

Malá Štupartská 5, Prague 1 (221 771 068/ www.metamorphis.cz). Metro Náměstí Republiky/ tram 5, 8, 14. **Open** 9am-midnight daily. **Main courses** 280-550 Kč. **Credit** AmEx, MC, V. **Map** p328 M3 🚳
Sedate and extremely capable, this family-run pasta café and pension has just one disadvantage: it's located directly on a main tourist route to Old Town Square. The cellar restaurant within is given a wonderful atmsphere by live jazz at night, though, and there is enough competition around these days that it's not necessarily overrun.

Modrá Zahrada

Národní třída 37, Prague 1 (224 239 055). Metro Národní třída/tram 6, 9, 17, 18, 22, 23. **Open** 11am-11.30pm daily. **Main courses** 120-280 Kč. **Credit** AmEx, MC, V. **Map** p328 L6 🚳
This is a popular and utilitarian pizza joint with a moody blue decor and art deco theme. At street level you'll find the futuristic bar, which has vanity tables

Eat, Drink, Shop

Eat, Drink, Shop

Aromi. *See p161*.

in the window for exhibitionists. One level up (the stairs are hidden at the back of the restaurant) the regulars gather from all around for cheap, pleasant pies – a safer bet than the salads, nearly all of which contain some kind of meat. It's a relaxing place and a bargain given the location. The service can be somewhat dizzy, though.

Other locations: Široká 114, Josefov, Prague 1 (222 327 171); Vinohradská 29, Vinohrady, Prague 2 (222 253 829).

Middle Eastern

Ariana
Rámová 6, Prague 1 (222 323 438/http://sweb.cz/ kabulrest/). Metro Náměstí Republiky/tram 5, 8. **Open** 11am-11pm daily. **Main courses** 220-460 Kč. **Credit** AmEx, MC, V. **Map** p328 M2 ⑫
A cosy little Afghan eatery with excellent, tender, spiced lamb and sumptuous vegetarian chalous. Familial service goes with the straightback chairs, rugs and brass lamps.

Byblos
Rybná 14, Prague 1 (221 842 121). Metro Náměstí Republiky/tram 5, 8, 14. **Open** 9am-midnight Mon-Fri; 11am-11pm Sat, Sun. **Main courses** 150-350 Kč. **Credit** AmEx, MC, V.
Map p329 N3 ⑬
Thought it may look generic, this little, affordable, unpretentious spot delivers top-drawer Lebanese mezes, with an excellent deal on the menu for two. Pizzas, pastas and such are served as well, but what really shines is the authentic Middle Eastern, from the tabbouleh to the baklava.

Yalla
Dlouhá 33, Prague 1 (224 827 375). Metro Náměstí Republiky/tram 5, 8, 14. **Open** noon-11pm daily. **Main courses** 120-240 Kč. **Credit** AmEx, MC, V. **Map** p329 N2 ⑭
Just a simple-looking couscous counter, but in Prague it stands out as a beacon of zesty, spicy, affordable fare. Healthy quick meals such as couscous, merguez sausages and stuffed sweet peppers with cheese add appeal to a busy street.

Seafood

Reykjavík
Karlova 20, Prague 1 (222 221 218/www.reykjavik. cz). Metro Staroměstská/tram 17, 18. **Open** 11am-midnight daily. **Main courses** 250-500 Kč. **Credit** AmEx, MC, V. **Map** p328 K4 ⑮
Blanched cod and perch are done to perfection with classic and Scandinavian sauces at what is a surprisingly high-quality restaurant for its location. Smack-bang on the main tourist route to Charles Bridge, the comfortably elegant restaurant still offers reasonable prices. The Icelandic owner has fish and lobster flown in and the local crowds lap it up. There's a street terrace in summer, but the upstairs loft offers the quietest seating for diners.

Vegetarian

Country Life
Melantrichova 15, Prague 1 (224 213 366). Metro Národní třída/tram 6, 9, 18, 22, 23. **Open** 9.30am-8.30pm Mon-Thur; 9.30am-3pm Fri; 11am-6pm Sun. **Main courses** 75-180 Kč. **No credit cards. Map** p328 L4 ⑯
Country Life is a Czech neohippie fave cafeteria with dirt-cheap, organically grown vegetarian fare. It specialises in massive DIY salads, fresh carrot juice, delectable lentil soup and crunchy wholegrain breads, but avoid the lunchtime crush.

World

Barock
Pařížská 24, Prague 1 (222 329 221). Metro Staroměstská/tram 17, 18. **Open** 10am-1am Mon-Thur; 10am-2am Fri, Sat; 10am-1am Sun; meals served until 10.45pm. **Main courses** 250-450 Kč. **Credit** AmEx, MC, V. **Map** p328 L2 ⑰
Come here for glam dining, a gleaming zinc bar, floor-to-ceiling windows and a credible sushi platter with suitably aesthetic nigiri. Reasonably priced breakfast menu and powerhouse lattes too.

Pravda
Pařížská 17, Prague 1 (222 326 203). Metro Staroměstská/tram 17, 18. **Open** noon-11pm Mon-Thur, Sun; noon-midnight Fri, Sat; kitchen closes 1hr before closing time. **Main courses** 250-850 Kč. **Credit** AmEx, MC, V. **Map** p328 L3 ⑱
Owner Tommy Sjöö, who helped bring fine dining to post-1989 Prague, runs this suitably airy and elegant restaurant. Chicken in Senegal peanut sauce vies against Vietnamese nem spring rolls and borscht, all done credibly. Cool and graceful service. *See also p157* **Still crazy**.

Nové Město

Americas

Banditos
Melounova 2, Prague 2 (224 941 096). Metro IP Pavlova/tram 6, 10, 11, 22, 23. **Open** 9am-12.30am Mon-Fri; noon-12.30am Sat, Sun. **Main courses** 180-380 Kč. **Credit** AmEx, MC, V. **Map** p331 N9 ⑲
There's an expat-friendly, café-style atmosphere to Banditos and the food, naturally, runs to Tex-Mex and south-western favourites. Try the spicy chicken sandwich, Caesar salad and cheeseburgers.

Don Pedro
Masarykovo nábřeží 2, Prague 2 (224 923 505). **Open** 11.30am-11pm daily. **Main courses** 180-350 Kč. **No credit cards. Map** p330 J9 ⑳
You won't find many Colombian restaurants in Prague, or indeed elsewhere in Eastern Europe, so it's just as well that Don Pedro is the real deal. Authentic zesty empanadas, spicy beef and potato

Eat, Drink, Shop

soup and gorgeously grilled meats are served up amid bright southern hemisphere colours. The oxtail cola guisada with yuca root is a favourite, and well worth the South American-speed service.

Jáma

V Jámě 7, Prague 1 (224 222 383/www.jamapub.cz).
Metro Můstek/tram 3, 9, 14, 24. **Open** 11am-
midnight Mon, Sun; 11am-1am Tue-Sat; kitchen
closes at 11.40pm. **Main courses** 100-260 Kč.
Credit AmEx, MC, V. **Map** p331 N7 **71**
Still a lunch and brunch fave after all these years, American-owned and outfitted Jáma has a prime patio space (and children's playground) out back and a bank of internet terminals by the door to boot. It's kept the loud college vibe that made its name, drawing Czech scenesters by day and young business types by night. Lunch specials and happy hour deals are a big pull, as is the Czech-Mex menu and well-poured Gambrinus. The video rental counter also does brisk business.

Picante

Revoluční 4, Prague 2 (222 322 022/www.picante.cz).
Metro Náměstí Republiky/tram 5, 8, 14. **Open** 24hrs
daily. **Main courses** 80-220 Kč. **No credit cards.**
Map p329 N3 **72**
Picante is a real surprise: an overlit, all-night, fast food counter that actually does the finest home-made salsas, steamed pork carnitas and soft maize tacos in town. Undoubtedly something heaven-sent for all the city's American expats.

Tulip Café

Opatovická 3, Prague 2 (224 930 019/www.tulip
cafe.cz). Metro Národní třída/tram 6, 9, 18, 22,
23. **Open** 11am-2am Mon-Thur, Sun; 11am-7am
Fri, Sat. **Main courses** 120-260 Kč. **Credit** MC, V.
Map p330 K8 **73**
Amazingly popular across the Czech and expat scenes, Tulip is a groovy café with back patio that offers imaginative American diner variations, but has serious service issues. The packs of American students don't seem to mind, though.

Asian

Hot

Václavské náměstí 45, Prague 1 (222 247 240).
Metro Muzeum/tram 11. **Open** 9am-midnight daily.
Main courses 180-450 Kč. **Credit** AmEx, MC, V.
Map p331 O7 **74**
Trendy, retro Thai and seafood, brought to a hungry public by capable Prague restaurateur Tommy Sjöö, and occupying the lobby of the newly made-over Hotel Jalta on Wenceslas Square.

Lemon Leaf

Na Zderaze 14, Prague 2 (224 919 056/
www.lemon.cz). Metro Karlovo náměstí/tram 7,
16, 17, 21. **Open** 11am-11pm Mon-Thur; 11am-
12.30am Fri; 1pm-12.30am Sat; 1-11pm Sun.
Main courses 180-320 Kč. **Credit** AmEx, MC, V.
Map p330 K8 **75**

Well-done Thai and Burmese in a warm, yellow and dark wood setting with bargain lunch specials have kept Lemon Leaf close to capacity since opening. No compromises for spice-phobic Czechs have been made with the tom ka kai or prawn curries.

Millhouse Sushi

Slovanský dům, Na příkopě 22, Prague 1 (221
451 771). Metro Náměstí Republiky/tram 5, 8,
14. **Open** 11am-11pm daily. **Main courses**
400-800 Kč. **Credit** AmEx, DC, MC, V.
Map p329 N4 **76**
This place is handy if you're in the shopping mall catching a film but it's not a place that'll have you saving your travel funds. However, the trendiest sushi bar in town does do maki and nagiri in lovely, quick fashion, it must be said.
Other locations: Sokolovská 84-86, Karlin, Prague 8 (222 832 583).

Siam Orchid

Na Poříčí 21, Prague 2 (222 319 410). Náměstí
Republiky/tram 5, 8, 14. **Open** 10am-10pm daily.
Main courses 120-320 Kč. **Credit** AmEx, MC, V.
Map p329 P3 **77**
Siam Orchid is an easy-to-miss family joint located up the stairs in a shopping passage. It also has the most authentic, unpretentious Thai food in town, including chicken satay and delicioius main courses of fried tofu with mung beans, and fiery chicken and cod curries, plus Thai beer.

SushiPoint

Na příkopě 19, Prague 2 (608 643 923/
www.sushipoint.cz). Metro Náměstí Republiky/
tram 5, 8, 14. **Open** 11am-11pm daily. **Main**
courses 180-350 Kč. **Credit** AmEx, MC, V.
Map p329 N5 **78**
SushiPoint is the latest place to be seen tossing back raw tuna and pickled ginger, with a crowd of spendy new, young Czech consumers who are fresh from the shopping malls all around.

Thanh Long

Ostrovní 23, Prague 1 (224 933 537). Metro
Národní třída/tram 6, 9, 18, 22, 23. **Open** 11.30am-
11pm daily. **Main courses** 120-250 Kč. **Credit**
AmEx, MC, V. **Map** p330 L7 **79**
Thanh Long is distinguished more by location and decor than a menu blanded down to suit Czech tastes: the position is central, the design deliriously over the top, including the revolving 'Lazy Susan' tables, pagoda lanterns and the huge moving-light painting in the back. This is an experience for all senses save the gustatory.

Continental

Červená Tabulka

Lodecká 4, Prague 2 (224 810 401/www.cervena
tabulka.cz). Metro Náměstí Republiky/tram 8, 26.
Open 11.30am-11pm daily. **Main courses**
120-300 Kč. **Credit** AmEx, MC, V.
Map p329 P2 **80**

Whimsical playschool decor and lava-grilled lamb, plus poultry comfort foods. Baked duck leg with bacon dumplings, apple and sauerkraut are cheerily served up alongside tasty skewered rabbit with cream and lime sauce.

Chaoz

Masarykovo nábřeží 26, Prague 1 (224 933 657). Metro Národní třída/tram 6, 9, 17, 18, 22, 23. **Open** noon-midnight daily. **Main courses** 130-270 Kč. **Credit** AmEx, DC, MC, V. **Map** p330 J8 ⑥①
The cuisine actually lives up to the lush art nouveau entrance on the Nové Město embankment. Risottos, roast duck and the Waldorf salad are standouts, while the salmon in pastry with wild rice does very well also.

Dynamo

Pštrossova 220-229, Prague 2 (224 932 020/ www.mraveniste.cz). Metro Národní třída/tram 6, 9, 18, 22, 23. **Open** 11.30am-midnight daily. **Main courses** 180-350 Kč. **Credit** AmEx, MC, V. **Map** p330 J7 ⑥②
This sleek designer diner typifies the renaissance sweeping through the area south of the National Theatre. Steaks and pasta just about keep up with the decor; don't miss the wall of single malt Scotches.

Hybernia

Hybernská 7, Prague 1 (224 226 004/www.hybernia praha.cz). Metro Náměstí Republiky/tram 3, 5, 8, 14, 24, 26. **Open** 9.30am-11.30pm Mon-Fri; 10.30am-11.30pm Sat, Sun. **Main courses** 120-310 Kč. **Credit** AmEx, MC, V. **Map** p329 O4 ⑥③
Having built a reputation for serving up impressive portions of hearty food with decent service Hybernia has earned a regular lunchtime crowd of wheeler dealers. It's next to the headquarters of the Social Democrat Party, but bodyguards and heads of government are less frequent visitors now that the conservatives are in power. The bouillabaisse is impressive, as is the ginger-marinated duck breast and gnocchi with Parma ham.

Czech

Celnice

V Celnici 4, Prague 1 (224 212 240). Metro Náměstí Republiky/tram 3, 5, 8, 24, 26. **Open** 11am-midnight Mon-Thur, Sun; 11am-1.30am Fri, Sat. **Main courses** 180-450 Kč. **Credit** AmEx, MC, V. **Map** p329 O4 ⑥④
The hippest of the Pilsner-licensed restaurants, Celnice is a mix of classic Czech, with updated fare like *kyselo*, or sauerkraut soup, pickled Prague ham and pastas, and a sleek, modern sushi bar with DJ dance fare at weekends.

Novoměstský Pivovar

Vodičkova 20, Prague 1 (222 232 448/www. npivovar.cz). Metro Můstek/tram 3, 9, 14, 24. **Open** 10am-11.30pm Mon-Fri; 11.30am-11.30pm Sat; noon-10pm Sun. **Main courses** 140-360 Kč. **Credit** AmEx, MC, V. **Map** p330 M7 ⑥⑤

One of the surprisingly few brew pubs in Prague, it's a vast underground warren with great beer and pub grub but also busloads of tourists and the inevitable slack service that goes with that.

U Pinkasů

Jungmannovo náměstí 16, Prague 1 (221 111 151/ www.upinkasu.cz). Metro Můstek/tram 6, 9, 18, 22, 23. **Open** *restaurant* 11am-1am daily. *Pub* 9am-2am daily. **Main courses** 120-300 Kč. **Credit** AmEx, MC, V. **Map** p328 M6 ⑥⑥
If you're here for the beer, then make a pilgrimage to the first (c1843) Pilsner pub. A century-and-a-half later it's still a smoky, packed, dependable source for gruff, authentic service and classic meat platters including leg of hare, and duck with red and white cabbage and potato dumplings.

Fast food

Gyrossino

Spálená 47, Prague 2 (no phone). Metro Národní třída/tram 6, 9, 18, 22, 23. **Open** 24hrs daily. **Main courses** 75-120 Kč. **No credit cards.** **Map** p330 L6 ⑥⑦
Actually two places, side by side, separated by a building entryway. The left half is a bakery, the right serves up roast chicken, falafel, kebabs and just-edible mini-pizzas.

U Rozvařilů

Na Poříčí 26, Prague 2 (224 219 357). Metro Náměstí Republiky/tram 3, 5, 8, 14, 24. **Open** 11am-11pm Mon-Fri; 11am-8pm Sat, Sun. **Main courses** 70-150 Kč. **Credit** AmEx, MC, V. **Map** p329 P3 ⑥⑧
This is a chrome-covered, mirrored version of that old pre-revolutionary classic, the workers' cafeteria. Servers in worn white aprons, harassed-looking customers in white socks and sandals, and soups, goulash, dumplings and *chlebíčky* (open-faced mayonnaise and meat sandwiches).

French

La Perle de Prague

Corner of Rašínovo nábřeží & Resslova, Prague 2 (221 984 160). Metro Karlovo náměstí/tram 7, 16, 17, 21. **Open** 7-10.30pm Mon; noon-2pm, 7-10.30pm Tue-Sat. **Main courses** 280-1,280 Kč. **Credit** AmEx, MC, V. **Map** p330 J9 ⑥⑨
Perched like an eyrie atop Frank Gehry's 'Fred and Ginger' building, the Pearl was once king of the hill. Patrons are from expense-account territory and the French cuisine is indeed fly, but is it really worth it? Even the views are a bit disappointing, with smallish recessed windows.

Le Bistrot de Marlène

Plavecká 4, Prague 2 (224 921 853/www.bistrot demarlene.cz). Metro Karlovo náměstí, then tram 7, 16, 17, 21. **Open** *Oct-Apr* noon-2.30pm, 7-10.30pm Mon-Sat. *May-Sept* noon-2.30pm, 7-10.30pm daily. **Main courses** 280-650 Kč. **Credit** AmEx, MC, V. **Map** p330 K12 ⑨⓪

Enchanting, market-fresh, traditional Franche-Comté cuisine in a sleek, modern room. Simple, expertly done pheasant, venison and boar are served alongside sea bass and spinach, filets mignons and chèvre salads. A cause for celebration among Prague foodies.

Universal

V Jirchářích, Prague 2 (224 934 416). Metro Národní třída/tram 6, 9, 18, 22, 23. **Open** 11.30-midnight Mon-Sat; 11am-11.30pm Sun. **Main courses** 180-320 Kč. **Credit** MC, V. **Map** p330 K7 ③

With old French advertisements on the wine-coloured walls, an interior inspired by train cars, servers who know their stuff and appealing daily

specials (cod in white sauce, flank steak and rolled veggie lasagne), Universal is hard to fault. And the sides are as impressive as the mains: delectable fresh spinach or roasted gratin potatoes done with flair.

Indian

Himalaya

Mikovcova 7, Prague 2 (224 231 581). Metro IP Pavlova/tram 6, 10, 11, 16, 22, 23. **Open** 11am-11pm Mon-Fri; noon-11pm Sat, Sun. **Main courses** 100-250 Kč. **No credit cards.** **Map** p331 O9 ③

Still crazy Tommy Sjöö

His **Barock** café on Prague's closest equivalent to Rodeo Drive, Parizska street, was once called a 'highly theatrical space' by a visiting stage designer. **Pravda**, across the road, invokes the old Russian propaganda sheet in its brand, while laying out posh, chandeliered, white-linen service and cuisine within. And the latest venture, **Hot**, has converted the lobby of one of Wenceslas Square's last die-hard socialist-decor hotels, the Jalta, into a scene-making dining room and bar with A-list guests, modular black appointments and elegant Thai food.

Tommy Sjöö, along with former partner Nils Jebens, has been behind most of the significant restaurant developments in Prague for well over a decade and he doesn't appear to be slowing down. Spinning new establishments off from existing ones seems to be a particular strength. One of Sjöö's former chefs, Lars Sjostrand, a fellow Swede, launched a shrine to Italian food, **Isabella**, in Old Town in 1995, which won rave reviews and did much to liven up quiet little U Milosrdnych street (No. 2, 224 819 957). Sjostrand launched a bar with creole food shortly afterward, Ellington's, jazzing up a formerly ho-hum expat drinking hole but, in the tough Prague marketplace, this one didn't take and has shut down.

Sjöö himself says he has no plans to launch another dining hotspot for the time being, preferring to concentrate on keeping his three existing places humming. That's no small feat in increasingly competitive Prague, where chefs are flown in every week to staff newly opened designer cafés and restaurants.

Sjöö's reputation for substance over flash sets his establishments apart (though that's not to say they're not flashy, but in an understated sort of way). More remarkable

than that, they remain affordable in a town where prices are often unrelated to quality.

What's been the key to keeping Barock, Pravda and Hot customers coming back? A protégé reveals that, despite the special buzz of all of Sjöö's ventures, there's no real magic; he's just married good business sense to his demanding rules for fresh, interesting ingredients. 'He seems easygoing. But he's a dragon,' says the chef with a note of admiration.

Eat, Drink, Shop

Radost FX Café. *See p159.*

While cheap Indian street eats are still a rarity in Prague, and those that exist are not on a par with the best of London, nevertheless Himalaya has won over expats and students. Lunch special Madras curries, biryanis and samosas (takeaway's best) have hopefully started a craze.

Mediterranean

Athina

Svobodova 11, Prague 2 (224 914 416). Tram 18, 24. **Open** 11am-11pm daily. **Main courses** 180-450 Kč. **Credit** AmEx, MC, V.

Not exactly central, but if you're in the area and fancy authentic Greek food in a humble taverna setting, Athina's the place. The tzatziki, tiropita and souvlaki are all mouth-watering delights.

Café Lamborghini

Vodičkova 8, Prague 1 (222 231 869/www. Ambi.cz). Metro Můstek/tram 3, 9, 14, 24. **Open** 8am-10pm Mon-Sat; 1-10pm Sun. **Main courses** 250-450 Kč. **Credit** AmEx, DC, MC, V. **Map** p330 M8 ❸

Burning rubber in the race to be Prague's hottest café, Café Lamborghini features a clean, streamlined space with slate grey accents and serves killer Italian coffee, imaginative salads with tropical fruit and gorgonzola, and the best pappardelle carbonara in town. Grind your own fresh parmesan and take in the colourful cast of casual-cool patrons.

Cafeterapie

Podskalská 3, Prague 2 (224 916 098). Metro Karlovo náměstí, then tram 7, 16, 17, 21. **Open** 10am-10pm Mon-Fri; noon-10pm Sun. **Main courses** 100-350 Kč. **No credit cards**.

Cafeterapie serves up delicious Mediterranean fare with a strong vegetarian showing plus big, crisp salads, tempeh and an impressive selection of good-value specials that make the most of seasonal ingredients. Situated as it is, just off the Vltava, this genial spot makes for a handy stop on an outing that takes you up to nearby Vyšehrad.

Cicala

Žitná 43, Prague 2 (222 210 375). Metro IP Pavlova/ tram 4, 6, 10, 16, 22, 23. **Open** 11.30am-10.30pm Mon-Sat. **Main courses** 250-550 Kč. **No credit cards**. **Map** p331 O8 ❹

The owner brings in fresh Italian wonders weekly, be it calamari or figs, presented like a work of art. An easily missed subterranean two-room eaterie on an otherwise unappealing street, Cicala is worth seeking out as a bastion of Prague's Italian community.

Credo

Petrská 11, Prague 2 (222 324 634). Metro Náměstí Republiky/tram 8, 26. **Open** 9am-midnight Mon-Fri; 10am-midnight Sat. **Main courses** 120-300 Kč. **No credit cards**. **Map** p329 P2 ❺

Credo is a surprisingly good lunch option that's conveniently situated just two blocks east of Old Town. Look at the menu and you can expect to see starters of gorgonzola-stuffed baked figs, arugula, caper and walnut salad, and main courses of creamy risotto and fillet of sole with Spanish rice.

Pizza Coloseum
Vodičkova 32, Prague 1 (224 214 914/www. pizzacoloseum.cz). Metro Můstek/tram 3, 9, 14, 24. **Open** 11am-11.30pm daily. **Main courses** 180-320 Kč. **Credit** AmEx, MC, V. **Map** p330 M7 ❾❻
Just off Wenceslas Square, this cellar's a top Prague pizzeria. Excellent bruschetta, flame-baked pizza and big, saucy pastas complement well-stocked wine racks and a familiar range of steak and fish.

Řecká Taverna
Revoluční 16, Prague 2 (222 317 762). Metro Náměstí Republiky/tram 5, 8, 14. **Open** 11am-midnight daily. **Main courses** 120-320 Kč. **Credit** AmEx, MC, V. **Map** p329 N2 ❾❼
Affordable, authentic Greek in a cheerfully tacky tavern across the street from Old Town. Stuffed vine leaves in tzatziki, spinach pie and saganaki cheese stand alongside savoury souvlaki and kebabs.

Rio's Vyšehrad
Štulcova 2, Prague 2 (224 922 156/www.rio restaurant.cz). Metro Vyšehrad/tram 7, 18, 24. **Open** 11am-midnight daily. **Main courses** 180-320 Kč. **Credit** AmEx, MC, V.
The cuisine and service will pass, with a good selections of salads, seafood and pasta, and a reasonable wine collection. But the main draw is the view from Prague's oldest hilltop castle ruins, a 12-minute metro ride south of the centre after a short walk.

Seafood

Alcron
Štěpánská 40, Prague 1 (222 820 038). Metro Můstek/tram 3, 9, 14, 24. **Open** 5.30-11pm daily. **Main courses** 400-1,200 Kč. **Credit** AmEx, MC, V. **Map** p331 N7 ❾❽
Once the haunt of Jazz Age stars, the name harks back to when the SAS Radisson hotel (*see p62*) – where the restaurant is located – was called the Alcron. At least now you won't get lost in the crowd: there are only seven tables available for diners over which seafood master chef Jiří Štift expertly casts pike-perch and savoury sauces.

Vegetarian

Radost FX Café
Bělehradská 120, Prague 2 (224 254 776/ www.radostfx.cz). Metro IP Pavlova/tram 4, 6, 10, 16, 22, 23. **Open** *Restaurant* 11.30am-3am daily. *Club* 10pm-4am Thur-Sat. **Main courses** 180-350 Kč. **No credit cards. Map** p331 P9 ❾❾
Prague's first vegetarian restaurant still has the latest opening hours around with all-night pastas, couscous and meatless Mexican food. It's of variable quality and the ornamental tables do bash your knees but it's as popular as ever, with a groovy, tassled backroom lounge. **Photo** p158.

U Govindy Vegetarian Club
Soukenická 27, Prague 2 (224 816 631). Metro Náměstí Republiky/tram 5, 8, 14. **Open** 11am-5pm Mon-Fri. **Main courses** 70-150 Kč. **No credit cards. Map** p329 O2 ❿⓿⓿
This Hare Krishna restaurant is extremely cheap and as basic as it gets. It offers a simple self-service vegetarian Indian meal for a mere 85 Kč. But at least it's a clean spot for sharing a table while seated on floor cushions (if this doesn't appeal, don't worry; there are real tables and chairs here too).

World

Soho Restaurant & Garden
Podolské nábřeží 1, Prague 2 (244 463 772). Tram 3, 16, 17. **Open** 11.30am-1am daily. **Main courses** 180-350 Kč. **Credit** AmEx, MC, V.
A short trek south of the centre, and don't wear jeans for the trip, but worth it for a modernist river terrace and mussels au gratin with parmesan or Chilean salmon sashimi starters. Gracious staff and a thoughtful, reasonable wine list as well.

Zahrada v opeře
Legerova 75, Prague 2 (224 239 685/www.zahrada vopere.cz). Metro Muzeum/tram 11. **Open** 11.30am-midnight daily. **Main courses** 220-480 Kč. **Credit** AmEx, MC, V. **Map** p331 P7 ❿⓿❶
The entrance to the Opera Garden is hard to find (at the back of the office building over it) but sumptuous feasts at this Czech and international dining room make it worth the effort. Tuna steak in filo is a delight, in keeping with the airy minimalist decor and the quietly gliding waiters.

Further afield

Americas

Artyčok
Londýnská 29, Prague 2 (222 524 110/www. artycok.cz). Metro IP Pavlova/tram 11. **Open** 11am-1am daily. **Main courses** 150-350 Kč. **Credit** AmEx, MC, V. **Map** p331 P9 ❿⓿❷
With passable Czech-Mex, Thai and tapas, Artyčok is a popular lunch venue for the offices all around. As much as the cuisine, a main attraction here is the terrace on a lovely street. That and the affordability – that is, for those not in a hurry.

Barracuda
Krymská 2, Vinohrady, Prague 2 (271 740 599/ www.barracuda-cafe.cz). Metro Náměstí Míru/ tram 4, 22. **Open** *Upstairs* 11.30am-midnight Mon-Fri; 5pm-midnight Sat, Sun. *Downstairs* 5-11.30pm Mon-Fri. **Main courses** 130-270 Kč. **Credit** AmEx, MC, V.
Once a top draw for Mexican food in Prague, Barracuda is definitely worth a visit if you're in the neighbourhood. The fajitas aren't exactly hot news any more, but the tacos are a hit. The atmosphere is welcoming.

Sonora

*Radhoštská 5, Prague 3 (222 711 029). Metro
Flora/tram 11.* **Open** 11am-midnight daily.
Main courses 120-260 Kč. **Credit** MC, V.
Map p333 D3 🔢

Some of the city's most inspired efforts in Mexican
food, complete with mole sauce, chips, salsa, taco salads, beef burritos and tasty quesadillas. All of which
are complemented perfectly by cheap Czech beer.

Balkan

Modrá řeka

*Mánesova 13, Vinohrady, Prague 2 (222 251 601).
Metro Muzeum/tram 11.* **Open** 11am-11pm Mon-Fri;
5-11pm Sat, Sun. **Main courses** 130-270 Kč. **No credit
cards. Map** p333 A3 🔢

It may be out of the way, to be sure, but think of this
experience as being a visit to the Yugoslavian home
you never knew you had. Muhamed Londrc and his
wife run this simple eatery, which might be mistak-
en for a pub were it not for the folk art hanging from
the walls. Customers are very nearly adopted as children, then stuffed senseless with home-made *somun*
bread and *Šarena dolma* (lamb-stuffed vine leaves
with peppers and onions).

Czech

Svatá Klára

*U Trojského zámku, Troja, Prague 7 (233 540 173/
www.svataklara.cz). Metro Nádraží Holešovice,
then bus 154, 191.* **Open** 6pm-midnight daily.
Main courses 280-480 Kč. **Credit** AmEx, MC, V.

This is an upscale, quality restaurant that produces
traditional Czech game dishes with a flair that
rewards adventurers who have trekked out to the
adjoining Troja Château *(see p129)* to take in the historic frescoes and formal gardens.

Včelín

*Kodaňská 5, Vršovice, Prague 10 (271 742 541).
Tram 4, 22, 23.* **Open** 11am-midnight Mon-Fri;
11.30am-1am Sat; 11.30am-11pm Sun. **Main
courses** 250-400 Kč. **Credit** V.

The Beehive is a well-named gathering spot for
up-and-coming Prague creative types, but without the
attitude that ruins most such places. The quick, ami-
able servers hustle from table to table bearing any of
three great Czech beers on tap – Kozel, Radegast and
Pilsner Urquell. The house special, gnocchi in spinach
sauce, is the hit of this little room, which is done up
with graphic-design magazine covers.

Žlutá pumpa

*Belgická 12, Prague 2 (608 184 360). Metro
Náměstí Míru/tram 4, 6, 10, 16, 20, 22.* **Open**
noon-1am Mon-Fri; 4pm-1am Sat, Sun. **Main
courses** 110-250 Kč. **No credit cards.**

The latest Prague trend, new angles on trad pubbing,
finds Czech-Mex expression at the Yellow Pump. It's
buzzy, colourful and local, but don't expect great service or remarkably memorable chow.

French

Café Atelier

*Na Kovárně, Prague 2 (271 721 866).
Metro Náměstí Míru, then tram 4, 22, 23.*
Open 11am-11pm daily. **Main courses**
180-580 Kč. **No credit cards.**

Often booked solid, Café Atelier is an incredible-
value French cuisine restaurant that's well worth
riding out of the centre for. The rabbit in *basquaise*
sauce and veal *osso-bucco* in orange sauce is served
up to customers in an intimate, modern space.
Fortunately the restaurant has opened a new terrace for warm-weather dining or sipping from one
of the city's best wine collections, which are priced
a good deal better than a lot of plonk. For dessert,
indulge in the chocolate mousse.

La Crêperie

*Janovského 4, Prague 7 (220 878 040). Metro
Vltavská/tram 1, 5, 8, 12,14, 25.* **Open** 9am-11pm
Mon-Sat; 9am-10pm Sun. **Main courses** 110-250 Kč.
No credit cards. Map p332 E3 🔢

Small in size but big in portions, the French-owned
La Crêperie serves sweet and savoury crêpes, for
very cheap prices. Seating is in a comfortable but
closet-sized basement, so this venue is probably not
ideal for office parties. To top the bill there is an
above average wine list, and fresh croissants.

La Lavande

*Záhřebská 24, Prague 2 (222 517 406). Metro
Náměstí Míru/tram 4, 6, 10, 16, 20, 22.* **Open**
noon-3pm, 7-11pm Mon-Fri. **Main courses**
280-880 Kč. **Credit** AmEx, MC, V.

A new arrival at the high end of Prague's culinary
scene, La Lavande offers quality cooking and service in a semi-casual French farmhouse atmosphere.
Recommended dishes include fresh gazpacho, goat's
cheese millefeuille, fried anchovies with coriander
and sour cream, beef Rossini, crunchy salad with
English bacon and grated parmesan.

Le Bistrot de Marléne

*Schwaigerova 3, Holešovce, Prague 6 (224 921 853/
www.bistrotdemarlene.cz). Metro Hradčanská/tram
20, 25.* **Open** 11am-2pm, 7-10.30pm Mon-Fri;
7-10.30pm Sat. **Main courses** 280-650 Kč.
Credit AmEx, MC, V. **Map** p332 A2 🔢

By the creator of the original, in Nové Město, this
elegant dining room serving the city's best rural
French food is at the Hotel Villa Schwaiger *(see p67)*.
Guests of the hotel are invited to eat here every night
if they wish. Visitors should definitely consider making a reservation to ensure a table.

Indian/Pakistani

Mailsi

*Lipanská 1, Žižkov, Prague 3 (222 717 783).
Tram 5, 9, 26.* **Open** noon-3pm, 6-11.30pm daily.
Main courses 250-350 Kč. **Credit** AmEx, MC, V.
Map p333 C2 🔢

Mailsi is quite simply a comfortable, friendly neighbourhood Pakistani restaurant – but it's the district's only one. Even though there's not much atmosphere, there is plenty of good, solid Pakistani food to be had, which goes down well in Žižkov, one of Prague's few truly ethnically mixed districts. The kebabs, dahl and other traditional dishes are all expertly prepared and spiced, and served up with fast and friendly gusto by competent waiting staff.

Mediterranean

Aromi

Mánesova 78, Prague 2 (222 713 222). Metro Jiřího z Poděbrad/tram 11. **Open** 11am-10pm Mon-Thur, Sun; 11am-11pm Fri, Sat. **Main courses** 280-680 Kč. **Credit** AmEx, MC, V. **Map** p333 B3 ⓲

One of Prague's best new Italian restaurants, thankfully located in quiet Vinohrady, off the tourist radar. Authoritative kitchen mastery meets low-key rough wood, brick interiors and fine presentation of everything from the six-seafood antipasti platter to veal on saffron risotto with thyme. Excellent wines, all fairly priced, from around Italy. **Photo** p152.

Grosseto Pizzeria

Jugoslávských partyzánů 8, Dejvice, Prague 6 (233 342 694/www.grosseto.cz). Metro Dejvická/tram 2, 20, 25, 26. **Open** 11.30am-11pm daily. **Main courses** 120-310 Kč. **No credit cards.**

With two booming locations, Grosseto does flame-cooked pizzas, most notably the four-cheese version – beware imitations elsewhere using anything called eidam or hermelín (generic Czech cheeses). The minestrone is hearty too, and the carpaccio in tomato sauce is perfect for sopping up with the complimentary fresh hot peasant bread.

Other locations: Francouská 2, Vinohrady, Prague 2 (224 252 778).

Puccelini

Tusarova 52, Holešovice, Prague 7 (283 871 134). Metro Vltavská/tram 1, 25. **Open** 11am-11pm Mon-Fri; noon-11pm Sat, Sun. **Main courses** 140-320 Kč. **Credit** AmEx, MC, V. **Map** p332 F2 ⓲

A fine Italian bistro in what is an otherwise semi-industrial Prague district. Adorned throughout with music scores and lamps hidden inside trumpets, Puccelini's wood-fired pizzas are dappled with excellent, punchy sauce. Baked stuffed aubergine and mozzarella, and potato-thyme soup are just as impressive.

Ristorante da Emanuel

Charles de Gaulla 4, Dejvice, Prague 6 (224 312 934). Metro Dejvická/tram 2, 20, 25, 26. **Open** noon-11pm daily. **Main courses** 180-480 Kč. **Credit** AmEx, MC, V.

With menu additions like swordfish carpaccio and pappardelle al cinghiale (mildly spiced ground boar), this little neighbourhood pasta joint always requires reservations. Expatriate Italians commute across Prague to eat at the tiny tables in an atmosphere of doting servers, terrible seaport decor and Charlie Chaplin signs to the loo.

Roca

Vinohradská 32, Prague 2 (222 520 060). Metro Náměstí Míru/tram 11. **Open** 10am-11pm daily. **Main courses** 160-320 Kč. **Credit** AmEx, MC, V. **Map** p333 A3 ⓲

Roca is a grand little Italian restaurant, complete with family and paisano regulars chatting away in the corners. Owners Roberta and Camilla, whose names each lend a syllable to this charming hole in the wall, oversee a particularly delicious pasta assortment served with delicate, creamy sauces, and some superior soups. The tender chicken scallopini and squid risotto nero are a treat.

Middle Eastern

Efes

Vinohradská 63, Prague 2 (222 250 015). Metro Náměstí Míru/tram 11. **Open** 11.30am-11pm Mon-Sat. **Main courses** 110-280 Kč. **No credit cards.** **Map** p333 B3 ⓲

Prague's finest Anatolian chow, with exotic, warming tastes like ayvar, which is a red peppers, chilli and garlic paste you spread on fresh sourdough, the tzatziki-like cacic and great vegetarian fare. Sonbahar kisiri is a cracked wheat mix of walnuts and olives, and the kizartma of caramelised aubergine and peppers does a quick job of seduction – certainly quite a bit quicker than the relaxed service. The kebabs served here are juicy and tender, and fine minced meat and Turkish spices feature in the mezes.

World

Akropolis

Kubelíkova 27, Vršovice, Prague 3 (296 330 913/www.palacakropolis.cz). Metro Jiřího z Poděbrad/tram 11. **Open** 10am-midnight Mon-Fri; 4pm-midnight Sat, Sun. **Main courses** 80-170 Kč. **No credit cards.** **Map** p333 C2 ⓲

As an eating destination, the Akropolis is no Michelin-star contender, but if you're clubbing here or rocking out in the attached concert space (see p235), a Czech chicken curry may indeed just do the job. Maybe order a fried, battered mushroom as a vegetarian option? Whatever you go for, just make sure you drown your food with plenty of beer while focusing on the surrounding environment, which is quite a striking dining room designed by surrealist artists. The service is laid-back to say the least, but the crowd is ever-lively. A good night out.

Mozaika

Nitranská 13, Prague 2 (224 253 011). Metro Jiřího z Poděbrad/tram 11. **Open** 11.30am-midnight Mon-Fri; 4pm-midnight Sat, Sun. **Main courses** 180-380 Kč. **Credit** AmEx, MC, V. **Map** p333 C4 ⓲

It might not be that easy to find, but Mozaika is a friendly local restaurant that offers solid value and decent comfort food. Try the hamburger with fresh mushrooms, served on a home-made spinach roll, or the hearty daily soup special and pork chops with baked potato and cherry sauce.

Eat, Drink, Shop

Cafés, Pubs & Bars

Prague's about bustle these days, but life still drifts back to the local.

Aloha Wave Lounge: great for an unpretentious drinking experience. *See p164.*

Eat, Drink, Shop

Czechs are deeply divided on the subject of drinking. Not, of course, on its advisability, but rather on its location. Where to sup tonight? The latest swanky bar, with zinc countertops and a packed crowd of the young, successful and pretty? Or the old neighbourhood *hostinec* with its cheap beer and cigarette smoke?

It's a perlexing dilemma. On the side of the pubs is a 500-year history of brewing, plus prices that have hardly risen since the early 1990s. Then again, so many cocktail bars are competing that there's always a new one: **Aloha Wave Lounge** is tropically over the top, while **Monarch** and **Le Terroir** set new standards on the wine learning curve. Then there are buzzy standbys **Tretter's** and **Alcohol Bar**.

Yet the magic words *pivo, prosím* (beer, please) still form a powerful incantation in the land that gave the world the famed Žatec hops. And there's no place better for pub crawling in terms of affordability and quality than Prague. You can savour the workhorses of *pivo* – Pilsner Urquell, Radegast, Staropramen and Gambrinus – just about anywhere. Then head for the speciality bars for less well-known Czech beer delights:

Letenský zámeček for Bernard, **U Černého vola** for Kozel, and so on. Even those without much on their menus will usually offer some trad beer grub like smoked meat platters and/or the magnificently smelly *pivní sýr* (beer cheese). How to decide? That's why weekends have two nights.

CAFÉ CULTURE

Café culture in Prague offers everything from imperial elegance to American experiments. The *kavárna* in Prague has long been at the centre of intellectual life and, with the secret police now gone, some new places have slipped right into this role, such as the delightfully Mitteleuropa-feeling **Café Dinitz**, while some classics have rebounded. The cosy **Café Montmartre** has bounced back from the bon vivant days when it hosted black masses during the 1930s. Whereas the **Slavia**, where dissidents like Václav Havel and Jiří Kolář once planned and plotted, has been slightly too cleaned up, alas. Meanwhile, expat caffeine addicts often get their fix at **Ebel Coffee House**, **Káva Káva Káva** and the **Globe Bookstore & Coffeehouse**.

Hradčany

U Černého vola

*Loretánské náměstí 1, Prague 1 (220 513 481).
Tram 22.* **Open** *10am-10pm daily.* **No credit
cards.** **Map** p326 B3 ①
One of the last authentic neighbourhood pubs in this
district, with murals that make it look like it's been
here forever; in fact, the Black Ox was built after
World War II. Its superb location, right above the
castle, made it a prime target for redevelopment in
the post-1989 building frenzy, but the rugged regulars bought it to ensure that local bearded artisans
would have at least one place where they could
afford to drink. The Kozel beer is perfection and,
although the snacks are pretty basic, they do their
job of lining the stomach for long sessions.

Malá Strana

Baráčnická rychta

*Tržiště 23, Prague 1 (257 532 461). Metro
Malostranská/tram 12, 22, 23.* **Open** *noon-
1am daily.* **No credit cards.** **Map** p327 E3 ②
A survivor from the days of old, this former hall of
barons and landlords has made only grudging nods
to the present, with designer lamps now illuminating
its heavy, communal tables. Czechs cling passion-
ately to an oasis of indigenous pub culture – immortalised in Jan Neruda's *Prague Tales* – that thrived
in Malá Strana from the 19th century onwards.
Behind a series of archways, the pub is split into
two: a small beerhall frequented by hardcore *pivo*
drinkers and a downstairs music hall.

Blue Light

*Josefská 1, Prague 1 (257 533 126/www.bluelight
bar.cz). Metro Malostranská/tram 12, 22, 23.*
Open *6pm-3am daily.* **No credit cards.**
Map p327 F3 ③
A cosy bar featuring occasional live jazz music,
jazzy sounds on the stereo and jazz posters all over
the dilapidated walls – perhaps they should have
gone all the way and called it Blue Note instead. By
day it's a good spot to sit with a friend, especially
when there's room at the bar. At night it gets more
rowdy and conversation becomes nigh impossible
but the vibe is certainly infectious. The bar stocks a
decent selection of malt whiskies.

Jo's Bar

*Malostranské náměstí 7, Prague 1 (257 531 422).
Metro Malostranská/tram 12, 22, 23.* **Open** *11am-
2am daily.* **No credit cards.** **Map** p327 F4 ④
A street-level adjunct to the rollicking downstairs
Jo's Bar & Garáž, Jo's Bar was once renowned for
being every backpacker's first stop in Prague and
the original source of nachos in the Czech Republic.
Founder Glen Emery has moved on and Jo's is under
new ownership. It's still a good place to meet fellow
travellers, but it lacks soul these days – as well as
the once-rare Mexican food menu and foxy servers.

Petřínské Terasy

*Seminářská zahrada 13, Prague 1 (257 320 688/
www.petrinsketerasy.cz). Metro Malostranská/tram 12,
18, 22, 23.* **Open** *noon-11pm Mon-Fri; 11am-11pm
Sat, Sun.* **Credit** AmEx, DC, MC, V. **Map** p326 D5 ⑤
One of two tourist traps on Petřín Hill, the Petřín
Terraces offers exquisite views of Prague Castle and
the city, expensive Krušovice and indifferent service.

St Nicholas Café

*Tržiště 10, Prague 1 (257 530 204). Metro
Malostranská/tram 12, 22, 23.* **Open** *noon-2am
Mon-Thur, Sun; noon-3am Fri, Sat.* **Credit** MC.
Map p327 E4 ⑥
An atmospheric vaulted cellar decked out with
steamer trunk tables and painted arches, St Nick's
café comes with Pilsner Urquell on tap. A mellow
but lively crowd gathers in the nooks for late
evening conversation about nothing in particular.
It's also good for giving the brew a rest and taking
up a glass of Havana Club rum. **Photo** p167.

Tato Kojkej

*Kampa park (no phone). Metro Malostranská/tram
22, 23.* **Open** *10am-midnight daily.* **No credit
cards.** **Map** p3327 G6 ⑦
A wonderfully run-down gallery café hidden on the
shore side of Kampa park, this former millhouse still
features a wooden water wheel. Inside is a long list

The best Pubs

For beer gardening

Letenský zámeček *(see p173)*, Park
Café *(see p174)* and U vystřeleného oka
(see p175).

For classic, unreformed pubbing

U Černého vola *(see p163)*, U Provaznice
(see p169) and U Medvídků *(see p169)*.

For literary creds

Duende *(see p165)*, Café Montmartre
(see p165), Shakespeare & Sons *(see
p175)* and Slavia *(see p169)*.

For local hangouts

U Zavěšeného kafe *(see p164)*,
U Sadu *(see p175)* and Pastička
(see p174).

For old Mitteleuropa cafés

Franz Kafka Café *(see p166)* and Kavárna
Obecní dům *(see p166)*.

For scenes that build late

Blue Light *(see p163)*, Chateau Rouge
(see p165) and Kozička *(see p166)*.

Chateau Rouge. *See p165.*

of cocktails – though the staff are not expert at making them – and a short one of cheap red wine. Sofas, second-hand chairs, abstract sculpture and a terrace are the trump cards. Sunday-night movies are fun.

U Malého Glena

Karmelitská 23, Prague 1 (257 531 717/www. malyglen.cz). Metro Malostranská/tram 12, 20, 22, 23. **Open** 10am-2am daily. **Credit** MC. **Map** p327 F4 ⑧

From looking at the rowdy pub at street level you'd never guess that the downstairs bar is one of Prague's top jazz holes. Tall Staropramen mugs are swung with gusto by expats and Czechs, the servers are as sexy as they get and there are large tables and benches, perfect for groups. Always an easygoing, affable vibe, but less noisy in the afternoons.

U Zavěšenýho kafe

Úvoz 6, Prague 1 (257 532 868/www.uzavesenyho kafe.com). Metro Malostranská/tram 12, 22, 23. **Open** 11am-midnight daily. **No credit cards.** **Map** p326 C3 ⑨

The Hanging Coffee Cup is a mellow, thoroughly Czech spot with plank flooring, traditional grub (onion soup and duck with sauerkraut) and a long association with artists and intellectuals. The name comes from a tradition of paying for a cup of coffee for someone who may arrive later without funds.

Staré Město

Alcohol Bar

Dušní 6, Prague 1 (224 811 744/www.alcoholbar.cz). Metro Staroměstská/tram 5, 8, 14. **Open** 7pm-2am daily. **Credit** AmEx, MC. **Map** p328 L3 ⑩

Clubby, with a wall of single malt whiskies, plus rums and tequilas from respected distillers. A New York-style sophistication pervades, the barmen are true gents and there are occasional groove DJs.

Aloha Wave Lounge

Dušní 11, Prague 1 (724 055 704/www.aloha praha.cz). Metro Staroměstská/tram 17, 18. **Open** 8.30pm-2am Tue-Fri, Sun; 8.30pm-4am Sat. **Credit** MC, V. **Map** p328 L2 ⑪

Just a maroon-tinged, surfboard-lined room at street level, with umbrella drinks dominating, but it conceals an underground bar, complete with thatched roof and dancefloor that's a laugh with a local crowd that doesn't take itself seriously. **Photo** p162.

Au Gourmand

Dlouhá 10, Prague 1 (222 329 060). Metro Staroměstská/tram 17, 18. **Open** 8.45am-7pm Mon-Fri; 9am-7pm Sat, Sun. **No credit cards.** **Map** p3328 M3 ⑫

Pretty as an art nouveau postcard, it's also the richest little French bakery in town, with savoury baguette sandwiches and quiches on one side, luscious pear tarts and Black Forest cakes on the other. Sit down at a wrought-iron table in the middle, surrounded by unique, fin-de-siècle tile interiors, and watch half of Prague slip in for a bite of sin.

Bakeshop Praha

Kozí 1, Prague 1 (222 316 823). Metro Staroměstská/tram 17, 18. **Open** 7am-7pm daily. **Credit** MC, V. **Map** p328 M3 ⑬

San Franciscan Anne Feeley launched this expat mainstay seven years ago and it hasn't looked back since. Zesty quiches, trad nut breads and peanut butter cookies have every Westerner in town ducking in.

Bar & Books

Týnská 19, Prague 1 (731 184 123/www.bar andbooks.cz). Metro Staroměstská/tram 17, 18. **Open** 5pm-4am daily. **No credit cards.** **Map** p328 M3 ⓮
Small, dim, hushed and oddly formal, this bar, patterned after a New York model, offers top-drawer cocktails, brandy, cigars and service in a library-like setting. Red leather benches and seats go along with red-jacketed hostesses. Old James Bond movies loop quietly on monitors above the bar.

Blatouch

Vězeňská 4, Prague 1 (222 328 643). Metro Staroměstská/tram 17, 18. **Open** noon-1am Mon-Thur; noon-3am Fri; 2pm-3am Sat; 2pm-midnight Sun. **No credit cards.** **Map** p328 L2 ⓯
Ever packed with students, artists and scribblers drinking cheap red wine, this gentle café is run by two sisters. A favourite among new bohemians, the Mudflower plays jazz and soul through the narrow, high-ceilinged space and up the metal stairwell to a cosy loft. The food is not recommended, though.

Bugsy's

Pařížská 10 (entrance on Kostečná), Prague 1 (224 810 943/www.bugsysbar.cz). Metro Staroměstská/tram 17, 18. **Open** 7pm-2am daily. **Credit** AmEx, MC, V. **Map** p328 L3 ⓰
Once the only source for proper cocktails in town, today Bugsy's attracts an older crowd, many suits and not a few hustlers, all soaking up its swish Pařížská location. Its claim to fame is the drinks list, including 200 cocktails, and bar staff good enough to mix them properly. Prices prohibit all but flush tycoons, but it's still packed most evenings.

Café Indigo

Platnéřská 11, Prague 1 (no phone). Metro Staroměstská/tram 17, 18. **Open** 9am-midnight Mon-Fri; 11am-midnight Sat, Sun. **No credit cards.** **Map** p328 K4 ⓱
A comfortable art café with a limited menu and cheap wine, the Indigo has an upbeat vibe, popular with students from nearby Charles University. There are huge streetside windows and the nicotine-addicted patrons produce an invariably friendly vibe and smoky atmosphere. Children's corner in the back.

Café Konvikt

Bartolomějská 11, Prague 1 (224 232 427). Metro Národní třída/tram 6, 9, 18, 22, 23. **Open** 9am-1am Mon-Fri; noon-1am Sat, Sun. **No credit cards.** **Map** p328 K6 ⓲
The Konvikt, a popular, well-lit Staré Město spot, attracts Prague's new generation of penniless creatives. Small sweets are served, but it's really just about drink, talk and smoke here.

Café Montmartre

Řetězová 7, Prague 1 (222 221 244). Metro Staroměstská/tram 17, 18. **Open** 9am-11pm Mon-Fri; noon-11pm Sat, Sun. **No credit cards.** **Map** p328 K5 ⓳

Czech literati like Gustav Meyrink and Franz Werfel all tippled here before it became a Jazz Age hotspot. Miscreants still gather around the threadbare settees and battered tables for late-night talk. **Photo** p170.

Chateau Rouge

Jakubská 2, Prague 1 (222 316 328). Metro Náměstí Republiky/tram 5, 14, 26. **Open** noon-4am Mon-No credit cards. **Map** p328 M3 ⓴
Wall-to-wall cruising and stoned young Americans, but also the most popular bar in town. Always loud, always happening. **Photo** p164.

Cream & Dream

Husova 12, Prague 1 (224 211 035). Metro Staroměstská. **Open** 11am-10pm daily. **No credit cards.** **Map** p328 K5 ㉑
Not a sex club, but an ice-cream shop, with admittedly sinful waffle cones stuffed with frutti di bosco or caramel. If you can make it past the gleaming freezer, a micro-bar awaits in the back.

Dahab

Dlouhá 33, Prague 1 (224 827 375/www.dahab.cz). Metro Náměstí Republiky/tram 5, 8, 14. **Open** noon-11pm Mon-Thur, Sun; noon-2am Fri, Sat. **No credit cards.** **Map** p329 N2 ㉒
A definitive Prague tearoom, resembling a candlelit harem with pistachio cookies, Turkish coffees and occasional belly dancing. Approach some of the 'Middle Eastern' buffet items with caution.

Duende

Karoliny Světlé 30, Prague 1 (604 269 731/www.duende.cz). Metro Národní třída/tram 6, 9, 17, 18, 22, 23. **Open** 1pm-1am Mon-Fri; 3pm-1am Sat; 4pm-1am Sun. **No credit cards.** **Map** p328 J6 ㉓
New bohemian in a nutshell, with affable regulars and low-budget Prague intellectuals from the publishing and film scenes. A second home to many, this Latin-flavoured café-bar is a good deal more than the sum of its parts: Russian mandolin-playing on Friday nights, bizarre movies screened on Sundays, tattered sofas and fringed lampshades. The walnut liqueur (*Ořechovka*) is a rare treat. **Photo** p169.

Ebel Coffee House

Týn 2, Prague 1 (222 895 788/www.ebelcoffee.cz). Metro Náměstí Republiky/tram 5, 8, 14. **Open** 9am-8pm daily. **Credit** AmEx, MC, V. **Map** p328 M4 ㉔
Serious coffees, courtesy of journalist and designer Malgorzata Ebel, who was one of Prague's first suppliers of good beans (more than 30 prime arabica stocked), plus passable quiches, bagels and brownies, served on a lovely cobbled courtyard. In short, a caffeine-junkie heaven and intimate wood-trimmed room where staff serve fine blends any way you like, with tables in Prague's most fashionable Staré Město courtyard for those good weather days.

Érra Café

Konviktská 11, Prague 1 (222 220 568). Metro Národní třída/tram 6, 9, 18, 22, 23. **Open** 10am-midnight daily. **No credit cards.** **Map** p328 K6 ㉕

Shooters

The *panák* – or 'little clown', as shots are known – is a serious business in the Czech drinking world. If you'll take a shot with someone and match them one for one all night, you're to be trusted and will have a lifelong friend. That is, if they remember who you are the next day.

Becherovka, a ubiquitous, sweetish, yellow herbal liqueur from Karlovy Vary, is drunk straight or cut with tonic, in which case it's known as *beton* – 'concrete'. Fernet, a bitter local liqueur inspired by Fernet-Branca, goes better with beer. This too can be lightened with tonic water to create a *Bavorské pivo*, or 'Bavarian beer' – which, of course, has no beer in it and is unknown in Bavaria. The cheapest ticket to oblivion, and thus favoured by local drunks, is *Tuzemský* rum, made from beets. With sugar, hot water and a slice of lemon it actually makes a good warming grog in winter. *Borovička* is a juniper brandy, more Slovak than Czech and not unlike Dutch Jenever, while *Slivovice* (plum brandy), if not home-made, is smooth and goes down a treat.

Absinthe, at a grand 70 proof, is banned in most countries. It's a wormwood distillate but contains a slightly smaller (and allegedly less brain-damaging) percentage of wood alcohol than the version that once pickled the best minds of Paris. A translucent green liquid, it tastes much like alcoholic shampoo.

The proper ritual is to soak a spoonful of sugar with absinthe then set the sugar alight in the spoon to caramelise it. When the fire goes out, dump the spoonful back into the glass and stir. Then make sure to hang on to your socks.

It's as if a copy of Czech *Elle* exploded in a Staré Město cellar – even the menu poses: salads of apple and walnut are artfully arranged for lunch, as are the garlic-sesame chicken baguettes and rich banana milkshakes. The service is great by Prague standards, but the chairs are less comfortable. There's a gay-friendly scene by night, with a permanent house-music soundtrack.

Franz Kafka Café
Široká 12, Prague 1 (222 318 945). Metro Staroměstská/tram 17, 18. **Open** 10am-8pm daily. **No credit cards. Map** p328 L3
Dim, old-world and almost austere, this little coffeehouse is a trip back in time: there's frosted glass, dark, deep wooden booths, old engravings of the Jewish Quarter (it's just around the corner from the Jewish Cemetery) and, naturally, lots of Kafka portraits. The decent coffee and convivial tables on the street make it a convenient stop when touring Josefov.

Kavárna Obecní dům
Náměstí Republiky 5, Prague 1 (222 002 763/ www.vysehrad2000.cz). Metro Náměstí Republiky/ tram 5, 14, 26. **Open** 7.30am-11pm daily. **Credit** AmEx, MC, V. **Map** p329 N4
Easily the most epic café space in town, this balconied, art nouveau sipping space with a grand piano is situated at street level in the magnificently restored Municipal House. Replete with elaborate secessionist brass chandeliers, odd characters and always a few grandes dames, there is certainly not a more memorable venue for an espresso in Prague. A must for any visitor.

Kozička
Kozí 1, Prague 1 (224 818 308/www.kozicka.cz). Metro Náměstí Republiky/tram 5, 8, 14. **Open** noon-4am Mon-Fri; 6pm-4am Sat; 6pm-3am Sun. **Credit** MC, V. **Map** p328 M3
A popular, unpretentious local – hard to beat if only for that reason – with homely nooks, mighty steaks served until 11pm and Krušovice on tap.

La Casa Blů
Kozí 15, Prague 1 (224 818 270/www.lacasablu.cz). Metro Staroměstská/tram 5, 8, 14. **Open** 11am-midnight Mon-Thur, Sun; 11am-2am Fri, Sat. **No credit cards. Map** p328 M2
Rug-draped chairs, street signs and tequila specials evoke Latin culture, helped by an authentic Mexican menu. Try the buzzer even if the door is locked – people often wheedle their way in past closing.

Le Terroir
Vejvodova 1, Prague 1 (602 889 118). Metro Národní třída/tram 6, 9, 18, 21, 22, 23. **Open** 11am-11pm daily. **Credit** AmEx, MC, V. **Map** p328 L5
Le Terroir is a standard bearer for the city's new wave of wine bars. There's a few warm starters on the menu, but a killer foie gras terrine, in an ancient cellar that's grand for sipping wine after dark.

M1 Secret Lounge

*Masná 1, Prague 1 (221 874 256). Metro
Staroměstská/tram 17, 18.* **Open** *6pm-4am
daily.* **No credit cards. Map** *p328 M3* ③①
A bit heavy on attitude but a late option with an
appealingly lurid style, M1 is just a bar with red velour
and wavy iron decor, but the crowd can be counted on
to get up to mischief. Stick to beer and shots.

Marquis de Sade

*Templová 8, Prague 1 (no phone). Metro Náměstí
Republiky/tram 5, 14, 26.* **Open** *4pm-3am daily.*
No credit cards. Map *p329 N3* ③②
Dark, decadent and known for sofas with the stuff-
ing knocked out, the Marquis is an institution.
Legendary expat owner JB Shoemaker is gone, but
little else has changed (except for the beer prices), so
bad behaviour is ever encouraged and way too much
absinthe is drunk. Prime seating is on the balcony.
The bar's nothing to write home about and the service gets pretty slack, but occasional live blues or
jazz compensate somewhat.

Molly Malone's

*U Obecního dvora 4, Prague 1 (224 818 851/www.
mollymalones.cz). Metro Náměstí Republiky/tram 5,
14, 26.* **Open** *11am-1am Mon-Thur, Sun; 11am-2am
Fri, Sat.* **Credit** AmEx, MC, V. **Map** *p328 M2* ③③
Prague's first Irish bar started an invasion that's
never slowed down. Complete with roaring log fire,
mismatched chairs and tables constructed out of old
beds and sewing machines, incessant Pogues in the
background and 'traditional Irish food', it attracts
backpackers and rowdy English businessmen. The
bar is great for propping up, the Guinness is excellent, the food is decent, and in winter there's a warm
and welcoming atmosphere.

Monarch

*Na Perštýně 15, Prague 1 (224 239 602/
www.monarchvinnysklep.cz). Metro Národní
třída/tram 6, 9, 18, 21, 22, 23.* **Open** *11am-7pm
Mon-Sat.* **Credit** AmEx, MC, V. **Map** *p328 K5* ③④
A great wine shop and wine bar with more than 25
varieties of cheese and a good selection of regional
sausage. The place to come for South American or
Californian imports, plus the best local vintages and
knowledgeable but friendly service.

Ocean Drive

*V Kolkovně 7, Prague 1 (224 819 089/www.
tretters.cz). Metro Staroměstská/tram 17, 18.*
Open *4pm-2am daily.* **Credit** AmEx, MC, V.
Map *p328 L3* ③⑤
The latest hotspot for well-mixed cocktails and well-
rehearsed chat-up lines, Ocean Drive has a gorgeous
clientele, tempting cocktails and a West Coast feel.

Pivnice u Pivrnce

*Maiselova 3, Prague 1 (222 329 404). Metro
Náměstí Republiky/tram 5, 8, 14.* **Open** *11am-
midnight daily.* **No credit cards. Map** *p328 K3* ③⑥
Old-fashioned Czech cooking in the Jewish Quarter.
Svíčková (beef in lemon cream sauce), duck with
sauerkraut and walls covered with crude cartoons.
Radegast beer is well tapped and nicely priced.

St Nicholas Café. *See p163.*

NEW TIME OUT
SHORTLIST GUIDES 2007

Barcelona
2007
WHAT'S NEW | WHAT'S ON | WHAT'S NEXT

London
2007
WHAT'S NEW | WHAT'S ON | WHAT'S NEXT

New York
2007
WHAT'S NEW | WHAT'S ON | WHAT'S NEXT

Paris
2007
WHAT'S NEW | WHAT'S ON | WHAT'S NEXT

Prague
2007
WHAT'S NEW | WHAT'S ON | WHAT'S NEXT

Rome
2007
WHAT'S NEW | WHAT'S ON | WHAT'S NEXT

The MOST up-to-date guides to the world's greatest cities

UPDATED ANNUALLY

WRITTEN BY LOCAL EXPERTS

Available at all major bookshops at only
£6.99 and from timeout.com/shop

Duende is where all the creatives hang out. *See p165.*

Eat, Drink, Shop

Radegast Pub

Templová 2, Prague 1 (222 328 069). Metro Náměstí Republiky/tram 5, 14, 26. **Open** 11am-12.30am daily. **Credit** AmEx, DC, MC, V. **Map** p329 N4 ⑰

Despite its central location Radegast remains defiantly unchanged. Apart from the absence of foreigners, its main attractions are the excellent beer and pub food – you could easily pay an extra 400 Kč in a swanky restaurant and not find a better goulash. Semi-enclosed tables give privacy, but the service can be a bit on the iffy side – orders have been known to get lost.

Slavia

Smetanovo nábřeží 2, Prague 1 (224 218 493/www.cafeslavia.cz). Metro Národní třída/tram 6, 9, 17, 18, 22. **Open** 8am-11pm daily. **Credit** AmEx, MC, V. **Map** p328 J5 ㊳

Karel Tiege and a struggling Václav Havel once tippled and plotted the overthrow of communism at the Slavia. They wouldn't recognise the place now. The new, art deco fixtures and crisp service were overdue but they're not the stuff of Jaroslav Seifert's classic poem *Café Slavia*. Still, it has castle views, a decent salmon toast and, of course, history.

Tretter's

V Kolkovně 3, Prague 1 (224 811 165/www.tretters.cz). Metro Staroměstská/tram 17, 18. **Open** 7pm-3am daily. **Credit** AmEx, MC, V. **Map** p328 L3 ㊴

With red walls, a blues singer on Mondays and over 50 cocktails created by owner Mike Tretter, this is a delightfully cosmopolitan scene, with beautiful, competent bar staff. Try the newest sensation, the Caipikahlua, at the grand old 1930s-style tiled bar, watching for film and music types in the crowd. The staff have earned several bartending and mixing awards at international competitions. **Photo** p173.

Týnská literární kavárna

Týnská 6, Prague 1 (224 826 023/www. knihytynska.cz). Metro Staroměstská/tram 17, 18. **Open** 9am-11pm Mon-Fri; 10am-11pm Sat, Sun. **No credit cards. Map** p328 M3 ㊵

Vinegary wine, watery coffee, stale pastries and students who couldn't love it more. They file in to smoke, cavort, sit on the patio in summer and get steadily wasted. An arty location with spacey staff.

U Medvídků

Na Perštýně 7, Prague 1 (224 211 916/www. umedvidku.cz). Metro Národní třída/tram 6, 9, 18, 22, 23. **Open** 11.30am-11pm Mon-Sat; 11.30am-10pm Sun. **Credit** AmEx, MC, V. **Map** p328 K6 ㊶

Noisy, over-lit and as friendly as they come, At the Little Bears has five centuries as a beerhall behind it. Having brushed off communism as a passing fad, the bar keeps the fine, cheap Budvar coming until you tell the waiter to finally stop. Don't be sidetracked by the modern bar to the left of the entrance (unless it's 2.30am or after and the main one's closed); the real thing is on the right. The food menu is a step up from pub grub.

U Provaznice

Provaznická 3, Prague 1 (224 232 528). Metro Můstek/tram 6, 9, 18, 21, 22, 23. **Open** 11am-midnight daily. **No credit cards. Map** p328 M5 ㊷

Café Montmartre. *See p165.*

Incredibly, this classic pub, with typical Bohemian fare (duck, smoked meat and dumplings), is friendly, buzzy, reasonably priced, yet within spitting distance of the Můstek metro and tourist throngs.

U Vejvodů

Jilská 4, Prague 1 (224 219 999/www.restaurace uvejvodu.cz). Metro Můstek/tram 3, 9, 14, 24. **Open** 11am-2am Mon-Thur, Sun; 11am-3am Fri, Sat. **No credit cards. Map** p328 L5 ㊸

Another brewery-owned mega-beerhall (it's one of Pilsner Urquell's), this vast pub caters to big tour groups – stick to the smaller front room to avoid them. But it does offer quick service and old-style wood interiors, accented by the obligatory huge copper beer vat lids. For a ye olde pub feel, fine brews and traditional pub fare, it's hard to beat.

U Zlatého tygra

Husova 17, Prague 1 (224 221 111). Metro Staroměstská/tram 17, 18. **Open** 3-11pm daily. **No credit cards. Map** p328 K5 ㊹

At the Golden Tiger was once the second home of Prague's favourite writer, the famously crotchety Bohumil Hrabal. But it has lost virtually all its appeal since its famous patron fell to his death from a hospital window in 1997. Tourists still besiege the place, however, which may explain the beer prices.

Nové Město

Café Archa

Na Poříčí 26, Prague 1 (221 716 117). Metro Náměstí Republiky or Florenc/tram 3, 24. **Open** 9am-10.30pm Mon-Fri; 10am-10pm Sat; 1-10pm Sun. **No credit cards. Map** p329 P3 ㊺

Theatre cafés are some of the coolest spots in Prague to catch a culture wave, owing to the city's long-held intense passion for the stage. This glass fish tank-type building, with dangling lamps as bait, has hooked a young, laid-back clientele with cheap drinks, pristine surfaces and posters and photographs from the theatre and rock worlds.

Café Dinitz

Na Poříčí 12, Prague 2 (222 314 071/www.dinitz.cz). Metro Náměstí Republiky/tram 3, 8, 24, 26. **Open** 8am-3am Mon-Fri; 9am-3am Sat, Sun. **Credit** AmEx, MC, V. **Map** p329 O3 ㊻

Roman Sorkin's stylish café is a local secret, with small, quality menus that match the classy retro decor. It's a favoured hangout for writers, who appreciate the well-shaken cocktails and jazz trios.

Café Louvre

Národní třída 20, Prague 1 (224 930 949/www. kavarny.cz/louvre). Metro Národní třída/tram 6, 9, 18, 22. **Open** 8am-11.30pm Mon-Fri; 9am-11.30pm Sat, Sun. **Credit** AmEx, DC, MC, V. **Map** p328 K6 ㊼

Popular since the 19th century, this lofty café somehow manages to get away with a garish cream-and-turquoise colour combination, perhaps because it leads to a fine back room with pool tables. Solid weekend breakfasts and vested waiters.

French Institute Café

Štěpánská 35, Prague 1 (222 231 782). Metro Můstek/tram 3, 9, 14, 24. **Open** 8.30am-7.30pm Mon-Fri. **No credit cards. Map** p331 N8 ㊽

An island of Left Bank-esprit, this convivial, smoky café is a crucial source of croissants, philosophy and strong espresso. The French Institute is a Gallic nerve centre, with an unapologetically Francophile art gallery downstairs and cinema adjoining. An elegant, prime posing space, with an open courtyard and a fair chance of starting an intellectual romance.

Fuzion

Vodičková 38, Prague 1 (224 215 156/www. fuzion.cz). Metro Můstek/tram 3, 9, 14, 24. **Open** 7am-8pm Mon-Fri; 10am-7pm Sat, Sun. **No credit cards. Map** p329 N6 ➍➒

Fuzion is the best place to go in the centre of town for healthy takeout or fast food options, with fresh sandwiches, crispy salads, premium coffee and toothsome sweets. The upstairs gallery makes a nice roost just off Wenceslas Square and the prices beat those of the nearby fast food places.

Globe Bookstore & Coffeehouse

Pštrossova 6, Prague 1 (224 934 203/www. globebookstore.cz). Metro Národní třída/tram 6, 9, 18, 22, 23. **Open** 10am-midnight daily. **Credit** AmEx, DC, MC, V. **Map** p330 K8 ➎➋

Far more than just a bookshop that serves coffee, the city's original expat bookshop-café has been pegged as the literary heart of post-revolutionary Prague – and blamed for encouraging all the wannabe Hemingways. The Globe still carries the burden graciously, offering a pleasant reading room and comfortable café surroundings to scribblers of novellas and postcards. Passable pasta salads and such do for food, easily surpassed by the tall lattes and enormous brownies. There's strong support for local writers, who do regular readings here. The internet terminals and bulletin board are lifelines for expats.

Jáma

V jámě 7, Prague 1 (224 222 383/www.jama pub.cz). Metro Můstek/tram 3, 9, 14, 24. **Open** 11am-1am daily. **No credit cards.** **Map** p331 N7 ➎➊

American-owned with a patio space out the back, Jáma still has the loud college vibe that originally made its name. Czech scenesters come here too, and lunch specials and happy hour deals are a big draw for the crowds, as are the Czech-Mex menu and the friendly, speedy waiting staff.

Jazz Café č.14

Opatovická 14, Prague 1 (no phone). Metro Národní třída/tram 6, 9, 18, 22, 23. **Open** 10am-11pm Mon-Fri; noon-11pm Sat, Sun. **No credit cards.** **Map** p330 K7 ➎➋

Always smoky and filled with second-hand knick-knacks and struggling students, the Jazz Café makes for a snug winter hideaway. Service is patchy and jazz is only on CDs, while very basic snacks do for victuals – *medovník*, or honey cake, is about it. But the *svařák*, or mulled wine, is warming indeed.

Le Patio

Národní třída 22, Nové Město, Prague 1 (224 934 402). Metro Národní třída/tram 6, 9, 18, 22, 23. **Open** 8am-11pm Mon-Fri; 10am-11pm Sat, Sun. **Credit** AmEx, MC, V. **Map** p328 L6 ➎➌

Opulent and well-stocked, with decadent sweets and serious coffee, this French-owned emporium of imported and locally made decorative art doubles as an atmospheric café that's open all day.

Pack

Ve Smečkách 21, Prague 2 (222 210 280/www. thepack.cz). Metro Muzeum/tram 4, 6, 10, 16, 22, 23. **Open** 9am-2am Mon, Fri; noon-2am Tue-Thur; 6.30am-2am Sat, Sun. **Credit** AmEx, MC, V. **Map** p331 N7 ➎➍

If you've always wondered what a Czech version of Hooters would look like, and are into buffalo wings and hangover breakfasts served by tanned girls who look like they're running a relay race, you're in luck.

Pivovarský dům

Lípová 15, Prague 2 (296 216 666/www.gastroinfo. cz/pivodum). Metro Karlovo náměstí/tram 4, 10, 16, 22. **Open** 11am-11.30pm daily. **Credit** AmEx, MC, V. **Map** p330 M9 ➎➎

Visit this modern microbrewery for the beer: the excellent traditional lager, possibly Prague's best *pivo*, or the various wheat, cherry, champagne and coffee varieties on offer. There's average Czech cuisine served if you need to soak up the beer.

Propaganda

Pštrossova 29, Prague 1 (602 975 083). Metro Karlovo náměstí/tram 6, 9, 17, 18, 22. **Open** 3pm-2am Mon-Fri; 5pm-2am Sat, Sun. **Credit** AmEx, MC, V. **Map** p330 K7 ➎➏

Just a friendly neighbourhood café and bar, but one invariably jumping with a lively young Czech crowd and occasional local celebrities.

Ridgeback

Žitná 41, Prague 2 (no phone). Metro IP Pavlova/ tram 3, 6, 14, 18, 22, 23, 24. **Open** 4pm-4am daily. **No credit cards. Map** p331 N8 ➎➐

A popular bar for those skateboard-toting young locals who like to carry on in a sweet-smelling haze until the sun comes up. Crowded, noisy and smoky, but it's got its devoted regulars.

Solidní nejistota

Pštrossova 21, Prague 1 (224 933 086/www. solidninejistota.cz). Metro Národní třída/tram 6, 9, 17, 18, 22, 23. **Open** 6pm-6am daily. **No credit cards. Map** p330 K8 ➎➑

A shrine to posing and pick-ups, Solid Uncertainty comes equipped with the now-standard blood-red interior and grill bar. Occasional live rock shows draw in the crowds.

U Fleků

Křemencova 11, Prague 1 (224 934 019/www. ufleku.cz). Metro Národní třída/tram 3, 6, 14, 18, 24. **Open** 9am-11pm daily. **Credit** AmEx, DC, MC, V. **Map** p330 K8 ➎➒

Yes, it's the city's most famous pub and it has indeed been brewing fine 13-degree dark beer on the premises for centuries. Unfortunately, the world and his wife know this, and troop in when visiting Prague. Be prepared for the long tables invariably filled with Germans swinging glasses to oompah music and don't necessarily accept the pricey Becherovka when it's suggested by your smiling waiter. Try the picturesque courtyard, which is shaded by cherry trees and enclosed by a graffitied wall and leaded windows.

U Kruhu

Palackého 6, Prague 1 (605 258 978). Metro Národní třída/tram 3, 9, 14, 24. **Open** 11am-10pm Mon-Fri; 4-10pm Sat, Sun. **No credit cards.** **Map** p330 M7 ⑥⓪
A smallish, dyed-in-the-wool Czech pub with well-tapped beer and a small patio space that's surprisingly tranquil considering it is only a block off Wenceslas Square. Hard to beat for a handy taste of surviving authentic pubbing.

Ultramarin

Ostrovní 32, Prague 2 (224 932 249/www.ultra marin.cz). Metro Národní třída. **Credit** AmEx, DC, MC, V. **Map** p330 L7 ⑥①
A cool combination of ancient townhouse and modern art bar, Ultramarin is one of the city's most stylish bars, if still alcoholically challenged. The atmospheric retro jazz on the sound system, Santa Fe chicken salad on the menu, and blond wood and mottled wall paint would be better complemented by classier cocktails and tastier wines. Still, it's the best option for chilled late-night refuelling.

U Sudu

Vodičkova 10, Prague 1 (222 232 207). Metro Karlovo náměstí/tram 3, 9, 14, 24. **Open** 1pm-2am Mon-Fri; 2pm-3am Sat; 3pm-1am Sun. **No credit cards.** **Map** p330 M8 ⑥②

Very local, very trashed and very worthwhile, U Sudu was originally a small, dark wine bar on the ground floor only. Over the years it's expanded into three Gothic cellars. The cellars have been claimed by students, while upstairs sees everyone from artists to business types to little old ladies. The wine is nothing to write home about, except when the *Burčák* (a half-fermented, traditional Czech wine punch; *see also p203*) arrives in September.

Velryba

Opatovická 24, Prague 1 (224 912 391). Metro Národní třída/tram 6, 9, 18, 22, 23. **Open** 11am-midnight daily. **No credit cards.** **Map** p330 K7 ⑥③
Starving student heaven, with perpetual blasting rock on the sound system, a fog of cigarette smoke, greasy, cheap grub and barely drinkable wine. The Whale combines clamorous front-room dining on pastas and chicken steaks with back-room chess, and a cellar gallery specialising in fringe art and photography. The bar only serves bottled Gambrinus.

Vesmirna

Ve Smečkách 5, Prague 1 (222 212 363). Metro Muzeum/tram 11. **Open** 8.30am-10pm Mon-Fri; 2-10pm Sat. **No credit cards.** **Map** p331 N8 ⑥④
On a back street but worth seeking out, this low-key coffeehouse serves fresh juices and light meals, using healthy and organic produce. The organic couscous with cheese and vegetables and the apple pie are hits with the lunchtime crowd.

Železné dveře

Křemencova 10, Prague 1 (224 932 052). Metro Národní třída/tram 6, 9, 17, 18, 22, 23. **Open** 7pm-5am daily. **No credit cards.** **Map** p330 K8 ⑥⑤

Made into runts

The Czech repertoire of words and phrases dedicated to describing states of drunkenness is seemingly bottomless. Overdoing it can be referred to as *zpumprdlíkovanej*, or made into a *pumprdlík*, which is basically a runt. And then, getting drunk is not unlike being hit – in fact, 'hit pretty well', or *ztřískanej*. When you've really had enough, '*mam vopici*', or 'I have a monkey', best sums it up. If someone's already nabbed that line, there's always '*zpitý pod čáru*', 'to be drunk under the line'; '*zlitej jak dán*', 'to be drunk as a Dane' (or even better, '*zlitej jak doga*' or 'drunk as a Great Dane'); '*být pod vobraz*', 'to be under the picture'; '*být na kaši*', 'to have turned to mush' (a favourite of teens). This often happens after 'drinking like a mushroom' or '*nasávat jak houba*'. Do so quickly enough and you'll find yourself throwing a sabre or '*hodit šavli*'

– or, if you prefer, a scythe or '*hodit kosu*'. That's vomiting, to the less imaginative.

Hopefully, before that stage one can at least enjoy 'being smoked out' (*zkouřenej*) or 'painted' (*zmalovanej*) or 'having a head like a searching balloon' (*mít hlavu jako pátrací balón*). Do try to maintain some composure, however, lest you 'swear like a cobblestone layer' (*nadávat jako dlaždič*).

You should be careful not to 'stick the axe in' or '*zaseknout sekeru hluboko*' lest you run up a big tab. Better to call it quits while you can still 'slither like a snail' or '*plazit se jako šnek*'. Just don't be surprised the following morning when your mind is found to be 'outside' or '*být mimo*' – that is, useless.

Worse still, you could find you have your 'brain swept up like leaves' (*nametený*) or, if you've really overdone it, have a 'head like a piece of broken glass' (*mít hlavu jako střep*).

This maze of underground rooms in Prague's ghetto of cool, the area south of the National Theatre, is a favourite with party animals and attracts an undiscriminating mob of students looking to get blitzed.

Zlatá Hvězda

Ve Smečkách 12, Prague 1 (296 222 292/www.sportbar.cz). Metro Muzeum/tram 4, 6, 10, 16, 22, 23. **Open** 11am-midnight Mon; noon-2am Tue-Thur; 11am-4.30am Fri; noon-4.30am Sat; noon-midnight Sun. **No credit cards. Map** p331 N8 ⑥⑥
A tattered interior, crap service and very average pizzas don't discourage the sports fans who gather here to watch the games on the battered big screens.

Further Afield

Dejvice

Café Orange

Puškinovo náměstí 13, Dejvice, Prague 6 (mobile 603 894 499). Metro Hradčanská. **Open** 10am-11pm Mon-Sat; 11am-3pm Sun. **No credit cards.**
Out of the way, but a discreet, warm space ideal for a secret rendezvous. The first daytime venue in Prague 6 with lattes, mozzarella ciabattas and street tables is on a quiet, hard-to-find square.

Holešovice

Fraktal

Šmeralova 1, Prague 7 (no phone). Metro Vltavská/tram 1, 8, 25, 26. **Open** 11am-midnight daily. **No credit cards. Map** p332 C3 ⑥⑦
An intense out-of-centre bar phenomenon, the friendly owners of this cosy little drinking hole with occasional live music and/or book launches have produced a trashy convivial place where anything goes. Mojitos and tequila gold with orange and cinnamon cocktails make notable accompaniments to the improved menu of inevitable Czech-Mex.

La Bodega Flamenca

Šmeralova 5, Prague 7 (233 374 075). Metro Vltavská/tram 1, 8, 25, 26. **Open** 4pm-1am Mon-Thur, Sun; 4pm-3am Fri, Sat. **No credit cards. Map** p332 C3 ⑥⑧
The easily missed entrance to this cellar tapas bar conceals a perpetual sangria party. Owner Ilona oversees the bar, serving up tapas such as marinated olives and garlic mushrooms. Bench-style seats line the walls and fill up fast and, in true Spanish style, things only really start hotting up after 1am.

Le Tram

Šmeralova 12, Prague 7 (233 370 359). Metro Vltavská/tram 1, 8, 25, 26. **Open** 8pm-6am daily. **No credit cards. Map** p332 C3 ⑥⑨
A French-owned hole-in-the-wall bar made up of old (you guessed it) tram parts. Other than that, and the bohemian sleep-starved students who tend to gravitate here, it's essentially the same cheap beer and Cuba Libres as everywhere else.

Tretter's. *See p169.*

Letenský zámeček

Letenské sady 341, Letná park, Prague 7 (233 375 604/www.letenskyzamecek.cz). Metro Hradčanská/tram 1, 8, 25, 26. **Open** *Beer garden* 11am-11pm daily. *Restaurants* 11am-11.30pm daily. **No credit cards. Map** p332 D4 ⑦⓪
A leafy enclave on the hill above the Vltava is arguably the city's finest summer beer garden. A local crowd gathers under the chestnut trees for cheap beer in plastic cups late into the evening. If you get hungry check out the adjoining Brasserie Ullman and Restaurant Belcredi, which have gone upscale with modern designer interiors, a dressy crowd and excellent Bernard beer on tap.

Un Chien Andalou

Korunovační 4, Prague 7 (731 221 167). Metro Hradčanská, then tram 1, 8, 15, 25, 26. **Open** 7pm-5am daily. **No credit cards. Map** p332 C3 ⑦①
Cool, dark and sofa-filled, this plush little place is a local secret, where live bands occasionally appear, usually as iconoclastic as the bar staff. Decent cocktails and wall-to-wall decadent atmosphere.

Výletná

Letenské sady 32, Prague 7 (no phone). Metro Hradčanská/tram 1, 15, 25, 26. **Open** 11am-1am daily. **No credit cards. Map** p332 D4 ⑦②
Situated just off the tennis courts in Letná park, this rustic little pub serves bargain barbecue fare on its terrace by summer and often gets taken over for parties and various events, sometimes stretching to literary readings, at other times of the year.

Smíchov

Káva Káva Káva

*Lidická 42, Prague 5 (no phone). Metro Anděl/tram
4, 7, 10, 14.* **Open** 7am-10pm Mon-Thur; 9am-10pm
Fri, Sat. **No credit cards**.
An LA-style coffee and muffin shop that can satisfy caffeine cravings ranging from Guatemalan arabica to Sumatra dark roast. Refreshingly laid back
for this newly smart district.

Kavárna v sedmém nebi

*Zborovská 68, Prague 5 (257 318 110). Tram 6, 9,
12, 22.* **Open** 10am-1am Mon-Fri; 2pm-1am Sat, Sun.
No credit cards.
A peaceful, arty café-bar, with a whimsical loft from
which to spy on those sipping from their cups in the
comfy junk-shop chairs below. This meeting place for
the local film community is half work of sculpture and
half living room. The menu is limited to coffee and
tea, along with *bábovka*, a Czech cake, *bundt*, toasted
sandwiches and crisps.

U Buldoka

*Preslova 1, Prague 5 (257 329 154). Metro Anděl/
tram 6, 9.* **Open** 8pm-4am daily. **No credit cards**.
At once old-world and modern, At the Bulldog is one
of the last classic pubs in the district. Well-tapped
Staropramen beer and excellent traditional grub go
with an international sensibility, quick service and
a cool dance club below deck. All-day specials of
halušky (Slovak gnocchi with bacon) and *guláš* soup
suit the light and dark beer, plus a nice collection of
Czech herbal liqueurs at the bar.

Vinohrady

Café Medúza

*Belgická 17, Prague 2 (222 515 107). Metro
Náměstí Míru/tram 4, 22.* **Open** 11am-1am Mon-
Fri; noon-1am Sat, Sun. **No credit cards**.
Map p331 Q11
On a quiet Belgická street you'll find one of the city's
cosiest, if threadbare, winter hideout spots, run by
two sisters who serve warming soups and mulled
wine to bookish regular patrons.

Café Metropole

*Anny Letenské 18, Prague 2 (222 254 457/
www.cafemetropole.cz). Metro Jiřího z Poděbrad/
tram 4, 10, 16, 22, 23.* **Open** 8am-midnight
Mon-Sat. **Credit** AmEx, MC, V. **Map** p333 A3
Café Metropole is an excellent bookstore café that
has its own wi-fi, improbably comfortable padded
café chairs, a good selection of wine on offer and
expert service, care of the New Yorker owner, a veteran of the Prague bar world.

James Bond Café

*Polská 7, Prague 2 (222 733 871/www.james
bondcafe.cz). Metro Jiřího z Poděbrad/tram 4, 10, 16,
22, 23.* **Open** 6pm-2am daily. **No credit cards**.
Map p333 B3

Café Metropole: take a sip.

This 007-inspired café didn't hold back when it came
to mod seating and bar surfaces, but its cocktails
aren't quite 'licensed to kill'. Service is a notch up
from many a bar. Good for a laugh and a light meal.

Kaaba

*Mánesova 20, Prague 2 (222 254 021). Tram
11.* **Open** 8am-10pm Mon-Sat; 11am-10pm Sun.
No credit cards. **Map** p333 A3
Filled with second-hand furniture, most of it fabu-
lous and redone in pastels, this neighbourhood café
is a haven for local creative idlers. The great windows on to the Vinohrady street outside and decent
wines by the glass from well-known domestic producers make it a good choice for long mornings of
lazing with magazines and cheap coffee.

Park Café

*Riegrovy sady 28, Prague 2 (no phone). Metro Jiřího
z Poděbrad/tram 11.* **Open** 11am-11pm daily. **No
credit cards**. **Map** p333 B3
One of the liveliest beer gardens in the district is
always crowded with old-timers, children, dogs and
expats. The beer is cheap and copious, and rock
bands liven it up for summer. Just watch where you
step, the dogs leave deposits.

Pastička

*Blanická 25, Prague 2 (222 253 228/www.pasticka.
cz). Metro Náměstí Míru/tram 4, 10, 16, 22, 23.*
Open 11am-1am Mon-Fri; 5pm-1am Sat, Sun.
No credit cards. **Map** p333 A3

The Little Mousetrap is a beloved neighbourhood hang that's always jumping with a mixed crowd that goes in for gab, grub, beer and cigarettes.

Potrefená husa

Vinohradská 104, Prague 3 (267 310 360). Metro Jiřího z Poděbrad/tram 11. **Open** 11.30am-1am daily. **Credit** AmEx, MC, V. **Map** p333 C3 ⑦
The kind of place that you'd find in every suburb of a Western city, the Wounded Goose is a runaway success in Prague. It offers a better menu and service than a lot of Prague restaurants – but that's not terribly difficult. Part of a national chain, it's nearly always packed with young professionals sipping Velvet beer and noshing on chicken wings and ribs while taking in cable TV sports.
Other locations: Kolinská 9, Prague 3 (267 310 360); Bilkova 5, Prague 1 (222 326 626).

První Prag Country Saloon Amerika

Korunní 101, Prague 2 (224 256 131). Metro Náměstí Míru/tram 11. 11am-midnight Tue-Fri; 5pm-midnight Sat; 6-11pm Sun. **No credit cards. Map** p333 C3 ⑥⓪
Head 'em up, move 'em out! Live Czech country-and-western bands – must be seen to be believed – fiddle nightly. Would-be cowboys and their gals crowd into the hardwood seating, tuck into steaks and admire the animal skins on the walls. The hardcore but incredibly friendly crowd here risked jail under the old regime for collecting Americana. *See also p240.*

Shakespeare & Sons

Krymská 12, Prague 10 (271 740 839/www. shakes.cz). Metro Náměstí Míru/tram 4, 22. **Open** noon-midnight daily. **Credit** MC, V.
An elegant bookstore and café a stone's throw from the Vršovice-Vinohrady border, Shakespeare & Sons offers a wide selection of mind fodder, as well as Bernard beer and good coffee. It's also clearly on the literary map, with readings, book launches and a thoroughly page-turning bohemian crowd.

Zvonařka

Šafaříkova 1, Prague 2 (224 251 990). Metro IP Pavlova/tram 6, 11. **Open** 11am-midnight daily. **No credit cards. Map** p331 Q12 ⑥①
A stylish new bar in a graceful old building that's been turned into one of the swankiest hotels in town. The terrace out back is a godsend, with its fine view of the Nusle Valley. There'a menu of traditonal Czech food for the hungry but the main reason to come here is to sip, chin-wag and look at the view.

Žižkov

Akropolis

Kubelíkova 27, Prague 3 (296 330 911). Metro Jiřího z Poděbrad/tram 11. **Open** 11.30-1am daily. **No credit cards. Map** p333 C2 ⑥②
Still the most popular bar in the district for the post-1989 generation, the Akropolis is a longtime Žižkov institution of drinking, indie music concerts and networking for arty types. It has four separate pubs on

site, each with its own crowd and vibe. The street-level Akropolis restaurant serves cheap and decent food with passable beer (*see p235*); the Kaaba Café is a small, well-lit place that's perfect for meeting a group of friends and getting a caffeine fix; the Divadelní Bar is a hot, intense vortex of DJ action and surreal woodcarvings; the Malá Scena, on the other hand, is a red-washed chill-out space with a post-industrial look and battered tables.

Blind Eye

Vlkova 26, Prague 3 (no phone). Metro Jiřího z Poděbrad/tram 11. **Open** 11am-5am daily. **No credit cards. Map** p333 B3 ⑥③
Blind Eye is a late-night hideout that's popular with the district's sleep-starved bohemians of all nationalities. The open but unfinished interior offers rambling conversations at the wavy iron-top bar, beer at a booth table or a cult movie of your choice from its built-in video rental. Great fun all round.

Park Café

Riegrovy sady, Prague 3 (222 717 247). Metro Muzeum/tram 11. **Open** 11am-midnight daily. **No credit cards. Map** p313 B2.
Children, dogs, beer and sunshine. Park Café is the biggest outdoor venue in the east end of central Prague, attracting people from three adjoining neighbourhoods, who are drawn by battered benches, the pleasant shade of chestnut trees and cheap Krušovice by the half-litre. Dogs run yapping between the tables, bands take to the stage on weekends and there are grassy knolls all around for more private moments.

U Sadu

Škroupovo náměstí 5, Prague 3 (222 727 072). Metro Jiřího z Poděbrad/tram 11. **Open** 10am-2am daily. **No credit cards. Map** p333 C3 ⑥④
U Sadu is a classic Czech pub-restaurant that's located in the heart of old-style Žižkov. It's popular with students and holds its own against the hundreds of earthy pubs around. The chilli goulash, schnitzels and fried cheese are a marvellously unhealthy treat, the Pilsner and Gambrinus are well tapped and service is thoroughly gruff. It doesn't get any more authentic than this. The kitchen is open late too, for Prague.

U vystřeleného oka

U božích bojovníků 3, Prague 3 (222 540 465). Metro Florenc, then bus 135 or 207. **Open** 4.30pm-1am Mon-Sat. **No credit cards. Map** p333 C1 ⑥⑤
Thoroughly surreal. The Shot-Out Eye sits beneath the ominous giant statue of General Jan Žižka, the renowned warrior whose battle injury inspired the gory name. Žižkov has more pubs than any other area of Prague, but this is definitely one of the best, at least for fans of garage rock and weird pieces of art. A three-level outdoor beer garden serves bargain-basement Měšťan, while the taps indoors flow non-stop to a soundtrack of local anarcho-rockers Psí Vojáci and a backdrop of grotesque paintings by the artist Martin Velíšek.

Shops & Services

Gear up and surf the tidal wave of post-totalitarian consumerism.

Get a snack while choosing a gift to take home at **Havelský Market**. *See p179.*

Eat, Drink, Shop

There was once a time when shopping in Prague told a tale of a cultural and commercial gulf between East and West, best exemplified by the horrified reaction of a shopping assistant to an item brought to the counter: 'It's the last one. If you buy it, we'll have to order more.'

These days, shopping in Prague is pretty much the same as in any Western city. This means that you'll be able to find what you want, but that some Czech idiosyncrasies have been worn out. Still, only people who never had to deal on a day-to-day basis with the idiocies and humiliations of communist-era customer service could mourn its passing. In its stead, visitors will now find that in the centre many shop workers speak some English and, although a court ruling recently upheld surcharges for credit card use, more and more shops will take plastic without looking at you like you've got a third head. Longer opening hours are in effect and not always just in the more touristy areas. But straying even a little outwards from the centre may still mean shops that close at noon on Saturdays and don't open at all on Sundays.

The majority of the big stores are multi-nationals, come in to spruce up the shopping scene. They've found a welcoming, shopping-crazed new generation of Czuppies waiting, especially eager for the clothing shops that sell inexpensive but trendy wares. The average Czech salary is still low compared to other, more senior, members of the European Union club, and retailers are mindful of their market. The shopping mall concept has taken off like a Prada sale, which is no small achievement in the dense urban area that is Prague. Larger malls are concentrated on the outskirts of the town, while smaller examples can be found at Palác Flora and Nový Smíchov Centrum.

With the influx of outsiders, some local shops are feeling the pinch, notably institutions like the neighbourhood *potraviny*. The massive hypermarkets, and even the more reasonably sized supermarkets, have been slowly easing these corner shops out of business.

While that may be all very well for the necessities of life, what about the essentials? The Louis Vuitton handbag, the Hugo Boss shirts, the Versace dress? Well, the Velvet Revolution wasn't just about ending 50 years of communist tyranny, it had the local fashionistas all a-tizzy too. These days, Czech fashion plates don't have to visit Paris or Milan for their dose of couture; a stroll down Old Town's most conspicuously consumptive streets, Celetná and Pařížská, will supply all the requirements of a properly tailored lifestyle. Want the style but don't have the dosh? Knock-offs of the brand names have followed right behind, doing good business with trend-loving locals who see no reason to pay for the real thing. Street markets are full of shoes, purses and the like, sporting the right look and the right label. These often turn up later at high-society events, adorning Czech celebs.

But you don't come to Prague for what you can find in any other European capital. No, the joys of Prague shopping are to be found off the main drag, down quiet alleyways and in dusty old shops. This is where you may still come across vintage prints and books, quaint lace and glass, or other treasures yet to be discovered. When entering a shop, the clerk will ask 'Máte přání?' ('Do you have a wish?'). While ringing up your purchases, he may ask 'Ještě něco?' ('Anything else?') or 'Všechno?' ('Is that all?'). If you want to know the price of an item, say 'Kolik to stojí?' to find out what it costs.

The best Shops

For Bohemian wearables
Belda Jewelry Design (see p187), Fashion Galerie No.14 (see p184), Modes Robes (see p187).

For catching the latest Czech rap craze
Bontonland Megastore, Maximum Underground (for both, see p194), Pohodlí (see p195).

For Czech-made natural goods
Dr Stuart's Botanicus (see p183), Manufaktura (see p192), Včelařské potřeby (see p193).

For designer specs
Eiffel optic (see p195), GrandOptical (see p196).

For unusual gifts
de.fakto (see p192), Hudební nástroje – Radek Bubrle (see p195), Qubus (see p192), Slovenská Izba (see p193).

SHOPPING AREAS

As is typical in most cities, avoid the central shopping areas unless you are desperate or in souvenir shopping mode. This especially applies to Hradčany and the area around Prague Castle. Staré Město is a little better, especially as you drift towards Nové Město. High fashion and high prices can be found on **Pařížská**, which is best hit on a sunny day for its tree-lined sidewalks and inviting outdoor cafés. Mall central, as well as many other chain stores, can be found along **Na příkopě**. **Wenceslas Square** can pretty much be skipped for shopping purposes but the streets on either side are excellent places for wandering, especially the further out you go. Beware of some shady characters, however, especially at night. Souvenir-seekers should stroll down any of the streets leading out from **Old Town Square**, as well as the **Malá Strana** area near **Charles Bridge**. Moving further out to **Karlín** and **Holešovice** will reward antique junkies, but just about every neighbourhood boasts a hidden surprise or two.

One-stop shopping

Department stores

Carrefour
Radlická 1, Smíchov, Prague 5 (257 284 111/ www.carrefour.cz). Metro Anděl/tram 4, 6, 7, 9, 10, 14. **Open** 7am-midnight daily. **Credit** AmEx, DC, MC, V.
A massive supermarket on the ground floor of the Nový Smíchov mall, the second floor is typical department store, with sections for clothing, household items, stationery and electronics. The supermarket has an excellent selection of just about everything: meats, cheeses, produce and wine. Lots of imported goodies too, as well as a decent-sized 'health' food section.
Other locations: Stodůlky, Prague 13 (251 173 111); Plzeňská 8, Smíchov, Prague 5 (257 284 111).

Kotva
Náměstí Republiky 8, Staré Město, Prague 1 (224 801 111). Metro Náměstí Republiky/tram 5, 8, 14. **Open** *Department store* 9am-8pm Mon-Fri; 10am-7pm Sat; 10am-6pm Sun. *Supermarket* 7am-8pm Mon-Fri; 9am-6pm Sat; 10am-7pm Sun. **Credit** AmEx, MC, V. **Map** p329 O4.
Kotva is centrally located, and strangely arranged almost like a market. The items get more varied as you move upwards, with cosmetics and luggage on the first floor, while clothing, sports equipment and furniture can be found on the upper floors.

Tesco
Národní třída 26, Nové Město, Prague 1 (222 003 111). Metro Můstek or Národní třída/tram 6, 9, 18, 21, 22, 23. **Open** *Department store* 8am-9pm

Mon-Fri; 9am-8pm Sat; 10am-8pm Sun. *Supermarket* 7am-10pm Mon-Fri; 8am-8pm Sat; 9am-8pm Sun. **Credit** AmEx, MC, V. **Map** p328 L6.

Always packed, and occasionally headache inducing, Tesco nonetheless probably has what you need. The basement is a grocery store, while the ground floor has cosmetics and beauty supplies, along with a small *potraviny* and some souvenirs and other gift items. Ascending through the building, you'll find the men's, women's and children's clothing floors, kitchen and other home needs, and, finally, electronic goods can be bought on the top floor.

Malls

A mall is a mall, and once you're inside you could be anywhere in the world. The newest is out in Chodov, a bit outside the centre, but very easily reached by metro. The dedicated mall rat should try the string of shopping centres that line Na příkopě: they may not offer inspired shopping but there's certainly plenty of it.

Černá růže

Na příkopě 12, Nové Město, Prague 1 (221 014 111). Metro Můstek/tram 3, 9, 14, 24. **Open** 10am-8pm Mon-Fri; 10am-7pm Sat; 11am-7pm Sun. **Credit** AmEx, MC, V. **Map** p329 N5.

Appropriately snuggled in next to a McDonald's, this fairly dull shopping centre has some fashion boutiques, some wine shops and a couple of other decent home furnishing offerings.

Myslbek Centre

Na příkopě 19-21, Staré Město, Prague 1 (224 239 550). Metro Můstek/tram 3, 9, 14, 24. **Open** 8.30am-8.30pm Mon-Sat; 9.30am-8.30pm Sun. **Credit** AmEx, MC, V. **Map** p329 N5.

Come to Prague and feel at home. Myslbek is where you'll find all the shops you know. Still, it's central, there's a good café on the top floor if you need refuelling, and the shops are reliable and will probably be able to supply what you need.

Nový Smíchov Centrum

Plzeňská 8, Smíchov, Prague 5 (257 284 111). Metro Anděl/tram 4, 6, 7, 9, 10, 14. **Open** 7am-midnight daily. **Credit** AmEx, MC, V.

This is a pleasant enough mall, complete with a Datart, H&M, Clinique and Sephora, among other name-brand stores. A branch of Carrefour is also located here, as is a third-level games arcade, spacious food court and cinema.

Palác Flóra

Vinohradská 149, Vinohrady, Prague 3 (255 741 700/www.palacflora.cz). Metro Flóra/tram 5, 10, 11, 16. **Open** 8am-midnight daily. **Credit** AmEx, MC, V. **Map** p333 C3.

Less crowded than Nový Smíchov Centrum, Palác Flóra is directly accessible from the metro station. There's something for everyone here, with trendy shops, big-name label stores, a supermarket and a dry-cleaner, as well as decent food offerings

– both of the fast and sit down type. It's the sort of mall you could enjoyably spend an afternoon in. Prague's IMAX theatre is also located here.

Slovanský Dům

Na příkopě 22, Nové Město, Prague 1 (221 451 400/ information 2421 1295/www.slovanskydum.cz). Metro Můstek/tram 3, 9, 14, 24. **Open** 10am-8pm daily. **Map** p329 N5.

Another dull offering on Na příkopě, the multiplex cinema is the biggest draw, along with a nice sushi restaurant. Some reasonable shops can be found, but otherwise there's nothing to write home about.

Markets

Prague doesn't have much in the way of outdoor markets, except around holiday time. The rest of the year it's mainly fruits and vegetables, along with the odd wooden or woven item. Christmas and Easter, however, see the squares come alive with a variety of holiday goodies. The Christmas markets in Old Town Square or Václavské náměstí are the best and, since it'll be chilly, you have the perfect excuse to warm yourself with a nice cup of steaming mulled wine – *svařené víno* or *svařák*.

Havelský Market

Havelská, Nové Město, Prague 1 (no phone). Metro Můstek or Národní třída/tram 6, 9, 18, 22. **Open** 7.30am-6pm Mon-Fri; 8.30am-6pm Sat, Sun. **No credit cards**. **Map** p328 L5.

Fruits and vegetables have been squeezed out by souvenirs, but there is still some fresh produce to buy. Lots of wooden items and toys, puppets and other tourist trinkets. Be sure to check out the sweet booths as well as the fresh flowers. **Photo** p177.

Market at the Fountain

Spálená 30, Nové Město, Prague 1 (no phone). Metro Národní třída/tram 6, 9, 18, 22. **Open** 7.30am-7pm daily. **No credit cards**. **Map** p330 L8.

Fruit and veg that look good, come in a reasonable number of varieties and have good prices attached make this market the place to buy your five-a-day. Apart from green stuff, there are scarves, sweaters and other random goodies on offer, the variety of which increases as the weather gets warmer. If you're trying to find the market, it's behind Tesco.

Antiques

There are dozens of antiques shops in Prague, but there are also numerous junk shops, selling everything from old irons and typewriters to prints by Alfons Mucha. If an antiques shop is on a main tourist route, you can be fairly sure that the prices are aimed at foreigners.

For cheaper and more unusual items, seek out a bazaar. Some are listed here, but more can be found in the *Zlaté stránky* (*Yellow Pages*) – look for the index in English at the back.

Eat, Drink, Shop

Take on a different identity at **Art Deco**. *See p181.*

Antique

Kaprova 12, Staré Město, Prague 1 (222 329 003).
Metro Staroměstská/tram 17, 18. **Open** 10am-7pm
Mon-Sat; 10am-6pm Sun. **Credit** AmEx, MC, V.
Map p328 J3.
Very impressive stuff, but you do pay for the quality on offer. There's some lovely glass and jewellery, and be sure to check out the fascinating religious items and the variety of pocket watches.

Antique Ahasver

Prokopská 3, Malá Strana, Prague 1 (257 531 404).
Metro Malostranská/tram 12, 18, 22, 23. **Open**
11am-6pm Tue-Sun. **Credit** MC, V. **Map** p327 F4.
Here you'll find antique formal gowns, traditional folk clothing, linens, mother-of-pearl hairpins, beaded purses, brooches and trays of charming oddments. The English-speaking sales assistants are always ready to supply a story and help you decide.

Art Deco

Michalská 21, Staré Město, Prague 1 (224 223 076).
Metro Staroměstská or Národní třída/tram 6, 9, 17,
18, 22, 23. **Open** 2-7pm Mon-Fri. **Credit** AmEx,
MC, V. **Map** p328 L5.
Dress-up fun! Vintage clothing and lots of jewellery, as well as an interestingly varied mix of other random goodies. The prices are good as well. **Photo**.

Bazar Antik Zajímavosti

Křemencova 4, Nové Město, Prague 1 (no phone).
Metro Národní třída/tram 6, 9, 18, 21, 22, 23.
Open 10am-6pm Mon-Fri. **No credit cards.**
Heavy on the glass, this is your typical bazaar. Tea cup fans will think they've found nirvana, but other shoppers can appreciate the linens and small collection of paintings and unique lamps.

Bric a Brac

Týnská 7, Staré Město, Prague 1 (224 813 240).
Metro Staroměstská or Náměstí Republiky/
tram 5, 8, 14, 17, 18. **Open** 10am-6pm daily.
Credit AmEx, MC, V. **Map** p328 M3.
Good things come in small, rammed-to-the-gills packages. Bric a Brac is the sort of place you visit, then find yourself returning to the next day to make sure you didn't miss anything. Street signs, jewellery and old cameras are only a few of the finds.

Hamparadi Antik Bazar

Pštrossova 22, Nové Město, Prague 2 (224 931 162).
Metro Národní třída/tram 6, 9, 18, 21, 22, 23.
Open 10.30am-6pm daily. **No credit cards.**
Map p330 K8.
Quirky treasures are scattered in and among the typical bazaar offerings of porcelain and glass. Be sure to take your time and browse carefully, so as not to miss any real finds. Toys and old advertisements add to the nostalgic motif.

Kubista

Dům u Černý Matky Boží, Celetná 34, Staré Město,
Prague 1 (224 236 378/www.kubista.cz). Metro
Náměstí Republiky/tram 5, 8, 14. **Open** 10am-6pm
daily. **Credit** MC, V. **Map** p329 N4.
How much more Prague can you get than a shop devoted to cubism? Original cubist porcelain and furniture, lovingly wrought re-creations and art books from the museum shop of the National Gallery's excellent museum of cubism at the House of the Black Madonna (*see p98*). **Photo** p182.

Modernista

Konviktská 5, Staré Město, Prague 1 (222 220
113/www.modernista.cz). Metro Můstek or
Národní třída/tram 6, 9, 18, 21, 22, 23. **Open**
2-6pm Mon-Fri; 11am-4pm Sat. **Credit** AmEx, MC,
V. **Map** p328 K6.
A cool shop. The pieces are cubist, art deco, functionalist and other –ists, all sleek and modern. It also showcases restored desk chairs and armoires from the early to mid-20th century, as well as reproductions from Czech architects and designers.

Bookshops & newsagents

The variety isn't that great and the prices charged are outrageous for locals, but English-language bookshops do exist in Prague. If you're dying for a read, check out one of the following. They're also a good place to chat with a fellow tourist or expat.

Anagram Bookshop

Týn 4, Staré Město, Prague 1 (224 895 737/www.
anagram.cz). Metro Náměstí Republiky/tram 5, 8,
14. **Open** 10am-8pm Mon-Sat; 10am-7pm Sun.
Credit DC, MC, V. **Map** p328 M3.
Good for hard to find books – especially used. Anagram also has an excellent selection of books on Prague and Central Europe.

Big Ben Bookshop

Malá Štupartská 5, Staré Město, Prague 1 (224 826
565/www.bigbenbookshop.com). Metro Náměstí
Republiky/tram 5, 8, 14. **Open** 9am-6.30pm Mon-Fri;
10am-5pm Sat; noon-5pm Sun. **Credit** AmEx, MC, V.
Map p328 M3.
If it's possible to buy it in Prague, here's where you should be able to find it. Big Ben Bookshop has an excellent children's section, multiple shelves of English-language newspapers and magazines, and friendly staff that knows the shop's stock. Come here for fiction, non-fiction, bestsellers and old favourites. Plus they'll order in products that you can't find in the store. The first stop for any bookworm.

Globe Bookstore & Coffeehouse

Pštrossova 6, Nové Město, Prague 2 (224 916 264).
Metro Národní třída/tram 6, 9, 18, 21, 22, 23.
Open 10am-midnight daily. **Credit** AmEx, MC, V.
Map p330 K8.
Probably the best-known expat hangout in Prague, the Globe should cover your reading needs and more. There's a simple restaurant at the back, internet access and lots of new and used books. An added bonus is its location in Nové Město, which makes it an excellent base for an evening of quirky dining and unique coffeehouse experiences. **Photo** p183.

Eat, Drink, Shop

Kubista: where everything is made up of angles. *See p181.*

Knihkupectví U Černé Matky Boží

Celetná 34, Nové Město, Prague 1 (224 222 349).
Metro Náměstí Republiky/tram 5, 8, 14. **Open** *Jan-Easter, Oct-Dec* 9.30am-7pm Mon-Fri; 10am-6pm Sat.
Easter-Sept 9.30am-7pm Mon-Fri; 10am-6pm Sat,
Sun. **Credit** AmEx, MC, V. **Map** p328 M4.
The location on Celetná is excellent, both for the
address and the architecturally notable building the
bookshop inhabits. You'll find English-language
books on the ground floor, along with puzzles, maps,
art prints and other gift goodies. Great coffee-table
books, as well as fun Prague gifts for children.

Trafika Můstek

Václavské náměstí, Nové Město, Prague 1 (no phone).
Metro Můstek/tram 3, 9, 14, 24. **Open** 8am-10pm
daily. **No credit cards. Map** p331 O7.
If it's an English-language periodical you're looking
for, this kiosk at the bottom of Wenceslas Square
should have it. If it doesn't, you are out of luck.

Old books & prints

Prague's second-hand bookshops are known
as *antikvariáty.* If you have the time and are
passing one, go in. You'll never know what
you'll find, from old communist coffee-table
books to dirt-cheap prints by unknown Czech
artists. *Antikvariáty* are also good for second-
hand novels in English.

Antikvariát Galerie Můstek

Národní 40, Nové Město, Prague 1 (224 949 587).
Metro Národní třída/tram 6, 9, 18, 21, 22, 23.
Open 10am-7pm Mon-Fri; noon-4pm Sat; 2-6pm Sun.
Credit AmEx, MC, V. **Map** p328 L6.
A discriminating *antikvariát* where you will find a
fine selection of antiquarian books and a reliable
stock of the major works on Czech art.

Antikvariát Kant

Opatovická 26, Nové Město, Prague 1 (224 934
219/www.antik-kant.cz). Metro Národní třída/
tram 6, 9, 18, 21, 22, 23. **Open** 10am-6pm Mon-
Fri; 10am-3pm Sat. **Credit** AmEx, MC, V.
Map p330 K8.
Antikvariát Kant has a varied mix of prints and
dust-encrusted tomes, along with quite a large, but
strange, selection of English books, and a huge, very
well-organised postcard collection. The prints on the
walls are varied, and the cheap books in the entryway are worth more than a passing glance.

Antikvariát Pařížská

Pařížská 8, Staré Město, Prague 1 (222 321 442).
Metro Staroměstská/tram 17, 18. **Open** 10am-7pm
Mon-Fri; 10am-6pm Sat, Sun. **Credit** AmEx, MC, V.
Map p328 L3.
An excellent shop, with fine, helpful staff, that spe-
cialises in maps and prints. There are some books,
antique stamps and postcards to add to the variety,
but it's the maps you'll want to see.

Computers

Apple Center Anděl
Nadrážní 23, Smíchov, Prague 5 (257 210 493/
www. appleobchod.cz). Metro Anděl/tram 6, 12, 20.
Open 10am-10pm Mon-Fri; 10am-7pm Sat; 2-7pm
Sun. **Credit** AmEx, MC, V.
The only Apple centre in town, the Apple Center
Anděl has a complete line-up of all things Mac,
including iPods, peripherals, software, iBooks and
the rest. Trained and helpful English-speaking staff.

HSH Computer
Nadrážní 42, Smíchov, Prague 5 (257 310 910/
www.hsh.cz). Metro Muzeum/tram 11. **Open** 9am-
6pm Mon-Fri. **Credit** MC, V.
Sales, service and rentals of a variety of big-name
brands including Compaq, HP, IBM and Toshiba.
Service centre: Gorazdova 5, Nové Město, Prague 2
(224 912 163). **Other locations**: Kotva, Náměstí
Republiky 8, Staré Město, Prague 1 (224 801 337);
Bílá labut, Na poříčí 23, Prague 1 (222 320 581).

Kinetik
Bělehradská 2, Vinohrady, Prague 2 (222 515 455/
www.macsource.cz). Metro IP Pavlova/tram 6, 11.
Open 9am-6pm Mon-Fri. **Credit** AmEx, MC, V.
Map p331 P10.
Previously called MacSource, it's a single-source
direct reseller of computer IT products and services.

Cosmetics & perfumes

You can, of course, find the usual lipsticks and
mascaras at any department store. The shops
listed below are a bit more specialised.

Body Basics
Myslbek Centre, Na příkopě 19-21, Staré Město,
Prague 1 (224 236 800). Metro Můstek/tram 3, 9,
14, 24. **Open** 9am-8pm Mon-Sat; 10am-7pm Sun.
Credit AmEx, MC, V. **Map** p329 N5.
Bathing emergency? Body Basics has got you cov-
ered. The store has its own line of body lotion and
some cosmetics, but really this is a place for the
votaries of Zeus, the (among other things) rain god:
there are shower and bath gels galore, in various ani-
mal, fruit and geometrical shapes, as well as poufs,
body scrubbers and bath salts.
Other locations: Marriott, V Celnici 10, Nové Město,
Prague 1 (228 818 55); Pavilon, Vinohradská 50,
Vinohrady, Prague 2 (222 097 105); Ruzyně Airport,
Ruzyně, Prague 6 (220 113 595); Nový Smíchov Centrum,
Plzeňská 8, Smíchov, Prague 5 (257 322 947).

Dr Stuart's Botanicus
Týn 3, Staré Město, Prague 1 (224 895 446/
www.botanicus.cz). Metro Náměstí Republiky/
tram 5, 8,14, 26. **Open** 10am-8pm daily.
Credit AmEx, MC, V. **Map** p328 M3.
Besides soap, lotions and bathing salts and gels,
Botanicus has herb-inspired oils, teas, honey and
foodstuffs. It's 100% Czech, with all ingredients
grown on a farm just outside of Prague. **Photo** p185.

Other locations: Lucerna, Štěpánská 61, Nové
Město, Prague 1 (224 221 927); Michalská 2, Staré
Město, Prague 1 (224 212 977); Veselská 663,
Letňany, Prague 9 (284 014 369); Centrum Černý
Most, Chlumecká, Prague 9 (281 917 726).

Lush
Kaprova 13, Staré Město, Prague 1 (603 164 362).
Metro Staroměstská/tram 17, 18. **Open** 10am-7pm
Mon-Sat; 2-6pm Sun. **Credit** AmEx, MC, V.
Map p328 J3.
The name says it all. This is the place to go to indulge
and spoil your body with outrageous creams, gels
and things to soak in. Lots of cool scents and dif-
ferent goops for different parts from head to toe.

Dry-cleaners & laundrettes

All the laundrettes in the city charge roughly
the same for washing and drying, so your
choice chiefly depends on location.

CleanTouch
Dlouhá 20, Staré Město, Prague 1 (224 819 257).
Metro Náměstí Republiky/tram 5, 8, 14, 26. **Open**
8am-7pm Mon-Sat. **No credit cards**. **Map** p328 M3.
CleanTouch offers dry-cleaning at reasonable prices
with a quick turnaround in modern surroundings.
Other locations: Na Rybníčku 1329, Vinohrady,
Prague 2 (296 368 500); Supermarket Delvita,
Jeremiášova 7A, Stodůlky, Prague 5 (5162 6371).

**Globe Bookstore
& Coffeehouse**. *See p181.*

Eat, Drink, Shop

Prague Laundromat

Korunní 14, Vinohrady, Prague 2 (222 510 180/ www.volny.cz/laundromat). Metro Náměstí Míru/ tram 4, 10, 16, 22, 23. **Open** 8am-8pm daily. **No credit cards. Map** p333 A4.

The self-proclaimed 'first internet-laundromat in Europe' will do everything your laundry needs, including dry-cleaning. The English-speaking staff provide service washes, but have been known to be a bit surly. Internet access, beer and coffee will help while away the hours in between wash cycles.

Electronics

Most basic electronic items can probably be found at either Tesco or Carrefour (for both, *see p178*). But if you need something specific, or hard to find, visit one of the places listed below.

Datart

Národní 60, Prague 1 (221 105 311/www.datart.cz). Metro Národní třída/tram 6, 18, 19, 22, 23. **Open** 9am-8pm daily. **Credit** AmEx, MC, V. **Map** p328 L6.

Come here for a new stereo, refrigerator, washing machine or any other electronic item your home may need. The store promises low prices and the staff for the most part are friendly and helpful.

Electro World

Řevnická 1, Zličín, Prague 5 (235 002 800). Metro Zličín. **Open** 9am-9pm daily. **Credit** MC, V.

Here's the big one for the silicon geeks: computers, digital cameras, HD TV, hi-fi, all the requirements for this binary age. If there's anywhere in Prague that has it, Electro World is the place, which makes the trek to the outskirts of town worthwhile. **Other locations:** Česlice, Obchodní 117, Prague Česlice (267 227 700); Černý Most, Chlumecká 1531, Prague 9 (281 028 555).

Fashion

Budget

Šatna

Konviktská 13, Staré Město, Prague 1 (no phone). Metro Národní třída/tram 6, 9, 18, 21, 22, 23. **Open** 11am-7pm Mon-Fri; 11am-6pm Sat. **No credit cards. Map** p328 K6.

Šatna is a second-hand clothing store that's small but neatly arranged, with all the items in great condition. There's a large men's section as well, which is sometimes hard to find in Prague.

Senior Bazar

Senovážné náměsti 18, Nové Město, Prague 1 (224 235 068). Metro Náměstí Republiky/tram 3, 5, 9, 14, 24, 26. **Open** 9am-5pm Mon-Thur. **No credit cards. Map** p329 P4.

You may get the evil eye from the regulars, but Senior Bazar is a Prague institution. It's one of the best second-hand clothes shops you'll find in the

city, and the variety and quality on offer are top notch. In short, it's the place to go when you're looking for something different that won't break the bank. **Other locations:** Karoliny Světlé 18, Staré Město, Prague 1 (222 333 555).

Costume & formal dress hire

Prague is a pretty dressed-up city, architecturally speaking, so you never know when the urge to do likewise with clothes may strike. Be sure, however, to make a reservation several days in advance and to take your passport along as proof of identity.

Barrandov Studio, Fundus

Kříženeckého náměstí 322, Barrandov, Prague 5 (267 072 210/www.barrandov.cz). Metro Smíchovské nádraží, then bus 246, 247, 248. **Open** 7am-3pm Mon-Fri. **No credit cards.**

This is the big daddy of dressing up: there are 240,000 costumes, 20,000 pairs of shoes and 9,000 wigs in stock. If you can't find something here, you should be staying at home. It's not cheap, but the selection and quality are outstanding.

Ladana Costume Rental

Opatovická 20, Nové Město, Prague 1 (224 930 234). Metro Můstek or Národní třída/tram 6, 9, 18, 21, 22, 23. **Open** 7.30am-8pm daily. **Credit** MC, V. **Map** p330 K8.

If you are lucky enough to be invited to a *ples*, or ball, while in Prague, Ladana has got what you need to make a grand entrance. There are all sorts of wedding and social gowns in stock, as well as period costumes, masks and Czech folk outfits.

Designer

While it may not be mentioned in the same breath as Paris or Milan, the Prague fashion scene continues to grow and improve. Communist couture left something to be desired, and the country is still playing catch-up, but more Czech designers are setting up shops and making names for themselves, both at home and abroad.

Fashion Galerie No.14

Opatovická 14, Nové Město, Prague 1 (no phone). Metro Národní třída/tram 6, 9, 18, 22. **Open** noon-7pm Mon-Sat. **Credit** AmEx, MC, V. **Map** p330 K8.

This is store is not for the budget conscious, but is definitely for the fashion plate. Each item is an original and the quality and the design of clothing are beautiful. There are mainly dresses on display, but some casual items are available, as well as jewellery to complete the ensemble.

Klára Nademlýnská

Dlouhá 3, Staré Město, Prague 1 (224 813 723/ www.klaranademlynska.cz). Metro Staroměstská/ tram 17, 18. **Open** 10am-7pm Mon-Fri; 11am-6pm Sat. **Credit** AmEx, MC, V. **Map** p328 M3.

For 100% Czech in a bottle… or a bar of soap, visit **Dr Stuart's Botanicus**. *See p183.*

Dressing for dark

Two weeks in Prague, two weeks in Paris. That's how Czech fashion designer Monika Drápalová stays fresh.

'I stay in Prague, but I like to work all over the world,' she says. 'I like to see and meet French designers, it's more of a fashion country than the Czech Republic and for me it's a challenge. It's good for inspiration.'

Though she only sells by special arrangement, working from her boutique in Prague 8, demand has never been stronger. Since earning her degree in fashion design from the Academy of Decorative Arts in Prague, Drápalová hasn't looked back. Her first big honour came in 1999 when she was named 'Designer of the Season' at the International 'Styl' fair in Brno. That led to an opportunity to open a studio in Lyon, France; she'd been operating Atelier Modrá in Prague since 1998. Before the high

fashion honours, though, Drápalová had been busy designing costumes for Czech films, television, theatre and singers.

'When I was young, I used to make clothes for young people, more sporty,' she says. 'But after my experience in France I started to focus on evening wear. I can express more with it.'

Drápalová does both custom work and her own designs and finds each one rewarding. 'I am sensitive to the person,' she says. 'I can express the personality of the woman. The other is only my ideas and my imagination. I have more freedom.'

All clothing starts with some sort of fabric, and that's what Drápalová likes best. 'I love thin and transparent material,' she says. 'I use special fabrics with laser copies of flowers; muslin, silk and satin; there are new high-tech fabrics that are interesting as well.'

Drápalová's Spring/Summer 2007 Collection is what she's focused on now. It's called 'Spoil Me' and is described as 'joyously nostalgic but playful' and uses a variety of fabric with 'motion and emotion'. She also would like to do a collection for the other half of the population. 'I have some ideas for a men's collection, but maybe not for Prague,' she says. 'But there may be a place for something new.'

So how does she see the Prague fashion scene? 'It's difficult to only work in the Czech Republic,' she says. 'You are influenced by the people who buy your clothing; there's a danger for you to lose your freshness. In Prague, we need more courage'.

Besides translating to 'blue' in English, the name of her studio, Modrá, is also the first letters of her first name and surname. Check **www.modra-fashion.cz** for more information.

Klára Nademlýnská sells cutting edge but wearable styles for women. The tailored items here are superior, her suits and separates wonderfully made. Enjoyable for just about anyone.

Tatiana
Dušní 1, Staré Město, Prague 1 (224 813 723/ www.tatiana.cz). Metro Staroměstská/tram 17, 18. **Open** 10am-7pm Mon-Fri; 11am-4pm Sat. **Credit** AmEx, DC, MC, V. **Map** p328 L3.
Designer fashions that are designed to be worn, Tatiana Kovarikova's clothing is a mixture of high fashion elegance and practicality. The perfect cut, beautiful styling and small details make each piece fashionable, yet functional.

Fur & leather

Kreibich Kožešiny & Rukavice
Michalská 14, Staré Město, Prague 1 (224 222 522/ www.kreibich.cz). Metro Staroměstská or Národní třída/tram 6, 9, 17, 18, 22, 23. **Open** 9.30am-6pm Mon-Fri. **Credit** AmEx, MC, V. **Map** p328 L5.
If it came from a dead animal, and you can cover your body with it, then this place has got it. Favoured by locals and tourists alike, it does a booming business once the mercury begins to drop. There are leather items too, including hats, coats and gloves. **Other locations**: Hybernská 30, Staré Město, Prague 1 (224 222 924).

Jewellery & accessories

Garnets and amber are the most popular jewels, but other unique and interesting gemstones can be found as well. The prices tend to be pretty much the same everywhere but quality can differ widely between stores, so it pays to look around and ask questions.

Belda Jewelry Design

Mikulandská 10, Nové Město, Prague 1 (224 933 052). Metro Národní třída/tram 6, 9, 18, 22. **Open** 10am-12.30pm, 1.30-6pm Mon-Thur; 10am-12.30pm, 1.30-5pm Fri. **Credit** AmEx, MC, V. **Map** p330 K7.

Unique, quality-crafted goods are the hallmark at Belda. These are pieces you won't find anywhere else, with the prices to match. A small selection, but the earrings, bracelets, rings and others are a refreshing change from the garnet- and amber-stuffed jewellery stores elsewhere.

Lingerie

Chez Parisienne

Pařížská 8, Staré Město, Prague 1 (224 817 786). Metro Staroměstská/tram 17, 18. **Open** 10am-7pm Mon-Fri; 10am-6pm Sat. **Credit** AmEx, DC, MC, V. **Map** p328 L3.

It's on Pařížská, so you have to pay for the location, but the lovely underthings will fit beautifully and they'll feel wonderful.

Dessous-Dessus

Králodvorská 7, Staré Město, Prague 1 (224 811 779). Metro Náměstí Republiky/tram 5, 8, 14. **Open** 10am-7pm Mon-Fri; 10am-6pm Sat. **Credit** AmEx, MC, V. **Map** p329 N3.

Variety is the name of the game here. Dessous-Dessus carries just about everything that can be hidden – or displayed – under your outer wear. Tights, available in a rainbow of colours, bras, panties, and lingerie ranging from the nearly naughty to nice. Pyjamas and chemises round out the selection. **Other locations**: Železná 547/3, Staré Město, Prague 1 (224 217 854).

Mid-range

Madeo Boutique

Vodičkova 28, Nové Město, Prague 1 (no phone). Metro Můstek/tram 3, 9, 14, 24. **Open** 10am-7pm Mon-Fri; 10am-3pm Sat. **Credit** AmEx, MC, V. **Map** p329 N6.

Constantly rotating stock helps keep this shop fresh. Primarily casual wear, and sometimes pricey, but check the sales racks for some good bargains.

Modes Robes

Benediktská 5, Staré Město, Prague 1 (224 826 016/www.cabbage.cz/modes-robes). Metro Náměstí Republiky/tram 5, 8, 14. **Open** 10am-6pm Mon-Fri; 10am-4pm Sat. **Credit** MC, V. **Map** p329 N3.

The interior is as much a reason to visit as the clothing inside this tiny shop. Designed by a local artist, Modes Robes has been selling unique clothing, accessories and art for more than ten years. Check out the wide selection of dresses: every body and every age will find something to flatter.

Vivienne Boutique

Rytířská 22, Staré Město, Prague 1 (221 094 314). Metro Národní třída/tram 6, 9, 18, 22. **Open** 10am-5.30pm Mon-Fri; 10.30am-3pm Sat. **Credit** AmEx, MC, V. **Map** p328 L5.

Tailored suits, casual tops, sweaters and jackets are the mainstay at Vivienne's. However, some sexy see-through items slip in as well. The selection is varied and unusual enough to ensure that you'll score something special.
Other locations: Královdvorská 5, Staré Město, Prague 1 (222 323 837).

Shoes

Stylish clothing may not always be easy to find, but in Prague you can ensure that your feet at least will look good: footwear stores are everywhere. You can find Italian imports, but Czech-made shoes, as well as other European offerings, are on offer at more reasonable prices.

ART

Narodni 36, Staré Město, Prague 1 (224 948 828). Metro Národní třída/tram 6, 9, 12, 18, 22, 23. **Open** 9.30am-7pm Mon-Fri; 9.30am-5pm Sat. **Credit** AmEx, MC, V. **Map** p328 L6.

Mainly women's shoes, heavy on the funky leather items and stiletto heels Czech women love to wear in any kind of weather. The store also carries brands like Camper, Doc Marten's and Adidas.

Baťa

Václavské náměstí 6, Nové Město, Prague 1 (224 218 133). Metro Můstek/tram 3, 9, 14, 24. **Open** 9am-9pm Mon-Fri; 8am-8pm Sat; 9am-8pm Sun. **Credit** AmEx, MC, V. **Map** p329 N6.

Baťa is a true Czech original – you could even justify your shoe purchase by counting it as a souvenir rather than footwear. Men's, women's and children's shoes are covered, in both fashion and sport styles. Baťa also does shoe repairs on the third floor, and there is a selection of luggage for sale.
Other locations: Jindřišská 20, Nové Město, Prague 1 (222 247 349); Moskevská 27, Vršovice, Prague 10 (271 721 860); Plzeňská 8, Smíchov, Prague 5 (251 512 847); Vinohradská 149, Prague 3 (255 740 028).

Humanic

Narodni třída 34, Nové Město, Prague 1 (224 920 295). Metro Můstek or Národní třída/tram 3, 6, 9, 14, 18, 22, 23, 24. **Open** 9am-8pm Mon-Fri; 9am-7pm Sat; 10am-6pm Sun. **Credit** MC, V. **Map** p328 L6.

This shop stocks the basic clothing requirements at prices most people can afford, with ranges suitable for men, women and children. Purses, wallets and hosiery are also available.

Eat, Drink, Shop

timeout.com

Over 50 of the world's greatest
cities reviewed in one site.

Shoe repairs

There are shoe repair shops in Baťa (see p187) as well as Tesco and Kotva supermarkets (for both, see p178). Failing that, check the Zlaté stránky (Yellow Pages) under 'obuv-opravy'.

Jan Ondráček

Navrátilova 12, Nové Město, Prague 1 (222 231 960). Metro Národní třída/tram 3, 9, 14, 24. Open 8am-6pm Mon-Thur; 8am-5pm Fri. No credit cards. Map p330 M8.
This central shoe repair shop offers all the services that you need to make your favourite pair last out that little bit longer.

Florists

Giving flowers is a big Czech tradition, so there's no shortage of florists in Prague. Nearby květinařství can be found on every block and clustered around metro stations. Any of these are likely to have what you need for most occasions, but if you're looking for something extra special, try the florist below.

Květinařství U Červeného Lva

Saská ulička, Malá Strana, Prague 1 (604 855 286). Metro Malostranská/tram 12, 22, 23. Open 9am-7pm Mon-Sat; 11am-7pm Sun. Credit MC, V. Map p327 G4.
This crowded little shop is fairly bursting with colour and variety. Dried flowers hang from the ceiling, while plants, cut flowers and wreaths cover every available square centimetre.

Food & drink

For classy eating in or a last-minute invite to a dinner party, the city's new wave of gourmand meccas should do the job.

Food delivery

Food Taxi

777 171 394/603 171 394/www.foodtaxi.cz. Open 10am-3.30pm, 5.30-10pm Mon-Fri; 11am-10pm Sat. No credit cards.
Order online or by phone from the menus of nearly 30 restaurants in Prague and have the food delivered directly to your door. Chinese, Mexican, Italian and International are the choices.

Tele Pizza

Klimentská 34, Staré Město, Prague 1 (222 311 383). Metro Náměstí Republiky/tram 5, 8, 14. Open 10am-2am Mon-Fri. No credit cards. Map p329 O2.
Promising incredible prices and perfect deep crust pizza, Tele Pizza rests its reputation on its traditional 'American-style' rich and chewy crusts. Added bonuses: there's no delivery charge in downtown, and pizzas are delivered in 30 minutes.

Specialist

Bakeshop Praha

Kozí 1, Staré Město, Prague 1 (222 316 823/ www.bakeshop.cz). Metro Staroměstská/tram 17, 18. Open 7am-7pm daily. Credit AmEx, MC, V. Map p328 M3.
Is there any more evocative smell than freshly baked bread? If so, we don't know it. Bakeshop Praha has a variety of baked goodies, in unique flavours and styles, that all make towards a great place to pick up something to go, or to sit down and have a coffee. Sandwiches, quiches and to-die-for muffins and cakes will also tempt your taste buds.
Other locations: Lázeňská 19, Malá Strana, Prague 1 (257 534 244).

La Bretagne

Široká 22, Staré Město, Prague 1 (224 819 672). Metro Staroměstská/tram 17, 18. Open 9.30am-7.30pm daily. No credit cards. Map p328 L3.
The Czech Republic may be a land-locked country, but piscivores take heart, fresh seafood can be found in Prague, and La Bretagne is your best bet. A variety of ice-packed, freshly caught imported fish is yours for the baking, sautéing or frying, as are other imported goodies like wine.

Country Life

Melantrichova 15, Staré Město, Prague 1 (224 213 366/www.countrylife.cz). Metro Můstek/tram 3, 9, 14, 24. Open 9.30am-6.30pm Mon-Thur; 10am-3pm Fri; 11am-6pm Sun. No credit cards. Map p328 L4.
The biggest and best-known health food store in the city. Tofu, fresh breads, organic items and bulk foods for the health-nuts. The accompanying buffet at the Melantrichova location is always a hit; the store on Jungmannova has a takeaway counter.
Other locations: Jungmannova 1, Nové Město, Prague 1 (257 044 419).

Cream & Dream

Husova 12, Staré Město, Prague 1 (224 211 035/ www.cream-dream.com). Metro Národní třída/ tram 6, 9, 18, 21, 22, 23. Open 11am-10pm daily. No credit cards. Map p328 K4.
You scream, I scream, we all scream for Cream & Dream. The yummiest ice-cream in town, the Italian-style gelato is made fresh on site. The combination of fresh fruit and rich cream equals a cool treat at anytime. If it's winter, get it with some coffee to balance your temperature.

Culinaria Praha

Skořepka 9, Staré Město, Prague 1 (224 231 017/ www.culinaria.cz). Metro Národní třída/tram 6, 9, 18, 21, 22, 23. Open 9am-6pm Mon-Fri; 10am-4pm Sat, Sun. Credit AmEx, MC, V. Map p328 L5.
Culinaria Praha is the place to come for all sorts of hard to find ingredients and imported foods. Ben & Jerry's ice-cream, Arizona Teas and Pam cooking spray have all been spotted. There's an excellent selection of Asian cooking products and kosher items as well as a sandwich, juice and coffee bar to eat in.

Saps and gems

Every jeweller worth their weight in carats offers them. Garnets and amber are impossible to miss among the crystal and stacking dolls in the tourist shops. But do you know anything about the history of these remarkable jewels, and how to ensure you're not getting ripped off? Read on.

The city of Turnov, north-east of Prague, is garnet central. This is where the original, and true, Bohemian garnets hail from. The Bohemian garnet is recognised by its fiery red colour and ability to reflect light. Its reputed curative effects include the ability to overcome sorrow, and to bring vitality and joy to the wearer. The jewel's popularity goes back to Rudolf II, who counted many garnet-encrusted pieces in his collection. Garnets were also used to decorate the dresses of Russian tsarinas in the 1800s.

Art Cooperative Granát, a production facility in Turnov, produces 3,500 different designs, and employs master craftsmen to create new ones every year. The garnets themselves are usually set in sterling silver, gold-plated silver, or 14- or 18-carat gold. Bear in mind that the Granát facility is the only legal mining operator in the country. You should always ask for a manufacturer's certificate when buying a jewel. True Bohemian garnets will also be marked with G, G1 or G2. The two Granát locations in Prague are both in Prague 1 (Panská 1, Staré Město, and Dlouhá 28, Nové Město).

And then there is, forever, amber. While it's often thought of as a gem, amber is an organic substance, the fossilised remains of prehistoric tree resin. Natural Baltic amber, sometimes called the gold of the north, has been used as an ornament and curative at least since Neolithic times, when it served as a symbol of the sun. Egyptians used to put amber in their tombs as a preservative, while Roman women would hold it in their hands, believing it to endow eternal youth. Some still swear amber can stave off depression, attract joy and promote healing. Amber made its way south to Bohemia along river trading routes from the Baltic Sea, where it soon found favour with commoners and royalty alike.

Fruits de France

Jindřišská 9, Nové Město, Prague 1 (222 511 261/ www.fdf.cz). Metro Můstek/tram 3, 9, 14, 24. **Open** 9.30am-6.30pm Mon-Fri; 9.30am-1pm Sat. **Credit** MC, V. **Map** p329 N6.

A foodie temple of imported goods and exotic fruit and vegetables, with the prices to prove it. There are two locations: visit the one on Jindřišská listed above if you're looking for fruits, vegetables or wine, while the Bělehradská store below has an excellent selection of fish and pâtés. **Photo** p191.
Other locations: Bělehradská 94, Vinohrady, Prague 2 (222 511 261).

Interlov Praha

Jungmannova 25, Staré Město, Prague 1 (224 949 516/www.interlov.cz). Metro Národní třída/tram 6, 9, 18, 21, 22, 23. **Open** 9am-5.30pm Mon-Fri. **No credit cards. Map** p328 M6.

Have the taste for some fresh boar, pheasant or rabbit? No gun required at this butcher. Exotic game, along with the spices and wine to go with it. For the less knowledgeable it sells recipe books; for the less adventurous, sausages.

Koruna Pralines Chocolaterie

V Jámě 5, Nové Město, Prague 1 (606 222 651). Metro Můstek/tram 3, 9, 14, 24. **Open** 9am-8pm Mon-Fri; 9am-6pm Sun, Sat. **Credit** MC, V. **Map** p330 M7.

The smell. It's what envelopes you as you enter the shop. Go there just for a nice sniff, but be sure to pick up a little something for your taste buds as well. All manners of milk, dark and white chocolate in all combinations mean something for everyone, be they a fruit or a nut. Try the Becherovka-filled chocolates. There is also a small but nice wine selection.

Maso Tomáš Turek

Jindřišská 23, Prague 1 (224 230 968). Metro Můstek/tram 3, 9, 14, 24. **Open** 8am-6pm Mon; 7am-6pm Tue, Wed, Fri; 7am-6.30pm Thur; 8am-12.30pm Sat. **No credit cards. Map** p329 N6.

Maso Tomáš Turek is a blast from the communist past, not in the sense of surly service, but of great fatty platters of *klobása*. The communists never did believe the health hype that red meat is bad for you and the husky, happy Czechs that fill the store would seem to back up the belief.

Shalamar

Lipánská 3, Žižkov, Prague 3 (603 495 260). Metro Jiřího z Poděbrad/tram 5, 9, 26. **Open** 10am-7pm Mon-Fri; noon-7pm Sat, Sun. **No credit cards. Map** p333 D2.

Being next door to a Pakistani restaurant, you can guess what imported goodies you'll find here. Basmati rice, lime pickles or a variety of other treats from the Subcontinent.

Teuscher

Malá Štupartská 5, Staré Město, Prague 1 (224 828 050). Metro Náměstí Republiky/tram 5, 8, 14. **Open** 10.30am-7.30pm daily. **No credit cards. Map** p328 M3.

Champagne- and Becherovka-filled truffles number among the fine Swiss chocolates on sale here. Chocoholics, and others, will find something unique and yummy to fill their tummies.

U Zavoje Cheese Shop

Havelská 25, Staré Město, Prague 1 (226 006 120). Metro Můstek/tram 6, 9, 12, 18, 22, 23. **Open** 9am-6pm Mon-Fri; 10am-4pm Sat, Sun. **Credit** AmEx, MC, V. **Map** p328 L5.

Say Brie. Say Gruyère. Say Mascarpone. Say it in the U Zavoje Cheese Shop and you'll get a big 'Ano!' in response. French, Swiss, Italian, Greek and Czech varieties are just some of the offerings, along with Italian sausages, Greek olives and dried tomatoes and spices. U Zavoje also has a cognac and cigar shop, as well as a wine shop at the same location.

La Vecchia Bottega

Na Perštýně 10, Staré Město, Prague 1 (224 234 629). Metro Národní třída/tram 6, 9, 18, 21, 22, 23. **Open** 9am-6pm Mon-Fri; 10am-4pm Sat, Sun. **Credit** AmEx, MC, V. **Map** p328 L6.

A small, long shop, the front half mainly has teas and honey, but the back is where you want to go for the Italian wines, pestos, pastas, vinegars and sweets. Downstairs are all the cooking utensils you could possibly shake a spoon at.

Supermarkets

Supermarkets can also be found in the aforementioned Tesco and Carrefour (for both, *see p178*).

Alberts

Václavské náměstí 21, Nové Město, Prague 2 (224 232 810). Metro Můstek/tram 3, 9, 14, 24. **Open** 9am-9pm daily. **Credit** AmEx, MC, V. **Map** p329 N6.

Conveniently located in a few metro stations, including Náměstí Republiky and Můstek, as well as elsewhere around town, Alberts will take care of all your meal or emergency snack needs.

Other locations: throughout town.

Delvita

Bělehradská 50, Nové Město, Prague 2 (222 562 292). Metro IP Pavlova/tram 4, 6, 11, 16, 22, 23. **Open** 9am-9pm daily. **Credit** MC, V.

More than two dozen branches across Prague make this one-stop market easy to find and easy to shop. Good bakery, so-so produce and a decent butcher.

Other locations: throughout town.

Wine & beer

Blatnička

Michalská 6, Staré Město, Prague 1 (224 233 612). Metro Národní třída/tram 6, 9, 18, 22, 23. **Open** 10am-6pm Mon-Fri. **No credit cards**. **Map** p328 L5.

Blatnička is a tiny place offering some tasty wines. It's a local favourite and you can even bring your own plastic bottle for staff to fill up. No corkscrew

Fruits de France. *See p190.*

Eat, Drink, Shop

Manufaktura.

Eat, Drink, Shop

is required. Many places keep *sudova vina* or jug wine on hand (which is cheaper wine kept in big barrels that can be dispensed into any container you bring to the shop) so be sure to ask if all you want is to refill your Coke bottle with something better.

Cellarius

Lucerna Passage, Štěpánská 61, Nové Město, Prague 1 (224 210 979/www.cellarius.cz). *Metro Můstek/tram 3, 9, 14, 24.* **Open** 9.30am-9pm Mon-Sat; 3-8pm Sun. **Credit** AmEx, MC, V. **Map** p331 N8.
A huge selection of wines is crammed into the small space of Cellarius. It's maze-like, so be sure to look both left and right so as not to miss anything. Lots of local vineyards as well as some good imports, including French, Bulgarian and Chilean wines.
Other locations: Budečská 29, Vinohrady, Prague 2 (222 515 243).

Galerie piva

Lažeňská 15, Malá Strana, Prague 1 (257 531 404). *Metro Malostranská/tram 12, 18, 22, 23.* **Open** 10am-6pm Mon-Sat. **Map** p327 F4
The Beer Shop stocks all the major Czech beers and dozens of the more interesting minors in bottles as well as just about every beer-imprinted mug. Good for the collector as well as the beer lover back home.

Monarch

Na Perštýně 15, Staré Město, Prague 1 (224 239 602/www.monarchvinnysklep.cz). Metro Národní třída/tram 6, 9, 18, 21, 22, 23. **Open** 11am-7pm Mon-Sat. **Credit** AmEx, MC, V. **Map** p328 L6.

Not only a shop but wine bar as well, Monarch offers more than 25 varieties of cheese for your perusing pleasure to accompany any offerings to Bacchus. This is the place to come if you are looking for South American or Californian imports.

Vinotéka u Svatého Štěpána

Štěpánská 7, Nové Město, Prague 2 (221 901 160). *Metro Muzeum/tram 3, 9, 14, 24.* **Open** 10am-7pm Mon-Fri. **Credit** AmEx, MC, V. **Map** p331 N8.
It's a smaller store, but there's a decent selection of both domestic and imported wines. Liqueurs and champagnes can be found here as well. Vinotéka u Svatého Štěpána also has gift bags and boxes, and very nice stemware and decanters.

Gifts

Garnets, crystal and wooden toys fairly jump out at you from every tourist shop you pass. The determined souvenir-seeker will find many goodies to lure their crowns and bring a smile for years to come.

Charita Florentinum

Ječná 4, Nové Město, Prague 2 (224 921 501). Metro Karlovo náměstí/tram 4, 6, 16, 22, 34. **Open** 8am-6pm Mon-Fri; 9am-1pm Sat. **No credit cards. Map** p330 J9.
All manner of religious goods can be found here including rosaries, candles and crucifixes. There are also tapes and CDs, and, around Christmas, a small but inspiring selection of nativity scenes.

de.fakto

Perlova 6, Staré Město, Prague 1 (224 233 815/ www.defakto.cz). Metro Můstek/tram 6, 17, 18, 22, 23. **Open** 10am-8pm Mon-Thur, Sun; 10am-9pm Fri, Sat. **Credit** AmEx, DC, MC, V. **Map** p328 L6.
A rewarding option for gifts and useful tokens from Prague, this cool boutique specialises in classy but functional designer kitchenware, gifts and loads of groovy little objets to stuff in your bag.

Manufaktura

Karlova 26, Staré Město, Prague 1 (221 632 480). *Metro Staroměstská/tram 17, 18.* **Open** 10am-8pm Mon-Thur, Sun; 10am-9pm Fri, Sat. **Credit** AmEx, DC, MC, V. **Map** p328 K4.
This place is a treasure trove of Czech-made goods. Manufaktura's motto is 'Inspired by Nature', and it does have quite a variety of items from its range of natural products. As an added bonus, next to each item is a brief description of the method and material used in constructing the piece. You can pick up placemats, tablecloths, handkerchiefs and the like. In particular, be sure to check out the blue print items. Blue print is a fabric dyeing technique used in Bohemia in the late 18th century.

Qubus

Rámová 3, Staré Město, Prague 1 (222 313 151/ www.qubus.com). Metro Náměstí Republiky/tram 5, 8, 14. **Open** 10am-7pm Mon-Fri. **No credit cards. Map** p328 M2.

From the über-cool Lomo cameras to the designer clocks and the weird ceramics, this freshly opened emporium of hipoisie is the place to catch and ride the latest Prague wave.

Slovenská Izba

Jilská 1, Staré Město, Prague 1 (224 947 130). Metro Staroměstská/tram 17, 18. **Open** 10am-12.30pm, 1.30-6pm Mon-Fri. **No credit cards. Map** p328 L5.

It hasn't been Czechoslovakia since 1993, but that doesn't stop some people from reuniting the country. Here you can discover all things Slovak, without the trip across the border. A large number of Slovak CDs are for sale, as well as books and Slovakian art items like ceramics and straw people.

Svara's Hexenladen

Jindřišská 7, Staré Město, Prague 1 (224 228 418). Metro Můstek/tram 6, 17, 18, 22, 23. **Open** 10am-6pm Mon-Fri. **Credit** AmEx, DC, MC, V. **Map** p329 N6.

For the practising Wiccan back home, Svara's Hexenladen offers a wide selection of oils, candles, stones and herbs representing a variety of traditions, including Celtic, Egyptian and New Age. Nearly all your Wicca and occult supplies can be found here, along with jewellery and books.

Včelařské potřeby

Křemencova 8, Nové Město, Prague 2 (224 934 344/www.beekeeping.cz). Metro Karlovo náměstí/tram 4, 6, 16, 22, 34. **Open** 9am-5pm Mon, Wed; 9am-6pm Tue, Thur; 9am-2pm Fri. **No credit cards.**

Bees are not included. However just about everything else that an apiarist either produces or needs is, from gloves and headgear, to honey and cosmetics. Certainly a gift to remember.

Hair & beauty

Looking for your basic trim? A *kadeřnictví* (hairdresser's) or *holičství* (barber's) should do the job for you, and the price is usually right. However, if a classy cut is more your style, visit one of the salons listed below. You'll pay a bit more, but by Western standards you'll still be cutting a bargain.

Powergifting

Shopping in Prague is, well, different. There's no great fashion scene, the markets are spotty in numbers, variety and quality, and you don't really want to spend your holiday in a mall, do you? So what's the shopaholic to do?

In a word, wander. You can still find unique Czech gifts and keepsakes, you just may need to work a little harder at it, and spend some extra time doing it.

Prague and the Czech Republic are best known for garnets and amber (*see p190* **Saps and gems**), marionettes, crystal and wooden toys. All make great mementos. Apart from the places mentioned below, be sure to try the humble *antikvariát*, or second-hand bookshop. These stores are invariably full of obscure Czech tomes, photos, maps, worker propaganda magazines and postcards. The more generic second-hand shop, the *bazar*, is everywhere too, and often rewards those willing to risk dusty shelves with amazing finds. World War I-era coffee grinder? Wehrmacht bayonet? Not a problem (though not best for carry-on transport). Get out of the centre for the best deals. **Nové Město**, around the Náměstí Republiky, and the **Malá Strana** area are more varied, but branching further out will reap you greater rewards. Try exploring the area of Prague 7 around **Letná park**. Walk west and south from **Wenceslas Square**. Or there are the areas around

Karlovo Náměstí and up **Vinohradská** in Prague 2 that are full of shops worthy of a Dickens novel.

For über-Czech, more practical, colourful stuff, we suggest **Manufaktura** (*see p192*). It might look touristy – a perception not helped by its being set in prime tourist locations including the departure lounge at Ruzyně Airport – but it is worth a second look. Loaded with locally made natural goods, every bar of herbal soap, candle and candleholder also tells the story of its history in Bohemia.

Dr Stuart's Botanicus (*see p183*) is another feel-good Czech chain with exclusively local wares. If you can stick a herb in it, Dr Stuart has, from soaps and shampoos to cooking oils and candles. Art is another excellent buy, and it doesn't have to be from a cheesy vendor on Charles Bridge. There are dozens of art galleries scattered around the city. One that features mainly Czech artists is **Gallery Left Bank** (Mišeňská 10, Malá Strana, Prague 1, 257 534 940, www.gallery-leftbank.com). Museum shops are worthwhile too, even if the city has far fewer good ones than it could; the **Museum of Decorative Arts** (*see p114*) and the **House of the Black Madonna** are the best (*see p98*). And, of course, never underestimate the power of Czech alcohol. A liqueur like Becherovka or a rare beer will keep the Prague memories flowing.

Eat, Drink, Shop

James Hair

Malá Štupartská 9, Staré Město, Prague 1 (224 827 373/www.jameshair.cz). Metro Náměstí Republiky/ tram 5, 8, 14. **Open** 8am-8pm Tue-Fri; 9am-5pm Sat. **No credit cards. Map** p328 M3.

Mostly English-speaking staff and cuts to write home about have made James Hair a much talked-about salon. The international stylist and his crew will do you up or make you over in style.

Libor Sula The Salon

Dušní 6, Staré Město, Prague 1 (224 817 575). Metro Staroměstská/tram 17, 18. **Open** 9am-9pm Mon-Fri; 11am-6pm Sat. **No credit cards. Map** p328 L2.

For award-winning hair, your best bet is Libor Sula. The salon has won numerous awards, including Czech and Slovak Hairdresser of the Year. The English-speaking staff will make sure that you leave looking like a winner yourself.

Thai World

Týnská 9, Staré Město, Prague 1 (224 817 247/606 116 272/www.thaiworld.cz). Metro Staroměstská/ tram 17, 18. **Open** 11am-9pm daily. **Rates** *Massage* 495 Kč/hr; 295 Kč/30mins. **No credit cards. Map** p328 M3.

The masseuses here will pull and push you back into shape. They offer traditional Thai massage (which focuses on pressure points in the body), reflexology, Swedish oil massage or combinations.

Household

Bauhaus

Budějovická 1A, Pankrác, Prague 4 (241 732 014/ www.bauhaus.cz). Metro Pankrác. **Open** 8am-8pm Mon-Sat; 8am-7pm Sun. **Credit** AmEx, MC, V.

DIYers will find themselves in handyman heaven. All your home repair needs, plus plants, art and a variety of household items.

Other locations: Ústecká 822, Chabry, Prague 8 (255 715 211).

IKEA

Skandinávská 1, Zličín, Prague 5 (251 610 110). Metro Zličín. **Open** 10am-8pm daily. **Credit** MC, V.

Yep, it's IKEA. Not much more to be said: if you've been in one, you've been in this one too. It's still the old standby when it comes to Czech decorating. As seems to be the case with IKEA branches everywhere, the place is usually packed solid, but at least you know what you will get.

Le Patio

Národní 22, Nové Město, Prague 1 (224 934 853). Metro Národní třída/tram 6, 9, 17, 18, 22, 23. **Open** 10am-7pm Mon-Sat; 11am-7pm Sun. **Credit** AmEx, MC, V. **Map** p328 L6.

Le Patio brings the world to Prague with a mixture of imported home furnishings.

Other locations: Pažižská 20, Staré Město, Prague 1 (222 320 260); Týn 640, Staré Město, Prague 1 (224 895 773).

Potten & Pannen

Václavské náměstí 57, Nové Město, Prague 1 (224 214 936/www.pottenpannen.cz). Metro Muzeum/ tram 3, 9, 14, 24. **Open** 10am-7pm Mon-Sat. **Credit** AmEx, MC, V. **Map** p329 N6.

All sorts of stuff to get your cooking juices flowing. Gourmets will love it, while people who want a good-looking kitchen can decorate with it. Kitchenaid appliances and dish sets too.

Key-cutting & locksmiths

It happens. Be prepared and have an extra set of keys at the ready. There's a *zamečnictví* at Tesco and at the bottom of the escalators at the entrance to the Alberts (*see p191*) near Kotva. If you didn't think ahead and need someone to help you out in a jam, try the business below.

Key Non-Stop

Dukelských hrdinů 7, Holešovice, Prague 7 (220 878 016). Metro Vltavská/tram 1, 5, 25, 26. **Open** 24hrs daily. **No credit cards. Map** p332 E3.

There can be few things more unsettling than being locked out of your apartment in a strange city. Key Non-Stop will come and get you back in and, yep, that non-stop really does mean 24-7.

Music

Records & CDs

Bontonland Megastore

Palác Koruna, Václavské náměstí 1, Nové Město, Prague 1 (224 235 356/www.bontonland.cz). Metro Můstek/tram 3, 9, 14, 24. **Open** 9am-8pm daily. **Credit** AmEx, MC, V. **Map** p329 N6.

Two floors of musical entertainment and one of video games makes Bontonland a must stop. All the newest releases, and huge sections of rock, country, jazz, etc are here. There's even a separate room for classical music, including a large opera section.

Disko Duck

Karlova 12, Staré Město, Prague 1 (221 213 696/ www.diskoduck.cz). Metro Staroměstská/tram 17, 18. **Open** noon-7pm daily. **Credit** MC, V. **Map** p328 K4.

Aspiring DJs can get their groove going here. More than 5,000 records spanning the musical worlds of hip hop, techno, jungle and beat. DJ equipment as well, including turntables, mixer and CD players.

Maximum Underground

Jilská 22, Staré Město, Prague 1 (222 541 333). Metro Můstek, Národní třída or Staroměstská/tram 3, 9, 18, 22, 23. **Open** 11am-7.30pm Mon-Sat; 1-7pm Sun. **No credit cards. Map** p328 L5.

Maximum Underground sells heavy music and also offers the appropriate bodily modifications to go with it, namely tattoos and piercings. This is the place to come to find all the alternative sounds that you can't get your hands on elsewhere.

Music shop-antikvariát

Národní třída 25, Nové Město, Prague 1 (221 085 268). Metro Národní třída/tram 6, 9, 18, 22. **Open** 10.30am-7pm Mon-Sat. **Credit** AmEx, MC, V. **Map** p328 L6.

Worth the climb up the stairs, the shop has a huge record selection along with some great used CDs from 50 Kč, with jazz and classical from 95 Kč.

Pohodlí

Benediktská 7, Staré Město, Prague 1 (224 827 026/www.etno.cz). Metro Náměstí Republiky/tram 5, 14, 26. **Open** 11am-7pm Mon-Fri; 10am-4pm Sat. **No credit cards. Map** p329 N3.

We are the world, man, and we have the music from all corners to prove it. This ethnic music store brings Indian and African music home to you, and offers some local Czech and Moravian goodies as well.

Musical instruments

Hudební nástroje – Radek Bubrle

Náprstkova 10, Staré Město, Prague 1 (222 221 110/www.nastroje-hudebni.cz). Metro Můstek or Staroměstská/tram 17, 18. **Open** 10am-6pm Mon-Fri; 10am-4pm Sat. **Credit** DC, MC, V. **Map** p328 J5.

Remarkably varied and organised second-hand instrument shop; the place to pick up an old Bohemian squeezebox (or clarinet, bongos, xylophone, sax, tuba and drums). Helpful staff are willing to advise both the professional and beginner – may also be able to assist with accessories.

Praha Music Centre

Soukenická 20, Nové Město, Prague 1 (226 011 111/www.pmc.cz). Metro Náměstí Republiky/tram 5, 14, 26. **Open** 9am-6pm Mon-Fri. **Credit** MC, V. **Map** p329 O2.

A bit more high-tech than the usual music shop, in addition to instruments Praha Music Centre sells speakers and the like. If you're looking for something that needs to be plugged in in order to play, this is probably your best bet.

Other locations: Revoluční 14, Staré Město, Prague 1 (222 311 693).

U zlatého kohouta

Michalská 3, Staré Město, Prague 1 (224 212 874). Metro Můstek or Národní třída/tram 3, 9, 14, 24. **Open** 10am-noon, 1.30-6pm Mon-Fri. **Credit** AmEx, MC, V. **Map** p328 L5.

Fancy a fiddle? This place has got them in bows, and even if you aren't in to playing, you should stop by to take a look at the beautiful craftsmanship that went into each violin. In addition to new instrument sales, it also offers restoration. **Photo** p196.

Opticians

Eiffel Optic

Na příkopě 25, Nové Město, Prague 1 (224 234 966/www.eiffeloptic.cz). Metro Můstek/tram 3, 9, 14, 24. **Open** 8am-8pm Mon-Fri; 9am-8pm Sat; 9.30am-7pm Sun. **Credit** AmEx, MC, V. **Map** p329 N5.

Eat, Drink, Shop

Visit **Pohodlí** and you'll leave with a slice of Prague not found in souvenir shops.

U zlatého kohouta: the perfect place to indulge in a fiddle. *See p195.*

This is the biggie in town, and almost always has some sort of sale going on. Thousands of frames, along with eye tests and contact lenses should have you seeing pretty in no time. There's an on-site optician and a one-hour express service.
Other locations: Ječná 6, Nové Město, Prague 2 (224 913 173); Jungmannovo náměstí 1, Prague 1 (224 232 744); Celetná 38, Staré Město, Prague 1 (225 113 302); Bělehradská 102, Nové Město, Prague 2 (222 512 431); Centrum Černý Most, Prague 9 (281 917 258); Palác Flóra, Prague 3 (255 742 006); Europark Štěrboholy, Prague 10 (272 701 775).

GrandOptical

Myslbek Centre, Na příkopě 19-21, Staré Město, Prague 1 (224 238 371/www.grandoptical.cz). Metro Můstek/tram 3, 9, 14, 24. **Open** 9.30am-8pm Mon-Fri; 10am-7pm Sat; 10am-6pm Sun. **Credit** AmEx, MC, V. **Map** p329 N5.
Designer brands, at a price. They're fast, they're good and they are all over the place, making it easy to find a branch. You can even occasionally find English-speaking staff as well.
Other locations: Shopping Park Praha-Zličín, Prague 5 (251 613 375); Metropole Zličín, Prague 5 (257 952 696); Nový Smíchov Centrum, Prague 5 (257 321 620).

Photocopying

Copy General

Senovážné náměstí 26, Nové Město, Prague 1 (224 230 020/www.copygeneral.cz). Metro Náměstí Republiky/tram 3, 5, 9, 14, 24, 26. **Open** 24hrs daily. **Credit** MC, V. **Map** p329 P4.

Copy General does more than just making copies. Binding and finishing services are available to customers as well as pick-up and delivery.
Other locations: Národní 11, Prague 1 (222 075 650); Jugoslávská 11, Prague 2 (221 181 181); Milady Horákové 4, Holešovice, Prague 7 (233 370 013); Na Bělidle 40, Smíchov, Prague 5 (257 316 653).

Photography

Camera shops & repairs

Foto Škoda

Palác Langhans, Vodičkova 37, Nové Město, Prague 1 (222 929 029/fax 222 926 016/www.fotoskoda.cz). Metro Můstek/tram 3, 9, 14, 24. **Open** 8.30am-8pm Mon-Fri; 9am-6pm Sat. **Credit** AmEx, DC, MC, V. **Map** p308 J6.
Sales, repairs, developing, supplies. Everything you could possibly want, need, desire or think you may have a use for. Excellent for the professional, but amateurs will be able to find what they need as well. Best selection of all things photography in Prague.

Jan Pazdera obchod a opravna

Lucerna, Vodičkova 30, Nové Město, Prague 1 (224 216 197). Metro Můstek/tram 3, 9, 14, 24. **Open** 10am-6pm Mon-Fri. **No credit cards**. **Map** p329 N6.
Practically a camera museum, full of beautiful old antique cameras and lenses. There's a small supply of film, batteries, and the like, but the store is best for your antique camera collection. Simple camera repairs can be done as well, be sure to ask. **Photo** p197.

Photo developing

Photo shops are rife all over the tourist areas, so finding a place to get your prints is never a problem, including your local *drogerie*. Quality is sometimes an issue, though, so if your snaps need to be picture perfect it might be worth taking them to Fotoplus.

Fotoplus

Na příkopě 17, Nové Město, Prague 1 (224 213 121). Metro Náměstí Republiky/tram 5, 14, 26. **Open** 7.30am-9pm Mon-Fri; 9am-7pm Sat; 10am-7pm Sun. **Credit** AmEx, MC, V. **Map** p329 N5.

Your best bet for photographic needs in the centre of town. One-hour photo and digital service makes those must have immediately photos a reality. You can pick up a photo album here too for something to do on the plane ride home.

Stationery & art materials

A nearby *papírnictví* should be able to handle your basic stationery needs, including pens, paper and envelopes. Tesco or Kotva (for both, *see p178*) also carry papers and pens, or try one of the shops listed below.

AKM Papírnictví

Vinohradská 151, Palác Flóra, Žižkov, Prague 3 (255 742 134). Metro Flora/tram 5, 10, 11, 16. **Open** 9am-9pm daily. **Credit** MC, V. **Map** p333 E3.

At AKM you'll find all sorts of office supplies as well as everything your kids need for school, from fine writing instruments to notepads. Get organised.

Altamira

Jilská 2, Staré Město, Prague 1 (224 219 950/ www.vytvarnepotreby.cz). Metro Národní třída/tram 6, 9, 18, 21, 22, 23. **Open** 9am-7pm Mon-Fri; 10am-5pm Sat. **No credit cards. Map** p328 L5.

Two locations around the corner from each other that have a selection of painting, sketching and other supplies. The Skořepka location has paper, paints, stencils and other materials for crafts like fabric painting and decorating glass, while the location on Jilská has fine artist supplies like canvases and easels. **Other locations**: Skořepka 2, Nové Město, Prague 1 (224 220 923).

Loco Plus

Palackého 10, Nové Město, Prague 1 (224 947 732). Metro Můstek/tram 3, 9, 14, 25. **Open** 8.30am-6.30pm Mon-Thur; 8.30am-6pm Fri; 9am-noon Sat. **No credit cards. Map** p330 M7.

A decent-sized store filled with paper supplies. Envelopes, notepads, binders, markers, pens and pencils, glues, etc. Disturbingly large selection of receipt books, but no stamps were spotted.

Papírnictví Týnská Ulička

Týnská ulička 10, Staré Město, Prague 1 (222 314 869/www.papirnictvi-tynska.cz). Metro Staroměstská/ tram 17, 18. **Open** 8am-6pm Mon-Fri. **No credit cards. Map** p328 M3.

Photographers will be in their element at **Jan Pazdera**. *See p196.*

A visit here will reveal more communist-era leftovers than a party convention the day after closing. If you're lucky, you might be able to purchase the last Havel lapel pin or Soviet cartoon character colouring book that's left in Prague.

Toys

You may not find many local children shopping at the stores below – they're at home busy with their computers and iPods just as they are in the rest of the world. But if you're looking for a selection of truly unique Czech toys, it's worth checking out the following places.

Beruška

Vodičkova 30, Nové Město, Prague 1 (no phone). Metro Můstek/tram 3, 9, 14, 24. **Open** 10am-6pm Mon-Fri. **No credit cards.** **Map** p329 N6.

Beruška is a small shop that's filled with toys for both younger and older children. Here you'll find a good selection of stuffed animals, clever wooden toys, and puzzles and games.

Sparky's Dům hraček

Havířská 2, Staré Město, Prague 1 (224 239 309/ www.sparkys.cz). Metro Můstek/tram 3, 9, 14, 24. **Open** 10am-7pm Mon-Sat; 10am-6pm Sun. **Credit** AmEx, MC, V. **Map** p328 M5.

A three-level behemoth of a toy store, with lots of good 'Czech' gifts as well as stuffed animals. The bottom floors are geared more to the younger set, with lots of wooden toys and games. The higher you go, the more you'll find for older children, including action figures and dolls, as well as games.

Teta Tramtárie

Jungmannova 28, Nové Město, Prague 1 (no phone/ www.tetatramtarie.cz). Metro Můstek or Národni třída/tram 6, 9, 18, 21, 22, 23. **Open** 7.30am-8pm daily. **Credit** MC, V. **Map** p328 M6.

Teta Tramtárie is a veritable heaven, and indeed haven, for the young; little ones and their parents will find a toy shop, a children's bookshop, a miniature movie theatre continuously showing children's films and cartoons (some in English), a puppet theatre, two pizza restaurants and an ice-cream parlour with a large indoor jungle gym.

Video rental

Planet DVD

Spálená 29, Nové Město, Prague 1 (224 930 888/ www.dvdplanet.cz). Metro Můstek/tram 3, 9, 14, 24. **Open** 10am-10pm Mon-Sat; 10am-6pm Sun. **Credit** MC, V. **Map** p330 L8.

High-tech all the way: peruse and reserve movies online and if the store is out of what you're looking for, staff will send you an SMS when it's in. Everything's done by computer – you can view your account and even see what movies you have rented to suss out your viewing patterns.

Video Gourmet

Jakubská 12, Staré Město, Prague 1 (222 323 364). Metro Náměstí Republiky/tram 5, 8, 14. **Open** 11am-11pm daily. **Credit** AmEx, MC, V. **Map** p329 N3.

Inside the lobby of American restaurant Red Hot & Blues (*see p144*), you can pick up your movie along with Duncan Hines cake and frosting mixes and some Orville Redenbacher popcorn. A visit here is an excellent cure for home-sickness.

Sparky's Dům hraček.

Arts & Entertainment

Festivals & Events	**200**
Children	**205**
Film	**210**
Galleries	**215**
Gay & Lesbian	**224**
Music	**228**
Nightlife	**241**
Theatre & Dance	**250**
Sport & Fitness	**256**

Features

Balls!	202
A long path to royalty	212
It matters	219
No summer blues	232
Still Crazy Monkey Business	234
Sound Czech	238
Still Crazy Tram from hell	242
Still Crazy The sex thing	249
Breaking barriers	255
Get in-line	260

Festivals & Events

Prague party city.

Before **Easter** eggs were chocolate they were, well, eggs. *See p201.*

The Czech winter, though not usually bitterly cold, tends to be long and grey, lending the town a grim, Kafka-esque cast. Which makes the coming of spring a truly joyous event in Prague. Czechs know the approximate day and certainly the order of appearance every new blossom, have their favourite summer weekend co-ordinated with 12 sets of friends months in advance, hunt down the mushrooms of autumn with alacrity and never miss a **St Nicholas's Eve** street party in winter. It's a whole different city with each season.

In April and May people seem to blossom along with the lilacs and chestnut trees, and emerge like moles into the sunlight. Beer gardens fill up even when the crowd is shivering at dusk. Off come the layers, as Stromovka park fills with runners training for the **Prague International Marathon**. Soon after, the **Prague Spring Festival** heralds the warm weather, as it has for half a century.

With the hot days of June and July, locals (including the staff of most cultural institutions, which go dark until September) tend to clear out to avoid the flood of tourists and head for the country. If you can get an invitation, you may get to experience the joy of the *chata* (cottage) and blueberry picking. The city bears its own sweet fruit during the summer months, though, with music festivals like the hip **United Islands of Prague** and the **Tanec Praha** modern dance performances.

In autumn symphonies, operas and balls return to town. With them comes **Prague Autumn** – and not a little of the sneak-attack libation known as *Burčák*. And, of course, with the tourists finally gone, Prague's citizens get their beautiful city back to themselves – just as it begins to fill with ice and smog.

Miserable though winter can be, it has its own rewards: the glorious spires that tower above Staré Město, Old Town, are an incomparable sight in the snow. The city may be a sleepy, grog-guzzling, grey and melancholy place, but its **Christmas markets** are enchanting. And, once the carp has been bashed into submission at the fishmongers' stands for the traditional festive supper, fireworks have people diving for cover in the same square on **New Year's Eve**.

TICKETS & INFORMATION

You can book for most ticketed events through **Ticketpro** (*see p230*), which accepts payments by credit card. Tickets are sometimes also available on the door, but it's advisable to phone ahead and note that credit cards are unlikely to be accepted at venues.

For up-to-the-minute listings check the *Prague Post* (www.praguepost.cz) or Prague TV (www.prague.tv) before and during your stay, as well as looking at organisers' websites for any special, one-off events.

Spring

Matejská pouť

Výstaviště, Holešovice, Prague 7 (220 103 204). Metro Vltavská/tram 5, 14, 25. **Admission** 30-50 Kč. **Date** Feb-Mar.

The St Matthew's Fair marks the arrival of warm weather with cheesy rides for the children at a run-down funfair at Prague's exhibition grounds, Výstaviště (*see p127*). Dodgem cars at 10 Kč a pop and the Ferris wheel bring out the juvenile in all.

Easter

Date Mar/Apr.

Men rush around the country beating women on the backside with willow sticks. Women respond by dousing the men with cold water but also by giving them painted eggs. Then everyone drinks a lot. This ancient fertility rite is rarely seen in Prague these days, but painted eggs and willow sticks (*pomlaska*) are on sale all over the city. **Photo** p200.

Witches' Night

Date 30 Apr.

A tradition that rolls the best of Hallowe'en and Bonfire Night into one package: *Pálení čarodějnic*, or Witches' Night, marks the death of winter and the birth of the new spring. Bonfires are lit to purge the winter spirits, an effigy of a hag is burnt – a relic of historical witch hunts – and the more daring observers of the custom leap over the flames. Most of the fires are to be found in the countryside, but occasionally there's a pyre in the capital, sometimes on Petřín Hill in Malá Strana.

Labour Day

Date 1 May.

There's little danger of being run over by a tank in Wenceslas Square these days, but May Day is still a good excuse for a demonstration. The communists, in an attempt to keep the faith alive, usually have a small rally in Letná park (*see p127*) and encourage pensioners to moan about the rigours of the free market. Prague's anarchists also sometimes hold an uncharacteristically orderly parade. **Photo** p203.

May Day

Petřín Hill, Malá Strana, Prague 1. Metro Malostranská/tram 6, 9, 12, 22, 23. **Map** p326 D6. **Date** 1 May.

Czech lovers of all ages, their sap rising, make a pilgrimage to the statue of Karel Hynek Mácha on Petřín Hill (*see p96*) to place flowers and engage in snogging. Mácha, who was a 19th-century Romantic poet, gave rise to many myths, several bastards and the epic poem *Máj* ('May'). It's actually a melancholy tale of unrequited love, but nobody lets that spoil their fun.

VE Day

Date 8 May.

The Day of Liberation from fascism is actually 9 May, which was the date when the Red Army reached Prague in 1945. In its eagerness to be a good Euro-citizen, however, the Czech government moved the celebration to 8 May, in line with the rest of the Continent. Flowers and wreaths are laid on Soviet monuments such as Náměstí Kinský in Smíchov, where a Soviet tank used to stand.

Prague International Marathon

Throughout the city, route varies (224 919 209/ www.pim.cz). **Registration fee** 300-600 Kč. **Credit** (online registration only) MC, V. **Date** May.

Runners from around the world now fly in for the biggest race of the year and have a city-wide street party afterwards, where more than just water is gulped by runners and a few thousand less healthy types. Those not up to the full 42km (26-mile) race still have a shot at the 10km (6-mile) race.

Prague Writers' Festival

Various venues (224 931 053/www.pwf.pragonet.cz). **Admission** varies. **Date** May.

A collection of Czech and international literati gather in Prague to read extracts, hobnob and compare their royalty contracts. This is your chance to observe Ivan Klíma's improbable hairdo and the quirks of other local literary lions.

Mezi ploty

Ústavní 91, near Bohnice Psychiatric Hospital, Prague 8 (272 730 623/www.meziploty.cz). Metro Nádraží Holešovice, then bus 200. **Admission** 200 Kč/day; 370 Kč/weekend. **Date** last weekend in May.

A unique festival, Mezi ploty brings together professional, amateur and mentally or physically disadvantaged artists, dancers and musicians for two days of events and performances in the grounds of the city's main psychiatric hospital.

Prague Spring

Hellichova 18, Malá Strana, Prague 1 (257 311 921/257 310 414/www.festival.cz). Metro Malostranská/tram 12, 22, 23. **Admission** varies according to venue. **Map** p327 F5. **Date** mid May-early June.

The biggest and best of Prague's music festivals begins on the anniversary of Smetana's death with a performance of his tone poem *Má Vlast* ('My Country'). The festival is hugely popular, drawing symphony orchestras and virtuosi from around the world, who perform at the city's finest venues, so book in advance if possible. *See also p233.*

Balls!

Though Czechs were considered a ruffian province under the Habsburgs, there are certain traditions from those days still relished by Praguers today. Balls are one of the biggest. Even the club kids you'll see in dreadlocks and army boots, when pressed, can probably waltz and foxtrot with the best of them.

That's because just about every high school student still goes through ballroom dancing training. And every village, town and hamlet in the country has its *ples*, as they're known, usually accompanied by a goodly amount of drink to help keep the knees fluid. In fact, the dances carried a bit of subterfuge with them before 1989 – and it wasn't because they were a surviving trapping of the bourgeoisie. In those days, pubs generally shut up tight at the dot of 10pm and balls were one of the few places to keep the party going until the wee hours.

Many balls are charity fundraisers, just like in the days of old, and are sponsored by some of the oldest civic associations and guilds around. There's the Moravian Ball, the Hunt Ball and the Fireman's Ball (Miloš Forman, before he emigrated to Hollywood, was even inspired to make a film based on this one, in which he sends up pompous local officials).

Tickets for balls run from 150 Kč for the humbler ones, up to a dizzying 2,000 Kč for events held at Municipal House or the other grand ballrooms.

Summer

Khamoro

Various venues (222 518 554/www.khamoro.cz). **Admission** free-200 Kč. **Date** May.

A festival that features concerts, seminars and workshops on Roma culture, focusing on the traditional side of Gypsy music, customs and art. The concerts, which are the biggest draw for visitors, run a surprisingly wide gamut from swing guitar jams to a Hungarian all-violin Roma orchestra.

Nine Gates

Various venues (www.9bran.cz). **Admission** free. **Date** June.

Nine Gates is a decade-old festival of Czech-German Jewish culture that features a week of great music from the likes of 7 Hippies, plus dance and classical music performances in some amazing venues such as the Wallenstein Gardens. **Photo** p204.

Respect

Various venues (222 710 050/603 461 592/ http://respect.inway.cz/). **Admission** from 120 Kč. **Date** June.

The world and ethnic music high point of the year features Balkan folk and Gypsy music, with performers such as Taraf de Haidouks, and its Prague counterparts. The organiser is Prague's main underground and ethnic music label, Rachot. Concerts are usually at the Akropolis (*see p235*).

Tanec Praha

Various venues (224 817 886/www.tanecpha.cz). **Admission** from 200 Kč. **Date** June.

Eagerly anticipated by audiences all year, Tanec Praha, or Dance Prague, is an international gala of modern dance that has become one of the more successful performance festivals in Prague. International participants perform in major theatres and venues across the city and sometimes conduct workshops and symposiums. *See also p254.*

United Islands of Prague

Various venues (www.unitedislands.cz). **Admission** varies. **Date** June.

Concerts and beer stands take over the Vltava riverfront, themes roughly by genre, featuring impressive performers both local and global, including the likes of Martin, Medeski & Wood and Placebo.

Summer Old Music Festival

Collegium Marianum, Melantrichova 19, Staré Město, Prague 1 (224 229 462/www.tynska.cuni.cz). *Metro Staroměstská/tram 17, 18.* **Admission** from 120 Kč. **Date** July.

Growing in popularity, this gala of Renaissance and baroque music, performed on period instruments and in historic settings, is one of the few native musical offerings during the summer holidays. It also attracts some of the highest-quality performers around.

Autumn

Mattoni Grand Prix

Staré Město (www.pim.cz). **Registration fee** 300-600 Kč. **Credit** (online registration only) MC, V. **Date** Sept.

This offshoot of the Prague International Marathon in May, although it has fewer crowds and a bit less pomp and ceremony, is still accompanied by music and enjoyable surrounding events. And it still fills Old Town streets with a 5km (3-mile) women's run and a 10km (6-mile) men's race.

Prague Autumn

Various venues (222 540 484/www.prazsky podzim.cz). **Admission** varies according to venue. **Date** mid Sept-early Oct.

Garnering more respect every year, the next best thing to Prague Spring is autumn's festival of world-renowned classical talents. Performances are held in the city's finest concert venues, including the splendid Rudolfinum (*see p218 and p230*).

Burčák arrives

Date late Sept-early Oct.

Burčák – a cloudy, half-fermented, early-season wine – arrives in Prague sometime in the autumn. It's a speciality of Moravia, where it would appear that the locals haven't got the patience to wait for their alcohol to finish ageing. Served straight from the barrel into special jugs, *Burčák* looks like murky wheat beer, tastes like cherryade and – drinker, beware – will sneak up on you if you don't treat it with proper respect.

Festival of Best Amateur & Professional Puppet Theatre Plays

Various venues (241 409 293). **Admission** varies according to venue. **Date** Oct.

Bohemia has a long tradition of puppet-making and this festival is a true celebration of Punch and his cousins. Puppets remain a big thing in the Czech Republic – some of the country's most innovative artists continue to use them, and a faculty at the university is devoted to the craft.

Anniversary of the birth of Czechoslovakia

Date 28 Oct.

The country no longer exists, but that's no reason to cancel a public holiday – so the people still get a day off. Lots of fireworks – as on every other possible occasion – and it takes forever to get a tram.

All Souls' Day

Date 2 Nov.

If there is one day in the year when you should visit one of the city's cemeteries, All Souls' Day, when people pray for deceased family members, is the day. Whole families turn out to light candles, lay wreaths, remember and pray. The best place to go is the enormous Olšany Cemetery (*see p133*).

Anniversary of the Velvet Revolution

Národní třída & Václavské náměstí, Nové Město, Prague 1. Metro Národní třída or Můstek/tram 3, 6, 9, 14, 18, 22, 23, 24. **Map** p328 L6. **Date** 17 Nov.

Surprisingly understated observances to commemorate the demonstration that began the Velvet Revolution. Flowers are laid and candles lit in Wenceslas Square near the equine statue and on the memorial on Národní třída near No.20.

Winter

Prague Jazz Festival

Various venues (222 211 275/www.agharta.cz). **Admission** varies according to venue. **Date** Feb-Oct.

One of the hottest jazz fests in Central Europe, the Prague Jazz Festival features world-class players like John Scofield and Viktoria Tolstoy. Sponsored by the AghaRTA club (*see p239*), the festival is small but persistent, carrying on throughout the spring, summer and autumn, with performances mainly at the Lucerna Music Bar (*see p236*).

St Nicholas's Eve

Around Charles Bridge & Staroměstské náměstí, Staré Město, Prague 1. Metro Staroměstská/tram 17, 18. **Map** p328 J4. **Date** 5 Dec.

Grown men spend the evening wearing frocks, drinking large amounts of beer and terrorising small children. They wander the streets in threesomes, dressed as St Nicholas, an angel and a devil, symbolising confession, reward and punishment. Rather than a red cloak, St Nicholas usually sports a long white vestment, with a white mitre and staff. The angel hands out sweets to children who have been good, while the devil is on hand to dispense rough justice to those who haven't.

Letná park. *See p201.*

Christmas

In the week leading up to the *Vánoce* (Christmas) holiday, the streets sport huge tubs of water filled with carp, the traditional Czech Christmas dish, and there are Christmas markets in Old Town Square and Wenceslas Square. The feasting and exchange of gifts happen on the evening of 24 December, when – apart from midnight Masses, the finest of which is at St Vitus's Cathedral (*see p77*) – pretty much everything closes down. Things don't start opening up again until the 27th.

New Year's Eve

Václavské náměstí & Staroměstské náměstí, Staré Město & Nové Město, Prague 1. Metro Můstek or Staroměstská/tram 3, 9, 14, 17, 18, 24. **Map** p329 N6. **Date** 31 Dec.

Bring your helmet? On New Year's Eve, or *Silvestr*, the streets are packed with a ragtag crowd of Euro-revellers, with much of the fun centred on Wenceslas Square and Old Town Square. Fireworks are let off everywhere and flung around with frankly dangerous abandon, then champagne bottles are smashed.

Anniversary of Jan Palach's death

Václavské náměstí, Nové Město, Prague 1. Metro Muzeum/tram 11. **Map** p329 N6. **Date** 16 Jan.

Jan Palach set himself ablaze on 16 January 1969 in Wenceslas Square to protest at the Soviet occupation that killed off the promise of cultural freedoms allowed the previous year during the brief Prague Spring. His grave at Olšany Cemetery (*see p133*) is adorned with candles and flowers all year round.

Wallenstein Gardens. *See p202.*

Many people visit Olšany or the memorial to the all-but-countless victims of communism (*see p117*) near the St Wenceslas statue to lay a few more.

Masopust

Akropolis, Kubelíkova 27, Žižkov, Prague 3 (www.palacakropolis.cz). Metro Jiřího Z Poděbrad/tram 11. **Map** p333 C2. **Date** mid Feb (7th Sun before Easter).

Traditionally, groups of 12 carollers accompanied by people in masks parade about in this whimsical celebration of what the rest of the world knows as Shrove Tuesday, the eve of Ash Wednesday (the original tradition seen in the Czech lands has the holiday on Sunday). According to custom, everyone who meets this procession should be invited to the evening feast, a great opportunity to stuff yourself with a freshly slaughtered pig and wash it down with rivers of beer. More manageable might be the version of the Masopust street party centred around Prague's Žižkov district, where a slate of activities revolves around the Akropolis club (*see p235*).

Out of town

Karlovy Vary International Film Festival

Hotel Thermal, IP Pavlova 11, Karlovy Vary (221 411 011/www.kviff.cz). **Admission** varies. **Date** July.

Every year a genteel Bohemian spa town finds itself the venue of the Czech version of Cannes. Despite, or because of this, the film festival draws an increasing crowd of international talent, filmmakers and even a few people with the power of the green light. But unlike festivals like Cannes, Berlin and Venice, the Karlovy Vary event is skewed towards audiences, offering thousands the chance to see films otherwise impossible to catch in the Czech Republic. There's an always interesting mix of home-grown features and great parties. *See p272* **Cue the lights.**

Barum Rally

Start/finish line: Interhotel Moskva, Práce náměstí 2512, Zlín (www.rallysport.cz/barum). **Admission** free. **Date** Sept.

A classic road race dating back decades, this still attracts drivers from across Europe and has recently been ranked one of the best. Moravian roads roar to life as amateur and pro drivers compete for the big *pohár*, the winner's cup. Autoklub Barum Zlín sponsors the event and an entry form in English can be downloaded from its website listed above.

Velká Pardubice Steeplechase

Pražská 607, Pardubice (www.pardubice-race course.cz). **Admission** 200-2,000 Kč. **No credit cards. Date** 2nd weekend in Oct.

The star steeplechase event in the annual calendar is also a controversial one: horses and riders are often injured on the difficult course. Celebrity horse people pour in from all over Europe, putting box seats at a premium. The website has ticket details.

Children

The best kind of fantasyland.

Children are invariably fascinated by Prague's picturesque old centre, and its fairytale qualities will seem perfectly natural to your little princes and princesses. From the dramatic gates of Prague Castle to the winding medieval streets of Staré Město and Josefov, it's a city that fires the imagination. Thankfully, it's also becoming a city that's more and more geared to the special needs of children. There are all sorts of suitable diversions, some quaint and low-tech like the **Zrcadlové Bludiště** (Mirror Maze; *see p96*), on picturesque Petřín hill, a favourite for generations of Czech children, while more high-tech developments include the cyber combat of **Laser Game**. The Czech Republic has a long tradition of **puppet theatre**, for adults and children, and other excellent outings include indoor jungle gyms at mini-mall **Teta Tramtárie** and **Jungleland**, **outdoor playgrounds**, a trip to **Prague Zoo** and a visit to the new **Sea World** aquarium.

When it's time to feed hungry little ogres, the good news is that an increasing number of restaurants can satisfy the whole family. One popular pizzeria, **Rugantino**, even lets children make their own pizza. More shops also cater to the needs of youngsters, and it's now possible to rent prams and car seats (*see p208*). Parents gagging for a night out will appreciate the host of babysitting agencies providing English-speaking care-givers too (*see p208*).

Finding a suitable area for baby-changing isn't always easy. **Mothercare** has one on the first floor, with two changing tables, a sink and a bottle warmer. **Nový Smíchov** shopping centre (*see p179*) has one on the first floor near the lifts and adult toilets, including toilets for toddlers – but be prepared to wait, as the mall is popular with mums. **Tesco** (*see p178*) has a changing table on the first floor. To use it, request a key from any cashier there. Teta Tramtárie also has facilities.

Sightseeing

Some attractions, such as the **Astronomical Clock** (*see p101*) and climbable towers like the **Petřín Tower** (*see p96*), **Old Town Bridge Tower** (*see p107*) and the **Powder Gate** (*see*

National Technical Museum. See p206.

Look for Nemo at **Sea World**.

p100), are as suitable for children as they are for adults. Note that most of the towers are closed during the winter months.

Museums

National Museum

Národni muzeum
Václavské náměstí 68, Holešovice, Prague 7 (224 497 111/www.nm.cz). Metro Muzeum. **Open** *Jan-Apr, Oct-Dec* 9am-5pm daily. *May-Sept* 10am-6pm daily. Closed 1st Tue of mth. **Admission** 110 Kč; 130 Kč family; free under-6s; free to all 1st Mon of mth. **No credit cards**. **Map** p331 P8.
Many of the displays in this natural history museum are a little dull, but children still seem to be fascinated by the stuffed animal exhibits on the top floor.

National Technical Museum

Národni technické muzeum
Kostelní 42, Holešovice, Prague 7 (220 399 111/www.ntm.cz). Metro Hradčanská or Vltavská/tram 1, 8, 25, 26. **Open** 9am-5pm Tue-Fri; 10am-6pm Sat, Sun. **Admission** 70 Kč; 150 Kč family. **No credit cards**. **Map** p332 D3.
Ideal for the transport-obsessed child, the National Technical Museum is a sure hit. It's full of original vehicles, some of which can be climbed on to afford a good look at the interiors, and the temporary exhibitions are interesting. A popular coal mine replica tunnels through the basement, and English-speaking tours can be arranged. **Photo** p205.

Sights

Prague Zoo

Zoologická zahrada v Praze
U Trojského zámku 3, Trója, Prague 7 (296 112 111/www.zoopraha.cz). Metro Nádraži Holešovice, then bus 112. **Open** *Jan, Feb, Nov, Dec* 9am-4pm daily. *Mar* 9am-5pm daily. *Apr-May, Sept-Oct* 9am-6pm daily. *June-Aug* 9am-7pm daily. **Admission** 90 Kč; 60 Kč children, students; 270 Kč family; free under-3s. **No credit cards**.
You'd never guess now that the floods of 2002 hit Prague Zoo hard. There was, however, a silver lining to the storm clouds for the resident animals. Numerous improvement projects that had been on the shelf were put into play not long after the waters receded. The temporary downside is that visitors can expect to encounter construction work at various places. Stromovka park is nearby, accessible via pedestrian bridge across the Vltava.

Sea World

Mořský svět
Výstaviště, Holešovice, Prague 7 (220 103 275/www.morsky-svet.cz). Metro Nádraži Holešovice/tram 5, 12, 17. **Open** 10am-7pm daily. **Admission** 150 Kč; 90 Kč children; 100 Kč concessions; 340-380 Kč family. **No credit cards**. **Map** p332 D1.
A trip underwater to see some sharks makes for a great break from musty castle tours. A soundtrack of waves crashing and seagulls crying gives the impression you've left this land-locked country. The aquarium has a collection of over 300 species.

Zrcadlové Bludiště

Mirror Maze
Petřín hill, Malá Strana, Prague 1 (257 315 212). Tram 12, 22, 23, then funicular to Petřín hill. **Open** *Jan-Mar, Nov, Dec* 10am-4.45pm Sat, Sun. *Apr, Sept* 10am-7pm daily. *May-Aug* 10am-10pm daily. *Oct* 10am-6pm daily. **Admission** 50 Kč; 40 Kč children. **No credit cards**. **Map** p326 C6.
It's not just children who enjoy seeing themselves distorted into all sorts of silly shapes, but they're the ones who are the most honest in their amusement. The mirror maze has been a staple of Czech childhoods for decades and it might well be the high point of your children's visit too. There's also a wax

diorama of the Swedes' unsuccessful 1648 attack on Charles Bridge. While you're on the hill, check out the Štefánik Observatory (*see p96*).

Activities & events

Boating
Slovanský Island & Charles Bridge, Staré Město, Prague 1. Metro Staroměstská/tram 17, 18. **Open** *Mar-Oct* 10am-6pm daily. **Rates** 80-120 Kč/hr. **No credit cards. Map** p330 J6/p328 J4.
Rowing or paddle boats can be rented at Novotného lávka, south of the Staré Město end of Charles Bridge, or at Slovanský Island, near the National Theatre. They're a great way to see the city.

Historic tram 91
296 124 901. **Open** *Apr-Nov* hourly, noon-6pm Sat, Sun & public holidays. **Fare** 25 Kč; 10 Kč children. **No credit cards.**
This quaint, wood-framed tram travels a loop from Výstaviště, trundling along the banks of Malá Strana, across the Legionnaires' Bridge to the National Theatre, up through Wenceslas Square and then back to Výstaviště via Náměstí Republiky. Hop on the antique at any stop along the route and see most of the city's sights in one go. *See p292.*

Horse-drawn carriages
Staroměstské náměstí, Staré Město, Prague 1 (no phone). Metro Staroměstská/tram 17, 18. **Rides** 10am-6pm daily. **Fare** 800-1,000 Kč/20min ride. **No credit cards. Map** p328 L4.
Hitch a ride on an old-time, horse-drawn carriage. Rides begin near the clock tower on Old Town Square and are offered during peak tourist months.

Matějská pouť
Výstaviště, Holešovice, Prague 7 (220 103 204). Metro Vltavská/tram 5, 14, 25. **Date** Feb-Mar. **Admission** 100 Kč. **No credit cards. Map** p332 D1.
A popular springtime carnival, Matějská pouť is generally a hit with children. For a month, the grounds of Výstaviště fairground (*see p127*) are jam-packed with rides, bumper cars and shooting galleries, and the air is filled with the pungent, evocative smells of doughnuts and candyfloss.

Prague Steamship Company
Pražská paroplavební společnost
Docked on the embankment below Palackého náměstí, Nové Město, Prague 1 (224 931 013/224 930 017/ www.paroplavba.cz). Metro Karlovo náměstí/tram 3, 4, 10, 16, 17, 21. **Open** Various times daily (call or check website for details). **Tickets** 80 Kč; 40 Kč children; free under-6s. **Credit** MC, V. **Map** p330 J10.
Great in combination with a trip to the Prague Zoo (*see p206*), which this steamship serves via the Vltava river, the PPS is a leisurely 75-minute ride along the river. The boat only operates from late March to November on this route, but the company also offers 55- and 90-minute sightseeing rides year-round. There are several cruises each day.

Entertainment & sport

Jungleland
Výmolova 298/2A, Radlice, Prague 5 (251 091 437). Metro Radlická. **Open** 9am-7pm daily. **Admission** 50 Kč for 90mins (accompanying adults free); 25 Kč disabled children. **No credit cards.**
Children aged one to 13 can burn off energy at this huge padded jungle gym, which features much more than your standard slide and box of plastic balls. Youngsters will have a blast climbing, balancing on a rope bridge, crawling under obstacles and navigating their way through the labyrinthine playground. Meanwhile, parents can relax at an elevated café, while there's a separate soft-play area for babies and toddlers.

Laser Game
Národní 25, Staré Město, Prague 1 (224 221 188). Metro Národní třída/tram 6, 9, 18, 21, 22, 23. **Open** 10am-midnight daily. **Admission** 149 Kč/ 15 mins. **No credit cards. Map** p328 L6.
If family tensions are running high, then work them out here with cyberblast pulse guns. Children are transformed into mini Terminators while running around a dark basement labyrinth, shooting laser guns at light sensors on their adversaries' belts to score a kill, while trying to dodge shots at their own belts. Adults not wanting to be brained should be mindful of low-clearance ceilings in the dark.

Teta Tramtárie
Jungmannova 28, Nové Město, Prague 1 (www.tetatramtarie.cz). Metro Mustek or Narodni trida/tram 6, 9, 18, 21, 22, 23. **Open** 7.30am-8pm daily. **Credit** V, MC. **Map** p328 M6.
Teta Tramtárie is a ball for children: an entire mini-mall of toy shop, children's bookshop, kid-sized cinema, with endless children's films and cartoons (some in English), puppet theatre, two pizza restaurants and an ice-cream parlour (*see p198*). By far the favourite is the large indoor jungle gym. Centrally located, pushchair-friendly, and with a baby-changing station and toilets adapted for small people.

Outdoor playgrounds

Happily, Prague finally has a good number of playgrounds newly fitted out with the latest swings, slides, merry-go-rounds and more – most generally have equipment suitable for toddlers too. Below are some of the more central ones, all of which are open from 8am until sunset daily.

Kampa
Malostranské nábřeží 1, Malá Strana, Prague 1. Metro Malostranská/tram 6, 9, 12, 20, 22, 23. **Map** p327 G6.
The walled playground on the side of Kampa park closest to the river (not to be confused with the nearby restaurant of the same name) is a consistent hit with the local children.

Kinského zahrada

Újezd 1, Smíchov, Prague 5. Metro Anděl/tram 6, 9, 12, 20.
Located just off Naměsti Kinský. To reach the playground, enter the park via the arched iron gate, then follow the pavement to the right.

Petřín hill

Újezd & Vítězná streets, Malá Strana, Prague 1. Metro Malostranská/tram 6, 9, 12, 20, 22, 23. **Map** p326 C5.
Walk up Petřín hill past the funicular stop (*lanová dráha*), then take the pedestrian bridge to the right. That path leads directly to the playground.

Puppet theatre

Puppet theatre has a rich history in Bohemia, having played a key role in the National Revival movement of the 19th century. The **National Marionette Theatre** (*see p253*) stages regular child-pleasing shows for foreigners, while a handful of theatres across the city host puppet performances. Another option is a non-verbal multimedia performance at the **Magic Lantern** theatre (*see p253*). For further information see the Theatre & Dance chapter. Current listings appear in the *Prague Post*, which also runs a column for children in summer, 'Child's Play'. If your little darling wants a marionette of his own, a number of quality puppet shops are along Jilská and Karlova streets in Staré Město. **Krásná Dišperanda** (Jilska 7, 224 235 579) is recommended.

Eating out

It's getting easier to eat out with children in Prague. More restaurants are providing highchairs upon request, though finding a suitable baby-changing area remains something of a challenge. However, be warned that restaurant owners often side with cigarette smokers and, under current law, are only obliged to provide non-smoking sections during peak hours. Still, **Pizzeria Rugantino** (Dušní 4, Staré Město, Prague 1, 222 318 172), minutes from Old Town Square, has friendly staff, provides crayons and paper, offers child-sized portions and has a non-smoking section. From 4pm to 6pm children can even make their own pizzas, but booking is essential.

The Staré Město branch of **Bohemia Bagel** (*see p137*), with its token play corner and quick, child-friendly food, remains a favourite of English-speaking parents. For dessert, treat your kids to a pilgrimage to fruit-ice heaven – also known as **Ovocný Světozor** (Vodičkova 39, Nové Město, Prague 1, 224 946 826), located in the Světozor passage, just off Wenceslas

Square. Don't be put off by the crowds, the service is quick. There are good sundaes and milkshakes available too.

Practicalities

Baby requirements

As in any European capital, disposable nappies and baby food are widely available. Any larger, full-service supermarket will stock all your basic baby supplies. For the basics, plus additional items like bottles, teats, nursing supplies, formula, lotions and so on, head to a hypermarket such as **Carrefour** or **Tesco** (for both, *see p178*), or to a pharmacy (*lékárna*). For late-night emergencies, each district in Prague has a 24-hour pharmacy. The Prague 1 *lékárna* is at Palackého 5 (224 946 982). It accepts credit cards on purchases over 300 Kč. Note there's a small surcharge on purchases after 7pm on weekdays, after noon on Saturday and all day Sunday.

If you're in need of clothes and other supplies for your sprog, try the following stores:

Baby Shop Sparky's

Slovanský dům, Senovážné náměstí 28a, Nové Město, Prague 1 (221 451 790). Metro Můstek/tram 3, 9, 14, 24. **Open** 10am-7pm daily. **Credit** AmEx, MC, V. **Map** p329 P4.
The upscale Sparky's stocks a wide variety of all things baby-related, including clothes, pushchairs, cots and toys. It specialises in the needs of babies up to 12 months old. Just outside the shop, you'll find Sparky's small, fenced-in play area.

Mothercare

Myslbek Pasáž, Na příkopě 19-21, Staré Město, Prague 1 (222 240 008). Metro Můstek/tram 3, 9, 14, 24. **Open** 9.30am-7pm Mon-Fri; 9am-6pm Sat; 11am-6pm Sun. **Credit** MC, V. **Map** p329 N5.
Everything for little ones, from pushchairs to clothes. There's also a spacious baby-changing area.

Baby gear rentals

Ajuty

Plzeňská 20, Smíchov, Prague 5 (257 320 032/ www.ajuty.cz). Metro Anděl/tram 4, 6, 7, 9, 10, 12, 14, 20. **Open** 9.30am-6pm Mon-Fri; 9am-noon Sat. **Credit** MC, V.
Pushchairs rent for 300-600 Kč per week. Car seats go for 385-420 Kč per week. A deposit is required.

Childminding

Large hotels usually offer a babysitting service. Otherwise, try the following, whose rates tend to be cheaper than the hotel rates. These agencies all provide sitters who speak English, but be prepared to pay the transport costs for sitters who stay after midnight. The website www.expats.cz has many forum posts and tips from expat parents as well.

Agentura Admina
Americká 10, Prague 2 (608 281 280/603 421 542). **Rates** 140-200 Kč/hr. **No credit cards.** **Map** p333 A4.
Apart from the usual babysitting options, Agentura Admina also offers the useful possibility of an indoor play area for short-term childminding.

Agentura Aja
603 886 736. **Rates** 100-150 Kč/hr. **No credit cards.**
Aja will book a sitter for any schedule and send them to you at rates of 100-150 Kč per hour, depending on the time of day and the number of children.

Agentura Pohoda
274 772 201/602 252 873/www.agpohoda.cz. **Rates** 130-150 Kč/hr. **No credit cards.**
Pohoda specialises in looking after non-Czech children, with a particular sideline working for the local film studios. The agency even looked after Bruce Willis's son and daughter when he was filming here.

Health

For sore throats, scuffed knees, or worse, call the following English-speaking care providers:

First Medical Clinic of Prague
První Pražská Zdravotní
Pankrác House, Lomnického 5, Pankrác, Prague 4 (234 630 111/emergencies 603 555 006/www.medicover.com). Metro Pražského povstání Náměstí/tram 3, 16, 17, 21. **Open** 8am-3pm Tue, Thur, Fri; noon-7pm Mon, Wed. **Credit** AmEx, MC, V.
A clinic that specialises in paediatrics.

Poliklinika na Národní
Národní třída 9, Nové Město, Prague 1 (222 075 120/emergencies 720 427 634/www.poliklinika. narodni.cz). Metro Národní třída/tram 6, 9, 18, 21, 22, 23. **Open** 8.30am-5pm Mon-Fri; by appointment Sat, Sun. **Credit** AmEx, MC, V. **Map** p328 L6.
Highly professional staff, including a paediatrician, and a central Nové Město location. Handy for crises.

Transport

In Prague children up to six years old travel free on public transport, while those aged 6-15 travel for half-price. On the metro, many stations lack escalators or lifts from ground level down to the entrance vestibule. Czechs are accustomed, however, to helping mums carry their strollers up or down the stairs. They may approach you offering help but if no one volunteers, don't be shy about asking – just say '*Pomoc, prosím*' ('Help, please'). If you're at a busy tram stop, it's a good idea to wave to the approaching driver to let him know you'll be getting on with a pram. People with prams must enter and exit by the tram's rear door; on buses, look for the pram sticker indicating which door to use. As you reach your stop, push the button above the door (not the red emergency one) to signal that you'll require a little extra time getting off.

Film

Roll the film festival.

Czech cinema operates on two very different planes: first there are the big-budget Hollywood films that use Prague as a prop, and then there are the shoestring films made by local auteurs, which nevertheless local audiences flock to see. Movies like Bohdan Slama's *Something Like Happiness*, Jan Hřebejk's *Beauty in Trouble* and the Czech-UK co-production *Shut Up and Shoot Me* by Steen Agro still keep rolling out despite dismal state funding. Czech filmmakers made headlines at Cannes in 2006 not for any film but by going on strike to protest at the Czech Parliament's refusal to pass a tax on cinemas, video rentals and commercial television stations to support the Czech film industry. Even so, there were 22 features competing for the local version of the Oscar, the Czech Lion, at the most recent awards' night; clearly, however little money there is, native filmmakers find a way.

Most Czech films don't export but they tend to play for extended runs in Prague, often with English subtitles and, helpfully, nearly all go on to DVD. Rental from shops is not difficult to arrange, even for foreigners.

Czech films, which used to have a near monopoly on local studio space, can seldom afford to rent the top-line facilities, so the newest flicks tend to be shot on location. Nonetheless, films like those mentioned above, domestic dramas like *Restart*, and even silly teen sex comedies like *Rafťáci* prove to be among the biggest domestic box-office draws. The latter film also shows another new trend in Czech filmmaking: product placement as a source of funding.

The first international splash of Czech filmmaking was *Ecstasy* (*Extáze*) in 1932, featuring a nude bathing scene with a young Hedy Lamarr. Until the mid 1960s, though, only a couple of Czech films, like Karel Zeman's 1958 *The Fabulous World of Jules Verne* (*Vynález zkázy*), took any international attention.

The Czech New Wave, between 1963 and 1968, brought Miloš Forman, Jiří Menzel and Ivan Passer to prominence. Menzel's *Closely Observed Trains* (*Ostře sledované vlaky*) won an Oscar in 1967. The Soviet-led invasion in 1968 put a damper on creativity for another 30 years. Recently, young filmmakers referred to as the Velvet Generation have been putting Czech cinema back on the international map with films like *Kolya*, *Divided We Fall* and *Loners*.

Glimpses of Prague turn up in better-funded Western fare as the city continues to prove its star quality. With the arrival of Bond in 2006 the city was truly put on the map as a major contender. Other recent Prague-made films include *Hostel*, *Last Holiday*, *Young Hannibal: Behind the Mask* and *The Illusionist*. Thus Praguers are very blasé about coming across World War II scenes on the way home from work or seeing a starlet at a local bar.

While cinema attendance, as in the rest of the world, is in decline, for those willing to plunk down for tickets the screens are plusher than ever. Not so long ago there was just one multiplex, Galaxie. Now there are a dozen, plus a fun, newish IMAX screen at Palác Flora. Most screenings are with the original soundtrack and Czech subtitles, which makes access easy unless you happen to be trying for a Chinese film without being a fluent speaker. Many of the single-screen cinemas that in the 1990s were sold out for the weekend by Friday afternoon are struggling to keep a handful of customers, but a few of the movie palace gems, like the Lucerna, keep hanging on. The art nouveau interior here makes for a welcome break from the assembly-line sterility of the multiplexes.

TICKETS AND TONGUES

While tickets for the multiplexes run at around 150 Kč, and more for special seating, the smaller theatres try to hold the line at 100 Kč.

There is generally a sign at the box office explaining what version the film is in. *Dabing* films are dubbed into Czech, but usually only children's films get this treatment. By and large, films are screened *s českými titulky*, or simply *č t* (with original soundtrack and Czech subtitles). Important Czech films are sometimes screened with English subtitles; look for *s anglickými titulky*.

Tickets have assigned seat numbers and you can usually pick your spot from a computer screen at the box office. To prevent arguments, be sure to find the row (*řada*) and seat (*sedadlo*) that are printed on the ticket.

Movie schedules are available in the *Prague Post*, as well as in a number of smaller but ever-changing Czech publications, usually available for free. Big posters at many tram stops and kiosks have a fairly complete schedule. All the multiplexes and many of the smaller art-house theatres have schedules online.

This may not be the *Beauty in Trouble* in Jan Hrêbejk's film. *See p210.*

Commercial cinemas

Bio-Illusion

Vinohradská 48, Vinohrady, Prague 2 (222 520 379/www.bio-illusion.cz). Metro Muzeum/tram 11. **No credit cards. Map** p333 C3.

Majoring mostly in recent Czech films, usually without English subtitles, this old-time movie palace has had a considerable facelift, with comfortable new seats and a full-service bar available for ticket holders. In an interesting, and environmental, twist, the bar uses furniture left over from a liquor company's advertising campaign, while the fairly comfortable seats in the theatre were recycled from the now-shuttered original Galaxie multiplex. When not showing new Czech titles, more recent art hits and better Hollywood films fill the schedule.

Blaník

Václavské náměstí 56, Nové Město, Prague 1 (224 032 172). Metro Muzeum/tram 11. **No credit cards. Map** p331 N7.

Still hanging on thanks to its prime location, this pleasant if plain single-screen theatre has undergone an extensive renovation and alternates between recent hit films and live theatrical productions.

Lucerna

Vodičkova 36, Nové Město, Prague 1 (224 216 972/ www.lucerna.cz). Metro Můstek/tram 3, 9, 14, 24. **Credit** DC, MC, V. **Map** p329 N6.

The art nouveau Lucerna is a reminder of cinemagoing's glory days. The elevated lobby bar has large windows that let you watch the 1920s-era shopping arcade, and, even better, somebody still occasionally tickles the ivories on the piano. What's more, the coat-check is still functioning, and you can still watch the films from the balcony. There is even a real curtain in front of the screen. Recently, the theatre has been moving to fewer Hollywood and more European films in its programming. **Photo** *p214.*

Perštýn

Na Perštýně 6, Nové Město, Prague 1 (221 668 432). Metro Národní třída/tram 6, 9, 17, 18, 22, 23. **No credit cards. Map** p328 L6.

The fairly large basement cinema has moveable tables and chairs, so seating is actually rather limited. The atmosphere is relaxed, but when it's full it can be hard to see the screen if people sit on the tables. The café has a limited selection of packaged snacks and beverages. It's a pity there's no real food, as the tables would be quite convenient.

Světozor

Vodičkova 39, Nové Město, Prague 1 (224 946 824). Metro Můstek/tram 3, 9, 14, 24. **No credit cards. Map** p329 N6.

One of the last holdouts for pure mainstream programming outside of the multiplexes.

Multiplexes

Cinema City Flora

Vinohradská 149, Vinohrady, Prague 3 (255 742 021-2/www.cinemacity.cz). Metro Flora. **No credit cards.**

A shopping-mall theatre, but it does have the city's only IMAX screen, capable of 3D-screenings.

A long path to royalty

Jiří Menzel, whose 1966 film *Closely Observed Trains* captivated the world with the indignities and fate of Czechoslovakia under the Nazis (and won the 1967 Best Foreign Film Oscar), missed out on the success and acclaim of contemporaries like Miloš Forman and Ivan Presser, both of whom went West to escape cultural repression. Menzel chose to stay on in Prague, living through the Soviet clampdown of 1968, which essentially sidelined his career for two decades.

After the Velvet Revolution of 1989 he finally got behind the camera again for the 1994 comedy flop *The Life and Extraordinary Adventures of Private Ivan Chonkin*. It would be 12 more years before he tried his hand at another feature project.

In 2006, however, elements finally came together for a film that's been anticipated for at least a decade: *I Served the King of England*, an adaptation of the novel by Czech literary lion Bohumil Hrabal.

Menzel's acolyte and sometime rival Jan Svěrák, who won an Oscar for the bittersweet comedy *Kolya* in 1996, also took up a camera again in the spring of 2006. *Bottle Return*, written by his comic actor father, Zdenek, marks the duo's first return to the big screen since 2001's World War II romance *Dark Blue World*. The elder Svěrák, as usual, plays a key role in the new feature, portraying a cash-poor retired teacher who takes a job at a supermarket recycling centre.

Jan, who differed strongly with his father over the script, was happy to finally settle on a new version that focuses more on characters and family than comic plot twists. 'My father can use his own experience with ageing,' the younger Svěrák told *Variety* about the project, 'and I like it very much. I think the story is working better now than in the previous editions.'

Menzel, who was involved in a bidding contest with Jan Svěrák over the *King of England* script, finally won the day in 2005 and, with a budget of an estimated $3 million, or triple the average cost of a Czech feature film, he went to work in locations in and around Prague.

During filming, the secretive Menzel only provided a glimpse of the process to journalists once, during which he downplayed expectations and complained of the pressure such a work entails. Indeed, Hrabal's novel has provided some of the most sought-after material in Czech filmmaking since the downfall of communism.

The old Hrabal, who lived various lives under the regime, from paper recycler to butcher, didn't make things easier by signing the rights away to two different parties.

In the end, though, the adaptation was done by his old friend Menzel, who had also adapted *Closely Observed Trains* from a Hrabal book. Somewhere the cantankerous novelist is surely smiling to himself.

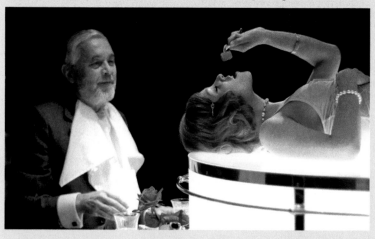

Cinema City Galaxie
Arkalycká 877, Háje, Prague 4 (reservations 267 900 567/schedule 296 141 414/www.cinemacity.cz). Metro Háje. **No credit cards**.
New management built a more modern Galaxie alongside the old one, which sits abandoned next door. Downtown ticket prices and film selection.

Multikino Ládví
Burešova 4, Kobylisy, Prague 8 (286 587 027/ www.multikinoladvi.cz). Metro Ládví/tram 24. **No credit cards**.
The new metro stop at Ládví has made this fairly cheap multiplex much easier to reach from downtown. Still, its location means that it seldom sells out and the café, one of the few places to go in its housing project neighbourhood, is popular.

Palace Cinemas Nový Smíchov
Plzeňská 8, Smíchov, Prague 5 (257 181 212/ www.palacecinemas.cz). Metro Anděl/tram 6, 9, 12. **No credit cards**.
The most popular multiplex in town. And if the 12 screens and 2,702 seats are sold out, across the street is Village Cinemas Anděl City.

Palace Cinemas Park Hostivař
Švehlova 32, Hostivař, Prague 10 (257 181 212/www.palacecinemas.cz). Tram 22, 26. **No credit cards**.
The first multiplex in the new wave of multiplex building has a slightly less ambitious schedule than its downtown cousins.

Palace Cinemas Slovanský dům
Na Příkopě 22, Nové Město, Prague 1 (257 181 212/www.palacecinemas.cz). Metro Náměstí Republiky/tram 5, 8, 14. **No credit cards**. **Map** p329 N5.
The most centrally located multiplex sometimes shows recent Czech films with English subtitles, or original-language versions of animated films that play elsewhere dubbed. The theatre also boasts a high-tech digital projector that can simulcast live concerts or show digital films. In January, the annual Febiofest takes over the whole complex.

Village Cinemas Anděl City
Radlická 3179, Smíchov, Prague 5 (251 115 100/ www.villagecinemas.cz). Metro Anděl/tram 6, 9, 12. **Credit** AmEx, DC, MC, V.
Hidden from the main street a bit, it is easy to miss this competing complex near Palace Cinemas Nový Smíchov, but it tends to be less crowded. The Gold Class screens offer reclining seats with a button to summon beverages from the concession stand. The tickets for the luxury seating are the priciest in town.

Art-house cinemas

Aero
Biskupcova 31, Žižkov, Prague 3 (271 771 349/ www.kinoaero.cz). Metro Želivského/tram 1, 9, 10, 16. **No credit cards**.
No cinema in Prague makes more of an effort than the 70-year-old Aero. It goes beyond the offerings of local distributors to get prints from all over. Luckily, the imports of foreign films often have English subtitles (with Czech translations broadcast to headsets). On occasion, filmmakers like Terry Gilliam and Paul Morrissey come along to introduce their films. The theatre is also home to several festivals. The cinema's bar has become a popular local hangout, but the noise sometimes filters into the theatre. Tickets can be booked in advance online.

Bio Oko
Františka Křížka 15, Holešovice, Prague 7 (233 382 606/www.kinooko.cz). Metro Vltavská/tram 5, 12, 17. **No credit cards**. **Map** p332 D3.
One of the few theatres with anything resembling a marquee, Oko has made a real stab at becoming one of the city's leading art houses. The pre-revolution feel has been replaced with a café and, thankfully, there are improved, padded seats in the theatre.

Evald
Národní třída 28, Staré Město, Prague 1 (221 105 225/www.evald.cinemart.cz). Metro Národní třída/ tram 6, 9, 18, 22. **No credit cards**. **Map** p328 L6.
The best downtown art house is rather small. The owners distribute films, so they often have exclusive bookings on some European art films, independent American films and Czech films, which are sometimes shown with English subtitles. Advance booking recommended for new films. There's no snack bar, but the theatre also has a fairly nice restaurant with Czech food specialities.

French Institute
Štěpánská 35, Nové Město, Prague 1 (221 401 011/ www.ifp.cz). Metro Můstek/tram 3, 9, 14, 24. **No credit cards**. **Map** p331 N8.
New and classic French films are shown in a full-scale, fairly comfortable basement cinema. About half the films have English subtitles. Tickets are an incredibly cheap 40 Kč. Don't even think of bringing food or beverages into the screening room.

MAT Studio
Karlovo náměstí 19, Staré Město, Prague 1 (224 915 765/www.mat.cz). Metro Karlovo náměstí/ tram 3, 4, 6, 14, 16, 18, 22, 24. **No credit cards**. **Map** p330 L9.
The smallest theatre in town. The intimate screening room shows a fair mix of offbeat films, Czech classics with English subtitles and rare selections from the vaults of Czech TV. The cinema's bar has some movie props and old posters from Czech films. Buy your tickets early – given the few seats available, the performances inevitably sell out.

Ponrepo
Bio Konvikt Theatre, Bartolomějská 11, Staré Město, Prague 1 (224 233 281 ext 31). Metro Národní třída/tram 6, 9, 18, 22. **Annual membership** 150 Kč. **Tickets** 40-60 Kč. **No credit cards**. **Map** p328 K6.

For some reason, the management at the screening room for the Czech Film Archive acts like it doesn't want you to see and enjoy old films. A photo ID is required, no exceptions, to see films. The schedule has Czech and Slovak films plus selected world classics. Be sure to check that the movie doesn't have a live Czech translation announced directly into the hall (denoted by *s překl*), since it will be impossible to hear the original soundtrack.

Světozor

Vodičkova 41, Nové Město, Prague 1 (224 946 824/ www.kinosvetozor.cz). Metro Můstek/tram 3, 9, 14, 24. **No credit cards**. **Map** p329 N6.

A new partner of the respected Aero rep house, the Světozor books consistently engaging and off-beat indie and global cinema, and has built up a loyal following in the process. This adds major convenience since the Aero is out of the centre, and the kino bar is invariably full of colourful characters.

Festivals & special events

Some film festivals have become relatively well established. Others tend to float a bit in terms of time and location, so be on the lookout for the occasional embassy-sponsored events. Most of these offer English-subtitled versions when possible. Interest in summer outdoor cinema is waning – the one at Střelecký Island has been going it alone recently. Look out for posters during the summer months.

Project 100

www.artfilm.cz. **Date** Jan-Feb.

Lucerna. See p211.

The programmes at the art houses are made up partly of films that come from this travelling festival. Approximately ten noted local film critics and scholars each choose what they think is an important film, either recent or classic, and the package then plays in Prague theatres in January and February before touring the country. After that, they turn up on arthouse schedules as often as their popularity allows.

Febiofest

221 101 111/www.febiofest.cz. **Date** late winter.

The multiplex at Slovanský dům houses the largest of the local festivals. The selection of films has a wide scope, with groups of films, both old and new, from all over the globe and on select topics. One constant problem, though, is that it is hard to tell which have English subtitles. Recent guests have included Roman Polanski and David Hemmings.

Days of European Film

224 215 538/www.eurofilmfest.cz. **Date** early Mar.

More than a decade old, this approximately ten-day festival displays films from European Union members and candidates in Lucerna and Aero. Many of the offerings have English subtitles, and a number of filmmakers come to introduce their works. A few of the films have gone into local distribution but most are just screened once or twice.

One World Human Rights Film Festival

www.oneworld.cz. **Date** early spring.

An increasingly popular festival of documentaries and features about human rights issues. The venues are spread out, but usually one of the theatres has films in English or with English subtitles.

Karlovy Vary International Film Festival

www.kviff.com. **Date** early July.

The main event for cinema is outside of Prague in the West Bohemian spa town of Karlovy Vary (*see p272* **Cue the lights**). This is the only film fest in the country accredited by the FIAPF, the group that sanctions the Cannes, Berlin and Venice festivals. High-profile guests including Robert Redford, Elijah Wood and Gus van Sant but the real joy is in the gathering of indie filmmakers, with parties almost as rewarding as the 230 or so screenings. Many films sell out, but if space allows they'll fit you in.

International Aviation Film

www.leteckefilmy.cz. **Date** Sept.

A relatively new festival features mostly classic war and action films. Guests have included famous pilots and war heroes. The festival seems to have settled at Village Cinemas Anděl City.

French Film Festival

221 401 011/www.ifp.cz. **Date** late Nov.

Not as arty as you might expect, since mainstream French comedies and crime films do appear, along with French stars introducing their films.

Galleries

Battling biennales.

What happens when biennales collide: **Prague Biennale 2**.

If one international biennale is good, two must be even better. To those uninitiated in the politics of the contemporary Czech art world, this might seem the rationale behind the city staging two concurrent biennales in the summer of 2005. The battling biennales – which cast themselves as 'underdog' and 'establishment' – divided the Czech art world bitterly, with calls for boycotts of the rival show, finger-pointing and myriad accusations.

The organisers of the low-budget 'underdog' biennale – the editors of Italian art magazine *Flash Art International* – were actually the first to come up with the concept of a biennial exhibition for Prague, staging 'Prague Biennale 1' in 2003 in the building where the Czech National Gallery houses its collections of modern and contemporary art. By 2005 the Prague Biennale had gone binary. The *Flash Art* editors had secured trademark status for '**Prague Biennale**' (www.praguebiennale.org), snaring the honour of staging an already name-branded biennale for the second time. Meanwhile, the National Gallery general director dubbed the upstart event the '**International Biennale of Contemporary Art**'.

Tellingly, former president Václav Havel lent his support to the *Flash Art*-led Prague Biennale 2, which, ousted from Veletržní palác, took up residence in an unpolished warehouse space in the working-class district of Karlín. Havel's long-time rival, current president Václav Klaus, threw his weight behind the National Gallery event, which drew financial support from state coffers and also aimed for a more polished look, in the soaring but sterile spaces of Veletržní palác.

Despite the squabbling, in the end the city of Prague won by establishing its credentials among international curators and artists as a town where contemporary art happens. And the public benefited by seeing scads of fresh art.

A further feather in the cap of Prague's reputation as a centre of contemporary-art happenings was what could be called an 'anti-biennale' that sprung up in 2006, which is an off-year for the other biennales. Called '**Tina B**' – an acronym for 'This Is Not Another Biennale' – it brought in intriguing art from near and far, while its curatorial aims were ambitious yet tightly focused. Such an effort both points out the absurdity of bickering biennales and proves

Municipal House Exhibition Hall.
See p218.

that there's enough elbow room for more modern art in this city of a hundred spires.

Apart from these mega international art events, Prague seems to have rediscovered the blockbuster exhibition. Prague Castle pulled out all the stops in 2006 to stage 'Charles IV: Emperor by the Grace of God', a celebration of art and culture during the reign of King and Holy Roman Emperor Charles IV and his heirs, the last of the Luxemburg line. It would have been the 'exhibition of the decade' if anyone other than schoolchildren had actually gone (it seems that the administrators of Prague Castle, worried that no one would come, gave nearly all the tickets to schools at huge reductions). But the show, the biggest ever at the castle, does bode well for future exhibitions.

There was plenty of support for contemporary art during the Havel era, but the current head of state, Václav Klaus, has redirected resources into projects deemed to be more 'in the national interest'. One example is the long-running and fascinating 'Story of Prague Castle', while the Charles IV show marks its apotheosis. The exhibition about the king first ran at New York's Metropolitan Museum of Art in autumn 2005, where it drew raves. The endeavour promises more cross-border co-operation in the lending of art works and co-organising major exhibitions with institutions from abroad.

The other big players in terms of having the means and space to stage major shows – the National Gallery and the Prague City Gallery – hew to their established curatorial paths.

The **National Gallery** is known for showcasing key artists in the nation's art history, like modernist Václav Špála and Czech patriot of the 19th century František Ženíšek, at the **Wallenstein Riding School**, while turning over the halls of Veletržní palác to a more varied mix of shows. There you'll find retrospectives of artists like Jiří Kolář and Zorka Ságlová, as well as exhibits by a roster of emerging and more-established Czech artists, spiced with occasional shows by foreign artists.

The **Prague City Gallery** (www.prague citygallery.cz) continues in its mission to support the upcoming generation of painters, often giving them their first big break by featuring them in a solo show at Old Town Hall. The City Gallery also shared responsibility with UMPRUM (the **Museum of Decorative Arts**; *see p114*) for another of the most important shows in recent years, 'Czech 20th-Century Photography', which sprawled across two venues run by the City Gallery and additionally filled the exhibition hall of UMPRUM.

It should be noted that the Prague City Gallery also organises its own biennial event:

the **Zvon Biennale of Young Artists**, which, like the other two biennales, runs in odd-numbered years. Focusing on young artists from the Czech Republic and Central Europe, the show has a more scholarly thrust. And while charting trends and advancing critical theory are important, the presentation itself can appear rather uneven if you don't read the catalogue essays.

But it is precisely the emerging young artists presented in Zvon and 'survey' shows like **Futura**'s 'Insiders' who are pumping fresh air into the Prague art scene. A handful seem to have unlimited energy, not only producing their own work, but also administering art galleries, sometimes while forging links with artists, curators and institutions from other lands.

The doyen among these indie spaces, at all of five years old, is **Galerie Display**. It's located in a graffiti-splashed storefront in the Holešovice district of Prague 7 – an area that is slowly burgeoning into an art centre, anchored by Veletržní palác. These artist-run spaces are demanding an ever-more-prominent place on the gallery map. Other efforts include **AM 180** in the Nusle district and **Karlín Studios** in the Prague district of that name, a former warehouse that encompasses a warren of exhibition spaces and studios.

At the same time, commercial galleries are joining together to rebuild the tradition of art collecting in this country, which was going strong during the First Republic but fizzled out under communism. Many gallerists point out that in the first post-communist years people were busy spending money on cars, home furnishings and holidays abroad. Now, they hope, it is time for the Czech middle classes to consider buying some art to hang over their new sofas, both for pleasure and as an investment. A beacon of this cause is the annual Art Prague art fair held every spring and growing more popular by the year. The gallerists themselves banded together in 2006 into the new Association of Gallerists of the Czech Republic, which grew out of the art fair.

Education of the art-buying public and nurturing the careers of contemporary artists are the twin aims of the handful of private galleries, including **hunt kastner artworks**.

But lest a visitor think that a commercial ethos is starting to edge out purer forms of expression, consider the 2005 winner of the annual Jindřich Chalupecký competition for under-35s. The award jury chose as the winning project the intangible social action by Kateřina Šedá (*see p219* **It matters**), whose work involved the rehabilitation of the artist's own grandmother and took place at an oilcloth-covered table in her kitchen in Moravia.

INFORMATION

For information on exhibitions, consult the *Prague Post, Kultura v Praze* (*Culture in Prague* – a listings booklet available in English from newsstands at some central locations) or *Atelier*, a Czech fortnightly broadsheet with an English summary and listings of exhibitions throughout the country. *Umělec* (*Artist*) magazine features reviews of recent shows and articles on the contemporary scene and is now available in separate English and Czech editions in some galleries and selected central newsstands. Websites with art listings include those run by the Prague Information Service (www.pis.cz) and Prague TV (www.prague.tv).

Most galleries and museums in Prague are closed on Mondays, and some smaller galleries take a holiday in August. It's always best to check that the one you want to visit hasn't closed temporarily for 'technical reasons'.

Exhibition spaces

Exhibition spaces are always coming and going in Prague as elsewhere, but the main organising bodies remain the National Gallery (*see p129*), Prague City Gallery (*see p217*) and Prague Castle (*see p76*).

Czech Museum of Fine Arts

Husova 19-21, Staré Město, Prague 1 (222 220 218/ www.cmvu.cz). Metro Staroměstská/tram 17, 18. **Open** 10am-6pm Tue-Sun. **Admission** 50 Kč; 20 Kč concessions. **No credit cards. Map** p328 K4.

Housed in an attractive block of renovated Renaissance townhouses, the Czech Museum of Fine Arts exhibits mainly 20th-century Czech art, with an increasing number of exhibitions by foreign artists like Karen LaMonte and overviews of contemporary art from other countries including Slovakia and Northern Ireland. The gallery also goes in for big exhibitions with overarching, sweeping themes, such as people, nature or technology, as well as holding special shows that are aimed at children around the time of the Christmas holidays. An ongoing cycle called 'Alternatives' is held in the atmospheric Romanesque cellar.

Galerie Rudolfinum

Alšovo nábřeží 12, Staré Město, Prague 1 (227 059 346/www.galerierudolfinum.cz). Metro Staroměstská/ tram 17, 18. **Open** 10am-6pm Tue-Sun. **Admission** 100 Kč; 50 Kč concessions; free under-15s. **No credit cards. Map** p328 J3.

The only space in the city that follows a European Kunsthalle model, the gallery in the 19th-century Rudolfinum concert building remains one of the best venues for catching Czech and international contemporary and modern art. It leans toward retrospectives of enigmatic modernists like Alén Diviš and Mikuláš Medek, major shows by artists of the middle generation like Petr Nikl and František

Skála, and, in contrast, shows of Chinese art. (If you're wondering how oriental art slipped in among all these Eastern Europeans, it's because this is an area of expertise of the gallery's director.) The Rasart series creates synergy among music, theatre and art.

House at the Stone Bell

Dům U Kamenného zvonu
Staroměstské náměstí 13, Staré Město, Prague 1 (224 827 526/www.citygalleryprague.cz). Metro Staroměstská/tram 17, 18. **Open** 10am-6pm Tue-Sun. **Admission** 90 Kč; 50 Kč concessions. **No credit cards. Map** p328 M4.

Operated by the Prague City Gallery, the House at the Stone Bell is a Gothic sandstone building on the east side of Old Town Square. It takes quite a show to outweigh the space itself, featuring as it does a gorgeous baroque courtyard and three floors of exhibition rooms, some of which have their original vaulting still in place. It favours retrospectives of Czech artists such as Toyen and Adolf Hoffmeister, and is also the traditional venue for the Zvon biennale of young Czech and Central European artists.

Kinský Palace

Staroměstské náměstí 12, Staré Město, Prague 1 (224 810 758/www.ngprague.cz). Metro Staroměstská/tram 17, 18. **Open** 10am-6pm Tue-Sun. **Admission** 100 Kč; 150 Kč family; free under-10s. **No credit cards. Map** p328 L3.

The National Gallery's renovated Kinský Palace, recently at the centre of a much-publicised restitution case, opened with a bang in 2000 with its polemical 'End of the World?' show, but it toned down its programme considerably and currently houses a long-term display of Czech landscape painting from the 17th through 20th centuries and photography from the 19th century to the present.

Municipal House Exhibition Hall

Obecní dům
Náměstí Republiky 5, Staré Město, Prague 1 (222 002 101/www.obecni-dum.cz). Metro Náměstí Republiky/tram 5, 8, 14. **Open** 10am-6pm daily. **Admission** 100 Kč for exhibitions. **Credit** AmEx, MC, V. **Map** p329 N4.

Even if you're not interested in any of the exhibitions here, it's worth coming just to see the building. Situated next to the Powder Gate, the Municipal House is a masterpiece of Czech art nouveau, fusing diverse influences into a harmonious whole. But the shows are generally worth visiting too. The exhibition rooms present varied displays, such as retrospectives of German photojournalist Werner Bischof and Decadent art in the Czech lands. But undoubtedly the best times to visit are when what's on display harmonises with the space itself. **Photo** p216.

Municipal Library

Mariánské náměstí 1 (entrance on Valentinská), Staré Město, Prague 1 (222 310 489/www.city galleryprague.cz). Metro Staroměstská/tram 17, 18. **Open** 10am-6pm Tue-Sun. **Admission** 100 Kč; 50 Kč concessions. **No credit cards. Map** p328 K4.

It matters

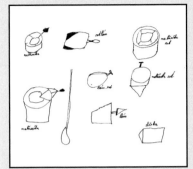

Like other awards for young artists, the **Jindřich Chalupecký Prize** for under-35s is closely watched and sometimes controversial. The winner in 2005 – Kateřina Šedá, a young artist from the Moravian capital of Brno and a recent graduate from the academy – was the most radical choice of winner in the award's 16-year history.

Šedá's project was a pigeonhole-defying 'social action' that actually did some good. Unlike most conceptual art, this 'happening' took place not in the public space, but in the intimate sphere of her own family.

Titled *It Doesn't Matter*, the project is unique on the Czech art scene, and perhaps in the world. It was prompted by the situation of her grandmother, who decided after she retired to retreat into a life of absolute idleness. Her existence revolved around sleeping and watching whatever happened to be on TV. She allowed her family to provide for all her needs, and made no effort to cook, clean, get dressed, bathe, or even click the remote control to a different channel. Her response to nearly every question by a family member was 'To je jedno' ('It doesn't matter)', a common Czech phrase that, taken to this extreme, became a declaration of her utter indifference to life.

Deciding to finally do something to change the situation, Šedá literally *drew* her grandmother out of her torpor. Šedá made a date to do a formal interview, and learned that her grandmother had found great satisfaction in her job as head of the stockroom for a hardware and housewares store for 33 years and, remarkably, could recall around 750 items from the shop's inventory. Šedá decided to put her

grandmother 'back to work' making drawings of all the items in order to 'reconstruct' the stockroom – starting with chisels of every description and running the gamut from scythes and sickles to dibbles and hoes – along with a hand-written inventory, specified down to every item's size in millimetres, with stock numbers and 1950s prices. During the course of their collaboration, the apathetic 'It doesn't matter' began to disappear from her grandmother's vocabulary.

The drawings themselves, though certainly possessing their own poignancy, cannot be considered as art. The art lies in the idea and its execution, the result of which is something so intangible yet transformative as the reawakening of her grandmother's connection with society. 'It is an elixir for her,' she says.

Established by former president Václav Havel together with visual artists Jiří Kolář and Teodor Pištěk, the Jindřich Chalupecký Prize at first went to artists prominent on the pre-1989 non-official art scene. In a sense, the award served to recognise the achievements and struggles of those artists who emerged and persevered amid the civic decay of socialism's final years.

With Kateřina Šedá, the generational break was made – and the award came full circle. Her genre-bending work developed with the support of her professor at the Academy of Fine Arts in Prague, Vladimír Kokolia – the very first Chalupecký laureate in 1990.

Šedá's selection as the Chalupecký winner may well signal a sea change in the way socially oriented art is viewed by post-communist Czech society, for whom it has retained the taint of the communist dictate that art should serve the socialist state.

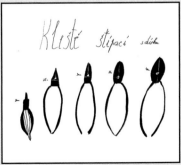

The extensive series of rooms in this venue situated above the Municipal Library and run by the Prague City Gallery provides an excellent showcase for large-scale exhibitions of historical importance, such as a sweeping show of Czech 20th-century photography and another one charting the medium's development in Germany. In 2005 it played host to the show of finalists for the Jindřich Chalupecký Prize, including the winner, Kateřina Šedá (see p219 **It matters**), rounding it out with young-artist award winners from other post-communist countries.

Old Town Hall

Staroměstské náměstí 1, Staré Město, Prague 1 (224 810 036/224 482 751/www.citygalleryprague.cz). Metro Staroměstská/tram 17, 18. **Open** *Ground floor* 11am-5pm Mon; 9am-5pm Tue-Sun. *City Gallery* 10am-6pm Tue-Sun. **Admission** 40 Kč; 20 Kč concessions. **No credit cards. Map** p328 L4.

There are two separate spaces for exhibitions within the Old Town Hall. The one entered from the ground floor generally presents a mixed bag of predominantly photographic shows, including the annual Czech Press Photo competition as well as celebrity portraiture and photojournalism. On the second floor, behind a forbidding door, is a space operated by the Prague City Gallery that specialises in introducing the youngest wave of Czech painters to the public through their first solo shows.

Wallenstein Riding School

Valdštejnská jízdárna
Valdštejnská 3, Malá Strana, Prague 1 (257 073 136/www.ngprague.cz). Metro Malostranská/tram 12, 18, 22, 23. **Open** 10am-6pm Tue-Sun. **Admission** 100 Kč; 50 Kč concessions. **No credit cards. Map** p327 G2.

No, it's not a school for equestrianism anymore. Part of the Wallenstein Palace complex and operated by the National Gallery, the Wallenstein Riding School space holds some of Prague's most popular and well-attended exhibitions. These include overviews of Czech artists like the National Revival-era patriot František Ženíšek, the modernist Václav Špála and the symbolist Max Švabinský.

Commercial, independent & private galleries

Like so much else in the city, Prague's roster of galleries is in the middle of rapid change. Among the ones that survive for more than a couple of seasons, some have very high standards, such as **Jiří Švestka Gallery**, which maintains an outstanding exhibition programme. Several non-profit spaces, whose funding doesn't hinge on appealing to mainstream tastes, are bringing a lot of the most interesting work to public attention. And a small but growing group of private galleries are endeavouring to nurture the market for Czech contemporary art.

AM 180

Bělehradská 45, Vinohrady, Prague 2 (605 407 320/731 177 641/www.am180.org). Metro Náměstí Míru/tram 6, 11. **Open** noon-7pm Mon-Fri; 11am-4pm Sat. **Admission** free. **No credit cards. Map** p331 P10.

This young space is the collective effort of a dynamic group of up-and-coming artists. Shows tend to be imaginatively titled and, even when the art is a tad unpolished, the artists exhibiting here often show great promise. Recently, more established Czech artists like Vacláv Stratil, Vladimir Skrepl and Tomáš Vaněk have been flocking to the gallery.

c2c

Za Strahovem 19, Strahov, Prague 6 (777 817 774/www.c2c.cz). Metro Hradčanská/tram 22, 23. **Open** 4-7pm Thur-Sat. **Admission** free. **No credit cards.**

Situated in the neighbourhood up behind the enormous Strahov stadium, c2c opened in late 2005 and is quickly establishing a reputation for experimental group shows that explore complex themes. The gallery name stands for 'Circle of Curators and Critics', and its exhibitions embody a focus on curatorship and critical theory.

Futura

Holečkova 49, Smíchov, Prague 5 (251 511 804/www.futuraprojekt.cz). Metro Anděl/tram 4, 7, 9. **Open** noon-7pm Wed-Sun. **Admission** free. **No credit cards.**

Futura has quickly risen to the top ranks of the Prague gallery circuit. A brilliantly renovated building houses multiple exhibition halls, ranging from white cubes to atmospheric cellar spaces, with a labyrinthine series of nooks devoted to video works and a Projekt Room presenting experimental shows by up-and-coming artists. It's proving to be a great place to see a blend of established Czech artists like Jiří David and Veronika Bromová and bright stars of European contemporary art such as Annika Larsson. Don't miss David Černý's provocative installation in the gallery's courtyard.

Galerie České pojišťovny

Spálená 14, Nové Město, Prague 1 (261 383 111/www.galeriecpoj.cz). Metro Národní třída/tram 6, 9, 18, 21, 22, 23. **Open** 10am-6pm daily. **Admission** free. **No credit cards. Map** p330 L8.

Finding České pojišťovny is half the fun: follow one of three passages (from Spálená, Purkyňova or Vladislavova streets) through a quiet courtyard with a pleasant café until you find the gallery. Opened in 2004 in an art nouveau building designed by Osvald Polívka, the gallery presents shows of mainly contemporary Czech photography, and painting by artists of the middle generation like Tomáš Cisařovský, Jaroslav Rona and Richard Konvička.

Galerie Display

Bubenská 3, Holešovice, Prague 7 (mobile 604 722 562/www.galerie.display.cz). Metro Vltavská/tram 1, 3, 8, 14, 25. **Open** 3-6pm Wed-Sun. **Admission** free. **No credit cards. Map** p332 A2.

Facing up to Islam at **Galerie Display**.

The Display's graffiti-splashed shopfront blends in perfectly to its urban surroundings and the gallery itself is a highly energetic player on the art scene. Opened in 2001, it is already a veteran among indie art spaces. In addition to a risk-taking exhibition programme, which often connects Prague audiences with young artists from other European countries, it also holds film screenings and discussion evenings with the artists themselves, useful if you want to ask them just what they had in mind.

Galerie Gambit

Mikulandská 6, Nové Město, Prague 1 (224 910 508/ www.gambit.cz). Metro Národní třída/tram 6, 9, 18, 21, 22, 23. **Open** noon-6pm Tue-Sat. **Admission** free. **No credit cards. Map** p328 K6.
You might have to squeeze to get into this waistcoat-pocket gallery but the beefed-up exhibition programme is worth breathing in for. It concentrates on small shows of new works by well-known names on the Czech scene – Michael Rittstein, Petr Nikl and Bedřich Dlouhý, for instance – while also presenting fresh young artists. The gallery also occasionally exhibits foreign artists and contemporary design.

Galerie Jelení

Drtinova 15, Smíchov, Prague 5 (737 407 353/ www.fcca.cz). Metro Anděl/tram 2, 12, 20. **Open** 3-6pm Tue-Thur. **Admission** free. **No credit cards.**
The Jelení kept its name when it moved from its previous location in Jelení Street to new quarters in Smíchov. Operated by the Foundation and Centre for Contemporary Art, it puts on a steady stream of experimental shows, including student exhibitions.

Galerie Kritiků

Jungmannova 31, Nové Město, Prague 1 (224 494 205/www.galeriekritiku.com). Metro Národní třída/tram 6, 9, 18, 21, 22, 23. **Open** 10am-6pm Tue-Sun. **Admission** 40 Kč; 20 Kč concessions. **No credit cards. Map** p328 M6.

An elegant space in the Adria Palace, with a grand pyramid skylight, Galerie Kritiků has proved itself to be a class act. It is particularly strong when it comes to group shows, while its offerings of international art often come from Japan.

Galerie Mánes

Masarykovo nábřeží 250, Nové Město, Prague 1 (224 930 754/www.galeriemanes.cz). Metro Karlovo náměstí/tram 17, 21. **Open** 10am-6pm Tue-Sun. **Admission** varies; free children. **No credit cards. Map** p330 J8.
The largest and most prominent of the Czech Fund for Art Foundation's network of galleries, Mánes is also a beautiful, if run-down, piece of 1930s functionalist architecture by Otakar Novotný. The riverside gallery usually hosts anything from international travelling shows to exhibitions of contemporary Czech artists like Lukáš Rittstein.

Galerie Miro

Strahovské nádvoří 1, Strahov, Prague 1 (233 354 066/www.galeriemiro.cz). Tram 22, 23. **Open** 10am-5pm daily. **Admission** ranges up to 150 Kč; often free for shows of contemporary artists. **No credit cards. Map** p326 A4.
Located in a deconsecrated church within the Strahov Monastery complex, the Miro specialises in shows of graphics by well-known artists from across the centuries like Goya and Dalí, but also stages shows of lesser-known contemporary European artists. Its owner, Miro Smolák, shot into the spotlight when he convinced star architect Daniel Libeskind to design a Dalí Museum for Prague. The model of the yet-to-be-built museum is on display at the gallery.

Galerie Montanelli

Nerudova 13, Malá Strana, Prague 1 (257 531 220/www.galeriemontanelli.com). Metro Malostranská/tram 12, 18, 22, 23. **Open** noon-6pm Mon-Fri. **Admission** free. **No credit cards. Map** p326 D3.

Located on the main pedestrian route to the castle, the Montanelli gallery specialises in established blue-chip Czech artists like Jitka and Květa Válová, and Běla Kolářová, as well as boosting the younger generation with group shows. The gallery has been co-operating with institutions in places such as Berlin to expose these artists to audiences abroad.

Galerie Václava Špály
Národní třída 30, Nové Město, Prague 1 (224 946 738/www.spalovka.nadace-cfu.cz). Metro Národní třída/tram 6, 9, 18, 21, 22, 23. **Open** 10am-noon, 12.30-6pm Tue-Sun. **Admission** free. **No credit cards. Map** p328 L6.

Until recently, you'd consistently find an interesting programme at this venue, run by the Czech Fund for Art Foundation. Sadly, it is now in the same boat as fellow foundation gallery Mánes, with only those shows that can afford the high rental fees able to secure a space on the roster.

Galerie Zdeněk Sklenář
Smetanovo nábřeží 4, Staré Město, Prague 4 (224 218 528). Metro Národní třída/tram 6, 9, 17, 18, 21, 22, 23. **Open** 1-6pm Wed-Sat. **Admission** free. **No credit cards. Map** p328 J5.

Overlooking the Vltava river, the Galerie Zdeněk Sklenář shows the latest works of the still-active senior generation of artists like Zdeněk Sýkora and Karel Malich. But younger artists, like Federico Diaz, are also at home here.

Gallery Art Factory
Václavské náměstí 15, Nové Město, Prague 1 (224 217 585/www.galleryartfactory.cz). Metro Můstek/tram 3, 9, 14, 24. **Open** 10am-6pm Mon-Fri. **Admission** 50 Kč. **No credit cards. Map** p329 N6.

Located in the former printing house of the main communist-era newspaper, the Art Factory is a spacious gallery that keeps much of the factory feel of the space's former function, with painted cement floors and some of the old industrial hardware as part of the interior architecture. One speciality of the gallery is shows by Slovak artists. The gallery also organises the annual Sculpture Grande outdoor exhibition of large-scale sculptures up and down Wenceslas Square and Na Příkopě.

hunt kastner artworks
Kamenická 22, Letná, Prague 7 (233 376 259/ www.huntkastner.cz). Metro Vltavská/tram 1, 8, 15, 25, 26. **Open** noon-5pm Thur, Fri; or by appointment. **Admission** free. **No credit cards.**

A new private gallery in a blossoming art neighbourhood in Prague 7, hunt kastner artworks established to nurture the careers of a stable of more than a dozen Czech contemporary artists like Tomáš Vaněk and Michael Thelenová, while at the same time helping to find collectors for their work and encourage the development of the fledgling art market in the Czech Republic.

Jiří Švestka Gallery
Biskupský dvůr 6, Nové Město, Prague 1 (222 311 092/www.jirisvestka.com). Metro Náměstí Republiky/ tram 5, 8, 14, 24. **Open** noon-6pm Tue-Fri; 11am-6pm Sat. **Admission** free. **No credit cards. Map** p329 P2.

Returned émigré Jiří Švestka has been specialising since 1995 in bold, internationally recognised Czech artists like Milena Dopitová, Krištof Kintera and Jiří Černický, and also exhibits international names like Tony Cragg in this former photography atelier.

Karlín Studios
Křižíkova 34, Karlín, Prague 8 (no phone). Metro Křižíkova/tram 8, 24. **Open** noon-6pm Tue-Sun. **Admission** free. **No credit cards.**

A vast complex in a renovated former factory building, Karlín Studios operates its own public gallery in addition to housing two private galleries, Entrance and Behémót. It also provides studio space for a select group of artists including Jiří David and Josef Bolf. It plans to hold a day of open doors twice a year, inviting the public into the precincts, normally off-limits, of the artists' studios.

Josef Sudek Atelier. *See p223.*

Nová síň

Voršilská 3, Nové Město, Prague 1 (224 930 255).
Metro Národní třída/tram 6, 9, 18, 21, 22, 23.
Open 11am-6pm Tue-Sun. **Admission** free. **No
credit cards. Map** p330 K7.
In the skylit space of this once-venerable gallery –
the proverbial white cube – the quality of exhibitions
has declined in recent years, with many artists renting out the space and curating their own shows. The
hope is that some day it will bounce back to its previous position as a serious player on the contemporary Czech art scene. Nonetheless, the space itself is
a draw for artists like Otto Placht, who selected the
venue for a month-long project to paint a floor-to-
ceiling mural in situ.

Photography galleries

In photography, the long and well-established
Czech tradition is carried on by practitioners
such as Jindřich Štreit, Pavel Baňka and, among
the younger generation, Markéta Othová and
the duo of Martin Polák and Lukáš Jasanský.
Try not to be confused by the trio of galleries
bearing the name Josef Sudek.

Galerie Velryba

Opatovická 24, Nové Město, Prague 1 (224 233 337)
Metro Národní třída/tram 3, 6, 9, 18, 21, 22, 23.
Open noon-9pm Mon-Fri; 11am-9pm Sat.
Admission free. **No credit cards. Map** p330 K8.
Handily located in the basement of the trendy
Velryba café, the gallery is the showcase for stu-
dents in the photography department of the Czech
film academy FAMU and, increasingly, photo
departments at other schools.

Josef Sudek Atelier

Újezd 30, Malá Strana, Prague 1 (251 510 760/
www.sudek-atelier.cz). Metro Malostranská/tram 9,
22, 23. **Open** noon-6pm Tue-Sun. **No credit cards.** 10
Kč; 5 Kč students. **No credit cards. Map** p327 F6.
This little gallery, where Josef Sudek long had one
of his photography studios, is accessible through a
residential building courtyard. Sudek maintained
both this studio and the one at Úvoz 24 for many
years, sleeping at whichever he chose during that
time. Select shows of quality art photography are
held in the intimate exhibition room, while Sudek
memorabilia is on view in a separate small room.

Josef Sudek Gallery

Úvoz 24, Hradčany, Prague 1 (257 531 489/
www.upm.cz). Metro Malostranská/tram 22, 23.
Open 11am-5pm Wed-Sun. **Admission** 10 Kč;
5 Kč students. **No credit cards. Map** p326 B3.
The father of modern Czech photography lived and
worked here from 1959 to 1976, and it once held a
collection of Sudek's own photography. These days
the exhibition schedule is organised by the Museum
of Decorative Arts (UMPRUM) and draws from the
museum's vast archives to make for shows of historical interest in the house's intimate rooms.

Josef Sudek House of Photography

Maiselova 2, Staré Město, Prague 1 (224 819 098/
www.czechpressphoto.cz). Metro Staroměstská/
tram 17, 18. **Open** 11am-6pm daily. **Admission**
20 Kč; 10 Kč concessions. **Credit** DC, MC, V.
Map 328 K3.
One of the three photography galleries in town bearing Sudek's name, although he did not actually work
or sleep here, this space just off Old Town Square
leans towards documentary pictures and reportage
from Czech photographers, with a steady stream of
fresh talent from abroad.

Langhans Galerie

Vodičkova 37, Nové Město, Prague 1 (222 929 333/
www.langhansgalerie.cz). Metro Můstek/tram 3, 9,
14, 24. **Open** noon-6pm Tue-Fri; 11am-4pm Sat.
Admission 60 Kč; 30 Kč concessions. **No credit
cards. Map** p329 N6.
This beautifully renovated building was once home
to the Jan Langhans Atelier, where anyone who was
anyone in interwar Prague had their portrait taken.
That rich tradition was recently reborn in this new
entry among photography galleries. The emphasis
is on historic shows, especially drawing on the
Langhans archives, mixed in with exhibits of work
by established and emerging photographers. A
recurring theme is memory, which has yielded some
haunting shows.

Leica Gallery Prague

(251 614 316/www.leicagallery.cz).
You wouldn't expect a notable gallery for documentary photography to find itself homeless, but
that's just what happened to the Leica Gallery when
the administrators at Prague Castle began renovations on the Old Burgrave's Palace where it was situated. But, following in the footsteps of many of the
best photographers from the past, the gallery has
not moaned but instead it's gone on the road, becoming a 'travelling gallery'. A particular stroke of bril-
liance was to invite Sebastio Salgado back to Prague
to show his series 'Workers' on a renovated train
that rolled throughout the Czech Republic before
moving on across the border. Look for the Leica
name on other innovative projects.

Prague House of Photography

Václavské náměstí 31, Nové Město, Prague 1 (222
243 229/www.php-gallery.cz). Metro Muzeum/tram
3, 9, 14, 24. **Open** 11am-6pm daily. **Admission**
30 Kč; 15 Kč concessions. **Credit** AmEx, MC, V.
Map p329 N6.
The peripatetic PHP seemed to have settled down in
a Staré Město courtyard until the devastating floods
in 2002 drowned its showroom. In Wenceslas Square
for the past several years, it has been planning a
move to a new permanent space on Revoluční street.
Still wrapped up in renovations and red tape at press
time, when it reopens it will be reborn as an institution with state funding, with enough space – some
2,600sq m (27,976sq ft) in two separate halls – to
stage major retrospectives and group shows.

Gay & Lesbian

Go wild in this country.

Though gays and girls will find no one taking any notice of them in Prague, they'll also notice the distinct lack of anything like a Gay Freedom Day parade. Folks seem content to remain in their orbits, or find themselves welcome at mainstream clubs, and food and drink venues, without the need to be out and proud. Certainly, no one troubles to hide their preferences (though the buzzers and metal doors on several of the ubiquitous underground cellar bars offer the fun of pretending). But there's no need for double lives: *Amigo*, a provocative gay guide to the city, is on sale at most newsagents – and polls show 90 per cent of Czechs are just fine with gays.

A number of gay bars feature big but harmless blokes at the door – despite the build-up, though, they're usually just bars. And it's worth venturing in, as many of these bars and some of Prague's gay cafés now hold warm-up parties for the big gay nights, and straight clubs, such as **Mecca** (see *p244*) and **Radost FX** (*see p245*), also have regular gay nights.

Prague's lesbian scene has been a much slower starter in comparison with the 'European Bangkok' of gay Prague, perhaps because it lacks the economic engine of prostitution. The Žižkov district's A-Club, once a girls' community hub, has sadly closed, but the scene seems to be maturing and relaxing, so that friendly gay bars like **TERmix** are as welcoming to lesbians as to the boys. Also, the community's well served by discussion boards at **www.expats.cz**. For gays, note that Czech-language pick-up sites like **www.xko.cz** and **www.xchat.cz** do have English-speaking users. An online escort service is available for men at **www.callboys.cz**.

The Czech Republic has a relatively low AIDS and HIV infection rate, owing mainly to the country's closed borders until 1989. Recent reports have put the number of HIV-infected people in the country at 807, but the actual infection rate is probably higher. Condoms are widely available in supermarkets, select clubs and in vending machines at some metro stations. For more information on health and helpful organisations, see the Directory.

The age of consent is 15 in the Czech Republic although, if money changes hands, the age rises to 18, and visitors have been busted that way. Most clubs with butterflies, or prostitutes, are run with discretion and supervision, as at **Drake's** and **Escape**. Others near the main rail station have no supervision and attract a less salubrious clientele and the interest of the police. By and large, though, the city is safe.

Do be aware that pickpockets favour clubs and darkrooms, and always discuss financial matters and boundaries before getting down to business. Most gay clubs are home to a varying number of prostitutes, so be prepared to accept or reject advances during your evening.

Spartacus, the international gay guide, is useful for planning, as are **www.planetout. com** or **www.gayguide.net**. Meanwhile, **Rainbow Travel** (www.rainbowtravel.cz) is a well-recommended accommodation agent.

HELP AND INFORMATION

The website **http://prague.gayguide.net** has up-to-date listings on Prague's gay scene.

Associations

Fiminismus Gender Studies

Gorazdova 20, Nové Město, Prague 1 (224 915 666/ www.feminismus.cz). Metro Karlovo náměstí/tram 3, 6, 14, 18, 22. **Open** by appointment. **Map** p330 J9.

The organisation's English website is currently under construction but is likely to become a useful resource for mainly lesbian activities.

Accommodation

Agencies

Prague Center Guest Residence

www.gaystay.net/PragueCenter. **Rates** 1,700-3,400 Kč. **No credit cards.**

Book via the website with Bob, the American owner, who rents some IKEA-inspired rooms and apartments, one with a fireplace. Some have shared bathrooms and living rooms, but service and locations are above average. Reservations required.

Toucan Apartments

www.gaystay.net/Toucan. **Rates** 1,800-5,800 Kč. **Credit** AmEx, MC, V.

This Dutch-owned agency has over 30 apartments available in Prague 1, 2, 3 and 10, all of which can be booked via the website. Some apartments are wood-beam attic niches, others are studios and a number have a washing machine – but all are simple, clean and comfortable, and the website offers information on nearby nightlife options. All staff are gay. Book ahead.

Hotels

Arco Pension

Voroněžská 24, Vršovice, Prague 10 (271 740 734/ fax 7174 0734/www.arco-guesthouse.cz). Metro Náměstí Míru/tram 4, 16, 22, 23. **Rates** (incl breakfast) 1,300 Kč double; 1,900 Kč apartment. **No credit cards.**

Occupying various addresses on the same street, Arco is a comfortable and relaxed collection of apartments, from fairly basic to quite luxurious. The main plus is the location and friendly restaurant, bar and internet café. Reservations are required.

Ron's Rainbow Guest House

Bulharská 4, Vršovice, Prague 10 (271 725 664/ mobile 604 876 694). Metro Flóra/tram 6, 7, 22, 24, 34. **Open** 9am-9pm daily. **Rates** 1,815-2,475 Kč/room. **Credit** MC, V.

The Rainbow comprises four comfortable apartments – one with a whirlpool – in residential Prague, bordering gay-centric Žižkov. Reservations required.

Bars

Non-Czech-speaking visitors may feel a tad neglected in the more local hangouts listed here, although the younger the crowd is, the more likely you'll find English spoken. If you're given a drink card upon entering a bar, don't lose it or you'll be charged a minimum of 1,000 Kč. Listed closing times generally tend to be ignored, depending on how much fun is being had.

Alcatraz

Bořivojova 58, Žižkov, Prague 3 (222 711 458/ www.run.to/alcatraz). Metro Jiřího z Poděbrad/tram 10, 11, 16, 51. **Open** 10pm-4am daily. **Admission** 80 Kč; 100 Kč party nights. **No credit cards.** **Map** p333 B2.

A hard-core leather and rubber venue in an appropriately dark though well-maintained cellar, with run-off troughs, slings, cages, equipment, darkrooms, cabins, videos and glory holes. Quite possibly everything you could imagine and then more, plus underwear and the occasional hard-core theme party.

Bar 21

Římská 21, Vinohrady, Prague 2 (724 254 048). Metro Náměstí Míru/tram 4, 10, 16, 22, 23, 51, 57. **Open** 4pm-4am daily. **Admission** free. **No credit cards. Map** p331 P8.

With a predominantly queer audience, this is a chilled-out bar in a cellar, close to the clubbing options. The music is dance-inspired, as is the young crowd, and Bar 21 is a hip place to spend a Friday night if you're not up to mad dancing and prefer to sit, chat and chew a light meal.

Drake's

Zborovská 50, Smíchov, Prague 5 (no phone). Metro Anděl/tram 6, 9, 12, 22, 57, 58. **Open** 24hrs daily. **Admission** 500 Kč. **No credit cards.**

For an older and more 'beefy' crowd, pay the (high) admission price and enjoy the myriad services and entertainments that are on offer for 24 hours each day, every day. Drake's can be slow at times during those 24 hours; a happening dance club bar it may not be, but a popular after-hours place it is. It is, after all, the grande dame of the Prague scene. There are video booths, daily strip shows at 9pm and 11pm, glory holes and an S&M dungeon.

Arts & Entertainment

Escape

V jámě 8, Nové Město, Prague 1 (mobile 606 538 111/www.escapetoparadise.cz). Metro Můstek/tram 3, 9, 14, 24, 58. **Open** *Disco* 9.30pm-3am daily. *Restaurant* 8pm-2am daily. **Admission** 50 Kč Fri, Sat. **No credit cards**. **Map** p330 M7.

Wall-to-wall hustlers, but if you enter as a couple you're not generally bothered. And they're well behaved because they're on staff, so not much risk of trouble, though some find the place a bit of a hard sell. Also, strippers, body paint, oil and live sex shows make an appearance.

Friends

Bartolomějská 11, Staré Město, Prague 1 (224 236 772/www.friends-prague.cz). Metro Národní třída. **Open** 4pm-5am daily. **Admission** free. **Credit** MC, V. **Map** p328 K6.

A relaxed, comfortable, grown-up sort of place, excellent for geting acclimatised to Prague's scene. Though originally around the corner, the new locale for the reopened Friends restores one of the longest-established and best-known gay watering hole names in Prague. This location takes the original comfy atmosphere and adds room for proper dancing, plus great sounds, lighting, even wi-fi. DJ parties Wednesday to Saturday.

Rudolf II Party Club

Slovenská 19, Vinohrady, Prague 2 (603 731 012). Metro Náměstí Míru/tram 4, 10, 16, 22, 23, 51, 57. **Open** 8pm-5am daily. **Admission** free. **No credit cards**.

A new venue, sometimes known as G Club, with a small dancefloor, mirror ball, DJ and wooden tables. A passable restaurant is on the ground floor. The club is downstairs behind the locked door – ring the bell.

Street Café

Blanická 28, Vinohrady, Prague 2 (222 013 116). Metro Náměstí Míru/tram 4, 10, 16, 22, 23, 51, 57. **Open** 9am-11pm Mon-Thur; 9am-4am Fri, Sat; 1-10pm Sun. **Admission** free. *Party nights* 50Kč. **No credit cards**. **Map** p333 A3.

A nondescript door leads to a cellar bar devoted to ladies – though no one is barred entry. Everyone seems to know each other or is getting to know each other, and fun dominates the slow grooves or the raunchy gyrations of table-top dancers – there's even a pole. It's a welcome addition to the city's lesbian scene.

Tingl Tangl

Karolíny Světlé 12, Staré Město, Prague 1 (224 238 278/www.tingltangl.cz). Metro Národní třída/tram 6, 9, 18, 21, 22, 23, 51, 54, 57, 58. **Open** 8pm-5am Wed-Sat. **Admission** 120 Kč. **No credit cards**. **Map** p328 J5.

A newish venue at an old address (U Střelce occupied these premises until the floods of 2002), Tingl Tangl serves a short menu of international cuisine upstairs and in the quiet courtyard. Downstairs you'll find the borderline-cliché cabaret and transvestite shows, which trade off with more unusual performers until the DJ takes over. Reservations are recommended.

Clubs

All the clubs we've listed in our nightlife chapter (*see p241*) offer cool nights of tunes and moves, where gays won't feel particularly noticed. But for decidedly gay options, try the following.

Angel

Kmochová 8 (corner of Grafická), Smíchov, Prague 5 (257 316 127/www.clubangel.cz). Metro Anděl/tram 4, 7, 9, 10, 58. **Open** 7pm-3am Mon-Thur, Sun; 7pm-6am Fri, Sat. **Admission** free Mon-Thur, Sun; 35 Kč Fri, Sat. **No credit cards**.

A mirror-balled, LP-decorated 1980s throwback of a dance club, and a very local hangout – hence the Czech and Slovak hits played on Friday nights. It's also out of the way and difficult to find, so take a taxi if Thursday's Karaoke Night appeals. Otherwise it's the admittedly popular weekend-long dance party.

Saints

Polská 32, Vinohrady (222 250 326/www. praguesaints.cz). Metro Náměstí Míru/tram 4, 10, 16, 22, 23, 51, 57. **Open** 5pm-2am Fri; 5pm-4am Sat; 5pm-1am Sun. **Admission** free. **No credit cards**. **Map** p333 A3.

A friendly, casual gay bar, as evidenced by the lack of the usual annoying buzzer and the welcoming, open atmosphere (dykes like it too) with a small but amusing dance space. The club also doubles as an information hub for the community in Prague (the website offers loads of gay accommodation and entertainment listings). Saints is run by British owners who excel at cocktails.

TERmix

Třebízského 4a, Vinohrady, Prague 2 (222 710 462/ www.club-termix.cz). Metro Jiřího z Poděbrad/tram 10, 11, 16, 51. **Open** 8pm-5am daily. **Admission** free. **No credit cards**. **Map** p333 B3.

Dedicated to the pure ideal of gay and lesbian drinks, dancing and sex, TERmix fulfils its obligations beautifully. Ring the bell and descend into the sleek and chic club, past the long glass bar, wide-screen TV, sofas and a car parked in the wall. The dancefloor is regularly packed as DJs throw on theme-night music: Latin and Czech hits are popular, while Thursday's Hot Night is a chilled get-together evening of candles and easy music. A chill-out room, make-out room and two darkrooms, cabins and a shower complete the facilities.

Cruising

Prague's long, hot summers tempt all towards outdoor escapades, and the metronome atop **Letná park** (*see p127*) beckons men and women with its rhythmic movements. Petřín Hill is no longer a popular cruising area, although the terrace at the hill's **Petřínské Terasy** restaurant (Seminářská zahrada 13, 290 000 457) remains a favoured spot. The nudist beach at the lake in **Šárka park** (*see p261*) has a gay

So good they... Oh, you know the rest. **Café Café**.

section – the area nearest the dam. The **Podolí** swimming pool (*see p262*) is a hotspot for hooking up, with its nude sunbathing galore, but note that families share the grounds. Prague's main train station **Hlavní nádraží** (*see p290*) is a seedy meeting point for male prostitutes and their mostly German clients.

Restaurants & cafés

See also Érra Café (*see p166*) and Pálffy Palác (*see p139*): both are popular with gays.

Café Café

Rytířská 10, Staré Město, Prague 1 (224 210 597/ www.cafe-cafe.cz). Metro Můstek/tram 6, 9, 18, 22, 51, 54, 57, 58. **Open** noon-11pm Mon-Fri; 10am-11pm Sat, Sun. **Main courses** 150-350 Kč. **Credit** MC, V. **Map** p328 L5.
This jam-packed café features large, old-fashioned murals and mirrors to improve the scoping action among the absurdly beautiful people who frequent it. Café Café attracts a gay crowd, but its Staré Město location makes it equally popular with anyone (so long as they're handsome) looking to hobnob, and the salads aren't bad either. Large windows and pavement tables make it a handy spot for assignation, planned or impromptu.

Downtown Café

Jungmannovo náměstí 21, Nové Město, Prague 1 (724 111 276). Metro Můstek/tram 6, 9, 18, 22, 51, 54, 57, 58. **Open** 10am-11pm Mon-Fri; 10am-midnight Sat, Sun. **Main courses** 150-350 Kč. **No credit cards**. **Map** p328 M6.

Being deliciously central, with delicious waiters (not all of whom are gay), Downtown Café is a popular place for all persuasions. Booths and tables fill the space around the central bar, which serves up sandwiches, baguettes, cakes, coffees and alcohol.

Saunas

Sauna Babylonia

Martinská 6, Staré Město, Prague 1 (224 232 304/ www.amigo.cz/babylonia). Metro Můstek/tram 3, 9, 14, 25. **Open** 2pm-3am daily. **Admission** 280 Kč full use. *Gym only* 60 Kč. **No credit cards**. **Map** p328 L6.
Babylonia is the most popular gay sauna in Prague, but some of the men here are clearly too young and too beautiful to be just hanging out.

Sauna Marco

Lublaňská 17, Nové Město, Prague 2 (224 262 833). Metro IP Pavlova/tram 4, 6, 11, 16, 22, 23. **Open** 2pm-3am daily. **Admission** 180-200 Kč. **No credit cards**. **Map** p331 O10.
Marco remains popular and not too crowded. A well-known meeting spot, it's also handy for the main gay clubbing options in the Vinohrady district.

Shops

Amigo Shop & Gay Info

U Půjčovny 954, Nové Město, Prague 1 (222 233 250/ www.amigo.cz). Metro Můstek/tram 3, 9, 14, 24, 58. **Open** 11am-7pm Tue-Sat. **Credit** MC, V. **Map** p329 O5.
All the sex aids you might need and the latest info.

Arts & Entertainment

Music

Rhythm, dissonance and counterpoint run deep in Czech society.

Czech Philharmonic: the best of an excellent orchestral bunch.

Classical & Opera

Classical music is the lifeblood of Prague, filling rehearsal halls and classrooms by day, and concert halls at night. Musicians are everywhere, toting instrument cases on and off trams, and performing in venues ranging from cramped, chilly church nooks to some of the grandest stages in Central Europe. There may be more star power in cities like Vienna and Berlin, but Prague's devotion to the tradition and practice of the musical arts remains unmatched.

For centuries, Prague has had a reputation as the conservatory of Europe, which is both good and bad news for visitors. The sheer amount of music in the city is astonishing, with major festivals and concerts supplemented by a wealth of excellent chamber ensembles and faculty and student recitals. Inevitably, though, the best singers and musicians leave Prague for countries where their training and skills can command much higher wages.

Still, much of what remains in Prague is first-rate. And the city's prestigious musical heritage attracts a steady stream of international stars like Jennifer Larimore and Rolando Villazón, and visiting orchestras like the Vienna Philharmonic and the London Symphony. Nor is the appeal and fare all mainstream classical; there are strong and developing baroque and modern music scenes. Add to that five major orchestras and three opera houses up and running on any given night, and the only question is how many performances you can squeeze in during your visit.

Among resident orchestras, the **Czech Philharmonic** (227 059 352, www.ceska filharmonie.cz) is top of the heap, a world-class ensemble with accomplished conductors and a wide repertoire that routinely draws rave reviews on tour. The **Prague Symphony Orchestra** (222 002 336, www.fok.cz) has lost some of its lustre in recent years, but has a very strong Russian repertoire, recently recording the complete Shostakovich symphonies under the baton of the composer's son Maxim.

The **Prague Philharmonia** (224 811 258, www.philharmonia.cz) is the hardest-working orchestra in town, backing most of the visiting opera stars and running an ambitious schedule of both chamber and orchestra concerts. With an expert assist from visiting French conductor Michel Swierczewski, a protégé of French composer Pierre Boulez, the Philharmonia has developed adventurous modern music programming as well.

The **Czech National Symphony Orchestra** (267 215 576, www.cnso.cz) has also pioneered interesting new paths, playing with unorthodox guests like American jazz musician and composer Chris Brubeck. And while the **Czech Radio Symphony Orchestra** (www2.rozhlas.cz/socr) is perhaps the least ambitious of the city's major ensembles, its longevity alone merits a listen – the orchestra marked its 80th anniversary at the 2006 Prague Spring Festival.

Prague Spring (www.festival.cz) is still the heavyweight among local music festivals, 60 years old in 2005 and a favourite among virtuoso performers like violinist Gil Shaham, singer Anne Sofie von Otter and pianist Garrick Ohlsson. Despite its age Prague Spring has kept up with the times, expanding its parameters in recent years to include contemporary musicians like jazz pianist Herbie Hancock and young sitar star Anoushka Shankar.

Prague Autumn (www.prazskypodzim.cz) offers a less substantial counterpoint, with a programme of predictable crowd-pleasers – Mozart arias, Beethoven symphonies and suites from popular operas like *Carmen*. The best news on the festival circuit is that summer is no longer the fallow period it once was. It used to be that at the end of June, every major orchestra and opera house shut down, and all the serious musicians left town for a two-month holiday. But in 2005, both the Prague Philharmonia and the Czech National Symphony Orchestra launched mini-festivals during July and August that provide a nice blend of the standard classical repertoire with the Czech masters, Smetana, Dvořák and Janáček.

The gem of summer festivals is the baroque concert series staged by **Collegium Marianum** (224 229 462, www.tynska.cuni.cz), Prague's premier baroque ensemble, in some of the city's most beautiful small halls. Also worth catching later in the autumn is the annual **Modern Music Marathon** at Archa Theater (www.archatheatre.cz), and the Martinů festival in early December (www.martinu.cz), which honours the lesser-known but excellent 20th-century Czech composer Bohuslav Martinů.

Prague's opera houses still live and die on the Czech repertoire, but have become more cosmopolitan in recent years. In a co-production with Deutsche Oper am Rhein in the spring of 2005, the National Theatre staged its first-ever production of Wagner's full *Ring* cycle. Meanwhile, the State Opera has shown a flair for unearthing overlooked gems like the other *La Bohème* (by Leoncavallo) and Verdi's *Sicilian Vespers*. Both houses are worth visiting for the sumptuous surroundings alone, though be advised that while National Theatre operas are usually performed with English subtitles, those at the State Opera – always sung in the original language – generally are not.

And no true fan of Mozart can leave Prague without a visit to the Estates Theatre, where the maestro himself conducted the première performance of *Don Giovanni* in October 1787.

TICKETS AND INFORMATION

Ticketpro (*see p230*) books for most of the big classical venues, with a small surcharge that's far less than many other agencies charge foreigners. If buying directly from the venue's box office, don't worry if a show is 'sold out'. Touts buy up all the remaining seats for popular shows, so just wait around the entrance until the last minute when the touts have to sell or lose their investment. Prices for concerts vary and some (in smaller churches) are free, but the cost is usually around 250 Kč to 600 Kč.

Information can be haphazard, but Bohemia Ticket International (*see below*) has an online calendar prepared months in advance and accepts bookings and credit card payment from abroad. Also keep an eye on the *Prague Post* (www.praguepost.com) for listings of current and forthcoming events. Prague has a tradition of subscription evenings, so you may find certain glittering occasions difficult to get into.

Bohemia Ticket International

Malé náměstí 13, Staré Město, Prague 1 (224 227 832/fax 224 237 727/www.ticketsbti.cz). Metro Můstek or Národní třída/tram 6, 9, 18, 22, 23. **Open** 9am-5pm Mon-Fri; 9am-1pm Sat. **No credit cards. Map** p328 L4.

This is the best non-travel agency for buying tickets in advance from abroad for opera and concerts at the National Theatre, Estates Theatre and State Opera, plus other orchestral and chamber events. **Other locations**: Na příkopě 16, Nové Město, Prague 1 (224 215 031).

Čedok

Na příkopě 18, Nové Město, Prague 1 (224 197 242/www.cedok.cz). Metro Můstek or Náměstí Republiky/tram 5, 8, 14, 26. **Open** 9am-7pm Mon-Fri; 9.30am-1pm Sat. **Credit** AmEx, MC, V. **Map** p329 N5.

Tickets for various events, with some concerts. **Other locations**: Václavské námesti 53, Nové Město, Prague 1 (221 965 243); Rytířská 16, Staré Město, Prague 1 (224 224 461).

Ticketpro

Old Town Hall, Staré Město, Prague 1 (224 223 613/www.ticketpro.cz). Metro Staroměstská/tram 17, 18. **Open** 9am-6pm Mon-Fri; 9am-5pm Sat, Sun. **Credit** AmEx, MC, V. **Map** p328 L4.
Advance booking for major concerts and various smaller events. The automated free phone number works for all branches – mostly found at Prague Information Service offices (*see p291*) and hotels. **Other locations**: Štěpánská 61, Lucerna, Nové Město, Prague 1 (224 818 080); Rytířská 31, Staré Město, Prague 1 (2161 0162); Václavské námstí 38, Rokoko, Prague 1 (224 228 455).

Principal concert halls

Municipal House

Obecni dům
Náměstí Republiky 5, Nové Město, Prague 1 (222 002 336/100/www.obecni-dum.cz). Metro Náměstí Republiky/tram 5, 14, 26. **Open** *Box office* 10am-6pm Mon-Fri. **Tickets** 150-1,100 Kč. **Credit** AmEx, MC, V. **Map** p329 O4.
A beautiful example of Czech art nouveau, the Municipal House is built around the Smetana Hall, home to the Prague Symphony Orchestra. The orchestra launches the Prague Spring Festival (*see p201*) here most years, a tradition going back half a century. Listen to Smetana variations on folk tunes while gazing at the ceiling mosaics of old Czech myths for an authentic Bohemian national cultural experience. *See also p118.*

Rudolfinum

Alšovo nábřeží 12, Staré Město, Prague 1 (227 059 309/352/www.rudolfinum.cz). Metro Staroměstská/tram 17, 18. **Open** *Box office* 10am-6pm Mon-Fri. Closed mid July-mid Aug. **Tickets** 200-1,100 Kč. **Credit** AmEx, MC, V. **Map** p328 J3.
One of the most beautiful concert venues in Europe, the Rudolfinum was built in the neo-classical style at the end of the 19th century and has two halls: the Dvořák Hall for orchestral works and major recitals, and the Suk Hall for chamber, instrumental and solo vocal music. Opinion is divided about the acoustics of the Dvořák Hall, but the stunning grandeur of the building's interior – plus the high standard of musicianship on offer – makes an evening here eminently worthwhile. *See also p218.* **Photo** p231.

Other venues

Venues for chamber music and instrumental recitals are legion, with practically every church and palace offering some concerts. The programming is mainly from the baroque and classical repertoire, with the emphasis on Czech music, and performances are usually of a high standard. Tickets for performances can generally be bought from the venue one to two hours before a performance is scheduled to start, while Bohemia Ticket International (*see p229*) also sells tickets for some events.

Basilica of St James

Bazilika sv. Jakuba
Malá Štupartská 6, Staré Město, Prague 1 (224 828 816). Metro Náměstí Republiky/tram 5, 14, 26. **Open** *Box office* 1hr before performance. **Tickets** 200-400 Kč. **No credit cards. Map** p328 M3.
St James's is a prime example of Czech baroque architecture, complete with resounding organ acoustics and an over-the-top façade above the entrance, depicting the Fall. In addition to large-scale sacred choral works, the music for Sunday Mass (usually 10am) is impressive. Concerts are held from Easter through until September.

Bertramka

Mozartova 169, Smíchov, Prague 5 (257 317 465/ www.bertramka.cz). Metro Anděl/tram 4, 7, 9, 10, 12, 14. **Open** 9.30am-5pm daily. **Tickets** 110-450 Kč. **No credit cards.**
The house where Mozart stayed when in Prague is now a museum devoted to him (*see p131*) that puts on regular concerts. Nearly all include at least one work by the Austrian, who has been adopted as a favourite son in the Czech musical pantheon.

Chapel of Mirrors

Zrcadlová kaple
Klementinum, Mariánské náměstí, Staré Město, Prague 1 (221 663 111/212). Metro Staroměstská/tram 17, 18. **Open** *Box office* 2hrs before performance. **Tickets** from 650 Kč. **No credit cards. Map** p328 K4.
This pink-marble chapel in the vast Clementinum complex (*see p105*) features all manner of Romantic, baroque and original chamber recitals and is seemingly an age away from the tourist hordes outside. Concerts here usually start at 5pm and 8pm.

Church of St Nicholas

Chrám sv. Mikuláše
Malostranské náměstí, Malá Strana, Prague 1 (224 190 991). Metro Malostranská/tram 12, 22. **Open** *Box office* 2hrs before performance. **Tickets** 250-450 Kč. **No credit cards. Map** p327 E3.
St Nicholas's is justly one of Prague's most celebrated churches, with a wonderful baroque interior. Irregular choral concerts and organ recitals are just as grand as the setting itself. *See also p90.*

Church of St Nicholas

Kostel sv. Mikuláše
Staroměstské náměstí, Staré Město, Prague 1 (no phone). Metro Staroměstská/tram 17, 18. **Open** noon-4pm Mon; 10am-4pm Tue-Sat. **No credit cards. Map** p328 L4.
The other St Nicholas hosts regular organ, instrumental and vocal recitals in a rather plainer setting. The emphasis is on baroque music. *See also p100.*

Rudolfinum. *See p230.*

Church of St Simon & St Jude

Kostel sv. Šimona a Judy
*Dušní & U Milosrdných, Staré Město, Prague 1
(222 321 352). Metro Staroměstská/tram 17.*
Open *Box office* 1hr before performance. **Tickets**
200-600 Kč. **No credit cards. Map** p328 L2.
Renovated with cunning trompe l'oeil work, this
deconsecrated church is now a full-time venue for
chamber music. The Prague Symphony Orchestra,
which also promotes selected ensembles, is responsible for the programming. Concerts start at 7.30pm.

Lichtenstein Palace

Lichtenštejnský palác
*Malostranské náměstí 13, Malá Strana, Prague 1
(257 534 205). Metro Malostranská/tram 12, 22.*
Open 10am-7.30pm daily. **Tickets** 30-100 Kč.
Credit MC, V. **Map** p327 F3.
The Lichtenstein Palace is the striking home of the
Czech Academy of Music. Regular concerts, which
usually start at about 7.30pm, are given in the
Gallery and in the Martinů Hall.

Lobkowicz Palace

Lobkovický palác
*Jiřská 3, Hradčany, Prague 1 (257 535 121). Metro
Malostranská/tram 22.* **Open** *Tours* 11am-1pm daily.
Tickets 390 Kč. **No credit cards. Map** p327 E2.

Concerts of baroque and Romantic chamber works
are held in the imposing banquet hall of the
Lobkowicz Palace, which boasts stunning frescoes
by Fabián Harovník. Concerts usually begin at 1pm
on Saturdays and Sundays.

St Agnes's Convent

Klášter sv. Anežky české
*U milosrdných 17, Staré Město, Prague 1 (221 879
270). Metro Staroměstská or Náměstí Republiky/
tram 5, 14, 26.* **Open** 10am-6pm Tue-Sun.
Tickets 250-550 Kč. **No credit cards.**
Map p328 M2.
The acoustics here may have their critics, but St
Agnes's Convent has a Gothic atmosphere and spe-
cialises in high-quality chamber music, with an
emphasis on Smetana, Dvořák and Janáček.
Definitely worth a visit. *See also p113.*

Opera

Estates Theatre

Stavovské divadlo
*Ovocný trh 1, Staré Město, Prague 1 (information
224 228 503/box office 224 215 001). Metro Můstek
or Staroměstská/tram 3, 9, 14, 17, 18, 24.* **Open**
Box office 10am-6pm daily. **Tickets** 30-1000 Kč.
Credit MC, V. **Map** p328 M4.

No summer blues

In between the Prague Spring and Prague Autumn festivals, there's Prague summer, which is traditionally the worst time of the year to hear classical music in the city. Just as the tourist crowds are peaking, the city's best orchestras and musicians are closing the doors and packing their bags for a long summer break.

But, having said that, the summer season is improving dramatically with the recent addition of two new festivals: **Prague Proms** and the **Prague Music Festival**. The former is a project of the Czech National Symphony Orchestra, specifically general manager Jan Hasenöhrl, who saw a need and decided to fill it.

'Summer is usually a black hole for quality classical music,' he says. 'We wanted to do something to help bring the level up to where it should be.'

Hasenöhrl programmed the debut 2005 Prague Proms with an eye toward attracting visitors, packaging concerts by the ethnicity of the programme and performers (American night, Japanese night, Italian night). The music was a tasty mix of serious fare (Verdi's *Requiem*) and crowd-pleasers (Ravel's *Bolero*), with an occasional shameless nod to tourist tastes like John Williams's music for *Star Wars*.

Former Prague Philharmonia director Ilja Šmid took the same tack with his Prague Music Festival, mixing in popular favourites with hefty doses of serious Czech composers and outstanding soloists like expatriate pianist Antonín Kubálek.

'They were very friendly classical concerts,' Šmid says. 'Anyone could attend and have a good experience.'

The results were hit-and-miss, but some of the concerts were as good as their better-known counterparts in the spring and autumn. And they were all light years better than the church ensembles and second-rate opera productions that have long been the staple of Prague summers. There were some good amenities as well. The Prague Music Festival offered a chance to hear visiting orchestras from cities like Teplice and Ostrava, which can be surprisingly good. And Prague Proms offered late-night jazz sessions after some concerts with notable local jazz stars.

Both festivals are in an expansionist mode, with the number of concerts growing every year, and they've agreed to run in different months so as not to compete with each other. And both are in it for the long haul.

'Prague needs this type of festival,' Šmid declared in 2005, forging ahead even after the government cut funding by more than half.

The summer season is not completely bleak otherwise. Prague's premier baroque ensemble, Collegium Marianum, puts on an excellent early music series every year. And celebrity violinist Jaroslav Svěcený stages virtuoso performances at the hard-to-reach but charming Chodov Water Fortress. Still, there's nothing like sitting in one of Prague's big concert halls and hearing a full orchestra blast away on some Dvořák or Mozart. That's been Prague's gift to Europe for centuries, and now summer visitors can sample it as well.

A shrine for Mozart lovers, this is where *Don Giovanni* and *La Clemenza di Tito* were first performed. The theatre was built by Count Nostitz in 1784; its beautiful dark-blue-and-gold auditorium was almost over-renovated after the Velvet Revolution. It began life as the Prague home of Italian opera but in 1807 became the German opera, with Carl Maria von Weber as its musical director (1813-17). Today much of the programming is given over to theatre, but there's still regular opera here – including, of course, *Don Giovanni*. See also p251.

National Theatre

Národní divadlo
Národní 2, Nové Město, Prague 1 (224 901 448/ www.narodni-divadlo.cz). Metro Národní třída/tram 6, 9, 17, 18, 22. **Open** *Box office* 10am-6pm daily. Closed July & Aug. **Tickets** 30-900 Kč. **Credit** AmEx, MC, V. **Map** p330 J7.

Smetana was a guiding light behind the establishment of the National Theatre, a symbol of Czech nationalism that finally opened in 1883 with a performance of his opera *Libuše*. The theatre concentrates on Czech opera, the core of the repertoire being works by Smetana and Dvořák (including lesser-known works such as Dvořák's *The Devil and Kate* and Janáček's *The Excursions of Mr Brouček*). Operas by non-Czech composers and some impressive ballets are also performed – generally five or six major new productions a year. See also p253.

State Opera

Státní Opera
Wilsonova 4, Nové Město, Prague 2 (224 227 266/ www.opera.cz). Metro Muzeum/tram 11. **Open** *Box office* 10am-5.30pm Mon-Fri; 10am-noon, 1-5.30pm Sat, Sun. **Tickets** 200-900 Kč. **No credit cards**. **Map** p331 P7.

The State Opera (originally the German Theatre) opened in 1887 and was regarded as one of the finest German opera houses outside Germany until World War II. After the war it changed its name to the Smetana Theatre and became the second house of the National Theatre. Today it's a separate organisation and presents consistently bold contemporary opera alongside standards from the Italian, German, French and Russian repertoires.

Festivals

The major event in the Prague music calendar is the Prague Spring Festival. Several summer festivals are also held out of town, for more information contact the Prague Information Service (*see p311*).

Opera Mozart

Žatecká 1, Staré Město, Prague 1 (224 819 324/ www.mozart.cz). Metro Staroměstská/tram 17, 18. **Open** 10am-8pm daily. **Tickets** 690-1,950 Kč. **Credit** AmEx, MC, V. **Map** p328 K3. **Date** July, Aug.

A heavily promoted production of *Don Giovanni*, which is performed by a travelling foreign troupe, moves into the Estates for the summer season. While not a bad rendition, it's aimed squarely at the tourist hordes and priced accordingly.

Prague Spring Festival

Festival office: Hellichova 18, Malá Strana, Prague 1 (257 310 414/www.festival.cz). Metro Malostranská/ tram 12, 22. **Tickets** from 200 Kč. **Credit** AmEx, MC, V. **Map** p327 F5. **Date** May, June.

Since the Velvet Revolution the Prague Spring Festival has had a much stronger international flavour and attracts first-class international performers. The festival typically opens with Smetana's patriotic cycle of symphonic poems, *Má Vlast* (*My Country*), and concludes with Beethoven's *Ninth*. Many of the major events sell out quickly. It's best to obtain tickets from the festival office rather than from ticket agencies, which add a hefty mark-up. The office opens one month before the festival and there are two price ranges available – one for tickets sold in Prague and one for those booked from abroad. If possible, get a Czech friend to buy them for you or wait until you get here.

Rock, Roots & Jazz

Prague's reputation for sex, drugs and rock 'n' roll (well, at least the first and last items) dates back to the heady days of 1968, just ahead of the Soviet crackdown, when the Velvet Underground were considered all but gods. Now, with drug use legal (caution: the Criminal Code definition of an arrestable offence is 'more than a little'), it seems every major band's got to have Prague on its European tour. Fringe acts, who know the city well, seem to gig here on

permanent rotation. And the city's lack of sonically perfect major halls means you'll catch these groups up close and personal at places like the threadbare **Lucerna Music Bar**, the cutting-edge **Archa Theatre**, with its intelligent and forward-looking booking philosophy, and the **Roxy**, where mixology and MCing reach their highest forms. Less frequent but still worthwhile venues include **Rock Café** or **Vagon**, a former hang of the very dissidents who risked jail to perform their VU-inspired rock, the Plastic People of the Universe.

And some good news for visitors: ticket prices are aimed at the Czech market, so seeing GZA or Medeski, Martin & Wood will cost you little more than a song.

On the dance scene things are less ideal for live music lovers. In the city centre, it's still a chancy business dropping into music clubs, and, with the exception of **N11**, you'll be hard-pressed to find a band playing accessible, danceable music. More than in most cities, DJs rule the scene these days, with live music left mainly to festivals, cover bands and jazz and blues clubs.

Fortunately, there are dozens of festivals each year, the best of them, like **Respect** (http://respect.inway.cz/; *see p202*), offering up world and Eastern European sounds you won't hear anywhere else, from Roma rock, to Tuareg and klezmer. And a few fine venues, like the **Akropolis** and the bunker-like **Klub 007**, still frequently book real bands, focusing on regional underground acts.

Czech rock doesn't export well and many of the iconic bands, like Už jsme doma and Psí vojáci, are acquired tastes with a bristling independence born of a long history of oppression. Bands like the Plastic People helped spark the Velvet Revolution, after all. Their descendants today, most notably Dan Bárta, can produce introspective, moody sounds, often tinged with jazz sensibilities, a current that runs deep in a country that once toasted Duke Ellington and Satchmo. More recent bands (*see p238* **Sound Czech**) are focusing on interesting alchemies, fusing Latin, Middle Eastern and funk elements with Czech and traditional rock. Hulking event-only spaces such as the industrial space **Abaton** make for great mega-parties, while festivals attract incredible talent, from Avishai Cohen for the Jazz at the Castle series, to Viktoria Tolstoy for the pretty-much permanently on Prague Jazz Festival (www.agharta.cz; *see p203*).

INFORMATION AND RESOURCES

Tickets should be booked in advance for big-name concerts, particularly at small venues, though at the funkier ones you'll need to buy directly from the venue.

The *Prague Post*'s pullout section 'Night & Day', online at www.praguepost.com, lists the hippest shows in town and carries a handy calendar of those upcoming in the next month or so for advance planning. Otherwise, fliers with the latest dope are invariably piled up at clubs like Radost FX, U Malého Glena or the Globe Bookstore and Coffeehouse. For digital, the venerable www.techno.cz/party still has the best intel around, usually with at least a bit of English text to help in deciphering directions and contacts.

Venues

Enormous gigs

Prague's largest venue, the 200,000-capacity Stadium Strahov has been graced in the past by President Havel's mates, the Rolling Stones. Shows are far more frequent at T-Mobile Arena, though the sound quality at both is poor.

Abaton

Na Košince 8 (off Povltavská), Libeň, Prague 8 (no phone/www.fanonline.cz/abaton). Metro Palmovka/tram 12, 14, 24.
The former Interplast factory is now the site of the city's most outrageous parties and concerts. Nights differ hugely and you might find the venue filled with sofas, bars and cigarette girls, and then at other times just fitted out with thundering amps and world music stars who come all the way from the Congo. Tickets and information about events are usually available at the Ticketpro website (log on to www.ticketpro.cz). Concerts generally start at around 8.30pm. A great night out.

Congress Centre

Kongresové centrum
5 května 65, Vyšehrad, Prague 4 (261 171 111/ www.kcp.cz). Metro Vyšehrad/tram 18, 24.
Once the pride of the Party, the former Palace of Culture has been renamed as the Congress Centre in an effort to leave behind its past as a communist convention facility. It has also had better sound and

Still crazy Monkey Business

Prague is wild for funk, as **Maceo Parker** can tell you. Since his first appearance in Prague in the early 1990s he's made the city an annual must in his schedule and maintains the crowd responses are like nothing he's ever seen.

Unwilling to wait for his yearly stopover, Czech pop star and producer Roman Holý got together with a few friends in 2000 to create the country's first big, brassy funk with lyrics in English, **Monkey Business** (*pictured*). From the first sold-out show, it was evident that they'd brought off the concept – thanks in part to guest appearances by the likes of former James Brown staffer Fred Wesley, and David Williams, a regular with Madonna and Michael Jackson.

But due credit must go to the band members themselves, who have managed to keep the tunes bright, tight and infectiously energetic for six years, with their crowd appeal only growing in that time. Although live shows are fairly rare, possibly due to the level of energy required and the cleaning bills on the white suits the band favours, they've been prolific at pressing albums and all are stocked in the Czech section of Bontonland (*see p194*) on Wenceslas Square.

Sony has also come on board as a label and Monkey Business's five albums all feature the sound and recording standards

you'd expect from a big city organisation backed by a major player. At the same time, there's no question that these albums have a natural, organic look and feel, revealing that the band still doesn't take itself too seriously. They also clearly aren't afraid to stick their necks out and will jump into material that's well outside the usual definitions of funk.

Why be In When You Could be Out, *Save the Robots*, *Resistance is Futile* and *Kiss Me on My Ego* feature guests like Hiram Bullock and Ray Davies, and they sell like hotcakes in the Czech Republic, while Monkey Business's four-DVD set, *Lazy Youth Old Beggars*, scored the Czech Music Award the year it came out. Those live shows that do get played tend to happen at the Lucerna Music Bar, the same venerable club that hosted Maceo. They invariably make the crowds go ballistic.

What's the chord they've struck? Lead singer Tonya Graves, a former teaching assistant from Peekskill, New York, who thought she was coming to Prague as a tourist back in 1995, confesses to be at something of a loss. Invoking the ghost of the Czech Tom Jones, she says, 'I'm not completely like Karel Gott – but I'm not the newest thing either.'

But even if she doesn't know why Czechs love her music, Graves is sensible enough not to monkey with the serious business of funk.

lights installed, but the concerts still tend to feel somewhat institutional – in the main hall, the over-stuffed seats allow no room for dancing.

Stadium Strahov

Diskařská 100, Břevnov, Prague 6 (233 014 111). Metro Karlovo náměstí, then bus 176 or tram 22 to Újezd, then funicular. **Map** p326 A6.

The biggest concert venue in town is a concrete monstrosity built before World War II without much to offer besides its ability to accommodate epic rock shows. To get there is a bit of a trek out of the centre of town, but a special bus service is laid on for the larger gigs. Look out for big names headlining.

T-Mobile Arena

Výstaviště, Za elektrárnou 319, Holešovice, Prague 7 (266 727 411). Metro Nádraží Holešovice/tram 5, 12, 17. **Map** p332 E1.

T-Mobile Arena is a skating rink when it's not a concert hall. Housed in a barn, it has all the acoustics you'd expect from such a compromise. But it remaians the only indoor spot in Prague that can accommodate thousands for a concert.

Small to middling gigs

Akropolis

Kubelíkova 27, Žižkov, Prague 3 (296 330 911/ www.palacakropolis.cz). Metro Jiřího z Poděbrad/ tram 5, 9, 11, 26, 55, 58. **Open** *Divadelní Bar* 7pm-5am daily. *Malá Scená Bar* 7pm-3am daily. **Concerts** 7.30pm. **Admission** from 90 Kč. **No credit cards**. **Map** p333 C2.

Akropolis is the heart of indie rock and world music in Prague. The club hosts series such as United Colours of Akropolis and Jazz Meets World to promote a rich array of artists and avant-garde acts, from throat-singing monks to Berlin klezmer. The downstairs Divadelní (theatre) Bar has nightly DJs on the decks, along with MCs, free of charge, while the Malá Scena features live jams and red-lit sofas. The main basement stage, which is a former cinema hall, boasts lights and sound as good as any in Prague, but headlines groups you won't witness anywhere else in the city. At street level you'll find a pub that has just-passable curries vastly surpassed by the Staropramen beer.

Batalion Music Club

28 Října 3, Staré Město, Prague 1 (220 108 147/ www.batalion.cz). Metro Můstek/tram 3, 9, 14, 24. **Open** 24hrs daily. **Concerts** times vary. **Admission** free. **No credit cards. Map** p328 M5.

A club with a worn-out sign (two signs, in fact, the other impersonating the Hard Rock Café, with which it has no connection) just off Wenceslas Square is not the place you'd expect to find edgy, enthralling bands. Correct! But Batalion is open all night, has fun, cheesy live rock, cheap beer and, if you don't mind the skate punks, can be a laugh.

Futurum

Zborovská 7, Smíchov, Prague 5 (257 328 571/ www.musicbar.cz). Metro Anděl/tram 6, 9, 12. **Open** 8pm-3am daily. **Concerts** 9pm. **Admission** from 100 Kč. **No credit cards.**

The former National House of the Smíchov district, a kind of local ballroom/lecture hall every major district once had, houses this club. Fully made over with powerhouse sound, video and a wavy bar, Futurum has been hosting more live music of late, usually Czech rock favourites such as Tony Ducháček and Garage.

Klub 007

Vaníčkova 5, Koleje ČVUT dorm 7, Strahov, Prague 6 (257 211 439). Metro Dejvická, then bus 143, 149, 217. **Open** 7pm-midnight Mon-Sat. **Concerts** 9.30pm. **Admission** 40-100 Kč. **No credit cards.**

Student dorm heaven – or hell, depending on how you look at it. If you can find this place (in the concrete basement of dorm, yes, 007), you'll never believe it could be a must on any international ska tour of Central Europe. But that it is, as you'll soon discover when the bands start up. As authentic a youth vibe as you'll find, complete with cheap beer in plastic cups – just mind the bass player doesn't knock your beer over during riffs as you're practically in each other's lap.

Lucerna Great Hall

Vodičkova 36, Nové Město, Prague 1 (224 225 440/ www.lucpra.com). Metro Můstek/tram 3, 9, 14, 24, 52, 53, 55, 56. **Concerts** 7-8pm. **Admission** 200-900 Kč. **Credit** AmEx, MC, V. **Map** p329 N6.

Run independently from the Lucerna Music Bar, this vast, pillared, underground performance hall hosts big-time acts from Maceo Parker to the Cardigans. Its art nouveau ballrooms, balconies, grand marble stairs and wooden floors add a palatial feel to rock shows. Though it feels big and the sound can echo, you're always reasonably close to the band. There are no regular box office hours so book ahead through an agent like Ticketpro (*see p230*).

Lucerna Music Bar

Vodičkova 36, Nové Město, Prague 1 (224 217 108/ www.musicbar.cz). Metro Můstek/tram 3, 9, 14, 24, 52, 53, 55, 56. **Open** 8pm-3am daily. **Concerts** 9pm. **Admission** 80 Kč; 80-300 Kč concerts. **No credit cards. Map** p329 N6.

An incredibly impressive list of rock, jazz and blues talents rolls through this neglected old cellar concert space. Artists who have performed here range from Kinsey Report to Richard Bona. But then this music bar has always featured greats, including the likes of Satchmo and Josephine Baker. Enter the venue from the faded 1920s Lucerna Passage just off Wenceslas Square and you'll descend into what's best described as a multi-level dive that boasts wood-panelled balconies. Frighteningly popular '80s disco nights take over on Fridays when there isn't a touring artist passing through.

Malostranská beseda

Malostranské náměstí 21, Malá Strana, Prague 1 (257 532 092). Metro Malostranská/tram 12, 22, 57. **Open** 5pm-midnight daily. **Concerts** 8.30pm or 9.30pm. **Admission** 80 Kč. **No credit cards. Map** p327 F3.

U staré paní. *See p240.*

Threadbare it may be, but this unimposing former lecture salon hosts the hottest local live acts in town. It's home to the Sto Zvířat, a popular Czech ska band, among dozens of other acts that play the back room on a regular basis. Bottled beer is the only drawback to an otherwise welcoming well-stocked bar. Weird pieces of art line the walls, surfaces are made up of battered wood and fantastic views through the windows that overlook Malá Strana's main square add to the appeal. Malostranská beseda also has a well-stocked jazz and alternative CD shop, which is open 11am to 7pm Monday to Saturday.

Meloun

Michalská 12, Staré Město, Prague 1 (224 230 126/ www.meloun.cz). Metro Můstek/tram 3, 9, 14, 24, 51, 52, 53, 54, 55, 56, 57, 58. **Open** 11am-3am daily. **Concerts** 9pm. **Admission** 80-100 Kč. **No credit cards. Map** p328 L5.

Ever packed with local pop and disco fans, the Meloun occasionally breaks the bad DJ habit with a good blues night. More often, it's album tracks better left in the pre-1989 community hall of a small Bohemian village. With occasional film screenings as well, this cellar pub covers all bases. For the summer, the attached garden pub offers traditional Czech schnitzels and the like.

N11

Národní třída 11, Nové Město, Prague 1 (222 075 705/www.n11.cz). Metro Národní třída/tram 6, 9, 18, 22, 51, 54, 57, 58. **Concerts** times vary. **Admission** 80-150 Kč. **No credit cards. Map** p328 L6.

One of the better sound systems and light racks makes this small club a good choice for taking in a pop-rock band. The venue is notable, being the immaculately restored headquarters of the *New*

Sound Czech

In a very real sense, all Czech bands are indies. Even those with songs in English generally don't export, though they have followings you'd almost call religious at home. And they seem quite comfortable with that as a rule.

The Prague sound, if there is one, tends to incorporate much of Western rock, soul and electronica, but mixes in darker elements, sometimes invoking Slavic folk, Renaissance madrigals and a major infusion of early Velvet Underground, which was worshipped during the crackdowns of 1968. A new generation continues to forge ahead, with fresh fusions and influences from world music, clubland and, frankly, rampant file-sharing driving things.

For an up-to-date sampling of what's out there, the formerly pirate **Radio 1** is a good source (you can listen to it online at www.radio1.cz). Interesting local and touring groups, DJs and MCs are interviewed and have their work played all day on Radio 1, which remains the city's most respected non-commercial rock station – just be ready to turn down all the non-commercial commercials.

The live music scene tends to orbit around the mother-ship of the **Akropolis** club (*see p235*) in the wild and woolly Žižkov district, where bands are deliberately nurtured. Tuesday evening shows, with an entrance fee of a nominal 20 Kč, are an invitation to new groups to perform and are always spontaneous. Free Monday nights at the **Roxy** (*see p239*) are also showcases for new talent, generally DJs or hybrids of digital and live sound.

Surprisingly enough, the **Bontonland Megastore** (*see p194*) in Wenceslas Square is a reliable source of new musical talent – CDs are so cheap to record and publicise in the Czech Republic that even the hungriest indie band has one and they're generally stocked here.

Good local bands to watch out for are **Nana Zorin** for upbeat electronica, **JAR** for packed club concerts of techno and **Chaozz** for something in between. Novelty acts abound too, of course, and one that has to be experienced to enjoy is **Moimir Papalescu and the Nihilists** (*pictured*). Something about the squeaking vocals of lead singer La Petite Sonja drives 'em wild every time, even if it doesn't translate on CDs. Another hot trendy boy band, **Chinaski**, packs in the girls. Pop singer **Lenka Dusílová** is the older counterpart for guys. Meanwhile, **Skyline** delivers more universal digital dance. Classic, loud rock carries on, of course, with veteran bands like **MiG21** (www.mig21.cz), **Priessnitz** (www.priessnitz.com) and **Support Lesbiens** (www.supportlesbiens.cz). Hip hop is a major influence for **Tatabojs** (www.tatabojs.cz), which raps about life in the pre-fab apartment blocks, while **Čechomor** (www.cechomor.cz) gets to Czech roots with an inspired blend of traditional folk music and modern rock.

Arts & Entertainment

Presence, a monthly opinion journal with roots dating back to the interwar First Republic. Sunday blues acts like Stan the Man keep the crowd on its feet. The attached restaurant and bar are friendly, capable and open late into the night.

Rock Café

Národní třída 20, Nové Město, Prague 1 (224 914 414/www.rockcafe.cz). Metro Národní třída/tram 6, 9, 18, 22, 51, 54, 57, 58. **Open** 10am-3am Mon-Fri; 5pm-3am Sat; 5pm-1am Sun. **Concerts** 9pm. **Admission** 90-150 Kč. **No credit cards.** **Map** p328 L6.

Sometimes booking rising local stars, Rock Café is one to watch, although it more often draws the backpacker crowd. Once a post-revolution rock pioneer, these days it's only occasionally a hot ticket and features endless rockumentary screenings and Czech 'revival' bands. Not much in the way of atmosphere.

Roxy

Dlouhá 33, Staré Město, Prague 1 (224 826 296/ www.roxy.cz). Metro Náměstí Republiky/tram 5, 14, 26, 51, 53, 54. **Open** 7pm-2am Mon-Thur; 7pm-4am Fri, Sat. *DJ events* from 10pm. *Live acts* from 8pm. **Admission** *DJs events* 100-250 Kč. *Live acts* 150-450 Kč. **No credit cards.** **Map** p328 L3.

Although dominated by digital dance tracks, the Roxy also hosts live acts, generally to accompany the digital stuff but occasionally standing alone. When it does, the band is usually impressive, with names such as Mad Professor, or a crazed local group like Ohm Square. The space itself is a wonder of a crumbling former movie house that attracts (and sponsors) artists of all genres, with the main proviso that they're weird. *See also p245.*

Vagon

Národní třída 25, Nové Město, Prague 1 (221 085 599/www.vagon.cz). Metro Národní třída/tram 6, 9, 17, 18, 22, 23. **Open** 6pm-5am Mon-Sat; 6pm-1am Sun. **Concerts** 9pm. **Admission** 60 Kč. **No credit cards.** **Map** p328 L6.

A smoky little cellar with bands playing, fresh, unrecorded rock, jam nights and reggae, both live and on the sound system. Vagon is just a student bar, but one with a love for chilled-out, dreadlocked hanging out. Don't miss the entrance, hidden as it is in a shopping passage.

Jazz & blues

Prague's jazz history stretches back to the 1930s, when Jaroslav Ježek led an adored big band as colleague RA Dvorský established a standard of excellence that survived Nazi and communist oppression. Karel Velebný, of the renowned Studio 5 group, continued that tradition after the war, while Czech-Canadian novelist Josef Škvorecký chronicled the eternal struggle of Czech sax men in book after book.

These days, the jazz scene occupies a lower echelon of the club world, but a corps of talented players works the city circuit – to such an extent that you'll find the same dozen top players in any venue you choose (watch for Jan Kořínek and Groove, and the inimitable Chicago blues sounds of the Rene Trossman band).

AghaRTA

Krakovská 5, Nové Město, Prague 1 (222 211 275/ www.agharta.cz). Metro Muzeum or IP Pavlova/ tram 4, 6, 10, 16, 22. **Open** *Club* 7pm-midnight daily. *Concerts* 9pm. *Jazz shop* 5pm-midnight Mon-Fri; 7pm-midnight Sat, Sun. **Admission** 100 Kč. **No credit cards.** **Map** p331 O8.

Named after Miles Davis's most controversial LP, this club off Wenceslas Square is one of Prague's best spots for modern jazz and blues. A fairly even mix of Czechs and foreigners mingles in the relatively small but comfortable space – which is perfect for sitting back and enjoying performances from Vibe Fantasy or Jiří Stivin. As at many Prague jazz clubs, there's a CD shop selling local recordings for between 150 and 400 Kč. Look out for releases on the club's own ARTA label.

Jazz Club Železná

Železná 16, Staré Město, Prague 1 (224 239 697). Metro Můstek/Národní třída/tram 6, 9, 18, 22. **Open** 7pm-2am daily. **Concerts** 9pm. **Admission** 150 Kč. **No credit cards.** **Map** p328 M4.

Live jams in a stony Old Town cellar, revived after being out of action for a time. It's a comfortably cool space where you can catch hot young players on the rise or a seasoned pro like František Kop, a Czech sax legend. The bar's still not much to look at but the hippie atmosphere is authentically free and the location can't be beat. Good acoustics and space too, considering the ancient architecture.

Reduta

Národní třída 20, Nové Město, Prague 1 (224 933 487/www.redutajazzclub.cz). Metro Národní třída/ tram 6, 9, 18, 22, 51, 54, 57, 58. **Open** *Box office* 5-9pm daily. *Club* 9pm-12.30am daily. **Concerts** 9pm. **Admission** 200 Kč. **No credit cards.** **Map** p328 J6.

Virtually unchanged since the Velvet Revolution, this old chestnut of a club steadfastly hangs on to its cramped, awkward seating, highly-priced beer and a coat-check guy who asks for your jacket, presumably in hopes of a tip. That Bill Clinton once played sax here to entertain Václav Havel hardly makes up for the high prices – though it's still certainly affordable by Western standards. Admittedly, some of the best musicians in town often sit in with the evening's band, and the club, unusually, has a good sound system and a proper baby grand piano.

U Malého Glena

Karmelitská 23, Malá Strana, Prague 1 (257 531 717/www.malyglen.cz). Metro Malostranská/ tram 12, 22, 57. **Open** 8am-2am daily. **Concerts** 9pm. **Admission** 100-150 Kč. **No credit cards.** **Map** p327 F5.

Music for free in the **Old Town Square**.

While U Malého Glena is easily the most crammed
club in town, patrons forget about the knee-bashing
tables the minute the bands start up in the tiny cellar space. The freshest jazz players in the country
have made Little Glenn's their home for nearly a
decade. The sound system has been improved and
so has the seating so squeeze in and order some
nachos from the pub at street level before the set
begins. Expect to see some excellent performances
from great Czech players like Robert Balzar or the
Wednesday night Chicago blues masters known as
the Rene Trossman Band.

U staré paní

Michalská 9, Staré Město, Prague 1 (224 228 090/
www.ustarepani.cz). Metro Můstek/Národní třída/
tram 6, 9, 18, 22. **Open** 7pm-2am daily. **Concerts**
9pm. **Admission** 150 Kč. **Credit** AmEx, MC, V.
Map p328 L5.

With a modern makeover but the same old cheap
wine and grub, the Old Lady has also kept tight hold
of the same hot players as ever, with jams that last
until dawn on a good Friday or Saturday night.
Conveniently, this is also a Staré Město hotel in a
great location. The best players in town tend to gravitate here to do their own thing after performing for
tourists at other venues. **Photo** p237.

Ungelt Jazz & Blues Club

Týn 2 (entrance on Týnská ulička), Staré Město,
Prague 1 (224 895 748/www.jazzblues.cz).

Metro Můstek or Náměstí republiky/tram 3, 5,
9, 14, 24, 26. **Open** 8pm-12.30am daily.
Admission 150-300 Kč. **No credit cards**.
Map p328 M3.

The highest-priced jazz club (drinks included) won't
catch much of a local crowd, but it's still pretty reasonable by Western standards. Having said that,
Ungelt offers a serious line-up of jazz, funk and
groove players in an atmospheric stone-walled space
that'll make you forget about the money.

Folk/country & western

The folk and country and western vein
runs surprisingly deep in the Czech lands.
The American cowboy lifestyle has been
romanticised here ever since Bohemians
settled in Prague, Texas, and 'trampers'
– avid hikers and campers – lustily sing old
campfire tunes when they escape from their
block housing and hit the countryside, often
without speaking a word of English.

První Prag Country Saloon Amerika

Korunní 101, Vinohrady, Prague 2 (224 256 131).
Metro Náměstí Míru/tram 4, 10, 16, 22. **Open**
11am-11pm Mon; 11am-midnight Tue-Fri; 5pm-
midnight Sat; 6pm-1am Sun. **Admission** 20 Kč.
No credit cards. **Map** p333 B4.
Still the place for an all-Czech cowboy fiddle jam.

Nightlife

Party like it's 1599.

Celnice. *See p242.*

Prague's reputation as the Amsterdam of the East is well deserved. These days it's definitely up all night, with whatever you've a hankering for generally available. In fact, it's been a party capital ever since the 16th century, when the somewhat eccentric Emperor Rudolf II moved the capital of the Habsburg Empire to Prague, and Bohemians, while often conservative by day, tend to go fairly wild after dark. There are a number of venues where you'll come up against some cut-throat competition for the hippest wardrobe prize and places where no one would notice if you arrived in your underwear. New venues are appearing constantly and some, like **Vertigo**, are worth a look but still evolving. Others personify a new generation of classy little dance spaces attached to successful restaurants and bars, such as **Celnice** and **Mecca**, which are both usually packed out. Also competing in this class are **Duplex**, **Zvonařka**, **Ultramarin**, **Solidní nejistota** and **Radost FX**. But generally, you'll find that beer is the only source of protein to be had while out late.

DJ culture reigns supreme in Prague, but it's a culture dominated by techno, as seen and heard at **Roxy** and Mecca, and the only

alternatives are usually those more mainstream venues that favour top-40 pop, such as **Klub Lávka** or **Double Trouble**. Clubs for danceable funk, soul or R&B are virtually non-existent. So it's a good thing that Radost FX comes through with at least one night a week that's not just for the early twentysomethings.

Closures and openings are a constant, as in the clubbing world everywhere. If anything, clubs are even more ephemeral in Prague since they tend to share buildings with residential spaces and Czechs are early risers – thus making for uneasy relationships between club managers and other residents. The other unique aspect of clubbing in Prague is a feeling of anarchy that could only be achieved in a place with virtually no safety regulations or PC culture. Bar-top stripping, crumbling walls and the rampant use of stimulants can all be found within blocks of each other in Staré Město on any Friday night.

Just remember that if you're caught with drugs, you're on your own. Czech police arrest anyone in possession of what they deem 'more than a little' of a controlled substance and the jails are full of people still not convicted of a thing. Gambling, however, is completely legal

Still crazy Tram from hell

Perhaps 'dreaded' is too harsh a word for the experience. But anyone without taxi money who is caught out 15 minutes after midnight, when the last metro trains are generally gone, certainly approaches with ambivalence their only remaining option for getting home: the night tram.

Though not entirely recommended, night trams are an option for those with a sense of adventure. Waiting at Lazarská and Spálená streets in Nové Město, squinting through the rain or graffiti at a schedule for a 50s-numbered tram, you may begin to feel like a lost soldier separated from his regiment behind enemy lines. If you have less than half an hour to wait, and the tram stops anywhere near your bed, you're in, well... one could call it luck.

Relief and revulsion vie for supremacy as the warm glow of an approaching car is spotted. The door opens, revealing a solid wall of humanity and a wave of smell. Stale alcohol, wet dogs, falafel aroma and body odour blast out like the bad breath of a jungle animal. Inebriated? Congratulations. Not being in full possession of your faculties is a distinct advantage.

All rules of personal space and politeness (not Prague's strong point at the best of times) are suspended. Force your way in, grab on to a pole and hold tight, as the driver takes the corner like he's at Le Mans. Don't even hope to get a seat. They're always full, occupied by scraggly, besotted street people. For some, the night tram is their only alternative to sleeping outside.

Younger, stronger riders somehow sleep while standing, hand gripping the pole above, head tucked into the crook of the elbow. Fortunately for travellers to the realm of Morpheus there's no way to fall – the press of bodies prevents that.

For the party crowd, it's just a cheap club on wheels. You'll hear them before you see them, the sounds of drunken outpourings mixing with the clink of beer bottles. Still, this lot only serves to enhance the generally loose and convivial atmosphere. Since it's the only way home, everyone is on the night tram – locals, tourists, expats – talking in a riotous polyglot babel.

The late hour and the alcohol intake fuel drama. Fist fights are rare – thankfully, there just isn't the space. The night tram does, however, provide stage space for heated arguments, intimate encounters and other happenings. Indeed, these steamy cars are rich laboratories of social science, revealing what makes Prague's citizens laugh or cry: warring couples produce sighs of relief as they disembark; drunken missteps or bad singing are seen as free entertainment; overheated heavy-petting sessions result in studied indifference; smiles and coos erupt when a dog of any kind is brought on board – the latter an instant feel-good for Czechs.

Perplexing by day (when did this route change?), a tram ride can be truly baffling at night, with pit stops between stops, nobody getting on or off, a warning buzzer (wake up!), then the car lurching on again. What's more, disembarking requires strategic planning, starting several stops ahead. Each time someone exits the show, edge closer to the door. When the big moment arrives, plunge ahead in a stream of 'pardons' and 'sorrys', nudge aside skate punks and a drunk or two, dive down the steps and leap out the door, praying it doesn't close on you. The night air never felt so good. Now, which way is home?

and high rollers will find the city has no shortage of casinos, though if you want to lose your money somewhere classy, we suggest the **Banco Casino**, **Palais Savarin** or the **Millennium**. Would-be beatniks and Charles Bukowskis, on the other hand, will find a plenitude of material in Prague's ubiquitous *herna* bars and many smoky dives lined with electronic one-armed bandits.

Note that any tram with a number in the 50s is a night tram. And, at the end of a long evening, taking a night tram is definitely an experience in itself (*see above* **Still crazy**).

Clubs

Celnice

V celnice 4, Nové Město, Prague 1 (224 212 240/ www.celnice.com). Metro Náměstí Republiky/ tram 5, 8, 14. **Open** *Restaurant* 11am-2am daily. *Club* 9pm-4am Thur-Sat. **Admission** *Men* 100 Kč. *Women* free. **Credit** AmEx, MC, V. **Map** p329 O3. With a space-age modern sushi bar and dance club in the cellar, what appears at ground level to be a fairly conventional restaurant (*see p156*) doubles as a dance venue and Czech party scene for the showy and successful. DJs spin happy house and the crowd dresses to kill, but it's a small space and can be dead some nights. Be buff or prepared to buy a lot of cocktails to get much attention. **Photo p241.**

Delta

Vlastina 887, Liboc, Prague 6 (233 312 443/ www.noise.cz/delta). Metro Dejvická, then bus 218/night bus 510. **Open** 7pm-midnight Thur, Fri. **Admission** from 100 Kč. **No credit cards.**
With solid local fringe rock credentials, but a location waaay out in the midst of suburban apartments on the city's north-western border, Delta is a club that attracts a neighbourhood crowd that's young, bored and aching to break out. A steady supply of uncommercial DJs and groups that were once banned by the communists, such as Echt!, perform irregularly.

Double Trouble

Melatrichova 17, Staré Město, Prague 1 (221 632 414/www.doubletrouble.cz). Metro Můstek or Staroměstská/tram 3, 6, 9, 14, 18, 22, 24, 52, 53, 55, 56, 57, 58. **Open** 5pm-6.30am daily. **Admission** free-180 Kč. **No credit cards.** **Map** p328 L4.
Looks like a lively scene at first, but only after venturing in do you see it's crammed with backpackers, happily paying heavily for drinks, admission and crap pop tracks. That said, they do seem to be enjoying themselves dancing on the bar and stripping off.

Duplex

Václavské náměstí 21, Nové Město, Prague 1 (224 232 319/www.duplexduplex.cz). Metro Můstek/tram 3, 9, 14, 24, 51, 52, 53, 55, 56, 58. **Open** *Café* 10am-midnight daily. *Restaurant* noon-midnight daily. *Club* 9.30pm-2am Tue-Thur; 9.30pm-5am Fri, Sat. **Admission** 150 Kč. **Credit** AmEx, MC, V. **Map** p329 N6.
The attitude here is so thick you can cut it with your stiletto heels, but if you have to experience a Wenceslas Square disco, this one's as good a candidate as any. Friday Funk 'n' Motion parties and go-go dancers come with the penthouse views, highly-priced drinks and hustlers. In April the Italian students who walk all over Staré Město in formation come in for landing here. Still, the programming has improved lately and the cuisine, while inconsistent, has won raves. Plus, there is a remarkable chill-out space on the terrace, where meals are also served.

Guru

Rokycanova 29, Žižkov, Prague 3 (777 155 103/ www.guruclub.cz). Metro Jiřího z Poděbrad/tram 5, 9, 26, 58. **Open** 11pm-5am daily. *Shows* 8pm or 9pm. **Admission** 30-200 Kč. **No credit cards.**
Very irregular programme and, in that sense, very Žižkov. With the right act, it can be a brilliant experience in a dive bar, but ask around before heading out unless you enjoy a gamble. A strange, worn-out, subterranean space with split-level dancefloor, balconies and dazed bar tenders. Staff ask for a deposit on glass beer mugs, which gives you an idea of how rowdy the crowds get.

Jo's Bar & Garáž

Malostranské náměstí 7, Malá Strana, Prague 1 (257 531 422). Metro Malostranská/tram 12, 20, 22, 23, 57. **Open** 9pm-2am daily. **Admission** 50-100 Kč. **Credit** AmEx, MC, V. **Map** p327 F3.
Another stone cellar dance club? Say it ain't so! The handiest one in Malá Strana can be a good time for brainless bouncing to the Red Hot Chili Peppers, but just as often there's nothing on at all except desultory beer drinking. Worth checking out if you happen to be in the neighbourhood.

Karlovy Lázně

Novotného lávka 1, Staré Město, Prague 1 (222 220 502/www.karlovylazne.cz). Metro Staroměstská/tram 17, 18, 53. **Open** *Café* 11am-4am daily. *Club* 9pm-5am daily. **Admission** 50-100 Kč. **No credit cards.** **Map** p328 J5.
Prague's unabashed commercial mega-club is in a former bathhouse next door to Charles Bridge. And it's every bit as original as you'd expect in that

Where's my drink? **Double Trouble.**

Mecca.

location. The four levels of Karlovy Lázně cover every baseline. Paradogs does techno on the fourth floor, Kaleidoskop does retro hits on the third, Discotheque does radio pop, and the MCM café, the only part of the club open by day, books occasional jazz and funk combos. Huge with teens.

Klub Lávka

Novotného lávka 1, Staré Město, Prague 1 (222 222 156/221 082 278/www.lavka.cz). Metro Staroměstská/tram 17, 18, 53. **Open** *Bar* 24hrs daily. *Disco* 9.30pm-5am daily. **Admission** 50-100 Kč. **Credit** AmEx, MC, V. **Map** p328 J5.

A lovely river terrace out back, go-go dancers, funk and disco tracks on the sound system, and all within spitting distance of Charles Bridge. All right, so there's no challenging digital music being played here but, in the black light, where everyone's underwear dances, no one seems to mind.

La Fabrique

Uhelný trh 2, Staré Město, Prague 1 (224 233 137). Metro Můstek or Národní třída/tram 6, 9, 18, 22, 53, 57, 58. **Open** 5pm-2.45am Wed, Thur, Sun; 5pm-3.45am Fri, Sat. **Admission** free. **Credit** AmEx, MC, V. **Map** p328 L5.

Disco lovers cram into this subterranean Staré Město club to hear pop, along with nightmarish DJs who love to announce things over the songs. Done up throughout in factory decor, it's a maze of rooms with a narrow entrance just off the Havelská fruit market.

Mánes

Masarykovo nábřeží 250, Nové Město, Prague 1 (224 931 112). Metro Karlovo náměstí/tram 17, 18, 53, 57, 58. **Open** 11am-11pm daily. **Admission** 50-150 Kč. **No credit cards. Map** p330 J8.

Mánes, a classy 1930s functionalist gallery, combines art (it is the Czech Fund for Art Foundation's most important exhibition space) with another, living, culture: it's a run-down riverside dance venue with an amazing location. For a while it specialised in Tropicana nights on Friday and Saturday, with hot mambo kings. These days, the programme is unpredictable, but a beer on the terrace (open until 11pm) is never a bad idea. *See also p221.*

Matrix

Konévova 13, Žižkov, Prague 3 (731 411 356/ www.matrixklub.cz). Metro Florenc, then bus 133 or 207. **Admission** free-120 Kč. **No credit cards. Map** p333 D1.

A former frozen meat plant, Matrix is a big teen scene for techno and good, grotty partying, with Gambrinus beer on tap. Occasional local DJ stars like Babe LN play, as do international bands willing to do nearly free shows, but generally it's a fringe line-up.

Mecca

U průhonu 3, Holešovice, Prague 7 (283 870 522/ www.mecca.cz). Metro Vltavská/tram 1, 3, 12, 25, 54. **Open** *Club* 10pm-6am Fri, Sat. *Restaurant* 10am-11pm Mon-Thur; 10am-6am Fri; 8am-6am Sat. **Admission** 100-300 Kč. **No credit cards. Map** p332 F2.

The biggest hit on the party scene, Mecca is a club for grown-ups. A disused factory made over into a stylishly modern, large-scale dance palace with respectable restaurant service, Mecca is worth a pilgrimage. Theme parties, a line-up of the city's top DJs and live jazz are the trophies. The C Lounge downstairs offers chill-out space and the most mellow of the club's three glossy bars.

Punto Azul

Kroftova 1, Smíchov, Prague 5 (no phone/www.
puntoazul.cz). Tram 6, 9, 12, 20, 57. **Open** 7pm-2am
daily. **Admission** free-50 Kč. **No credit cards.**
A club so far underground that you'll need canaries
just to test the air. Despite the name, there's nothing
Spanish about the place; it's just a student drinking
dive on every wirehead's map, notwithstanding the
fact that the techno dance space isn't much bigger
than a circuit board. Nevertheless, a consistent
groove is achieved through a line-up of the city's
more avant-garde house DJs.

Radost FX

Bělehradská 120, Nové Město, Prague 2 (224 254
776/www.radostfx.cz). Metro IP Pavlova/tram 4,
6, 10, 11, 16, 22, 51, 56, 57. **Open** 8.30am-4am
Mon-Fri; 11am-6am Sat, Sun. *Club* 10pm-4am Thur-
Sat. **Admission** 120-250 Kč. **No credit cards.**
Map p331 P10.
The original house party in Prague is going strong
after more than a decade in service. Radost FX still
offers the best all-night mix you'll find in the city: a
combination of creative veggie café, spaced-out
back-room lounge, and small but slick downstairs
club featuring absurdly glam theme parties, which
provides a first-class venue for endless fashion
shows, local stars of house and techno, and, very useful after a heavy night, one of the best Sunday
brunches to be had in town (*see p159*). **Photo** p247.

Roxy

Dlouhá 33, Staré Město, Prague 1 (224 826 296/
www.roxy.cz). Metro Náměstí Republiky/tram 5, 8,
14, 53. **Open** 7pm-2am Mon-Thur; 7pm-4am Fri, Sat.
Party nights 10pm-5am. **Admission** *DJ nights* 100-
250 Kč. *Live events* 150-450 Kč. **No credit cards.**
Map p328 L3.
The run-down Roxy is Prague's top destination for
house, R&B and jungle, thanks in large part to one
of Central Europe's best party organisers, David
Urban. Star acts no other club could afford, from
Arrested Development to Transglobal Underground,
get talked into doing Roxy shows, in addition to local
kings of the decks. Meanwhile, the Galerie NoD fills
out the venue with multiple floors of edgy, non-commercial culture and fringe art. Free Mondays pack
the place with kids. *See also p239.* **Photo** p248.

Sedm vlků

Vlkova 7, Žižkov, Prague 3 (222 711 725/www.
sedmvlku.cz). Metro Jiřího z Poděbrad/tram 5, 9, 26,
55, 58. **Open** 5pm-3am Mon-Sat. **Admission** free.
No credit cards. Map p333 B2.
Newly redone with surrealist art, low light and
bendy ironwork, the Seven Wolves remains one of
the hippest bar-cum-club spaces in the party mecca
that is the Žižkov district. With hot-and-cold running jungle on the decks, there's basically just beer
for quality libation, but that's fairly standard in
Prague clubs. The crisp sound system is another
reason this club has stolen some of the thunder
from the more established clubs around, such as
the neighbouring Akropolis (*see p235*).

Solidní nejistota

Pštrossova 21, Nové Město, Prague 1 (224 933 086/
www.solidninejistota.cz). Metro Národní třída/
tram 6, 9, 17, 18, 22, 23, 51, 52, 53, 54, 55, 56,
57, 58. **Open** 6pm-6am daily. **Admission** free.
No credit cards. Map p330 K8.
Solid Uncertainty is the most shameless meat market
in Prague, with the world-weary bar staff manning
the taps at the centre of the room, around which every
creature looking to hook up rotates, scanning the possibilities. If the new Prague aquarium (*see p206*) is
closed, this is a good spot to watch the sharks. The
grill is open late into the night, but it looks like the
beefy doormen are the only ones who use it.

Tropison cocktail bar

Náměstí Republiky 8, Staré Město, Prague 1 (224
801 276). Metro Náměstí Republiky/tram 5, 8, 14,
53. **Open** 8pm-3am Mon-Wed; 8pm-5am Thur, Fri;
7pm-5am Sat; 6pm-3am Sun. **Admission** free-100
Kč. **No credit cards. Map** p329 O4.
All right, the service and uninspiring menus aren't
likely to tempt you here, but wait until you see the
view from the terrace. Then there's the chance to
boogie on the grave of communism (this was a communist department store once) at the silly Latin
dance parties. Put it down as a maybe.

Vagon

Národní 25, Staré Město (221 085 599/www.
vagon.cz). Metro Národní třída/tram 6, 9, 17, 18,
22, 23, 51, 52, 53, 54, 55, 56, 57, 58. **Open** 6pm-
5am Mon-Sat; 6pm-1am Sun. **Admission** free-100
Kč. **Map** p328 L6.
A smoky cellar bar that is consistently packed with
high-spirited young locals, despite the limitations on
space and oxygen content.

Vertigo

Havelská 4, Staré Město (774 744 256/www.vertigo-
club.cz). Metro Můstek/tram 3, 6, 9, 14, 18, 22, 23,
52, 53, 55, 56, 57, 58. **Open** 9pm-4am daily.
Admission free. **Map** p328 L5.
Three levels of capable café and clubbing space,
with decent DJs, decor, lights and sound. Despite all
that, it's easily overlooked and can be deadish.

U Bukanýra

Na Františku embankment (near Čechuv Bridge),
Staré Město, Prague 1 (777 891 348/www.
bukanyr.cz). Metro Staroměstská/tram 17, 18.
Admission free-100 Kč. **No credit cards.**
Map p328 L1.
A floating barge party, but programming can be iffy.
House-music DJs maintain sway when At the
Buccaneer is operating, but it's not unheard of for it
to be dark for weeks. Worth checking on, since it's
right in the centre and good fun if you're in luck.

U Buldoka

Preslova 1, Smíchov, Prague 5 (257 329 154/www.
ubuldoka.cz). Metro Anděl/tram 4, 6, 7, 9, 10, 12,
14, 20, 52, 58. **Open** 11am-midnight Mon-Fri; noon-
midnight Sat, Sun. **Admission** 30-50 Kč.
No credit cards.

With well-tapped Staropramen beer and excellent traditional grub, the Bulldog is a classic cheap Czech pub that cleverly manages to conceal a groovin' music club downstairs. The space is done up in the prevailing retro style, with the usual crew of Czech DJs: Loutka, Tráva and Liquid A.

Újezd

Újezd 18, Malá Strana, Prague 1 (no phone). Metro Malostranská/tram 6, 9, 12, 20, 22, 23, 57, 58. **Open** *Bar* 2pm-4am daily. *Café* 6pm-4am daily. *Pub* 8pm-4am daily. **Admission** free. **No credit cards.** **Map** p327 F6.

In its earlier days as Borát, this three-storey madhouse was an important venue for the alternative music crowd. Today, with its surrealist ironwork decor, a young Czech crowd in dreads and thick, smoky atmosphere, Újezd is home to some loud, badly amplified Czech rock tracks, battered wooden chairs in the café upstairs and shouted conversation in the bar below. And the venue is not an iota less popular for it.

Ultramarin

Ostrovní 32, Nové Město, Prague 2 (224 932 249/ www.ultramarin.cz). Metro Národní třída/tram 6, 9, 17, 18, 22, 23, 51, 52, 53, 54, 55, 56, 57, 58. **Open** 10.30am-4am daily. **Admission** free. **Credit** AmEx, MC, V. **Map** p330 J7.

Lesser-known DJs rock the small stone cellar space and critical mass seems to be easily achieved, making Ultramarin an engaging place to stay up late and get sweaty. At street level it's an art bar with a small menu of salads, Czech-Mex food and seating made from designer materials like layered cardboard. You'll find a grown-up crowd and it's in a handy location, just streets from Staré Město.

U zlatého stromu

Karlova 6, Staré Město, Prague 1 (222 220 441/ www.zlatystrom.cz). Metro Staroměstská/tram 17, 18, 53. **Open** *Club* 8pm-6am daily. *Restaurant* 24hrs daily. **Admission** 80 Kč. **Credit** AmEx, MC, V. **Map** p328 K4.

Here's one of the strangest combinations in the Staré Město area: a non-stop disco, striptease, bar, restaurant and hotel. Descend into the cellar labyrinth of bad pop and strippers, and you could end up in a peaceful outdoor garden or a recessed nook ideal for that profound conversation about God and sex. The upstairs café has a full menu plus coffee and drinks.

Wakata

Malířská 14, Holešovice, Prague 7 (233 370 518/ www.wakata.cz). Metro Vltavská/tram 1, 8, 25, 26, 51, 56. **Open** 5pm-3am Mon-Thur; 5pm-5am Fri, Sat; 6pm-3am Sun. **Admission** free. **No credit cards.** **Map** p332 D2.

A down-and-dirty teenage wasteland, this bar can deliver great jungle mixing, but more often it feels like you've unwittingly stepped out of Prague and onto the set of a cheap horror film. At least it stays open way past official hours, has motorcycle seats for bar stools and is, errm, away from it all.

XT3

Pod plynojemem 5, Libeň, Prague 8 (284 825 826/ www.xt3.cz). Metro Palmovka/tram 1, 3, 8, 10, 12, 19, 24, 52, 54, 55. **Open** 4pm-2am daily. **Admission** free-40 Kč. **No credit cards.**

XT3 features breakbeat, lots of smoke and cheap beer – all packed into a venue foreigners won't stumble upon. Don't forget your skateboard, and bring Czech teen friends if you want to blend in.

Zvonařka

Šafaříkova 1, Vinohrady, Prague 2 (224 251 990). Metro Náměstí Míru/tram 6, 11, 56. **Open** 11.30am-midnight Mon-Fri; noon-midnight Sat, Sun. **Admission** free-200 Kč. **Credit** MC, V.

What was once a popular Czech pub has had the hyper-modernist makeover and now looks a bit like a cruise ship inside. The circular bar and blue-and-silver motifs set the stage for high-energy parties when the place is busy. Still, should you pine for a memory of old Prague, there's a terrace that looks out over the city's southern suburbs. And, when the DJs aren't up to much, at least the food's reliable.

Gambling

Gambling is big business in Prague – and seems to get bigger every year. First came the *hernas* ('gambling halls', which are essentially bars full of one-armed bandits). Then came the bigger casinos that now line Wenceslas Square. Regulation is questionable, so, if you want to roll the dice, stick with the respectable international chains, which are geared towards tourists, encourage small-time betting and have fairly relaxed atmospheres. The *hernas* cater mostly to locals, pay a maximum of 300 Kč for a 2 Kč wager and operate on a legally fixed ratio of 60 to 80 odds.

Casinos

Banco Casino

Na příkopě 27, Nové Město, Prague 2 (221 967 380/ www.bancocasino.cz). Metro Náměstí Republiky/tram 5, 8, 14, 24, 26, 52, 53. **Open** 24hrs. **Credit** MC, V. **Map** p329 N5.

Classy enough to serve as a set in the last Prague-shot Bond flick, *Casino Royale*, the Banco is a reputable, plush establishment with private salons and high-tech slots for those not into green felt.

Millennium

V celnici 10, Nové Město, Prague 1 (221 033 401). Metro Náměstí Republiky/tram 5, 8, 14, 24, 26, 52, 53. **Open** 3pm-4am Sun-Thur; 3pm-5am Fri, Sat. **Credit** MC, V. **Map** p329 O3.

Plush, classy and palatial, the Millennium looks like an appropriate playground for any passing super spies. It's part of a spick-and-span hotel and retail complex just east of Staré Město. Free drinks for players add to the fun if you can keep your head.

Radost FX the parts other clubs cannot reach. *See p245.*

Palais Savarin

Na příkopě 10, Nové Město, Prague 1 (224 221 636/ www.czechcasinos.cz). Metro Můstek/tram 3, 5, 8, 9, 14, 26, 51, 52, 53, 55, 56, 58. **Open** 1pm-4am daily. **Credit** DC, MC, V. **Map** p329 N5.

One of the best established operations in town, with candelabras and baroque frescoes, it's a world apart from most of the betting rooms on Wenceslas Square. Just about worth a look even if you don't gamble – but if you do, drinks are on the house. American roulette and stud poker are offered along with all the traditional games of chance. Bets from 20 Kč to 5,000 Kč.

Herna bars

Herna Můstek

Inside Můstek metro station, Nové Město, Prague 1 (no phone). Metro Můstek/tram 3, 9, 14, 24, 52, 53, 55, 56, 58. **Open** 24hrs daily. **No credit cards.** **Map** p329 N6.

Most *herna* bars are pretty seedy, but this one, inside Prague's main metro station, is not too threatening.

Adult clubs

Czech lawmakers enjoy skirting the issue of prostitution – although pimping is illegal, the law does not address prostitution directly. Clubs and hundreds of patrons certainly do, however, with the women in most of the strip clubs working legally as independent contract entertainers with 'private dances' in private rooms widely available. It's all pretty safe and hygienic, and most of the clubs these days will refund your entry fee if you opt for the extra services packages. Stag party favourites include **Darling Club Cabaret** and **Desire Cabaret**. As in such clubs anywhere, the house truly cleans up on the hugely inflated drink prices, with strippers encouraged to ask for them from customers.

Big Sister

Nádražní 46, Smíchov, Prague 5 (257 310 043/ www.bigsister.net). Metro Smíchov/tram 12, 52. **Open** 6pm-3am daily. **Admission** 290 Kč; couples free. **Credit** MC, V.

The most astounding new wave in Prague's booming sex business, Big Sister nakedly cashes in on the *Big Brother* phenomenon, but puts its live internet cameras inside a free brothel (excluding admission) in which all the punters agree to be on the web in exchange for one hour of gratis action once inside.

Cabaret Atlas

Ve Smečkách 31, Nové Město, Prague 1 (296 326 042). Metro Muzeum/tram 4, 6, 10, 16, 22, 51, 53, 55, 56, 57, 58. **Open** 7pm-7am daily. **Admission** 200 Kč. **Credit** MC, V. **Map** p331 N8.

Striptease, a crowd of businessmen who can expense the drinks and whirlpools at a mere 2,500 Kč per half hour – and that's just for starters.

Roxy. *See p245.*

Still crazy The sex thing

Finding one's socially responsible gender role is not at the top of Prague's party generation agenda. In fact, it's a bit shocking, even in this day and age, to see what Bohemians get up to when they're out on the town.

Of course, nightclubbing has always been a sexy business and some countries in Central and Eastern Europe clearly have different sensibilities about sexiness (or outright sex) in semi-public. Nude sunbathing doesn't merit a second glance in Prague, and public parks in Hungary, Slovakia and Germany, come the warm weather, are filled with lusty activities. On a hot day, sitting on the grass, you'd be thought awfully odd not to drop your top, whatever your gender.

Never a particularly religious society to begin with, these days things are only getting naughtier in the city. One canny local mogul figured out a way to combine the booming internet porn business with Praguers' penchant for partying and established www.madsexparty.com – formerly known as www.wamsexorgy.com, as in 'wet and messy' (subsites include www.drunksexorgy.com and www.partyhardcore.com).

This site, predicated on inviting dozens of young female students to Prague parties where admission and booze is free, draws hundreds of future nurses, teachers and probably IT marketing mavens to a club where porn actors start doing their stuff. Far from being shocked, the attendees generally jump in, spraying each other with champagne and getting into epic food fights. Presumably, their parents don't have high-speed internet access.

More out in the open are the monthly parties at club Face to Face on the Vltava island opposite the Holešovice district (Ostrov Štvanice 1125, Holešovice, Prague 7, 607 180 331). Subtly dubbed Sex Appeal (www.sexappeal.cz) and sponsored by the Czech porno magazine *Leo*, the parties pack in crowds by the hundreds. In addition to having one of the biggest dancefloors in town, the parties tend to attract hordes of beautiful young things, who are served by waiters and waitresses wearing mainly gold body paint. The partygoers are also grabbed by *Leo* models and, much to the amusement of most of the people watching, stripped.

Captain Nemo

Ovocný trh 13, Staré Město, Prague 1 (224 210 356). Metro Náměstí Republiky/tram 5, 8, 14, 53. **Open** 8pm-5am Mon-Thur, Sun; 4pm-6am Fri, Sat. **Admission** 300 Kč. **Credit** MC, V. **Map** p328 M4.
This is a handy Staré Město club that employs mainly local talent and goes for a nautical theme, though it's not clear that anyone's noticed yet.

Caroica

Václavské náměstí 4, Nové Město, Prague 1 (296 325 314). Metro Můstek/tram 3, 9, 14, 24, 51, 53, 55, 56, 57, 58. **Open** 9pm-4am Mon-Thur; 5pm-4am Fri-Sun. **Admission** 200-500 Kč. **Credit** AmEx, MC, V. **Map** p329 N6.
Deep under Wenceslas Square in what looks like an imperial bedroom, Caroica was formerly one of the city's best jazz holes. The baroque red-and-gold setting has remained, but new management has launched a cabaret: dancers with top hats and canes alternate with strippers in what could almost be called entertainment appropriate for a date – though with the usual high drink rates.

Darling Club Cabaret

Ve Smečkách 32, Nové Město, Prague 1 (no phone/ www.kabaret.cz). Metro Můstek/tram 3, 9, 14, 24, 51, 53, 55, 56, 57, 58. **Open** noon-5am Mon, Tue, Thur; 8pm-5am Wed; noon-6am Fri, Sat. **Admission** 200 Kč. **Credit** AmEx, MC, V. **Map** p331 N8.

The biggest bacchanalia in town and a stopover for travelling 'entertainers' from all over, Darling wins patrons with two plush bars, dizzying drink prices and loads of improbably beautiful women.

Desire Cabaret

V jámě 8, Nové Město, Prague 1 (296 338 539/ www.desire-cabaret.cz). Metro Můstek. **Open** 5pm-5am daily. **Admission** 350 Kč. **Credit** AmEx, MC, V. **Map** p330 M7.
The latest up-and-coming strip club with massage (and more), where entry gets you access to a dozen women guaranteed to laugh at your jokes.

Goldfingers

Václavské náměstí 5, Nové Město, Prague 1 (224 193 571). Metro Můstek/tram 3, 9, 14, 24, 51, 53, 55, 56, 57, 58. **Open** 9pm-4am daily. **Admission** 450 Kč. **Credit** AmEx, MC, V. **Map** p329 N6.
Welcome to Prague's version of a Vegas revue, with a theatrical setting and dizzy dancers. And it's strictly dancing, so all's fairly innocent in the end, perhaps to the disappointment of the stag parties.

Satanela

Vílová 9, Strašnice, Prague 10 (274 816 618). Metro Strašnická/tram 7, 19, 26, 51, 55. **Open** noon-midnight daily. **Admission** varies. **No credit cards.**
Whips and chains, lab coats and fetish.

Arts & Entertainment

Theatre & Dance

The play's the thing.

Socially and politically, the Czech Republic is still struggling to shake off the last vestiges of communist rule. But, culturally, the country has leapt into the modern world, and in no areas more dramatically than theatre and dance, which were heavily censored and suppressed during the communist era.

The best time to see contemporary dance in Prague is the spring and early summer, when twin festivals provide showcases for the cream of home-grown talent. **Czech Dance Platform**, held in April, reprises the best of the previous year's offerings, which typically include performances by winners of the Sazka Prize, awarded annually for the most promising new Czech dancer. In June, **Tanec Praha** juxtaposes new Czech works with headliner performances by visiting dance troupes.

Autumn brings another festival twin bill: **Four Days in Motion** selects a new and unorthodox site every year, like an abandoned factory, to stage avant-garde dance and physical theatre pieces. **Konfrontace** offers similar fare in more traditional venues, with an emphasis on visiting companies.

But you don't need a festival to sample contemporary dance. Experimental venues like **Galerie NoD**, **Alfred ve Dvoře** and **Ponec** offer a steady stream of performances by visiting and local artists throughout the year. **Divadlo Komedie** periodically offers new dance pieces by major choreographers; watch in particular for the excellent Déja Donné. And if an established foreign contemporary dance troupe is touring Europe, a stop at the **Archa Theatre** will be on its itinerary.

If your tastes run more to classical ballet, the National Theatre ballet company (which performs at both the **National** and **Estates** theatres) and the State Opera's resident company offer a steady diet throughout the year, ranging from standards like *Swan Lake* to original works like the State Opera's *Má Vlast*, set to Smetana's anthemic music. Generally speaking, the National Theatre pieces tend to be more polished and sophisticated, and the State Opera productions more bold and colourful. The one must-see is anything by t he brilliant choreographer Jiří Kylián.

If it seems there's a theatre on every block in the city, that's not a mistaken impression; Prague has a long and dynamic theatrical tradition that manifests itself in hundreds of stages, ranging from bare wooden platforms in subterranean redoubts to the grandiloquent National Theatre. Most of the productions are in Czech, but the amount and variety of English-language theatre is growing each year.

The star of the city's English-language scene is **Švandovo Divaldo**, a refurbished theatre in the city's up-and-coming Smíchov district that's managed to retain its friendly, funky atmosphere in smart new surroundings. At any given time, Švandovo has eight to ten plays in its repertoire, about half of which are staged with English titles. This has opened up a whole new world for expats and tourists, making accessible works like Václav Havel's *Beggar's Opera*. Intermittently, the theatre also stages interesting concerts and conversation nights with visiting celebrities like Lou Reed. And it boasts a great street-front pub.

If you're in Prague during the summer, consider a visit to one of the 'Shakespeare at the Castle' performances. There's no concession for English speakers, but in most cases the work is so well known that you don't need titles to follow what's going on. There's no experience like watching *Hamlet* staged in a real castle as twilight turns to darkness and church bells in the nearby courtyard toll ominously.

Finally, for family fun, don't forget black light and puppetry (*see p253* and *p254*).

TICKETS AND INFORMATION

Many box office clerks have at least a rudimentary command of English, but you're better off buying tickets through one of the central agencies. These accept credit cards (unlike many venues), you can book via their websites or by telephone in English, and there are numerous outlets throughout the city. Bohemia Ticket International (*see p229*) is the best agency for making advance bookings from abroad for the National Theatre, Estates Theatre and State Opera. Ticketpro (*see p230*) also sells tickets for some events.

Ticket touts cluster at the National Theatre, Estates Theatre and State Opera. You can often get into sold-out (*vyprodáno*) performances, at a price. Wait until the last bell for the best deal.

For the latest theatre and dance listings, pick up a copy of the *Prague Post* or drop into your nearest branch of the Prague Information Service (*see p311*) or its website, www.pis.cz.

National Theatre. *See p253.*

Czech theatres

Alfred ve Dvoře Theatre

Divadlo Alfred ve Dvoře

Františka Křížka 36, Holešovice, Prague 7 (233 376 997/www.alfredvedvore.cz). Metro Vltavská/tram 1, 5, 8, 12, 17, 25, 26. **Open** *Box office* 1hr before performance. **Tickets** 130 Kč; 80 Kč students. **No credit cards. Map** p332 D3.

A curious and appealing modern building constructed inside a residential courtyard. Physical, visual, non-verbal and experimental theatre play here, as well as some dance and mime artists. Some performances and programme notes in English.

Archa Theatre

Divadlo Archa

Na Poříčí 26, Nové Město, Prague 1 (221 716 333/ www.archatheatre.cz). Metro Náměstí Republiky or Florenc/tram 3, 8, 24, 26. **Open** *Box office* 10am-6pm Mon-Fri; 2hrs before performance. **Tickets** 100-300 Kč. **Credit** AmEx, MC, V. **Map** p329 O3.

The superb Archa Theatre brings international avant-garde luminaries of contemporary dance, theatre and music to its versatile space. It also features the cream of the Czech new wave crop – such as Filip Topol, Petr Nikl and the Agon Orchestra. Most visiting performances are in English, and often the physical theatre pieces need no translation.

Divadlo Komedie

Jungmannova 1, Nove Mesto, Prague 1 (224 222 484/224 238 271/www.divadlokomedie.cz). Metro Můstek/tram 3, 9, 14, 24. **Open** *Box office* 10am-6pm daily. **Tickets** 70-300 Kč. **No credit cards. Map** p328 M6.

Since 2002 this progressive theatre has been home to the Pražské komorní divadlo (Prague Chamber Theatre ensemble), whose productions bring to life a mainly Czech-language body of work covering contemporary Czech, Austrian and German drama. The ensemble itself was founded in 1998 and has gone on to present many performances at European theatre festivals. Co-productions with guest productions also add colour and freshness.

Estates Theatre

Stavovské divadlo

Ovocný trh 1, Staré Město, Prague 1 (information 224 901 448/box office 224 902 322/www.nd.cz). Metro Můstek/tram 3, 9, 14, 24. **Open** *Box office* 10am-6pm daily. **Tickets** 30-1,000 Kč. **Credit** MC, V (for advance sales only). **Map** p328 M4.

Opened in 1783, this wonderful, baroque wedding cake of a building is one of the two venues for the National Theatre company (along with the National Theatre itself). The Estates hosts a rotating schedule of prestigious ballet, modern dance and opera productions. Most of the operas but very little of the drama will have English titles.

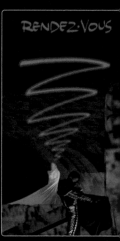

Galerie NoD

1st Floor, Dlouhá 33, Prague 1 (224 826 330/
www.roxy.cz). Metro Staroměstská or Náměstí
Republiky/tram 5, 8, 14. **Open** 1pm-1am Mon-Sat.
Tickets 60-80 Kč. **No credit cards. Map** p328 L3.
Best described as 'very Prague', Galerie NoD is a
proper artists' hangout that's decked out in surrealist decor and that stages off-centre theatre events,
experimental music and comedy nights. It also houses an art gallery and hip internet café-bar. Supported
by the Linhart Foundation, a major funder of Czech
alternative culture, it offers radical, although therefore sometimes hit-and-miss, work.

National Theatre

Národní divadlo

Národní 2, Nové Město, Prague 1 (224 901 448/
www.nd.cz). Metro Národní třída/tram 6, 9, 17, 18,
22. **Open** Box office 10am-6pm daily. **Tickets**
30-900 Kč. **Credit** AmEx, MC, V. **Map** p330 J7.
Appropriately enough, the National Theatre is an
architectural ode to Slavic myth. It was first completed in 1881, funded completely by public subscription, and then promptly burned down. The
public, not to be put off, dug into their wallets once
more and the rebuilt theatre reopened in 1883 to the
strains of Smetana's opera *Libuše*, commissioned for
the occasion and based on the tale of the prophet
who envisaged Prague. Productions include drama,
ballet and operas, usually (but not always) in their
original language, and usually with an English
translation projected above the stage. You can
reserve tickets through the theatre website up to
three months in advance but they must still be
bought at the box office – with a 20% surcharge for
reserving on the internet if you book more than 30
days before curtain. Many visitors are drawn to see
the playhouse itself. Tours are available daily.
Programmes in English and German. **Photo** p251.

Ponec

Husitská 24A, Žižkov, Prague 3 (224 817 886).
Metro Florenc, then bus 133 or 207. **Open** Box
office 6-8pm performance days. **Tickets** 140-250 Kč.
No credit cards. Map p333 A1.
What was once a cinema is now the home of the
Tanec Praha (Dance Prague) association, which is
dedicated to producing new contemporary dance
work in the theatre, as well as the annual, well-
regarded festival of the same name (*see p254*). Both
local and international dance work can be seen. Book
a ticket a week ahead and, for a fee, the Ponec can
provide babysitting services.

State Opera

Státní opera

Wilsonova 4, Nové Město, Prague 2 (224 227 266/
www.opera.cz). Metro Muzeum/tram 11. **Open** Box
office 10am-5.30pm Mon-Fri; 10am-noon, 1-5.30pm
Sat, Sun. **Tickets** 200-900 Kč. **No credit cards.**
Map p331 P7.
As elegant and sumptuous a building as the other
large venues, the State Opera nevertheless offers less
grand programming than its big-budget counterpart,

the National Theatre. The children's ballets are excellent, however, and generally well worth a visit for
their Central European charm and humour, although
the modern classical dance and opera productions
are sometimes lacking in real innovation and style.
Programmes in English and German.

Švanda Theatre

Švandovo divadlo

Štefánikova 57, Smíchov, Prague 5 (234 651 111/
www.svandovodivadlo.cz). Metro Anděl/tram 6, 9.
Open Box office 2-7pm daily; 2-9pm performance
days. **Tickets** 100-240 Kč. **No credit cards.**
A brand-new addition to the scene, the Švanda
Theatre retains its old world charm amid the
updates, and stages everything from alternative
modern Czech productions to Czech adaptations of
English-language classics and contemporary works.
The theatre is also a lively venue for music and lectures. A tiny studio in the theatre's stone vaulted
basement is still more offbeat.

Theatre on the Balustrade

Divadlo Na zábradlí

Anenské náměstí 5, Staré Město, Prague 1 (222 868
868/www.nazabradli.cz). Metro Staroměstská/tram
17, 18. **Open** Box office 2-4pm, 4.30-8pm Mon-Fri;
2hrs before performance Sat, Sun. **Tickets** 100-290
Kč. **No credit cards. Map** p328 J5.
Founded in 1958, the Theatre on the Balustrade lay
the groundwork for Czech Theatre of the Absurd. It
was the focus of much secret police attention prior
to 1989, when it harboured such dissidents as Václav
Havel and New Wave filmmaker Jiří Menzel. Havel's
celebrated play *The Garden Party* premièred here,
and his works are still part of the repertoire.

Black light theatre

The luminous 'black light' tradition has been
all the rage here since Czech performers blew
the audience away at the World Expo '58 in
Brussels. Modern practitioners use fluorescent
paint, black lights, dance, pantomime and a
large dose of kitsch to aim at tourists, generally
without text – or, if there is text, it tends to be
offered in several languages. 'Black light' is
sometimes referred to as 'Magic Lantern'
after the venue that helped popularise it.

Black Light Theatre of Jiří Srnec

Černé divadlo Jiřího Srnec

Reduta, Národní Třída 20, Staré Město, Prague
1 (257 921 835/box office 224 933 487). Metro
Národní třída/tram 6, 9, 18, 22, 23. **Open** Box
office 9am-7.30pm daily. **Tickets** 490 Kč. **No**
credit cards. Map p328 L6.
The founding father of Czech black light theatre and
co-author of productions at Laterna Magika, Jiří
Srnec has been putting on work for 40 years. His
shows, staged here and then moving from theatre to
theatre, are the true item in a genre that's normally
all kitsch grotesque and sentimentality.

Arts & Entertainment

Image Theatre

Divadlo Image

Pařížská 4, Staré Město, Prague 1 (222 314 448/222 314 548/www.imagetheatre.cz). Metro Staroměstská/ tram 17, 18. **Open** *Box office* 9am-8pm daily. **Tickets** 400 Kč. **No credit cards. Map** p328 K2.

With more dancing, modern jazz and pantomime than some black light theatres, the shows at the Image Theatre epitomise the modern style of black light. There are three to four productions per month, and clips from all the performances are medleyed in a monthly 'Best of Image' production.

Magic Lantern

Laterna Magika

Nová Scéna, Národní třída 4, Nové Město, Prague 1 (224 931 482/www.laterna.cz). Metro Národní třída/tram 6, 9, 17, 18, 22, 23. **Open** *Box office* 10am-8pm Mon-Sat. **Tickets** 300-600 Kč. **No credit cards. Map** p328 L6.

Famous for pioneering the Magic Lantern style, this company's glossy, high-tech multimedia productions are professional, though no longer at the cutting edge; more slick modern dance than traditional black light theatre, but still with an emphasis on visual tricks. The company's home is the Nová Scéna, the glass addition to the National Theatre.

Puppet theatre

Puppetry is not just for children in Bohemia – it formed an intrinsic part of the Czech National Revival in the 1800s. Though much puppet theatre is aimed at tourists, high-quality Czech puppeteers and productions appear frequently and continue to develop the medium. The Dragon Theatre (Divadlo Drak) and Cakes & Puppets (Buckty a Loutky) troupes put on inspired shows that should not be missed.

National Marionette Theatre

Národní divadlo marionet

Žatecká 1, Staré Město, Prague 1 (224 819 322/ www.mozart.cz). Metro Staroměstská/tram 17, 18. **Open** *Box office* 10am-8pm daily. **Tickets** 490 Kč. **Credit** AmEx, MC, V. **Map** p328 K3.

A somewhat touristy company, the National Marionette Theatre presents unchallenging, but popular and skilful, productions of *Don Giovanni*.

Theatre Minor

Divadlo Minor

Vodičkova 6, Nové Město, Prague 1 (222 231 351/ www.minor.cz). Karlovo náměstí/tram 3, 9, 14, 24. **Open** *Box office* 9am-1.30pm, 2.30-8pm Mon-Fri; 11am-8pm Sat, Sun. **Tickets** 80-120 Kč. **No credit cards. Map** p329 N6.

A lively and progressive Czech puppet theatre for both children and young adults. All directors and designers are contemporary guest artists invited from the worlds of opera and film as well as puppet theatre. Clown performances and productions are without words and therefore good for foreigners.

Festivals

Czech Dance Platform

Various venues (www.divadloponec.cz). **Tickets** 100-400 Kč. **No credit cards. Date** Apr.

Now into its second decade, Czech Dance Platform collects the best in Czech and Slovak dance and movement theatre every spring.

Four Days in Motion

Čtyři dny v pohybu

Various venues (www.ctyridny.cz). **Tickets** 100-200 Kč. **No credit cards. Date** Oct.

An annual festival of dance and visual theatre that brings practitioners of experimental international movement theatre and multimedia performance to an assortment of makeshift theatres inside industrial spaces around Prague. Recent festivals have been located creatively in spaces such as a former sewerage plant and an ancient sports complex. An English programme is available and there are some English-language productions.

Konfrontace

Confrontations

Various venues (www.dejadonne.com/confrontations). **Tickets** 100-250 Kč. **No credit cards. Date** Oct.

For lovers of the best in avant-garde dance, Konfrontace comes as a real treat. Focusing on the recent work of respected and idiosyncratic individuals from Europe and the USA, it brings the best of what's new in physical performance to Prague.

Mezi ploty Festival

Areál PL Bohnice, Ústavní 91, Bohnice, Prague 8 (272 773 727/www.meziploty.cz). Metro Nádraží Holešovice, then bus 152 or 200. **Tickets** 100-200 Kč. **No credit cards. Date** late May, Oct.

The Mezi ploty twice yearly two-day theatre, music and art festival is staged in the grounds of the Bohnice mental hospital on the outskirts of Prague. It features performances by top Czech theatre companies, but nothing for English speakers.

Prague Fringe Festival

Various venues (www.praguefringe.com). **Tickets** 100-200 Kč. **No credit cards. Date** June.

The city's newest theatre festival combines the best of Czech and international companies in a host of standard and unusual venues, such as the catacombs of Vyšehrad. As with the other 36 fringe festivals worldwide, any company is welcome to apply, so the result is an unpredictable cocktail – anything from cabaret to multimedia. There are some English-language productions and a full English programme.

Tanec Praha

Dance Prague

Various venues (www.tanecpha.cz). **Tickets** 150-250 Kč. **No credit cards. Date** June.

Dance Prague is the biggest and longest-running dance event in Prague, featuring world-renowned companies as well as lesser-known Czech and international dance and dance-theatre troupes.

Breaking barriers

Great theatre abounds in Prague, a city with a strong dramatic tradition. Unfortunately for visitors, very little of it is staged with an English-language audience in mind. But with a little bit of luck and good timing, you can sample some of the city's best cutting-edge theatre just a brief tram ride from the city centre, at Švandovo divadlo.

Švandovo runs a full repertoire of classical and contemporary productions, many of which are performed with English subtitles. For theatre buffs, it's a great opportunity to see how the Czechs interpret Molière and Shakespeare, or to see works like Václav Havel's *Beggar's Opera* in their proper cultural setting. And there's plenty of popular fare like *The Lieutenant of Inishmore* and *Elton John's Glasses* too.

Švandovo has a storied history. It's the third-oldest theatre in Prague (only the Estates and National theatres have been operating longer), established in 1881 by impresario Pavel Švanda as a home for his touring drama troupe. Over the decades it endured numerous artistic and political changes, as some of the name changes – Intimate Theatre, Realistic Theatre – suggest. After a long period of neglect, it went through massive renovations in the early 1990s and reopened in 2002.

The remodelling included a major technical upgrade that didn't disturb the art deco architectural touches or change Švandovo's funky atmosphere. You can relax in what feels like an informal throwback to the 1930s while enjoying state-of-the-art lighting and sound facilities in two theatre spaces – a main hall that seats 300, and a basement studio for 60. And there's a great street-front pub.

The best travelling avant-garde troupes tend to appear at Archa, but the city's resident companies are at Švandovo. And because much of their work tends to be physical theatre, you don't need subtitles to enjoy groups like Teatr Novogo Fronta or Farma v Jeskyni (Farm in the Cave). This is also a great place to catch puppet theatre for adults, most notably by Buckty a Loutky (Cakes and Puppets), which has no fear of taking on an epic like *Gilgamesh* or an American icon like Sylvester Stallone's *Rocky*.

If there's a music night on while you're in town, these are also worth catching. The programmes vary widely, from 20th-century classical works performed by ensembles from the Prague Philharmonia to Ondřej Havelka and his Melody Makers, an unlikely Czech take on the big bands of the 1940s. Švandovo also runs occasional speaker's nights featuring English-language celebrities. In the autumn of 2005 fans literally hung from the balcony to watch a conversation between Václav Havel and Lou Reed.

For pomp and star power, nothing beats a night at the National or Estates theatres. But for a bracing dose of Prague's up-and-coming theatre generation, or just a great night of entertainment, Švandovo is the ticket.

Sport & Fitness

Lean, mean Czechs are fighting their way back to glory.

Despite the communist-era sponsorship of sports being long dead, Czech sport remains strong. For a nation of only 10.2 million people, the profile of the country's sportsmen and sportswomen is remarkably high. Football star Pavel Nedvěd and teammates electrified the nation in summer 2006 with the Czech Republic's first qualification for a World Cup in over a decade, although the team's subsequent elimination in the first round dampened the celebrations. Alongside Nedvěd, a younger generation of star players has proven that Czech talent can succeed even in the sometimes cruel free market.

Similarly, young Czech players continue to flood into North America's top ice hockey league, the NHL, and the national team remains a force to be reckoned with, even if it hasn't been able to repeat its success in the 1998 Winter Olympics. And 2004 witnessed a milestone: Prague hosting the World Ice Hockey Championships, a big step forward for the sport. It was the biggest international sports event the country has hosted since the Velvet Revolution. Meanwhile, the newly completed multipurpose Sazka Arena, home of the ice-hockey side, HC Slavia Praha, provides a worthy addition to Prague's sporting infrastructure. There's even talk of a bid for the Summer Olympics in 2020.

But it's not all good news. The harsh realities of being a small player in a post-communist world have hit some sports hard. The country no longer boasts tennis superstars to rival Ivan Lendl, Martina Navrátilová or Jana Novotná, and Prague has been stripped of its ATP tournament. Similarly, the country that gave the world running legend Emil Zátopek is rebuilding after its recent lean spell in athletics (but did manage to pick up four medals, including gold for skiing, in the 2006 Winter Olympics in Turin). Quite how the sporting landscape will be changed by the ongoing shift from state-sanctioned, club-based sporting activities to more diverse, individualistic pursuits (anything from bungee jumping to golf) remains to be seen. In the meantime, the passion for obscure Czech sports, such as cycle ball, or *kolová*, is still going strong – that's football on bicycles for anyone not in the know.

From a visitor's point of view, however, the change is definitely good news. Whereas Prague's sporting facilities were once a closed shop, catering mainly to clubs of serious athletes, there's now a wide range of facilities across the city that are open to everyone.

Spectator sports

Football

AC Sparta Praha

Toyota Arena, Milady Horákové 98, Holešovice, Prague 7 (220 570 323/www.sparta.cz). Metro Hradčanská/tram 1, 8, 15, 25, 26. **Admission** *European games* 400-1,000 Kč. *League games* 60-200 Kč. **No credit cards**. **Map** p332 B3.
Though its dominance of the domestic league has been challenged of late by provincial upstarts such as Slovan Liberec and Baník Ostrava, AC Sparta remains the team to beat in the Czech football league. Despite this, Sparta is a poor relation in European

Delroy's Gym. *See p258.*

competition in comparison to teams like Barcelona and Juventus, but this hasn't stopped the team from pulling off some mighty upsets against wealthier and more famous opponents. Their 18,500-capacity stadium, known as Letná, is the country's best and hosts big international matches.

FK Viktoria Žižkov

Stadion FK Viktoria Žižkov, Seifertova 130, Žižkov, Prague 3 (222 722 045/www.fkviktoriazizkov.cz). Tram 5, 9, 26. **Admission** 60 Kč. **No credit cards. Map** p333 B2.
Despite dismal support, 'Viktorka' has enjoyed several impressive seasons in the past, along with significant redevelopment of its compact stadium. For the time being, however, the team is back in the second division and showing few signs of health.

SK Slavia Praha

Stadion Evžena Rožického, Strahov, Prague 6 (233 081 751/www.slavia.cz). Bus 143, 149, 176, 217. **Admission** 70-200 Kč; free children under 140cm. **No credit cards.**
For all its proud history, abundant talent and romantic ideals, SK Slavia struggles to maintain a distant second place behind Prague rivals Sparta, and is forced to play at Strahov's soulless Evžen Rožický stadium while their 'Eden' home in Vršovice undergoes reconstruction.

Horse racing

The Chuchle racecourse offers a regular chance to spend a day at the races. A highlight of the Czech sporting calendar is the Velká Pardubice steeplechase, the world's longest race, which is held at Dostihový spolek.

Chuchle

Radotínská 69, Radotín, Prague 5 (257 941 431/ www.velka-chuchle.cz). Metro Smíchovské nádraží, then bus 129, 172, 241, 243, 244, 255. **Tickets** 100-350 Kč. **No credit cards.**
Flat racing. The season runs from April to October, but takes a summer rest for the months of July and August. The races start at 2pm on Sundays.

Dostihový spolek

Pražská 607, Pardubická, 110km (68 miles) east of Prague (466 797 111/www.pardubice-racecourse.cz). Metro Florenc, then ČSAD bus to Pardubice. **Tickets** 110-1,200 Kč. **No credit cards.**
The Velká Pardubická steeplechase is held here on the second Sunday in October. The facilities are basic, with outdoor seating and indoor monitors for watching the action, plus a handy selection of dilapidated bars and restaurants. For those wanting to take a punt, betting works in a similar way to the British system, with two agents accepting minimum bets, of 20 Kč and 50 Kč respectively. You can bet to win (*vítěz*) or place (*místo*), or you can bet on the order (*pořadí*). Regular race meetings are also held every Saturday from May to October.

Ice hockey

HC Slavia Praha

Sazka Arena, Ocelářská ulici, Vysočany, Prague 10 (www.sazkaarena.cz). Metro Českomoravská. Tram 8, 19. **Open** *Box office* 90mins before games. **Admission** 140-1,150 Kč; 0.35 Kč children under 135cm. **No credit cards.**
Slavistas rejoiced in 2003 when their team won the championship for the first time in its history. Visitors to the tiny arena, known as 'Eden' to locals, would be hard-pressed to identify it as the home of national champions but, for sound and fury, it's hard to beat. Don't expect comfort, however: the arena is unheated and it's usually standing room only, but downing a few beers may help to ease the pain.

HC Sparta Praha

T-Mobile Arena, Za elektárnou 419, Holešovice, Prague 7 (266 727 443/www.hcsparta.cz). Tram 5, 12, 14, 15, 17. **Open** *Box office* 9am-noon, 1-5.30pm Mon-Fri. **Admission** 50-160 Kč. **No credit cards.**
Sparta's home ice rink, like Wembley Arena, was state-of-the-art when it was built, but today it's showing signs of wear and tear. The team itself, though, is well financed and always competitive. The large arena doesn't really come alive until the play-offs; regular season games are often poorly attended, yet the Sparta boys were the 2006 champs. Tickets can be bought in advance from the box office at entrance 30 or online through Ticketpro (*see p230*).

Active sports

Bungee jumping

K Bungee Jump

Nechánice 263, Eastern Bohemia, 75km (47 miles) south of Prague (777 250 126/608 768 168/ www.bungee.cz). Rates 700-800 Kč/jump. **Open** *June-Sept* 11am-5pm Sat, Sun. *Groups* by arrangement. **No credit cards.**
Come to Prague, jump off a bridge. Obvious, huh? And, during the summer, this company based south of Prague will enable you to do just that, with regular weekend plummeting sessions from Zvíkovské podhradí, a bridge high over the Vltava. Call ahead.

Climbing

Boulder Bar

V jámě 6, Nové Město, Prague 1 (222 231 244/ www.boulder.cz). Metro Můstek/tram 3, 9, 14, 24. **Open** 8am-10pm Mon-Fri; noon-10pm Sat; 10am-10pm Sun. **Rates** 70 Kč/2hrs. **No credit cards. Map** p330 M7.
Note that Prague's only bar with a climbing wall was closed for reconstruction as we went to press but is scheduled to reopen in autumn 2006. Worth checking the website for the status before heading here in your rock boots. When open, it's a popular place to tackle the cliffs in the back.

Sport Centrum Evropská

José Mártiho 31, Vokovice, Prague 6 (220 172 309/ www.sportcentrumevropska.cz). Metro Dejvická, then tram 20, 26. **Open** 7am-11pm daily. **Rates** 80 Kč/hr. **No credit cards.**

A popular and impressive indoor climbing wall within the expansive environs of Charles University's sports faculty. Booking is essential.

Cycling

City Bike

Králodvorská 5, Staré Město, Prague 1 (776 180 284/www.pragueonline.cz/citybike). Metro Náměstí Republiky/tram 5, 8, 14. **Open** Apr-Oct 9am-7pm daily. **Rates** *Rental* 100 Kč/hr; 700 Kč/day. *Tours* 250-600 Kč. **No credit cards. Map** p329 N3.

Cycle tours of the city, three times a day: 11am, 2pm and sunset. Reasonable rental fees too.

Fitness centres

In addition to the following, the central Marriott hotel also has a good gym (*see p63*).

Cybex

Hilton Prague, Pobřežní 1, Karlín, Prague 8 (224 842 375/www.cybexprg.cz). Metro Florenc/ tram 8, 24. **Open** 6am-10pm Mon-Fri; 7am-10pm Sat, Sun. **Admission** 600-900 Kč/day; 250 Kč under-15s. *Squash* 600 Kč/hr. **Membership** 3,960 Kč/mth; 19,900 Kč/6mths; 35,000 Kč/yr. **Credit** AmEx, MC, V.

It's based in the Hilton, so you pretty much know what to expect: a swanky, state-of-the-art fitness centre that also offers spa and beauty treatments.

Delroy's Gym

Zborovská 4, Smíchov, Prague 5 (257 327 042/ www.delroys-gym.cz). Metro Anděl/tram 4, 7, 10, 14. **Open** 7am-10pm Mon-Fri; 9am-10pm Sat, Sun. **Admission** *Gym* 100 Kč/9mins; 1,400 Kč/20 visits. *Taebo* 110 Kč/class. *Thai kick boxing* 120 Kč/class. *Karate* 150 Kč/class. *Thai kick boxing for children* 100 Kč/class. *Fit kick boxing for women* 120 Kč/90mins. **No credit cards.**

Delroy's specialises in martial arts but offers courses ranging from aerobics to self-defence. **Photo** p256.

Fitness Club Inter-Continental

Náměstí Curieových 43, Staré Město, Prague 1 (296 631 525/www.intercontinental.com/prague). Metro Staroměstská/tram 17. **Open** 6am-11pm daily. **Admission** *Gym* 290 Kč/90mins. *Pool, sauna & hot tub* 400 Kč/2hrs. *Turbo solarium* 20 Kč/min. *Yoga, Pilates, aqua aerobics* 250 Kč/class. **Credit** AmEx, MC, V. **Map** p328 K2.

Popular among the rich and moderately famous, this posh workout palace in a similarly posh hotel features good cardio machines and eager trainers.

HIT Fitness Flora

Chrudimská 2, Žižkov, Prague 3 (267 311 447/ www.hitfit.net). Metro Flora/tram 5, 10, 11, 16. **Open** 7am-11pm Mon-Fri; 8am-11pm Sat, Sun.

Admission *Gym* 110 Kč. *Solarium* 7 Kč/min. *Squash* 200-380 Kč. *Aerobics, Pilates, boxing, spinning* 100-120 Kč/class. **No credit cards.**

The HIT Fitness Flora is a well-equipped, modern and reasonably priced gym that is conveniently located not too far from the centre of town.

Go-karting

Kart Centrum

Výpadová 1335, Radotín, Prague 5 (602 757 475/ 602 612 492/www.kart-centrum.cz). Bus 172 or 244 from Smíchovské nádraží to Přeštínská. **Open** 3pm-midnight Mon-Fri; 11am-midnight Sat, Sun. **Rates** *Mon-Thur* 150 Kč/hr; *Fri-Sun* 200 Kč/hr. **No credit cards.**

A colourful and cheerfully tacky indoor go-karting centre in far-flung Radotín, Kart Centrum claims to be Europe's largest. There's even a water feature.

Golf

Once shunned by the communists, golf continues to gain in popularity among the country's business classes, but Prague itself is relatively poorly served. The city has only one course, the Golf Club Praha. Outside the city, in Central Bohemia, there are 18-hole courses in Poděbrady (Golf Club Poděbrady, 325 610 982, www.golfpodebrady.cz), Karlštejn (Golf Resort Karlštejn, 311 604 999, www.karlstejn-golf.cz) and Konopiště (Golf Resort Konopiště, 317 784 044, www.gcko.cz).

Erpet Golf Centrum

Strakonická 4, Smíchov, Prague 5 (257 321 177/ www.erpet.cz). Metro Anděl, then tram 12, 14, 20. **Open** Jan-Mar, Nov, Dec 8am-11pm daily. Apr-Oct 7am-midnight daily. **Rates** *Golf simulators* 300-400 Kč/hr. *Squash* 120-300 Kč/hr. *Tennis* 250-600 Kč/hr. **Membership** 18,000 Kč/yr. **Credit** AmEx, MC, V.

An indoor golf centre catering to the new-money set. Golf simulators offer the only 18-hole course in Prague's city limits (virtual, of course). There are also squash courts and tennis in the summer.

Golf Club Praha

Plzeňská 401, Smíchov, Prague 5 (257 216 584/ www.gcp.cz). Metro Anděl, then tram 7, 9, 10. **Open** 8am-dusk daily. **Rates** 400-600 Kč/9 holes; 900-1,100 Kč/18 holes. **Credit** MC, V.

A nine-hole course and driving range on a hilltop. The course can get very dry in the summer.

Horse riding

Velkostatek Tetín

Equestrian Centre
Tetín, Central Bohemia (602 633 775). **Rates** *Group lessons* 670 Kč/50mins. *Private lessons up to 4 people* 800 Kč/50mins. *Trail riding* 600 Kč/hr. **No credit cards.**

This Canadian-Austrian centre offers English language lessons, plus trail riding. Phone ahead.

Watching the birdies at **Erpet Golf Centrum**.

Get in-line

It's a long way from California, and nearly as far to the beach, yet in-line skating is the summer sport for many Czechs. The question is, why? Could it be the Czech fascination with ocean and beach culture? Or the public affinity for skimpy clothing? Whatever the answer, it's certainly not a general aptitude for skating. Despite being a nation with a great ice hockey culture, skates with wheels seem to present a whole new challenge.

It's not that Czechs are altogether bad skaters. But they have no fear. Generally, if you see a rollerblader, it's a good idea to take evasive action. Even if they look like they can skate, that doesn't mean that they know how to stop. In ice hockey, rink barriers take care of this problem.

Without argument, in-line skating is a great way to see the city's parks in summer and a convenient way to work off the carb- and fat-loaded Czech diet. Many parks now offer tracks with equipment rentals just for this purpose, perhaps because rollerbladers significantly outnumber runners. Although the local marathon boasts a pretty good turnout, casual running is still considered somewhat overrated. But classic Czech inventiveness

has the answer: why run on feet when you can run faster and smoother on wheels?

Because the authorities rightfully consider rollerblading to be a dangerous sport, the city regulates where it's legal. Shopping malls and public transport are out, we're afraid. And you're taking your life into your own hands if you try it on the city streets. Czech drivers aren't exactly known for courteousness and accident figures are staggering.

The parks that allow skates are quite pleasant, fortunately. Some, like Letná in Holešovice, offer magnificent views of Prague. Although none of these even remotely resembles the boardwalks of Venice Beach, at the least there's plenty of California tan to be spotted wheeling around.

Another popularity factor is the invariable proximity to alcohol. Virtually all blading tracks feature some sort of a refreshment stand, where beer and more is not only offered but – as in so many other places in the city – positively encouraged. This trend presents another good reason to get out of the way of rollerbladers in the parks. But remember, if you do decide to try it yourself, don't forget the knee, elbow and wrist pads.

Ice skating

USK Praha Hotel Hasa

Zimní stadion
Sámova 1, Vršovice, Prague 10 (271 747 128).
Tram 6, 7, 24. **Open** 9-11am Mon, Tue, Thur, Fri;
9-11am, 4-5.30pm Wed; 10am-noon Sat, Sun.
Admission 50 Kč. **No credit cards.**
Though still open as we went to press, the future of this big ice skating hall remains uncertain. It would be a great pity if it should eventually close since the facilities and, more to the point, the large expanse of ice, are good enough to attract figure skating and ice hockey teams. The rest of the time it's available to the public to try out jumps and spins.

Zimní stadion Štvanice

Ostrov Štvanice 1125, Holešovice, Prague 7
(602 623 449/www.stvanice.cz). Metro Florenc or
Vltavská/tram 5, 8, 12, 14, 17. **Open** 10.30am-noon
Mon; 10.30am-noon, 3.30-5pm Wed, Fri; 10.30am-noon,
3.30-5pm, 8-9.30pm Sat; 9-11am, 2.30-5pm, 8-10pm
Sun. **Admission** 100 Kč. *Skate rental* 80 Kč.
No credit cards.
A somewhat rickety-looking structure that houses two ice rinks, with reasonably generous opening hours, on an island in the Vltava.

In-line skating

See above Get in-line.

Ladronka In-Line Park

Ke Kotlářce & Plzeňska streets, Břevnov, Prague 6
(no phone/www.ladronka.cz). Metro Anděl, then bus
191 to stop U Ladronky. **Open** 2-9pm Mon-Fri;
noon-9pm Sat, Sun. **Rates** 120 Kč/hr incl. pads.
No credit cards.
The best spot for in-line skating in the city.

Letná K2

Milady Horákové & U Vorlíků streets, Holešovice,
Prague 7 (no phone/www.inlinespecial.cz). Tram 1,
8, 25, 26. **Open** noon-8pm daily. **Rates** 50Kč/hr.
No credit cards.
Good selection of in-line rentals on offer just across from Letná, a popular skating park.

Jogging

Prague's infamous pollution makes jogging, even in the parks of the central part of the city, a relatively serious health hazard. But if you must run, try one of the following areas, which are far enough from the worst of the pollution to make the endeavour somewhat less risky.

Arts & Entertainment

Divoká Šárka
Nebušice, Prague 6. Metro Dejvická, then tram 20, 26 or bus 119, 218.
Challenging, hilly trails for joggers, with bulbous rock formations and thick forests. The reservoir at the west end of the park attracts hordes of people in summer. Šárka is most easily accessible from Evropská, towards the airport.

Stromovka
Holešovice, Prague 7. Metro Nádraží Holešovice, then tram 5, 12, 14, 15, 17. **Map** p332 C1.
The most central of Prague's large parks. After the initial sprint to avoid the Výstaviště crowds, you can have the meadows to yourself.

Parachuting

Paraškola Impact
Dolní 12, Nusle, Prague 4 (261 225 431/www. paraskolaimpact.cz). Metro Muzeum, then tram 11. **Rates** *Basic course* 1,900 Kč. *Tandem jumps* 3,200 Kč. *Jump & video* 4,400 Kč. **No credit cards.**
Perhaps not the ideal name for nervous, novice skydivers, but nevertheless Impact is a well-established parachuting school that offers basic and advanced courses along with tandem jumps.

Skyservice
Kunětická 2, Nové Město, Prague 2 (724 002 002/ www.skyservice.cz). Metro Muzeum, then tram 11. **Rates** *Basic course* 2,000 Kč. *Tandem jumps* 3,200 Kč. **No credit cards. Map** p333 A2.
You can't skydive in New Town: the above listing is for the Prague office of a firm that organises jumps from airfields in Příbram or Prostějov.

Pool

Billard Centrum
V cípu 1, Nové Město, Prague 1 (224 009 235/ www.billardcentrum.cz). Metro Můstek. **Open** 11am-2am daily. **Rates** *Pool* 99 Kč/hr. *Snooker* 120 Kč/hr. *Ten-pin bowling* 150-250 Kč/hr. **Credit** MC, V. **Map** p329 N5.
An endearingly seamy pleasure palace on a back street not far from Wenceslas Square, Billard Centrum offers an impressive range of bar-room pursuits.

Harlequin
Vinohradská 25, Vinohrady, Prague 2 (224 217 240). Metro Muzeum, then tram 11. **Open** 2pm-4am daily. **Rates** 111 Kč/hr. **No credit cards. Map** p333 C3.
Play serious pool late into the night or unwind with one of Prague's best selection of arcade games.

Shooting

AVIM Praha
Sokolovská 23, Karlín, Prague 8 (222 329 328/ www.avim.cz). Metro Florenc/tram 8, 24. **Open** *Sept-June* 10am-10pm daily. *July, Aug* 2-10pm daily. **No credit cards.**

A shooting range close to the centre of town. If you want English-language assistance, phone ahead first and ask for George.

Skateboarding

Aside from the Mystic Skate Park, skaters head to the pavilion next to the National Theatre ticket office (*see p232*) and the area around the metronome in Letná park (*see p127*).

Mystic Skate Park
Ostrov Štvanice 38, Holešovice, Prague 7 (222 232 027/www.mysticskates.cz). Metro Florenc or Vltavská/tram 5, 8, 12, 14, 17. **Open** *Oct-Apr* noon-9pm daily. *May-Sept* 9am-10pm daily. **Rates** *BMX, in-line skates* 80-120 Kč. *Skateboard* 50-80 Kč. **No credit cards. Map** p332 E4.
A popular skate park on Štvanice Island in the Vltava, which has also hosted the internationally known Mystic Skate Cup for the past 12 years.

Skiing & snowboarding

While not perfect for skiers (there's a distinct lack of mountains), the winter is sufficiently cold to guarantee snow at higher elevations, so ski resorts do exist. Although most of the Czech Republic's winter resorts offer equipment rental, it's also possible to secure skis and boards in advance in the capital. Both of these shops also offer repairs.

Happy Sport
Národní obrany 16, Dejvice, Prague 6 (728 148 287/www.happysport.cz). Metro Dejvická/tram 2, 8, 20, 26. **Open** 9am-6pm Mon-Fri; 9am-1pm Sat. **No credit cards.**
Happy Sport's snowboard rentals start at 220 Kč per day, with ski rentals at 70 Kč per day, though you'll also have to pay insurance of 20-40 Kč and leave a deposit of 1,500-3,500 Kč, depending on the package. **Other locations:** Beranových 127, Letňany, Prague 9 (286 920 113); Na Pankráci 1598, Pankrác, Prague 4 (241 403 961).

Sport Slivka
Újezd 40, Malá Strana, Prague 1 (257 007 231). Metro Malostranská, then tram 12, 20, 22, 23. **Open** 10am-6pm Mon-Fri. **Credit** MC, V. **Map** p327 F6.
Good, reasonable rentals for skiers – a complete package costs 200 Kč per day.

Squash
See also p258 Erpet Golf Centrum.

Squash & Fitness Centrum Arbes
Arbesovo náměstí 15, Smíchov, Prague 5 (257 326 041/www.squasharbes.cz). Metro Anděl, then tram 6, 9, 12, 20. **Open** 7am-11pm Mon-Fri; 9am-10pm Sat, Sun. **Rates** 150-340 Kč/hr. **No credit cards.**
A smart fitness centre with four squash courts and a reasonably central location.

Arts & Entertainment

Squashové centrum

Václavské náměstí 13-15, Nové Město, Prague 1 (224 232 752/www.asbsquash.cz). Metro Můstek/ tram 3, 9, 14, 24. **Open** 7am-11pm Mon-Fri; 8am-11pm Sat, Sun. **Rates** 150-450 Kč/hr. **No credit cards. Map** p329 N6.

Three courts and a central location draw Prague's business community to this underground facility.

Swimming

Pool facilities have markedly improved since 1989, when hygiene was a genuine concern for swimmers. These days, a more significant problem is selecting a pool that isn't block-booked by swimming clubs or jam-packed with hysterical children and amorous teenagers. If you prefer open-air swimming, dam reservoirs are usually murky as soup but wildly popular among the locals, especially the one at Šárka park. Other options are hotels that have fitness centres with pools (*see p42*).

Divoká Šárka

Nebušice, Prague 6 (no phone). Metro Dejvická, then tram 20, 26 or bus 218, then 5min walk. **Open** May-mid Sept 9am-7pm daily. **Admission** 20 Kč; 10 Kč children. **No credit cards.**

An outdoor pool in an idyllic setting with a comfortable lawn area on which to lounge.

Hotel Axa

Na Poříčí 40, Nové Město, Prague 1 (222 323 967). Metro Florenc or Náměstí Republiky/tram 3, 8, 24, 26. **Open** 6-9am, noon-1pm, 5-10pm Mon-Fri; 9am-9pm Sat, Sun. **Admission** 1 Kč/min (100 Kč deposit). **No credit cards. Map** p329 O3.

The pool in this hotel is a good length and is free from hordes of shrieking children in the morning. There are decent sauna facilities available too (100 Kč per hour; 200 Kč deposit).

Plavecký Stadion Podolí

Podolská 74, Podolí, Prague 4 (241 433 952/ www.pspodoli.cz). Metro Palackého náměstí, then tram 17, 21. **Open** 6am-9.45pm (last entry 9pm) Mon-Fri; 9am-7.45pm (last entry 7pm) Sat, Sun. **Admission** *Indoor* 80 Kč/90mins; 45 Kč children. *Outdoor* 120 Kč/day. **No credit cards.**

Prague's biggest (and perpetually packed) swimming centre lies in the south of the city, along the river. A survivor from the old regime, it features outdoor lap swimming open year-round plus a 50m indoor pool that attracts serious swimmers.

Ten-pin bowling

Billard Centrum (*see p261*) also has an alley.

Bowling Bar Kingpin

Milady Horákové 109, Dejvice, Prague 6 (224 396 264). Metro Hradčanská/tram 1, 15, 18, 20, 25, 26. **Open** noon-2am daily. **Rates** 300 Kč/hr before 6pm; 400 Kč/hr after 6pm. **No credit cards.**

Ignore the intimidating graffiti-covered exterior and check out the smart interior: three Brunswick lanes at reasonable prices, complete with ultra-violet lighting and glow-in-the-dark bowling balls.

Bowling centrum RAN

V Celnice 10, Nové Město, Prague 1 (221 033 020/ www.bowlingran.cz). Metro Náměstí Republiky/tram 3, 5, 14, 24, 26. **Open** noon-2am daily. **Rates** 330-450 Kč/hr. **No credit cards. Map** p329 O3.

Eight professional AMF lanes tucked away underneath the Marriott hotel (*see p63*).

Tennis

The Czech Republic has long been renowned for its tennis stars – notably, Ivan Lendl, Martina Navrátilová, Hana Mandlíková and Jana Novotná. Although Lendl and Navratilova defected to the West, they're still national heroes. The sport has struggled to come to terms with post-communist economics, but while participation no longer reaches communist-era levels of fanaticism, there remains plenty of interest.

1. ČLTK

Ostrov Štvanice 38, Holešovice, Prague 7 (222 316 317/www.cltk.cz). Metro Florenc or Vltavská/tram 5, 8, 12, 14, 17. **Open** 7am-midnight daily. **Rates** 360-600 Kč/hr. **No credit cards.**

Ten outdoor clay courts, three of which are floodlit, plus sparkling indoor facilities (four hard courts, two clay courts) that have been newly reconstructed since 2002's floods. Booking is essential.

Tenisový klub Slavia Praha

Letenské sady 32, Holešovice, Prague 7 (233 374 033). Metro Hradčanská, then tram 1, 8, 15, 25, 26. **Open** *Jan-Mar, Nov, Dec* (indoor only) 7am-10pm daily. *Apr-Oct* 7am-9pm daily. **Rates** *Indoor* 600 Kč/hr. *Outdoor* 300-350 Kč/hr. **No credit cards.**

Eight floodlit outdoor clay courts, plus a tennis bubble for the winter months on Letná plain.

Yoga

Aruna Singhvi

Soukenická 7, Nové Město, Prague 1 (222 318 230). Metro Náměstí Republiky/tram 5, 8, 14. **Rates** 400 Kč/2hr session. **No credit cards.**

Dr Singhvi offers classical and Ashtanga hatha yoga tuition for all levels in English, Czech and German, and organises weekend retreats.

Jógacentrum Blanická

Blanická 1, Vinohrady, Prague 2 (224 253 702/ www.joga.cz/praha). Metro Náměstí Míru/tram 11. **Open** 7.30am-7.30pm Mon-Thur; 7.30am-4pm Fri. **Rates** 145-160 Kč/session. **No credit cards. Map** p333 A4.

The Blanická centre offers a huge range of yoga classes, mainly in Czech, plus information on other yoga centres across Prague.

Trips Out of Town

Getting Started	**264**
Day Trips	**266**
Overnighters: Town	
& Village	**276**
Overnighters: Country	**284**

Features

Cue the lights   272

Terezín. *See p275.*

Getting Started

Czech out.

Everyone's done Prague by now. Bragging rights these days go to those who, like the Czechs, venture out into ancient castle towns and impossibly quaint villages for a spot of the simpler life. It's an easily accessible land of rolling hills, ruins and hamlets that specialise in time travel. So leave behind the growing noise, exhaust fumes and stress of Prague – if only for a short break – and hit the highways of greater Bohemia and Moravia.

The trains of the former Eastern bloc are an excellent resource: a survivor of communist times, they may be somewhat shabby and overheated, but they're also cheap, efficient and scenic, and they go just about everywhere. Alternatively, cars can be rented for around 600 Kč a day if you shop around (*see p295*) and buses, which are also very cheap, go everywhere that the trains don't – though their drivers may cost you in other ways if you're prone to nerves. But any of these modes of transport will take you into the heartland of Central Europe and expose you to people and places totally apart from that of the capital. You're likely to learn far more about modern

Czech life by joining the locals, hiking through the countryside or pottering around a small town for an afternoon than you ever could from Old Town tours, relentless Mozart concerts and kitschy beerhalls.

Our suggested excursions are divided into the following categories: **Day trips** are places that are feasible to get to even if you had one too many beers the night before and don't make it out of bed until mid morning. As well as some picturesque towns, we've also included a selection of classic central Bohemian castles. The overnighters are places worth making more of an effort for – bearing in mind both the journey time and how much there is to see and do when you get there. We've subdivided these longer trips into **Overnighters: Town & Village** and **Overnighters: Country**. Most destinations that are listed have been included with ease of access by public transport in mind. We've also included highlights of the Czech Republic's wine country, which lies in the eastern province of Moravia and is well suited to a driving tour. If you want a city break with minimal effort, try one of the trips to **Terezín** (see *p275*), **Karlštejn** (see *p266*) or **Karlovy Vary** (see *p269*) available through Čedok (see *p311*). Rafting and cycling trips can also be arranged through Central European Adventures (Jáchymova 4, Staré Město, Prague 1, 222 328 879, www.members.tripod.com/cea51).

If you're thinking of staying overnight at any of these destinations, the tourist offices listed in the following chapters should be able to help you book accommodation. Private houses all over the country also offer rooms for tourists, which can be a chance to savour something of small-town real life.

A TOUR OF THE COUNTRY

Divided into the provinces of **Bohemia** in the north-west and **Moravia** in the south-east, the terrain of the Czech Republic offers surprisingly diverse countryside. Graced with wooded hills and little valleys, Moravia is prettiest in autumn, when a leisurely week could be spent vineyard-hopping, combing through the region's caves, and getting your music and culture fix in **Brno**, the Czech Republic's second city (see *p276*).

North Bohemia, despite inheriting a sad legacy of pollution from heavy industry, also offers the beautiful **Český ráj** (Czech Paradise; see *p284*), which is a playground for hikers and clean-air addicts. Here striking sandstone cliffs line the banks of the **Labe** (Elbe) river.

Green, mountainous southern Bohemia, with its carp ponds and dense woods, attracts pilgrims from spring to autumn, and quaint, ancient towns like **Kašperské Hory** (see *p286*) and **Český Krumlov** (see *p278*) make great jumping-off points for hikes, road trips and mushrooming expeditions.

In West Bohemia, the stars still shine as they touch the earth during the Karlovy Vary International Film Festival (see *p272* **Cue the lights**), but the hilly landscape around the famed spa towns is enchanting at any time of year, with spruce forests and hot springs.

Getting around

By bus

Many inter-city bus services depart from **Florenc** coach station (see *p291*). Bus services are more frequent in the morning. It's worth checking the return times before you leave, as the last bus back may depart disappointingly early (often before 6pm). A few buses also leave from **Nádraží Holešovice** station (see *p291*). The state bus company **ČSAD** (Křižikova 4, Karlín, Prague 8, 900 144 444, www.vlak-bus.cz) covers most destinations. It's best to pick up tickets a day beforehand for popular weekend

trips, and note that you'll need a local friend to get any use out of the Czech-only information line, which operates 24 hours, but costs 14 Kč per minute. A number of private services now offer competitive prices and times, and arguably better service and coaches.

By car

There are just a few motorways in the Czech Republic, although more are planned, so drivers are often confined to local roads. Petrol stations (some marked by a big *benzín* sign) are ubiquitous these days and now come fully stocked with microwaveable junk food and coffee machines. Petrol comes in two grades, super and special; the latter is recommended for most West European cars. Unleaded is called natural and diesel is nafta. The speed limit is 50kph (31mph) in built-up areas, 130kph (81mph) on motorways, and 90kph (56mph) everywhere else. If you have an accident, call the **Emergency Road Service** on 1240. Prices for car hire vary widely depending on whether you're renting from an international or local company (see *p295*).

By train

Trains often follow more scenic routes than buses but cover less ground and usually take longer. There are four main railway stations in Prague, but no real fixed pattern as to which destinations they serve. **Hlavní nádraží** (see *p290*) is the most central station and one of two principal departure points for international services, as well as some domestic services. Timetables can be obtained at the information windows (don't queue at a *mezinárodní* info window unless you want an international train). **Nádraží Holešovice** (see *p291*) is also principally used for international services. As a rule, **Masarykovo nádraží** (see *p290*) serves most destinations in northern and eastern Bohemia. Domestic routes to the south and west leave from **Smíchovské nádraží** (see *p291*). Train travel is priced by the kilometre and, despite recent price hikes, is still a bargain.

Hitchhiking

The usual rules of courtesy and common sense, especially for women, apply to hitchhiking within the Czech Republic. It's a time-honoured method of transport, particularly among students. As with hitching a ride in any country, travel with a friend and position yourself just outside the city limits with a sign bearing your destination of choice. You should offer to help with petrol money, though your money will most likely be waved away.

Day Trips

Forward to the past.

Castles

The Czech Republic's position at the crossroads of Europe and the meeting point of empires comes down to one thing in the end to many visitors: castles. The country is pockmarked with them. Find a rocky outcrop, preferably by the bend in a river, and you can all but guarantee that someone sometime will have built a redoubt on top. Another welcome consequence of this armoury of castles is the easy accessibility of some striking fortresses that are all within day trip distance of the city. Around an hour's train journey or drive from Prague will land you at the foot of the palatial **Karlštejn**, the architecturally impressive **Konopiště** (for both, *see below*) or the Gothic grandeur of **Křivoklát** (*see p268*).

Karlštejn

Jutting up like the royal crown it is, **Karlštejn** was once Charles IV's summer palace, perched over a lush bend of the Berounka river some 30 kilometres (19 miles) to the south-west of Prague. But it's said by castle aficionados that Karlštejn looks better from without than from within. Indeed, it was largely rebuilt in neo-Gothic style in the 19th century, but its interiors were sadly neglected.

Owing to its proximity to Prague, Karlštejn is also the Czech Republic's most visited castle, so it inevitably comes with some jostling, courtesy of uncoached tour parties. The approach to the fort is an obstacle course of overpriced snack bars and hawkers of postcards, crystal and lace. At least this 14th-century stronghold, former home to the royal jewels, offers spectacular views to reward visitors for the short but strenuous hike up to the castle entrance from the train station. And one rewarding feature when you get inside is the **Holy Rood Chapel**, its walls adorned with semi-precious stones and painted wooden panels by Master Theodoric, Charles IV's court portrait artist. There's also an altar with a diptych by Tomaso da Modena. Unfortunately, the remaining rooms can't match the chapel's splendour.

Karlštejn makes for an easy and convenient trip from Prague, but it's probably one best done early or late in the season.

Karlštejn Castle

Karlštejn (311 681 617/274 008 154/ www.hradkarlstejn.cz). **Open** *Mar, Nov, Dec* 9am-noon, 1-3pm Tue-Sun. *Apr, Oct* 9am-noon, 1-4pm daily. *May, June, Sept* 9am-12.30pm, 1-5pm daily. *July, Aug* 9am-12.30pm, 1-6pm Tue-Sun. Last tour 1hr before closing. **Admission** *Castle tour* 220 Kč; 120 Kč children, students. *Castle tour (incl Chapel)* 300 Kč; 150 Kč children, students. **No credit cards.**

There are two tours of the castle in English, but they are thoroughly tedious in any language. The second tour includes the Holy Rood Chapel but must be booked ahead and only runs July to mid November.

Where to eat

Koruna

Karlštejn 13 (311 681 465). **Open** *Jan, Mar-Dec* 10am-10pm daily Tue-Sun. **Main courses** 190 Kč. **Credit** AmEx, MC, V.

The Koruna pub is a local favourite frequented by the village's enthusiastic beer drinkers.

U Janů

Karlštejn 90 (311 681 210). **Open** *Jan, Mar-May, Sept-Dec* 11am-5pm Tue-Sun. *June-Aug* 11am-10pm Tue-Sun. **Main courses** 160-180 Kč. **No credit cards.**

A cosy, old-fashioned place with antlers hanging from the ceiling, a pleasant terrace garden and assorted schnitzels and goulash.

Getting there

By car

Karlštejn is 30km (19 miles) south-west of Prague. Take the E50-D5 or Route 5 towards Plzeň, then leave the motorway at exit 10 and follow the signs for Karlštejn.

By train

Trains leave Prague's Smíchovské nádraži or Hlavní nádraži stations for Karlštejn about every hour. The trip takes about 40mins. It's a 10min walk from the station up to the village, and a further 15mins from there up to the castle.

Konopiště

With more architectural appeal than Karlštejn and of equal historical significance, **Konopiště** is an exceptional castle in a land that's studded with hundreds. Built with seven French-style tower fortifications defending a rectangular bailey, Konopiště's contents are more stirring

Where archdukes go to play. **Konopiště**.

Trips Out of Town

than most as well, particularly the fantastic collection of weapons and the gruesomely extensive display of hunting trophies.

The castle, which dates from the 14th century, was refurbished by the Habsburgs as a hunting lodge to satisfy the predatory passions of its most famous occupant, Archduke Franz Ferdinand. He resided here with his Czech wife, Sophie, who was shot along with him at Sarajevo in 1914. The assassination, aside from the minor detail of triggering World War I, spoiled Ferdinand's accession to the throne to which he was heir. As you meander through his decadent digs it will become apparent that he, nevertheless, managed to do quite a bit of damage to the local fauna during his curtailed time on this earth. Ferdinand slaughtered nearly every kind of animal imaginable from the surrounding Sázava river woods and, incredibly, the countless trophies here represent only one per cent of the total collection. He supposedly felled an average of 20 animals a day, every day, for some 40 years.

The tour takes in sedate rooms featuring collections of wooden Italian cabinets and Meissen porcelain. A second tour of the castle, requiring a separate ticket, takes you through the archduke's private chambers, the chapel and a Habsburg version of a gentlemen's club. The castle has large grounds in which the peacocks and pheasants aren't affixed to a wall. Bears pace incessantly in the dry moat, oblivious to their unluckier brethren within.

Konopiště's popularity is second only to that of Karlštejn, so expect lots of coach parties. If you can, get there early.

Konopiště Castle

Konopiště (317 721 366/274 008 154/www.zamek-konopiste.cz). **Open** *Apr, Oct* 9am-noon, 1-3pm Tue-Fri; 9am-noon, 1-4pm Sat, Sun. *May-Aug* 9am-noon, 1-5pm daily. *Sept* 9am-noon, 1-4pm daily. *Nov* 9am-noon, 1-3pm Sat, Sun. **Admission** 180 Kč; 100 Kč concessions. 300 Kč English-speaking guide. **Credit** MC, V.

Getting there

By bus

Buses leave from Florenc station nearly every 45mins; the trip lasts a little over an hour.

By car

Konopiště is 35km (22 miles) from Prague. Go south on the D1 and exit near Benešov, following the signs for Konopiště.

By train

Hourly trains to Benešov from Hlavní nádraží take about an hour. The castle is a 2km (1.25-mile) walk from the station, or you can catch one of the infrequent buses.

Křivoklát

Křivoklát manages that unusual feat of being a living Gothic fortress. It does this, despite being founded nearly 900 years ago in 1109, by functioning as a kind of living museum to medieval life and crafts, with the resident artists and craftsmen operating a smithy and offering the resulting wares for sale. All the products are produced by ancient and authentic carpentry, ceramics and weaving techniques. It's also the perfect counterpoint to the tourist hordes that descend on overcrowded Karlštejn. Just inconvenient enough to remain peaceful, Křivoklát boasts one of the finest interiors in the country, featuring a magnificent knights' hall and royal hall plastered in late Gothic paintings and sculptures.

The drive to Křivoklát, while protecting it from too many visitors, is in fact part of the reason for visiting in the first place, following as it does the course of the Berounka river past fields, meadows and a forested hill before the castle dramatically appears, standing atop the de rigueur (for castles) lofty promontory.

Křivoklát was originally a Přemyslid hunting lodge, which was converted into a defensible castle at the beginning of the 12th century by King Vladislav I. Fires followed, along with a spate of rebuilding by the Polish King Vladislav II Jagellon, whose trademark 'W' can be seen throughout the castle. A fine altarpiece in the chapel portrays Christ surrounded by sweet-looking angels holding medieval instruments of torture. A more varied selection awaits in the dungeon, where you'll find a fully operational rack, a thumbscrew and the Rosary of Shame (a necklace made of lead weights), along with the Iron Maiden. The castle's enormous Round Tower dates from 1280. English alchemist Edward Kelley was confined here for three years after Rudolf II tired of waiting for him to succeed in turning base metals into gold. Kelley managed to wangle his release, but failed to produce the gold, and was imprisoned in a different castle where he later died, supposedly from the injuries suffered while trying to escape.

Křivoklát Castle

Křivoklát (313 558 120/www.krivoklat.cz). **Open** *May-Aug* 9am-noon, 1-5pm Tue-Sun. *Apr, Sept* 9am-noon, 1-4pm Tue-Sun. *Oct, Dec* 9am-noon, 1-3pm Tue-Sun. **Admission** *Long tour* 150 Kč; 80 Kč concessions. *Short tour* (tower only) 80 Kč; 40 Kč concessions. **No credit cards.**

Two English-language castle tours set off every half-hour up to one hour before closing time. However, for the tours to run, there has to be a minimum of five English speakers willing to take part – or a smaller number willing to pay for the cost of five tickets.

Where to eat

Hotel u Dvořáků
Roztoky 225, Křivoklát (313 558 355). **Open**
10am-11pm daily. **Main courses** 150 Kč.
No credit cards.
This is the only real place to eat near the castle. It
serves a decent menu of the usual Czech fare.

Getting there

By bus
Direct buses leave from opposite the Hradčanská
metro stop twice a day. The journey takes about 1hr
20mins.

By car
Křivoklát is 45km (28 miles) from Prague. Take
the E50-D5 in the direction of Beroun. Turn off at
junction 14 and follow the Berounka valley west, as
if going to Rakovník.

By train
Direct trains to Křivoklát are infrequent, so take one
to Beroun, which leaves from Smíchovské nádraží or
Hlavní nádraží about every half-hour (journey time
around 45mins), and change at Beroun for Křivoklát
(a further 40mins).

Towns

Although you might not immediately realise
it, there's more to life outside Prague than
castles. With the spa town of **Karlovy Vary**
(*see below*), the fascinating silver mines of
Kutná Hora (*see p270*), postcard-perfect
Mělník (*see p271*) or the dark wartime history
of **Terezín** (*see p275*) to pick from, Bohemia's
and Moravia's towns make for ideal trips out of
the capital – the only problem is having to
choose which one to fit into your day.

Karlovy Vary

The promenades and colonnades of this West
Bohemian town evoke the feeling of its past as
a celebrated spa destination. Aristocrats and
artists from Russia to the capitals of Western
Europe once trekked to Karlsbad, as it was
known until last century, for luxurious cures
and to hobnob. Though the streets are quiet
these days, and it's almost too pretty in a
picture postcard sort of way, **Karlovy Vary** is
surely the grandest and most venerated of the
nation's collection of natural hot springs. The
number of Russian visitors has jumped hugely
of late, outnumbering the usual crowd of
Germans. Things hot up even further during
the midsummer **Karlovy Vary International
Film Festival** (*see p272* **Cue the lights**),

when this assortment of boulevards and
thermal fountains becomes the Hollywood
Boulevard of Central Europe. And while it
may be best known as a cineaste's festival,
with endless screenings of new and avant-
garde films, that's not to say there aren't
plenty of opportunities to indulge in some
excited celebrity-spotting too.

Local lore has it that Karlovy Vary began its
ascent to steamy fame and fortune in 1358 when
one of Charles IV's hunting hounds leapt off a
steep crag in hot pursuit of a more nimble stag.
The unfortunate dog fell to the ground and
injured its paw, then made a miraculous recovery
as it limped through a pool of hot, bubbling
water. (Everyone say 'ahhh'.) Experts were
summoned to test the restorative waters and
declared them to be beneficial for all kinds of
ills. From that moment onwards, Karlovy
Vary's future was ensured.

The Ohře river runs through the centre
of town and disappears beneath the hulking
Hotel Thermal (IP Pavlova 11, 359 001 111,
www.thermal.cz, 1,800-2,580 Kč double),
which stands as a fascinating symbol of the
communist notion of luxury, especially when
contrasted with the gracious elegance of the
Grand Hotel Pupp. As for the town itself, the
garish boutiques and inescapable wafer shops
may not be your idea of relaxation – but you
can always retreat to the parks, which are
adorned with busts of some of the spa's more
famous guests, or self-medicate with a few
Becherovkas – the famous local herbal liqueur
that works magic with its base of the region's
pure spring water.

Vojenské State Baths
Lázně 3, Mlýnské nábřeží 5 (353 119 111). **Open**
7am-3pm Mon-Sat. **Admission** 400 Kč. **Credit**
AmEx, MC, V.
Not as plush as the Pupp baths, naturally, but you'll
get a thorough and renewing treatment here, admin-
istered by no-nonsense pros.

Where to stay & eat

Grand Hotel Pupp
Mírové náměstí 2 (353 109 630/www.pupp.cz).
Open *Harfa baths* 8am-3pm Mon-Sat. *Castle baths*
7.30am-7.30pm daily. *Grand restaurant* noon-3pm, 6-
10pm daily. **Rates** 4,890-6,500 Kč single; 6,300-7,800
Kč double; 10,000-12,000 Kč suite; apartments up to
38,000 Kč. **Main courses** 350-600 Kč. **Credit**
AmEx, MC, V.
If you splurge on this lavish hotel – said to be the
finest in the country – ask for a room that has not
yet been refurbished; several have been rather
unsympathetically 'modernised'. If you're feeling
flush, the elegant restaurant is worth a visit, as is
the hotel spa, the Harfa and Castle Baths.

Promenáda

Tržiště 31 (353 225 648/www.hotel-promenada.cz).
Rates 1,990-2,490 Kč single; 1,340-1,690 Kč double;
5,960-6,960 Kč apartments. **Main courses** 200-350
Kč. **Credit** AmEx, MC, V.
This respectable restaurant, still something of a rarity in Karlovy Vary, is a cut above the usual goulash-and-dumplings places – with reasonably quick service, freshwater trout and steaks. If you can't afford the Pupp's dining room, then try dinner here.

Resources

Čedok

Dr Davida Bechera 21-23 (353 222 994/353 223 335). **Open** 9am-6pm Mon-Fri, 9am-noon Sat.
No credit cards.
Information and tickets for events and concerts other than the film festival. For the difficult task of obtaining tickets for the festival, *see p272* **Cue the lights.**

Tourist information

*Information Centre of town of Karlovy Vary,
Lázeňská 1 (353 224 097).* **Open** *1 Apr-15 Nov*
9am-7pm Mon-Fri; 10am-6pm Sat, Sun. *16 Nov-31
Mar* 9am-5pm Mon-Fri; 10am-5pm Sat, Sun.
No credit cards.
The staff here are helpful, multilingual and have information and tickets for all local events, except, of course, the Karlovy Vary International Film Festival. You don't think you can just roll up and buy tickets from the tourist office, do you?

Getting there

By bus

Buses run at least every hour from Prague's Florenc station starting at 8am (journey time about 2hrs 30mins). The private bus service Asiana (841 111 117, www.asiana.cz) also runs a bus hourly from Florenc metro and bus station, the Dejvická metro and Ruzyně Airport.

By car

Karlovy Vary is 130km (81 miles) west of Prague on the E48.

By train

Trains leave Prague's Hlavní nádraží three times a day (journey time about 4hrs).

Kutná Hora

The soaring, twin peaks of **Kutná Hora's** cathedral are visible for miles around the town, testifying to its former role as a key source of wealth in Bohemia. An ancient gem that has served as a movie set more than once, Kutná Hora's fame and status were secured in the late 13th century with the discovery of silver. A Gothic boom town was born, and for 250 years Kutná Hora was second in importance only to Prague in this part of the nation.

However, all this might not be readily apparent when you get off the train. Don't worry, and don't be put off by the blighted concrete tower blocks that cluster around **Sedlec** station like bad teeth. The UNESCO-designated World Heritage Site old centre is only a couple of kilometres (1.25 miles) away to the south-west. But before carrying on there you might want to stop at Sedlec's incredible bone chapel, the **Ossuary**, where 40,000 skeletons, arranged in myriad forms, have been used as decoration and statuary. The Cistercian abbey, which was founded in 1142 and now houses a tobacco factory, established the ossuary a few hundred metres north of the church on Zámecká so that the monks might have an appropriate memento mori.

To get from Sedlec to Kutna Horá's old centre either walk or take a short bus ride (catch the bus marked 'Centrum') and you'll find yourself at the town's crowning glory, the **Cathedral of St Barbara**. Designed in Peter Parler's workshop, it's a magnificent 1388 building with an exterior that outclasses even Parler's St Vitus's Cathedral in Prague. St Barbara was the patron saint of silver miners and their guild emblems decorate the ceiling of the building. For an idea of what life was like in a medieval mine, head to the Hrádek or Little Castle. Here, the **Czech Silver Museum** kits you out in protective suits and hard hats for a trip down into the tunnels.

Cathedral of St Barbara

Kostel sv. Barbory
Barborská (327 512 115). **Open** *Nov-Mar* 10am-noon, 1-4pm Tue-Sun. *Apr, Oct* 9am-noon, 1-4.30pm Tue-Sun. *May-Sept* 9am-6pm Tue-Sun. **Admission** 30 Kč; 15 Kč children. **No credit cards.**
A Gothic marvel.

Czech Silver Museum & Medieval Mine

České museum stříbra
Barborská 28 (327 512 159/www.cms-kh.cz).
Open *Apr, Oct* 9am-5pm Tue-Sun. *May, June,
Sept* 9am-6pm Tue-Sun. *July, Aug* 10am-6pm
Tue-Sun. *Nov* 10am-4pm Tue-Sun. Last entry 90mins before closing time. **Admission** 60-130 Kč; 30-80 Kč consessions; 400 Kč tours in English.
No credit cards.
If you want to see the silver mine, a guided tour is compulsory. Booking is advisable.

Sedlec Ossuary

Kostnice Zámecká (327 561 143). **Open** *Nov-Mar* 9am-noon, 1-4pm daily. *Apr-Sept* 8am-6pm daily. *Oct* 9am-noon, 1-5pm daily. **Admission** 35 Kč; 20 Kč children. **No credit cards.**
The Ossuary is a gruesome collection of human bones, arranged over the ages into fantastic shapes and chandeliers by monks as a reminder of the eventual fate of all flesh.

Where to eat

Harmonia
Husova 105 (327 512 275). **Open** 10am-11pm daily.
Main courses 70-180 Kč. **No credit cards**.
Harmonia serves up good, traditional Czech food on
a beautiful terrace.

Resources

Tourist information
*Tourist Information Kutná Hora, Sankturinovský
dům, Palackého náměstí 377 (327 515 556/327 512
378).* **Open** *Apr-Sept* 9am-6pm daily. *Oct-Mar* 9am-
5pm Mon-Fri; 10am-4pm Sat, Sun. **No credit cards**.
The helpful staff here can arrange for stays in private houses as well as providing the usual range of
tourist-related information.

Getting there

By bus
Buses leave 11 times a day from Florenc station
(journey time about 75mins).

By car
Kutná Hora is 70km (44 miles) from Prague. Head out
through Žižkov and follow signs to Kolin to Route 12;
then change to road 38 to Kutná Hora. A scenic
alternative is Route 333 via Říčany, further south.

By train
Trains run from Hlavni nádraži or Masarykovo
nádraži daily and take 50mins. The main Kutná Hora
station is actually located in Sedlec. Local trains meet
express trains coming from Prague and take visitors
into Kutná Hora proper.

Mělník

An important town in the transplanting of
viniculture from France to the Czech lands,
Mělník is a quiet little hamlet within easy
reach of Prague, offering pastoral views
from its impressively restored castle. Just 33
kilometres (20 miles) north of Prague, the town
also features yet another bizarre ossuary to go
with its bucolic appeal. And, opera buffs note,
the castle vineyards produce Ludmila wine,
which is the tipple that Mozart supposedly
drank while he composed *Don Giovanni*.

The main sights are concentrated near
the lovely **castle**, now more château than
stronghold. It occupies a prime position on a
steep escarpment overlooking the confluence
of the Vltava and Labe rivers, which was the
inspiration for Smetana's anthem to Bohemia,
Ma Vlast ('My Country').

Although a settlement has existed here
since the tenth century, it was Charles IV who

Why Smetana loved his country. **Mělník**.

Cue the lights

In the film business they say do Cannes for the deals and visit Venice for the glitz. Karlovy Vary's just for film lovers.

KVIFF, as everyone calls the **Karlovy Vary International Film Festival**, is admired by directors worldwide who tire of being hermetically sealed from real audiences at the posh festivals. In Karlovy Vary backpackers are welcome – in fact, they're normally in the audience. After those with tickets are seated, the backpackers are often slipped in to sit in the aisles.

Despite this, KVIFF, which runs in the first week of July, is in the same industry class as Berlin, Cannes, Locarno, San Sebastian and Venice, the elite A-category festivals. And it's got to be the only one where just about anyone can score a ticket for any screening, with the possible exception of opening and closing nights. Usually for well under 100 Kč.

So how do you get your ticket? Ah, the eternal question. As much as public access to the films is deliberately maintained, this is, after all, a Czech festival; naturally there's got to be a complicated ticketing system involved.

You might think it would be a good idea to book through the internet. Think again. Although the festival website is indeed brimming with gossip, complete screening schedules, interviews and a downloadable festival newspaper in PDF format you can't prebook (or even reserve) your tickets online.

In fact, tickets can only be bought with cold, hard cash at the festival headquarters, the hulking Hotel Thermal, in person, once the festival has actually started. Which adds a

introduced vines to the region from his lands in Burgundy. He also established a palace for the Bohemian queens, who would come here to escape Prague until the end of the 15th century.

The castle was rebuilt during the 16th and 17th centuries, when it lost much of its medieval character as a fort as it was transformed into something more like a palace. Recent restitution laws have returned it to the ownership of the Lobkowicz family – once among the most powerful in Bohemia before being driven into exile – from whom the property was expropriated by the communists.

You can tour the castle's interior and, even better, take a separate tour round the splendidly gloomy wine cellars, wherein viniculture is followed, appropriately enough, by tastings and a chance to walk over an arrangement of thousands of upturned bottles.

Opposite the castle is the late Gothic **Church of Ss Peter and Paul** (Kostel sv. Petr a Pavel). The ossuary in the crypt consists of skulls and bones piled to the ceiling. Two

speakers precariously balanced on top of a stack of femurs broadcast a breathless English commentary delivered in Hammer horror style, accompanied by Bach organ music. The site was established as a burial place for plague victims in the 16th century and sealed off for the next few hundred years. However, in 1914 a professor from Charles University cracked open the vault and brought in his students to arrange the 15,000 skeletons he found within. The end result includes the Latin for 'Behold death!' spelled out in skulls, and a cage displaying the remains of people with physical deformities.

The main square below the castle, **Náměstí Míru**, is lined with typically Bohemian baroque and Renaissance buildings. The fountain dates from considerably later.

Mělník Castle

Svatováclavská 19 (315 622 127/www.lobkowicz-melnik.cz). **Open** 10am-5pm daily. **Admission** *Castle tour* 70 Kč; 50 Kč children. *Wine-tasting tour* 110 Kč. **No credit cards.**

certain thrill of the chase, of course, to the uncertainty of travelling thousands of miles in order to see a film that you haven't even got tickets for.

There's a different ticketing system every year and almost as much fun as the festival and the attendant parties is figuring out how to get in to see something. The festival authorities seem to have settled on a card system (thereby entitling everyone to wear their piece of plastic around their necks on a nifty keepsake lanyard) under which you can at least buy a fixed number of tickets one day before screenings and a package of extras for a set price once you arrive and register. The cost usually ranges from 200 Kč for a one-day pass to 1,000 Kč for the whole nine days. In addition, the card gets you into several fest-only areas, such as the Thermal basement bar, Peklo (or Hell), and you're also entitled to go in free at the last minute to any screenings that are not sold out.

If you'd like more tickets than that, you simply buy them – but be advised you may be told you can only purchase one per movie per pass. Also, the Czechs being big on promptness, you may not get in at all, even with a ticket, if you're not present 10-15 minutes before start time.

Which leaves only the sleeping and eating arrangements to sort out.

The festival, helpfully, has a housing desk located right on the ground level of the Thermal (just follow the thematic displays that lead in), with hundreds of rooms listed, the accommodation varying from dormitories that are little more than barracks to small pensions and hotels.

If, like most people, you feel more comfortable with at least some idea of where you'll be crashing when you arrive, you can at least book a room in advance via the Good Bed Agency (Kříženeckého náměstí 322, Prague 5, 267 073 456, www.goodbed.cz).

After that, it's pretty much a free-for-all. Schmooze with the national film contingent from a small country and you're bound to get into some great parties. If you can wangle it, try to get into those at the Grand Hotel Pupp, but you'll probably have fun even at Lázně 1, one of the town's famous mineral spas that's converted into a throbbing techno nightclub for the duration of the festival.

Typically about 60 per cent of the 10,000-plus festival passes are sold to the general public, the rest of the tickets going to journalists, filmmakers and industry types.

So come out to Karlovy Vary and live a little dangerously. Who knows? You may end up talking residuals with the likes of Robert Redford, Sharon Stone, Michael Douglas, Morgan Freeman, Lauren Bacall...

Ossuary

Kostnice

Church of Ss Peter & Paul (315 622 337). **Open** 9.30am-12.30pm, 1.15-4pm Tue-Fri; 10am-12.30pm, 1.15-4pm Sat, Sun. **Admission** 25 Kč; 15 Kč children. **No credit cards.**
Proving that ossuaries are not solely a medieval Czech fixation, this was devised 80 years ago.

Where to eat

Castle vinárna

Svatováclavská 19 (315 622 121). **Open** 11am-6pm Tue-Sun. **Main courses** 195-575 Kč. **Credit** AmEx, MC, V.
The Castle vinárna is the swankiest dining room in town: the crockery is embossed with the insignia of the Lobkowicz family, the vaulted walls are painted a delicate peach colour and it's one of the better restaurants in the whole region.

Restaurace Stará Škola

Na vyhlídce 159 (no phone). **Open** 11am-11pm daily. **Main courses** 190 Kč. **No credit cards.**

Restaurace Stará Škola is a basic restaurant, close to the Church of Ss Peter and Paul, that does a decent plate of steak and chips with a more than decent backdrop: the terrace has a beautiful view over the surrounding countryside and the confluence of the Vltava and Labe rivers.

Resources

Tourist information

Náměstí Míru 30 (315 627 503). **Open** *May-Sept* 9am-5pm daily. *Oct-Apr* 9am-5pm Mon-Fri.

Getting there

By bus

There are roughly 15 departures a day from Prague's Holešovice metro and train station (journey time 50mins).

By car

Mělník is 33km (21 miles) from Prague. Head north out of Prague on Route 608; follow signs to Zdiby, then Mělník on Route 9.

The culture of death. **Terezín**.

Terezín

Originally known as Theresienstadt, when it was built as a fortress town in 1780 on the orders of Emperor Joseph II to protect his empire from Prussian invaders, **Terezín** was briefly given its old name back when the Nazis took it over in 1941. It was here that Red Cross inspectors, visiting as a result of Danish pressure to ascertain what had happened to Danish Jews, were duped with propaganda into believing that it was a model resettlement site when in fact the entire town was functioning as a holding camp for Jews en route to death camps further east. Of 140,000 men, women and children who passed through Terezín, 87,000 were sent east, most of them to Auschwitz. Only 3,000 of these were to return alive. Another 34,000 people died within the ghetto of Terezín itself.

Now little more than a Czech army barracks town, Terezín's atmosphere is still distinctly eerie, with lifeless, grid-pattern streets. The Nazis expelled the native population, few of whom chose to return after the war.

The **Ghetto Museum** screens documentary films of wartime life here in several languages. Possibly the most chilling contains clips from the Nazi propaganda film, commonly called *The Führer Gives a Town to the Jews* although its correct title is *Terezín: A Documentary Film of the Jewish Resettlement*, part of the sophisticated strategy to hoodwink the world. Red Cross officials visited the camp twice and saw a completely staged, self-governing Jewish community with a flourishing cultural life. A Jewish prisoner, Kurt Gerron, directed the film. After shooting the film, most of the cast, and the director himself, were deported to Auschwitz and killed.

The harrowing ground-floor exhibition of artwork produced by the children of Terezín has now been removed to Prague's Pinkas Synagogue. Upstairs there is a well laid-out exhibition on the Nazi occupation of Czechoslovakia. Decrees of discriminating measures against Jews are detailed – including, in a telling detail of the systematic dehumanisation of the Jews by the Nazis, the certificate that a customer in a pet shop intending to buy a canary was required to sign, which promised that the pet would not be exposed to any Jewish people.

A 15-minute walk back down the Prague road brings you to the **Small Fortress**, which was built at the same time as the larger town fortress. The Gestapo established a prison here in 1940, through which 32,000 political prisoners passed. Some 2,500 died within its walls. The approach to the Small Fortress passes through a cemetery containing the graves of 10,000 Nazi victims with, in the middle, a giant wooden cross.

The whole fortress is now a museum, and a free map (available from the ticket office) assists exploration of the Gestapo's execution ground and of courtyards and cells, some of which held more than 250 inmates at a time. The former SS commander's house is now a museum with displays detailing the appalling physical condition the inmates endured.

Ghetto Museum

Muzeum ghetta
Komenského 411, Terezín (416 782 225/www .pamatnik-terezin.cz). **Open** *Nov-Mar* 9am-5.30pm daily. *Apr-Oct* 9am-6pm daily. **Admission** *Museum* 160 Kč; 130 Kč children, students. *Museum & Small Fortress* 180 Kč; 140 Kč children, students. **No credit cards.**

Small Fortress

Malá pevnost
Malá pevnost, Terezín (416 782 225). **Open** *Nov-Mar* 8am-4.30pm daily. *Apr-Oct* 8am-6pm daily. **Admission** 180 Kč; 140 Kč children, students. **No credit cards.**
Guided tours run for groups of ten-plus. It is best to book ahead.

Where to eat

Light meals can be had in the former guards' canteen inside the entrance to the Small Fortress.

Atypik

Máchova 91, Terezín (416 782 780). **Open** 9.30am-9pm Mon-Fri; 11am-9pm Sat; 11am-6pm Sun. **Main courses** 100Kč. **Credit** AmEx, MC, V. The best bet for a goulash within Terezín town.

Hotel Salva Guarda

Mírové náměstí 12, Litoměřice (416 732 506/ www.salva-guarda.cz). **Open** 11am-11pm Mon-Thur, Sun; 11am-1am Fri, Sat. **Main courses** 150 Kč. **Credit** AmEx, DC, MC, V. A traditional restaurant, serving decent Czech cuisine.

Resources

Tourist information

Náměstí ČS armády 179, Terezín (416 782 616). **Open** 8am-5pm Mon-Thur; 8am-1.30pm Fri; 9am-3pm Sun.

Getting there

By bus

Buses leave Florenc station once every hour (journey time 60-75mins).

By car

Terezín is 50km (31 miles) north west from Prague. Join Route 8 or the E55 at Holešovice, via Veltrusy, and follow it to Terezín.

Trips Out of Town

Overnighters: Town & Village

Hip little Brno is a low-key Prague, with crypts and clubbing; the wine country's a treat; and ancient towns put you in the middle of your own legend.

Brno

Compact, party-loving and spiked by tall medieval spires, the town of **Brno** is a cultural and visual oasis in the middle of the otherwise placid rolling hills and plains of Moravia, the Czech Republic's eastern half. Its population of 400,000, which is almost half that of Prague, makes it the republic's second city and it has a lot more going for it than just cathedrals, crypts and cobbled streets. A thriving cultural scene and nightlife nearly as varied as Prague's add up to an engaging but easygoing city without the capital's pretensions.

Having originated as a ford across the Svratka river – the city's name is derived from the old Slavonic word for mud – around 1100, Brno prospered from its location on important trade routes and swiftly became the capital of the Great Moravian Empire of old before it was annexed by the Czechs.

The transfer thoroughly Catholicised the city and Brno's greatest treasures today reflect that. Rising above the old centre of town is the vertiginous **Petrov Cathedral**. Although the cathedral is a bit of a disappointment on the inside, it balances atop a suitably dramatic hill in defiance of heresy. Its 'noon' bells sound at 11am, a tradition that originated during the Swedish siege of Brno, when the town was supposedly saved by an ingenious monk who knew that the attackers had decided to fight only until noon and then move on.

The **Capuchin Crypt**, just below Petrov Cathedral and adjoining the former coal market, **Zelný trh**, features a sobering confrontation with what awaits us all: death. Through the action of constant draughts, several of the nobles and monks who were buried in the crypt have been mummified and they are now on display, many still in their original garb. If you haven't yet exceeded your squeamishness quota, further lugubrious sights await in the 13th-century fortress of **Špilberk**, on a hill even higher than Petrov's, across Husova from the old centre. Here you can visit the labyrinth of dungeons, the casemates, where Emperor Joseph II had various prisoners suspended on the dank and dreary walls. Thankfully, they are no longer on display.

Back in the fresh air, Brno's streets revive you with their engaging possibilities for turning up the unexpected around every corner. Centuries-old pubs such as Pegas, as well as the fruit and veg market on Zelný trh and half a dozen impressively ornate baroque churches are within strolling distance of the main square, **náměstí Svobody**. A sight that almost every tourist sees is the **Dragon of Brno** – actually an overstuffed crocodile – hanging outside the tourist information bureau. It is said to be the gift of a Turkish sultan who rather exaggerated its status – hence the name.

The club scene in Brno is alive with its own particular vitality and the influence of local talents is typified by Iva Bittová, an avant-garde singer/violinist. You might even run into a local musician or performance artist at **Spolek**, the city's newest bookshop-café, which is also a good spot to try Moravia's greatest claim to fame: the delectable white wines.

For information on trips to the **Moravský kras**, or Moravian Caves, near Brno, *see p287*.

Capuchin Crypt

Kapucínská krypta
Kapucínské náměstí (542 213 232/www.volny.cz/kapucini.brno). **Open** *15 Feb-Apr* 9am-noon, 2-4.30pm Tue-Sat; 11-11.45am, 2-4.30pm Sun. *May-Sept* 9am-noon, 2-4.30pm Mon-Sat; 11-11.45am, 2-4.30pm Sun. *Oct-15 Dec* 9am-noon, 2-4.30pm Tue-Sat; 11-11.45am, 2-4.30pm Sun. Closed 15 Dec-14 Feb. **Admission** 40 Kč; 20 Kč concessions. **No credit cards.**

Špilberk Castle

Špilberk 1 (542 123 611/www.spilberk.cz). **Open** *Casemates* May-Sept 9am-6pm daily. Oct-Apr 9am-5pm Tue-Sun. *Observation tower* May-Sept 9am-6pm Tue-Sun. Apr-Oct 9am-5pm Sat, Sun. **Admission** 50-120 Kč; 30-60 Kč concessions. **No credit cards.**

Petrov Cathedral

Katedrála sv. Petr a Pavla
Petrov 9 (543 235 031). **Open** *Crypt* 11am-5pm Mon-Sat; 11.45am-5pm Sun. **Admission** 35Kč. **No credit cards.**

Trips Out of Town

Brno 900 years ago.

Nightlife

Charlie's Hat
Kobližná 12 (542 214 459). **Open** 11am-4am
Mon-Thur; 11am-5am Fri; noon-5am Sat; 3pm-4am
Sun. **No credit cards.**
A handy labyrinth of bars and a patio with DJ action
and local bands blaring forth.

Krokodýl fashion club
Kounicova 1 (732 307 766/www.krokodylclub.cz).
Open 8pm-2am Mon-Thur; 8pm-6am Fri, Sat.
No credit cards.
American, European and African hits.

Where to eat & drink

Restaurant Pegas
Jakubská 4 (542 210 104). **Open** 9am-midnight
Mon-Sat; 10am-10pm Sun. **Main courses** 150 Kč.
Credit AmEx, DC, MC, V.
A classic, grand-scale beerhall with its own brew,
served in wheat and cinnamon varieties. Foodwise,
expect schnitzel and goulash galore, credibly done.

Šermířský klub L.A.G.
Kopečná 50 (543 237 068). **Open** 11am-2pm,
3.30pm-midnight Mon-Fri; 5pm-midnight Sat, Sun.
Main courses 170 Kč. **No credit cards.**
The waiters, who come garbed in medieval tunics at
this ye olde Moravian inn, serve up massive stuffed
potato pancakes. It is also the headquarters of the
local historic sword-fighting club.

Spolek
Orlí 22 (542 219 002). **Open** 10am-10pm Mon-Sat;
1-10pm Sun. **No credit cards.**
A short walk from the bus station, this bookshop-
café is a hip but unpretentious hangout.

Where to stay

Hotel Amphone
*Třída kapitána Jaroše 29 (545 428 310/www.
amphone.cz).* **Rates** (incl breakfast) 990 Kč single;
1,490 Kč double. **Credit** AmEx, MC, V.
Although it's not situated in a particularly enchanting building, Amphone is one of the most convenient
and friendly hotels in Brno.

Hotel Royal Ricc
*Starobrněnská 10 (542 219 262/www.romantic
hotels.cz/royalricc).* **Rates** (incl breakfast) 3,200-3,500
Kč single; 3,500-4,000 Kč double; 6,500 Kč single
suite; 7,000 double suite. **Credit** AmEx, MC, V.
The Hotel Royal Ricc is set in some particularly luxurious Renaissance-era quarters, with timbered ceilings, stained-glass windows and staff who take their
job as being to make your stay enjoyable. Modern
amenities nicely balance the historic trappings.

Resources

Tourist information
*Tourist Information Brno, Radnická 8, Brno (542
211 090).* **Open** Oct-Mar 9am-5pm Mon-Fri; 9am-
5pm Sat; 9am-3pm Sun. *Apr-Sept* 8.30am-6pm
Mon-Fri; 9am-6.30pm Sat, Sun. **No credit cards.**
Staff here can book rooms at hotels and pensions.

Getting there

By bus
Buses leave Prague for Brno every half hour, from
Florenc station. The trip takes around 2hrs 30mins.

By car
Brno is 110km (77 miles) east of Prague. Take
the E50/E65 motorway directly to Brno.

Trips Out of Town

Second only to Venice. **Český Krumlov**.

By train

Trains leave from Hlavní nádraží 15 times a day and take about 3hrs 30mins.

Český Krumlov

Český Krumlov is a beloved escape from Prague. Its rocky setting in the foothills of the **Šumava mountains** makes it ideal for sport activities and hiking – all of which can be co-ordinated through the tourist information centre (*see p279*) – while the town itself has both a fine castle to explore and a lively, lovely centre, with a delectable beer of its own. It's dominated by an enormous and well-cared-for **castle complex**, which seems to grow straight out of a rocky escarpment, overlooking beautiful countryside, gabled inns and pubs overflowing with fine dark Eggenberg and Budvar, the local brews.

In 1992 the tiny town so impressed UNESCO with its beauty that it was declared second in importance only to Venice on the World Heritage list. Krumlov's fantastic pink Renaissance tower rises high above the town, idyllically positioned on a double loop of the Vltava river on the eastern edge of the forested region. The streets below are a labyrinth of cobbled alleyways filled with medieval architecture, craft shops and homely eateries.

The castle is one of the most extensive complexes in Central Europe, with 40 buildings in five courtyards. Founded before 1250, the fortress was adopted by the Rožmberk clan in 1302. As the family's wealth and influence increased, it was transformed into a palace.

Cross the dry moat to enter, noting the bored bears that roam below. The tower was redone as a whimsical pink-and-yellow Renaissance affair in 1591, topped with marble busts and gold trimmings. The five-tiered **Plášťový Bridge** is equally spectacular, linking sections of the palace perched on two steep escarpments. For the best view descend to the **Stag Gardens** (Jelení zahrada) and look upwards. In summer, the extensive formal garden is one of the venues that hosts the **Český Krumlov International Music Festival**, which features everything from classical ensembles to costumed period performances to Roma music.

The highlights of the castle tour include a gilded carriage built in 1638 to convey presents to the Pope, and the Mirror and Masquerade Halls, both of which are triumphs of the arts of stucco and trompe l'oeil.

On the opposite side of the Vltava from the Castle district (Latrán) is **Nové Město** (New Town), laid out a mere seven centuries ago. On Horní street is the impressive **Church of St Vitus** (Kostel sv. Víta), c. 1439, the long tower of which is visible from all parts of town.

But it's not just a tourist town. Residents work in graphite mining, at the Eggenberg Brewery or at the nearby paper mills. Before World War II, Český Krumlov was part of the predominantly German-speaking Sudetenland and so was annexed by Hitler in 1938. The majority of the region's German-speaking inhabitants were expelled in 1945 and the town's centuries-old bicultural life came to an end.

Note that castle entry is only with the hour-long tour. Last visit an hour before closing.

Trips Out of Town

Český Krumlov Castle

Zámek 59 (380 704 711/www.castle.ckrumlov.cz).
Open *Castle* Apr-Oct 9am-5pm Tue-Sun. June-Aug
9am-6pm Tue-Sun. *Tower* Apr-Oct 9am-4.30pm Tue-
Sun. June-Aug 9am-5.30pm Tue-Sun. **Admission**
80-100 Kč; 50 Kč concessions. **Credit** MC, V.

Český Krumlov International Music Festival

*Various venues (Auviex 241 445 404/www.
auviex.cz).* **Admission** varies according to venue.
Date Aug.

Where to eat, drink & stay

Hospoda Na louži

Kajovská 66 (380 711 280). **Open** 10am-11pm
daily. **Rates** 1,350-2,300 Kč. **Main courses** 150 Kč.
No credit cards.
A good place to sample south Bohemian cuisine, Na
louži is an old-fashioned and central pub with traditional food and walls covered in tin signs. The
rooms are a bit like your granny's spare room, with
creaky floors but wall-to-wall charm.

Hotel Růže

Horní 154 (380 772 100/www.hotelruze.cz). **Open**
Restaurants 7am-10pm daily. **Rates** 2,400-4,600 Kč
single; 3,800-6,100 Kč double; 5,300-7,800 Kč suite.
Main courses 350-700 Kč. **Credit** AmEx, MC, V.
A restoration of this towering Renaissance pile, a
former Jesuit college, has created one of the country's most luxurious hotels. The carved wood furnishings, ceiling beams, three restaurants, cellar bar
and amazing views fit in with the town perfectly.
The modern attractions feel almost out of place but
they're all there: a fitness centre and pool, business
amenities, top-notch service and a disco.

Hotýlek a Hospoda u Malého Vítka

Radniční 27 (380 711 925/www.vitekhotel.cz). **Rates**
(incl breakfast) 900-1,200 Kč single; 1,200-1,650 Kč
double; 2,100-2,950 Kč suite. **Credit** MC, V.
A restored Renaissance inn just off the main square
of the city's Vnitřní Město district. Children and pets
welcome. A lobby pub sells light snacks.

Pension Ve věži

*Pivovarská 28 (380 711 742/www.ckrumlov.cz/
pensionvevezi).* **Rates** (incl breakfast) 900-1,200 Kč
double. **No credit cards.**
Phone well ahead to reserve one of the four rooms
inside this fortress tower with metre-thick walls.

Resources

Tourist information

*Tourist Information Český Krumlov, Náměstí
Svornosti 2 (380 704 622).* **Open** *July, Aug* 9am-
8pm daily. *June, Sept* 9am-7pm daily. *Apr, May,
Oct* 9am-6pm daily. *Nov-Mar* 9am-5pm daily.
No credit cards.
In addition to finding rooms, staff can book canoe
and boat tours down the Vltava.

Vltava Travel Agency

Kájovská 62 (380 711 978/www.ckvltava.cz). **Open**
Jan-Mar 9am-noon, 12.30-5pm Mon-Sat. *Apr-Dec*
9am-noon, 12.30-5pm daily. **Credit** MC, V.
The staff here can book rooms, horse rides, canoe
trips and numerous other activities in the area.

Getting there

By car

Český Krumlov is 136km (85 miles) from Prague.
Either leave on the Brno motorway (D1-E50) and
then take the E55 at Mirošovice past Tábor and
České Budějovice, then the 159 road; or go via Písek
leaving Prague on Route 4, towards Strakonice.

By train

The trip from Hlavní nádraží takes 3hrs 30mins and
includes a change at České Budějovice.

By bus

Buses leave Prague for Český Krumlov 6 times a day,
from Florenc bus station. The trip takes 2hrs 50mins.

Olomouc

Fairly remote, located some 280 kilometres
(174 miles) east of Prague in the heart of
Moravia, **Olomouc** has a picturesque town
centre – a UNESCO World Heritage Site – and
a willingness to stay up late, unlike other pretty
old Czech hamlets, thanks to its university
students. Strolling through the main squares
(the town has three, cascading downhill from
Václavské náměstí to **Horní náměstí** to
Dolní náměstí) of an evening, you'll see
parties heading to the latest happening bar
or club, such as **Barumba**.

Otherwise, the town is a quiet, friendly
escape from Prague or a good stopoff on the
way to Poland, the **Jeseniky mountains** or
the impressive nearby **Bouzov Castle**. Dating
back at least to 1017, Olomouc was a prize city
in the Czech Přemyslid land grab that ended
the Great Moravian Empire. During the Hussite
wars, the town, like much of Moravia, sided
with the Catholics, saw Hussite rebels executed
on its squares and was rewarded with a dozen
handsome churches.

The **Old Town** (Staré Město) is defined by
a bend of the Morava river and is criss-crossed
by tiny lanes that twist up to **St Wenceslas
Cathedral**. No doubt it was the last thing
Václav III saw before he was murdered in the
chapter house in 1306. It later inspired an
11-year-old Mozart to compose his *Sixth
Symphony*. The neighbouring **Přemyslid
Palace**, with foundations dating back to 1204,
is an evocative pile with Romanesque windows
but no other pulse-quickening contents.

Don't miss the socialist realist makeover of
the **Town Hall Astronomical Clock Tower**

Trips Out of Town

on Horní náměstí, which includes a mosaic of a scientist discovering means of better living for all through chemistry.

St Wenceslas Cathedral

Kostel sv. Václava
Václavské náměstí (585 224 236). **Open** 9am-6pm daily. **Admission** free.
The towering spire of this neo-Gothic wonder more than merits the hike to the city's uppermost square.

Nightlife

Barumba

Mlýnská 4 (777 799 607). **Open** 7pm-3am Mon-Thur; 9pm-6am Fri, Sat. **Admission** free-120 Kč. **No credit cards.**
Barumba is a combination internet café, split-level student bar and dance club, which often has DJs and live acts from Prague on its programme. It's a major scene at weekends.

Where to eat, drink & stay

Arigone

Univerzitní 20 (585 232 351/www.arigone. web.worldonline.cz). **Rates** (incl breakfast) 1,690 Kč single; 1,990 Kč double; 2,990 Kč suite. **Open** *Restaurant* 6am-midnight daily. **Main courses** 60-300 Kč. **Credit** DC, JPC, MC, V.
Arigone, a restored townhouse hotel with raftered ceilings and warm service, also boasts a popular restaurant and bar.

Restaurace U Kapucínů

Dolní náměstí 23 (585 222 700). **Open** 10am-10pm Mon-Tue, Sun; 10am-11pm Fri-Sat. **Main courses** 200-350 Kč. **Credit** MC, V.
With regional cuisine well-done and frothy pints on tap, Restaurace U Kapucínů supplies just the basics on atmosphere, but it's good and cosy.

Resources

Tourist information

Town Hall, Horní náměstí (585 513 385/www. olomoucko.cz). **Open** 9am-7pm daily. **No credit cards.**
The staff here can book rooms and arrange tours to Bouzov Castle just outside town. You can also pick up full listings of concerts, clubs, and food and drink in the area.

Getting there

By bus

Four buses depart Prague's Florenc station for Olomouc daily. The trip takes about 3hrs 30mins.

By car

Olomouc is 280km (174 miles) east of Prague. Take the E50/E65 south-east towards Jihlava and Brno, merging on to the E462 south of Brno and on to Olomouc.

By train

Trains leave hourly from Hlavní nádraží and take about 3hrs to reach Olomouc.

Tábor

Though it's hard to imagine this friendly little town as a key military stronghold against the superior Habsburg forces, that's just what it was some 600 years ago. A band of religious radicals founded Tábor in 1420 following Jan Hus's execution. Led by the one-eyed general Jan Žižka, 15,000 Taborites battled the Catholic forces for nearly 15 years. Their policies of equal rights for men and women and common ownership of property did not endear them to the ruling classes, and the Taborites were eventually crushed by more moderate Hussite forces under George of Poděbrady. A statue of Žižka sits astride a hill overlooking Prague; Tábor honours him with a more modest sculpture in its main square.

The **Hussite Museum** features more, though it's almost entirely in Czech – a highlight is Žižka's unusual military innovation, a crude sort of tank consisting of cannons balanced on a wagon. The museum also runs tours of the underground passages (used as stores and refuges during the Hussite wars) in much of the centre. The main square, **Žižkovo náměstí**, is the spoke from which labyrinthine streets and alleys radiate. Their confusing layout was a ploy to befuddle Tábor's enemies.

Hussite Museum

Náměstí Mikuláše z Husi 44 (381 252 242). **Open** *Apr-Oct* 8.30am-5pm daily. *Nov-Mar* 8.30am-5pm Mon-Fri. **Admission** *Museum* 60 Kč; 30 Kč concessions. *Tunnel tours* 40 Kč; 20 Kč concessions. **No credit cards.**

Where to eat & drink

Beseda

Žižkovo náměstí (381 253 723). **Open** 10am-10pm daily. **Main courses** 150-300 Kč. **Credit** MC, V.
Bohemian bureaucrats like their beer, and this beer-hall that is actually within the town hall serves the usual meat platters, warming soups and dumplings.

Where to stay

Hotel Dvořák

Hradební 3037 (381 251 290/www.geneahotels.cz). **Rates** 2,050-2,250 Kč single; 2,250-2,850 Kč double; 2,950-4,500 Kč suite. **Credit** AmEx, MC, V.
The newest and most stylish accommodation in Tábor is set square in the town's old heart, with great service, an impressive kitchen, and amenities such as a sauna, fitness centre and massage that were previously unknown in places of this size.

Tábor.

Černý leknín

Příběnická 695 (381 256 405). **Rates** (incl breakfast) 1,290 Kč single; 1,550 Kč double. **Credit** MC, V.
A quaint Gothic villa that provides Tábor's cosiest accommodation.

Resources

Tourist information

Infocentrum, Žižkovo náměstí 2 (381 486 230/ www.tabor.cz). **Open** *May-Sept* 8.30am-7pm Mon-Fri; 10am-4pm Sat, Sun. *Oct-Apr* 9am-4pm Mon-Fri.

Getting there

By bus

About 6 buses depart Prague's Florenc station and Praha Roztyly for Tábor daily (journey time 2hrs).

By car

Tábor is 82km (51 miles) south of Prague. Take the D1 south-east towards Jihlava and Brno, exiting at junction 21 to motorway 3 south.

By train

Trains depart from Hlavní nádraží and the journey takes about 1hr 35mins or the train to Vienna from Prague stops in Tábor.

Telč

Lovely, deathly quiet and with an incongruous surrealist art collection in its palace, **Telč**, while maybe not a prime destination in itself, is worth the trip if you're passing through the region on the way to Krumlov or Tábor. With a main square chock-full of immaculately preserved Renaissance buildings, still partly enclosed by medieval fortifications and surrounded by lakes, Telč is yet another Czech town that is on UNESCO's World Heritage list. The rhomboid central square dates back to the 14th century, with a delicate colonnade delineating three sides of the meeting place. This and the photogenic gabled houses were added in the 16th century by Zachariáš of Hradec. A trip to Genoa and a fortuitous marriage to Katerina of Wallenstein gave this Renaissance man the inspiration and means to rebuild the town following a devastating fire in 1530. Each of the pastel-hued buildings has a different façade adorned with frescoes, sgraffito or later baroque and rococo sculptures.

On the narrow end of the square stands the onion-domed 17th-century Jesuit church on one side and the Renaissance castle on the other, their exteriors the work of Italian architect Baldassare Maggi, hired by Zachariáš in 1552 to spruce up his new home. The coffered ceilings of the Golden and the Blue Halls, and the monochrome trompe l'oeil decorations that cover the Treasury are among the finest Renaissance interiors in Central Europe.

The Marble Hall exhibits fantastic armour, while the African Hall contains a collection of hunting trophies.

The castle also houses a small municipal museum, which features an ingenious 19th-century mechanical nativity crib and a permanent exhibition of works by the Moravian surrealist Jan Zrzavý (1890-1977). The castle's peaceful gardens stretch down to the lake and make for a lovely afternoon walk.

Telč Castle

Státní zámek (567 243 943). **Open** *Apr, Oct* 9am-noon, 1-4pm Tue-Sun. *May-Aug* 9am-noon, 1-5pm Tue-Sun. **Admission** 70-80 Kč; 35 Kč concessions. **No credit cards**.

Tours are conducted in Czech but you can pick up a detailed English text at the ticket counter.

Where to eat

Šenk pod věží

Palackého 116 (567 243 889). **Open** 11am-10pm daily. **Main courses** 150 Kč. **No credit cards**.

Of the various restaurants in Telč, this is the most charming place to eat. It serves good Czech fare, and has friendly staff and a terrace.

Where to stay

Hotel Celerin

Náměstí Zachariáše z Hradce 43 (567 243 477/ www.hotelcelerin.cz). **Rates** 1,000-1,100 Kč single; 1,350-1,600 Kč double. **Credit** AmEx, DC, MC, V.

A romantic and friendly restored hotel of 12 rooms on the town's main square.

Pension Privát Nika

Náměstí Zachariáše z Hradce 45 (567 243 104). **Rates** from 400 Kč single; 700 Kč double. **No credit cards**.

Comfortable and good value, the Pension Privát Nika, a family-owned hotel, may be somewhat unprepossessing but it is nonetheless friendly.

Resources

Tourist information

Tourist Information Telč, Náměstí Zachariáše z Hradce 10 (567 112 407). **Open** *May, Sept* 8am-5pm Mon-Fri; 10am-5pm Sat, Sun. *June-Aug* 8am-6pm Mon-Fri; 10am-6pm Sat, Sun. *Oct* 8am-5pm Mon-Fri; 10am-4pm Sat, Sun. *Nov-Apr* 8am-5pm Mon, Wed; 8am-4pm Tue, Thur; 8am-3pm Fri. **No credit cards**.

The staff here can book accommodation, plus fishing, horse riding and hunting expeditions for around 300 Kč to 500 Kč for a day excursion.

Getting there

By bus

Buses leave several times daily from Florenc bus station and twice from Roztyly. The journey takes just under 4hrs.

By car

Telč is 150km (93 miles) south-east of Prague. Head out of Prague in the direction of Brno on the E50/D1 motorway. At Pávov follow the signs to Jihlava; at Třešť follow signs to Telč.

Telč me to the river, drop me in the water.

Trips Out of Town

Overnighters: Country

What are you waiting for? There's Czech paradise in them there hills, lakes and valleys.

If you go down to the woods today, you're sure of a big **Sumava**.

Spring and summer send Czechs to every lake, meadow and wine cellar outside of Prague, as does just about every fine weekend. Berry-picking, snoozing in the grass and jumping into lakes are all part of the ritual, and all can be done easily in the densely forested mountains of the **Šumava region**, near **Kašperské Hory** or **Český Krumlov** (*see p278*).

The great outdoors is a favourite getaway and, though it's often basic, renting a cottage is the best form of accommodation to be had – camping is technically prohibited in the Šumava region. Alternatively, you could always pitch a tent at one of the campsites in **Český ráj** (*see below*), a lush area of lakes, woods, rocks and castles.

The Czech-language *Šumava* by Miloslav Martan is a handy, somewhat decipherable guide that contains trail maps along with pictures of regional flora and fauna, while a new agency, **Česká Pohoda**, can arrange stays at rustic country cottages at rates significantly lower than those that even small town inns charge. So, if your head needs clearing, take the cure and hit the back roads.

Česká Pohoda

Pod sokolovnou 693, Prague 4 (241 402 222/777 048 638/www.ceskapohoda.cz). Metro Pražského povstání, then bus 193. **Open** 10am-4pm Mon-Fri. **Rates** (per person) 1,000-3,000 Kč/wk. **No credit cards.**
This agency can organise stays in cabins in some of the prettiest corners of Bohemia. The majority involve roughing it, but the lovely surroundings are worth the sacrifice.

Český ráj

Easier to reach than Šumava, and hence more crowded, **Český ráj** is still Czech paradise (in case you think we're making extravagant eschatological claims, that's what the name means). Its lake, castles, woods and rock formations draw hundreds of fans in warm weather. As Central European wildernesses go, this picturesque region – a protected national park – is very nearly worthy of the name, even if it is concentrated in a small area. Though accessible by road, the best way to explore it is on foot; even reluctant amateurs can cross the region in two days.

The neighbouring towns of **Jičín** and **Turnov** provide a good base from which to begin your exploration, as signposted trails can be followed almost from the town centre of each. A good way to see Český ráj is to get the train to one town and then hike over to the other for the return train journey.

The greatest concentration of protruding rocks is to be found around **Hrubá skála**: follow any of the marked footpaths from the village and you'll soon find yourself surrounded by these pockmarked giants. The **Hotel Zámek** and **Hotel Štekl** make the best bases for exploring the region. The most useful map is the *Český ráj Poděbradsko*, which is available at any decent Prague bookshop.

Supreme among ruined castles in the area is **Trosky** (the name means 'ruins'). Its two towers, built on dauntingly inaccessible basalt outcrops, form the most prominent silhouette in the whole region. The taller, thinner rock goes by the name of Panna (the Virgin), while the smaller one is Bába (Grandmother) – feminine appellations that are somewhat misleading given Trosky's hulking muscular mass. In the 14th century Čeněk of Vartemberk undertook a monumental feat of medieval engineering by building a tower on top of each of the two promontories, with interconnecting ramparts between them. The towers remained virtually impregnable through the medieval, pre-gunpowder, period, as they could only be reached by an ingenious wooden structure that could be dismantled in times of siege, leaving invaders with the choice of scaling the impossibly steep rocks or, more likely, beating a hasty retreat. In the 19th century Trosky Castle became a favourite haunt of Romantic poets, painters and patriots. Now you too can climb to the base of the tower for outstanding views of the countryside.

From 1 April until 31 October climbers can scale the sandstone pinnacles in the region. Simply pay the 45 Kč entry fee at any park attendant's booth – you'll need to bring your own climbing gear, however, as there's nowhere to rent equipment.

Trosky Castle

Rovensko pod Troskami (481 313 925/www. trosky.cz). **Open** *Apr, Oct* 8.30am-4pm Sat, Sun, public hols. *May-Aug* 8.30am-6pm Tue-Sun. *Sept* 8.30am-4pm Tue-Sun. **Admission** 40 Kč; 25 Kč concessions. **No credit cards. Photo** p286.

Where to eat & stay

There are plenty of places close to every main tourist sight that offer filling, if uninspiring, traditional Czech food.

We've listed convenient hotels below, but if you want to sleep out, there are campsites – although most people just seem to pitch their tent on any appealing plot of land. Those who do prefer the convenience of a campsite should try Autocamp Sedmihorky, or Podháj (no phone) just north-west of Hrubá skála on the Libuška creek, which has the same rates and season as Sedmihorky.

Autocamp Sedmihorky

Turnov (481 389 160/162/www.campsedmihorky.cz). **Open** year-round. High season 1 Apr-31 Oct. **Rates** *Tents* from 30 Kč/night. *Cars* from 30 Kč/night. *Trailers* from 50 Kč/night. *Additional charge* 25 Kč/adult; 20 Kč/child. **No credit cards.**
This campsite is convenient for exploring the sandstone rocks and as a starting point for hopping on the 268km-plus (167 miles) of cycling tracks. You can also rent bungalows for up to seven people from 200 Kč per night.

Hotel Štekl

Hrubá skála, Turnov (481 389 684). **Open** *Restaurant* 8am-10pm daily. **Rates** (incl breakfast) 680 Kč single; 890-1,300 Kč double. **Main courses** 150 Kč. **Credit** AmEx, MC, V.
A decent dining room with views over the surrounding valleys. The hotel is well worn and far from plush but perfectly serviceable.

Hotel Zámek

Castle Hrubá skála (481 659 111/www. hrubaskala.cz). **Open** *Restaurant* 10am-10pm daily. **Rates** 1,250 Kč single; 1,960 Kč double. **Main courses** 250 Kč. **Credit** AmEx, MC, V.
Fabulous location, good prices and fantastic views from the ivy-covered turret rooms. The food in the restaurant here is traditional Czech, with service that's a bit better than in Prague.

Getting there

By bus

Buses go every 30mins from Černý Most metro station (Line C) to Jičín. If you opt not to walk from here (which would be an ambitious hike), catch a bus to Hrubá skála-Borek. Buses from Prague's Florenc station go daily to Turnov, where you change for a train to Doubravice. From there it's a 20min walk to Hrubá skála.

By car

The Český ráj area is about 90km (56 miles) north-east of Prague. Follow signs to Mladá Boleslav and join the E65 via Route 10 to Turnov. Jičín is 23km (14 miles) south-west of Turnov. Hrubá skála and Trosky are both just off Route 35, which is the Turnov–Jičín road.

Trosky Castle. *See p285.*

By train

Five trains a day leave Hlavní nádraží for Turnov. There are local connections from Turnov to Hrubá skála and Malá skála. A local train plies the line between Jičín and Turnov.

Kašperské Hory

Thoroughly isolated and ensconced in the **Šumava National Forest** (www.ckrumlov. cz/uk/region/soucas/t_napasu.htm), yet only a two-hour drive from Prague, **Kašperské Hory** is an idyllic little town that was built on gold mining, which was guarded by the nearby fortress of **Kašperk**. With performing knights and damsels, and cold 11-degree beer, the ruins make for a worthwhile five-kilometre (three-mile) hike from the town centre.

Once part of the Sudetenland annexed by Hitler, the soothingly quiet country here is now on the edge of one of the largest forest reserves in Central Europe with a vast area of 685 square kilometres (264 square miles) protected. The massif is one of the oldest in Europe and its large woods are home to deer, eagles, otter and lynx, as well as being the source of the Otava and Vltava rivers. For those wishing to explore, the forest, which is on the UNESCO Biosphere Reserve list, is criss-crossed with marked trails. The area gets a lot of rain, so be prepared.

Dining on river fish and Staropramen is your reward upon your return from the mountain trials. For a second day, particularly for those suffering from blistered feet and an excess of trees, another option is the **Šumava Museum**, featuring stuffed versions of any wildlife species you may have missed in the woods plus dusty historic and glass-making exhibits.

In the surrounding countryside, horse riding is a local passion; the accommodating **Aparthotel Šumava 2000** can set you up for a day in the saddle.

Šumava Museum

Muzeum Šumava
Náměstí 140 (376 582 530/376 582 609). **Open** *May-Oct* 9am-5pm Tue-Sat; 9am-noon Sun. **Admission** 30 Kč. **No credit cards**.
Excellent collection of Bronze Age and medieval relics, plus local flora and fauna.

Where to stay

Aparthotel Šumava 2000

Náměstí 8, Kašperské Hory (376 546 910/fax 376 546 910/www.sumava2000.cz). **Rates** (per person) 820-1,180 Kč. **Credit** AmEx, DC, MC, V.
Modern, equipped with a sauna and happy to set you up with hiking maps, trekking gear or horse riding.

Pension Soňa

Karlova 145, Kašperské Hory (376 582 454/728 736 777). **Rates** (per person) 250-270 Kč. **No credit cards**.
Basic but friendly family-run guesthouse that is near the central square.

Resources

Tourist information

Městské informační centrum, Náměstí 1, Kašperské Hory (376 503 411/376 503 412/www. sumavanet.cz/khory). **Open** *Jan-Aug* 7.15am-noon, 12.30-5pm Mon, Wed; 7.15am-noon, 12.30-4pm Tue, Thur, Fri. *Oct-Dec* 7.15am-noon, 12.30-5pm Mon, Wed; 7.15am-noon, 12.30-4pm Tue, Thur; 7.15am-3pm Fri. **No credit cards**.

Getting there

By bus

Nine buses from Na Knížecí (Metro Anděl, line B) leave for Vimperk or Sušice, where you need to change for Kašperské Hory.

By car

Kašperské Hory is 120km (75 miles) from Prague. Take motorway 4 south 90km (56 miles) to Strakonice. From here, take road 22, about 18km (11 miles) west to Horažďovice, then road 169, which is another 20km (12.5 miles) south-west to Sušice. From here take road 145 and follow it 19km (12 miles) south to Kašperské Hory.

Moravský kras

The stars of the Czech Republic's many cave systems (*jeskyně*) are the ones north of the Moravian capital of Brno (*see p276*). Busloads of children and even pensioners (the rarefied air is touted as a cure for allergies and asthma) go on the guided tours through the chilly limestone caves – a welcome respite in the hot months, but remember to bring a jumper. As this is a phenomenally popular summer attraction, long queues are inevitable.

The **Moravský kras** (Moravian Caves), comprising a series of 400 holes, is by far the most concentrated and accessible network of caves in the Czech Republic. Best visited as a day trip from Brno, these are limestone caves, created over 350 million years by the erosive action of acidic rainwater and underground streams. The **Kateřinská, Sloupsko-Šošůvské** and **Balcarka** caves are all within striking distance of Brno.

If you're looking to do all your caving in one go, your best bet is the **Punkevní jeskyně**, which is the largest cave in the country. Some three kilometres (two miles) of the cave's 12-kilometre (7.5-mile) length are open to the public. Passages of stalactites give way to the colossal **Macocha Abyss**: 140 metres (459 feet) deep, it was formed in part by the collapse of the ceiling of a cave further below. The tour then sends you down the narrow tunnels by boat. Visiting is a distinctly up-close experience: the passages are barely wide enough for the boats, and you'd likely be impaled by a stalactite if you stood up.

Arrive early in peak season as tours can sell out by mid morning. It's even better to reserve a place by phone, as queues can be long.

There are other attractions easily accessed by car. The most popular is the spectacular Gothic castle of **Pernštejn**; others include the Napoleonic battlefield of **Austerlitz** (Slavkov) and the **Alfons Mucha Museum** (515 322 789, closed Jan-May, Nov-Dec, Mon) housed in the Renaissance château of **Zamek Moravský Krumlov** (515 321 064, www.mkrumlov.cz).

Moravian Caves

Moravský kras
Skalní mlýn (516 413 575/www.cavemk.cz). **Open** Punkevni jeskyně *Jan-Mar* 8.40am-2pm Tue-Sun. *Apr-June* 10am-3.50pm Mon, 8.20am-3.50pm Tue-Sun. *July, Aug* 10am-5pm daily. *Sept* 10am-3.50pm Mon, 8.20am-3.50pm Tue-Sun. *Oct* 8.20am-3.40pm Tue-Sun. *Nov, Dec* 8.40am-2pm Tue-Sun. Other caves Feb-Oct. **Admission** *Punkevni jeskyně* (incl chairlift to entrance & boat ride) 100 Kč adults; 80 Kč concessions. *Other caves* 50 Kč adults; 20 Kč students; free under-6s. **No credit cards**.

Where to eat & stay

Hotel Skalní Mlýn

Skalní Mlýn (516 418 113). **Open** *Restaurant* 7am-11pm Mon-Fri; 8am-11pm Sat, Sun. **Main courses** 150 Kč. **Rates** (incl breakfast) 980 Kč single; 1,320 Kč double. **Credit** AmEx, MC, V.
A popular place and the best base for the caves – plus there's a reasonable restaurant.

Resources

Tourist information

Tourist Information Brno, Old Town Hall, Radnická 8, Brno (542 211 089). **Open** *Oct-Mar* 9am-6pm Mon-Fri; 9am-5pm Sat; 9am-3pm Sun. *Apr-Sept* 8.30am-6pm Mon-Fri; 9am-6.30pm Sat, Sun. **No credit cards**.
The staff here can book rooms in and around the town and can also supply you with maps, brochures and other information.

Getting there

By bus

Buses run roughly every hour between Brno and Prague (journey time 2hrs 30mins). From bus station Florenc.

By car

Brno is 202km (126 miles) south-east of Prague. The D1 motorway runs all the way to Brno. The caves are 22km (14 miles) north-east of Brno.

By train

Trains to Brno from Prague run hourly and take 3-4hrs. About 12 trains a day leave Brno for the nearby town of Blansko. Local buses then take you onwards to the caves. A tourist train travels between the Punkevni caves and the centre of Skalni Mlýn, synchronised with the opening hours, from which the other three caves are accessible.

Staring into the abyss. **Balcarka Cave.**

Directory

Getting Around	**290**
Resources A-Z	**296**
Vocabulary	**313**
Further Reference	**314**
Index	**316**
Advertisers' Index	**322**

Features

Travel advice	297
Weather report	311

Directory

Getting Around

Arriving & departing

By air

Prague's only airport, the expanded and modernised **Ruzyně**, is 20 kilometres (12.5 miles) north-west of the city centre and unfortunately it is not directly accessible by metro or tram. Some of the more expensive hotels offer a pick-up service from the airport if you book ahead, and a regular public bus service runs back and forth. For information in English on arrivals and departures call 239 007 576; for other airport information call 239 007 007.

CONNECTIONS TO THE CITY

Taxis are regulated but still often charge very high prices, and the firm with the current airport contract is known for hiring particularly keen drivers. The ride (about 20 to 25 minutes) should cost around 500 Kč to the centre of Prague. The price consists of 26 Kč boarding fee and the charge should be 17 Kč per kilometer. Check at the airport information kiosk for the going rate to your destination. For an honest taxi driver you could try taking your luggage to the customs depot (where people accept air-freighted shipments from abroad) and phoning one of the reputable taxi services that we list to come and fetch you, such as AAA or Profi (see p293). Note that neither company will pick you up at the regular Arrivals/ Departures area.

EXPRESS AIRPORT BUS

The private bus service ČEDAZ (220 114 296) runs transport between the airport and Metro Dejvická and Náměstí Republiky for 90 Kč (6am to 9pm daily). The white vans leave from outside the Arrivals terminal. The friendly, English-speaking Prague Airport Shuttle (602 395 421, www.prague-airport-shuttle.com) service provides door-to-door transport, as well as transport in Prague and throughout the Czech Republic. After hours, night bus No.510 departs from the airport to Divoká Šárka, from where you can catch night tram No.51 to the centre of the city.

LOCAL BUS

Four local buses run from the airport to metro stations about every 20 minutes from 5am to midnight. Bus **No.119** departs from the airport to Metro Dejvická (green Line A), bus **No.108** goes to Metro Hradčanská (green Line A) and bus **No.179** connects to Metro Nové Butovice (yellow Line B). You can also catch bus **No.100** in front of the main terminal for an express service to the Zličín metro stop on the yellow Line B, which enters the city from the south. This is the cheapest, slowest and most crowded alternative. If you have lots of bags, you'll need to buy extra tickets for them. The buses depart from the stands in front of Arrivals. There you'll find orange public transport ticket machines (you'll need 20 Kč in change). There are also ticket machines and an information office in the airport lobby. For ticket details, see p291.

By rail

International trains arrive at the Main Station (Hlavní nádraží, sometimes called Wilson Station or Wilsonovo nádraží) and Holešovice Station (Nádraží Holešovice). Both are on the red Line C of the metro. Caution: it is easy to get off at Holešovice thinking that it is the main railway terminus. If your train stops at both, wait for the last stop.

The centrally located **Main Station** is a beautiful art nouveau building, with communist-period lower halls. It has several food stalls and a PIS (Prague Information Service) office in the main hall. There are also public showers and a 24-hour left luggage area in the lower hall. At night the station becomes a home for homeless people, drug addicts and hustlers, so it's not a good idea to hang around there or in the small park nearby – locals have nicknamed it Sherwood Forest as so much illegal redistribution of wealth goes on here. Enough said.

24-hour rail infoline

221 111 122
Telephone the above number for national and international timetable information. English is spoken. For ticket prices, call 840 112 113.

Hlavní nádraží

Main Station
Wilsonova, Nové Město, Prague 2 (972 241 883). Metro Hlavní nádraží/tram 5, 9, 11, 26.
Map p329 P5.

Masarykovo nádraží

Masaryk Station
Hybernská, Nové Město, Prague 1 (224 611 111/221 111 122). Metro Náměstí Republiky/tram 3,

5, 14, 24, 26. **Open** International ticket office 7.30am-6pm daily. **Map** p329 Q4.

Nádraží Holešovice

Holešovice Station
Vrbenského, Holešovice, Prague 7 (220 806 790). Metro Nádraží Holešovice/tram 12, 25.
Map p332 E1.

Smíchovské nádraží

Smíchov Station
Nádražní, Prague 5 (221 111 122). Metro Smíchovské nádraží/tram 12.

By coach

Florenc coach station may be the least pleasant place in Prague. However, it's on two metro lines (yellow Line B and red Line C) so it's relatively easy to make a quick getaway. Late arrivals can take the night tram or a taxi or stay in one of the hotels on nearby Na Poříčí. The 24-hour coach infoline charges 14 Kč per minute.

Florenc station

Křižíkova 4, Prague 8 (infoline 900 144 444/www.csad.cz/ www.uan.cz/www.florenc.info). Metro Florenc/tram 8, 24.

Getting around

Walking is the best way to see the relatively compact centre of Prague. Every twist of the city's ancient streets reveals some new curiosity. If you're going further afield, the city has an excellent, inexpensive and almost 24-hour integrated public transport system that will get you just about anywhere you want to go. But in winter, you may have to put up with some noisome co-passengers who treat them as rolling bedrooms. **Driving** in Prague takes some getting used to and it really isn't worth the bother if you're only going to be here on a short visit. **Taxis** are ubiquitous but unreliable – pretty cheap if you find an honest driver; ruinous if you let one rip you off.

The communists dammed the Vltava so thoroughly that there isn't any real freight or passenger traffic on the river– just pleasure cruises. An assortment of eccentric conveyances – including horse-drawn carriages, bike-taxis and a Disney-esque electric train that takes tourists up to the castle and back – can all be found in Old Town Square.

INFORMATION

There are bus and/or tram connections and usually taxi stands at every metro station, and all of Prague's railway stations are connected to the metro network.

The Prague Public Transport company, DP, runs around the clock. Day service is from about 5am to about ten minutes past midnight daily. Peak times are 5am to 8pm Monday to Friday. From midnight to 5am, night buses and trams take over. English-language content, downloadable maps, the latest route changes and incredibly arcane facts about public transport are on the DP website (www.dp-praha.cz). Metro, tram and bus lines are indicated on most city maps. Timetables can be found at every tram and bus stop. The times posted apply to the stop where you are – which is highlighted on the schedule. If your destination is listed below the highlighted stop, you are in the right place.

Prague Public Transit Company (DP) Information Offices

Ruzyně Airport *(220 115 404)*. **Open** 7am-10pm daily.
Ruzyně Airport Terminal Sever *(296 667 072)*. **Open** 7am-10pm daily.
Muzeum metro station *Nové Město (296 191 817)*. **Open** 7am-9pm daily. **Map** p331 O7.
Můstek metro station *Nové Město (222 646 350)*. **Open** 7am-6pm Mon-Fri. **Map** p328 M5.

Nádraží Holešovice metro station *Holešovice (296 191 817)*. **Open** 7am-6pm Mon-Fri.
Černý Most metro station *Černý Most (222 647 450)*. **Open** 7am-6pm Mon-Fri.
Anděl metro station *Smíchov (2264 6055)*. **Open** 7am-6pm Mon-Fri.
Employees usually have at least a smattering of English and German, and are unusually helpful. They provide free information booklets and sell tickets, maps, night transport booklets and individual tram and bus schedules (cash only).

FARES AND TICKETS

Tickets (*jízdenky*) are valid for any mode of transport (metro, bus, tram, even the funicular). Most locals have passes (*see p292*), which are probably the easiest option for visitors too as you can't buy a ticket on board trams or buses.

Ticket machines are only found in metro stations and dispense dozens of types of tickets. Only two need concern you, though. A **14 Kč ticket** buys a single 20-minute ride on any transport above ground, or one ride of up to five stops on the metro. It is not valid for use on night transport, the Historical Tram or the funicular. A **20 Kč ticket** lasts for 75 minutes at peak times (5am-8pm Mon-Fri) and 90 minutes during off-peak periods (8pm-5am Mon-Fri and all of Sat, Sun, public holidays), allowing unlimited travel throughout Prague, including transfers between metros, buses and trams.

Babies in buggies, children under six, handicapped people, small bags and skis ride for free. Children aged six to 15, large items of luggage and other sizeable items require a half-price ticket. Enormous bags and, quote, 'items that stink or look disgusting' aren't allowed on Prague public transport.

The orange ticket machines themselves are marvels of Czechnology. They are covered with buttons marked with prices. Press once for the ticket you want, twice if you want two tickets (and so on) and then press the 'enter' button. Insert the total amount in coins (change is given) and wait an agonisingly long time while the machine's screeching mechanism prints out each ticket individually.

If you're here for anything other than a quick visit it's worth stocking up on tickets in advance. You can buy them at most tobacconists, DP information offices (*see p291*) and PIS offices (*see p311*), or anywhere displaying a red-and-yellow DP sticker.

Stamp your ticket (face up in the direction of the arrow) in the machine as you board a bus or enter the 'paid area' of the metro. There are no guards or gates, but plain-clothes inspectors (*revizoři*) carry out random ticket checks. They can sometimes be merciless and have little understanding of English. They also have a reputation for choosing those public transport routes where tourists are most likely to be found (such as tram No.22), hoping to come across a lot of confused foreigners who either don't know they should stamp their tickets or buy the ticket of wrong value. The penalty for buying the wrong ticket, or failing to stamp the right one, is 500 Kč or 950 Kč if you fail to produce the money on the spot. For obvious reasons, it's always wise to demand a receipt if you are fined. Most ticket outlets also sell transit passes, which allow unlimited travel on the metro, trams and buses. The **24hr pass** can also be purchased from automatic ticket machines. To validate a short-term pass, fill in your full name and date of birth on the reverse and then stamp it as you would an ordinary ticket. The pass is valid from the time it was stamped. A 24-hour pass costs

80 Kč, a 72-hour pass is 200 Kč, a 168-hour pass (seven days) is 280 Kč and a 360-hour pass (15 days) is 320 Kč.

Residents usually have long-term passes valid for a month or longer, available at the DP windows and at the Karlovo náměstí metro station. You will need a recent passport photo and some ID. **Long-term passes** cost 460 Kč for one month, 1,260 Kč for three months and 4,150 Kč for the year. There's also a 'gliding' coupon valid for any 30- to 90-day period, so you needn't wait till the end of the month in order to start a pass.

In terms of **disabled access**, public transport is still difficult to use, as are Prague's ancient and often cobbled streets, but there are lifts at the following metro stations – although at some you'll need help to operate the lift: Dejvická, Muzeum, Strašnická and Skalka (green Line A); Zličín, Stodůlky, Luka, Lužiny, Hůrka, Vysočanská, Kolbenova, Hloubětín, Rajská zahrada, Nové Butovice, Smíchovské nádraží and Černý Most (yellow Line B); Nádraží Holešovice, Hlavní nádraží, Florenc, Muzeum, IP Pavlova, Vyšehrad, Pankrác, Roztyly, Chodov, Opatov, Háje, Ládví, Kobylisy and Budějovická (red Line C).

There are two bus routes that are served only by kneeling buses. Bus No.11 starts in Bryksova and runs via Černý Most, Florenc, Náměstí Republiky and IP Pavlova to Chodov. The No.13 runs from Zličín via Hradčanská, Náměstí Republiky and Nádraží Holešovice to Sidliště Ďáblice.All of the newer, boxier trams also kneel, but there's no counting on just when one is going to come along. You can find out which lines use the newer cars at DP information offices (*see p291*).

Metro

Prague's metro network, with a total length of 55 kilometres (34 miles) running through 53 stations along three lines, is a scaled-down copy of the grandiose Moscow metro. The stations are well lit and clearly signposted; trains are clean and frequent. A digital clock on each platform informs you of the time elapsed since the last train came along (though the time until the next arrival would be more useful). The metro comprises three lines: the green Line A (Skalka–Dejvická); the yellow Line B (Černý Most–Zličín); and the red Line C (Ládví–Háje).

Transfers (*přestup*) are possible at three stations: Muzeum (between Line A and Line C), Můstek (between Line A and Line B) and Florenc (between Line B and Line C). The metro runs from 5am to midnight daily. Trains come every two minutes at peak times, and every five to ten minutes off-peak. For a metro map, *see p336*.

Trams

An electric *tramvaje* service began in Prague in 1891 and trams have been the preferred method of transport for most Praguers ever since.Trams come every six to eight minutes at peak times and every ten to 15 minutes during the rest of the day. With the newer, boxier trams, you may find you need to press the green button to open the doors.The best tram lines for seeing the city are the No.22, from the castle to Národní třída and beyond, and the Historic Tram (the No.91), from the Výstaviště in Prague 7 through Malá Strana, across to the National Theatre, through Wenceslas Square, Náměstí Republiky and back to Prague 7. The Historic Tram runs on Saturdays, Sundays and holidays from Easter to the middle of November and leaves Výstaviště every hour from noon to 5.35pm. The ride takes 40 minutes, and tickets cost 25 Kč for adults and 10 Kč for children.

Buses

Since 1925, *autobusy* in Prague have provided transport to the places where no other form of public transport is able to go. They run from about 5am to midnight, after which time ten night bus lines take over (*see below*). Buses run every five to 18 minutes during peak times and every 15 to 30 minutes at other times.

Bus infoline
900 144 444. **Open** 24hrs daily. Calls cost 14 Kč per minute. The operators speak English.

Night trams/buses

Night buses and trams run about every 40 minutes, from midnight to about 4.30am. Every night tram (they all have numbers in the 50s) stops at Lazarská crossroads on Spálená. There's no central stop for night buses (Nos.501 to 512), but many stop at the top of Wenceslas Square (near Metro Muzeum) and around the corner from Metro IP Pavlova. You can buy a guide to night transport – showing all lines, times and stations – at the DP information offices (*see p291*) for about 10 Kč.

Funicular railway

The funicular (*lanovka*) runs for half a kilometre from the bottom of Petřín Hill at Újezd (around the corner from the tram stop of the same name), stops midway at Nebozízek (at the restaurant of the same name) and continues to the top of Petřín Hill. It runs every ten or 15 minutes between 9am and 11.30pm daily and costs 20 Kč for adults and 10 Kč for

children. Transport passes are valid, but beware: a recent scam by ticket sellers and inspectors netted thousands of crowns – don't get on board without buying a ticket and getting it stamped in the yellow machine, even if you have to move a clerk out of the way in order to do so.

Water transport

The Prague Steamship Company had a monopoly on river traffic all the way back in 1865 – and the company still provides most boat services on the river today. You'll find them, as well as other companies plying sight-seeing and booze cruises, and rowing boats for hire, along the right bank of the Vltava.

Prague Steamship Company
Pražská paroplavební služba
Rašínovo nábřeží, Nové Město, Prague 2 (224 930 017/224 931 013/www.paroplavba.cz). Metro Karlovo náměstí/tram 3, 16, 17. **Map** p330 J10.

Taxis

The appalling reputation of Prague's taxi drivers has prompted City Hall to introduce strict guidelines in an effort to ensure that tourists, and their dollars, return to the city. But even with this municipal effort, the odds are high that you will still get ripped off. The drivers waiting at ranks in obvious tourist locations are generally crooks, so avoid them. It's a far better bet to hail a moving cab or to call one of the services listed below. Make sure that you are using an authorised taxi – it should be clearly marked, with its registration number and fares printed on the doors and a black-and-white checked stripe along the side. If the driver doesn't turn on the meter, insist he does. If he won't, get out straight away

or agree on a fee to your destination. Do neither, and the driver will demand a ruinous fare at the end of your journey; he may even resort to violence in order to collect it. Ideally, your taxi experience should go something like this: the driver does not turn on the meter (*taxametr*) until you enter the cab. When he does, 34 Kč appears as the initial amount. While you are driving within Prague, the rate is set at '1' and should never be more than 25 Kč per kilometre. When your ride is over, the driver gives you a receipt (*účet* or *paragon*). (If he doesn't, you are theoretically not required to pay the fare.) Few drivers will actually provide a receipt unless you ask. Honest cabbies print one out on the agonisingly slow machine; rip-off merchants will write you one out on a pad. At press time, the maximum taxi rates allowed by a directive of the City Hall were: 34 Kč (if you hail a cab) or 25 Kč (if you call to book), plus 5 Kč per minute for waiting (because of a passenger request or traffic) and no more than 25 Kč (if hailed) or 20 Kč (if you booked by phone) per kilometre for normal rides. However, fares are scheduled for a slight increase.

Cab companies
AAA
222 333 222, 221 102 211, 221 111 111, 14014/ www.aaataxi.cz.
If you're using a mobile (*see p310*), use the numbers below for cheaper calls: T-Mobile 603 331 133; Eurotel 602 331 133; Oskar 777 331 133.
ProfiTaxi
261 314 151/800 118 294.
Halo Taxi
244 114 411/www.halotaxi.cz.

Taxi complaints
Živnostenský odbor
Vodičkova 18, Prague 1 (221 097 111/222 231 640). Metro Můstek/tram 3, 9, 14, 24. **Open** 9am-5pm Mon-Fri.

Rail services

Trains are generally useful only for travelling from town to town in the Czech Republic, not within Prague. *See p290.*

Driving

The worst days for driving are Friday and Sunday, when people who don't know the difference between the clutch and the brake pedal pack their families into new Škodas for a weekend trip to their summer cottage. Watch out for the Czech tendency to stop in the middle of junctions on a red light. One unwelcome result of the Velvet Revolution is the horrendous traffic in the city centre that has accompanied rising incomes. Unless you have a Czech residence permit you'll need an international driver's licence (ask a motoring organisation in your home country, such as the AA or AAA, how to apply). Traffic regulations in the Czech Republic are similar to those in most European countries. However, note that there is zero tolerance for drinking and driving – drivers are not allowed to drink any alcohol at all; ditto for drugs. The use of seat belts is required in the front and – if the car is equipped with them – back seats (though most Czechs will laugh at your faint-heartedness if you belt up). Children under 12 and anyone under 18 who is shorter than 150 centimetres (4 feet 11 inches) cannot ride in the seat next to the driver unless they sit in approved safety seats and there's no airbag in the front seat. Small children must be in approved safety seats whether they're placed in the front or the back seat. Trams, which follow different traffic lights to cars, always have the right of way. You must stop behind trams when passengers are getting on and off at a stop

where there is no island, and you should avoid driving on tram tracks unless the road offers no alternative. The speed limit for cars and buses is 90kph (56mph) on roads, 130kph (81mph) on motorways and 50kph (31mph) in towns and villages. Motorcyclists, along with their passengers, must wear protective helmets and eyegear, and the speed limit for motorcycles is 90kph (56mph) on roads and motorways and 50kph (31.25mph) in the villages and towns.

You are required to notify the police of any accident involving casualties or serious damage to a car.

Breakdown services

Autoklub Bohemia Assistance

Autoklub České republiky *Opletalova 29, Nové Město, Prague 1 (224 230 506/222 241 257/www.aba.cz).* **Open** 8am-4.30pm Mon-Fri. **No credit cards.**
Call 1240 or 266 193 247 for 'ABA': 24-hour, seven-day-a-week emergency road service.

Central Automobile Club Prague

Ústřední automotoklub *Na Stráži 9, Michle, Prague 4 (261 104 111/www.uamk.cz).* **Open** 8am-4pm Mon-Fri. **No credit cards.**
Call 1230 or 261 220 220 (Renault Assistance) for the 'Yellow Angel' 24-hour emergency road service.

Fuel stations

Leaded fuel (octane 90) is called Special, leaded fuel (octane 96) is known as Super and unleaded fuel (95D) is called Natural. Super Plus 98 and diesel fuel are also widely available. A booklet listing all the petrol and service stations (and some car parks) in Prague is available from PIS offices (*see p311*). Many service stations remain open 24 hours a day.

Insurance

If you are driving your own car, you will need to have international proof of insurance (known as a Green Card; contact your motoring organisation) and pay an annual toll for using the Czech roads. If you hire a car, insurance and toll should be taken care of for you. Otherwise, the toll sticker – which should be displayed on the windscreen – is 200 Kč for 15 days, 300 Kč for 2 months or 900 Kč for a year. It can be bought at post offices, most border-crossing points and petrol stations.

Parking

Prague wasn't designed for cars and parking in the city can be a nightmare. Watch out for the special zones reserved for area residents and businesses, and make sure you don't park in them yourself. If you park illegally, your car can be towed away (call 158 to get it back) or clamped and it will cost you around 1,000 Kč to retrieve – more if there's a delay. If you're new in town, the best option is to use a car park, ideally one that has 24-hour security.

Parking meters

Coin-operated parking meters dispense tickets. Display them face up on the dashboard, visible through the windscreen. Streets in Prague 1 are separated into three types of parking. Blue zones are reserved for local residents and companies. Orange zones are for stops of up to two hours and cost a minimum of 10 Kč for 15 minutes and 40 Kč for one hour; and green zones are for stays of up to six hours and cost 15 Kč for 30 minutes, 30 Kč for an hour and 120 Kč for six hours. Ignore the restrictions at your peril.

Rideshare

A great way to cut the stress, while riding a lot more directly and comfortably than in a bus, sharing rides is a well-organised process at Prague's main rideshare centre.

Town to Town Agency

Národní třída 9, Prague 1 (tel/fax 222 075 407/www.spolujizda.cz). Metro Národní třída/tram 6, 9, 17, 18, 22, 23. **Open** 9am-6pm Mon-Fri; 10am-4pm Sat. **No credit cards. Map** p328 L6.
Pay a nominal deposit and you're set, with complete online listings of the rides offered and the passengers seeking rides, organised by destination, with times and prices.

Vehicle hire

Renting a car can be pretty expensive in Prague, with many Western firms charging higher rates than they would back home. It is definitely worth shopping around, as many small local firms charge far less than the big boys. When renting a car, be sure to bring your international driver's licence, passport and credit card with you. The agency should provide you with a green insurance card, which you will be asked to show if you are stopped by police or drive across the border. Arrange your rental a few days in advance to be sure that you get the car you want.

In addition to the places listed below, American Express (*see p305*), Čedok (*see p311*) and Student Agency (*see p309*) arrange car rental.

A Rent Car

Washingtonova 9, Nové Město, Prague 1 (224 211 581). Metro Muzeum/tram 11. **Open** 7am-7pm daily. **Rates** 2,300-4,800 Kč per day. **Credit** AmEx, DC, MC, V. **Map** p329 P6.
Other locations: Ruzyně Airport, Prague 6 (224 281 053/220 140 370); Shopping Mall Millenium Plaza, V Celnici 10, Prague 1 (224 211 587).

Avis

Klimentská 46, Staré Město, Prague 1 (221 851 225-6/810 777 810/fax 221 851 229/www.avis.cz). Metro Florenc/tram 3, 8. **Open** 8am-4.30pm Mon-Fri; 8am-2pm Sat; 10am-2pm Sun. **Rates** from 2,300 Kč per day. **Credit** AmEx, DC, MC, V. **Map** p329 Q1.
Other locations: Ruzyně Airport, Prague 6 (235 362 420).

Alimex

Tusarova 1548/39, Holešovice, Prague 7 (233 350 001/800 150 170/www.alimexcr.cz). Metro Vltavská/tram 1, 3, 25. **Open** 8am-6pm daily. **Rates** from 450 Kč without VAT per day for a Škoda Fabia covered with company ads or from 890 Kč without VAT per day for an unmarked one. **Credit** AmEx, DC, MC, V.
Other locations: Ruzyně Airport, Prague 6 (220 114 860)

Budget

Čistovická 100, Řepy, Prague 6 (235 325 713/235 301 152/www.budget.cz). Tram 22, 25. **Open** 8am-4.30pm Mon-Fri. **Rates** from 1,900 Kč per day. **Credit** AmEx, DC, MC, V.
Other locations: Ruzyně Airport, Prague 6 (220 113 253); Hotel Inter-Continental, Staré Město, Prague 1 (296 630 595).

Central Rent a Car

Eliášova 6, Dejvice, Prague 6 (222 245 905/602 618 177 24hr service/www.rentcentral.cz). Metro Můstek /tram 3, 9, 14, 24. **Open** 9am-8pm Mon-Fri; 9am-7pm Sat; 11am-7pm Sun. **Rates** from 990 Kč per day. **Credit** AmEx, DC, MC, V.

European Inter Rent/Europe Car Rental

Pařížská 28, Staré Město, Prague 1 (224 810 515/224 811 290/www.europcar.cz). Metro Staroměstská/tram 17, 18. **Open** 8am-8pm daily. **Rates** from 2,012 Kč per day; 3,333 Kč per 2 days. Reduced price on longer rentals. **Credit** AmEx, DC, MC, V. **Map** p328 K2.
Other locations: branches can be found in most of the major cities in the Czech Republic.

Hertz

Karlovo náměstí 15, Nové Město, Prague 2 (222 102 424/www.hertz.cz). Metro Karlovo náměstí/tram 3, 4, 6, 14, 16, 18, 22, 23, 24, 34. **Open** 8am-8pm daily. **Rates** from 2,113 Kč per day; 3,499 Kč for 2 days. **Credit** AmEx, DC, MC, V. **Map** p330 L10.

Cycling

Frankly put, pedalling in Prague is hellish. There are no cycle lanes, drivers are oblivious to your presence and pedestrians yell at you if you take refuge on the pavement. Mountain bikes are best, as the wide wheels shouldn't get stuck in the tram tracks. Prague does, however, have plenty of parkland inside and outside the city. On public transport, bikes are allowed in the last carriage of metro trains.

Bicycle hire

City Bike

Králodvorská 5, Staré Město, Prague 1 (mobile 776 180 284/www.pragueonline/bike). Metro Náměstí Republiky/tram 5, 8, 14. **Open** *Apr-Oct* 9am-7pm daily. **No credit cards. Map** p329 N3.
Cycle tours of the city, three times a day: 11am, 2pm and 5pm. Reasonable rental fees: 700 Kč per day.

Walking

By far the best way to get around Prague's compact centre is on foot. The excellent pocket-sized map *Praha do kapsy* is available at most newsstands. It is generally safe to walk anywhere at any time – using common sense and appropriate caution in the wee hours, of course. Prague does not (yet) have any 'bad' areas that you should generally avoid. Beware of bad drivers, though – they've only begrudgingly begun to stop for pedestrians at crossings because a recent law compels them to do so.

Directory

Resources A-Z

Addresses

Czech buildings have two numbers posted on them, one in red, which is used in city records only, and one in blue, which denotes the address used for letters and callers (and is the one used in this guide). The street name comes first, followed by the street number, then, on a new line, a district code and district number, followed by the country, thus:

Jan Novak
Kaprova 10
11 000 Praha 1
Czech Republic

Age restrictions

The legal age for driving in the Czech Republic is 18, as it is for drinking and smoking, though it's virtually unheard of for clubs, bars and shops to ask for proof of age. The age of sexual consent for both straights and gays is 15.

Attitude & etiquette

Praguers sometimes seem stand-offish at first, as people do in many cities, especially in the service sector. But Czechs will quickly warm to you if you attempt to speak even a word or two of their language. Generally speaking there's a culture of shyness and a tradition of avoiding confrontation at all costs, and Czechs are understated to say the least about expressing happiness. To fling a few more wild generalisations into the mix, Czech people tend to melt at the sight of children and dogs, are sexually liberal, deeply reverent about Czech beer and the country itself, and fiscally and gastronomically conservative.

Business

Resources & organisations

British Embassy Commercial Section

Na příkopě 21, Nové Město, Prague 1 (222 240 021-3/fax 222 243 625/www.britain.cz). Metro Můstek/tram 3, 9, 14, 24. **Open** 9am-noon, 2-5pm Mon-Fri. **Map** p329 N5.

Czechinvest

Štěpánská 15, Nové Město, Prague 2 (296 342 500/infoline 800 800 777/fax 296 342 502/www.czech invest.org). Metro Můstek/tram 3, 9, 14, 24. **Open** 8am-4.30pm Mon-Fri. **Map** p331 N8.
This Czech government agency encourages large-scale direct foreign investment and assists in joint ventures. Staff can research Czech contacts in fields of interest.

Economic Chamber of the Czech Republic

Hospodářská komora ČR Freyova 27, Prague 9 (296 641 111/296 646 112/fax 296 646 221/www.komora.cz). Metro Hlavní nádraží, then tram 5, 9, 26. **Open** 8am-4pm Mon-Fri.
The Chamber of Commerce provides background information on Czech industrial sectors, companies and economic trends.

Enterprise Ireland

Tržiště 13, Malá Strana, Prague 1 (257 531 585/fax 257 532 224). Metro Malostranská/tram 12, 22. **Open** 9am-1pm, 2-5pm Mon-Fri. **Map** p327 E4.

Prague Stock Exchange (PX)

Rybná 14, Staré Město, Prague 1 (221 831 111/www.pse.cz). Metro Náměstí Republiky/tram 5, 8, 14. **Open** 8am-4.30pm Mon-Fri. **Map** p329 N3.
PX trades about 50 companies in its top-tier listing. The big banks are among forty odd brokerages that can place orders. Liquidity is good, though insider trading has been a problem in the past.

US Embassy Foreign Commercial Service

Tržiště 15, Malá Strana, Prague 1 (257 531 162/fax 257 531 165/www.buyusa.gov). Metro Malostranská/tram 12, 22, 23. **Open** 9am-noon daily. **Map** p327 E4.

Accountancy firms

The major international accountancy firms are well established in Prague and offer a full range of services. There are also hundreds of local companies that offer book-keeping and payroll services.

Deloitte & Touche

Nile House-River City Prague, Karolinská 2, Prague 8, Karlín (246 042 500/www.deloitte.com). Metro Křižíkova. **Open** 8am-8pm Mon-Fri.

KPMG

Pobřežní 1A, Prague 8 (222 123 111/www.kpmg.cz). Metro Křižíkova. **Open** 9am-5pm Mon-Fri.
Smaller and more personal than the other agencies, KPMG is known for its financial planning and technical expertise.

PriceWaterhouse Coopers

Kateřinská 40, Nové Město, Prague 2 (251 151 111/www. pwcglobal.com). Metro IP Pavlova/tram 4, 6, 10, 11, 16, 22, 23. **Open** 9am-5pm Mon-Fri. **Map** p331 N10.
Accounting specialists whose auditors have a good reputation internationally and in Prague.

Banking

Anyone can open a bank account in the Czech Republic, although some banks will require you to pay in a minimum deposit. Corporate bank accounts require special paperwork. Banks generally charge high fees and current accounts do not pay interest. Most banks have some English-speaking staff. Service is improving, but still expect long queues, short opening hours and lots of burdensome paperwork. Czech banks usually cater to individual account holders, while international banks are largely geared to corporate accounts, but usually offer at least some traditional banking services. The five main Czech banks are Česká spořitelna (ČS), Československá obchodní banka (ČSOB), Komerční banka (KB), HVB Bank and Živnostenská banka.

Česká spořitelna

Rytířská 29, Staré Město, Prague 1 (224 101 630/800 207 207 toll free/www.csas.cz). Metro Můstek/tram 3, 9, 14, 24. **Open** 9am-6pm Mon, Thur; 9am-5pm Tue, Wed; 9am-4pm Fri. **Map** p328 L5.
Geared toward domestic savings accounts. Operates a large cashpoint (ATM) network throughout the city.
Other locations: Václavské náměstí 16, Prague 1 (224 422 666).

Citibank

Evropská 178, Dejvice, Prague 6 (233 062 211/www.citibank.cz). Metro Dejvická/tram 20, 26. **Open** 8.30am-5pm Mon-Fri.

HVB Banka

Náměstí Republiky 3, Prague 1 (221 112 111/www.hvb.cz). Metro Náměstí Republiky/tram 5, 8, 14. **Open** 8.30am-4.30pm Mon-Thur; 8.30am-3.30pm Fri. **Map** p329 N4.

Computer rental & leasing

For repairs/supplies, *see p183*.

APS

Rujanská 1223, Prague 4 (224 215 147/www.aps.cz; in Czech only). Metro Opatov. **Open** 9am-5pm Mon-Fri. **Credit** MC, V.
Flexible PC leasing options.

MacSource/ CompuSource

Bělehradská 68, Nové Město, Prague 2 (221 501 511/fax 222 515 456/www.macsource.cz). Metro IP Pavlova/tram 6, 11. **Open** 9am-5pm Mon-Fri. **Credit** AmEx, MC, V. **Map** p331 P10.

Both PC and Macintosh computer equipment are available for leasing and rental, on short and long term contracts.

Apple Center Anděl

Nádražní 23, Prague 5 (257 210 493/www.appleobchod.cz). Metro Anděl/tram 4, 7, 9, 10, 12, 14, 20. **Open** 10am-6pm Mon-Sat.
If you're stuck for an iPod cable or iBook RAM, this is the place.

Couriers/messengers

DHL

Aviatická 1048/12, Ruzyně Airport, Prague 6 (toll free 800 103 000/220 300 111/www.dhl.cz). **Open** *Telephone bookings* 24hrs daily. **Credit** AmEx, MC, V.
Offers a daily pick-up service until 6.45pm on weekdays, 3pm on Saturdays.

FedEx

Na Radosti 399, Zličín, Prague 5 (toll free 800 133 339/www.fedex.com). Metro Budějovická. **Open** *Telephone bookings* 8am-7.30pm Mon-Fri; 8am-1pm Sat. **Credit** AmEx, MC, V.

Messenger Service

Libínská 3127, Prague 5 (220 400 000/fax 220 400 000/www.messenger.cz). **Open** *Telephone bookings* 24 hrs daily. **Credit** AmEx, MC, V.
Cycle couriers. One-hour collection and two-hour delivery on local jobs. Also delivers outside Prague.

Estate agents

Finding reasonably priced and adequate office space can be challenging. Estate agents tend to push expensive properties to maximise their commission. Make sure that any space has cable internet access lines and isn't due for noisy or disruptive repairs. If parking is important, choose a space out of the centre.

Apollo

Na Zájezdu 11, Prague 10 (224 222 587/fax 224 222 641/www.apollosro.cz). Metro Flora. **Open** 9am-5.30pm Mon-Fri.
Lease and sale of commercial and private real estate. Financial and development consulting.

Praha-Nexus Europe

Jana Masaryka 6, Prague 2 (236 040 221-2/www.nexus-e.cz). Metro Náměstí Miru/tram 4, 22, 23. **Open** 9am-5.30pm Mon-Fri. **Map** p331 Q12.
Serves small and medium-sized businesses.

Interpreting & translating

Prague has dozens of good translation companies, with most offering services in all the major European languages along with many non-European languages.

Travel advice

For up-to-date information on travelling to a specific country – including the latest news on safety and security, health issues, local laws and customs – contact your home country government's department of foreign affairs. Most have websites packed with useful advice for would-be travellers.

Australia
www.dfat.gov.au/travel

Canada
www.voyage.gc.ca

New Zealand
www.mft.govt.nz/travel

Republic of Ireland
www.irlgov.ie/iveagh

UK
www.fco.gov.uk/travel

USA
www.state.gov/travel

Directory

Translation rates are usually determined by the page (there are reckoned to be 30 lines per page at 60 characters per line).

Artlingua

Myslíkova 6, Prague 2 (224 917 616/fax 224 921 715/www. artlingua.cz). Metro Karlovo Náměstí/tram 17. **Map** p330 K8. Specialises in legal and financial documents.

TaP Servis

Jungmannova 22, Prague 1 (224 226 629/fax 224 211 443/ www.tapservis.cz). Metro Můstek. **Map** p328 M6.

Law firms

There are dozens of local and international law firms that can help establish a company and provide the standard range of legal services. Local firms tend to have a better grasp of the more arcane elements of Czech law, while international firms offer better linguistic skills and more polish (at a price). For a local lawyer, contact the Czech Chamber of Commercial Lawyers.

Cameron McKenna

Karolíny Světlé 25, Prague 1 (296 798 111/fax 221 098 000/ www.law-now.com). Metro Národní třída or Můstek/tram 6, 9, 17, 18, 22, 23. **Open** 9.30am-6pm Mon-Fri. **Map** p328 J5/6. Cameron McKenna claims to have the largest network of law offices in Central Europe.

Čermák, Hořejš & Myslil

Národní třída 32, Nové Město, Prague 1 (296 167 111/fax 224 946 724/www.cermakhorejs myslil.cz). Metro Národní třída/ tram 6, 9, 17, 18, 22, 23. **Open** 9am-5pm Mon-Fri. **Map** p328 L6. Local firm specialising in patent and other types of corporate law.

Czech Chamber of Commercial Lawyers

Kaňkův palác, Národní 16, Nové Město, Prague 1 (221 729 011/www.cak.cz). Metro Národní třída/tram 22, 23, 18. **Open** 8am-4.45pm Mon-Thur; 8am-3.30pm Fri. **Map** p328 L6.

Haarmann Hemmelrath

Ovocný Trh 8, Staré Město, Prague 1 (224 490 000/fax 224 490 033/www.haarmann hemmelrath.com). Metro Můstek/tram 3, 9, 14, 24. **Open** 8am-7pm Mon-Fri. **Map** p328 M4. Offers advice on privatisation, acquisitions, labour code, foreign investment and other issues.

Office hire

Business Centrum Chronos

Václavské náměstí 66 (entrance at Mezibranská 23), Nové Město, Prague 1 (296 348 111/fax 222 211 327/www.chronos.pha.cz). Metro Muzeum/tram 11. **Open** 8am-6pm Mon-Fri. **Map** p331 O7. Offers temporary office space, phone and secretarial services.

Regus

Vyskočilova 1A/1422, Prague 4 (244 026 111/fax 244 026 200/ www.regus.com). Metro Budějovická. **Open** 9am-6pm Mon-Fri. Can provide short-term offices and conference rooms, as well as access to the internet and email.

Photocopying

See p196.

Recruitment agencies

Adecco

Spálená 10, Prague 1 (224 948 084/fax 224 946 500/www. adecco.cz). Metro Národní Třída/ tram 6, 9, 18, 22, 23. **Open** 9am-6pm Mon-Fri. **Map** p330 L8. One of several international head-hunting agencies. Fills positions in all sectors of the economy and focuses also on temporary help.

AYS

Krakovská 7, Prague 1 (222 210 013/www.ays.cz). Metro Muzeum/ tram 11. **Open** 8am-6.30pm Mon-Fri. **Map** p331 O8. A wide range of professions, and good for secretarial and administrative support.

Helmut Neumann International

Štětkova 18, Prague 4 (244 096 379/www.Neumann-inter.com). Metro Vyšehrad. **Open** 8am-6pm Mon-Thur; 8am-4pm Fri.

One of several international head-hunting agencies. Fills positions in all sectors of the economy.

Consumer

There is a Czech Office of Consumer Protection, but it doesn't have English-speaking services or a hotline and it's largely ineffective, so it's best to adopt a philosophy of Buyer Beware. Shops may allow you to exchange faulty goods but are not generally willing to refund money.

Customs

There are no restrictions on the import and export of Czech currency, but if you're carrying more than 350,000 Kč out of the country, you must declare it at customs. The allowances for importing goods are:

● 200 cigarettes or 100 cigars at max. 3g each or 250g of tobacco;

● 1 litre of liquor or spirits and 2 litres of wine;

● Medicine in any amount for your own needs.

If you want to export an antique, you must have a certificate stating that it is not important to Czech cultural heritage: ask when you purchase.

Customs Office

Celní ředitelství pro Prahu a Středočeský kraj *Washingtonova 1621, Nové Město, Prague 1 (261 334 383/ www.cs.mfcr.cz). Metro Muzeum/ tram 11.* **Open** 7am-3.30pm Mon-Fri. **Map** p331 O7. **Other locations:** Ruzyně Airport, Prague 6 (220 113 100).

Disabled access

According to the law, all buildings constructed after 1994 must be wheelchair-friendly. Reconstructed buildings, however, need not provide wheelchair access, though many do voluntarily. Even so, it is no picnic to be in

Prague in a wheelchair. There are few ramps. Most hotels provide no wheelchair access and only five railway stations in the entire country are wheelchair-friendly. The guidebook *Přístupná Praha* (*Accessible Prague*), available from the Prague Wheelchair Association, contains maps of hotels, toilets, restaurants, galleries and theatres that are wheelchair-friendly. For travel information, *see p292*.

Prague Wheelchair Association

Pražská organizace vozíčkářů *Centre for Independent Living (Centrum samostatného života), Benediktská 6, Staré Město, Prague 1 (224 827 210/www.pov.cz). Metro Náměstí Republiky/tram 5, 8, 14.* **Open** 9am-4pm Mon-Fri. **Map** p329 N3.
This organisation is run by the disabled for the disabled. In addition to its *Accessible Prague* guidebook, it provides helpers and operates a taxi service and an airport pick-up service. Service is limited and should be ordered as far in advance as possible. It can also rent wheelchairs if people have any problem with their own.

Electricity

Electricity is 220 volts with two-pin plugs almost everywhere. Bring continental adaptors or converters with you, as they are expensive here when they are available at all.

Embassies

All embassies and consulates are closed on Czech holidays (*see p312*) as well as their own national holidays. For other embassies, you will need to consult the *Zlaté stránky* (*Yellow Pages*) under 'Zastupitelské úřady'.

American Embassy

Tržiště 15, Malá Strana, Prague 1 (257 530 663/emergency number 257 532 716/www.usembassy.cz). Metro Malostranská/tram 12, 22, 23. **Open** 9am-noon Mon-Thur. **Map** p327 E4.

Australian Trade Commission & Consulate

Na Ořechovce 38, Prague 6 (224 310 743). Metro Dejvická, then tram 20, 26. **Open** 9am-1pm, 2-5pm Mon-Fri.

British Embassy

Thunovská 14, Malá Strana, Prague 1 (257 402 111). Metro Malostranská/tram 12, 22. **Open** 8.30am-noon Mon-Fri; *telephone enquiries* 9am-9pm Mon-Fri. **Map** p327 E3.

Canadian Embassy

Muchova 6, Dejvice, Prague 6 (272 101 800/fax 272 101 890/www.canada.cz). Metro Hradčanská/tram 18, 22. **Open** 8.30am-12.30pm Mon-Fri. **Map** p332 A3.

Emergencies

All numbers are toll-free.
Emergencies 112
First aid 155
Czech police 158
Fire 150
See also the Health, Helplines and Police sections.

Gay & Lesbian

Prague is a generally tolerant city and an increasingly popular destination for gay and lesbian travel, though the proximity of Germany, a major market for sex tourism, has resulted in a boom in the commercial side of the scene.

Help & information

The encyclopaedic online resource Gay Guide (http://prague.gayguide.net) has the most complete and up-to-date information available in English on the scene, accommodation, legalities and practicalities.

Health

Prague isn't the healthiest place on earth to live. The Czech diet is fatty, pork-laden and low on fresh vegetables. The Czechs top world beer-consumption charts and are unrepentant smokers. The city also has serious smog problems and an archaic public sanitation system to contend with.

All of which makes Prague great for hypochondriacs. The damp climate creates a haven for various moulds that can be hell for anyone with allergies. Salmonella thrives in a favourite Czech lunch item, mayonnaise meat salads that sit out for hours.

But if you do get ill, the chronically underfunded socialised healthcare system will undoubtedly soon have you feeling worse. If you have health insurance, the doctors will try to rack up points for the care they give – sometimes overdoing it – which they redeem for money from the health insurance companies. In general, if you pay cash (which is universally accepted), you'll get far better treatment than the locals who must rely on the state system.

Medical facilities are usually open from 7.15am to 6pm on weekdays only. It's usually best for expats to find a GP (*rodinný* or *praktický lékař*), dentist (*zubní lékař*) and paediatrician (*dětský lékař*) close to their home or workplace. Many Czech doctors will speak English or German, especially at larger facilities like hospitals (*nemocnice*) and medical centres (*poliklinika*).

Accident & Emergency

Canadian Medical Care

Veleslavínská 30, Prague 6 (235 360 133/emergency 724 300 301/www.cmc.praha.cz). Metro Dejvická/tram 20, 25, 26. **Open** 8am-6pm Mon-Fri. **Credit** DC, MC, V.
Established general practice clinic with paediatricians, gynaecaologists, cardiologists and other specialists, and on-site labs for many common tests.

Medicover Clinic

Pankrác House, Lomnického 1705, Prague 4 (234 630 111/ emergency 603 555 006/call centre 1221/www.medicover.cz). Metro Pražského povstání. **Open** 7am-7pm Mon-Fri; 9am-noon Sat. **Credit** AmEx, MC, V.
With a professional international staff, Medicover honours Central Health Insurance Office temporary insurance (*see p301*).

Motol Hospital

Fakultní nemocnice v Motole V Úvalu 84, Smíchov, Prague 5 (224 431 111/224 431 111/ emergency 224 438 590-8/155 toll-free/www.fnmotol.cz). Metro Hradčanská, then 108, 174 bus. **Open** 24hrs daily. **Credit** AmEx, MC, V.
Emergency treatment, plus a hospital department dedicated to the care of foreigners.

Na Homolce Hospital

Nemocnice Na Homolce Roentgenova 2, Smíchov, Prague 5 (257 271 111/emergencies 257 272 191/paediatrics 257 272 025/emergencies 257 272 043/ www.homolka.cz). Tram 4, 7, 9/167 bus. **Open** *Emergency* 24hrs daily. *Paediatric department* 8am-4pm daily. **Credit** AmEx, MC, V.
Provides English-speaking doctors and 24-hour emergency service. Care can be excellent but given the state of the Czech public healthcare system, a private clinic is more advisable. Home visits are possible if needed.

Complementary medicine

Czechs have a long history of herbal cures and many of them have embraced traditional Eastern medical practices with enthusiasm. Thus the average pharmacy, or lékárna, will stock dozens of teas for everything from menstrual cramps to bronchitis but you will need to bring a Czech friend along to decipher the labels. Check the *Zlaté stránky* (*Yellow Pages*) (there's an English-language index at the back) for 'Health Care – Alternative Medicine'.

Contraception & abortion

Condoms are widely available in Prague and stocked at many grocers. Abortion is legal and can be arranged through most clinics.

Dentists

Many of the Western clinics have dentists on staff but the following one, a private practice, is also well recommended.

Dental Emergencies

Palackého 5, Nové Město, Prague 1 (224 946 981). Metro Můstek/ tram 3, 9, 14, 24. **Open** 7pm-6.30am Mon-Fri; 7am-6.30pm, 7pm-6.30am Sat, Sun. **No credit cards.** **Map** p330 M7.

Medicover Clinic

Pankrác House, Lomnického 1705, Prague 4 (234 630 111/ emergency 603 555 006/call centre 1221/www.medicover.cz). Metro Pražského povstání. **Open** 7am-7pm Mon-Fri; 9am-noon Sat. **Credit** AmEx, MC, V.

Motol Hospital

Fakultní nemocnice v Motole V Úvalu 84, Smíchov, Prague 5 (224 433 681/224 431 111/ emergency 224 436 107-8/155 toll free/www.fnmotol.cz). Metro Hradčanská, then 108, 174 bus. **Open** 24 hours daily. **Credit** AmEx, MC, V.

Opticians

Most Western clinics (*see p299*) have referral services with opticians, although glasses shops, such as Eiffel Optic (*see p195*) also have licensed opticians on staff who can determine your prescription.

Pharmacies

Many central pharmacies (*lékárna* or *apothéka*) have been doing business in exactly the same place for centuries and have gorgeous period interiors that are worth

seeking out even if you're bursting with health. Over-the-counter medicines are only available from pharmacies, which are usually open from 7.30am to 6pm on weekdays, though some operate extended hours. All pharmacies are supposed to post directions to the nearest 24-hour pharmacy in their window, though this information will be in Czech. Ring the bell for after-hours service, for which there will usually be a surcharge of approximately 30 Kč.

24-hour pharmacies

Belgická 37, Vinohrady, Prague 2 (222 519 731). Metro Náměstí Míru/tram 4, 6, 16, 22, 23. **No credit cards.** **Map** p311 M9.
Palackeho 5, Nové Město, Prague 1 (224 946 982). Metro Můstek. **No credit cards.** **Map** p 331 Q11.

STDs, HIV & AIDS

ČSAP (Česká společnost AIDS Pomoci)/Lighthouse (Dům Světla)

Malého 3, Prague 8 (224 810 345/AIDS help line 800 800 980/www.aids-pomoc.cz). Metro Florenc/tram 8, 24. **Open** *Volunteers available* 9am-4pm Mon-Fri.
ČSAP is the Czech organisation for AIDS prevention and for the support of people with HIV or AIDS. In addition to a 24-hour hotline, it runs the House of Light, which is a hospice for HIV-infected individuals who would otherwise have nowhere to go. Donations are very welcome.

Women's health

Bulovka Hospital

Budinova 2, Libeň, Prague 8 (266 081 111). Metro Palmovka/tram 12, 14. **Open** 24hrs daily. **No credit cards.**
Housed within a huge state hospital complex, the privately run MEDA Clinic is favoured by British and American women. Prices are reasonable, the gynaecologists speak English along with some other languages and the facilities are clean and professional.

Dr Kateřina Bittmanová

Mánesova 64, Vinohrady,
Prague 2 (office 222 724 592/
603 551 393/home 272 936 895).
Metro Jiřího z Poděbrad/tram 11.
Open 7am-4pm Mon-Fri. **No**
credit cards. Map p333 B3.
Dr Bittmanová speaks fluent
English. She runs a friendly
private practice and, what's more,
is on call 24 hours a day. Her fee
for a general examination is 900
Kč; a smear test costs an
additional 450 Kč.

Podolí Hospital

Podolské nábřeží 157, Podolí,
Prague 4 (296 511 111). Tram
3, 16, 17. **Open** 24hrs daily.
No credit cards.
The Podolí Hospital has
obstetricians and gynaecologists
who speak English. With modern
facilities and good neo-natal care,
this is where most of Prague's
pregnant expatriates choose to
give birth.

RMA Centrum

Dukelských hrdinů 17, Holešovice,
Prague 7 (233 372 614). Tram
4, 12, 14, 17, 26. **Open** 7am-5pm
Mon, Tue; 7am-7pm Wed; 7am-
6pm Thur; 7am-1pm Fri. **No**
credit cards. Map p332 E3.
An alternative medicine centre
offering homeopathy, acupuncture
and acupressure, traditional
Chinese medicine and massage
as well as gynaecology and
mammography. There's also a
sauna and beauty salon.

Helplines & crisis centres

Helplines generally run around
the clock, but of course that
doesn't mean they'll speak
English. You have a better
chance of catching an English-
speaker if you call during
regular office hours. For AIDS
crisis helplines, *see p300*.

Alcoholics Anonymous (AA)

Na Poříčí 16, Nové Město, Prague
1 (224 818 247). Metro Florenc or
Náměstí Republiky/tram 5, 8, 14,
26. **Sessions** at 5.30pm daily.
Map p329 Q2.
Twelve-step programmes. Anyone
with alcohol problems is welcome
to call or attend. English spoken.

Crisis Intervention Centre

Centrum krizové intervence –
Psychiatrická léčebna Bohnice.
Ústavní 91, Prague 8 (284 016
111/www.plbohnice.cz). Metro
Nádraží Holešovice, then 102, 177,
200 bus. **Open** 24hrs daily.
The biggest and best-equipped
mental health facility in Prague.
Lots of outreach programmes.

Drop In

Karolíny Světlé 18, Staré Město,
Prague 1 (tel/fax 222 221 124/
222 221 431 non-stop helpline/
www.dropin.cz). Metro
Staroměstská or Národní
třída/tram 6, 9, 17, 18, 22, 23.
Open 9am-5.30pm Mon-Thur;
9am-4pm Fri. **Map** p328 J5/6.
Focusing on problems related to
drug addiction, including HIV
testing and counselling, this is
an informal clinic. Call or just
drop in 24 hours a day.

ID

Spot checks of foreigners'
documents are not unheard
of so it is best to carry ID. A
photocopy of your passport is
usually sufficient. Bars and
clubs virtually never ask for ID
but you may be asked to show
a passport if changing money.

Insurance

Foreigners are technically
required to present
documentary evidence of
health insurance to enter the
Czech Republic, though in
practice it is rarely asked for.
Nationals of a country with
which the Czech Republic
has a reciprocal emergency
healthcare agreement are
exempt. These countries are
the United Kingdom, Greece
and most of the republic's
former allies in the ex-Warsaw
Pact countries. Visitors
requiring a visa will have to
provide proof of insurance
with their application,
however. The relevant bodies
will issue visas to foreigners
only for as long as they have
valid health insurance.

Všeobecná zdravotní
pojišťovna (Central Health
Insurance, VZP), the main
health insurance provider in
the Czech Republic, provides
affordable policies to foreigners
for urgent care coverage for up
to a year. Due to its massive
debts and delayed payments
it isn't favoured by some
doctors, however.

Most state clinics and
hospitals, and a few private
ones, accept VZP.

If you have your own travel
insurance, make sure that it
covers Central and Eastern
European countries.

Central Health Insurance Office

Všeobecná zdravotní pojišťovna
Tyršova 7, Nové Město, Prague 2
(221 972 270/www.vzp.cz). Metro
IP Pavlova/tram 4, 16, 22. **Open**
8am-4pm Mon-Thur; 8am-1pm Fri.
Map p331 O10.
VZP is the main provider of health
insurance in the Czech Republic,
offering reasonable rates for short-
term coverage, issued in terms of
30-day periods.
Other locations: Na Perštýně 6,
Staré Město, Prague 1 (221 668
103); Orlická 4, Žižkov, Prague 3
(221 753 114).

Property insurance

Insuring personal belongings
is always wise and should be
arranged before leaving home.

Internet

Most of the upper-end hotels
provide dataports these days,
and there are internet cafés all
over Prague. Try the Globe
Bookstore & Coffeehouse
(*see p181*).

If you have access to a
modem line and a laptop,
ask your ISP whether it has a
Prague dial-in or a reciprocal
arrangement with a local
provider. Alternatively, if you
are a frequent traveller or plan
on a long stay, you could set
up an account with a local
ISP. The number of companies
offering internet access here is

Directory

growing and services are improving all the time. The standard rate for individual accounts, usually including unlimited browsing time and email but not call charges, starts at about 500 Kč a month. Corporate and leased lines are also available and rates rise according to the connection speed and number of accounts.

The main ISP in Prague is listed below. Alternatively, a list of Czech providers is available at the Czech-language search engine Seznam (www.seznam.cz).

Telenor/Nextra

V Celnici 10, Nové Město, Prague 1 (296 355 122/hotline 296 355 703/www.nextra.cz). Metro Náměstí Republiky/tram 5, 8, 14. **Open** 8am-5am Mon-Fri. **No credit cards. Map** p329 O3.
Born as the humble Terminal Bar, long since closed, the ISP side of the business was bought up and went corporate and is now Prague's leading service provider. It offers dial-up services, web hosting and design. Standard rates are generally friendly and reliable (but occasionally rather flaky) service.

Language

The Czech language was exiled from officialdom and literature in favour of German for much of the history of Bohemia, until the national revival in the 19th century saw its return as the national language. Today Czech is spoken throughout Prague, though most places of business, at least in the centre, should have some English-speaking staff. German may help you in speaking to some older Czechs, and many middle-aged people speak Russian, which was taught compulsorily in schools before the Velvet Revolution.

Czech is a difficult but rewarding language to learn in that it helps penetrate the wall put up by rather shy Czechs. They invariably light up upon hearing even the most

stumbling attempts at speaking their mother tongue by a foreigner. For essential vocabulary, *see p313*.

Left luggage

There are left luggage offices/lockers at Hlavní nádraží (*see p290*) and Nádraží Holešovice (*see p291*) stations and Florenc bus station (*see p291*).

Legal help

See lawyers listed under Business or contact your embassy (see Embassies).

Libraries

For a full list of Prague's libraries, ask at the National Library or look in the *Zlaté stránky* (*Yellow Pages*) under 'knihovny'. Admission rules vary – generally, you don't need to register to use reading rooms, but you do to borrow books, and for this you'll need your passport and sometimes a document stating that you are a student, teacher, researcher or a resident of Prague. Most libraries have restricted opening hours or close during July and August.

British Council

Politických vězňů 13, Nové Město, Prague 1 (221 991 160/www.britishcouncil.cz). Metro Muzeum/tram 11. **Open** 9am-6pm Mon-Fri. **Map** p329 O6.
The interior of the British Council's new location, Bredovský Dvůr, was designed by the celebrated Czech architect Eva Jiřičná. The new classrooms are designed in line with the latest technology and come with all manner of gadgets. The reading room is stocked with all the major British newspapers and magazines, plus there are free internet terminals available. The library is packed with materials and aids for TEFL and TESL teachers, but most of the literature in its collection now resides at the Městská knihovna, or City Library (*see below*). The video selection is varied and the free screenings can be excellent.

City Library

Městská knihovna v Praze
Mariánské náměstí 1, Staré Město, Prague 1 (222 113 555/www.mlp.cz). Metro Staroměstská/tram 17, 18. **Open** 9am-8pm Tue-Fri; 10am-5pm Sat. **Map** p328 K4.
The City Library is spacious, calm and state of the art. You'll find an excellent English-language literature section bolstered by 8,000 books and magazines from the British Council. An impressive music and audio collection also awaits, along with plenty of comfortable spaces for studying, scribbling and flipping through tomes. To borrow books (if you are staying in the Czech Republic less than six months) you will need your passport and 1,000 Kč for a cash deposit.

National Library

Národní knihovna v Praze
Klementinum, Křížovnické náměstí 4, Staré Město, Prague 1 (221 663 111/fax 221 663 261/www.nkp.cz). Metro Staroměstská/tram 17, 18. **Open** 9am-7pm Mon-Sat; main reading room 9am-10pm Mon-Sat). **Map** p328 J4.
A comprehensive collection of just about everything ever published in Czech and a reasonable international selection, housed in a confusing warren of occasionally gorgeous halls. This state-funded library has an ancient system of ordering books based on filling in little leaflets and throwing them in a box, which is emptied every two hours. The orders are brought after another hour (or a day if it isn't stored on site). Foreigners may only take books as far as one of the reading rooms. Hours vary for different reading rooms.

Lost property

Most railway stations have a lost property office (*Ztráty a nálezy*). If you lose your passport, contact your embassy (*see p299*).

Central Lost Property Office

Karolíny Světlé 5, Staré Město, Prague 1 (224 235 085). Metro Národní třída/tram 6, 9, 17, 18, 22. **Open** 8am-5.30pm Mon, Wed; 8am-4pm Tue, Thur; 8am-2pm Fri. **Map** p328 J5/6.

Media

Business, financial & news publications (English)

Business Central Europe

A monthly economics and business magazine published by the owners of *The Economist* magazine. It covers the whole of Central Europe and the former Soviet Union with regular stories on the Czech Republic.

Czech Business Weekly

Prague-based business magazine with extensive coverage of the markets and financial trends in the Czech Republic.

Central European Economic Review

A monthly regional overview published by the *Wall Street Journal* that, as you would expect given its provenance, tends to focus its coverage on the financial, banking and capital markets.

Fleet Sheet

www.fleet.cz
A daily one-page digest of the Czech press offering good coverage of major political and financial events. It is sent out as a fax each morning.

Newsline Radio Free Europe

www.rferl.org
Dry but highly informative daily overview of events in Eastern Europe and the countries that once formed the Soviet Union. It is produced in co-operation with the Prague-based radio station, Free Europe/Radio Liberty. Newsline's information is also available as an email service or it can be accessed from RFE's comprehensive website.

Radio Prague E-News

www.radio.cz
Czech state radio offers free email copy of daily news bulletins in English, Czech and other languages. The informative website comes with plentiful links to other internet-based sources of information.

General interest (English)

New Presence

This is the English-language version of *Nová přítomnost*, a journal dating back to inter-war Bohemia that offers a liberal and stimulating selection of opinion writing, some translated from its original Czech, by both local and international writers. It's not easy to find, but still worth seeking out for an in-depth look at the Czech Republic. Try the Globe Bookstore & Coffeehouse or Big Ben Bookshop (for both, *see p181*).

Prague Post

www.praguepost.com
The principal English-language weekly in the Czech Republic has come a long way in recent years with cultural coverage that betters that of many papers in larger cities of the former Eastern bloc, events calendar, business and trend features, plus a lively opinions section.

Transitions online

www.tol.cz
A fascinating internet-only magazine covering current events in Central and Eastern Europe, the Balkans, and the former Soviet Union. A Czech non-profit magazine dedicated to independent journalism, *Transitions Online* is based in Prague and uses a network of locally based correspondents to provide unique, cross-regional analysis.

Czech newspapers

Blesk

The extremely popular *Blesk* ('Lightning') is a daily tabloid packed full of sensationalised news, celebrity scandals, UFO sightings and a smattering of busty page-three girls.

Hospodářské noviny

The Czech equivalent of the *Financial Times*, this daily covers capital markets, exchange rates and business. Required reading for Czech movers and shakers.

Lidové noviny

An underground dissident paper in the communist days, *Lidové noviny*'s finest hour came in the early 1990s. Today the paper is still well-respected in some right-wing and intellectual circles, but commercialism has taken a toll.

Mladá fronta Dnes

A former communist paper, this has been the country's leading serious newspaper for several years. It now offers fairly balanced national and international news, and a reasonable level of independent opinion. The reporting and editing, however, can be poor.

Právo

The former Communist Party newspaper (the name means 'Justice'; it used to be *Rudé Právo* – 'Red Justice') has become a respectable, left-leaning daily with an equally respectable circulation.

Respekt

A scrappy weekly paper, *Respekt* takes a close look at the good, the bad and the ugly effects of the Czech Republic's transformation to a market economy. Not only does it ask the questions other newspapers don't but it also has some cutting-edge cartoons.

Sport

Daily sports paper with scores just decipherable to non-Czech speakers. Predictably heavy on European football, ice hockey and tennis; it also gives results from the NBA and NFL.

Czech periodicals

Elle

The local *Elle* fails to stand up against its Western counterparts, but does successfully appeal to both teens and middle-aged women, with flashy fashion spreads and interviews.

Reflex

Reflex is a popular, low-rent style weekly with glossy format, some interesting editorial and some very boring design.

Živel

A cyberpunk mag with a slick design and a sub-culture slant – like a cross between the *Face* and *Wired*. It's got a small circulation, so is more likely to be found in bookshops than at newsagents, and publishes irregularly.

Directory

Listings

Annonce

A classified ad sheet into which bargain-hunting Czechs delve to find good deals on second-hand washing machines, TVs, cars, etc. *Annonce* is also a good flat-hunting tool. Place your ad for free, then simply wait by the phone – it works.

Culture in Prague

An exhaustive monthly calendar of all categories of events held throughout Prague and the republic. Published mainly in Czech, it's also available in English at Wenceslas Square bookshops. Considerably easier to decode than *Kulturní přehled* (*see p311*). Notoriously unreliable movie listings.

Literary magazines

Though many have folded over the past few years, a whole pile of literary magazines is still published in Prague, in both Czech and English. You should be able to track down most of them at the Globe Bookstore & Coffeehouse or Big Ben Bookshop (for both, *see p181*). The Czech-language *Revolver Review*, supposedly published quarterly (but distinctly irregular), is a hefty periodical with samizdat (underground culture) roots. The *RR* presents new works by well-known authors along with lesser-known pieces such as pet favourites such as Kafka. *Labyrint Revue*, a monthly magazine, and *Literární noviny*, a weekly, are the other two main Czech publications offering original writing and reviews of new work. *Labyrint* also has music and art reviews.

English publications tend to come and go. The best and most widely known is *Trafika*, a 'quarterly' – tending to lapse to an 'occasionally' – showcase for international writers. Although it has recently been out of action, *Trafika*'s editors may yet revive this early and respected pioneer.

The *Prague Review*, formerly the *Jáma Review*, is a slim quarterly of plays, prose and poetry from Czechs and Czech-based expats. Its editors – who have included such Czech literary heavyweights as Bohumil Hrabal, Ivan Klíma and Miroslav Holub – subtitle the volume 'Bohemia's journal of international literature'.

Foreign press

Foreign newspapers are available at various stalls on and around Wenceslas Square and at major hotels. The *International Guardian*, *International Herald Tribune* and the international *USA Today* are available on the day of publication. Most other papers arrive 24 hours later.

Television

ČT1/ČT2

There are two national public channels. ČT1 tries to compete with TV Nova, but is out of its depth financially. ČT2 serves up serious music (including lots of jazz greats), theatre and documentaries to the small percentage of the population that tunes in. ČT2 sometimes broadcasts English-language movies with Czech subtitles on Monday evenings– Woody Allen flicks are popular, as are Monty Python classics. It also airs *Euronews*, an English-language pan-European programme, on weekdays usually at 12am and on weekends at 7.30am.

Prima TV

A Prague-based regional broadcaster that has been lamely following the lead of TV Nova but is slowly being revamped by new foreign partners from the West. The last resting place of (dubbed) US action serials.

TV Nova

One of the first private television stations in Eastern Europe. Funded by Ron Lauder, son of Estée, Nova TV looks like US television with lots of old Hollywood films and recycled sitcoms dubbed into Czech. Appallingly successful.

Radio

BBC World Service (101.1 FM)

English-language news on the hour plus regular BBC programming, with the occasional Czech and Slovak news broadcast. For 30 minutes a day at around teatime it transmits local Czech news in English, courtesy of Radio Prague.

Expres Radio (90.3 FM)

A newer station winning an increasing audience with fresh programming and alt pop.

Radio Free Europe

Prague is now the world headquarters for RFE. It still beams the same old faintly propagandist stuff, mainly to the Middle East now, from its HQ at the former Czechoslovak Federal Assembly building, next to the National Museum.

Radio Kiss (98.0 FM); Radio Bonton (99.7 FM); Evropa 2 (88.2 FM)

Pop music, pop music and more pop music.

Radio 1 (91.9 FM)

Excellent alternative music station that plays everything from Jimi Hendrix through world music of various ethno origins to techno. Unpredictable, however, with occasional evenings of call-in story reading in Czech. The Friday evening calendar show with Tim Otis has everything the hip party-goer needs to know.

Radio Prague (92.6 FM & 102.7 FM)

Daily news in English, plus interviews, weather and traffic. Nothing too inspired, but this is a well-established station with some history behind it.

Money

Currency

The currency of the Czech Republic is the *koruna* or crown (abbreviated as Kč). One crown equals 100 hellers (*haléřů*). Hellers come as small, light coins in denominations of

50. There are also 1, 2, 5, 10, 20 and 50 Kč coins in circulation. Notes are issued by the banks in denominations of 50, 100, 200, 500, 1,000, 2,000, and 5,000 Kč. At the time of going to press, the exchange rate was running at approximately 41 Kč to the pound, or around 22 Kč to the US dollar. It's obviously impossible to predict exchange rates in the future, but recently they have been fluctuating, largely upwards, so it's probably wise to convert only as much as you need in the short-term.

After the end of communist hegemony in Eastern Europe, the crown became the first fully convertible currency behind what had been the Iron Curtain. A bizarre indicator of its viability is the number of convincing counterfeit Czech banknotes in circulation. If someone stops you in the street asking if you want to change money, it's a fair bet he'll be trying to offload dodgy notes – and a complete certainty that he's scamming.

Cash economy

The Czech Republic has long been a cash economy, and such conveniences as cash machines (ATMs), credit cards and cheques (travellers' cheques included) are not nearly as ubiquitous here as they are in EU countries or the US. However, the situation is changing fairly rapidly and, particularly in Prague, it's not difficult to find ATMs that will pay out cash on the major credit and charge card networks such as Maestro, Cirrus and Delta. Look for the symbol that matches the one on your card and use your usual PIN number. Many classier shops, and restaurants, especially around Wenceslas Square and the Old Town, take credit cards and travellers' cheques in a major currency such as dollars or euros.

Loss/theft

Komerční banka (*see below*) is a local agent for MasterCard and Visa; call the numbers given in case of loss or theft. For lost/stolen AmEx cards, the number is 222 412 241, Diners Club 267 314 485 and to report missing travellers' cheques, it's 222 800 224 for American Express and 221 105 371 for Travelex.

Banks & currency exchange

Exchange rates are usually the same all over, but banks take a lower commission (usually one to two per cent). Unfortunately, they are only open during business hours (usually 8am-5pm Monday to Friday).

Bureaux de change usually charge a higher commission for changing cash or travellers' cheques, although some (such as those at the Charles Bridge end of Karlova street) may only take one per cent.

Bear in mind that this means little if you're getting a poor exchange rate.

Opening an account

At some banks, such as ČSOB, there is no requirement to deposit a minimum amount of funds in order to open an account and foreign currency accounts are available without the high fees once charged.

Money transfer

To get money fast, try the American Express office or, in the case of a serious emergency, your embassy. The Na příkopě branch of ČSOB processes transfers faster than other Czech banks.

American Express

Václavské náměstí 56, Nové Město, Prague 1 (222 800 224). Metro Můstek or Muzeum/tram 3, 9, 11, 14, 24. **Open** 9am-7pm daily. **Map** p329 N6.

Cardholders can receive their mail and faxes here and have personal cheques cashed, but can't cash third-party cheques.

Československá obchodní banka (ČSOB)

Na příkopě 14, Nové Město, Prague 1 (261 351 111/www. csob.cz). Metro Můstek or Náměstí Republiky/tram 3, 5, 9, 14, 24. **Open** 8am-5pm Tue-Thur; 8am-4pm Fri. **Map** p329 N5.

Specialises in international currency transactions and offers exceptionally professional service, if long waits for transfers from abroad.

Komerční banka

Na příkopě 33, Nové Město, Prague 1 (222 432 408/infoline 800 111 055/www.kb.cz). Metro Můstek or Náměstí Republiky/tram 3, 5, 9, 14, 24. **Open** 9am-6pm Mon, Wed; 8am-5pm Tue, Thur, Fri. **Map** p329 N5.

The country's largest full-service bank, with a large network of branches throughout the Czech Republic. The ATM network accepts international credit cards and is a MasterCard (Eurocard) and Visa agent. Its card emergency number is 224 248 110.

Živnostenská banka

Na příkopě 20, Nové Město, Prague 1 (224 121 111). Metro Můstek/tram 3, 5, 9, 14, 24. **Open** 8.30am-5pm Mon-Fri. **Map** p329 N5.

This old trading bank, which is housed in one of the most beautiful buildings in Prague, has long experience in working with foreign clients, and most staff speak a reasonable level of English.

Natural hazards

Deer ticks are known to transmit encephalitis in Central and Eastern Europe, for which a vaccine is available at many clinics. Ticks found should be smothered in soap or Vaseline, then removed by twisting in an anti-clockwise direction.

Lightning strikes are quite prevalent during Bohemia's muggy summer but they pose little hazard unless you are on open ground at high elevations.

Directory

Air quality in Prague has improved but pollution regulation is poorly enforced and the incidence of cancer is well above Western Europe's.

Numbers

Dates are written in the British order, not the American: day, month, year.

When writing figures, Czechs put commas where Americans and Britons would put decimal points and vice versa, thus ten thousand Czech crowns is written as 10.000 Kč.

Opening hours

Standard opening hours for most shops and banks are from 8am or 9am to 5pm or 6pm Monday to Friday. Many shops are open a bit longer and from 9am to noon or 1pm on Saturday. Shops with extended hours are called *večerka* (open until 10pm or midnight) and 'non-stop' (open 24 hours daily). Outside the centre, most shops are closed on Sundays and holidays. Shops frequently close for a day or two for no apparent reason; some shops close for an hour or two at lunch; and some shops and many theatres close for a month's holiday in August. Most places have shorter opening hours in winter (starting September or October) and extended hours in summer (starting April or May). Castles and some other attractions are only open in summer.

Police & security

Police in the Czech Republic are not regarded as serious crimefighters or protectors of the public and are just barely considered keepers of law and order. Their past as pawns for the regime, combined with a present reputation for corruption, racism and incompetence, has prevented them from gaining much in the

way of respect. If you are the victim of crime while in Prague, don't expect much help – or even concern – from the local constabulary.

For emergencies, call **158**. The main police station, at Na Perštýně and Bartolomějská, is open 24 hours daily. In theory, an English-speaking person should be on call to assist crime victims with making a report, but in practice any encounter with the Czech police is likely to be slow, unpleasant and ineffective.

Legalities

You are expected to carry your passport or residence card at all times. If you have to deal with police, they are supposed to provide an interpreter for you. Buying or selling street drugs is illegal, and a controversial Czech drug law outlaws the possession of even small quantities of drugs. The legal drinking age is 18, but nobody here seems to pay any attention to this.

Prague's pickpockets concentrate in tourist areas like Wenceslas Square, Old Town Square and Charles Bridge and are particularly fond of the Slavia and tram No. 22 from Malostranské náměstí to Prague Castle. Keep an eye on your handbag or wallet, especially in crowds and on public transport. Seedier parts of Prague include some of Žižkov, parts of Smíchov, the park in front of Hlavní nádraží (the main train station), and the lower end of Wenceslas Square and upper end of Národní třída.

Postal services

Stamps are available from post offices, newsagents, tobacconists and most places where postcards are sold. Postcards as well as regular letters (up to 20 grams) cost 11 Kč within Europe and 20 Kč for airmail outside Europe.

Packages should be wrapped in plain white or brown paper. Always use black or blue ink – never red, or, horrors, green – or a snippy clerk will refuse to accept your mail. Even oddly shaped postcards are known to have been refused by the rule-obsessed Czech Post.

Post offices are scattered all over Prague. Though they are being thoroughly modernised, many have different opening hours and offer varying degrees of service, and all are confusing. Indeed, the system designating what's on offer at which window is perplexing, even for some Czechs.

The Main Post Office on Jindřišská in Nové Město, Prague 1, offers the most services, some available 24 hours a day. Fax and international phone services are in the annexe around the corner at Politických vězňů 4. Some services, such as poste restante (general delivery) and EMS express mail, are theoretically available at all post offices, but are much easier to use at the main office on Jindřišská.

You can buy special edition stamps and send mail overnight within the Czech Republic and within a few days to Europe and the rest of the world via EMS – a cheaper but less reliable service than commercial couriers.

Packages

To send or collect restricted packages or items subject to tax or duty, you must go to the Customs Post Office (*see p307*). Bring your passport, residence permit and any other ID. For incoming packages, you will also need to pay duty and tax. The biggest queues at the Customs Post Office form between 11am and 1.30pm.

Outgoing packages should be wrapped in plain white or brown paper. If they weigh more than two kilogrammes (4.4 pounds), are valued upwards of 30,000 Kč or contain 'unusual contents' such as medicine or clothing, they must officially be cleared through the Customs Post Office, but in practice this is not usually necessary.

Uninsured packages of up to two kilos don't need to be declared and can be sent from any post office – they're treated as letters (400Kč to the UK; 560 Kč to the US), and you don't need your passport. Up to four kilos the consignment is treated as a package, but if you don't want to insure it, it doesn't usually need to be declared and can be sent from a post office (457 Kč-505 Kč to the UK; 715 Kč-881 Kč to the US). If the package is heavier or you would like to insure it, take it to the Customs Post Office and declare it. Take your passport.

Useful postal vocabulary

letters: *příjem – výdej listovin.*
packages: *příjem – výdej balíčků* or *balíků.*
money transactions: *platby.*
stamps: *známky* – usually at the window marked *Kolky a ceniny.*
special issue stamps: *filatelistický servis.*
registered mail: *doporučeně.*

Main Post Office

Hlavní pošta
Jindřišská 14, Nové Město, Prague 1 (221 131 111/infoline 800 104 410). Metro Můstek/tram 3, 9, 14, 24. **Open** 2am-midnight daily. **No credit cards. Map** p329 N6.

Masarykovo nádraží

Hybernská 15, Nové Město, Prague 1 (222 219 714). Metro Náměstí Republiky/tram 5, 8, 14. **Open** 8am-8pm Mon-Fri; 8am-noon Sat. **Map** p329 O4.

Customs Post Office

Celní Pošta
Plzeňská 139, Smíchov, Prague 5 (257 019 111). Metro Anděl, then tram 4, 7, 9. **Open** 7am-3.30pm Mon, Tue, Thur, Fri; 7am-6pm Wed. **No credit cards.**

Religion

There are plenty of churches in Prague, but services in English are held only at these churches:

Anglican Church of Prague

Klimentská, Nové Město, Prague 1 (284 688575). Metro Náměstí Republiky/tram 5, 8, 14. **Services** 11am Sun. **Map** p329 Q1.

Church of St Thomas

Josefská, Malá Strana, Prague 1 (257 530 556). Metro Malostranká. **Services** 6pm Sat, 11am Sun (in English). **Map** p327 F3.
Catholic Mass.

International Baptist Church of Prague

Vinohradská 68, Žižkov, Prague 3 (731 778 735/www.ibcp.cz). Metro Jiřího z Poděbrad/tram 11. **Service** 11am Sun. **Map** p333 C3.

International Church of Prague

Peroutkova 57, Smíchov, Prague 5 (296 392 231/www.volny.cz/jx-studio). Metro Anděl, then bus 137 or 508. **Services** 10.30am Sun.

Prague Christian Fellowship

Ječná 19 (entry at back of house), Prague 2 (224 315 613). Metro Karlovo Náměstí. **Services** 4.30pm Sun. **Map** p330 L9.

Safety & security

Prague has historically been a crossroads between Europe and Asia and a major transit point for goods both legal and otherwise, and the people who traffic and buy them. Penalties for even minor drug possession are severe, so it's best not to take chances.

The street crime in the city consists mainly of pickpockets, not violent crime, though many practitioners are experts. They are easy enough to avoid, however, if you stay away from crowds at major tourist attractions and remain as alert as you would in any major city.

A favourite target of family pickpockets, who create diversions while mobbing you in a group, is the 22 tram during late spring and summer, especially between Malostranské náměstí and Prague Castle.

It's always a good idea to use your room safe, if you have one. Thus, rather than carrying all your holiday money, only sufficient for the day is kept on your person and liable to loss. Keep a separate record of the numbers of any travellers' cheques and credit cards, along with contact information for reporting their loss.

Smoking

Smoking is not allowed on public transport in Prague but that's about the only place in the city that people don't light up and puff away like lab beagles. A new anti-smoking law is in effect but has had little practical effect. Basically, restaurants must have non-smoking areas but smoke still gets in your eyes.

Study

Charles University

Founded in 1348 by King Charles IV, Charles University (Univerzita Karlova) is the oldest university in Central Europe, and the hub of Prague's student activity. Its heart is the Carolinum, a Gothic building on Ovocný trh near the Estates Theatre, home to the administration offices. Other university buildings are scattered all over the city.

Several cash-hungry faculties now run special courses for foreigners. Contact the relevant dean or the International Relations Office during the university year (October to May) for information on courses and admissions procedures. It is best to enquire in person at the university as the staff can be difficult to reach by phone.

Below is a selection of popular offerings. For courses outside Prague, contact the British Council (*see p302*).

Charles University

International Relations Office, Universita Karlova, Rektorát, Ovocný trh 3-5, Staré Město, Prague 1 (224 491 302/fax 224 229 487/www.cuni.cz). Metro Staroměstská or Můstek/tram 3, 9, 14, 17, 18, 24. **Open** 9am-5pm Mon-Fri. **Map** p328 M4.

FAMU

Smetanovo nábřeží 2, Staré Město, Prague 1 (221 197 211/221 197 222). Metro Staroměstská or Národní třída/tram 6, 9, 17, 18, 22, 23. **Open** noon-4pm Mon, Wed; 10am-1pm Tue, Thur. **No credit cards.** **Map** p328 J5.
Famous for turning out such Oscar-winning directors as Miloš Forman, Prague's foremost school of film, TV and photography runs several English courses under its Film For Foreigners (3F) programme and Cinema Studies, including summer workshops (in co-operation with NY University, Washington, Miami and Boston), six-month and one-year courses in aspects of film and TV production and a BA in photography.

Institute of Language & Professional Training

Ústav jazykové a odborné přípravy Univerzita Karlova, Vratislavova 10, Nové Město, Prague 2 (224 990 411/fax 224 990 440/www.ujop.cuni.cz). Metro Karlovo náměsti/tram 3, 16, 17, 21.
Fees 1yr course of training for future study at universities 125,000 Kč; 1yr course of Czech 95,000 Kč; 6wk session 20,000 Kč; intensive semester 46,000 Kč; individual lesson 530 Kč for 45 mins. **Open** *Oct-Dec* 10am-2pm Tue-Thur. *Feb-May* 10am-2pm Tue-Thur. **No credit cards.**
Aimed at preparing foreign nationals who want to embark on degree courses at Czech universities, this branch of Charles University offers Czech-language training in the form of a one-year course (ie ten months of teaching) or intensive Czech-language courses for a semester, or individual classes.

School of Czech Studies

Filozofická fakulta, Univerzita Karlova, náměstí Jana Palacha 2, Staré Město, Prague 1 (221 619 381/www.ff.cuni.cz). Metro Staroměstská/tram 17, 18. **Open** 9-11am, 1-3pm Mon-Wed; 11am-3pm Thur; 9-11am, noon-2pm Fri. **Fees** 68,000 Kč per 2-semester year for Czech Studies programme; Czech language courses start at 28,000 Kč. **No credit cards.** **Map** p328 J3.
The School of Czech Studies runs year-long courses during the academic year, offering a mix of language instruction and lectures in Czech history and culture (Czech Studies programme). Czech-language classes are available for beginner, intermediate and advanced speakers.

Summer School of Slavonic Studies

Filozofická fakulta, Univerzita Karlova, Náměstí Jana Palacha 2, Staré Město, Prague 1 (221 619 381/http://lsss.ff.cuni.cz/english/). Metro Staroměstská/tram 17, 18. **Open** by appointment only. **Fees** 15,000 Kč (course fee and trips only); 33,000 Kč (includes dorm accommodation & meals). **No credit cards.** **Map** p328 J3.
This one-month summer course, held yearly in August, is designed for professors and advanced students in Slavonic studies. It's best to apply by post.

Other courses

Anglo-American College

Lázeňská 4, Malá Strana, Prague 1 (257 530 202/www.aac.edu/www.aavs.cz). Metro Malostranská/tram 12, 18, 22, 23. **Open** 9am-5pm Mon-Fri. **Fees** 44,300 Kč per 5-course semester; 11,200 Kč per 1-course semester. **No credit cards.** **Map** p327 F4.
A Western-accredited private college offering Western-style degree courses in business, economics, the humanities and law. While the entire syllabus and all the classes are in English, the student body itself is a mix of Czechs, Slovaks and various foreign nationals. There are limited course offerings during the summer session.

Prague Center for Further Education

Pštrosova 19, Nové Město, Prague 1 (257 534 013-14/www.prague-center.cz). Metro Národní třída/tram 6, 9, 18, 21, 22, 23. **Open** 9.30am-6pm Mon-Fri. **Fees** 2,600-5,600 Kč per course. **No credit cards.** **Map** p330 K8.
Provides Prague's international community access to English-language learning. Dynamic and interactive courses in everything from Czech film history to wine tasting, plus sundry other Prague-related subjects.

Language courses

Many schools offer Czech-language instruction. If you prefer a more informal approach, place a notice on one of the boards at the Charles University Faculty, the Globe Bookstore (*see p181*), Radost FX (*see p244*) or anywhere else where young Czechs and foreigners meet. Many students and other young people are happy to offer Czech conversation in exchange for English conversation. But since Czech grammar is difficult most serious learners need some systematic, professional instruction to master the basics.

Akcent International House Prague

Bítovská 3, Kačerov, Prague 4 (261 261 638/fax 261 261 880/www.akcent.cz). Metro Budějovická. **Fees** 3wk intensive 7,800 Kč; standard 20wk course 5,500 Kč. **No credit cards.**
A co-op run and owned by the senior teachers, both Czech and foreign, this school has a good reputation for standards and quality. Choose a three-week intensive course (60 hours instruction) or a more relaxed five-month (one semester) course (two hours weekly). All classes have a maximum size of six. A bit out of the way, but worth the travel.

ARS Linguarum

Londýnská 41, Nové Město, Prague 2 (224 266 744/fax 224 266 740/www.arslinguarum.cz). Metro IP Pavlova. **Open** 9am-

4.30pm Mon-Fri. **Fees** 350-370 Kč per lesson. **No credit cards**. **Map** p331 P9.
Courses of Czech are run for English, German, French, Russian, Spanish and Italian speakers and are scheduled individually, beginning and ending at any time during the course of the year. Intensive classes include 20 lessons a week and are charged 350 Kč per lesson. Standard courses of two 90-minute lessons a week are charged up to 370 Kč per hour and run in classes of up to ten students. Instructors are both Czech and foreign. Textbooks, tapes, videos and other material developed in-house are provided by ARS Linguarum.

Ulrych Language Studio
Benešovská 21, Prague 10 (267 311 300/fax 271 733 551/www.ulrych.cz). Metro Náměstí Míru/tram 10, 16. **Open** 8.30am-5pm Mon-Fri. **Fees** 670 Kč per 60-min lesson; 1,000 Kč per 90-min lesson. **No credit cards**.
This language school is ideal for companies; the price includes overall testing every half a year. The client can choose between intensive courses including 20 hours' teaching a week or standard courses running twice a week.

LBS
Vinohradská 184, Prague 3 (267 132 127/www.lbspraha.cz). Metro Flora/tram 10, 16. **Fees** 8am-5pm Mon-Fri. **Fees** 440 Kč per 45 mins. **No credit cards**.
A medium-sized language school with reasonable prices and very pleasant staff with professional attitudes, that is generally recommended by its former students. Intensive courses of 8 to 12 lessons a day have 20% discount. A programme including an intensive week course followed by a three-month standard course of two 90-minute lessons a week is the most popular.

Lingua Viva
Křemencova 10, Nové Město, Prague 1 (222 922 292/fax 224 921 142/www.linguaviva.cz). Metro Národní třída/tram 6, 9, 18, 21, 22, 23. **Open** 9am-7pm Mon-Thur; 9am-noon Fri. **Classes** of 5-9 students. **Fees** 72-hr course

(5 mths) 5,650 Kč; intensive 64-hr course (1 mth, summer only) 4,650 Kč; individual lesson 405-472 Kč 45mins, 540-630 Kč 60mins. **No credit cards**. **Map** p330 K8.
Small, independent Lingua Viva is something of an upstart in comparison to the other language schools, with better rates and more informal instruction than most.

State Language School
Státní jazyková Škola
Školská 15, Nové Město, Prague 1 (Slavonic languages & Czech for foreigners 222 230 016/fax 222 232 236/www.sjs.cz). Metro Můstek/tram 3, 6, 9, 14, 17, 18, 22, 23, 24. **Open** 12.30-3.30pm Tue; 12.30-6.30pm Wed; 12.30-3.30pm Thur, Fri. **Fees** intensive 14,760 Kč; standard 4,065 Kč; summer 7,000 Kč. **No credit cards**. **Map** p330 M7.
The largest and cheapest language school in Prague is state run and teaches just about every language under the sun. The Czech for Foreigners department offers both intensive courses (16 hours weekly for five months) and standard courses (four hours weekly for five months) during the normal school year, as well as shorter intensive summer courses (20 hours weekly for one month). Classes tend to start very large, but many students drop out over the course of the term, leaving a smaller, more dedicated, but reasonably priced class.

Student travel

GTS
Ve Smečkách 33, Nové Město, Prague 1 (222 211 204/296 211 717/call centre 844 140 140 or 257 187 100/www.gtsint.cz). Metro Muzeum/tram 3, 9, 14, 24. **Open** 9am-7pm Mon-Fri; 10am-3pm Sat. **Credit** AmEx, DC, MC, V. **Map** p331 N8.
The best place for ISIC card-holders to find cheap student fares. Especially good international flight bargains, as well as occasional deals on bus and train travel. GTS also offers travel insurance and issues ISIC cards – though, annoyingly, only to applicants who have ID from local institutions.
Other locations: Bechyňova 3, Dejvice, Prague 6 (224 325 235/fax 224 325 237).

Student Agency
Ječná 37, Nové Město, Prague 2 (224 999 666/fax 224 999 660/www.studentagency.cz). Metro IP Pavlova/tram 4, 6, 11, 16, 22, 23, 34. **Open** 9am-6pm Mon-Fri, 9am-1pm Sat. **Credit** MC, V. **Map** p330 L9.
Cheap flights, buses and trains outside the Czech Republic, especially for ISIC holders. Also offers Allianz travel insurance and issues ISIC cards, visas, working permits for programmes abroad, and international phone cards.
Other locations: Ruzyně Airport, departure hall, plane tickets only (222 111 909/fax 222 111 902)

Telephones

Virtually all of the public coin telephones that still take 2 Kč coins are perpetually broken; the rest run on telephone cards, which come in denominations of 50 to 150 units and can be bought at newsstands, post offices and anywhere you see the blue-and-yellow Český Telecom sticker. Local calls cost 3.20 Kč (lasting two minutes from 7am to 7pm weekdays, and four and a half minutes from 7pm to 7am weekdays, all day weekends and public holidays and Sundays). International calls, which are horrendously expensive unless you use a Trick card (*see p310*), can be made from any phone box or more easily at a private booth at the Main Post Office (*see p307*).

The international dialling code to the Czech Republic is 420. To call abroad from Prague, dial the prefix 00, the country and the area codes (for UK area codes omit the 0) and then the number. The prefix for the United Kingdom is 44, for America and Canada it's 1 and for Australia 61. If you use the prefix 952 00, then the country code, then the number, you will be connected on a digital line at a significant discount.

Since September 2002 all numbers in Prague have been

Directory

on digital switchboards. All fixed lines were amended so phone numbers always have nine digits. If you come across an old Prague fixed line number starting in 02 followed by eight digits, omit the zero and you should theoretically be able to get through. If it's followed only by seven digits you may have to call the information on 1180, tell them the old number and they'll give you the current one. Most operators speak some English. The *Zlaté stránky* (*Yellow Pages*) also has an English-language index at the back.

Český Telecom – Czech Telecom

Olšanská 5, Žižkov, Prague 3 (800 123 456 toll free/www.telecom.cz). Metro Želivského/tram 5, 9, 16, 19. **Open** 8am-4pm Mon-Fri. **Map** p333 E2.

Trick Cards

Pre-paid long distance phone cards are on sale at newsagents' stands for 200 Kč up to 300 Kč. One unit is worth 4 Kč. The length of the unit differs with the time of the call and the destination to which the call is being made. During the busiest hours on a weekday between 7am and 7pm one unit lasts 35 seconds, at weekends and public holidays it lasts 82 seconds. Access the lines from any public or private phone via a code number.

Faxes

You can send faxes from the Main Post Office (*see p307*) from 7am to 8pm daily (counter No.2, look for post fax). To Great Britain as well as the US you pay 63 Kč for the first page plus 28 Kč for each additional page.

You can receive a fax marked clearly with your name at the Main Post Office (fax 221 131 402). You are charged 16 Kč for a maximum of five pages, 2 Kč for each additional page.

Mobile phones

Competition has led to improved services and lower rates in the Czech Republic but since January 2004 22 per cent VAT has been imposed on telecommunication services so prices have increased accordingly. Despite the popularity of mobile phones – Czechs are obsessed with them, and more than 70 per cent of the population, including infants and people over the age of 65, own one – it sometimes seems that more energy goes into marketing mobile phones than providing good service and coverage. The three main companies are listed below – they offer different payment schemes and coverage areas, so it's best to get details before deciding. They are also the only companies in town who rent out phones short-term – at highly expensive rates. Cheap phones can be bought second-hand, but guarantees are slim to nil. If you are here for a short time, pick up a combination SIM and pre-paid card for your phone.

All three companies use both the 1,800 MHz and 900 MHz wavebands, which means that owners of all standard UK mobiles can use them as long as they have a roaming facility (which may need to be pre-arranged). US tri- and quad-band GSM mobile phones will work in the Czech Republic as well as the rest of Europe.

EuroTel

Vyskočilova 1442/1b, Prague 4 (267 011 111/www.eurotel.cz). Metro Českomoravská/tram 8. **Open** 8am-6pm Mon-Fri; 9am-1pm Sat. **No credit cards.** The leading provider of mobile phone services and a subsidiary of the national telephone monopoly Český Telecom.

T-Mobile

Tomíčkova 1244, Prague 4 (24hr service 603 603 603/www.t-mobile.cz). Metro Roztyly. **Open** 8am-6pm Mon-Fri. **No credit cards.**

Providers of T-Mobile, the main rival to Eurotel. English-language help and loads of different service packages are available at T-Mobil shops all over the city.

Vodafone

Vinohradská 167, Prague 10 (800 777 777 toll free/www.vodafone.cz). Metro Strašnická/tram 17, 18. **Open** 9am-8pm Mon-Fri; 9am-2pm Sat. **No credit cards.** Providers of the newest mobile phone service – Vodafone has cheaper rates under some packages but spotty coverage, especially outside Prague.

Time

The Czech Republic is on Central European Time (CET), one hour ahead of the UK, six ahead of New York and nine ahead of Los Angeles, and uses the 24-hour clock. The Czechs are prompt, and you should never be more than 15 minutes late for a meeting.

Tipping & VAT

Czechs tend to round up restaurant bills, often only by a few crowns, but foreigners are more usually expected to leave a ten per cent tip. If service is bad, however, don't feel obliged to leave anything. Service is often added on automatically for large groups. Taxi drivers expect you to round the fare up but, if you've just been ripped off, don't give a heller.

A value-added tax of 19 per cent has been slapped on to retail purchases for years in the Czech Republic but only as recently as 2000 was a system set up to reimburse non-resident foreigners' VAT payments. You can claim a refund at the border or at Ruzyně Airport in the departure hall at the customs desk on the left. You'll need your shop receipt, passport and a VAT refund form, which staff can supply. Purchases of over 1,000 Kč are eligible if taken out of the country within 30 days of sale.

Toilets

Usually called a 'WC' (pronounce it 'veh-tseh'), the word for toilet is *záchod* and there is sometimes a charge for using one of about 5 Kč. Calls of nature can be answered in all metro stations from at least 8am to 8pm, and at many fast-food joints and department stores. 'Ladies' is *Dámy* or *Ženy*, 'Gents' *Páni* or *Muži*. Czech public lavatories, located primarily in metro or train stations, are often locked and are generally insalubrious so you're better off finding one in a restaurant or hotel.

Tourist information

The English-language weekly *Prague Post* carries entertainment sections along with survival hints. Monthly entertainment listings can be found in *Kulturní přehled* (in Czech), *Kultura v Praze* and its shorter English equivalent *Culture in Prague* (see Media). The Prague Information Service (PIS; *see below*) publishes a free monthly entertainment listings programme in English.

Bear in mind that the use of the international blue-and-white 'i' information sign is not regulated, so the places that are carrying it are not necessarily official.

The best map for public transport or driving is the widely available *Kartografie Praha Plán města* (a book with a yellow cover), costing about 100 Kč, though for central areas the co-ordinates are sometimes far too vague. Check you've got the latest edition. For central areas the free map from Prague Information Service is useful.

Čedok

Na příkopě 18, Nové Město, Prague 1 (224 197 111/800 112 112/www.cedok.cz). Metro Můstek/tram 3, 5, 8, 9, 14, 24. **Open** 9am-7pm Mon-Fri; 9.30am-1pm Sat. **Map** p329 N5.

The former state travel agency is still the biggest in the Czech Republic. A handy place to obtain train, bus and air tickets, and accommodation information.

PIS (Prague Information Service)

Pražská informační služba *Betlémské náměstí 2, Prague 1 (general info 12444/www.pis.cz). Metro Můstek/tram 3, 4, 8, 9,14, 24.* **Open** *Apr-Oct* 9am-7pm Mon-Fri; 9am-6pm Sat, Sun. *Nov-Mar* 9am-6pm Mon-Fri; 9am-5pm Sat, Sun. **Map** p328 K5.

PIS provides incredibly wide-ranging, free information, maps and help with a smile. **Other locations**: Hlavní nádraží (Main Railway Station), Wilsonova, Nové Město, Prague 1 (224 239 258); Old Town Hall, Staroměstské náměstí, Staré Město, Prague 1 (224 482 202/224 482 018); Charles Bridge – Malá Strana-side Tower (summer only).

Visas

Requirements can change frequently, but at press time citizens of the US, UK and other EU members and most other European countries did not need a visa to enter the Czech Republic for stays of up to 90 days – just a valid passport with at least six months to run by the end of their visit. Under a recent law aimed at preventing illegal residence by foreigners, however, border crossings can get complicated if you don't prepare. Foreigners who do need a visa to enter the Czech Republic, including at press time Canadians, Australians, New Zealanders and South Africans, can no longer get theirs at the border but must apply at a Czech embassy outside the Czech Republic (but not necessarily in their home country). The process may take weeks, so early planning is critical.

Even visitors who don't require a visa may now be asked for proof that they have sufficient finances, pre-arranged accommodation and international health insurance.

Automated, extremely confusing visa information is available in English at the Foreigners' Police in Prague (*see p312*) or at the Ministry of Foreign Affairs (224 181 111/www.mzv.cz). You are technically required to register at the local police station within 30 days of arriving (if you are staying at a hotel this will be

Weather report

Average daytime temperatures, rainfall and hours of sunshine in Prague.

	Temp (°C/°F)	Rainfall (mm/in)	Sunshine (hrs/day)
Jan	-5 to 0/22-32	26/1.0	2
Feb	-4 to 3/25-37	20/0.8	3
Mar	-1 to 8/30-46	27/1.1	5
Apr	3 to 13/37-56	35/1.4	6
May	7 to 18/45-65	64/2.5	8
June	10 to 21/51-70	71/2.8	9
July	12 to 23/53-74	81/3.2	9
Aug	12 to 23/53-73	72/2.8	8
Sept	9 to 17/48-63	47/1.8	6
Oct	4 to 13/40-56	29/1.1	4
Nov	0 to 6/32-43	29/1.1	2
Dec	-3 to 2/26-36	22/0.9	1

Directory

done for you). If you are from one of the countries whose residents are allowed only 30 days in the Czech Republic, you must obtain an extended visa (confusingly called an exit visa, or výjezdní vízum) from the Foreigners' Police office to allow you up to 90 days in total.

Longer stays

The other option if you want to stay longer is a residence permit (občanský průkaz), which isn't easy to get and must be obtained from a Czech embassy abroad.

The Czech police conduct periodic crackdowns on illegal aliens. They're usually aimed at Romanians, Ukrainians, Vietnamese and other nationals considered undesirable, though a few Brits and US citizens get caught. Even so, many expats reside here illegally. Some avoid dealing with the above requirements by leaving and re-entering the country. Border police are getting wise to the trick, however, and it can't be relied on. If you try it, be sure to get the required stamp in your passport as you leave and re-enter by saying razítko prosím (stamp please).

Foreigners' Police

Cizinecká policie
Sdružení 1, Praha 4 (info 974 820 935). Metro Pankrác. **Open** 7.30am-11.30am, 12.15-3pm Mon, Tue, Thur; 8am-12.15pm, 1-5pm Wed; 7.30am-11.30pm Fri. **Other locations**: Olšanská 2, Žižkov, Prague 3.

Weights & measures

Czechs use the metric system, even selling eggs in batches of five or ten. Things are usually measured out in decagrams or 'deka' (10 grams) or deciliters or 'deci' (10 centilitres). So a regular glass of wine is usually two deci (abbreviated dcl), and ham enough for a few sandwiches is 20 deka (dkg).

When to go

Spring

Hotel prices rise, but Prague's most awaited season sees the city shaking off the hibernation of a long, cold, cloudy winter. While it's not unheard of for snow to linger as late as early May, temperatures are often perfect for strolling.

Summer

Praguers usually leave for their country cottages (chatas) and abandon the city to the tourist hordes, leaving hotel bargains but many closed venues. Summers are warm (rarely hot) and prone to thundery showers. The days are long, and it stays light until 10pm.

Autumn

Can be the prettiest time of year, with crisp cool air and sharp blue skies, but can also be the wettest. September is a good month to visit the city, with hotel prices falling but castles still open. The streets are once again jammed with cars, the parks full of children, and the restaurants busy. The days grow shorter alarmingly quickly. By the end of October, the sun sets at around 5.30pm.

Winter

Street-side carp sellers and Christmas markets help break the monotony of the long, cold, grey winter, rooms are at their most affordable (except during the holidays) and snow makes Prague so beautiful that you forget the gloom that blankets the city. Sadly, bright, white snow is rarely accompanied by a clear blue sky. Many Prague residents still burn coal for heating, which doesn't help.

Public holidays

New Year's Day, 1 Jan; Easter Monday; Labour Day, 1 May; Liberation Day, 8 May; Cyril & Methodius Day, 5 July; Jan Hus Day, 6 July; Statehood Day, 28 Sept; Czech Founding Day, 28 Oct; Struggle for Freedom Day, 17 Nov; Christmas, 24-26 Dec.

Women

Traditional gender roles are firmly entrenched in the Czech Republic and feminism is still not taken very seriously, but nevertheless some women's organisations do exist. Most tend to emphasise women's rights as an integral part of human rights, rather than enter any debate about that tricky word 'feminism'.

Ženské Centrum in Prague 2 (Gorazdova 20, 224 917 224) consists of two organisations: proFem focuses on protection of women against violence, and the Centre for Gender Studies deals with women's rights in general, organising seminars and educational campaigns. The Gender Studies Library (224 915 666) has some material in English.

Working in Prague

To work legally in the Czech Republic, you need a work permit and the necessary residency permit (confusingly termed a 'Temporary Visa for over 90 Days'). Unless you already have the residency permit, only available from Czech embassies and consulates outside the republic, usually after a long wait, there's little hope of finding legal work.

Work permits

If you do have the residency permit, and are to be employed by a Czech company, the company needs to obtain a work permit for you. You'll need to give evidence of qualifications and in some cases proof of relevant work experience, all accompanied by official notarised translations.

Useful addresses

The Prague Post's web page (www.praguepost.com) contains a mini-guide to the Kafka-esque process of living and working in the city and its classifieds often feature advertisements from service agencies that are willing to help for a fee.

Vocabulary

For Czech food and drink vocabulary, see p148 **What's on the menu?**

Pronunciation

a	as in gap
á	as in father
e	as in let
é	as in air
i, y	as in lit
í, ý	as in seed
o	as in lot
ó	as in lore
u	as in book
ú, ů	as in loom
c	as in its
č	as in chin
ch	as in loch
ď	as in duty
ň	as in onion
ř	as a standard r, but flatten the tip of the tongue making a short forceful buzz like ž
š	as in shin
ť	as in stew
ž	as in pleasure
dž	as in George

The basics

Czech words are always stressed on the first syllable.
hello/good day *dobrý den*
good evening *dobrý večer*
good night *dobrou noc*
goodbye *nashledanou*
yes *ano* (often *o* or just *jo*)
no *ne*
please *prosím*
thank you *děkuji*
excuse me *promiňte*
sorry *pardon*
help! *pomoc!*
attention! *pozor!*
I don't speak Czech *nemluvím česky*
I don't understand *nerozumím*
Do you speak English? *Mluvíte anglicky?*
sir *pán*
madam *paní*
open *otevřeno*
closed *zavřeno*
I would like... *Chtěl bych...*
How much is it? *kolik to stojí?*
May I have a receipt, please? *účet, prosím*
Can we pay, please? *zaplatíme, prosím*

where is... *kde je...*
go left *doleva*
go right *doprava*
straight *rovně*
far *daleko*
near *blízko*
good *dobrý*
bad *špatný*
big *velký*
small *malý*
no problem *to je v pořádku*
Do you have any light food here? *Máte nějaké lehké jídlo?*
Cool piercing! *dobrej piercing!*
It's a rip-off *to je zlodě_jina*
I'm absolutely knackered *jsem úplně vyfluslý*
The lift is stuck *výtah zůstal viset*
Could I speak to Václav? *mohl bych mluvit s Václavem?*

Street names, etc

In conversation most Prague streets are referred to by their name only, leaving off *ulice*, *třída* and so on.
avenue *třída*
bridge *most*
church *kostel*
gardens *sady* or *zahrada*
island *ostrov*
lane *ulička*
monastery, **convent** *klášter*
park *park*
square *náměstí* or *nám*
station *nádraží* or *nádr*
steps *schody*
street *ulice* or *ul*
tunnel *tunel*

Numbers

0	*nula*
1	*jeden*
2	*dva*
3	*tři*
4	*čtyři*
5	*pět*
6	*šest*
7	*sedm*
8	*osm*
9	*devět*
10	*deset*
11	*jedenáct*
12	*dvanáct*
13	*třináct*
14	*čtrnáct*
15	*patnáct*
16	*šestnáct*
17	*sedmnáct*
18	*osmnáct*
19	*devatenáct*
20	*dvacet*
30	*třicet*
40	*čtyřicet*
50	*padesát*
60	*šedesát*
70	*sedmdesát*
80	*osmdesát*
90	*devadesát*
100	*sto*
1,000	*tisíc*

Days & months

Monday	*pondělí*
Tuesday	*úterý*
Wednesday	*středa*
Thursday	*čtvrtek*
Friday	*pátek*
Saturday	*sobota*
Sunday	*neděle*

January	*leden*
February	*únor*
March	*březen*
April	*duben*
May	*květen*
June	*červen*
July	*červenec*
August	*srpen*
September	*září*
October	*říjen*
November	*listopad*
December	*prosinec*

Spring	*jaro*
Summer	*léto*
Autumn	*podzim*
Winter	*zima*

Pick-up lines

What a babe! *To je kost!*
What a stud! *Dobrej frajer!*
Can I walk you to the pig slaughter? *Můžu tě doprovodit na zabijačku?*
Do you want to try my goulash? *Chceš ochutnat můj guláš?*
I love you *Miluju tě*
Another drink? *Ještě jedno?*

Put-down lines

What are you staring at? *Na co čumíš?*
Shit your eye out! *Vyser si oko!*
That pisses me off! *To mě sere!*
You jerk! *Ty vole!*
You bitch! *Ty děvko!*

Further Reference

Books

Literature & fiction

Brierley, David
On Leaving a Prague Window
Readable but dated thriller set in post-communist Prague.

Chatwin, Bruce *Utz*
Luminous tale of a Josefov porcelain collector.

Hašek, Jaroslav
The Good Soldier Švejk
Rambling comic masterpiece set in World War I, by Bohemia's most bohemian writer.

Havel, Václav
The Memorandum; Three Vaněk Plays; Temptation
The President's work as playwright.

Hrabal, Bohumil
I Served The King of England; Total Fears
The living legend's most Prague-ish novel, *I Served the King of England* tracks its anti-hero through a decade of fascism, war and communism. *Total Fears* is a lush new translation by the respected Twisted Spoon Press.

Kundera, Milan *The Joke; The Book of Laughter and Forgetting; The Unbearable Lightness of Being*
Milan Kundera's tragi-comic romances are still the runaway bestselling sketches of Prague.

Ledgard, Jonathan *Giraffe*
A Cold War thriller about very tall animals. Perfectly Prague.

Meyrink, Gustav *The Golem*
The classic version of the tale of Rabbi Loew's monster, set in Prague's Jewish Quarter.

Neruda, Jan *Prague Tales*
Wry and bittersweet stories of life in 19th-century Malá Strana, from Prague's answer to Dickens.

Škvorecký, Josef *The Engineer of Human Souls*
The magnum opus of the chronicler of Czech jazz.

Topol, Jáchym
Sister City Silver
A long-awaited translation of three noir novellas by one of the city's leading young writers.

Wilson, Paul (ed) *Prague: A Traveller's Literary Companion*
An excellent collection of stories organised to evoke Prague's sense of place.

Kafka

Kafka, Franz *The Castle; The Transformation & Other Stories; The Trial*
Kafka classics.

Anderson, Mark M
Kafka's Clothes
Erudite and unconventional book encompassing Kafka, dandyism and the Habsburg culture.

Brod, Max
Franz Kafka: A Biography
The only biography by someone who actually knew the man.

Hayman, Ronald
K: A Biography of Kafka
Widely available, dependable.

Karl, Frederick *Franz Kafka: Representative Man*
A thorough and thoughtful account of the man and his work.

History, memoir & travel

Demetz, Peter
Prague in Black and Gold
Thoughtful exploration of prehistoric to First Republic life.

Garton Ash, Timothy *The Magic Lantern: The Revolution of 1989 Witnessed in Warsaw, Budapest, Berlin and Prague; History of the Present*
Oxford academic's on-the-spot 1989 history and his look back a decade later, painfully explore the morality of the Velvet Revolution.

Rimmer, Dave
Once Upon a Time in the East
Communism seen stoned and from ground level.

Ripellino, Angelo Maria
Magic Prague
Mad masterpiece of literary and cultural history, which celebrates the city's sorcerous soul.

Sayer, Derek
Coasts of Bohemia
Phenomenally well-researched and witty account of the millennium-long Czech search for their national identity.

Shawcross, William *Dubček*
Biography of the Prague Spring figurehead, updated to assess his role in the 1989 Velvet Revolution.

Essays & argument

Čapek, Karel
Towards the Radical Centre
Selected essays from the man who coined the word 'robot'.

Havel, Václav
Living in Truth; Letters to Olga; Disturbing the Peace
His most important political writing, his prison letters to his wife, and his reflections.

Miscellaneous

Holub, Miroslav
Supposed to Fly
This collecion of poetry by this former dissident was inspired by his youth in war-torn Plzeň.

Iggers, Wilma
A Women of Prague
Fascinating – lives of 12 women, across 200 years.

Sís, Petr *Three Golden Keys*
Children's tale set in Prague, with wonderful drawings.

Various eds *Prague: 11 Centuries of Architecture*
Solid and substantial.

Film

Many of the following films can be viewed on video at, or rented from, Virus Video (*see p180*) or found periodically at film festivals or video shops.

Ecstasy (Extáze)

Gustav Machatý (1932)
Known primarily for its groundbreaking nude scene with the nubile actress who would later be known as Hedy Lamarr, this imagistic film depicts a girl frustrated with her relationship with an older man.

The Long Journey (Daleká cesta) *Alfred Radok (1949)*
Banned by the communists for 20 years, this film depicts the deportation of Jews to concentration camps.

The Great Solitude (Velká samota) *Ladislav Helge (1959)*
The Great Solitude is one of the few pre-new wave movies that goes deeper than farm-tool worship, this film focuses on how tough it is to be a rural party official.

**The Shop on Main Street
(Obchod na korze)** *Ján
Kadár & Elmar Klos (1964)*
Set during World War II in the
Nazi puppet state of Slovakia, it's
about an honest carpenter who
must act as the person 'Aryanising'
a button shop run by an old Jewish
woman. Winner of the 1966 Oscar
for Best Foreign Film.
**Intimate Lighting (Intimní
osvětlení)** *Ivan Passer (1965)*
Possibly the most delightful film
of the Czech New Wave, which
tells of the reunion of two old
friends after many years.
**Larks on a String
(Skřivánci na niti)**
Jiří Menzel (1969)
This tale of forced labour in
the steel mills of industrial
Kladno deals with politics a bit,
but love – and libido – somehow
always triumph. Banned soon
after its release, the film was not
shown again until 1989 – when
it won the Berlin Film Festival's
Golden Bear.
The Ear (Ucho) *Karel
Kachyňa (written by Jan
Procházka) (1970)*
The full force of surveillance
terror and paranoia is exposed
in this chilling film, whose
origins go further back than the
communists to Kafka. The film
was banned instantly.
Otesánek
Jan Švankmajer (2000)
Švankmajer updates a classic
Czech myth about a childless
couple who adopt an insatiable
baby made from tree roots.
**Divided We Fall
(Musíme si pomáhat)**
Jan Hřebejk (2001)
The Oscar-nominated tale of a
small Czech village in wartime
and its residents' confrontations
with moral decisions.
Želary *Ondřej Trojan (2004)*
This World War II melodrama
nominated for Best Foreign Film
Oscar tells the story of a nurse
hiding out in a village.

Music

**Dan Bárta: Entropicture
(Sony)**
Dan Bárta, the soulful reigning
prince of Czech pop rock takes
a thoughtful turn with some
respected jazz men about town.

**Ecstasy of St Theresa:
In Dust 3 (EMI)**
Jan P Muchow creates a
textured digital background
for the provocative vocals of
Kateřina Winterová.
**Rok Ďábla (Sony
Music/Bonton)**
This soundtrack from the hit
film of the same name presents
the songs of beloved Czech folk
balladeer Jarek Nohavica in a
completely new light.
**Various: Future Sound
of Prague (Intellygent)**
Reliable series of the best of house
and ambient sounds heard around
the city's most plugged-in clubs.

Homegrown classics
Czech Serenade *Antonín
Dvořák, Josef Suk, Vítězslav
Novák, Zdeněk Fibich, Leoš
Janáček (Supraphon)*
The pantheon of great Czech
composers, in performances by
a range of artists including the
Czech Philharmonic and a gallery
of top-class chamber players,
mostly digitally recorded. The
works incorporate old Czech
and Moravian folk influences.
**Jan Ladislav Dusík: Piano
Concerto, Sonatas**
*Jan Novotný, Prague Chamber
Philharmonic, conducted by
Leoš Svárovský (Panton)*
The Prague Chamber
Philharmonic delivers the energy
that has set it apart from the city's
larger orchestras in these excellent
recordings of Dusík's 'Concert
Concerto for Piano and Orchestra'
in E flat major, 'Op 70' and two of
his more lyrical sonatas, the F
Sharp minor 'Op 61' and the A flat
major 'Op 64'. Novotný's playing
is particularly expressive.
**Martinů, Bohuslav: Double
Concerto** *Orchestre National de
France (Teldec/Erato)*
This lyrical composition, performed
with sensitivity by soloists Jean-
François Heisser and Jean Camosi,
and conducted by James Conlon,
provides a toothsome taste of the
rarely heard modernist Czech
composer at his best.
Pavel Šporcl *Pavel Šporcl
(Supraphon)*
This unorthodox Czech violin
virtuoso has won over audiences
with his deft treatment of
Smetana, Dvořák, Janáček and
Martinů. This is his star debut.

**Zdeněk Fibich:
Symphony No 1 in F
major, Symphony No 2 in
E flat major, Symphony
No 3 in E minor**
This is a set of symphonies by the
little-known romantic Czech
composer now receiving a well-
deserved revival. Performed by
the Czech Philharmonic Orchestra
under Karel Šejna, it includes two
excellent shorter works.

Websites

Czech-English Dictionary
www.slovnik.cz
Millions of words translated from
English, German, Italian, French
and Spanish to Czech and back.
Czech Techno
www.techno.cz
The party-list link contains
the original, authoritative list
of what's on in the dance clubs
all over town.
www.idos.cz
Searchable online train and bus
timetables for every city and town
in the Czech Republic.
Expats.cz
www.expats.cz
Online bulletin board with handy
classifieds, tips on residency,
apartment hunting and jobs.
Prague TV
prague.tv
Tune in for outlandish columns,
food and drink tips, links to maps
and the beer counter.
The Prague Post
www.praguepost.com
Prague's main English-language
weekly reports on the issues,
trends and culture with useful
tourist information pages.
**Prague Information
Service**
www.pis.cz
Comprehensive source for city
events with well-organised pages
of general tourist information.
**Radio Free Europe/
Radio Liberty**
www.praguemonitor.cz
A witty daily roundup of all the
latest links to English-language
news and features related to the
Golden City.
Time Out Prague Guide
www.timeout.com/prague
Shameless self-promotion it may
be, but here's where you'll find the
best of what's new in Prague.

Directory

Index

Note: Page numbers in **bold** indicate chapters and main references; page numbers in *italics* indicate photographs.

abortion 300
absinthe 166, *166*
AC Sparta Praha 127, **256**
accessories shops 187
accident & emergency 299-300
Accommodation 42-70
agencies 45, 225
best hotels 42
booking 42
by price category
budget 47, 50-53, 59-61, 65, 68-70; *deluxe* 45, 47, 53, 61-62, 66; *expensive* 45, 47-49, 53-55, 62, 66-67; *moderate* 45-47, 49-50, 55-59, 63-65, 67
gay & lesbian 225
hostels 53, 61, 65, 70
hotel bars 46
palaces 59
prices 43
see also p320
Accommodation index
accountancy firms 296
addresses 296
Adria Palace 118
age restrictions 224, 296
AIDS & HIV 224, 300
airport 290
transport to/from 290
Alchemy 34
alcohol
shooters 166
shops 191-192
see also beer; wine
All Souls' Day 203
Amadeus 72, 75, 90
amber 190
American Embassy 299
amusement parks 127
Anniversary of Jan
Palach's Death 204
Anniversary of the Birth of
Czechoslovakia 203
Anniversary of the Velvet
Revolution 203
antiques shopping 179-181
aquariums *see* zoos &
aquariums
Archa Theatre 250, 251
Archbishop's Palace 85
Architecture 27-33
art nouveau 32
Baroque 29-31
communist 33
early Romanesque 29
Gothic 29
modernist 32-33
neo-classical 31
post-communist 33
Renaissance 29

revivalist 31-32
walk, Staré Město 103
see also castles & ruins;
churches, cathedrals &
cemeteries
Art
art materials shops 197-198
Art Prague art fair 217
commercial art/galleries
217, 220
contemporary
art/galleries 215-217
exhibition spaces 218-223
Jindřich Chalupecký
Prize 219
walk, Staré Město 103
Astronomical Clock **101-103**, 205
Austerlitz (Slavkov) 287

Baba Villas 130
baby requirements 208
babysitting agencies 205, 208
Ball Game Court 82
ballroom dancing 202
banks 296-297, 305
Barrandov 131
bars *see* cafés, pubs & bars
Bartolomějská 109
Barum Rally 204
Basilica of St James 98, 230
Basilica of St Margaret 130
Becherovka 166
Beer 37-39
hostinec (neighbourhood
pub) 136, 162
microbreweries 38-39, 171
shops 191-192
see also cafés, pubs &
bars
Belvedere 81-82
Belvedere Palace 29, 81
Benes, Edward 15, 16, 17
Benes, František 86
Bertramka 131, 230
Bethlehem Chapel 108-109, *109*
Bethlehem Square 108
Betlémské náměstí 108
bicycles & cycling 295
bicycle hire 295
cycle tours/trips 258, 265
Bilek Villa 86
Bilek, František 86
black light theatre 253-254
Black Tower 81
boating 209, 293
Bohemia Ticket
International 229
books about Prague
bookshops 35, 175, **181-182**
Borovička 166
Botanical Gardens 126
Brahe, Tycho **84**, 86, 101

breakdown services 294
Břevnov Monastery 130
breweries *see* beer
Bridge of Intelligence 132
British Council 302
British Embassy 89, 299
Brod, Max 35
Bubeneč 127
budget clothes shops 184
bungee jumping 257
Buquoy Palace 92
Burčák arrives 203
Bursík, Martin 22-23
buses & coaches
airport services 290
coach station 291
inter-city 265
business 296
Byzantine era 10

Café Montmartre 105, 162, **165**, *170*
Cafés, Pubs & Bars 162-175
best pubs 163
café culture 162
gay & lesbian 225-226
hotel bars 46
see also p321 cafés, pubs
& bars index
camera shops & repairs 196
camping & campsites 284, 285
Canadian Embassy 299
Carolinum 102
cars & driving 291, **294-295**
Barum Rally 204
parking 294
trips out of town 265
vehicle hire 295
casinos 241-242, 246-248
Castle Steps 81
castles & ruins **266-269**, 271-272, 275, 285, 286, *286*, 287
see also Prague Castle
Cathedral of St Barbara 270
cathedrals *see* churches,
cathedrals & cemeteries
caves *see* Moravský kras
CD & record shops 194-195
Čedok 229-230
cemeteries *see* churches,
cathedrals & cemeteries
Černin Palace 86
Česká Pohoda agency 284
Česká Typografie building 33
Český Krumlov **278**, 284
Český ráj 284-286
Chapel of Mirrors 230
Chapel of the Holy Rood 76
Chapel of St John of the
Laundry 92
Charles Bridge 29, *106*, **107**, 127

Charles IV, Holy Roman
Emperor **11**, 75, 76, 77, 79, 83, 96, 100, 101, 107, 108, 113, 124, 217, 266, 269, 271-272, 307
Charles University 307-308
chemists 300
childminding services 208-209
Children 205-209
activities & events 207
eating out 205, 208
entertainment & sport 207
health 209
outdoor playgrounds 207-208
practicalities 208-209
sightseeing 205-207
toy shops 198
transport 209
Christmas 204
markets 200, 204
Church of Our Lady Before
Týn 29, 101
Church of Our Lady
Beneath the Chain 93
Church of Our Lady of the
Snows 118
Church of Our Lady
Victorious 96
Church of SS Peter & Paul
132, 272, 273
Church of St Giles 109
Church of St Havel 107
Church of St Joseph 90
Church of St Ludmila 132
Church of St Nicholas
(Malá Strana) 29, **88-89**, **90-91**, *92*, 230
Church of St Nicholas
(Staré Město) 100, 230
Church of St Saviour 105
Church of St Simon & St
Jude 231
Church of St Thomas 90, 91
Church of St Wenceslas
133
Church of the Sacred Heart
32-33, 133
Church, the 19
churches, cathedrals &
cemeteries 23, 29, 75, 76-77, 79, 82, 85, 90-91, 92, 93, 96, 98, 101, 105, 107, 109, 110, 112-113, 118, 123, 124, 126, 130, 132, 133, 204, 230, 270, 272 , 273
as classical music venues 230
Cigler, Jakub 125
City Library 302
Civic Democratic Party
(ODS) 20, 23
Clam-Gallas Palace 103-105
classical music 228-233
Clementinum 29, 105
clerics, state employment of
19

climate 311, 312
climbing *see* rock climbing
clothes shops 184-186
clubs *see* nightlife
coffee 162
Collegium Marianum 229
communist era **16-20**, 17,
    19, 118, 124, 250
complementary medicine
    300
computer rental & leasing
    297
computer shops 183
Congress Centre 132, 234
consumer protection 298
contraception 300
Convent of St Agnes of
    Bohemia *see* St Agnes's
    Convent
cosmetics shops 183
costume hire 184
cottage rental 284
Counter-Reformation **12**,
    29, 85, 91
country & western music
    venues 240
countryside 265
couriers & messengers 297
credit cards 305
currency exchange 304-305
customs 298
cycling *see* bicycles &
    cycling
cycling trips 265
Czech Academy of Music
    231
Czech Academy of Sciences
    121
Czech Dance Platform 250,
    254
Czech language &
    pronunciation 302
    study institutes 308-309
    translation &
        interpretation services
        297-298
    vocabulary & phrases
        313
    for drunkenness 172
    in restaurants 148-151
    pick-up/put-down lines
        313
    postal 307
Czech Museum of Fine Arts
    218
Czech National Symphony
    Orchestra 229
Czech Philharmonic 228,
    228
Czech Radio Symphony
    Orchestra 229
Czech Silver Museum &
    Medieval Mine 270

Dalibor Tower 81
dance *see* theatre & dance
Dancing Building, 27, 33,
    123
Danube House 33
Days of European Film 214
dentists 300
department stores 178-179
designer clothes shops 184-
    186

DHL 297
Dientzenhofer Summer
    House 82
disabled access 292, 298-
    299
Divadlo Na zábradlí 105,
    253
Divoká Šárka 131, 261
Dlouhá 113
Domeček 86
Drápalová, Monika 186
driving *see* cars & driving
drugs (illegal) 24, 241
dry-cleaners 183-184
Dubček, Alexander 17, 18,
    19, 117, 125
DVD/video rental 198, 210
Dvořák, Antonín 123, 132
Dvořák Museum 123, 124

Easter *200*, 201
electricity 299
electronics shops 184
embassies 299
emergencies 299
entrepreneurialism 24
estate agents 297
Estates Theatre 31, 108,
    229, **231-232**, 250, **251**
etiquette & attitude 296
Euro Palace 33
European Union, entry into
    20

fairgrounds 127
fashion shops 184-188
Faust House 123
faxes 310
Febiofest 214
Federal Assembly building
    27, 117
FedEx 297
Ferdinand, Archduke
    Franz 268
Festival of Best Amateur &
    Professional Puppet
    Theatre Plays 203
Festivals & Events 200-
    204
    autumn 202-203
    film 214, 272-273
    literary 35
    music
        classical & opera 201,
        229, 233
        rock, roots & jazz 202,
        203, 233
        spring 201
        summer 202
    theatre & dance 250, 254
    winter 203-204
Film 210-214
    art-house cinemas 213
    commercial cinemas 211
    Czech films 314-315
    dubbing 210
    festivals & special events
        214, 272-273
    multiplexes 211-213
fitness centres 258
florists 188
folk music venues 240

food & drink
    delivery/take-away 188
    specialist shops 188-191
    supermarkets 191
    see also alcohol; cafés;
        pubs & bars;
        restaurants
football 256-257
forests 286
formal dress hire 184
Former Ceremonial Hall
    110, 112
Four Days in Motion 250,
    254
Freedom Union 23
French Film Festival 214
fuel stations 294
funicular railway 293
funk music 234
Further Afield 127-134
    accommodation 66-70
    cafés, pubs & bars 173-
        175
    Dejvice & further west
        130-131
    Holesovice, Letná &
        Troja 127-129
    Jižní Město & Háje 134
    restaurants 159-161
    Smíchov & Barrandov
        131
    Vinohrady & Žižkov 132-
        133
    Vyšehrad *130*, 131-132
Futura gallery 217, **220**

Galerie Display 217, 220-
    221, *221*
Galerie Mánes 33, 121-123,
    221
Galerie Miro 221
Galerie Rudolfinum 218
Galleries 215-223
    commercial, independent
        & private 220-223
    exhibition spaces 218-220
    photography galleries
        223
    see also museums &
        galleries
gambling 241-242, 246-248
gardens *see* parks &
    gardens
garnets 190
Gay & Lesbian 224-227
    accommodation 225
    associations 225
    bars 225-226
    clubs 226
    cruising 226-227
    help & information 299
    restaurants & cafés 227
    saunas 227
    shops 227
Gehry, Frank 33, 123
Ghetto Museum, Terezin
    275
gift shops 192-193
Giraffe 36
Globe Bookstore &
    Coffeehouse 123, **171**,
    181, *183*
go-karting 258
Golden Lane 81, *82*

golf 258, *259*
Golz-Kinsky Palace 29, 101
Gorbachev, Mikhail 19
Gottwald, Klement 17, 19,
    86, 101, 134
Grand Hotel Evropa 32, *62*,
    63, 117
Green Party 22-23
Gross, Stanislav 19, 23
gyms 258

Habsburg Empire **12**, **15**,
    79, 81, 129, 202, 241, 268
hairdressers 193-194
Háje 134
Hasek, Jaroslav 35
Havel, Václav 34, 75, 79,
    105, 117, 125, 162, 169,
    215, 217, 250, 314
Havelsky Market *177*, 179
health 299-301
    children's 209
    helplines & crisis centres
        301
    women's 300-301
High Synagogue 109
hiking 284, 285, 286
historic tram 91 207
Historical Museum 81
History 10-21
    Byzantine era 10
    communist era **16-20**,
        17, 19, 118, 124, 250
    Counter-Reformation **12**,
        29, 85, 91
    European Union, entry
        into 20
    Habsburg Empire **12**,
        15, 79, 81, 129, 202,
        241, 268
    key events timeline 20
    NATO membership 20
    Přemyslid dynasty **10**,
        72, 131
    Reich Protectorate 16-17
    Soviet Invasion of 1968
        18, *18*, **20**, 125, 204
    Thirty Years' War **12-
        13**, 88, 90, 130
    Velvet Revolution **10**, 20,
        34, 101, 115, 117, 125,
        178, 233
    World War I **15**, 79, 134,
        268
    World War II **15-16**,
        100, 102, 123, 126, 275
Hitler, Adolf 15, 16, 76, 286
HIV & AIDS 224, 300
Hlavní nádraží 32, 117, 227,
    265, **290**
Holešovice 127
Holidays, public 25-26
horse riding & racing 204,
    257, 258
horse-drawn carriages 207
hospitals 299-301
hostels 53, 61, 65, 70
hotels *see* accommodation
House at the Golden Ring
    102, **114**
House at the Stone Bell 29,
    101, 102, **218**
House of the Black
    Madonna **98-100**, 102

House of the Lords of
Kunštát and Poděbrady
109
household shops 194
Hrabal, Bohumil 35
Hradčanské náměstí 85
Hradčany 75-87
accommodation 45-47
cafés, pubs & bars 163
restaurants 137-138
Hrubá skála 285
Hunger Wall 96
Hus, Jan 11, *13*, 15, 101,
108, 109
Jan Hus Monument *100*,
101
Hussite Church 133
Hvězda Hunting Lodge
130-131

ice hockey 256, 257
ice skating 260
identification (ID) 301
in-line skating 260
insurance 301
International Aviation Film
214
International Biennale of
Contemporary Art 215
internet cafés 301-302
interpreting 297-298

Jan Hus Monument *100*,
101
jazz & blues venues 239-
240
jazz festival 203
Jesuit Church of St Ignatius
123
jewellery shops 187, 190
Jewish Cemetery 133
Jewish community 109-113
during World War II 15,
16, 110, 275
Jewish writers 35
synagogues & cemeteries
109-110, 112-113, 133
travel agency 110-112
Jewish Museum 110, 112
Jewish Town Hall 109
Jičín 285
Jindřich Chalupecký Prize
219
Jiří Švestka Gallery 220
Jižní Město 134
jogging 260-261
John Lennon Wall **92**, 94,
97
Josef Sudek Atelier 94, *222*,
223
Josef Sudek Gallery 223
Josef Sudek House of
Photography 223
Josefov 109
Joseph II 31, 75, 81, 87, 89
Jungleland 205, 207

Kafka, Franz 16, 35, 65, 81,
90, 101, 103, 110, **111**,
133, 166, 314

Kampa Island 91-92
Kampa Museum 92, 94
Kampa Park 92, *93*
Karlova 103, 105
Karlovo náměstí 123
Karlovy Vary 269-270
Karlovy Vary International
Film Festival (KVIFF)
204, **214**, 269, **272-
273**
Karlštejn Castle 266
Karlův most 29, *106*, **107**
Kašperské Hory 284, 286
Kaunitz Palace 88
Kepler, Johannes 84
key events timeline 20
key-cutting shops 194
Khamoro 202
Kinský Palace 218
Klaus, Václav 20, 22, 23,
22, 215, 217
Klausen Synagogue 110,
112
Knights of the Cross
Square 105
Konfrontace 250, 254
Konopiště Castle 266-268,
267
Koruna Palace 33, **117**
Kotva department store 33,
178
Křivoklát Castle 268-269
Křížovnické náměstí 105
Kutná Hora 270-271
Kylián, Jiří 250

Labour Day 201
lamp-post, Cubist *33*, 118
language *see* Czech
language
Lapidárium 127
Laser Game 205, 207
Laterna Magika **121**, 208,
253, **254**
laundrettes 183-184
law firms 298
leather & fur shops 186
Ledebour Gardens 81
Ledgard, Jonathan **36**, *36*
left luggage 302
legal help 302
Leica Gallery Prague 223
Lennon Wall *see* John
Lennon Wall
Leppin, Paul 35
lesbian scene *see* gay &
lesbian
Letná park 31, **127-129**,
201, *203*, 226
libraries 187, 218-220, 302
Lichtenstein Palace 89, 231
lingerie shops 187
Literary Prague 34-36
books about Prague
bookshops 35, 175, 181
Czech writers 34-35, 314
festivals 35
see also Kafka, Franz
Little Square 103
Lobkowicz Palace 81, 96,
231
locksmiths 194
Loretánské náměstí 86
Loreto, The 31, *85*, **86-87**

Lorraine cross 107
lost property 302
Lucerna cinema 211, *214*
Lucerna Great Hall 236
Lucerna Music Bar 203,
234, 236
Lucerna shopping passage
117, *119*
Lunapark 127, 129

magazines & periodicals
303-304
Magic Latern **121**, 208,
253, **254**
Main Station *see* Hlavní
nádraží
Malá Strana 88-97
accommodation 47-53
cafés, pubs & bars 163-
164
restaurants 138-144
Malé náměstí 103
malls 179
Malostranské Square &
around **88-91**, 93
Maltézské Square *89*, 93
Mánes gallery 33, 121-123,
221
marathon *see* Prague
International Marathon
Market at the Fountain
179
markets 179
Christmas 200, 204
Martinic Palace 29
Masaryk train station 118,
265, **290**
Masaryk, Jan 16, 17, 86
Masaryk, Professor Tomáš
15, *15*
Masarykovo nádraží 118,
265, **290**
Mašín group 14, *14*
Masopust 204
massage parlours 194
Matejská poutt 201, 207
Mattoni Grand Prix 202
May Day 201
measurements 312
media 303-304
Mělník 271-273, *271*
Mělník Castle 271-272
Menzel, Jiří 250
metro 292
Meyrink, Gustav 35
Mezi ploty Festival 201,
254
Michna Palace 93
Miniatures Museum 87
Minute House 101
Mirror Maze 96, 97, 205,
206-207
mobile phones 310
Modern Music Marathon
229
money 304-305
Monkey Business 234, *235*
Moravian Caves 286-287,
287
Moravsky kras 286-287,
287
Morzin Palace 90
Mostecká 88
Mozart Museum 131

Mozart, Wolfgang
Amadeus 108, 131, 230,
232, 233
see also Amadeus
Mucha Museum 124
Municipal House 25, *27*, 32,
100, 102, **118**, 166, **230**
Exhibition Hall *216*, 218
Municipal Library 218-220
Museum of Communism
124
Museum of Decorative Arts
see UMPRUM
Museum of the City of
Prague 124
Museums & Galleries
art, fine House at the
Golden Ring 114;
House of the Black
Madonna 98; Mucha
Museum 124; National
Gallery 217; National
Gallery Collection of
19th-, 20th- & 21st-
Century Art 129;
Prague Castle Picture
Gallery 82; Sternberg
Palace 85; Zbraslav
Château 131
communism Museum
of Communism 124
*decorative arts &
crafts* UMPRUM 114;
Prague Jewellery
Collection 97
ethnographic Náprstek
Museum 109 *history*
Museum of the City of
Prague 124 *Jewish*
Jewish Museum *law &
order* Police Museum
126 *music & musicians*
Dvořák Museum 124;
Mozart Museum 131
natural history
National Museum 115,
206 *toys &
amusements*
Miniatures Museum
87; Toy Museum 85
*science, technology &
transport* National
Technical Museum
129, 206
Music 228-240
classical & opera 228-233
concert halls 230-233
festivals 229, 233
rock, roots & jazz 233-
240
Czech bands 238
venues 234-238, 239-240
shops 194-195

Na Kampě 91-92
Nádraží Holešovice 127,
265, **291**
Náměstí Jana Palacha 113
Náprstek Museum 108, 109
National Gallery 217
National Gallery Collection
of 19th-, 20th- & 21st-
Century Art 127, 129

National Library 302
National Marionette
  Theatre 208, **253**
National Memorial *131*,
  133, 134
National Museum 32, **115**,
  206
National Revival
  movement 31, 35, 132,
  208, 254
National Technical
  Museum 127, *205*, 206
National Theatre **31-32**,
  121, *126*, 229, **232**, 250,
  251, **253**
National Theatre ballet
  company 250
NATO membership 20
natural hazards 305-306
Nazi occupation 15, 16, 75,
  79, 86, 100, 101, 102, 113,
  115, 125, 214, 275
Němcová, Božena 35, 121
Neruda, Jan 94, 132, 163
Nerudova 89, *90*
New Castle Steps 89-90
New Town Hall 29, 123
New Town *see* Nové Město
New World 86
New Year's Eve 200, 204
newsagents 181-182
newspapers 303, 304
Nezval, Vítězslav 35
Nightlife 241-249
  adult clubs 248-249
  clubs 242-246
  gambling 246-248
  gay & lesbian clubs 226
  nudity & sex 227
Nine Gates 202, *204*
Nové Město 115-126
  accommodation 61-65
  cafés, pubs & bars 170-
    173
  restaurants 153-159
Nový Svět 86
nudity & sex 227
  adult clubs 248-249
  porn industry 24
numbers 306

office hire 298
Old Castle Steps 81
Old Jewish Cemetery 110,
  112-113, *112*
Old Town Bridge Tower
  107, 205
Old Town Hall 101-102,
  105, 220
Old Town *see* Staré Město
Old Town Square 100-101,
  101, 179, *240*
Old-New Synagogue 29, *32*,
  109, **110**
Olsany Cemetery 133, 134,
  203, 204
One World Human Rights
  Film Festival 214
opening hours 306
  museums & galleries 218
Opera Mozart 233
opera music 228-229, 231-
  233
opticians 195-196, 300

orchestras 228-229
Orthodox Cathedral of SS
  Cyril and Methodius 124,
  126
ossuaries 270, 272-273

palaces as accommodation
  59
Palach, Jan 113, 134, 204
parachuting 261
Paradise Gardens 81, 90
Pařížská 109
parking 294
parks & gardens 81, 90, 92,
  126, 127, 131, 261
Paroubek, Jiří 23
perfume shops 183
Pernštejn castle 287
Petřín Hill **96-97**, 208
Petřín Tower **96**, **97**, 205
petrol stations 294
pharmacies 300
photography
  galleries 223
  shops/developing 196-
    197
Pinkas Synagogue 110, 113
Pivovar U Bulovsky 39
playgrounds, outdoor 207-
  208
poetry festival 35
police & security 306
  secret police 92, 108
Police Museum 124, 126
pool bars 261
porn industry 24
postal services 297, 306-307
Powder Bridge 76, 81
Powder Gate *see* Powder
  Tower
Powder Tower, 29, 76, **79**,
  98, *99*, **100**, 118, 205
Prague Autumn Festival
  200, 202, 229
Prague Biennales 215, *215*
Prague by numbers 26
Prague Card 72
Prague Castle 29, 31, 32,
  75-80, 88, 89, 90, 217
  Archbishop's Chapel 77
  archaeological research
    83
  Bohemian Chancellery 79
  Chapel of St Wenceslas
    77
  Chapel of the Holy Rood
    76
  Diet chamber 79
  first & second
    courtyards 75-79
  Golden Portal 77
  Great Tower 77
  map 77
  Old Royal Palace 79
  Picture Gallery 76, 82
  St George's Convent 79,
    82-85
  St Vitus's Cathedral **75**,
    76-79, *80*, 83, *83*
  Shakespeare at the Castle
    performances 250
  third courtyard 79
  tombstone of St John of
    Nepomuk 79

Vladislav Hall 79
Prague Center Guest
  Residence 225
Prague City Gallery 217,
  220
Prague Fringe Festival 254
Prague 4 suburb 134
Prague House of
  Photography 223
Prague Information Service
  118, **311**
Prague International
  Marathon 200, 201
Prague International
  Poetry Festival 35
Prague Jazz Festival 203
Prague Jewellery Collection
  97
Prague Philharmonica 229
Prague 6 suburb 130
Prague Spring Festival 200,
  201, 229, 230, **233**
Prague Steamship
  Company 207
Prague Symphony
  Orchestra 118, **228-229**,
  231
Prague 10 suburb 132
Prague Writers' Festival
  35, 200, 201
Prague Zoo 129, 205, **206**,
  207
Precious Legacy Tours 110-
  112
Přemyslid dynasty 10, 72,
  131
priests, state employment
  of 19
prints, rare 182
Project 100 214
public holidays 25-26
public transport 291-293
  disabled access 292
  fares & tickets 291-292
  information 291
  night buses/trams 242,
    293
  see also buses &
    coaches; taxis; trains
  water transport 293
  with children 209
pubs *see* cafés, pubs & bars
puppet theatre 203, 205,
  208, 254

radio 304
rafting trips 265
record & CD shops 194-195
recruitment agencies 298
Reich Protectorate 16-17,
  115
religion 24, 307
Renaissance, the 29
Respect festival 202, 233
Restaurants 136-161
  best 136
  by cuisine
    Americas 138, 144,
      153-155, 159-160
    Asian 137, 138, 144,
      155 *Balkan* 138-139,
      160; *Continental* 139-
      141, 144-147, 155-156
    Czech 137-138, 141-

143, 147-148, 156,
  160 *Fast food* 156
French 149, 156-157,
  160 *Indian/Pakistani*
  149, 157-158, 160-161
  Jewish 150
  Mediterranean 143,
  150-153, 158-159, 161
  Middle Eastern 153,
  161 *Seafood* 143,
  153, 159 *Vegetarian*
  153, 159 *World* 143-
  144, 153, 159, 161
  child-friendly restaurants
  205
  gay & lesbian 227
  menu, the 148-151
  tipping & VAT 137, 310
  vegetarians 136, 137, 153,
  159
  see also cafés, pubs &
  bars; *pp321*
  Restaurants index
Rezidence Lundborg 49, 93
rock climbing 257-258, 285
rock music venues 233-239
rollerblading *see* in-line
  skating
Rotunda of St Martin 132,
  132
Rotunda of the Holy Cross
  29, 108
Royal Garden 81
Royal Route 98
Rudolf II **12**, *12*, 79, 82, 84,
  85, 113, 127, 241
Rudolfinum 32, 103, 113,
  218, **230**, *231*
Galerie Rudolfinum 218
ruins *see* castles & ruins
running 260-261
Ruzyně airport 290

safety & security 306, 307
St Agnes's Convent 29, 102,
  113, **114**, 231
St George's Basilica *28*, 29,
  79
St George's Convent 79, 82-
  85
St Martin's Rotunda 29, 132
St Matthew's Fair 201
St Nicholas's Eve 200, 203
St Vitus's Cathedral **75**, **76-**
  79, *80*, 83, 83, 101, 204
Sárka park 226, **261**
saunas, gay & lesbian 227
Schönborn Palace 96
Schwarzenberg Palace 29,
  85-86
Sea World 205, 206, *206*
secret police 92, 108
Šedá, Kateřina 219
Sedlec Ossuary 270
Senovážé Námestí 118, *122*
service in restaurants 136
sex & nudity 227
  adult clubs 248-249
  porn industry 24
shoe shops 187-188
shooters (alcoholic) 166
shooting 261
Shops & Services 177-
  198

best shops 178
gay & lesbian 227
shopping areas 178
sightseeing tips 72-74
Singing Fountain 82
Sjöö, Tommy 157
skateboarding 261
skiing & snowboarding 261
Slavín 132
Small Fortress, Terezín 275
Smíchov 131
restaurants 138-144
Smíchovské nádraží 265, **291**
smoking 307
Social Democrats 22, 23
Soviet Invasion of 1968 18, *18*, 20, 125, 204
spa towns 269
Spanish Synagogue 110, 113
Sport & Fitness 256-262
active sports 257
spectator sports 256-257
squash courts 261-262
Stalin 17, 31, 134
Staré Město 98-114
accommodation 53-61
cafés, pubs & bars 164-170
Northern Staré Město 113
restaurants 144-153
Southern Staré Město 107-108
State Language School 309
State Opera 117, 229, **232-233**, **253**
stationery shops 197
statistics 26
STDs 300
Štefánik Observatory 97
Sternberg Palace 85
Strahov Monastery **86**, **87**, *87*, 97
Strahov Monastery Library 31, 87
Stromovka 127
study 307-308
suburbs *see* further afield
Sudek, Josef 94, 223
Šumava Museum 286
Šumava National Forest 286
Šumava region 284, *284*
Summer Old Music Festival 202
supermarkets 191
Svandovo divadlo 250, 255, *255*
Svěrák, Jan 212
swimming pools 262
synagogues & cemeteries 109-110, 112-113, 133

Tanec Praha 200, **202**, 250, 253, **254**
tax 310
taxis 291, 293
to/from airport 290
telephones 309-310
television 304
temperature 311, 312
Templová 98

tennis 262
ten-pin bowling 262
Terezín *274*, 275
Teta Tramtárie 205, 207
Theatre & Dance 250-255
Black light theatre 253-254
Czech theatres 251-253
English-language theatre 250, 255
festivals 250, 254
puppet theatre 254
Theatre on the Balustrade 105, **253**
theft 305
Thirty Years' War 12-13, 88, 90, 130
Thun-Hohenstein Palace 90
tickets
festivals 201
music events 229, 230
theatre & dance 250
Ticketpro 108, 117, 201, 229, **230**
time 310
Tina B 215
tipping & VAT 310
toilets 311
Tomin, Lukás 35
Topol, Jáchym 35
Toucan Apartments 225
tourist information 311
Toy Museum 81, 85
toy shops 198
trains & railways 290, 291, 294, 265
funicular railway 293
trips out of town 265
trams 292-293
night tram 242, 293
translating 297-298
transport *see* cars &
driving; public transport
travellers' cheques 305
Trips Out of Town 264-287
day trips 266-275
getting started 264-265
hitchhiking 265
overnighters
country 284-287
town & village 276-283
rafting & cycling trips 265
transport 265
Troja Château 129
Trosky Castle 285, *286*
Turnov 285
Tuzemský rum 166

UMPRUM (Museum of
Decorative Arts) 113,
114, *114*, 217
United Islands of Prague
festival 200, 202
universities 307-308

Václavské náměsti 100-101,
101, 179, *240*
VAT 310
VE Day 201

vehicle hire 294
Veletržni palác 127
Velká Pardubice
Steeplechase 204, 257
Velvet Revolution **10**, 20,
34, 101, 115, 117, 125,
178, 233
Anniversary of 203
video/DVD rental 198, 210
Villa Amerika 31, 124
vineyards & viniculture
271, 272
Vinohrady 132
visas 311
Vitkov Hill 133
Vltava river *121*
Vojan's Gardens 90
Vojenské State Baths 269
Vyšehrad *130*, 131-132
Výstaviště 127, 129

walks & walking 291, 295
guided tours 72
hiking 284, 285, 286
suggested routes
Malá Strana 94-95
Staré Město (art &
architecture) 102-103
see also hiking

Wallenstein Gardens **90**,
91, 94, 202, *204*
Wallenstein Palace 29, 117,
90
Wallenstein Riding School
94, 217, **220**
weather 311, 312
websites 315
weights & measures 312
Wenceslas II 37
Wenceslas IV 11, 79
Wenceslas Square **115-117**, *116*, **125**, *125*, 178
Wenceslas, 'Good King' 11,
75, 77
when to go 311, 312
where to stay *see* accommodation
Wilson Station *see* Hlavní
nádraží
wine shops 191-192
Witches' Night 201
women 312
health 300-301
safety & security 307
working 312
World War I 15, 79, 134,
268
World War II **15-16**, 100,
102, 123, 126, 275
writers, Czech 34-35, 314

yoga 262
youth hostels 53, 61, 65, 70

Zamek Moravský Krumlov
287
Zbraslav Château 131
Žižkov 128, 133

Žižkov Tower 33, **133**,
133, **134**
Žofin cultural centre 121
zoos & aquariums 31, 129,
206
Zrcadlové Bludiště 96, 97,
205, 206-207
Zvon Biennale of Young
Artists 217

Accommodation

A&O Hostel Prague 70
Alchymist Grand Hotel &
Spa 47
Alpin penzion 68
Ambassador Zlatá Husa 61
Ametyst 68
Andante 63
Andel's Hotel Prague 66
Apostolic Residence 55
Arco Pension 225
Arcotel Hotel Teatrino 66
Aria Hotel *43*, 47
Bellagio Hotel Prague 55,
56
Best Western Kampa Hotel
49
Betlem Club 59
Blue Key 50
Bohemia Plaza 67
Botel Admiral 68
Botel Albatross 59
Carlo IV 63
Casa Marcello 53
Černá Liška 56
Charles University Dorms
65
City Penzion 68
Cloister Inn 56
Clown & Bard 70
Corinthia 67
Diplomat Hotel Praha 67
Dorint Don Giovanni 67
Dům U velké boty 45
Floor Hotel 56
Four Season Hotel Prague
53
Golden Horse House 47
Grand Hotel Bohemia 53
Grand Hotel Evropa *62*, 63
Hostel Boathouse 70
Hostel Sokol 53
Hotel 16 U sv. Kateřiny 65
Hotel Abri 68
Hotel Adria Prague 63
Hotel Anna 68
Hotel Černy Slon 59
Hotel Čertovka 49
Hotel Elite 63
Hotel Hoffmeister 47
Hotel Josef 56, *58*
Hotel Liberty 57
Hotel Mejstřík Praha 57
Hotel Metamorphis 57
Hotel Neruda 45
Hotel Opera 63
Hotel Palace Praha 61
Hotel Paříž Praha 57
Hotel Pod Věži 49
Hotel Questenberk 46
Hotel Rott 55
Hotel Savoy 45
Hotel Tosca 68
Hotel Třiska 68

Hotel U Klenotníka 57
Hotel U Prince 57
Hotel Villa Schwaiger 67
Hotel Waldstein 49
Hotel William 50
Hotel Yasmin 62
Ibis Praha City 70
Inter-Continental Praha 58
Iron Gate 53
Janáček Palace Hotel 49
Jerome House 65
Julian 70
K+K Fenix 61
Klub Habitat 65
Marriott 63
Mercure Prague Centre Na Poříčí 63
Miss Sophie's Prague 70
Mövenpick Hotel 67
987 Prague 65
Pachtův Palace 55
Palais, Le 66, *69*
Pension Corto II 46
Pension Dientzenhofer 53, *55*
Pension Vyšehrad 70
Prague Hilton 66
Radisson SAS Alcron 62
Renaissance Prague Hotel 65
Residence Nosticova 49
Residence Řetězova 58
Rezidence Lundborg 49
Romantik Hotel U raka 45
Ron's Rainbow Guest House 225
Sir Toby's Hotel 70
Travellers' Hostel 61
U Červeného Lva 46
U Červeného Lva II 46
U Karlova mostu 50
U krále Jiřího 61
U krále Karla 46
U Křiže 50
U Medvídků 61
U Páva 50, *51*
U Šuterů 65
U Tří Bubnů 58
U Tří Pštrosů 50
U Zlaté Studně 50, *52*
U zlaté studny 58
U žluté boty 47
Ventana Hotel 59
Zlatá Hvězda 47

Cafés, Pubs & Bars

Akropolis 175
Alcatraz 225
Alcohol Bar 164
Aloha Wave Lounge *162*, 164
Au Gourmand 164
Bakeshop Praha 164
Bar & Books 165
Bar 21 225
Baráčnická rychta 163
Blatouch 165
Blind Eye 175
Blue Light 163
Bodega Flamenca, La 173
Bugsy's 165
Café Archa 170
Café Café 227, *227*

Café Dinitz 170
Café Indigo 165
Café Konvikt 165
Café Louvre 170
Café Medúza 174
Café Metropole 174, *174*
Café Montmartre 165, *170*
Café Orange 173
Casa Blú, La 166
Chateau Rouge *164*, 165
Chien Andalou, Un 173
Cream & Dream 165
Dahab 165
Downtown Café 227
Drake's 225
Duende 165, *169*
Ebel Coffee House 165
Erra Café 165
Escape 226
Fraktal 173
Franz Kafka Café 166
French Institute Café 170
Friends 226
Fuzion 171
Globe Bookstore & Coffeehouse 171
Jáma 171
James Bond Café 174
Jazz Café č.14 171
Jo's Bar 163
Kaaba 174
Káva Káva Káva 174
Kavárna Obecní dům 166
Kavárna v sedmém nebi 174
Kozička 166
Letenský zámeček 173
M1 Secret Lounge 167
Marquis de Sade 167
Molly Malone's 167
Monarch 167
Ocean Drive 167
Pack 171
Park Café 174
Park Café 175
Pastička 174
Patio, Le 171
Petřínské Terasy 163
Pivnice u Pivrnce 167
Pivovarský dům 171
Potrefená husa 175
Propaganda 171
První Prag Country Saloon Amerika 175
Radegast Pub 169
Ridgeback 171
Rudolf II Party Club 226
St Nicholas Café 163, *167*
Shakespeare & Sons 175
Slavia 169
Solidní nejistota 171
Street Café 226
Tato Kojkej 163
Terroir, Le 166
Tingl Tangl 226
Tram, Le 173
Tretter's 169, *173*
Tynská literární kavárna 169
U Buldoka 174
U černého vola 163
U Fleků 171
U Kruhu 172
U Malého Glena 164
U Medvídků 169
U Provaznice 169

U Sadu 175
U Sudu 172
U Vejvodů 170
U vystřeleného oka 175
U Zavěšenýho kafe 164
U Zlatého tygra 170
Ultramarin 172
Velryba 172
Vesmirna 172
Výletná 173
Železné dveře 172
Zlatá Hvězda 173
Zvonařka 175

Restaurants

Akropolis 161
Alchymist *137*, 139
Alcron 159
Allegro 150
Amici Miei 150
Ariana 153
Aromi *152*, 161
Artyčok 159
Athina 158
Banditos 153
Bar Bar 139
Baráčnická rychta 141
Barock 153
Barracuda 159
Bellevue 144
Bistro de Marlène, Le 156
Bistrot de Marlène, Le 160
Bohemia Bagel 138
Brasiliero 144
Byblos 153
C'est La Vie 139
Café Atelier 160
Café Colonial, Le 147
Café El Centro 143
Café Lamborghini 158
Café Savoy 143
Cafeterapie 158
Čelnice 156
Červená Tabulka 155
Chaoz 156
Chez Marcel 149
Cicala 158
Country Life 153
Cowboys 138
Credo 158
Crêperie, La 160
Cukrkávalimonáda 139
DaMúza 147
David 139
DeBrug 144
Don Giovanni 150
Don Pedro 153
Dynamo 156
Efes 161
Francouzská restaurace 149
Giardino, Il 143
Gitanes 138-139
Grosseto Pizzeria 161
Gyrossino 156
Hergetova Cihelna 143
Himalaya 157
Hot 155
Hungarian Grotto 139
Hybernia 156
Jáma 155
Kampa Park *138*, 143
King Solomon 150
Klub Architektů 144
Kogo Pizzeria & Caffeteria 151

Kolkovna 147
Lavande, La 160
Lemon Leaf 155
Maestro 151
Mailsi 160
Malý Buddha 137
Metamorphis 151
Millhouse Sushi 155
Modrá Řeka 160
Modrá Zahrada 151
Mozaika 161
Na Verandách 141
Nagoya 138
Nostress *142*, 147
Novoměstský Pivovar 156
Orange Moon 144
Palffy Palác 139
Perle de Prague, La 156
Petřínské Terasy 141
Picante 155
Pivnice u Pivrnce 147
Pizza Coloseum 159
Pizzeria Rugantino 208
Pravda 153
Provence, La 144
Puccelini 161
Radost FX Café *158*, 159
Rasoi Restaurant/Bombay Café 149
řecká Taverna 159
Red Fish 144
Red Hot & Blues 144
Restaurance po Sečuánsku 144
Reykjavík 153
Rio's Vyšehrad 159
Ristorante da Emanuel 161
Roca 161
Scene, La *141*, 147
Siam Orchid 155
Siam-l-San 144
Soho Restaurant & Garden 159
Sonora 160
Square 143
Stoleti 147
Střelecký ostrov 143
SushiPoint 155
Svatá Klára 160
Thanh Long 155
Tulip Café 155
U Bakaláře 147
U Cisařů 137
U Govindy Vegetarian Club 159
U Karlova mostu 143
U Malířů 139
U Maltézských rytířů 139
U Medvídků *145*, 148
U Modré kachničky 148
U Patrona 141
U Pinkasů 156
U Radnice 148
U Rozvařilů 156
U Sádlů 148
U Sedmi Švábů 143
U Ševce Matouše 137
U Zlaté studně 141
Universal 157
V Zátiší 147
Včelín 160
Veranda, La 147
Yalla 153
Zahrada v opeře 159
Žlutá pumpa 160

Advertisers' Index

Please refer to the relevant pages for contact details

Casino Poker Room   **IFC**

In Context

Black Light Theatre Image   **8**
Moser   **24**

Where To Stay

Residence Nosticova/Alchymist   **40**
HotelConnect   **44**
Hotel Jalta   **44**
Aria Hotel/Golden Well Hotel   **48**
House at the Big Boot   **54**
Hotel Ametyst   **54**
Hotel Liberty   **54**
Hotel Metamorphis   **60**
Hotel Athena Palace   **60**
Residence Řetězová   **64**
Airport Cars   **64**

Sightseeing

Museum of Communism   **78**
Dům Vín   **78**
AAA Radio Taxi   **78**
Franz Kafka Museum   **104**
Mucha Museum   **104**
Pilsner Urquell Brewery Museum   **104**
Hotel Josef/Maximilian Hotel   **120**
Carbon Neutral Flights   **120**

Restaurants

Lví Dvůr   **140**
U modré kachničky   **140**
Patriot-X   **146**
U Mudre Ruže   **146**
Brasserie M   **154**
Jama   **154**

Pubs & Bars

Time Out Shortlist Guides   **168**

Shops & Services

Galerie Jakubská   **176**
Big Ben Bookshop   **176**
timeout.com   **188**

Theatre & Dance

Laterna Magika   **252**

Directory

Casino Palais Savarin   **288**
Time Out Guides   **IBC**

Place of interest and/or entertainment	▢
Railway stations	▢
Metro stations	Ⓜ
Parks	▢
Pedestrian zones	▢
Churches	✚
Steps	▬
Area name	JOSEFOV
Tram routes	—

Maps

Trips Out of Town	324
Prague Overview	325
Street Maps	326
Street Index	334
Prague Metro	336

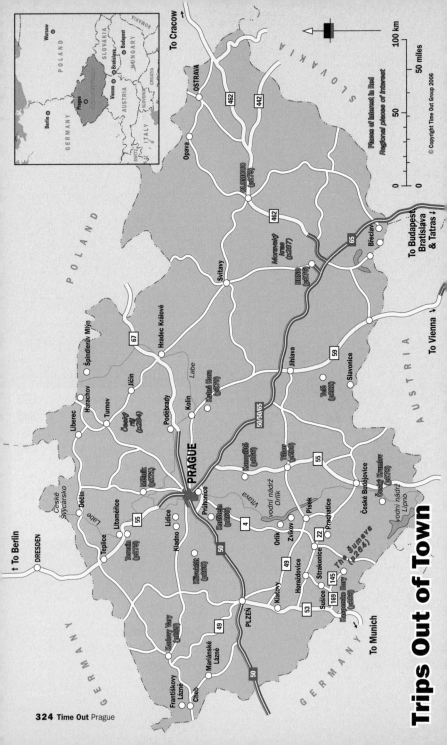

Trips Out of Town

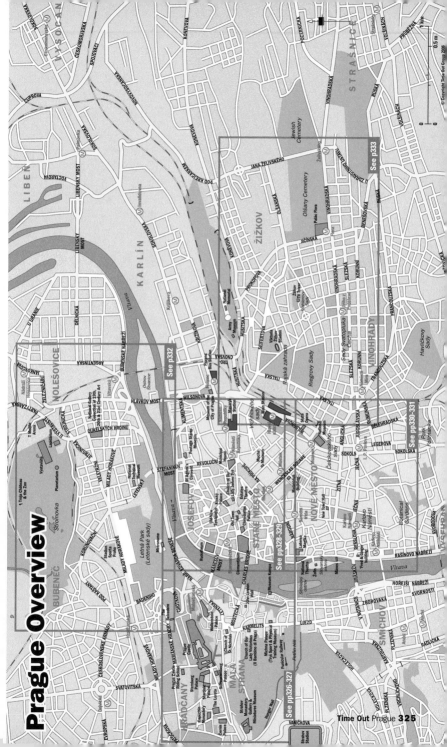

Prague Overview

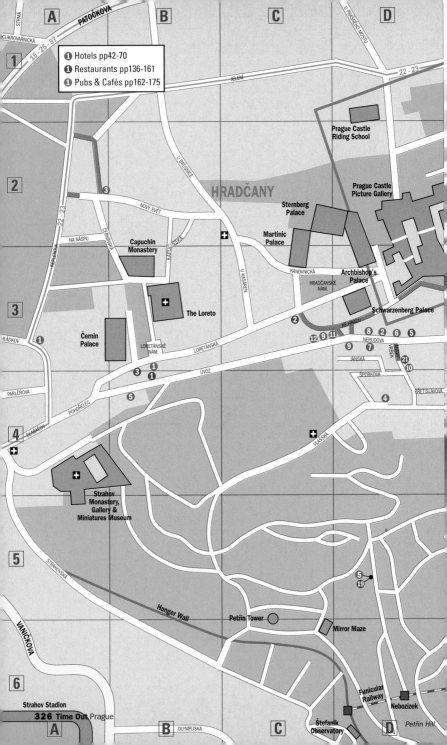

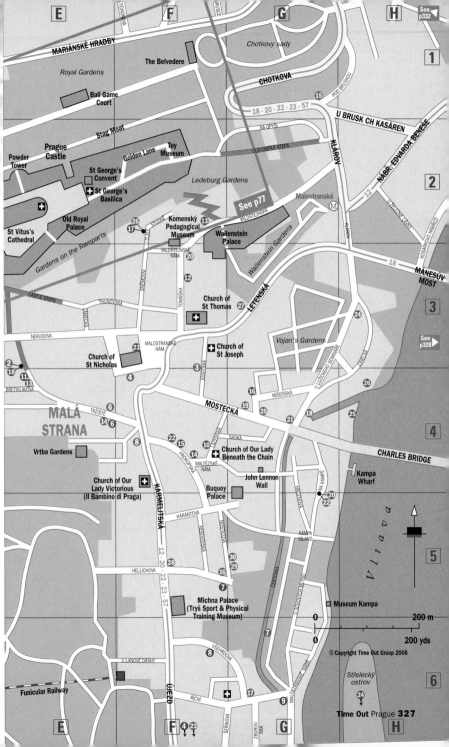

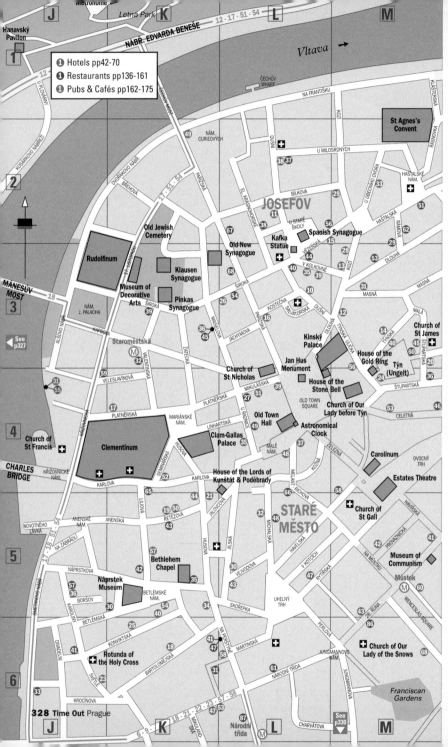

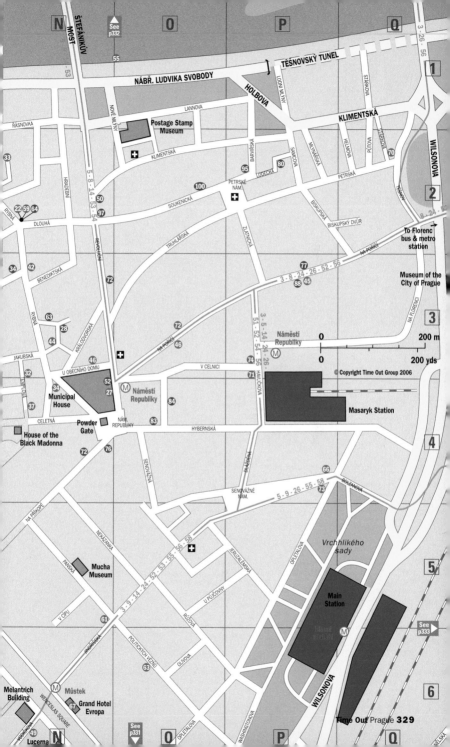

N O P Q

ŠTEFÁNIKŮV MOST

TĚSNOVSKÝ TUNEL

See p332

NÁBŘ. LUDVIKA SVOBODY

HOLBOVA

KLIMENTSKÁ

WILSONOVA

55

53

ŘÁSNOVKA

33

NOVÉ MLÝNY

LANNOVA

Postage Stamp
Museum

KLIMENTSKÁ

HRADEBNÍ

5 · 8 · 14 · 53 · 54

50

97

RYBNÁ

22 59 64

DLOUHÁ

BARVÍŘSKÁ

LODNÍ MLÝNY

STÁRKOVA

HELMOVA

PTÁLÚV

70

95

LODECKÁ

80

PETRSKÉ
NÁM.

SAMCOVA

MLYNÁŘSKÁ

PETRSKÁ

100

SOUKENICKÁ

ZLATNICKÁ

BISKUPSKÁ

BISKUPSKÝ DVŮR

To Florenc
bus & metro
station

34 42

BENEDIKTSKÁ

TRUHLÁŘSKÁ

NA POŘÍČÍ

Museum of the
City of Prague

RYBNÁ

63

28

KRÁLODVORSKÁ

NA POŘÍČÍ

72

77

3 · 8 · 24 · 26 · 52 · 56

88 45

Náměstí
Republiky

3

44

46

51 · 52 · 54 · 55

JAKUBSKÁ

32

TEMPLOVÁ

U OBECNÍHO DOMU

46

72

72

V CELNICI

74

71

HAVLÍČKOVA

3 · 5 · 14 · 24 · 26

M

0   200 m

0   200 yds

© Copyright Time Out Group 2006

37

52

27

M Náměstí
Republiky

84

Masaryk Station

Municipal House

CELETNÁ

Powder
Gate

NÁM.
REPUBLIKY

83

HYBERNSKÁ

House of the
Black Madonna

72

76

SENOVÁŽNÁ

66

73

OPLETALOVA

BOLZANOVA

SENOVÁŽNÉ
NÁM.

5 · 9 · 26 · 55 · 58

NA PŘÍKOPĚ

NEKÁZANKA

5 · 9 · 26 · 52 · 53 · 55 · 58

Vrchlického
sady

5

PANSKÁ

Mucha
Museum

JERUZALÉMSKÁ

U PUČOVNY

Main
Station

See
p333

V CÍPU

61

3 · 9 · 14 · 24 · 52 · 53 · 55 · 58

RŮŽOVÁ

POLITICKÝCH VĚZŇŮ

OLIVOVA

63

Melantrich
Building

M Můstek

67

Grand Hotel
Evropa

See
p331

VÁCLAVSKÉ NÁMĚSTÍ

WILSONOVA

N

49

Lucerna

WASHINGTONOVA

OPLETALOVA

N O P Q

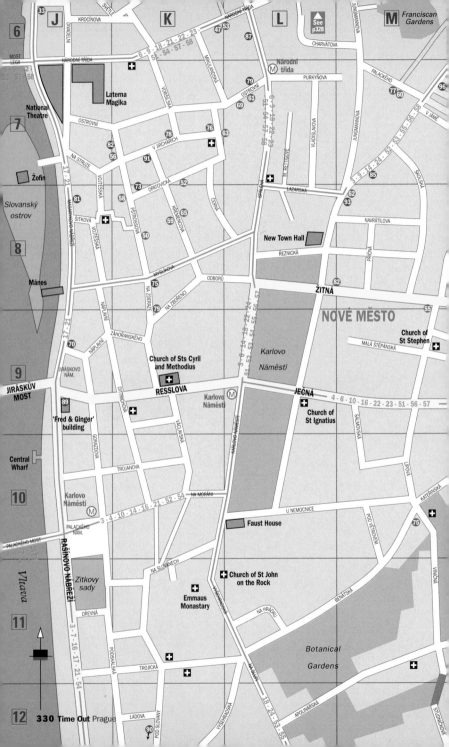

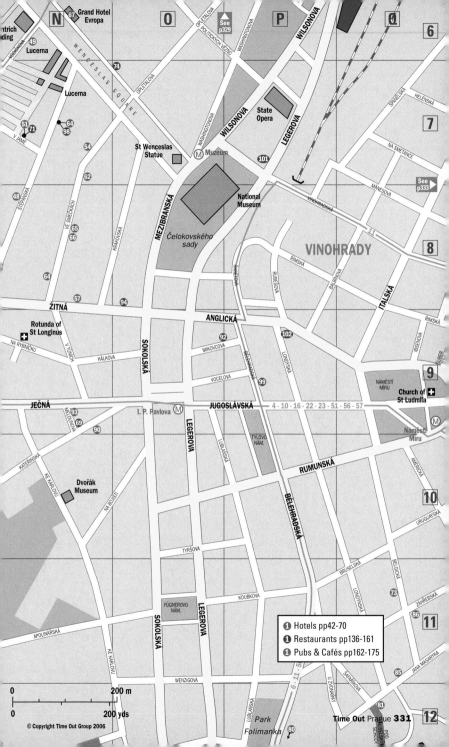

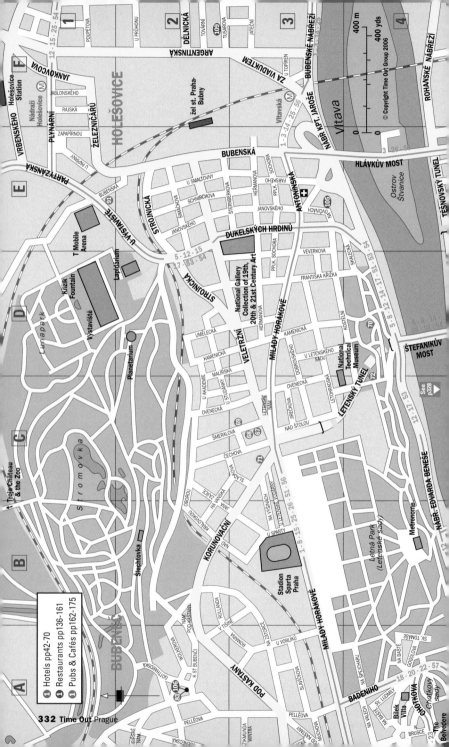

ŽIŽKOV

VINOHRADY

Olšany Cemetery

Palác Flora

Church of the Sacred Heart

Hussite Church

Church of St Ludmila

National Memorial

Jan Žižka Statue

Army Museum

Žižkov TV Tower

Mahlerovy Sady

Viktoria Žižkov Stadion

Rajská zahrada

Riegrovy Sady

Sady Svatopluka Čecha

Main Station

See p331

Hotels pp42-70
Restaurants pp136-161
Pubs & Cafés pp162-175

© Copyright Time Out Group 2006

400 m
400 yds

Street Index

17. Listopadu - p328 K2/3
28. Října - p328 M5/6
Alšovo Nábřeží - p328 J3
Americká - p331 Q10, p333 A4
Anenská - p328 J5/K5
Anenské Náměstí - p328 J5
Anglická - p331 O9/P9
Anny Letenské - p333 A3
Antonínská - p332 E3
Apolinářská - p330 L12/M11, p331 N11/O11
Argentinská - p332 F1/2/3
Badeniho - p332 A4
Balbínova - p331 P8/9/Q8, p333 A3
Baranova - p333 D3
Bartolomějská - p328 K6
Barvířská - p329 P1/2
Basilejské Náměstí - p333 F1
Bělehradská - p331 P9/10/11/12
Belgická - p331 Q10/11, p333 A4
Benátská - p330 L11/M10/11
Benešovská - p333 E4
Benediktská - p329 N3
Betlémská - p328 J6/K5
Betlémské Náměstí - p328 K5
Bílkova - p328 L2
Biskupský Dvůr - p329 P2/Q2
Biskupská - p329 P2/Q2
Blahníkova - p333 C1/2
Blanická - p333 A3/4
Blodkova - p333 C3
Bořivojova - p333 B2/C2/D2/3
Boleslavská - p333 D3/4
Bolzanova - p329 Q4, p333 A1
Boršov - p328 J5
Bratří Čapků - p333 E4/F4
Břehová - p328 K2
Břetislavova - p326 D4, p327 E4
Bruselská - p331 P11/Q10/11
Bubenečská - p332 A2
Bubenská - p332 E1/2/3
Bubenské Nábřeží - p332 F3
Budečská - p333 B3/4
Celetná - p328 M4, p329 N4
Charles Bridge - p327 H4, p328 J4
Charvátova - p328 L6/M6, p330 L6/M6
Chelčického - p333 D2/E2
Chlumova - p333 C1/2
Chodská - p333 B4
Chopinova - p333 B3
Chotkova - p327 G1, p332 A4
Chvalova - p333 C2
Cihelná - p327 H3/4
Cimburkova - p333 C1
Cukrovarnická - p326 A1
Čajkovského - p333 C2
Čáslavská - p333 D3/4
Čechův Most - p328 K1/2
Čechův Wharf - p328 L1
Čechova - p332 C2
Čerchovská - p333 B3
Černá - p330 K7/8
Černínská - p326 A2/B3
Českobratrská - p333 D1
Dalimilova - p333 C1
Dělnická - p332 F2
Dittrichova - p330 K9/10

Divadelni - p328 J6, p330 J6
Dlážděná - p329 P4
Dlabačov - p326 A4
Dlouhá - p328 L3/M2/3, p329 N2
Dobrovského - p332 C3/D3
Domažlická - p333 E1
Dřevná - p330 J11
Dušní - p328 L2/3
Dukelských Hrdinů - p332 E3
Dvořákovo Nábřeží - p328 J2/K2
Dykova - p333 C4/D4
El. Krásnohorské - p328 L2/3
Farského - p332 E3
Fibichova - p333 C2/3
Francouzská - p333 A4/B4
Františka Křižka - p332 D3/4
Fügnerovo Náměstí - p331 O11
Gogolova - p332 A4
Gorazdova - p330 J9/10
Gotthardská - p332 A2
Ha Vanská - p332 B2/C2
Hájkova – p333 E1
Hálkova - p331 N9/09
Harantova - p327 F5
Haštalská - p328 M2
Haštalské Náměstí - p328 M2
Havelkova - p333 B2
Havelská - p328 L5
Havířská - p328 M5
Havlíčkova - p329 p3/4
Heřmanova - p332 D3/E3
Helénská - p331 Q7, p333 A3
Hellichova - p327 F5
Helmova - p329 Q2
Hládkov - p326 A3
Hlávkův Most - p332 E4
Holbova - p329 P1
Hradčanské Náměstí - p326 C3/D3
Hradešínská - p333 C4/D4
Hradebni - p329 N2
Hradecká - p333 E3/4
Hroznová - p327 G4/5
Husinecká - p333 B1
Husitská - p333 A1/B1/C1
Husova - p328 K4/5
Hybernská - p329 O4/P4
Ibsenova - p331 Q9, p333 A4
Italská - p331 Q8/9, p333 A2/3
Jablonského - p332 F1
Jáchymova - p328 L3
Jagellonská - p333 C3/D3
Jakubská - p329 N3
Jalovcová - p328 K5/L5
Jana Masaryka - p331 Q11/12
Jana Zajíce - p332 B2/3/C2
Jana Želivského - p333 F1/2
Jankovcova - p332 F1
Janovského - p332 E2/3
Jánská - p326 D3
Jánskývršek - p326 D3
Jatečni - p332 F3
Ježkova - p333 B2
Ječná - p330 L9/M9, p331 N9
Jelení - p326 C1
Jeronýmova - p333 C1
Jeruzalémská - p329 O5/P5

Jeseniova - p333 D1/E1/F1
Jičínská - p333 D2/3/E3
Jilská - p328 L5
Jindřišská - p329 N6/O5
Jiráskův Most - p330 J9
Jiráskovo Náměstí - p330 J9
Jirečkova - p332 C3
Josefská - p327 F3/4
Jugoslávská - p331 O9/P9/Q9, p333 A4
Jungmannova - p328 M6, p330 M6/7
Jungmannovo Náměstí - p328 L6/M6
K Brusce - p327 F1, p332 A4
K St Bubenči - p332 A2
Kamenická - p332 D2/3
Kanovnická - p326 C3
Kaprova - p328 J3/4/K3/4
Kapucinská - p326 B2/3
Karlovo Náměstí - p330 L8/9/10
Karmelitská - p327 F4/5
Karoliny - p328 J5/6
Kateřinská - p330 M10, p331 N9/10
Ke Hradu - p326 C3/D3
Ke Karlovu - p331 N10/11/12/O12
Keplerova - p326 A2/3
Klášterská - p328 M1
Kladská - p333 C4
Klárov - p327 G2/H2
Klimentská - p329 O2/P1/Q1
Kožná - p328 L4
Kolinská - p333 D3/4
Komenského Náměstí - p333 D1
Koněvova - p333 D1/E1
Konviktská - p328 J6/K6
Korunní - p333 A4/B4/C4/D4
Korunovační - p332 B2/3/C3
Kosárkovo Nábřeží - p327 H2/3, p328 J2
Kostečna - p328 L3
Kostelní - p332 D3/4
Kostnické Náměstí - p333 C1
Kouřímská - p333 F4
Koubkova - p331 P11
Kozí - p328 M1/2
Krakovská - p331 N8/O7/8
Královdvorská - p329 N3
Krásova - p333 B1/2/C2
Křemencova - p330 K7/8
Křišťanova - p333 D2/3
Křižovnická - p328 J4
Křižovnické Náměstí - p328 J4
Křížovského - p333 B3/C3
Krkonošská - p333 B3
Krocínova - p328 J6/K6, p330 J6/K6
Kubelikova - p333 B2/C2
Kuněticka - p333 A2
Ladova - p330 K12
Lannova - p329 O1
Laubova - p333 C3
Lazarská - p330 L8
Lázeňská - p327 F4
Legerova - p331 O9/10/11/12/P6/7
Letenská - p327 G3
Letenské Náměstí - p332 C3
Letenský Tunel - p332 C3/4/D4
Letohradská - p332 C3/D3

Libická - p333 D3/4
Lichnická - p333 A2
Liliová - p328 K5
Linhartská - p328 K4/L4
Lipanská - p333 C2/D2
Lípova - p330 M10
Lodecká - p329 P2
Lodni Mlýny - p329 P1
Londýská - p331 P9/10/Q10/11
Loretánská - p326 Bb/C3
Loretánské Náměstí - p326 B3
Lužická - p333 B4
Lublaňská - p331 O9/10/P10/11/12
Lucemburská - p333 C3/D3
Lukášova - p333 D1
Lupáčova - p333 D2
M. Rettigové - p330 L7
Maiselova - p328 K3/L3
Malá Štěpánská - p330 M9
Malá Štupartská - p328 M3/4
Malé Náměstí - p328 L4
Malešická - p333 E1/F1
Malířská - p332 D2/3
Malostranské Nábřeží - p327 G6
Malostranské Náměstí - p327 F3
Maltézské Náměstí - p327 F4
Mánesův Most - p327 H3, p328 J3
Mánesova - p331 Q7/8, p333 A3/B3/C3
Mariánské Hradby - p327 E1/F1
Mariánské Náměstí - p328 K4
Martinská - p328 L6
Masarykovo Nábřeží - p330 J7/8/9
Masná - p328 M3
Melantrichova - p328 L4/5
Melounova - p331 N9
Mezibranská - p331 O7/8
Michalská - p328 L5
Mikovcova - p331 O9/P9
Mikulášská - p328 L4
Mikulandská - p328 K6, p330 K6/7
Miličova - p333 C1/2
Milady Horákové - p332 A3/B3/C3/D3
Milešovská - p333 C3
Míšeňská - p327 G4
Mlynářská - p329 P2
Moravská - p333 B4
Most Legii - p330 J6
Mostecká - p327 F4/G4
Muchova - p332 A3
Myslíkova - p330 J8/K8/L8
Na Baště - p332 A4
Na Bojišti - p331 N10/O10
Na Florenci - p329 Q3, p333 A1
Na Františku - p328 L1/M1
Na Hrádku - p330 L11
Na Kampě - p327 G4/5
Na Můstku - p328 M5
Na Moráni - p330 K10
Na Náspu - p326 A2
Na Opyši - p327 G2
Na Ovčínách - p328 M2
Na Příkopě - p329 N4/5
Na Parukářce - p333 E1/F1

Na Perštýně - p328 L6
Na Poříčí - p329 O3/p3/Q2/3
Na Rybníčku - p331 N9
Na Slovanech - p330 K10/11
Na Slupi - p330 L11/12
Na Smetance - p331 Q7, p333 A3
Na Struze - p330 J7
Na Valech - p332 A4
Na Výšinách - p332 B3/C3
Na Zábrádlí - p328 J5
Na Zájezdu - p333 D4/E4
Na Zátorce - p332 A3/B3
Na Zbořenci - p330 K8/9
Na Zderaze - p330 K8/9
Na Šafránce - p333 D4
Na Špejcharu - p332 A4
Na Švihance - p333 B3
Nábřeží Kpt. Jaroše - p332 E3/F3
Nábřeží Edvarda Beneše - p327 H1/2, p328 J1/K1/L1, p332 B4/C4/D4
Nábřeží Ludvika Svobody - p329 O1/P1
Nad Štolou - p332 C3
Nad Královskou Oborou - p332 B2/C2
Náměstí Barikád - p333 E1
Náměstí Curieových - p328 K2/L2
Náměstí J. Palacha - p328 J3
Náměstí Jiřího Z Poděbrad - p333 C3
Náměstí Pod Kaštany - p332 B2
Náměstí Republiky - p329 N4/O4
Náměstí W. Churchilla - p333 B1/2
Náměstí Míru - p331 Q9, p333 A4
Náplavní - p330 J8/9
Náprstkova - p328 J5/K5
Národní Třída - p328 L6, p330 J6/7/K6/L6
Navrátilova - p330 M8
Nebovidská - p327 F5
Nekázanka - p329 N4/5/O5
Nerudova - p326 D3, p327 E3
Nitranská - p333 C4
Nosticova - p327 F5
Nové Mlýny - p329 N1/O2
Novotného Lávka - p328 J5
Nový Svět - p326 B2
Odborů - p330 K8/L8
Olšanská - p333 E2/F2
Olšanské Náměstí - p333 D2
Old Town Square - p328 L4
Olivova - p329 O6
Olympijská - p326 B6
Ondříčkova - p333 B3/C3
Opatovická - p330 K7/8
Opletalova - p329 O6/P5/6, p331 O6/7, p333 A1
Orebitská - p333 B1/C1
Orlická - p333 D3
Ostrovní - p330 J7/K7/L7
Ovenecká - p332 C2/3
Ovocný Trh - p328 M4
Palackého - p330 M7
Palackého Most - p330 J10
Palackého Náměstí - p330 J10
Panská - p329 N5
Pařížská - p328 K2/L3
Parléřova - p326 A4
Partyzánská - p332 E1
Patočkova - p326 A1/B1
Pelléova - p332 A2/3

Perlová - p328 L5/6/M6
Perunova - p333 D4
Petrská - p329 P2/Q2
Petrské Náměstí - p329 P2
Pisacká - p333 E3/4
Pitterova - p333 F2
Platnéřská - p328 J4/K4/L4
Plynární - p332 E1/F1
Pod Bruskou - p327 G1/H1
Pod Kaštany - p332 A2/3
Pod Nuselskými Schody - p331 Q12
Pod Slovany - p330 K12
Pod Větrovem - p330 M10
Podskalská - p330 J11/K12
Pohořelec - p326 A4
Politických Vězňů - p329 O6, - p331 O6/P7
Polská - p333 A3/B3
Poupětova - p332 F1
Pplk. Sochora - p332 D3/E3
Přemyslovská - p333 D3
Příčná - p330 M8
Příběnická - p328 J4/K4
Pštrossova - p330 K7/8
Půtova - p329 Q1/2
Prokopova - p333 C1/D1/2
Prokopská - p327 F4
Provaznická - p328 M5
Purkyňova - p330 L7
Rašínovo Nábřeží - p330 J10/11
Radhošťská - p333 D2/3
Rajská - p332 F1
Rámová - p328 M2/3
Resslova - p330 K9
Revoluční - p329 N2/3
Roháčova - p333 C1/D1/E1
Rohanské Nábřeží - p332 F4
Rokycanova - p333 D1/2
Rollanda - p332 B2
Romaina - p332 A3
Rubešova - p331 P8
Rumunská - p331 O10/P10/Q10, p333 A4
Ruská - p333 E4/F4
Růžová - p329 O5/6/P6
Rybná - p329 N2/3
Rytířská - p328 L5/M5
Řásnovka - p328 M2, p329/N1
Řehořova - p333 B1
Řetězová - p328 K5
Řeznická - p330 L8
Říčanská - p333 D4
Říční - p327 F6
Římská - p331 P8/Q8/9, p333 A3/4
Řípská - p333 C4
Salmovská - p330 M9/10
Salvátorská - p328 L3
Samcova - p329 P2
Saská - p327 G4
Sázavská - p333 B4
Schnirchova - p332 E2/3
Seifertova - p333 B2/C2
Seminářská - p328 K4
Senovážná - p329 O4
Senovážné Náměstí - p329 P4
Sibiřské Náměstí - p332 A2
Skalecká - p332 D4/E4
Skořepka - p328 L5
Sládkova - p332 C3
Sladkovského Náměstí - p333 C2
Slavíčkova - p332 A3
Slavíkova - p333 B3/C3
Slezská - p333 A4/B4/C4/D4/E3/4
Smetanovo Nábřeží - p328 J5/6
Sněmovni - p327 F3
Sokolská - p331 O9/10/11/12
Soukenická - p329 O2

Spálená - p330 L7/8
Srbská - p332 A3
Stárkova - p329 Q1/2
Strahovská - p326 A5
Strmá - p326 A1
Strojnická - p332 D2/E2
Studničkova - p330 M12
Sudoměřská - p333 D2/3
Sv. Ludmily - p332 A4
Sv. Tomáše - p332 A4
Světlé - p328 J5/6, p330 J6
Šafaříkova - p331 Q11/12
Šeříkova - p327 F6
Ševčíkova - p333 C2
Šimáčkova - p332 E2
Široká - p328 K3/L3
Šitková - p330 J8
Školská - p330 M7/8
Škrétova - p331 P8
Škroupovo Náměstí - p333 C3
Šmeralova - p332 C2/3
Španělská - p329 Q6, p331 Q6/7, p333 A2/3
Šporkova - p326 D4
Šrobárova - p333 E4/F4
Štefánikův Most - p329 N1, p332 D4
Štěpánská - p331 N7/8
Šternberkova - p332 E2/3
Štítného - p333 C1/2
Štupartská - p328 M4
Šubertova - p331 Q9, p333 A4
Šumavská - p333 B4
Těšnov - p329 Q2
Těšnovský Tunel - p329 P1/Q1, p332 E4
Templová - p329 N3/4
Thunovská - p327 E3/F3
Tomášská - p327 F3
Tovární - p332 F2
Třebizského - p333 B3
Tržiště - p327 E4/F4
Trocnovská - p333 B1
Trojanova - p330 J10/K10
Trojická - p330 K11
Truhlářská - p329 O2/3
Tusarova - p332 F2
Tychonova - p327 F1
Tylovo Náměstí - p331 P9/10
Tyršova - p331 O10/P10
Týnská - p328 M3
Týnská Ulička - p328 M3
U Akademie - p332 C2/D2
U Brusk Ch Kasáren - p327 H1/2
U Brusnice - p326 B1/2
U Kanálky - p333 B3
U Kasáren - p326 C3
U Lanové Dráhy - p327 F6
U Letenské Vodárny - p332 B3/C3
U Letenského Sadu - p332 D3
U Lužického Semináře - p327 G3/4/H3
U Milosrdných - p328 L2/M2
U Nemocnice - p330 L10
U Obecního Domu - p329 N3
U Obecního Dvora - p328 M2
U Půjčovny - p329 O5/P5
U Papírny - p332 E1
U Plovárny - p328 J1
U Průhonu - p332 F2
U Prašného Mostu - p326 D1
U Radnice - p328 L4
U Rajské Zahrady - p333 B2
U Smaltovny - p332 E2/3
U Sovových Mlýnů - p327 G5/6
U Sparty - p332 B3
U Stadiunu - p333 F1/2

U Staré Školy - p328 L2
U Studánky - p332 C2/D2
U Topíren - p332 F3
U Tržnice - p333 B4
U Vodárny - p333 C3/4
U Vorlíků - p332 A3
U Výstaviště - p332 E1/2
U Zásobni Zahrady - p333 E1/F1
U Zdravotniho Ustavu - p333 F3/4
U Železné Lávky - p327 H2
U Zlaté Studně - p327 F2
U Zvonařky - p331 P11/12
Uhelný Trh - p328 L5
Újezd - p327 F6
Umělecká - p332 D2
Uruguayská - p331 Q10, p333 A4
Úvoz - p326 B3/4/C3
V Celnici - p329 O3/p3
V Cípu - p329 N5
V Jámě - p330 M7, p331 N7
V Jircháří - p330 K7
V Kolkovně - p328 L3/M3
V Kotcích - p328 L5
V Tůních - p331 N9
V Tišíně - p332 A2/B3
Václavská - p330 K9/10
Valdštejnská - p327 G2
Valdštejnské Náměstí - p327 F3
Valentinská - p328 K3/4
Vaničkova - p326 A5/6
Varšavská - p333 A4
Ve Smečkách - p331 N7/8
Vejvodova - p328 L5
Velehradská - p333 C3/D3
Veleslavínová - p328 J4/K4
Veletržní - p332 C3/D3
Veverkova - p332 D3/E3
Vězeňská - p328 L2/3/M2
Viničná - p330 M10/11
Vinohradská - p331 P8/Q8, p333 A3/B3/4/C3/D3/E3/F3
Vita Nejedlého - p333 C2
Vlašimská - p333 E4
Vlašská - p326 C4/D4
Vladislavova - p330 L7
Vlkova - p333 B2/C2
Vocelova - p331 O9/P9
Vodičkova - p329 N6, p331 N6
Vojtěšská - p330 J7/8
Voršilská - p330 K7
Vozová - p333 B2
Vrbenského - p332 E1/F1
Všehrdova - p327 F6/G6
Vyšehradská - p330 K11/12/L11/12
Washingtonova - p329 P6, p331 O7/P6
Wenceslas Square - p328 M5/6, p329 N6, p331 N6/7/O7
Wenzigova - p331 O11
Wilsonova - p329 P6/Q1-6, p331 P6/7, p333 A1/2
Wolkerova - p332 A2
Za Viaduktem - p332 F3
Záhřebská - p331 Q11
Záhořanského - p330 K9
Zámecká - p327 E3
Zapapírnou - p332 E1
Zborovska - p327 G6
Zikmunda Wintra - p332 A3
Zlatnická - p329 P2/3
Žatecká - p328 K3/4
Železná - p328 L4/M4
Železničářů - p332 E1/F1
Žerotinova - p333 D1/E1
Žižkovo Náměstí - p333 D2/3
Žitná - p330 L8/M8, p331 N8/9

Prague Metro

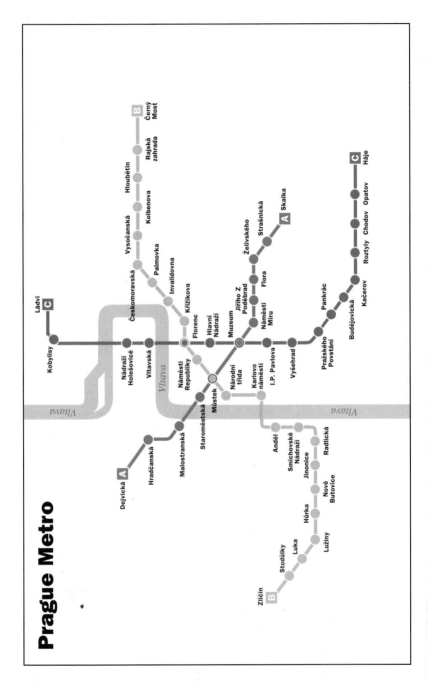